The Posthumous Works of ... John Howe, Ed. by J. Hunt

John Howe

Nabu Public Domain Reprints:

You are holding a reproduction of an original work published before 1923 that is in the public domain in the United States of America, and possibly other countries. You may freely copy and distribute this work as no entity (individual or corporate) has a copyright on the body of the work. This book may contain prior copyright references, and library stamps (as most of these works were scanned from library copies). These have been scanned and retained as part of the historical artifact.

This book may have occasional imperfections such as missing or blurred pages, poor pictures, errant marks, etc. that were either part of the original artifact, or were introduced by the scanning process. We believe this work is culturally important, and despite the imperfections, have elected to bring it back into print as part of our continuing commitment to the preservation of printed works worldwide. We appreciate your understanding of the imperfections in the preservation process, and hope you enjoy this valuable book.

THE

POSTHUMOUS WORKS

OF THE LATE

REV. JOHN HOWE M.A.

THE

POSTHUMOUS WORKS

OF THE LATE

REV. JOHN HOWE, M. A.

WITH A MEMOIR.

EDITED BY

THE REV. JOHN HUNT.

IN FOUR VOLUMES,

VOL. III.

CONTAINING

THE PRINCIPLES OF THE ORACLES OF GOD.

PART I. CONTINUED.
1. THE DOCTRINE OF THE TRINITY, IN FOUR LECTURES.
2. THE DIVINE ATTRIBUTES, IN NINE LECTURES.
PART II.
1. THE DECREES OF GOD, IN EIGHT LECTURES.
2. THE WORK OF CREATION, IN SEVEN LECTURES.
3. THE CREATION OF MAN, IN FIVE LECTURES,
4. THE FALL OF MAN, &c., IN FOURTEEN LECTURES.
5. THE JUSTICE OF GOD VINDICATED, IN EIGHT LECTURES.

LONDON:

PUBLISHED BY FRANCIS WESTLEY, 10, STATIONERS'-COURT, AND AVE-MARIA-LANE;

AND SOLD BY WAUGH AND INNES, EDINBURGH; AND CHALMERS AND COLLINS, GLASGOW.

1832.

THE PRINCIPLES

OF

THE ORACLES OF GOD,

In Two Parts.

NEVER BEFORE PUBLISHED.

PART I.

CONTAINING

I. An introduction, proving the necessity of their being taught, in two lectures, on Heb. 5. 12.

II. The existence of God, manifest from the creation, in four lectures, on Romans 1. 20.

III. The divine authority of the scriptures, in five lectures, on 2. Timothy 3. 16.

IV. The unity of the Godhead, in two lectures, on James 2. 19.

V. The trinity of persons in the divine essence, in four lectures, on John 5. 7.

VI. The attributes and perfections of the divine being, in nine lectures, on Matthew 5. 48.

LECTURE XIII.*

1 John 5. 7.

For there are three that bear record in heaven, the Father, the Word, and the Holy Ghost: and these three are one.

I INTEND no long discourse upon this subject, nor longer than may consist with the design of going over the several heads of religion, in as plain a manner, and in as short a way as I can. It would very ill agree with such a design, to insist upon, and discourse upon all the several texts of Scripture arguments and objections this way and that, which are wont to be ventilated upon this point. All that can be expected, according to the course I have proposed to use, will be barely to represent that which I take, and which (I hope) we generally agree to be the truth in this matter, in as few and as plain words as is possible. If one should take the large course, which some (it may be) would expect, it would be to make one particular subject the business of a long life's time, and would be to turn this place into a theatre of contentious disputations rather than serious instructions, tending only to gratify vain minds, rather than to edify the sober mind.

I shall not need to stay at all upon the particular controversy about this text, the authenticity of it, which, it is true, is disputed: but upon that account only, that some copies have been found not to have it. But for such as are in doubt thereupon concerning it, I need do no more than recommend them

* Preached, March 27. 1691.

(amongst others) to what hath been most judiciously, and, indeed, very charitably written as to that matter by Dr. Hammond, in his annotations on the New Testament, where he hath, with equal judgment and charity, represented how it is very easily supposable that in the transcribing of some copy or another, two verses coming here together, this seventh and eighth that do begin and end, both of them, somewhat alike, the eye of the transcriber might fall upon the latter, and so write without looking back to the former. A very obvious supposition, and a great deal more probable (as it is a great deal more charitable) than to suppose that either side, in the time of the Arian controversy, did design a corruption of the Scripture text; I say, it is a great deal more rational, (as it is more charitable) because indeed it had been a very foolish thing, merely out of favour to one side, to have corrupted the Scripture in that one particular place, leaving other scriptures to stand as they were that speak so fully the same thing, as that 28 Math. 18. 19. and that John 10. 30. " I and my Father are one." It is not likely there should be a designed corruption, where the loss of reputation would be so very great, and the gain and advantage so very little; but we have reason enough to be satisfied that the most ancient copies have it as we here find.

And for the way of managing the discourse upon this subject, I shall not offer at that which some have done, the demonstrating a Trinity in the Godhead in a rational way, as that which some have supposed sufficiently evident by rational light; and which some have made it their business to evince, (both Poiret and others before him,) and with no contemptible endeavour. But whether such do demonstrate their point yea or no, it is to me a very strong demonstration of the strange imbecility of the human mind, that some should think it rationally demonstrable, that, that cannot but be, which others take to be rationally demonstrable cannot be. This, I say, it is a great demonstration to me of; and I do believe that they who do read the other writings of Poiret and others, who think the Trinity rationally demonstrable, and read the writings of Socinus and others, his followers, who think the contrary, will apprehend in other matters, Poiret to be as rational a man as ever Socinus was, or any that followed him. Compare the writings of the one and the other, in other matters; and then I say, it is a strong demonstration, and that which doth require our very serious thoughts, of the imbecility of the minds of men, and how little the confident pretences to rational demonstrations, by interested persons, engaged and dipped in a party this way and that, are to be relied upon, when some very highly rational men shall undertake to demonstrate, that it is impossible this should be; when others as rational as they, shall undertake to demonstrate it is impossible not to be. That is, that there could have been no such thing as creation nor indeed any action in the Deity, and consequently, no Deity at all if there were not a Trinity in it. That is, if there were not an eternal mind which, when there was nothing else, should like an intellectual sun turn its beams inward upon itself, and so by consequence, beget an eternal action, its own eternal image, and that there must be an eternal love between that mind begetting, and the mind begotten: and there you have the Trinity in the Deity.

But this I insist not on; only that it may appear that it is not impossible: and I hope that all pretence that it is, will in due time, and easily vanish. It is so plainly revealed in Scripture, that there is a Trinity in the Godhead, that we may very well take it upon the word of him that reports it to us, and who best (we may be sure) understands his own nature. Take it, I say, amongst those things of God, which are only to be known by the Spirit of God; as there are things of a man, that are only known by the spirit of a man that is in him: (as the apostle speaks; 1 Cor. 2. 14.) and if the mind and spirit of every particular man, have its own particularities known only to itself, till the man is pleased to reveal and make them known, sure it is very little strange that the divine Being should have his peculiarities too, not otherwise knowable than as he is pleased to reveal them. And if he plainly reveal to us, that there is a Trinity in the Unity of his nature, then surely, to sober inquirers and learners, the business is done.

As to the latter part of the verse, I shall not need to insist upon it, "these three are one," having, I hope, sufficiently evinced to you the Unity of the Godhead from another text. And I chose to do it from another text rather, that had that expression in it which this hath not. For this doth not expressly say, these three are one God, but it doth say, these three are one. But having already proved to you that the Godhead is but one, it leads us with so much the more clearness (having asserted the doctrine of the unity of the Godhead to be true) to apprehend, that it must be the truth of this place, and so shall have occasion but to repeat concerning that which we have already proved, but not to prove it any more. And therefore, the plain contents of this scripture you may take thus— that there is a Trinity in the Deity, or—if you will, a little more largely—that there are three which we cannot more fitly express or conceive of, than by the name of persons, in the only one Godhead. And,

I. I shall evince the *truth* of this doctrine.

And now to let you see that this is reasonably given you, as the sense and meaning of this place, I shall proceed by some gradual steps: and,

1. To prepare my way, let you see that this is spoken here in this place; it is the doctrine of this place. So that if it can be made appear to be in itself true, we shall have all the reason in the world to conclude, that it is fitly represented as the doctrine held forth in this text. And for the truth of the thing, we shall come to consider from other places afterwards. And,

(1.) It seems very reasonable, inasmuch as we otherwise ascertained that there is but one God, that the one thing wherein the three persons mentioned are said to be united, is the Godhead. "These three are one." One what? It is most reasonable to understand the meaning is, that they are one God, though this be not expressed in the text. For it is very plain, from what hath been already said, that the Godhead can be but one. And when it is said, there are three in heaven that are all one, that one thing which they are said to be, must needs be God, or the Godhead wherein they are said to unite; especially the Father being said to be one of the three, concerning whose Godhead there is no doubt.

(2.) It is very plain, (upon supposition that the three mentioned in the text do unite, or are united in the Godhead,) the meaning must be, that they are one God and no more; that is, that the one God which they are said to be, is but one, is one God and no more. There can be no reason imagined why it should be said they are one, if the intendment were not that they were only one; or that that thing which they are said to be, is but one. To say the Godhead is one, it must always mean one exclusively, that is, that there is no other God but that, that one. And so, that is the thing that these three do unite, or are united in: not one witness, it is not a being united in their end: that cannot be meant here: for it is manifest that the apostle doth vary the form of expression in the following verse, where it is said, "These three agree in one;" all to one purpose, all to one design, all giving one and the same testimony concerning Christ, concerning that Jesus who was descended and come down into this world. But here it is said in the text, they are one, are one thing, not one person, and therefore, it doth signify that they do agree, or do unite and meet in that wherein it is never intended to say or intimate that they differ: that is, in essence they are united, but not in personality. If it had been a person that was spoken of, then it would have been proper enough, to have spoken of it under the notion of things. But inasmuch as it is the essence, and not the person, that is here intended, therefore it is said, one thing: if we would read the words literally, it is, "these three are one thing," that is the meaning of them and so they should be rendered.

(3.) Hereupon it is very rational to conclude, that when it is said, there are three that are united in this one thing, that it must also be understood, they are three and no more, as by one is meant only one, so by three is meant only three. Whereupon,

(4.) It must with equal reason be concluded, that these three which are three, and no more, must needs be some eminent three, and of some very eminent order. And do but pause here a little, and see if light do not spring into your minds about this matter: when it is said there are three (it being by parity of reason to be understood, three and no more) in heaven, Pray what three in heaven can there be, that are three, and no more, of one eminent order, but they must be three divine persons? Bethink yourselves of it a little: it cannot be three angels, for then it cannot be said, there are three and no more in heaven: and you have not heard of any higher creatures than angels, any superior order of creatures above angels, of which there are three and no more: and it cannot be three Gods, because the Godhead is but one; there is but one God and no more. Then I beseech you, What is there left? It is not three angels, it is not three of any sort of creatures superior to angels, of whom there are three and no more. And the Father is here mentioned as one of them, of whose Godhead there can be no doubt: and then pray consider, What can these three be? Not three creatures, not three Gods; therefore, they can be nothing but three persons, three substances in the Godhead. Thus then you are gradually led on to see, that this is the plain doctrine of the text, and if you can be convinced that there is in it, *veritas rei, the truth of the thing,* there will be no doubt at all but that it is *veritas loci, the truth of this place.*

2. And that is it I now come to, that is, to evince to you *veritatem rei, the truth of the thing,* that there is a Trinity in the Godhead, that there are three that are all of them this one God. And, I shall (with all possible brevity) labour to prove it to you positively, from other scriptures and scripture-considerations, and then—shew you the unreasonableness of

what is pretended against it, how irrational the pretence is against such a thing. That is, that there should be three who in some one respect are truly to be said and called three, and in some other respect are as truly to be called, or said to be but one. But,

(1.) I come to the positive proof. And because, concerning the personality and deity of the Father there is no question; there is none that will contend with us about that matter, therefore our business will relate to the other two. And concerning them, that is, the Word (as he is here called) and the Holy Ghost, I shall endeavour to evince to you these two things—that they are persons, and—that they are divine persons.

[1.] That they are persons. And here (as I have told you) we have not a fitter notion under which to conceive of them, nor a fitter word in our tongue by which to express or speak of them. Not that we can think, that person being afterwards to be clothed with the notion of divine, can be the same thing with God as with us; because it is impossible any thing can have one common notion to him and to us. That would be altogether inconsistent with the perfection, the universal perfection of the divine Being, to suppose that any notion could be common to him and the creature. For then, he should not comprehend all entity in himself, if there were a notion common to him and to us; for that must import something superior to both, and that were comprehensive of both, and so it would make God but a part of being. Therefore, the word person as any other word whatsoever, that is wont to be applied to, and spoken of God and of us, must be spoken of us but analogically, not univocally, not as if it signified the same thing when it is spoken of him, and when it is spoken of us. And therefore, we are not to judge of a divine person by a human person, or by a created person. The difference is infinite, and the distance is infinite between God and any creature. So any thing that is spoken of him must infinitely differ from whatsoever may be spoken of us under the same name. Therefore, when we speak of a person, among creatures, as signifying an intelligent *suppositum, being,* neither *suppositum* nor intelligent can be the same with him and with us. His intellect and ours differ infinitely: and it is so little known how individuations are made among creatures, that it is infinitely more impossible how they are made with God. But that being premised, that these two, the Word and the Holy Ghost are so spoken of in Scripture, as that we have no other way of conceiving otherwise than that they must be spoken of as persons; this I shall endeavour to evince.

First. As concerning the Word, I only premise that which is in itself evident, that by the Word here, and the Son of God elsewhere, must be meant the same thing. As is plain in the first of St. John's Gospel: "In the beginning was the Word:" that which is called the Word there, is called the Son of God presently after, in the same chapter: "The Word was made flesh and dwelt among us, (and we beheld his glory, the glory as of the only begotten of the Father,) full of grace and truth." The Word and the Son are all one. Then, what is there and elsewhere called the Word sometimes, and sometimes Son, or the Son of God, that must needs mean what we can conceive of no otherwise than under the notion of a person. That is, we find the action, from time to time, ascribed to this Word, or this Son, of an intelligent agent, of one that did act understandingly and with design. And we can have no better signification of a person, no clearer notion of one than that is. He is constantly spoken of as an intelligent agent; and concerning that, there can be no difficulty, nor indeed is there any controversy between us and our antagonists, concerning his personality; only they will have him to be but a human person, which we shall in its own place consider by and by. And,

Secondly. Concerning the Holy Ghost, that he also is a person, or such a one as we can conceive of under no other notion than that of a person; that is, as acting intelligently and with design: even so is he most apparently spoken of, from time to time, in Scripture. Hereupon it is said, He bears witness in heaven; as he did in heaven, and from thence, testify concerning Christ, that he was the Son of God, to be heard and obeyed and submitted to as such; and as a dove, descended in visible glory upon him from the heavens. This speaks the act of an intelligent, designing cause on his part, as to what he did in testifying, and so he is very frequently spoken of, as coming for such and such a purpose. "When he is come he shall convince the world." John 16. 7, 8. And (which is most observable) in several parts of these chapters, of the 14. 15. and 16th of that gospel, even there, where he had been spoken of under the name of the Spirit before, when one would expect, in correspondence to that name spirit, it would have been said, *it*, it, being neutral, a word of the neuter gender, it is said *he*; when *he* is come, not when *it* is come, he shall convince the world of sin: yea, and even the very laws of grammar and syntax are waved, as if it were on purpose to hold out this one thing to us, that the Holy Ghost was a person, an intelligent Being, working and acting with design: for when we have the word spirit, presently *he* doth follow upon it: and at a very great distance, in one place, (several verses being interposed) from any other antecedent but spirit. Indeed, in the 14. and 15th chapters, there was the comforter as well as the spirit, to which *he*, might have reference: but still, spirit was the nearer antecedent. But you will find, in the 16th chapter, the 13. and 14th verses, that there is no antecedent for many verses together, besides spirit, and afterwards immediately subjoined *he*, and not *it*, on purpose to signify (and we cannot imagine what it should be to signify besides) the personality of the Holy Ghost. And it is a very unreasonable supposal, that in the form of baptism which we have, Matth. 28. 19. " Go ye, teach all nations, baptizing them, in the name of the Father, and of the Son, and of the Holy Ghost;" that the two first should be persons, (as they are confessed on all hands to be) and that there should be put in the same order with them a quality, as our antagonists would teach us to conceive concerning the Holy Ghost, baptizing them in the name of the Father, and of the Son, and what? of a quality, in the third place. That is, that when the design manifestly was there to state the Object of all practical religion, of the whole of our Christianity, into the believing whereof we are to be baptized, there should be a transient quality put into conjunction with those two great persons, the Father and the Son. Surely, it needs but to stay and to pause here a little, to have light irresistibly strike into the mind of any one that will do so, that will consider how unreasonable it is to imagine, when the design is manifestly to represent and state the entire object of whole Christianity, that is, the Father, the Son and the Holy Ghost, that the two first of these are persons, and the third but a quality. Therefore, that being very plain,

[2.] The second thing that needs to be evinced is, that they are divine persons, and much is done towards that already. It appearing they are persons, they cannot be created persons, they cannot be angels, of which it can be said there are three and no more. But we hear of no intervening order of creatures, above angels and below God. And then what should they be, since they are persons, (as is plain) but divine persons, that do subsist in the Godhead? And to evince this a little more distinctly, but very briefly,

First. Concerning the Word, or the Son, (which you see are both of them names of the same person) how expressly is he often said to be God? In that mentioned first of John, nothing can be spoken more openly nor in plainer words. " In the beginning was the Word, and the Word was with God, and the Word was God." And Psalm 45. 6. " Thy throne O God is for ever and ever," which the author to the Hebrews (chap. 1. 8.) allegeth to be plainly said to the Son; "And to the Son he said, Thy throne, O God, is for ever and ever." So Romans, 9. 5. "Of whom, as concerning the flesh, Christ came, who is over all, God blessed for ever." And that, 1 John 5. 20. "And we know that the Son of God is come, and hath given us an understanding, that we may know him that is true; and we are in him that is true, even in his Son Jesus Christ. This is the true God and eternal life:" most fitly spoken of the Son who was to be the spring of life to us, according to what had been said a little above in the same chapter, "This is the record, that God hath given us eternal life, and this life is in his Son. He that hath the Son hath life; and he that hath not the Son hath not life."

It is, I know, alleged with a great deal of triumph by some of the adversaries, that he is excluded in another place from being the true God, and that that should not be said of him, when we are told, (John. 17. 2.) "This is life eternal, that they might know thee the only true God, and Jesus Christ, whom thou hast sent." If the Father only be true God, then the Son is not. But the inconsequence of this will easily appear to them that shall but consider, how the word *only* is placed. It is placed so as to assert the predicate, and not the subject in the latter proposition. It is not said, Thou only art the true God, and so, that doth not exclude the Son at all. The Father is the only true God, and the Son is the only true God, and the Holy Ghost is the only true God. But it cannot be said that either the Father only is the true God, or the Son only is the true God, or the Holy Ghost only is the true God: but they are each of them that God which is the only true one, and of which there is but one and no more. Do but observe that the word *only* affects not the subject spoken of, but the thing affirmed, or spoken of that subject. The case is but like this, as if I should use these words, "This is the only London." It may be true for ought we know, that there is no other London, but this which is famously called so by that name, but if one should say, "This only is London," that is, this place where we are, and there the *only* should limit the subject, that were false; for there are thousands of places in London as well as this, there are a great many assemblies in London, a great many places of worship and societies besides this: but we may say, "This is the only London," so the difference is plain to any that will consider it.

I might insist much more largely, (but it is not needful to say every thing that might be said in a plain case,) concerning the Son, to prove his divine personality by most manifest attributes of Deity, given him over and over in Scripture, as " The First and the Last :" creating power, as " Him by whom the world was made, and by whom he made the world," which is over and over said of him. Col. 1. 15. Heb. 1. 3. John 1. beginning. And universal knowledge, Omnisciency, heart knowledge ; "Thou knowest all things, thou knowest that I love thee." But then,

Secondly. Concerning the divine person of the Holy Ghost, that he also is God ; that doth sure, carry convictive light with it to any that do consider, that when the form of baptism is given (as was said) with design to state the whole object of our religion, "The Father, the Son, and the Holy Ghost" are mentioned together; and there can be no object of religion but God, none but a divine person: and we find the Holy Ghost frequently mentioned, upon the same account, as one of those eminent three. How many places are there (it were endless to name them) where these three are brought in together, as it were purposely to signify that they were *ejusdem ordinus, of the same order;* and that we are to conceive of each of them under the same notion, that is, that of Deity, of the Godhead in God. Look but to that 1 Pet. 1. 2. Rom. 1. 4, 5. 2 Thes. 2. 13, 14 : and a great many places besides, where these three are brought in still together. As if it were purposely to signify their being of one order, and as having, in distinct respects, a concern in our great affairs ; those that relate to our salvation and blessedness. Besides, that it must be a great prevarication, to understand that place otherwise than as expressing the Holy Ghost to be God: Acts 5. 3, 4. " Why hath Satan filled thine heart to lie unto the Holy Ghost ?—thou hast not lied unto man, but unto God." And certainly if he were not God, it were the most dangerous thing in all the world, to have him represented to us as if he were : and so tempt men to pay the homage of divine worship to a creature. It is never to be imagined, that there would have been such a snare laid before us, to lead us into so dangerous a mistake as that: things would have been spoken more cautiously, if he had not been God, than, when it was just said before, " Why dost thou lie against the Holy Ghost ?" so immediately to say, " Thou didst not lie to man but unto God." It is not to be thought, (the thing being so full of danger) to place the notion or homage of the Deity upon any thing to which it doth not belong, that there should have been such incautiousness used, or so little caution, as directly to lead and train persons into so perilous a mistake. But besides all this, to put the matter out of all doubt : whereas, they that will have the Holy Ghost not to be

God, being urged, "What is he then?" do say, "He is the mighty power of God, a certain mighty *vis emissa*, a divine *power* that *issues from* God for the working such and such effects." As for this conceit, pray do but consider the matter thus, Is the Holy Ghost indeed not God, but the power of God? Why this power which it is said to be, is either a created power, or an uncreated one. If it be an uncreated power, He is God, for every thing that is uncreated is God: if he be then a created power, the created power of God, or the power of God, but created, then it seems God did, without power, create this power, and was without power till he had created it: so that he did the act of creation (which is an act of omnipotency) when he was impotent. It supposes, first, an impotent God, and then supposeth him, when he was impotent, to create his own power; that is, when he was without all power, he did that act which requires an infiniteness of power, to wit, to create. I know nothing that carries clearer evidence with it, than this doth, that the Holy Ghost cannot be that created power which these persons pretend to; or cannot be divine power distinct from God, from the very essence of God. Every thing of God is God, and cannot be otherwise. If he were the power of God and not God, he must have been created power, by God; that is to say, God did create omnipotent power, being before impotent; for this it plainly comes to.

Thus far, I think, it is with some competent clearness evident, that these three, the Father, the Word, and the Holy Ghost, (concerning the first, as you have heard, there is no question) are persons; they are that which we cannot conceive of otherwise than under the notion of persons: and they are divine persons, so that there are three divine persons that do subsist in the Godhead, that is but one. So you have this, as the doctrinal truth of this place, and as the real truth in itself, positively evidenced to you.

What is to be said by way of objection against it, we shall next come to. Only upon the whole matter, it seems to me, that there needs a great deal more of humility and reverence and seriousness and fear of the Lord, over-awing the spirits of men, to apprehend this to be the plain doctrine of Scripture, than of further argument in the case. And that will more appear by considering how irrational the pretence is, that this is a thing rationally impossible, that there should be such three, that are but one God. Nothing indeed, would be plainer than that the same cannot be three and one, in one and the same respect: but, that they may be three in one respect, and but one in another respect, we may make appear to be no impossible thing, and that there is nothing of harshness in it, nay, whereof we have parallel instances, (as far as there can be a parity between God and creatures) that occur to us every day. So that one would wonder how men can stumble in so plain a way, and when there is nothing indeed in view that should occasion it, besides their having indulged themselves, I fear, too much liberty to prevaricate in their own minds, and reasonings before, and then they think it reasonable to justify error by erring always, by never retracting, or by endeavouring to make men believe, that things suggested to them as true, are impossible to be true.

LECTURE XIV.*

3. But now to come to the third part of the proposed work, to vindicate the truth of this doctrine laid down, in the proposition, as to what is objected, and alleged against it, which summarily and generally is but this one thing, into which all results; That it is contrary to the common reason of men, and such as doth in itself imply a contradiction, that three should be but one. And thereupon it is determined by the leader of them, Socinus himself, that if any thing do appear to be never so plainly contained in Scripture, if yet also it do appear to imply a contradiction, or to be contrary to natural reason, any, whatsoever violence, ought rather to be put upon the Scriptures than to admit it. And this goes therefore, with the men of that way, for a principle, that whatsoever seems to be repugnant to their reason, or to imply a contradiction, ought to be rejected, though never so plainly expressed in Scripture, or contained therein.

Now first, I shall say here somewhat to this principle in the general, by which these men do steer themselves in this, and all matters of religion besides. And then secondly, I shall say somewhat in the particular application of it in this case, and shew how very untruly it is alleged here, that this is a doctrine repugnant to the common reason of man, and which doth carry a contradiction in itself.

(1.) As to the principle in general, I shall in short say these things to it:

[1.] That if we can be certain, that any thing is repugnant to the reason of man, as it is such and doth in itself imply a

* Preached April the 10th, 1690.

contradiction, it ought to be rejected even in duty to God, and as a piece of homage to him. We do owe that homage to our Maker, as the God of truth, to reject every thing that we are sure is contrary to the common reason of man, which he hath put into him, which is truly and purely reason, and which belongs to the Spirit, unto which by the inspiration of the almighty God, that understanding is given, which distinguishes him from the fowls of the air, and the beasts of the field. We do owe it as a homage to the Author of our nature, to reject whatsoever is manifestly contrary to that reason, and which is in itself a contradiction. First, because he is most confessedly the *primum verum, the first truth.* And as all the beams of the sun, in whatsoever way they do shine to us, whether directly, or by never so various refraction, we are sure are all from the sun; so whatsoever rational dictate, that we are most certain, or can be sure is such, which we find arrive to us, we cannot but be sure that it is from the Father of lights, from whom can issue nothing but light; nothing opposite to light or truth: and secondly, That it is impossible we can in duty, or as a homage to God, believe a contradiction, any thing that carries a contradiction in itself, because the highest and primary reason upon which I am to admit any thing for truth, is as it is a production of the first truth, as hath been told you. But I am certain, the same thing cannot be true and false; and therefore, as a deference to God, I cannot have greater reason to believe it, than I have to disbelieve it. If it carry a contradiction in it, and is pretended to be from God, I cannot believe it for any reason, but for the same reason, I am bound to disbelieve it. There is not more weight in one end of the scale than there is in the other: and so it cannot be believed in that case, as a piece of duty unto God: and thereupon, we are as ready to reject every thing, we are sure is contradictory and repugnant to a manifest dictate of reason, as they can be. But,

[2.] If any thing be plainly contained and expressed in the word of God, that seems repugnant to our reason, we are then certain that the seemingness and semblance is false, because we cannot be surer of any thing than that God is true, and that he can never be deceived himself, nor deceive us: that both verity and veracity are most essential to him; and that it is repugnant to his nature, either to be ignorant of any thing, or to lie unto us in any thing. And therefore,

[3.] When there is this competition between any plain words of Scripture and a seeming dictate of reason, we are to censure the latter by the former, and not the former by the latter: we are to measure the rational dictate, by the divine word, and not the divine word by the seeming rational dictate. And especially,

[4.] When that thing is spoken often in Scripture, in the divine word, and in varied forms of speech, which have all the same manifest sense and meaning, and are not, without the most notorious violence, capable of another. And (which will be the ground of this last mentioned assertion) when,

[5.] That word being professedly and declaredly given us as a rate to measure our sentiments as well as our practices by. If therefore, we should oppose that which seems to us a rational dictate, to the plain expressions of that word, we make that which is to be ruled, the rule; we do in that case regulate our rule, and do not admit that the rule should regulate us. We judge the law, (as the apostle James's expression is, in a case that hath reference to practice, and the case is the same in reference to sentiments, and our judgments of things,) which is certainly very great insolency: that when God, in compassion to the darkness and blindness of our minds, gives us such a rule, a light shining in a dark place unto which we are told, we should do well to take heed, we should reject this rule, and say, we can do better without it, reject this light, and say, we can see better without it. As if one should, out of mere good will, offer himself as a guide to a bewildered traveller that knows nothing of his way, and this traveller should at all turns be controverting with his guide, and say, I know the way and how to steer my course better than you; which would be as well the highest insolency as ingratitude, supposing that guide to be very highly superior and very kindly condescending to do that office in such a case. And again,

[6.] There is yet the more ground for this, when there is among men, and even among wise, and learned, and rational men, a very great division about what is a rational dictate in this case, and what is not. This makes the determination which I have given, to be so much the more reasonable, and makes the pretence on the other hand so much the more absurd, that that should be given for a dictate of common reason wherein most rational men do disagree, at least, therein, as rational men as these pretenders, are of a quite contrary mind: and that cannot be so clear a dictate of common reason, wherein even the most rational men do disagree, and sure then, in that case, one would be glad to be determined by a divine word. And I add,

[7.] That the reason of man, in this our present state, even in things of much inferior concernment, is very dubious and uncertain, in matters wherein religion is not concerned, and so wherein the minds of men are not apt to be perverted by ill inclination, as in the matters of religion they are. For though it be very true, that it is natural for men to be of some religion, yet it is as true and as evident, that there is an aversion and antipathy in the minds and spirits of men against true religion, against sincere, living religion. And if the reason of man be a very dubious, uncertain thing, even when there is nothing to bias one this way or that, as it is in thousands of instances that might be given most apparently; much more cause have we in matters of religion, and of this nature, not to over attribute unto it. In philosophical matters, wherein men's minds cannot, through prejudice be swayed this way or that, and wherein it is no one's interest that this side be true rather than that side, yet there are the greatest difficulties imaginable in determining what is reason and what not, what is true and what not, as all the controversies in philosophy do shew: and some, wherein it is the hardest matter imaginable, even to the greatest wits that have ever been in the world, to free themselves from the appearance of contradiction, which side soever they had in the controversy. As it is most notorious, to any that know any thing in philosophy, about the *compositum continuum*, whether the *continuum*, that is, a body doth consist of parts always divisable, or of indivisable parts; so that bring it to the minutest thing imaginable, even if it be to the breadth of a hair, whether it be still perpetually divisible or indivisible. It is plain, take one side or the other in that question, and hitherto all the wits in the world have not found how, freely and clearly, to disentangle themselves from contradiction in saying, this is always divisible; or it is sometimes impossible to be divided any further, and the apprehension of that doth (I must acknowledge) greatly lower my reverence to that which goes under the notion of a rational dictate, when in such a case as that of any, the minutest thing you can imagine, even the breadth of a hair, no man shall be able to assert either it is always divisible or sometime indivisible, without entangling himself in such appearances of contradiction as from which, the greatest wits that have ever been, have not been able to shew us the way of being extricated. And when there is such a division, even among the masters of reason, the highest pretenders to it; this is a rational dictate, saith the one side, the quite contrary is a rational dictate, saith the other side, even in this very business of the Trinity itself: whilst some with loud clamour cry out against it as impossible to be, others on the other hand, take upon them to demonstrate it to be utterly impossible that it should not be; that there could be no creation, no Creator if there were not a Trinity.

These things being said in reference to that principle in the general, I now come,

(2.) To the application of it to this objection; that is, that this is a doctrine, (say some) to common and rational principles, contradictious in itself, that three should be one.

That we may speak to this with the more clearness, we shall —consider what it is, from Scripture, we assert concerning this matter, and then—shew how unreasonably this is pretended to be repugnant to reason, or to imply any thing of a contradiction.

[1.] What it is we do from Scripture assert in this matter, and what we do not. For we must distinguish here, between plain Scripture doctrine and the bold determinations of some schoolmen. We do not think we are obliged to justify every determination of a confident and presuming schoolman, as if it were divine writ. But what from Scripture we do affirm is, That there are three in the Godhead, that these three are some way distinguished from one another, otherwise they could not be three, there were no pretence to call them three. We find they have distinct names; that is plain—the Father, the Word or Son, and the Spirit or the Holy Ghost, over and over. But there must be somewhat of distinction among themselves, otherwise there were no pretence to call them three, if they were no way distinguishable.

Again, we do affirm they are so far distinguished from one another as, that can be said concerning one which cannot be said concerning the other. As when we say, "The Word was made flesh," (which you know the Scripture speaks,) the meaning is, not that the Father was made flesh, or the Spirit was made flesh, but that the Son was made flesh. When it is said, (as it often is,) that the Spirit or the Holy Ghost is sent by the Father, or the Son, the meaning is, not that the Father sends himself, or that the Son sends himself. Therefore, they are so far distinct from one another as, that is said of the one which cannot be said of the other. But then, how much greater the distinction is, we pretend not to say, because the Scripture doth not say it. Only this we do say, We can think of no notion by which they are so fitly distinguishable as that of personality, as that of their being distinct persons; that we do find plainly said concerning one of them, the Father, (who is so called in that Heb. 1. 3.) that the Son is the express image of his person. So we render the word *hypostasis* fitly and aptly enough. And they being so frequently mentioned together, as we find they are, it doth naturally suggest to us, that there should be a suppositality. And concerning the personality of the Son too, there is no question; but as concerning the Holy Ghost, he being so frequently spoken of under the notion He, and, (as was noted to you) the gender varied on purpose, contrary to strict grammar, we ought also, to conceive of him, under the notion of a person: though at the same time (we have told you) it is impossible that the notion of a person should be the same with God and amongst men, and that for the reason which hath been mentioned to you. Only, we have nothing by which more fitly to conceive it, than by this notion. Then, so much as this, being what we do affirm and assert to be the doctrine of the Scriptures, and to be Scripture in this case, then, I say,

[2.] This is very unreasonable and pretenceless, to affirm that this is contradictious in itself, or any way opposite or contrary to the plain dictates of reason. For where should the contradiction lie? It is only pretended to lie in this, that the same thing cannot be three and one. And it is easily admitted, that the same thing cannot be three and one, in the same respect wherein they are but one. But nothing hinders, but that the same may be, in different respects, that is, in those respects wherein they are three, they are not only one: in that respect wherein they are but one, they cannot be three. But, that in divers respects, the same thing may be three and one, or that there may be a trinity, a triad, in one and the same thing, the instances are so many, so plain and so notorious in other inferior things, that it is absurd and unreasonable to pretend this to be contradictious, or contrary to the dictate of nature. Let us go to the most obvious thing that can be thought of. If I should go no further but only to give you an instance of this book which I have here in my hand, it hath its breadth, its length and its thickness, as you all easily see and apprehend, but its breadth is not its length, nor is its length its thickness, neither of these are one another, yet all the same book: that is, this thing which is so long, so broad and so thick is this book. If we speak of a man, he is a very vegetative creature, and he is a sensitive creature, and he is a rational and intelligent creature, and yet, it is most plain, vegetation is not sensation, nor sensation intellection. The sun, it hath belonging to it, light and heat and motion: that luminous body is the sun, that califective body is the sun, and that moving body is the sun. These three are all but one sun: and yet there are three in it as is evident. The world is full of instances of the like nature. We can hardly think of any sort of things wherein this may not be exemplified. And whereas, the greatest quarrel is about personality, there is nothing more plain than that one and the same man may sustain three persons, the person of a father, the person of a son, and the person of a magistrate, and the like. Many persons may be sustained by one and the same man; the notion of person, in the strict and common sense, being only taken for the circumstances of their state and condition who are spoken of, and not as denoting this or that particular essence; and so to be a man, and this or that person is not all one: and so to be God, and this or that person in the Godhead is not all one. The same man may endure, and may *sustentare*, may put on, and may bear, several persons: and so it is no repugnancy to reason at all that the same God do so too. And therefore, this pretence of the irrationality or contradictiousness of this doctrine, doth itself want a pretence; there can be really no ground for it. And so much hath been so far said, by some of the late zealous contenders in this case the other way, that they are brought to say and publish, that truly he must be a madman that will say there cannot be three persons in the same God. That we find published not long ago: so far doth that pretence vanish, that this doctrine must be rejected as being irrational and contradictory. And if we would take the notion of person and personality, in the most strict and scholastic sense, it would be with very great arrogance that they must pretend this doctrine (taken even in that sense) to be contrary to a common, rational dictate, when as it is so very well known first, that the very notion of individuation or personality, suppositality, or more generally personality, in reference to rational beings, is one of the most disputed things in the world. And how absurd is it to say, that this or that is opposite to a common rational dictate, about which, (as was said before,) the most learned men, and the highest pretenders to reason have constantly disagreed. There must first, before this can be said, some one common notion of personality and individuation be fixed, which all men must assent to, as soon as ever they hear it, that must command assent to it in every man's mind. But about these things there is the greatest disagreement, and hath constantly been, ever since the name of a schoolman or metaphysician hath been known in the world. And then, secondly, besides that, there is so great a disagreement among schoolmen and metaphysicians, about the notions of suppositality, personality and individuality, that they who will conclude this to be against a rational dictate, must be able to evince, that the notion of personality must be the same with us and with God, which it will be impossible for them ever to evince, and the contrary whereof (as hath been said) is demonstrable. That is, were it ever so certain that there cannot be three finite persons partaking the same finite nature, it will be hence no consequence, that there cannot be three infinite persons partaking the same infinite nature, or communicating in the same infinite nature: no reason, for a parallel cannot be drawn so much as with a plausible pretence, between what is finite and what is infinite, in this case.

But to shut up all that I intend, as to the polemical part of this discourse, I shall only leave these few things, which will plainly represent to us that this doctrine may be conceived, and hath not that difficulty in it which commonly hath been thought. As,

First. It is out of all question that God is but one, can be but one. And,

Secondly. That whatsoever is necessarily, is God. Whatsoever is in being, from a necessity in nature, is God; than which no principle can be plainer. And,

Thirdly. That whatsoever is by dependance on the divine will, is creature; whatsoever is not of necessity, but by mere dependance on the divine will, that is all creature. "Thou hast created all things, and for thy pleasure they are and were created."

Fourthly. If therefore, we do suppose the Son and the Holy Ghost to be from the Father, by a necessity of nature, an eternal necessity of nature, and not by dependance upon his will, they will not be creatures, because nothing is creature but what depends upon the will and pleasure of the Creator. And if they be not creatures, what are they then? Then they must be God, and yet both of them from the Father too: for all that do assert the Trinity, do acknowledge the Father to be *fons trinitatis, the fountain of the Trinity:* and if from this fountain, the Son be one way, and the Holy Ghost be another way, both from the Father; that is, the Son from the Father immediately, and the Holy Ghost from the Father and the Son, and this, not by choice, but by an eternal necessity of nature, here is this doctrine as easily conceivable as any that I know of whatsoever, that lies not within the compass of our manifest demonstration. And my business is not now to demonstrate to you that thus it is, but that it is very easily conceivable that thus it may be. That is, that the Son and the Holy Ghost may be from the Father, and that we are sure they are from him by an eternal necessity of nature, and not by choice. It is not by his pleasure they are and were, but by eternal necessity of nature they are from him as he is originally from himself. That is, they are always and eternally in that nature which is self-originate. And here is no contradiction, nor the least appearance or shadow of it in all this.

And thus far now, hath our labour been taken up as to this subject, about the truth of it: that is, to prove and to vindicate it. Our next business, which only remains, will be about the importance of it, the great usefulness of it, and the mighty weight and stress that lie upon it. At present I leave this with you, that I know nothing more needful to clear our apprehensions, and make our minds very calm and serene, in reference to this doctrine of the Trinity than first, high, adoring thoughts of God, and secondly, mean thoughts of ourselves. If we can but think highly enough of God, and meanly enough of ourselves, and how unmeet and incompetent such moles and worms of the earth as we are, must needs be to make an estimate of his nature, and how things are with him, otherwise than he is pleased graciously and freely to declare to us concerning himself, there will be nothing then in all this doctrine that we shall stumble at, nothing that we shall receive with difficulty, and nothing but what we may receive with great use and advantage to ourselves.

LECTURE XV.[*]

Therefore, now for the *importance* and *use* of this doctrine, much may be conceived of that, if it be considered how the stamp and impression of a Trinity doth run through the world. A noted writer, of our time, hath said very much to that purpose, of which I shall say but little. Take the whole universe of created beings and you have every where a Trinity instamped. It is observable enough in that great triad, the several things conceivable under each member, of nature, morality and religion. But it is with religion that we are concerned, and wherein the practice of it doth principally appear, and is most considerable. Our religion you do know, objectively considered, is made up of doctrines to be believed, and of duties to be done, and of benefits to be sought, and these are comprised in those three noted summaries, the creed, the decalogue, and the Lord's prayer. In these three, there is some impression and resemblance of the Trinity in the divine nature. That is, of that power and of that wisdom and knowledge, and of that benignity and love, which are the three great most noted principles we have to conceive of, and that we cannot but distinctively conceive of, we cannot otherwise

[*] Preached April 17. 1691.

conceive of, than as distinct in the simple union of the Godhead; and which may probably enough correspond to, and be the very notion of, Father, Son, and Spirit.

Why now, if we consider doctrinals in the first place, the doctrines that do make up the first and most noble part of the scheme of religion, you know how they all depend upon, and are reduced to, the notions that are given us of the Father, Son and Holy Ghost; upon these three heads hangs the frame of Christian doctrine. That is, of the Father considered as God Creator; and of the Son considered as God Redeemer; and of the Holy Ghost considered as God Sanctifier. Which three great works of God, though it be true that they do each of them owe themselves to the concurrence of each of the persons according to that known maxim, *opera Trinitatis ad extra sunt indivisa:** which is undoubtedly a true and clear one: yet each of these is appropriated to each of the persons severally, not exclusively, but eminently. And that we may understand that aright, when it is said, the Father creates, it is to be understood eminently, not exclusively, of the Son and the Holy Ghost; and so as to the rest. When we profess to believe in God as the Creator of heaven and earth, that is, in God the Father, as he is the first Fountain of all being, uncreated and created too; why though that be plainly said, yet it is as plainly said, that without the Word was nothing made; and that by him, that is, the Word, even he—who is said to be " the brightness of his Father's glory and the express image of his person," the worlds were made: and that they were made by the Spirit of his mouth; and that the Spirit did move upon the waters, that is, upon the fluctuating chaos, which we must suppose to have been first made, before things were made out of it: and that it was first made is the most demonstrable thing, in all the world; otherwise, it were, itself, a necessary and self original being, and so God; the notion of God would not be all-comprehending, or there would be something *præter Deum, besides God*, originally and naturally, and of itself. So again, as to the work of redemption, that was designed by the Father, but wrought by the Son, and applied by the Holy Ghost. These are plain things and abundantly evident in Scripture as, if I should turn from text to text, you would see. But I must suppose you to understand it already. You cannot then but see the mighty importance of this doctrine of the Trinity in our religion. We shall have occasion to press that further by and by. But now hereupon, I shall, for putting a period to the discourse on

* The Holy Trinity, in external operations, is not divided.

this subject, subjoin several instructions in reference hereto. As,

1. That we should all learn to adore the wonderful divine condescension, that he should so far unveil himself, and make known so much of the things of his own nature and being, to such despicable beings as we. We can never wonder enough at this. Indeed, I have many times considered, it is a very instructive thing, that so many of the pagans should discover so very reverential thoughts of God, upon this account, and under this notion, as they apprehend his Being to be inscrutable, unsearchable, as that inscription on one of their temples doth import, "I am he that was, and he that is, and he that shall be, and no one hath ever unfolded my veil." Such reverential apprehensions, had they (however they came by them,) of the inscrutableness and occultness of the Divine Being, that there were such arcana, such secrets veiled from all eyes, that could never possibly be looked into. Now that God should take such poor creatures as any of us are, and let us see so far into the veil, that, whereof we could have had no certain apprehensions, if he had not told us, how wonderful is it! Though some have made it very much their business, (after they had got the hint from Scripture concerning the Trinity,) to shew how rational it was; not only to shew how consistent it was with reason, (which is a very justifiable undertaking and a great piece of right done to our religion,) some carry the matter higher, (as I told you,) and undertake to demonstrate it to be necessary, and that we cannot conceive of the nature of God, and of that great work of his, the creation of the world, in reference to one another otherwise. But this is to strain beyond what the exigency of the case doth require. It may however, (by that improvement I have already made of it too,) serve somewhat to rebuke the proud confidence of that sort of men, who represent this doctrine as contrary to a common, rational dictate, the common sense and reason of mankind. That is most insolently pretended when, as (unless they will assume to themselves that there can be no such thing as a rational dictate, that is not stamped at their mint) I say, unless they would assume that to themselves, it must appear very incongruous to pretend that such a thing is impossible to be, when others at the same time, (who may for ought I know lay as good a claim to that of being the men, and that wisdom shall die with them as they can,) should say with so much confidence, it is impossible not to be; and that there could be no such thing as a Creator and a creation, if it were not so.

But waving this disquisition, since it is most certainly not impossible in itself, it is very adorable that God should come, and so graciously discover to us that so it is; when we see how useful it is, and how expedite a frame of religion it lays open before us: that he should discourse to such children, such weaklings as we, at that rate concerning his own nature; "I will tell you how things are with me: now in the Godhead these are co-existent from all eternity, Father, Son and Spirit: and this I would not have hid from you; I would have you to be possessed with right notions and apprehensions of my nature thus far, that thus it is with me, and in me." You would wonder that a great and wise prince should take upon him to discourse his arcana with a peasant, a mean, ignorant peasant. But we do not enough wonder at this condescension of God, upon this ground, that we do not enough set ourselves to consider the distance between God and creatures, and what mere nothings we are to him, and that when we have the most exalted thoughts that our minds are capable of, concerning any created being whatsoever, and then descending to the meanest sort of creatures we can think of, the distance is not only greater, but it is still infinitely greater between the great God and us. What then have we left to do, but to fall down and wonder, fall down and adore, and cry out, "Whence is it to us that thou shouldest let us know so much of thyself?" that whereas, the things of God are never to be known distinctly, otherwise than as the Spirit of God doth reveal them, that Spirit of God should be the Author to us, of such a revelation as this, which we have contained in the Bible, concerning this great and most important mystery.

2. Let us learn this too, not to think it a small matter, now that we are informed that there is in the Godhead, Father, Son and Spirit; that all three should so far concern themselves as we find they do, and be so constantly concerned as they are about our affairs. If all the potentates on earth should concern themselves about the life of one single fly, it were not so strange a thing, it were not so great a stoop. We should consider with ourselves over and over, What am I? what am I, and what is my life, that the eternal Father, and the eternal Son, and the eternal Spirit, should all concern themselves from eternity about me? And again,

3. It should further instruct us into this, to fasten the apprehension deep in our souls, of the great concernment of the doctrine, that it may lie with weight upon us, as a seal that doth not make impression unless it be pressed on; that we should endeavour and intend more to press on this doctrine, this truth upon our own souls, that it may make the proper,

due impression, that we may be delivered up into the mould and form of it: as the expression is, Rom. 6. 17. And to that purpose, let us bethink ourselves, how miserably (where this doctrine is not entertained) the scheme of Christianity, and the Christian religion are scattered and torn by the want, or by the denial of it. This apprehension should urge us so as that the doctrine should lie with greater weight and pressure upon our spirits, because where it is not received, away go the great limbs of Christian religion. The Deity of the Son of God, that is abandoned and cashiered: well, and what then becomes of our religion? Do you not think yourselves concerned in this matter? What! Are you willing to venture your souls otherwise than in the hands of a Divine Saviour, when you know yourselves to be sinners, to be guilty creatures? Do you think it will answer the exigency of your case, to have an atonement made for you of no greater value than if one mere man were made a sacrifice for another? And if that would do, suppose one man were as good as another; why inasmuch as all are sinners, when he goes to satisfy another's sin, who shall satisfy for his sin? Or how shall he satisfy for his own? And suppose an innocent man should be made on purpose (as it is supposed in this present case) to be a sacrifice; that is still but man for man. It is true, he hath no sin of his own to satisfy for, but suppose he could satisfy for the sin of another man, there must then, be as many innocent men created as there are guilty men, at that rate. But would not you be loath to hazard your souls upon such conceits as these? and to quit your hold of a mighty God for your Saviour? of this assurance, that he who is to be your Saviour is known by the name of "the mighty God, the everlasting Father, and the Prince of Peace?" Would you be content to abandon this, that he is to be your Saviour who is God blessed for ever; who before the worlds were made was with God; and in time was made flesh, and dwelt among us; that word that was with God, and that was God, and by which all things were made, without which nothing was made, that was made, was made flesh? An amazing thing it is to me, how men that pretend to believe the divine authority of the Bible, can disentangle themselves from such a place as this, "The Word was made flesh." They that will have Jesus Christ never to have been, no such person ever to have been, before he was born of the Virgin Mary, I would then know of them, "What was that, that was made flesh?" It was the word that was made flesh; there was somewhat before this flesh was made, or it was nothing, that was made flesh. And every one that understands the ordinary use of this expression (flesh) knows it doth not signify the person of a man, but the whole of a man, not the body only: for when it is said, "in his sight there shall no flesh be justified," what is the meaning of that? That the bodies of men shall not be justified? Surely not. But thus, from not believing this doctrine, proceeds the denial of that great and noble propitiation, once for all made for the sins of men, under the proper notion of a propitiation or an expiatory sacrifice to atone for sin, and take away guilt. Again hereupon,

The eternal priesthood of the Son of God is evacuated and reduced to a nullity: and all upon this, that an alterity cannot be conceived in the Godhead. Not that there is therein, *Aliud et aliud, one diverse from another*, but that there is there *personæ altera et altera, one person distinct from another*. But because this is not apprehended, nor will be apprehended, therefore, say they, There can be no such thing as a propitiatory sacrifice, such as we, such as the Scripture, such as the gospel doth most expressly speak of, that is, of him who was God offered up unto God. For, say they, There is but one person in the Godhead; and a satisfier and a satisfied, must be two persons, there must be in such a case an alterity of persons *personæ altera et altera*, and so they truly reason. He that doth satisfy and he that is satisfied must be two persons: this is most certain, but they, not admitting the alterity of persons, therefore exclude the whole doctrine. And then,

That mighty power that is to go forth from the Divine Spirit, for the breaking of the bands of iron, and the rescuing of captive souls out of the devil's power; to turn men from darkness to light, and from the power of Satan unto God, all that is reduced to nothing too. And so there is no other Christianity left in the world but a certain sort of self-sprung religion: no power but that which I can be the author of to myself, what I have of mine own: or else if they will have more, they do speak altogether unintelligibly and contrary to the plain sense of things: that is, they will not have the Holy Ghost to be a distinct person in the Godhead, but (as they call it) the power of God, meaning a quality. But I take what hath been said against that, to be truly as plain demonstration as can be used in any case whatsoever. The Holy Ghost is called the divine power. Comply with them so far, then say I, This divine power is either created power or uncreated. If this divine power be created, then they must suppose God, while he was without power to create power; that is, that God being first impotent, created power and became omnipotent. But if they will say, It is an uncreated power, then they say what we say: then it is God: the Holy Ghost is God. But he is God so as he is capable of being sent, and sent of the Father, and so that he must be a distinct person in the Godhead. But the stress of all that mighty affair which is to be wrought in the souls of men, when they are sanctified; of children of the devil, and friends of hell, to be made children of God, and meet to be partakers of an inheritance with them that are sanctified, with the saints in light: all that mighty work that is to be done by an Almighty Spirit, must be proportionally diminished as the cause is diminished, as the agent is diminished and reduced, by their doctrine, to a mere creature. Therefore, I say, labour to apprehend deeply, the mighty importance of this doctrine, and to fix the apprehensions of it, and to have it wrought in your souls, that so such a truth may no more be capable of being torn away from thence than one faculty of your souls can be torn from another. And,

4. Labour to savour and relish such truth, this truth, this doctrine, labour to get the savour and relish of it into your souls; that is, to receive this truth in the love of it. It is a matter of dangerous importance, when truth of this kind which concerns the vitals of religion, is received merely as an airy notion, and is not digested, doth not enter and sink deep into our hearts, and that which must entertain and admit there: even into the very centre of our souls must be the love of it. "They received not the truth in the love of it, that they might be saved." 2 Thess. 2. 10. And what became of that matter? When they did so lightly adhere to divine truth as one doth to a thing that he doth not love, or that is not united to his soul by love, they easily suffered their souls to be cheated of it: and then, for their not loving this truth, (it being a thing most highly criminal not to love divine truth, not to love so great and sacred a thing) God gave them up to strong delusions, to believe lies, that they all might be damned who received not the truth, but had pleasure in unrighteousness. Such truth they could take no pleasure in, but they could take pleasure in unrighteousness. "Let them go," saith God, "the way that the inclinations of their own wicked hearts carries them to." There is that kindred, that alliance between the soul and truth, that there is a violence done to both if they be severed, and if the soul do not inwardly love truth, as that which is most nearly allied to it. They that are after the Spirit do savour the things of the Spirit, as they that are after the flesh do savour the things of the flesh. And this is the way to become most stable christians, when souls and truth come to be united and knit together in love, meet-

ing in one and the same common centre, and even in this as the centre; as you may see in that place which I will recommend to your present perusal, and future serious thoughts. Colos. 2. 2. Saith the apostle, " I would, that ye knew what great conflict I have had for you, (as he introduceth it to them by what he saith in the foregoing verse) that your hearts might be comforted, being knit together in love, and unto all riches of the full assurance of understanding, to the acknowledgment of the mystery of God." And what is comprehended in this mystery of God? that is, of the Father and of Christ; it is generally expressed first, "the mystery of God," and then particularly, "of the Father and of Christ." The former *and*, is not copulative but exigetical: "To the acknowledgment of the mystery of God, and," that is, even, or to wit, of the Father and of Christ. That is, the mystery of God doth comprehend these two. The Holy Ghost is not always mentioned, being expressly enough so in many other texts. But here is the very sum of our religion in this mystery, "the mystery of God," to wit, "of the Father and of Christ;" two particular expressions including the general one, from both which, (as other scriptures sufficiently instruct us,) the Holy Ghost issues forth, as the great and mighty Agent to accomplish all the great things, which by Christian religion are to be effected in the world. And this was the apostle's deep concern on the behalf of these christians. "You cannot imagine," saith he, "what conflict I have about these things; that you might be strong christians:" and how? "That you may be knit together in love, unto the riches of the full assurance of understanding," all loving together, all agreeing together to love the same truths, the same doctrines, and thereby to have it incorporated, inwrought into you, that you may be able to say, "I can as soon suffer limb to be torn from limb, as suffer such truth as this to be torn away from my soul:" that that is to be bought and never to be sold, never to be parted with on any terms, "What! part with that? or be indifferent towards that? or let my mind hover or be in suspense? why it is my very life, my life lies here: shall I in the midst of a tempestuous sea, being safely brought to a firm and stable rock, quit my rock and go to floating again amidst the raging waves?" So will any man reckon in this matter, that hath any care or concern for his soul. Again,

5. You may hence learn, how we are to eye God in our transacting the great business of covenanting with him; that is, as God the Father, God the Son, and God the Holy Ghost; which that initial seal of the covenant doth plainly enough dictate, when we are required to be baptized in the name of the

Father, and of the Son and of the Holy Ghost. When I enter into covenant with God to take him for my God, if I am first solemnly to do it yet; or if I am with solemnity, from time to time, to renew my covenant, we must consider how we are to do it; we must not think of taking God abstractly or taking one person alone. But we must take God the Father, and God the Son, and God the Holy Ghost for our God. Do not think your baptism signifies nothing, when it is directed to be administered in that order, in the name of the Father, the Son and the Spirit. So you are to consider with yourselves, "I am to be a devoted one, I am a devoted one, and must continue so, to God the Father, God the Son, and God the Holy Ghost." A wonderful thing that we should be a congregation of such persons dwelling on earth, who have these names named upon us, that such a claim should be laid from heaven to us, I claim every one of you for mine, for mine, saith the Father, you were baptized in my name; and so the rest. Why should we not walk up and down this world with this sense on our minds, with this thought often renewed, often impressed upon us?

LECTURE XVI.*

6. It lets us see how we are to understand the relation that results from such a covenant between God and us, whereby we become related to God the Father, God the Son, and God the Holy Ghost, and they become related to us: you have heard under what distinct notions, principally, but not exclusively, each of the persons is related to us. The Father as Creator, not excluding the Son and Spirit: the Son as Redeemer, not excluding the Father and Spirit, the Spirit as Sanctifier, not excluding the Father and Son. We have shewn you concerning each of these, that creative power (according as the Scripture teacheth us to conceive) is from the Father, as the Fountain, through the Son as the way of its conveyance, (in respect whereof some speak of a natural mediatorship belonging unto the Son of God before the ordinate one) and by the agency of the Holy Ghost, who is represented as the immediate Agent in all the operations of God towards the creature, whether in the sphere of nature or of grace. And we are to look upon the Son as under the notion of the Redeemer, but so as to understand that this redemption

* Preached April 24, 1691.

was designed by the Father, and is applied by the Holy Ghost: and upon the Holy Ghost as the Sanctifier, and yet still to understand that this his sanctifying work was pre-determined by the Father, procured by the Son, and effected by himself. When therefore, we are to consider God as related to us as our God, ("this God is our God, he will be our guide even unto death") we must take in and bring together each of these notions, and conceptions concerning him; we must take in the conceptions of each of the persons, " God the Father, God the Son, and God the Holy Ghost is my God." Somewhat agreeable to what the ancient philosopher saith, concerning relatives, *Relata sunt quorum totum esse est ad aliud*; that is, *relatives are such things, the whole of which appertains to another.* Why so? All that is conceivable in the Divine Being is, in this case, all to us. The fulness of God is to be considered with relation to us so far as is needful. so far as we are capable: he doth not reserve himself from us in any thing of it. How admirable a thing is this! How great and high thoughts ought we to have concerning the privilege state of our case! Indeed, there is nothing that we have to consider of this God, or to look after the knowledge of, to answer the curiosity of a vain mind; but every thing or any thing that may answer the necessity of a perishing soul, of a soul that must otherwise be miserable and lost. Whatsoever is requisite to our real felicity and blessedness, we may look to all that is in God as determined by a special relation unto us. " As I am such (saith God) I am such entirely yours, all for you, wholly yours." Therefore, did the everlasting covenant that comprehends and conveys all this, yield such solace to the soul of dying David, 2 Sam. 23. 5. "Thou hast made with me an everlasting covenant ordered in all things and sure, for this is all my salvation and all my desire." ' I care for nothing beyond this.' The great thing that the covenant doth convey, is God: and by it, it is, that God the Father, Son and Spirit do become related to us as ours, if once we do take hold of the covenant, if once we put in our claim, and do but lay the ground by that act of our own interest: our claimable interest doth depend upon that; that very act of taking, accepting, "laying hold" as the expression is in that 56 Isaiah, for the encouragement of poor strangers that might possibly apprehend they were quite cut off from God. "No, let the sons of the strangers that take hold of my covenant encourage themselves; that makes me theirs: I am theirs, if they do but lay hold; it is but take and have," as afterwards, in this chapter where the text is, it is said concerning the Son especially, "He that hath the Son hath life, and he that hath not the Son hath not life." And he hath him who hath once taken him. Again,

7. This serves specially to instruct us concerning our application to God in prayer. That is, that we must still comprehend in our thoughts, Father, Son, and Spirit together; the Father, Word, and Holy Ghost, as it is expressed in the text. I know and have particularly understood from some, that they have been full of dubious, perplexing thoughts, how to steer aright in their applications to God, making their solemn addresses so as to run into neither of those things which they have pretended to have been, both of them, their fear and confusion: on the one hand, by not ascribing distinctly to each of the persons what they should; or blasphemy on the other hand, by ascribing what was not due; what was not to be ascribed. But our way is very plain, if we do but consider what the Scriptures say concerning these three substances in the Godhead, and what copies it sets us of applying ourselves hereupon. That is, to the eternal Father, through the eternal Son, by the eternal Spirit; so we ought to apply ourselves, and here is nothing to lead us into confusion or indistinction of thoughts in so doing. It is plain we have the Father always represented as the original Foundation of all light, all life, all being, all excellency, all perfection, whether created or uncreated. He is then a most adequate terminative Object of our worship in such application and supplication. We go properly to the Fountain of all good. Whither should we go else? But he is (especially to those that have been in delinquency and transgression) inaccesible: we need a mediator: there could no mediator answer the exigency of our case, that was not God as well as man: we need a Divine Mediator, a God Mediator, we cannot expect that God should do any thing for us but for the sake of God, or for his sake who was God: so we are always taught to apply ourselves, to direct our addresses: and so we are to expect the answers of them: that is, that prayer must ascend through Christ, and that blessings are to descend through him. "Blessed be the God and Father of our Lord Jesus, who has blessed us with all spiritual blessings in heavenly places," through him. Eph. 1. 3. And we are to suppose that whatsoever is done for us, in answer to our prayers, when they are accepted, it must be by the agency of the Holy Ghost. The state of our case is such, as to require an infinite almighty Agent to work in us, and to work for us, the things that are necessary to our present support, and to our final blessedness. And we are hereupon, taught by our Lord himself, in respect to the final and terminative Object of

such worship, (that of prayer for instance) to pray unto the Father; "Our Father which art in heaven"—so we are taught to pray. "I bow my knees unto the Father of our Lord Jesus Christ." Ephes. 3. 14. Yea, and so our Lord Jesus Christ did pray himself: "I will pray the Father and he shall give you another Comforter." John 14. 16. "Father forgive them; for they know not what they do." Luke 23. 24. And to him he renders solemn acknowledgment by way of thanksgiving. "I thank thee, O Father, Lord of heaven and earth." Matth. 11. 25. And when he did so, (as we find his was a very praying life, in the days of his flesh, here in this world,) it is very vainly and foolishly alleged that then he must, according to our doctrine and notion, be supposed to pray to himself: it is a very vain and idle pretence. And so I find indeed, that the arguments of that sort of adversary, that is, they that do impugn the divinity of the Son of God, tend to prove, generally, nothing but that which we never deny, that is, that Christ was man. This is the thing that by many arguments they set themselves most industriously to prove, which none of us deny, that Christ was man. Who doth doubt it? But they would thence conclude that because he is man, therefore he could not be God; which is their absurd and foolish consequence, when we know it was so plainly, so very plainly said, that the Word which, in that text, is said to be with God, is also said to be God: and the same Word is said to be made flesh, to be incarnate, to have assumed and taken on flesh: that is, not as if it did, in becoming flesh, cease to be what it was before, but did only add an assumed nature to a divine; and therefore, there being two natures now meeting together in that one person, it was no way unintelligible, but that he should do that in the one nature which was impossible he should do in or by the other. That is, as man he did grow, and as a man he did die, and as man he did pray, whenas God he could do none of these. But he that was God did do these things, though not as he was God. He that was God, did lay down his life, as in that 3rd. chapter of this epistle, verse 16. "Hereby perceive we the love of God, that he" (that same he that was God) "laid down his life for us." And so he that was God, shed his blood for us. Acts 20. 28. "Feed the flock of God (his church) which he hath purchased with his own blood;" his own, who was God; though as God, we know he could neither bleed nor have blood. But whereas, the Son of God, as he was the Son of God and God, did pray, and praying, apply himself to the Father, so are we to do, to pray, and in praying, apply ourselves to the Father as we are led by that great example. But then, we being nothing but creatures, we have the whole Deity in view as the Object of our worship and addresses. But not the Deity, abstractly considered, but the Deity as subsisting in these three persons. The Deity abstractly considered, in the case of our Lord himself, was neither the Object, nor the Subject of prayer; God, as God, did neither pray nor was prayed unto by him; did not pray, for it was the man, the man Christ that prayed; nor abstractly, nor merely as God, was he the Object of prayer: but as the Godhead did subsist in the person of the Father, so did the man Christ apply himself to him, and so could in no sort be said to pray to himself, in praying to him. But now, I say, we who are nothing but creatures, we have the entire Godhead, not abstractly, but as subsisting in three persons, to apply ourselves unto, and those persons conceived of, according to the order they are represented to stand towards one another, and to be related one to another. As we told you already, when we pray to the Father, as the final and terminative Object of our prayers, we are at the same time, to conceive the Son as through whom the prayer is to be transmitted, together with the answer, the good we are to expect and pray for: and the Holy Ghost, as by whose power to pray, and by whose power the answer of prayer is to be effected too. And so it is God that our prayers must respect, God to whom, God through whom, and God by whom. Pray to God, through God and from God, and so our prayer hath every way to do with God. Our prayer, as it is to be through the mediation of Christ, so both it and its answer are to be wrought by the Holy Ghost: we are in that great and sacred work of praying, to deliver up ourselves to the conduct of the Holy Ghost, and so we are to do in the whole of our course. "As many as are the sons of God they are led," *oracled* (as that word signifies, Rom. 8. 14) "by the Spirit of God." Which Spirit is a Spirit of adoption, (as it afterwards follows,) the Spirit that belongs to the state of worship, as they are sons, that teaches them to cry "Abba Father." And because they are sons, he hath sent the Spirit of his Son into their hearts, as it is said in that parallel place, Gal. 4. 6. And we are required to pray alway in the Spirit. Ephes. 6. 18. And in the Holy Ghost: 20th verse of the epistle to Jude. "Praying in the Holy Ghost, keep yourselves in the love of God, looking for the mercy of our Lord Jesus Christ unto eternal life."

Put all this together, and then every prayer of ours, ought to respect each person in the Godhead. That is, it ought to be to God, through God, and from God: even as the answer, it is to be in the same order, originally God's answer, through Christ, and by the Holy Ghost. And so we run into no confusion, when we suffer ourselves to be governed by Scripture light. And we can be in no danger of incurring the guilt of blasphemy: for we do not ascribe to any of these persons more than the Scripture doth plainly teach us to ascribe. And as our Saviour saith concerning himself, so may we concerning each of these persons: when the Scripture saith so and so, and doth attribute such and such things to them, will any one say, that he blasphemes that saith, that the eternal Father is God, or the eternal Son is God, or the eternal Spirit is God? Scripture most expressly saying these things as words can speak them. And again,

8. This should further teach us how to steer our whole course in this world: our business here on earth, ought to be (in the main of it) religion: we ought to make religion our business. The business of religion, while we are in this imperfect state, is only a motion Godward. The religion of the way, is coming to God. So that any one who is sincerely religious and Godly, will be able to make answer to this question, What is the main business of your life? This true answer he can make, "My main business is to make towards God, I am aiming at God, tending towards God, as one that hath been removed and set at a distance from him, and so am to be brought back to him." It was this, Christ died for, the just for the unjust, to bring us to God. Now this being the state of our case, we are distant from him, in nearness to whom consists our duty and felicity. When we are to take and direct our course Godward, we must have a final term for our motion: "Whither are you going?" "Why my course is tending and directed Godward." This motion must have for its ultimate term, God the Father. This is the sense and language of an inquiring soul, when once it comes to understand what the Scripture doth so plainly reveal; that there are in the Godhead, Father, Son and Holy Ghost. Their sense, I say, is what we find expressed, John 14. 8. "Shew us the Father and it sufficeth us:" "do but shew us the Father, and we have enough: our great inquiry is after the Father, the Fountain and Original of all things, in whom is our life and our only hope." "Well," saith our Saviour (meeting that genius and sense of such an inquirer) "I know where you would be, and who you are seeking: and have you so long known me, and are ignorant of the Father? Come, I will be your Conductor, I will be your Guide, no man cometh to the Father but by me." And therefore, as there must be a final term of this motion, so there must be a way leading thereto. "Why, I am the way, the truth and the life, (John 14. 6.) no man cometh unto the Father, but by me." What is consider-

able in all motion, is especially considerable in this. In every motion there must be a final term, and there must be a way to move in. The Father, he is the final term—the Son, he tells us, he is the way. But then there must be a third thing, there must be an acting, moving principle besides, and that must be the Holy Ghost, and can be no other. It is by that one Spirit that all who shall approach to God must have access to him, even to him the Father, considered under the notion of the Father. Jews and Gentiles have been wont (as that was the noted distinction) to divide the world. Now we find both spoken of in the same context, Ephes. 2. His business was to make them nigh who were afar off. The Gentiles were afar off, the Jews were comparatively nigh: now Christ was to make them nigh too, and both of them were to have access by one and the same Spirit to the Father: from the 18th to the 18th verse. Whoever have a mind to return, to come back to God, (from whom, in the common apostacy, all have made a defection and cut themselves off,) here is the course and method of their proceedure, they must propound to themselves God the Father, (the Fountain of all life and blessedness) to whom they must come, to whom they must be bending and directing their course, and to whom they must guide their course in the way he hath prescribed, and that is, by his own Son: "No man cometh to the Father (saith our Saviour) but by me." And they must be acted on in this way towards that final term and end, by the power of the Holy Ghost. There can be no motion without the concurrence of such a third, unto which there is a correspondency here. That is, no man can move, but he moves somewhither towards some term, nor can he move, but it must be in some way. Nor again, can he move but it must be from some motive principle, that carries him through this way to that end. And so you may easily represent to yourselves the business of your lives here in this world. My business is from day to day, to tend towards the eternal Father by the eternal Son and under the conduct and influence of the eternal Spirit. These are obvious and useful instructions, in reference to the doctrine that hath been opened to you from the text, that do more directly concern and relate to the subject we have thus far been upon.

But there is somewhat else, in reference to the present purpose, upon this subject, which is collateral, and will be of use to us, however, to take notice of too. Our great design upon this text, was to observe to you, that there are such a three in the Godhead; three and no more, as we have observed and insisted, of one certain order, Father, Son, and Spirit, that do subsist in the Godhead, which is but one. But the apostle doth here not only take notice what they are, that are thus in heaven, but what also they do, how they are employed, amidst the glory of the heavenly state. And he tells us they "bear record in heaven: the Father, the Word and the Holy Ghost, and these three are one." You see who the witnesses are, in the words of the text, and may see, a little lower, what is the matter of their testimony, (as I was hinting to you but now) that is, in sum, the truth of the Christian religion, or the whole constitution of the Mediator. This is the record, (as it is presently subjoined) that God hath given us eternal life, and that this life is in his Son. He hath an infinite fulness of life to convey, to communicate, and to diffuse through a desolate world, a world lost in death and darkness. And how is it to be conveyed? in what way is it to be communicated? Why it is all treasured up in his Son, he hath constituted and appointed a Mediator, that in him it might be deposited, and that by him and through him, it might be transmitted and made to diffuse itself, and flow amongst lost and perishing souls. This was the matter of this testimony. Why let us take so much of instruction from hence,

That since those Three glorious Three that are in heaven, are bearing record to the truth of our religion, of Christianity, that is, that God hath a design to communicate life to lost and perishing souls, and hath treasured up that life in order to this communication in his Son: since this is their record, their testimony, I pray let us take care that we duly receive it. Be afraid of slighting that testimony, the matter whereof, is of so great importance to ourselves, and the Authors whereof, are the three glorious Persons in the Godhead, so venerable and so great Ones. When they are said to bear record in heaven, or to testify in heaven, the meaning is, not that their testimony is performed in heaven terminative, but originaliter, that is, these witnesses do testify from heaven, concerning this matter which is of so great importance to the sons of men on earth. And pray see that we receive their testimony, as after it follows; If the testimony of a man (who is of any credit) ought not to be slighted; the testimony of God is greater. We have the testimony of God the Father, God the Son, and God the Holy Ghost, concerning this one thing, that there is a design of saving sinners, and giving life to them through his Son, and that this life is only in this way to be communicated and conveyed to perishing and undone souls: what an awe should this lay upon our souls that are perishing! And it is to us, that this salvation is offered. They are dead themselves, as the apostle's expression is, "You are dead, but your life is hid with Christ in God." This being the state of our case, tremble at the thought of slighting such a record, such a testimony, that proceeds from these three great Witnesses that do bear record in heaven. That is, the Father testifies concerning his Son, "This is my beloved Son in whom I am well pleased:" The Son, that eternal Word, testifying concerning the man to whom he united himself, replenishing that man with a divine glory, so as that glory descending from heaven, and accompanying him in his descent from heaven, shone visibly in him as the glory of the only begotten Son of the Father, full of grace and truth. For he, at the same time when, after his descent, he had united himself with flesh is said to be the Son of Man, who came down from, and who is in, heaven. John 3. 13. He was therefore. testifying from heaven, and was actually in heaven, when also he was actually united with this man on earth. And the Holy Ghost, he testifying from heaven, by descending on this same man, in visible glory like a dove and lighting upon him. Thus, here was God the Father, testifying from heaven, and the eternal Word testifying, and the ever blessed Spirit testifying, from heaven, and their testimony meeting all in one point, namely, that Christ the Mediator is he by whom life is to be conveyed from the God of all grace unto undone, perishing, lost souls.

And consider in reference to this further, that as this is a testimony to us, it is our concernment, and is incumbent on us so to comport ourselves as that it may finally prove a testimony for us, and not a testimony against us. This testimony is directly to us, that is, that this is God's appointed way for saving lost souls and bringing of them to life and blessedness, and consequently, according as the design of this testimony is comported with or not, it will be either for us or against us. For us, if it can be recorded at last concerning us, such and such have had the gospel preached unto them, Christ hath been offered, God hath been offering himself in Christ; and they have obeyed the gospel, they have complied with the call, they have received the Son of God. Oh! how great a thing would it be to have a record in heaven for that? How did Job solace himself in this, "My record is in heaven." When you can appeal to the records in heaven touching transactions between God and you, and you can say, "Lord, thou didst make an offer to me of thy Son, thou didst require me to receive him as my Lord and Saviour; I have done so, I appeal to thee whether it be not recorded above, let the records of heaven be searched, see, whether I be not recorded a believer, one that hath resigned up my soul to God in Christ by the power of the eternal Spirit, to be entirely and absolutely his for ever. O! how blessed a thing will it be to have such a record in heaven concerning you and for you? He that knows all things knows that such a one hath received Christ in truth, such a one hath truly believed, such a one loves the Lord Jesus in sincerity."

And how fearful, by consequence, will it be to have it recorded in heaven against you " So long, so many days, so many years hath such a one lived under the gospel,—so often hath a Christ been tendered to him, and been refused by him, and there he stands in the records of heaven, a refuser of the grace of God, refuser of his Christ, despiser of the great salvation, that hath been published and proclaimed and " begun to be spoken by the Lord himself, and was confirmed by them that heard him, God bearing them witness by divers miracles and gifts of the Holy Ghost."

And besides, that we are thus to take notice of what is doing above; how these Three employ themselves, their bearing record in heaven, consider too (and therewith I shall shut up all) where it is that this work is doing, that these Three are bearing this record in heaven. Let us consider a little, and take this instruction from it, that it very ill becomes us to alienate ourselves from heaven and disregard the affairs and concerns of heaven. For we find that our affairs and concernments who dwell on earth are minded in heaven. In heaven there is a concern about such poor, wretched creatures as we upon earth. It is very unworthy dealing if we live here upon earth, groveling in the dust of it, and very seldom think any thought of heaven. When, in heaven, by that glorious Triad above, we see our concernments while we are upon earth are not forgotten, are not disregarded. These great and glorious Ones in heaven, are taken up about our affairs. Sure it should provoke us to look upwards much and often, adoringly. It should suggest from time to time this thought to us, that the intercourse between heaven and earth is not cut off. Still (as abject creatures as we are in this our low estate) these glorious persons above are concerned about us. Certainly, it should be often considered by us, that we have mighty attractives to draw our minds and thoughts upwards, God the Father, God the Son, and God the Holy Ghost still bearing a record from heaven to us about things that are of the greatest and highest concernments for us to mind.

And it should, in fine, provoke us to have aspirings upwards, towards the blessedness and perfection of the heavenly state. In heaven, these three bear record, the Father, the Word, and the Holy Spirit. Who can think of this, and not say, "O that I were there! O that I were there! Then will this glorious mystery of the Trinity lie open to my view." It is in that seat of the divine glory that these Three are performing this kind office towards the poor children of men, even amidst the light and glory of the heavenly state. The time will come that we may hope to ascend, and be caught up into this region of light, and in that light to see light, so that as whatsoever is dark and obscure and unknown, and unrevealed, concerning this glorious Three and One, will be done away. When once we ascend and get up thither into the regions of light and bliss, where the glory of the Eternal Being doth display itself, we shall then know as we are known: we cannot know now but in part, and see but in part, but we shall then know perfectly and fully, and as we are known; so far as the capacity of created nature can admit. O! how pleasant should our aspiring upward to these Three be, where they do thus testify and bear record. How often should we be directing our thoughts and spirits, and the longing of our souls towards these regions of light and bliss, saying within ourselves, "When shall a period be put to the time of my converse with bats and moles in this base earth? when shall I hear the divine voice from the throne of glory that shall say to me, Ascend and come up hither, and see the things whereof thou hast hitherto but heard by the hearing of the ear?"

LECTURE XVII.*

Matt. v. 48.

Be ye therefore perfect, even as your Father which is in heaven is perfect.

NEXT to the doctrine of the Trinity, comes (according to proper theological order) that of the Divine Attributes or Perfections, most fitly to be considered. After the discourse of the Trinity which we have showed you subsists in the Godhead, we have chosen this text, both as it serves to confirm, and as it serves to regulate, that foregoing doctrine.

First, As it serves to confirm it. For when we are so plainly told that "there are three that bear record in heaven;" and that the great Object of our religion, and whereto we are most solemnly to be devoted, is represented to us as three, the Father, the Son, and the Holy Ghost; supposing such a triad as you see in the Godhead, you can suppose it under no other notion than that of a very great and high perfection belonging thereunto. And that, therefore, it must greatly intrench upon the perfection of the Godhead, and unspeakably diminish it, if there should be any attempt or offer made to diminish and detract from that sacred number. It could not but be a horrid maim to the very Object of our religion: and against any such disposition thereunto, or to do any thing, or to admit of any thought into our minds that may have that tendency, it would fortify us greatly, to have the belief well fixed in our minds of the perfection of the Godhead. And,

* Preached May the 8th, 1691.

Secondly, It serves to regulate that doctrine of the Trinity too: that is, to direct us to understand it so as may consist with the other perfections of the Godhead; where we are sure it is impossible there can be any war, or that there should not be the highest and most perfect agreement. We must so conceive of the Trinity in the Godhead, and the perfections that we are here and elsewhere taught to ascribe unto it, as that these may manifestly accord with one another. And for that purpose, we must conceive of the divine perfections as the Scripture doth direct us, according as God himself speaks of them; allowing his word to be our measure, in making our estimate and judgment concerning them. They that take another course, and pretend to discover to us the incomprehensible nature of God, by methods and measures of theirs' secluding this, and opposing it in any kind, truly we have a great deal more reason to be astonished at their confidence than we have to admire their knowledge; as if they could make a better discovery and a clearer representation of God to us than he himself. But if we do understand the divine perfections according to those plain and express measures which he hath given us in his word, or which he enables us to collect, as we are reasonable creatures, from what he hath said in his word concerning himself and them, it would then withhold us from any such exorbitant conceptions concerning the Trinity of persons in the Godhead, as shall not be easily reconcileable with the doctrine of his perfections, according as he hath represented and stated it himself.

And upon that account, shall we apply ourselves to consider so much concerning the perfections of the Godhead, as this scripture will give us a general ground for. Indeed to speak of the several perfections and attributes that do belong to the Divine Nature, distinctly and at large, would be the work of a life's time; and very little agree with what I have designed, the expounding and opening to you the principles of religion, in as short a time as I can. Therefore, I have pitched upon this text, designing to sum up all under it, which I think requisite to say concerning the excellencies and perfections of the Divine Being, which we commonly speak of under the name, his attributes. You may take the ground of discourse thus,

That all the excellencies which are requisite to make up the most absolute perfection, belong as attributes to the nature of God; or as so many attributes to be ascribed to God. This, some may possibly apprehend will be but to do what hath been done already, and to do it over again. That is, when in proving to you the existence of the Deity, we shewed that we are to conceive of him under the notion of a Being absolutely perfect. It is true, it was impossible to demonstrate his existence without forelaying that notion of God. And that is suitable to what the laws of method do require, in treating of any subject whatsoever. That is, if there be occasion to put the question *an sit*, whether such a thing be or not and to prove the existence of it, first, and before we come to that inquiry, to inquire *quid sit*, and what it is. To open the nature of such a thing, there must be first some general notion assigned and laid down of that whose existence we would prove, and about which the first inquiry was made *an sit*, whether it be yea or nay. Otherwise, in attempting to prove that, we may as well prove any thing else, if we do not give such a notion of it as will distinguish it from another thing.

But now after we have done so, it comes properly of course then, to proceed to a more narrow inspection into the nature of such a thing. And so the order of tractation did require it should be in this present case. That is, when we were to inquire concerning the existence of the Deity, first to put you in mind, what you and all must be supposed to apprehend concerning the thing we inquired about, that is, a Being of absolute perfection in the general: and we can have no other notion of God but as a Being absolutely perfect. That being done, and it having been evinced to you that there is such a Fountain-Being from whence whatsoever perfections we do behold, and come under our notice among the creatures, must have descended and been derived, inasmuch as whatsoever we behold, and take notice of, that comes under any notion of perfection with us at all, is not nothing, and therefore could not come from nothing, and therefore must be first in a fountain from whence it came. When by this means, I say, we have plainly evinced, that there is one Being which hath all perfection originally in itself; and thereupon shewn that Being to be a fit Object for religion, and to be worshipped by us, and to whom duties and exercises of religion ought to be performed, and that this can be done acceptably no way but agreeable to his own will; thereupon we were put upon an inquiry, how that will of his might be understood and known: and having found that it was discovered (with that design and to that purpose that he might be duly and acceptably worshipped) in that word that bears his name, thence we come regularly and of course, to speak of things particularly and more expressly concerning him (whereof we have had some general notions before) which are contained in this Book, and which this word will help us to a more distinct knowledge of. And therefore now, in speaking to the proposition laid down, we are to consider the subject of it: "your heavenly Father," and then we are to consider the thing affirmed concerning this subject: He "is perfect."

I. For the former, the subject of this affirmation, we must consider in what sense (as there will be occasion to take notice of by and by) he can be spoken of under the name of a subject. Scholars know how to distinguish between a subject of predication, and a subject of inhæsion. He can be no subject of inhæsion, as you will see presently. But a subject concerning which, this or that may be affirmed or spoken, that is the only thing which we can truly and properly mean when we speak of God under that name or term. But whereas he is here mentioned as our " Father which is in heaven," (as our Saviour directs he should be prayed unto, in that comprehensive system of petitions that he himself was pleased to give his disciples, "Our Father which art in heaven,") we must distinguish between Christ's calling him Father himself and his teaching us to call him so, or his speaking of him as our Father. When Christ himself calls him "Our Father," he calls him so as he was: and so he doth speak himself, when he speaks of his having come from, his having descended from the Father. He could mean by the term "Father," nothing else but the first person in the Trinity. But when he speaks of him as our Father and directs us so to speak of him, or to speak to him, we do not need so to limit that term "Father," in reference to us, for we may fitly enough consider the whole God in the paternal relation to ourselves. Concerning the Father there is no doubt, for so our Saviour hath taught us to conceive and speak, "I go to my Father and your Father, My God and your God," John 20. 17. And even the Son is spoken of as our "everlasting Father." Isaiah 9. 6. And all the children of God are said to be born of his Spirit, and to be begotten thereby. John 3. 1. And suppose we should look upon Father, here, strictly as a personal name or title, yet so we must consider the Divine Nature as subsisting *fontaliter,* or as in a *fountain* in that person: and it is that person as having that nature eminently and originally and firstly in him; even that same nature that is common to each of the persons. And so it is not the person as the person, but as having the Divine Nature in it, which is the subject here spoken of. "Your Father which is in heaven is perfect." The Godhead or the nature of God subsisting as in the Fountain, in the Father: and that same nature which is also common with him to the Son and to the Holy Ghost. But then,

II. For that which is affirmed or spoken of this subject, He "is perfect." How are we at a loss when we come to speak of this divine perfection! "I have seen an end" (saith the Psalmist) "of all perfection, but thy commandments are, or thy commandment is exceedingly broad." Even so much of divine perfection as is expressed that one way (in the divine word) is of so exceeding vast a latitude as to represent itself as the matter of the highest wonder to a very enlarged and comprehensive mind, that had exceeded the bounds of all other perfection and already gone beyond them all. I have seen an end of all perfection, but how vast a perfection beyond all that do I perceive in thy divine word, wherein there are yet but some sunbeams, some glimmerings of the perfection of the Divine Nature! Indeed when we go about to speak of such a subject as this, or to think of it, we may even fear to meet with such a rebuke as that, Job 38. 2. "Who is this that darkens counsel by words without knowledge?" Can we think, by searching to find out God? Can we find out the Almighty unto perfection? Job 11. 7. Somewhat, the case requires should be said, of what we can say and conceive but little of. Something, the exigency of our case doth require; that we labour, all of us, to be informed concerning one with whom we have so much to do, and in whose hands all our great concerns do lie.

For the word that is used here, *"perfect,"* and the words in the learned languages that we are referred to by these penmen, they do (as all words must do) fall most inconceivably short of the thing. Words cannot but be poor, and labour under a penury when they are expressive of any thing of God. Alas! They can go but a little way in it.

The words that we have here to do with more immediately, do carry in them a kind of diminishing and lessening intimation of coming to a state, or having come to a state that is higher and more excellent, from a state that was meaner and lower; in which the subject spoken of is (as it were) supposed to have been before, according to the general and indefinite use of such words. As the Greek word τελειος that is here used, refers to a word that signifies *an end*, and so carries an intimation with it, as one had but then attained an end which he was aiming at, and tending towards before, which implies such a diminution as can by no means be admitted concerning God. As when any one doth then suppose himself to have arrived at an eternal sort of perfection, when he hath compassed an end that he was about. "I work this day, and to-morrow, and the third day I shall be perfect;" finish a work I was engaged in, which is but an external sort of perfection. The word (for want of being more expressive) is borrowed and employed here, in a case of very transcendent height above that. And so for the Latin word *perfectio*, or *perfectus*, it carries an intimation with it as if the thing spoken of were, now at length, thoroughly made that which before it was not. Such expressions do (through the natural poverty of speech and language) lessen and diminish greatly the thing that should be represented and set forth by them.

But to consider the thing itself, (as we may be capable to open to you somewhat of the divine perfections) there are two things to be done in reference hereto. We shall note to you, some things more generally that do concern the divine perfections indefinitely considered: and then shall (though briefly) come to consider some of the particular perfections themselves, which we are more specially concerned to take notice of, that are comprehended under those generals.

1. There are some things more generally to be laid down concerning the divine perfections, or excellencies, or attributes; you may call them which of these you will, fitly enough. And,

(1.) There is this to be considered concerning them, that there are of these divine excellencies or perfections, which we are taught to attribute to God, some that are altogether incommunicable ones. There are some that are incommunicable; that is, that have not so much as a name common to him, and to us, by which they are to be signified and spoken of. As there is his Self-subsistence, his All-sufficiency, his Eternity and his Immensity. These are attributes, or perfections of the Divine Nature that are not so much as common in name to him and to us; so appropriate to him, that there is nothing known by the same name that can be said of us. And there are some of his attributes and perfections that are communicable, that is, which under one and the same name, may be spoken of him and of us, of him and of the creature. As his wisdom; there is also such a thing among men: and his power; they have some power: and his goodness; they have some goodness: and so his justice, his holiness, and his truth: these are divine perfections that are spoken of under one and the same name, concerning him and concerning some of his creatures. That is one thing that you have in general to note; as concerning the incommunicable attributes of God, they have not so much as the same name with him and with us: for there is nothing in us, to which such names do agree: All-sufficiency, immensity, eternity, omnipotency, self-existence and the like. But the other (as was said) are signified by words applicable to somewhat in us, as to be wise, to be good, to be just, to be powerful and the like. And,

(2.) In the next place, you must note, that for those divine attributes and perfections which are communicable, it is only the name that is common to that thing in him, and that thing in us, which is expressed thereby. It is true that there is the same name but not the same nature. There is a likeness, a similitude, but not an identity, or a sameness. Take heed of apprehending, or imagining any such thing between the divine wisdom, or the divine power, or the divine goodness, that are uncreated, and that which is created; and so of his holiness, his justice and the like. We are not to think there is a sameness of nature, though there be the same names used in such perfections as these, as they are found to be in God, and as they are found to be in us, or in the creature: for it is impossible that the nature which is infinite, and the natures which are finite can be the same. An infinite nature and a finite nature must needs differ infinitely, and therefore can by no means be the same nature. Wherefore, all that is said in this case, in reference to us, when God is pleased to derive and communicate from himself unto those whom he regenerates, that which is called the Divine Nature; it is only said of it,—that it is his image, and his likeness, that is conveyed or communicated: it is only somewhat like God or the image of God that is impressed upon, and wrought into the soul. We must take heed of thinking that it is the same nature, as they have thought and blasphemously spoken, who have talked of being godded in God; as if the very nature of God was under such a name as this, transmitted into the creature. And again,

(3.) We must understand these perfections, or excellencies of the Divine Nature to be his very nature itself, and not to be any accidental thing superadded thereunto. We must not conceive that such divine perfections as wisdom and power and goodness and the like, are additions to the nature of God: but they are his very nature itself. There can be no such thing as an accidental supervention to the Divine Nature; but every thing that is in God must be conceived to be God. He is essential wisdom and goodness and truth, and is not these things by accident, as men may be, so as to have those things separable from their nature; no, nor can his nature, indeed, be so much as conceived without them. We are not to look upon them as accidents, either as separable or inseparable from his nature, but as being essentially included in it. And this is most evident, upon the account we have showed you; and the thing speaks itself in demonstrating to you the existence of the Godhead, that that Being whose existence we were to demonstrate, is self-existent, existing always by and from itself without depending, without being beholden to any thing from whence it was. Now what is so self-existent is existent necessarily; that is, it owes its own existence to that peculiar excellency of its own nature, to which it is repugnant, and impossible not to exist. Now, whatsoever doth exist necessarily, so that its non-existence should be altogether impossible (which is the peculiar manner of the Divine existence) that must needs be unalterable. What is necessary, must be eternally or invariably necessary, and without any mutation: and nothing can be superadded to another but must infer a mutation: any addition would make an alteration. Therefore, none of these perfections are additions to God; for then they would make a change; but that which is necessarily what it is, never admits of any change, neither by addition nor subtraction any ways.

(4.) You must take this general note farther, that it is hence consequential, that the excellencies and perfections of the Divine Nature are in him, in perfect simplicity. That is, if none of them do differ from the Divine Nature, then it is impossible they should differ from one another; they cannot really differ one from another in themselves. It is true, indeed, that by our imperfect way of conceiving things, through the narrowness and incomprehensiveness of our minds, which cannot take in all things at once, we are fain to admit distinct notions which are wont to be called inadequate notions, concerning the Deity. We can conceive of such and such excellencies but by parts, but by little and little. It is but a small portion we can take up of him in the whole, and but very little after all. And therefore, all we are fain (looking upon the glorious and ever blessed Deity) to conceive, is an unknown wisdom in him, and an unknown goodness, and an unknown holiness and the like. Not as if these things did more really differ in him than one and the same face, (as one aptly expresseth it) doth really differ in itself because a great many glasses are placed against it, that do themselves differ from one another, and are variously figured and cut, do seem to represent divers faces. There is, I say, no more of real difference in these perfections from one another, as they are in God, than there would be in that case of so many real things that are reflected by so many glasses, where the difference of the reflected image doth proceed from the glasses, and not from the original which is one and the same to them all. And that we may preserve the notion entire of the Divine Simplicity, it is easy to be demonstrated to them that shall consider—that if there be not a most perfect simplicity in the Divine Nature, so as that the several excellencies belonging thereto be really in him, one and the same thing, then these excellencies could not meet there but by composition; they would make a composition in the Divine Nature if they were there with real difference. But such a composition in the Divine Nature is altogether impossible, upon these two accounts. First, If there were such a composition there must be supposed a causation: if the Divine Nature were compounded, it would be inferred it were caused; and so God were not the first Cause of the first being: and, Secondly, (though one would think that nothing should need to be added after that, it being plain, nothing can be prior to God,) If there were a composition there would also be a limitation, and so these perfections of the Divine Being would not be infinite, and consequently they must be perfections altogether disagreeable, no way agreeing to the Divine Nature. It cannot but be that he must be infinitely wise, infinitely good, infinitely powerful, and the like. But he should not be so, if these things did really differ in him from one another; for whatsoever doth really differ from one another, doth limit that other from which it differs. If there be an infiniteness in goodness, or an infiniteness in power, or an infiniteness in knowledge, we cannot suppose many infinites; there cannot be more infinites than one; and therefore it is but one and the same thing that is all these. Whatsoever you do design to the one, you must detract from the other. And if you should suppose two infinites, you do thereby suppose neither to be infinite, but both to be finite. That therefore, you must fixedly retain, as a general rule, that the several excellencies and perfections of the Divine Nature, are in him, in most perfect simplicity, and so do not differ in him, as one thing differs from another. Only the Divine Nature and Being itself, as it hath all excellency and perfection in it doth, when it comes to cast an aspect upon us and upon our minds, appear as various, though in itself it is most simply one. And again,

(5.) You must further note this, that the negative attributes of the Divine Being do always imply somewhat positive. There are some things ascribed to God in negative terms, which must be understood to have a positive sense and meaning, under those terms. As when it is said of God, he is immortal, which is a negative term, it implies the most infinite and undecaying fulness of life. And so when it is said of God, that he is invisible, though that be a negative term, such a being as cannot be seen, the meaning is, that his being is of that high and glorious excellency as not to be liable and subject to so mean a thing as the sight of our eye; it is too fine, too bright and glorious for so mean and low a faculty to reach unto. And,

(6.) You must note this, that any particular excellency that men attribute or ascribe to God, it must always be understood to be ascribed to him in the highest pitch of perfection, and not with that diminution wherewith we behold the shadow of such things to be accompanied in the creature. And therefore, we must take heed of debasing the excellencies of the Divine Nature, by confining, concerning them, to that which only gives some faint representation of them among us. We speak of several things that are real excellencies among the creatures; as quickness of sense, to be able presently to feel whatsoever is noxious and hurtful: this sense of pain, is in the creature a perfection; but we are not to conceive any such thing in God: but we are to conceive that which is transcendent in him, that comprehends in itself the power of giving such and such perfections to the creature; so as that those things are eminently, constantly, only in him which, speaking of this and that particular perfection, is in a distinct, formal notion in the creature. We must not say, that this or that we behold in the creature is in him, but some transcendent excellency that doth virtually and eminently comprehend it; as when the Psalmist tells us, "He that planted the eye, doth he not see? and he that formed the ear doth not he hear? and he that teacheth man knowledge doth not he know?" we are not to think that there is such seeing, or such hearing with God, or any kind of sensation as is with us: but there is that transcendent excellency in him, that doth eminently contain all these in a far more glorious manner than we can conceive. These things, it is fit we should note generally, concerning the divine attributes, or perfections, as a ground for somewhat more distinctly, though very briefly, concerning these attributes, or perfections of God, particularly considered.

But before we pass from this discourse, of what is of more general import concerning them, give me leave to suggest somewhat to you that may be of present use, and that may influence practice, and tend to better the hearts and spirits of us, who are now called to hear about such a subject; "Your Father which is in heaven is perfect." So our Lord, who was a Teacher come forth from God, on one of his great errands, doth direct us to conceive concerning him. I pray let our thoughts stay here a little, and meditate, and pause awhile; both on this Subject here spoken of, and that which is affirmed concerning this Subject.

[1.] The Subject spoken of, "Your Father which is in heaven," This NAME, "Your Father," should carry a very attractive sound with it to every ear, and to every heart among us. It is very unfit that we should, any of us, sleep and slumber under the mention of this name, this title given to God, "your Father." Let us bethink ourselves: Can we call God Father? It is a thing to be thought on—with much caution, and then, if that hath produced any effect, and reached any good issue with us, it ought to be thought on—with high consolation.

First. With great caution. "Your Father which is in heaven is perfect:" when we find that some are addressed by our blessed Lord, with the supposed capacity of bespeaking God as their Father, would it not strike cold to any man's heart, that should have cause to think, "Am not I excluded? Am not I one of them that may not dare to take such a name into my mouth and apply it to him, to call him my Father? Doth not my own heart smite me, that I assume so much to myself as to say, God is my Father?" There were those that briskly and boldly pretended to it in our Lord's time. "We are not born of fornication, we have all one Father, even God," say some of these petulent hearers. John 8. 44. It ought to be seriously considered, "What Godlike thing have I in me to bespeak me his child, or that may give me the confidence to call him my Father? What childlike dispositions do I find in me towards him? Is there that trust that becomes a child, that love, that dutifulness, that study to please him?" Let us consider whether we can call him Father, and our hearts not smite us, and tell us inwardly, this is a title that belongs not to thee to give. But if we can find it doth, it is a thing to be considered as with great caution.

Secondly. With high consolation afterwards. Can I indeed say, that he is my Father? What then can I have to complain of? what have I to fear? what have I to desire? what have I to crave beyond what this contains, and carries in it? And pray take heed of diminishing so great a thing to yourselves. Have you, upon a strict inquiry, reason to look upon yourselves as one of that regenerate seed which is peculiar and appropriate to God? carries his signature, his stamp, his image? It is then a very unworthy thing to your Father, to let your spirits sink. It should greaten your minds, it should make you to say within yourselves, "Then am I to live far above the world, it is base, for the children of such a Father to live mean, and lie low, and to grovel in the dust; and to let his own heart despond and sink within him, upon the less grateful aspect and appearances of things from this world. For alas! what is this world to me, if God be my Father?" And, "Your Father, which is in heaven is perfect." You must consider how this our Father is in heaven; not as confined there, not as if heaven did confine him, whom the "heaven of heavens cannot contain." And we should thereupon consider, that truly if heaven do not confine him, this earth ought not to confine me. If he be my Father, there should be no exclusive limits between him and me. If he be my Father, so in heaven as that though he hath his throne, the theatre of his glory, his court, and his retinue there above, yet he doth also diffuse a vital and essential presence throughout the creation, so as that this earth itself is not excluded, "Whither shall I flee from thy presence? If I ascend up into heaven thou art there; If I traverse the seas, wherever I come, there thou art." Psalm 139. 7. I say, if heaven doth not contain him, but that he reacheth this earth too, I should thereupon think this earth should not so confine me, but I will reach him, and apply myself to him, and converse and lead my life with him. And since heaven is represented as the seat of his most glorious residence, we should always think ourselves to have concerns lying there above. I am not to be limited then to this base low earth, if I have a Father in heaven. It is intolerable hereupon, that we should live here upon earth, if we had renounced and quitted all claim to heaven, never looking up thither. What! Do we forget that our Father is there? There he dwells in glory, there he beholds the dwellers upon earth, and looks into the very inmost motions of our thoughts, and workings of our spirits, from day to day, and from moment to moment; if he see a mind carried after vanity all the day long, will he not say, "What! Is such a one, one of the offspring of heaven, but hath no business there, who never minds any thing but this base earth?" Shall he have cause to observe this concerning us, and thus to judge and censure us from day to day? "These are the children of the earth, sons of the earth, they have nothing to do in heaven, they never look up thither." Such words standing here in the Bible, " Your Father which is in heaven is perfect;" methinks they should make strange impressions upon our spirits when we come to look on them and seriously consider them.

[2.] And then what is affirmed concerning this Subject, (though I must not spend time upon that now,) he is perfect, every way perfect. We may yet, by the way, see what ground of reproof there is here for us, that we so little adore, and so little imitate this perfection. That God is not greater in our eyes when we are beholding him, and considering, that whatsoever our minds can conceive of excellency, we find it in him in the highest perfection, and yet we adore him not, we take no notice of that glorious One, how sad is the case when even this itself is a continual increase of guilt upon us, that we know so much of God, that a poor creature should have cause to say, "I should have been far more innocent if I had known less, and been less capable of knowing God. I might have been an innocent creature, in comparison, if I had not known so much." To know him to be so perfectly holy and not to imitate him, to know him to be so good and not to trust him, to love him, to depend upon him and to seek union with him; to know him to be so perfect, and content myself with my own imperfection, when according to this rule of our Lord we should be " perfect as our Father which is in heaven is perfect."

LECTURE XVIII.*

2. But I come now to give, in the second place, some more distinct account of some, at least, of the more eminent of the attributes of God. And I shall begin with that which must be understood as comprehensive of all the rest, and that is, of the DIVINE ALL-SUFFICIENCY.' This is the summary perfection of God; his All-sufficiency. And as the verse where the text lies, saith " Be ye perfect as your Father in heaven is perfect," so elsewhere, is the Divine All-sufficiency represented to us as the ground and pattern of that perfection which is required in us. Gen. 17. 1. "I am God All-sufficient: walk before me and be thou perfect." The word there used is, in some translations, rendered All-mighty, in others, All-sufficient, *El-Shaddai*. They indeed seem to me, to give the more congruous account of the etymology of that word that do read it All-sufficient, deriving it not from *Shadda* that signifies to destroy, to lay waste, which yet, is comprehended no doubt (that is the power of doing so) in the notion of Almightiness, but rather deriving it from a word that signifies sufficiency with the pronominal particle he: He that is sufficient, God that is sufficient, *El-Shaddai* or that is self-sufficient. And he is so self-sufficient either understanding it to be a sufficiency arising from himself or a sufficiency serving for himself. Either way he is self-sufficient; by a sufficiency that speaks him to be All to himself, a sufficiency arising and springing up within himself, or a sufficiency to himself, as having enough in himself to enjoy without being beholden, without depending upon any thing without himself. And such All-sufficiency spoken of God must needs mean, He that is of himself, sufficient for himself, must needs be sufficient for all the creation besides.

* Preached May 15, 1691.

If of himself there be a sufficiency in him for all his own perfections, there must be a sufficiency for all that communication that the creature can any way stand in need of. This is that attribute, that comprehensive one, that we shall in the first place say somewhat to.

And I shall say the more of this, because it is so vastly comprehensive as hath been said, and as the matter is plain in itself that it is. It is the same thing that is meant by that fulness that we find again and again, in Scripture, attributed to God, that πληρωμα του Θεου, "That you may be filled with all the fulness of God." Ephes. 3. 19. Not that there needs any great fulness to fill us. A very little thing will do it; and it signifies nothing to the vastness of the plenitude of the ocean, that a nut shell or a minute vessel may be filled; but it is the greatness of the expression that I here note, "the fulness of God;" how vast, how immense, how profound an abyss must that be! In Ephes. 1. 23. we read of the "fulness of him that filleth all in all;" that filling fulness: it is another fulness that is meant there in that form of expression where, most condescendingly, the church of Christ in this world is spoken of as his fulness. But whose fulness is it? The "fulness of him that filleth all in all." Even he, notwithstanding his vast and boundless self-fulness doth yet vouchsafe to be filled in respect of that union that he is pleased to take a people out of this world into, with his own blessed Self. We read (Col. 2. 9.) of "all the fulness of the Godhead" dwelling in flesh, as it were, embodied in flesh, which we must understand still is the same fulness when it is deposited, when it is, as it were, so disposed for communication. It is not another fulness from the original Divine Fulness, but the same under a new relation wherewith it now comes to be clothed. As when also, in that Col. 1. 19. it is said, "It pleased the Father that in him should all fulness dwell," fulness and all fulness, that it should dwell in him. It did dwell indeed in him originally and naturally in the person of the Son, but now it dwells in the Mediator, that being so lodged and settled, (as it were) it now lies ready for communication to indigent creatures, necessitous creatures, empty creatures; such as we are, empty of every thing that is good, and of the desert of every thing that is so; and only designed and fitted by natural designation as so many "vessels of wrath" to be filled with wrath. Now all the fulness of God comes to be posited and clothed with that relation, to put on that aspect, with reference to us, that according to our need, measure and capacity it is all for us. "It pleased the Father, that in him should all fulness dwell," with such a design that he might fill the sacrifice first, that was offered up, as you find the context speaks,—(Col. 1. 19, 21.) "that he might make peace by the blood of his cross and reconcile all things to himself:" and then, that he might fill the souls which that sacrifice had been accepted for, in the virtue of it, opening its own way to flow in to us. And another expression you have of this same perfection, (the All-sufficiency and plenitude of the Godhead) to wit, that of his being "All in all." A most Godlike phrase, wherein God doth in his own word speak so of himself, speaks like himself, at the rate of a God, with divine greatness and majestic sense. It is used with reference to the divine operations, 1 Cor. 12. 5. "There are diversities of operations, but it is the same God which worketh all in all." But it is also spoken of the Divine Being with reference to his existence; He is All in all; or as in the mentioned place, (Ephes. 1. 23) "filleth all in all." In the final state when all the great designs of God are compassed and brought about, then is he more entirely, fully and immediately to be All in all. He will be more conspicuously so then: he is now so indeed, as it hath not escaped the notice of heathens themselves, who tell us, that whatsoever we see is Jupiter, and whatsoever we are moved by, is Jupiter: that one universal mind doth work through all the universe and mingles itself with the vast body of the creation. So is Christ, in whom is all the fulness of God, (as was told before) he is said to be "All in all." Here is an All in an all, a comprehending all and comprehended all; that is, an uncreated All, and a created: the latter, contained in the former, the former, containing the latter, in-wrapping it, infolding it, diffusing itself any where throughout it, and in all, and over all, and through all. And indeed, that created all, is a little, most contemptible little all, in comparison of the all-comprehending, uncreated fulness, that involves the other in as great a disproportion as you may suppose an atom, a little mote or particle of dust comprehended in the whole earth, or a minute drop in the vast ocean, that swallows it up and runs through it and through it; so is the all of this creation (as great as it may appear to our little narrow minds and thoughts) swallowed up in the uncreated All, so as that in comparison of that, it is nothing. All nations come under this notion, but "as the drop of a bucket, and the small dust of the balance, and lighter than nothing," as confessing it impossible to speak diminishingly enough of the littleness of the creature, in comparison of the Divine All, "less than nothing." Indeed, simple nothing cannot vie with all fulness, with the immense plenitude of substantial beings. But that, that seems to be newly stept forth out of nothing, that, it may be, will pretend to vie, and therefore that is so much the more despicable, even more despicable than mere nothing: mere nothing hath no competition with it to that vast plenitude and fulness of Being. But there may seem somewhat of competition in that which is just stept forth out of nothing: and therefore, that is despised as less than nothing; for mere nothing is not so despicable as that which is just risen out of nothing when it is brought into any kind of compare with the infinite, immense All.

But to speak yet a little more particularly and distinctly concerning this most perfect All-sufficiency and fulness of God, (as it can be possible to us to speak and hear of so great a thing) I shall speak somewhat to the nature of it, what sort of fulness or plenitude this All-sufficient, perfect fulness is. And then—speak somewhat of the purposes which it answers and is most apt to answer.

1. Somewhat of the nature of it. And for that, our best way of opening and unfolding it will be to consider these two things, namely, what it contains, and—after what peculiar it doth contain what it must be understood to carry in it: that is, the contents and the properties of this fulness: what it contains and with what peculiar and distinguishing characters it doth contain it.

(1.) For the contents of this most absolute and perfect fulness of God, All-sufficient fulness; it contains all that we can think, and indeed all that we cannot think. It contains all being, and all life, all motive and active power, all knowledge and all wisdom, and all goodness; every thing that is excellent, valuable and desirable in all the kinds, and in all the degrees of perfection conceivable, in reference thereunto. I shall not speak more distinctly now, in reference to that head, because under other heads that we are afterwards to speak a little (though but a little) particularly to, there will be more occasion to discourse of these severally. But we come,

(2.) To consider of the characters of this fulness, the properties of it, whereunto it must be understood to contain what it doth contain. And so,

[1.] It is a self-original fulness, a fulness that ariseth from itself. It is the highest fountain itself, and not fed from any higher, which is the signification of that title, or that name by which God was pleased to make himself known to Moses, " I Am," and a little more largely " I Am that I Am." A name so expressive of this plenitude and fulness of being and all-perfection of God; so aptly and naturally expressive thereof, that it hath obtained naturally, easily in the pagan world, as that inscription testifies in the temple, which I formerly named, "I am that which I was, and that which is, and that which shall be, and let any man at his peril disclose my veil." And we are told by some of the ancients in the Christian church, that the notions which Plato doth so abound with, he learnt in Egypt, and came by them, it is most probable, and as they think, as having been communicated from some of the Israelites to some of the Egyptian priests with whom he afterwards conversed, that is, with those of them to whom those traditions came some centuries of years afterwards. And that this fulness is self-original, or self-originate, they must always apprehend, who do apprehend that any such thing as Deity could only be of itself, from itself. A Being of that sort and kind, as unto which not to be, was always repugnant; and so that it owes whatsoever it is, or whatsoever it hath in itself, to that peculiar excellency of its own nature, which was always necessary to it, to be what it is; can receive nothing *aliunde*, from without, and can lose nothing, or suffer no detraction of what it is, or hath already belonging to it. This is "I Am," the stable and permanent Being that is by itself what it is. That then, is the character under which we are to conceive of this divine fulness, of this perfect All-sufficiency; that it is self-originate: he being the perpetual, everlasting Spring and Fountain of it to himself. "With thee is the fountain of life." Psal. 36. 9. There, being is in its first Fountain, and life is in its first Fountain. To that, all things else that be and live, and that have any thing of motive and active power, they participate all from hence; "In him we live and move and have our being," as the apostle expresseth it, Acts 17. 28. For which he there quotes a pagan poet; and likewise for that in the adjoining words, "we are all his offspring."

[2.] We are to conceive concerning this Divine Fulness, that it is immense as well as self-originate. He is infinite, unbounded: and that it must needs be for the same reason, because it is self-originate: for causation speaks limitation, whatsoever causeth another, limits it: and that which is uncaused must be unlimited, *omnis limitatis est causata;* that which doth impart and communicate to another doth measure and bound its own communication: and from whence any thing hath that which it doth derive from another, thence it hath the bounds and limits of that which is derived. The limits of the derivation proceed from the original. Therefore it is plain whatever is uncaused must be unlimited, and so this fulness of God being self-originate without any superior cause, must needs be immense and infinite without bounds and limits. There is nothing to bound and limit, but he existing necessarily, when all things else do exist contingently, and by dependance upon his will and pleasure, it could not be but that he must engross all being, all life, and all perfection in himself, because there was nothing else existing besides or before that which did exist necessarily, that is himself, by which what was in him could not be any way limited. Therefore, so we are to conceive of the Divine Fulness—that it is immense. It is then a perfection here spoken of God, which is not particular of this or that special kind, but which is most properly absolute and universal, to wit, of all kinds taken together, with all the several degrees that can come within the compass of each several kind. So metaphysicians are wont to distinguish of perfection, into that which is simple or absolute, and that which *sui generis*, of its own particular kind, that which hath all that belongs to that kind in it, may be said to be perfect in its own kind. That which hath the essence and properties of gold may be said to be perfect gold, and especially if it be pure from dross and doth exclude every thing that is alien from it, if it be pure. That is the notion of pure : *purum est quod est plenum sui, that is pure that is full of itself*, and hath no admixture of any thing alien from it. So may a thing be said to be perfect in its own particular kind, when it is full of itself and when it is free from admixture of any thing else. But the Divine Nature (as is evident) is infinite and immense ; is not perfect of this or that particular kind, but of all kinds whatsoever ; that is, of all that is excellent and valuable ; yea, every thing of all being, being included and comprehended in it. Not formally, for that would make God and the creature all one, but eminently and transcendently, that is, it being in the divine power to determine whether any thing besides should be extant, or not extant. And so he is the Root of being to every thing that is, and the Spring of life to every thing that lives, and the Fountain of all excellency to every thing that can partake of it. And therefore, his perfections or fulness is not of this or that particular kind ; if it were so, it were a limited fulness, a bounded fulness : but it is a fulness that comprehends all kinds together eminently, and transcendently in itself. As the root of the tree doth comprehend all the branches, that is, virtually, it comprehends that virtue in it, and transmits that which extends to all the branches, and as the very seed did virtually contain the whole tree once in itself ; so all the creation was contained in God, before it, by his appointment and command, stood forth into actual being. And,

[3.] It is hereupon an immutable Fulness. This divine fulness admits of no alteration, either by augmentation or diminution. It can neither be made more nor less than it is: either, would make a change, and no change can have place in that Being which is necessary. The Divine Being and all that plenitude and fulness that belongs to it, being self-original, it must be necessary; it could spring from no other, therefore, it must be of itself what it is: and no other imaginable reason can be assigned why such a Being doth exist, but only that peculiar excellency of its own nature, to which it was repugnant not to exist. Hereupon therefore, this is the only necessary Being, and that which is necessarily what it is, can never be other than what it is, can never vary, and therefore that " Father of lights (as the blessed God is mentioned under that name, James 1. 17.) is without variableness or shadow of turning." Without so much as the umbrage of a change, there is not the shadow of variation with him. But before the creation was he was the same, and through all the successions of time when that creation is in being, he is still the same: and if the creation should drop back again into nothing he were the same. Unto that which is necessarily what it was first, nothing can supervene, because it hath its whole being necessarily, so that there can be no addition to it: and then there can be no detraction from it, no diminution, because it hath what it hath necessarily: it is essential to be what it is. And therefore,

[4.] This plenitude of God, must be everlasting, this, All-sufficiency, this perfection, must be eternal. For if there can be no variation in any, the least degree, much less is it conceivable there should be a cessation of the whole Being. A variation in any, the least degree, is altogether impossible to that which is necessarily what it is: and thereupon the eternal permanency of it in the same state must needs be consequent. Hence those amazing expressions about the Divine Being, " from everlasting to everlasting thou art God." Psalm 90. 2. Set yourselves to contemplate God; you must needs yield yourselves to be lost and swallowed up in your minds upon the contemplations of that which is " from everlasting to everlasting." And so that most emphatical expression, of his inhabiting eternity; " Thus saith the high and lofty One that inhabiteth eternity, I dwell in the high and holy place." Isaiah 57. 15. But before that, he was his own place, and indeed all the creation is rather vested in him, than he in any thing. Before time was, or any creature was, he had nothing to inhabit but his own eternity, that is, his own eternal Self: for eternity and the eternal One are the same thing.

Thus you have some account of the nature of the all-sufficient, perfect fulness of God, both from the contents and properties or perfections thereof; what it contains, to wit, all being, all life, all motive power, all wisdom, all knowledge, and whatsoever excellency besides you can conceive, or all that is conceivable, and indeed, all that is unconceivable by any created mind. And then, under what characters, as it is a self-originate fulness, an immense fulness, an unalterable fulness, incapable of any augmentation or diminution, and as it is an everlasting fulness.

2. The next thing is to shew you what purposes this perfect, All-sufficient fulness of God may answer. And indeed, it answers all that is any way desirable should be answered, or that it were to be wished should be answered. For,

(1.) It answers the corresponding purpose of its own felicity, to be an everlasting felicity to himself, where there is the only correspondency, that it is any way possible it should otherwise be; should any way be found between the fruitive faculty and the object. Here is an immense and boundless object for an immense fruitive faculty: nothing could satisfy God but God: there is a capacity not otherwise to be filled up. It was to be answered by nothing but himself, and therefore we must not suppose that there are any additions any way to that felicity from any thing without himself. He only enjoys himself and takes pleasure in his own designs. When he hath designs upon such poor creatures as we, he only pleaseth himself in himself, in his bountifulness, the benignity and the kindness of his own design. When he did, (he must be supposed to have done) even in the days and ages of eternity always retain with himself a design, "I will raise up such and such creatures;" such in particular as any of us; "I will in their proper time and season raise them up out of nothing, on purpose to take them into a communion and participation with me in my own felicity, my own blessedness." What is it he was pleased with? was it that he loved us or delighted in us? He was self-pleased with the kindness and benignity of his own design: not that any thing in us could draw his eye, his love, or his delight, but his kindness and goodness therein was its own reason. He sheweth mercy because he will shew mercy. It was not that one was better than another, but from that goodness of his that is invariable, and can never be better than himself, the complacency that it was always apt to take in its own designments,

From hence it is, that he hath any such thing as delectation in a creature, only as he hath freely placed a design and made it terminate upon such a one, and so is pleased in that kindness and goodness which he hath in himself, and not in any delectableness that was previously in the object. For as to that, there was no more in one than another, and if it were for that reason as such, then it must have followed that all would have a like participation in the felicity of the Divine Being. But this is the eminent, great purpose that the divine All-sufficient fulness serves for, even for his own eternal and invariable felicity. Whence he hath so frequently the title and name of "the ever-blessed God;" his own blessedness being his very essence, or essential to himself; so that he was never to be known under another name, or conceived of under another notion, than as the blessed One, the Fountain of all blessedness; "The glorious gospel of the blessed God," saith the apostle, 1 Tim. 1. 11. And "the blessed and only Potentate." 1 Tim. 6. 15. And "the God and Father of our Lord Jesus Christ, who is blessed for evermore." 2 Cor. 11. 31. And so of Christ as he is God, he is said to be "over all, God blessed for ever." Rom. 9. 5. "Blessed for ever," that is, only in himself as the only correspondent and adequate object of his own fruition. And,

(2.) His most perfect Divine Fulness, appears to have been sufficient for the creation of this world: and (which is but doing the same thing continually) preserving it ever since it was created, even until now; not only bringing it into being, a rude mass of being; but settling and conserving of order in it, and that variety and distinction of creatures, which we behold and which indeed we must suppose to be the only effect of the All-sufficient perfection of a God. The very being of such a world speaks his power; but the order that is in it and the variety of creatures wherewith it is replenished, and the continued preservation of those distinct kinds and species through so many successive ages; so that what this or that plant is, or at least was, so many thousand years ago, it continues to be the same, a thing of the same kind; in the same rank or class of being still as it was. All this is by the All-sufficient, perfect fulness of a Deity that could answer such a purpose as this, to make such a mass of created beings exist and arise out of nothing; and that so much of order and distinction of kinds should obtain and be preserved even in this natural world, through so many successive ages unto this day. It was this that the perfect All-sufficiency of God did, and doth continually serve for. And,

(3.) For the government of the intelligent world; so that wheresoever he hath intelligent creatures he can, by bare touches upon the mind, steer them and act them this way and that at his own pleasure: make great numbers of people at once to agree in one and the same design, all of them; as God did touch their minds in making Saul, king. And that is one instance that shews what is done throughout all the world, and all other ages, where all minds lie under the agency and influence of one supreme, universal Mind. And otherwise, how were it possible that all should conspire and agree to serve the same purpose and do the same thing. And again,

(4.) This perfect, All-sufficient Fulness serves for the defeating of the designs of his enemies; so that he can with the greatest facility and ease, consume adversaries with a fire not blown, and make them "perish like their own dung:" and blow upon them with the breath of his nostrils and make every thing of opposition vanish when he will. And thereupon, as being perfectly Master of his own designs and having every thing in his own power with the times and seasons and ways of doing them, he lets enemies run on, foreseeing still at a distance their day that is coming. He knows their day is coming, and in the mean time sits in heaven and laughs at them, "the Most High hath them in derision:" them who say "Come, let us break their bands asunder and let us cast away their cords from us:" as it is in the 2nd Psalm.

(5.) It answers the purpose of sustaining and preserving his own, the people that he hath collected and chosen out of this world to be peculiar to himself, the whole community of them and every particular soul belonging to that community so as to lose none of them. He bears them up and carries them through all the temptations and conflicts and trials and exercises that they meet with here, in a sojourning state and in a warfaring state, so as that they are kept by his mighty power through faith unto salvation. And then,

(6.) And lastly, this perfect and All-sufficient Fulness serves for their final satisfaction and blessedness, when they shall be brought into that region, into his "presence, where there is fulness of joy, and to his right hand where there are pleasures for evermore." Psalm 16. 11. And that which is felicity enough for himself, will surely be enough for them too.

LECTURE XIX.*

But now in the next place I shall speak further to you of some of the most eminent and noted of those attributes and perfections of God which are comprehended in this general one, and concerning the order of speaking to them, I shall not be much solicitous. Some distinguish them into negative and positive. But that distinction I reckon less material; because that those they call negative ones are so only verbally, there being somewhat most really positive, that is comprehended under such negative terms, as infinite and immortal and immense and the like. They are usually distinguished into communicable and incommunicable, as hath been occasionally told you already; the former whereof, being those attributes of God of which there is some image and resemblance under the same name among the creatures.

The INCOMMUNICABLE ATTRIBUTES are those whereof there is no direct resemblance among the creatures, nor the very name thereof justly or properly to be given to any among them or to any thing that is to be found among them. And for this distinction of the divine attributes, they speak very properly and congruous to the nature of the thing, who tell us, that in the description of God, the former sort of these attributes (the communicable ones) do serve to express his nature more generally, or serve to supply the room of a *generus* in a definition. And that the incommunicable attributes serve to supply the place of a *difference* in a definition restraining (as it is the business of a difference to do) that general nature, that is presupposed.

And others again distinguish these several ways, that is, some do call every thing a divine attribute, which may be any way affirmed concerning God. When some others of them do only mean by a divine attribute, that which is affirmed concerning him, (as the logicians are wont to speak) "*Loquiter quid,*" not "*in quo;*" as when it is said, "God is a Spirit," that they do not reckon a divine attribute which is only to answer the question, What he is? But those things only are to be called attributes, or divine perfections, that do speak more distinguishably concerning his nature, to shew what a one he is, or what a peculiar sort or kind of being he is. And so for one class of divine attributes some reckon his natural properties which do some way specify his nature.

* Preached June 12, 1691.

And then for the second kind, the faculties which, (according to our way of conceiving things) we must attribute to him. And then for a third sort, the exercises that do reside in those several faculties, and for a fourth, those that do imitate the affections that are in us belonging to the rational nature, as it is to be found with us, such as love, anger, desire, delight or the like.

I do not think fit indeed that we should tie ourselves to any such distribution. What I mentioned before, of communicable attributes and incommunicable, carries its own evident reason with it, and its own light to every one that observes things. There are some divine excellencies whereof there is an image and resemblance in the creatures fitly mentioned, under the same name in him and in them, though they do not signify the same thing in them as they do in him, but only the image or resemblance of such a thing. And then there are those that are *incommunicable*, and which neither in name nor in likeness can agree to the creature. This is a very plain distinction, obvious to any one that considers.

For his *incommunicable attributes* they are such as these, and I shall but only mention them. As,

1. His SIMPLICITY, absolute uncompoundedness, all excellencies and perfections meeting, and being united in him, in the absolute unity of his own Nature without division, without composition and without mixture.

2. His IMMUTABILITY, by which he is always invariably, eternally what he is. "I Am what I Am," without "shadow of turning," (as the apostle James's emphatical expression is) there being not so much as the shew of a change.

3. His SELF-EXISTENCE, or (which is all one) his necessary existence, or the necessity of his existence. That perfection of the Divine Nature, by which he is so, as that it is simply impossible for him not to be, or ever not to have been, his essence involving existence in it, so as it is not with any thing besides; for as to any created being, it may be, or it may not be; it may exist or not exist. But it is peculiar to the Divine Being to exist necessarily, so as that it cannot but exist: that is the same thing with self-existence, not existing from another, but existing only from himself. And,

4. His INFINITENESS, which comprehends divers things in it; for the infinity of the Divine Being, it is either extrinsical or intrinsical: extrinsical as it imparts some kind of relation to somewhat *ad extra*, or without, and so the extrinsical infiniteness of God is two fold: that which respects time and that which respects space. That which respects time is eternity,

and that infinitely exceeds all the measures of time. Consider God's duration in reference to time, and his duration is eternal, which is founded in his self-existence, or his necessary existence, was told you before. His being, is of that peculiar kind or hath that peculiar excellency belonging to it that could never not be; and therefore must exist from eternity, and must be to eternity. This is his extrinsical infiniteness in reference to time. And there is his infiniteness in reference to space, which is extrinsical too. It is somewhat supposed without, or besides himself; though but supposed or but imagined. All that space which the Divine Being doth occupy and possess: and this is his immensity. In reference to time, his infiniteness speaks eternity, in reference to space his infiniteness speaks immensity, that which some understand to be his omnipresence. And indeed, it is mostly so, but not wholly, for omnipresence even as presence is a relative term, and refers to somewhat with which it may be said to be present, and so the divine presence can refer to nothing besides himself, without the compass of the created universe, for there is nothing without that, that he can be present to. But his immensity hath an infinitely further reference, that is, to all the boundless, imaginable space (only imaginable) through which the Divine Being diffuseth itself. For not only is it truly said concerning him. He fills heaven and earth, "Do not I fill heaven and earth? saith the Lord." Jer. 23, 24. But also, "the heaven, and the heaven of heavens cannot contain him," as it is said in that seraphical prayer of Solomon at the dedication of the temple "Will God indeed dwell with men on the earth, whom the heaven of heavens cannot contain?" And so his infiniteness in reference to space, it doth, without any limits, go beyond and transcend this vast created universe, be that as vast as it can be supposed to be: and it must be supposed to be very vast indeed, by all that do set themselves to consider what is by human indication or inquiry to be found most considerable, and who allow themselves the liberty ever to think of that vast extent of created being, in comparison whereof not only our earth is but a point, but even that vortex that covers this part of the world to which the earth belongs, is but a mere point, that which contains our sun, and the other planets; all that is but a mere point in comparison of the rest of the universe. Consider that, and the vast extent thereof, and you must yet consider, all this is but a mere point in comparison of the vast amplitude of the Divine Being, concerning which we are to conceive there is not any point of conceivable space any where, but there the Divine Being is, and still infinitely beyond it. And indeed, it is fit we should give great scope to our thoughts, that we may as far as possible conceive in this respect worthily and greatly concerning that God whom we serve and whose name we bear, and to whom we profess to be devoted ones.

But then there is his intrinsical infiniteness besides, that is, his infiniteness considered not with reference to any thing without him, but in reference to what he is in himself. And so it signifies the unfathomable profundity and depth of his essence, including all being itself, in all the kinds, in all the degrees, and in all the perfections thereof; so as that there is no being of any kind, or of any sort, which his being doth not some way or other comprehend, virtually at least: his, being the radical Being from which all other beings spring.

Concerning these Incommunicable Attributes, or perfections of the Divine Being, I shall say no more to you than only to give you this summary and short account that I have given, because in our demonstrating the existence a God it was impossible not to speak to these things: that was a thing not to be done without mentioning such things as these, even somewhat too in a way of demonstration, that demonstrating of them we might give some account of the Being whose existence we are to demonstrate. But now there are sundry other divine attributes that I shall speak a little more distinctly to, and which lie under that other head of

Communicable Attributes, and which therefore are more familiar, and ought to be so to ourselves, as having some image, some resemblance of them, under the same names, in us; all, either have, or ought to have; some indeed have and cannot but have a resemblance in every intelligent creature, yea (and further than so) in every animate creature. And for those that fall under a moral consideration, they are such as ought to be in us, though they be not. These perfections of God are distinguished into natural, intellectual, and moral; or of his nature, mind, and will.

First. I shall consider his natural perfections: and,

1. I shall begin with that perfection of the Divine Nature whereof there is in us some kind (and ought to be in other kinds) a resemblance or image under the same name. And that is, the DIVINE LIFE, the life of God. I do not mean it now in that sense wherein it is a thing either derived to us, or prescribed to us. As in the one or the other, or both of these senses, that expression must be used and understood, (Eph. 4. 18.) " being alienated from the life of God through the ignorance that is in them, and because of the blindness of their hearts," speaking of the Gentile world, and those

Ephesians themselves, while as yet they were in a state of gentilism. I do not, I say, speak of that life now which God requires us to live, and which he makes his own children to live. But I speak of that life which he lives himself; and in respect whereof he is so frequently in Scripture called " the Living God," that excellency of his Being, which he many times attests, to add weight and solemnity and emphasis unto his protestations to men, to assure them that this is so, or not so, or that this or that he doth, or doth not, or will do, or will not do. " As I live, saith the Lord, I have no pleasure in the death of the wicked." And so, upon sundry like occasions, that form of protestation is used by him: "As I live I will do so or so, or it is so and so;" which intimates this, to be a most glorious excellency of the Divine Being, and that which he lays a mighty stress upon himself, and would have us to do so too. It is that which should highly raise our thoughts and apprehensions of the Divine Being, to consider him as the living God: and therefore the properties of that life by which he lives, (after the general conception of life itself,) would be worth our while a little to stay upon. We can have no other general conception of life, but that it is a self-active principle. It speaks a sort of self-activeness in the subject wherein it is: and so, being spoken of God, it attributes that to him in the highest perfection that can be thought, and indeed doth suppose it to be in him, in a perfection infinitely beyond what we can conceive: that is, that he is by the excellency of his own Being, a perpetual fountain of life to himself. It is that which is included in the notion of a spirit, though it is not expressive of all that is signified by that notion. It is but an inadequate conception of what is carried in the notion of a spirit. A spirit, it is, as such, (though that be not all) a self-active being, a being of self-actuating vigour, that can move itself within itself. And that is the most full and distinct conception that we have of life. But taking that for the general conception, there are peculiar excellencies of the Divine Life, that distinguish it from life any where else. As,

(1.) His is absolutely self-originate. No other life is so; but his is absolutely self-originate. All other life is derived, participated, even such creatures to which life is essential, yet their life is but participated; for admit, life is essential, (as it is to all created spirits as such) yet inasmuch as their being is participated and derived, so is their life too; and their being, being a spiritual being, (though a created being) life is so essential to it, for if it ceaseth to live it ceaseth to be, and so its life and being are not separable things. It is not so with that life which our bodies do partake of; even in ourselves, our bodies and our souls have two very distinct sorts of life, our bodies have but a borrowed life, a united life which they borrow from the soul that is within them, and unto which they are united. That soul may retire and part, and then the body dies, and yet it is the same body that it was before: so that if it cease to live, it doth not thereby cease to be. These bodies of ours may cease to live, though not cease to be, because their life is a borrowed life from another: they have it from the soul. But the soul, that hath life in itself, essential to it; so that it cannot cease to live, but it must cease to be. But though it be so, yet its essence and life are but derived from that great Original Life, and from that great Original Being whose life we now speak of. He is the well-spring of life, (psalm 36. 9.) "With thee is the fountain of life." It is equally impossible, as was said before, for him either to cease to live, or cease to be; whereas to us this impossibility is only supposed, it is only a suppositive impossibility. If we should cease to live, we should cease to be too, in reference to these souls of ours. But it is positive as to God, that he can neither cease to live nor cease to be. His is therefore an absolute self-original Life. He hath life in himself, or by himself, as that expression is, John 5. 26. "As the Father, (who we are told is our Father) which is in heaven is perfect," perfect in this respect, hath life in himself, a perpetual spring of life within himself, so hath the Son life in himself, as he is God, and as he is God-man; life to communicate and derive from himself to quicken whom he will, as it is in that context. And then,

(2.) This life of God, as it is a self-original, so it is a self-communicative life; it is a self-communicating life. Not in the same kind, but it doth contain in itself eminently that life which it makes others to live, which it imparts unto creatures. Indeed they cannot live that same life, for life being essential unto him in whom it originally is, to communicate his life were to communicate his essence, and so we make the creature, God which is impossible. But he contains eminently in himself that life by which, formally, he makes the creature live. And so in that respect, the Divine Life, is self-communicative, causual, efficient, making those to live to whom he doth impart it. With him is the well-spring of life. Now these two things are carried in the notion of a fountain: 1st. That there be a perpetual spring in it, and 2nd. that there be a communication and eflux, a deriving of streams from that spring. These two things are carried in the very notion of a fountain. And so as he is the well-spring of life it imports,

[1.] That life that is in him to be self-original, he is the perpetual Spring of it, in himself and to himself. And then,

[2.] Self-communicative, continually deriving streams issuing and flowing out to the creatures, so as to quicken whom he will, as it is said, " the Son doth, in that," John 5. 20. And

[3.] This life of God is an indeficient life; a life that cannot decay, a life that cannot fail, a life that cannot languish, life always in the highest perfection, every thing in God being God, and therefore no more capable of diminution or decay, than the being of God is, which, as you have heard, is a necessary being, and therefore can never be otherwise than as he is, never more perfect, nor ever less perfect. And,

[4.] It is universal life. The life which belongs to the Divine Being, is universal; that is, it carries all kind of life eminently in it, not formally but eminently. You know that there is a great variety of the kinds of life among the creatures; but all comes from one Fountain, and therefore that life which doth belong to the blessed God himself, it must be a universal sort of life, a universality of life, all kinds of life are summed up there, not formally but eminently, there being no kind of life that is lived by any creature, from the most excellent to the most mean and abject, but the power of giving it, the power of imparting it, being in himself who is the Original of life: he hath it within his own power to make that creature live this or that sort of life suitable to the capacity of its own nature, and it is observable to this purpose, that in that passage, Psalm 42. 8. where the psalmist saith, "my prayer shall be to the God of my life;" in the Hebrew it is plural, to the God of my lives. And you know, a man (and more may be said in this kind concerning a holy man, a saint) lives several sorts of lives, as he lives a vegetative life, first the life of a plant, and then the sensitive life; the life of an animal, and then the rational life; the life of a man, and then, if he be a saint, as you know the Psalmist was, a holy life. Now all these lives are comprehended together in this one Fountain. " My prayer shall be to the God of my lives." It is he that makes me live all these several ways that I do live. As I live the life of a plant, I have it from him: as I live the life of an animal, I partake that life from him: as I live the life of a man, a rational creature, I still partake that life from him; and as I live the life of a saint, a holy man, I partake that life from him too, which carries the nearest resemblance with it of his own life.

And thus we are to conceive of our Father which is in heaven, to be perfect in respect of this high and glorious excellency of life; self-original life, self-communicative life, indeficient life and universal life, that contains all sorts and kinds of life eminently in itself.

And now to make some *Use* of this subject of the *life of God*, how highly should this raise our thoughts concerning that God whose name we bear, concerning our Father that is in heaven. It must highly serve to recommend him to us,

1. As the Object of our worship. What a glorious object of worship have we! How may our souls solace themselves every time we go to worship in the contemplation of this, "I am going to worship the living God!" So he is pleased to distinguish himself from the false gods, by this same epithet of the living One. Therefore, we have living and true, put together distinctly concerning him. 1 Thes. 1. 9. "To serve the living and true God." And it is with reference to the consideration of him as the glorious Object of our worship, that the apostle speaks of him, in Acts 14. 15. when those ignorant barbarians, among whom he was, would have done worship unto him and Barnabas, he runs in among them and saith "Sirs, why do you these things? We also are men of like passions with yourselves, and preach to you that you should turn from these vanities to the living God, who made heaven and earth and all things therein. "Our business is to bespeak you to be worshippers of the living God alone." Thus doth the word magnify him above the inanimate, senseless deities of the pagan world, who were wont to worship stocks and stones and the works of their own hands; and bow down and pray to a god that could not save. And how should we magnify to ourselves the Object of our worship, under this notion, and admire and bless God that he hath revealed himself to us, so as we are not left altogether ignorant whom we are to worship, that we do not worship altogether we know not what. We know the Object of our worship carries in it the reason of its own being worshipped, which renders it a rational worship. He is the living and so the true God whom we worship.

2. How highly should it recommend him to us as the Object of our trust. "Therefore we labour and suffer reproach, because we trust in the living God who is the Saviour of all men, especially of them that believe. 1 Tim. 4. 10. and chap. 6. 17 "Charge them which be rich in this world that they trust not in uncertain riches but in the living God, who giveth us richly all things to enjoy." How heart satisfying an Object of trust have we in this respect, considering God as the living God, the Fountain of an indeficient, never failing self-original and universal life, in all the excellencies and perfections of life.

3. What an Object of fear have we even in this conception of God, or from this divine attribute. "It is a fearful thing to fall into the hands of the living God." Heb. 10. 31. A man may be angry with me, and he dies and then his anger dies with him; but it is a fearful thing to fall into his hands who never dies, the hands of the everlasting God. Who would not value his favour as that wherein stands life? It should mightily raise our apprehensions concerning God to conceive of him so. And,

4. It highly recommends him to us as the Object of our imitation. For this is one of the divine excellencies or perfections, whereof there is a *mimesis*, a resemblance under the same name in us. We do all of us live (as was said) several sorts of lives wherein we do resemble God. But we should most of all resemble him in a holy life, such of us who are raised from death to life, or shall be so. And herein it is the duty of every believer to resemble him. This is matter of precept, a thing capable of being put into a command. It is no matter of duty to us to imitate him in the other kinds of life, but in this kind of life it is matter of duty to imitate him in it, that is, in the perfection of that life which is therefore called the life of God, because it is prescribed us by God, enjoined us by God and it is that wherein we are to imitate God. And therefore, it is called, even as it is in us, "the life of God." Ephes. 4. 18. Others not yet reconciled to God, not brought home, but remain in their natural, unconverted state, they are " alienated from the life of God through the ignorance that is in them because of the blindness of their hearts." We are to consider God, the living God, as the Object of our imitation: and therefore, should reflect with just severity upon ourselves; "Do we pretend a relation with the living God, and say he is our God? O! then what mean our dead prayers, our dead duties, our dead hearts! that we let them be dead, and do not strive and wrestle and contend with them. to get them up to this raised perfection of life wherein we are to resemble God, and to express a visible conformity to him!" It is a severe rebuke which is put upon the Sardian church. "Thou hast a name to live and art dead." It is plain, he doth not speak of a total death, or as if there was nothing of spiritual life among them, for in the next words he saith, " be watchful and strengthen the things that remain which are ready to die." There were great degrees of deadness, but strengthen (saith he) the remains of life, " the things that remain that are ready to die," and see how it is enforced, " for I have not seen thy works perfect before God." Your heavenly Father is in this

respect perfect, as he is the living God, as life is in him in the highest pitch of perfection and excellency: "but I have not found your works perfect before me, as your heavenly Father is perfect;" therefore, "strengthen the things that remain that are ready to die;" that your life may shine in lustre and glory more suitably and conformably unto the divine life, unto the life of God himself. But now,

LECTURE XX.*

2. In the next place I shall go on to speak somewhat concerning the POWER OF GOD which is another natural perfection in him, and is next of kin to the life of God. Once have I heard this, twice hath it been spoken, that power belongeth unto God, as in that 62 Psalm 1, verse. It is in him as in its native seat and subject. It belongs unto him. Nothing is more appropriate, more peculiar to God than power: and it so belongs to him as it can to no other. If we speak of strength, lo, he is strong: (as the expression is in Job) implying all created power is not to be spoken of in comparison with him. All other power is not to be named power, not worthy to bear that name. "Your heavenly Father is perfect" in this, as well as other respects: power is with him in perfection; the perfection of power belongs to him.

And here, concerning the power of God, I shall give you some instances and some properties of it.

(1.) Some instances of it. As,

[1.] That it hath been the sole, productive cause of this great creation. Consider all this vast creation as resolved back again into nothing: and then consider it all springing up out of nothing (as it were) at once. How vast a power is this! Whatsoever in all the whole universe of created things you see or hear of, or can think of; all this is raised up out of nothing by the divine power. To bring any thing out of nothing, how vast a power would it require! how far surpassing any human, any created power! If you could but suppose all the powers in all the world, if the whole creation were to be combined and united together only for this one single purpose, to make one single atom, the least that can be thought to be raised out of nothing, you would easily apprehend it would never be. If all the world were assembled to contrive and unite their power to make a grain of dust out of nothing, they must all confess it

---

* Preached June 26, 1691.

infinitely above them. Then to have so vast a creation as this made to arise out of nothing, at once from nothing come to being, how should it overwhelm us to think of it; all that we now behold in being, and so far beyond, so inconceivably beyond what we can behold it to be. This earth of ours, as spacious as it is, is but a mere point, compared with our own vortex; but a part, but a little corner of the creation, and that but a mere point in comparison with the rest of the universe; and all this spoken out of nothing into being by the great Creator: the word of Divine Power but saying, "Let it be," and it was. Lift up your eyes on high, as the prophet's direction is, Isaiah 49. 18. and think who hath created all this: when you behold the sun, and moon, and stars, the vast expanse of the heavens, and all the ornature thereof. And again,

[2.] There is the continual sustentation of this world, once created and made, which is the same momently expense of power; for all created being, if not continually sustained must, by its own natural mutability, every moment be dropping into nothing. So that here is the same power put forth as if a new world were created every moment. And then,

[3.] That all the motion that is any where to be found, throughout the whole universe continually proceeds so from it, that the divine power is the continual spring of it. A wonderful thing to think of! We are apt to have our thoughts soon excited and awakened concerning the divine power when we see some wonderful instance of it fall out, besides the ordinary course. When we behold the effects of some violent wind and impetuous tempest; if we see trees torn up by the roots, houses shattered down, all to pieces, mountains torn asunder, the bowels of the earth ript open, we straightway think these to be great instances of a mighty power. But the power is incomparably greater that works continually and every moment in all the motion that is any where through the universe, in the most still, and silent, and steady and composed way. The power that continually, but silently turns about the mighty orbs of heaven, and the great luminaries that are in it, and, as some think, this very earth itself, in that still, unobserved way that we can take no notice of, which if it be, is incomparably less than that the so inconceivably greater body of the sun should be moved in so inconceivably greater a space, so much larger in circuit, so vastly large, with that celerity that must answer what we expect and see every day. What must that power be that goes forth in this? Such motion of the heavenly bodies that we find move the sun, and moon, and other planets, besides all the innumerable stars, multitudes whereof are so unspeakably greater than the body of the sun, and that so vastly greater than this earth of ours: and all these continually turned about by a motive power: which because it is steady and constant we are therefore so stupid as not to take notice of it, or adore what is doing by it every moment, without failure, without stop, even for one moment. We are to blame that we do not more use our thoughts this way, to aggrandize to ourselves the greatness of him that made all things, and us little inconsiderable parts of them all. And again,

[4.] That this power doth work constantly and steadily with nature in a natural way, and extraordinarily, whensoever he will to whom it belongs, against nature. Here is what doth demonstrate it to be the exceeding greatness of his power, it is vastly great, as it co-operates with nature, as it works with nature. And how vastly great doth it appear as it counterworks nature in several respects, and at his pleasure whose power it is. It was great power that could make such a thing as fire to burn, to seize and prey upon other matter, and devour and consume it. But how much greater power doth it require to make fire not to burn, to bind up the natural tendency of it, as in the instance of the three children. It was a great power to make that great element of water to flow along every where as he hath assigned its receptacles and channels; and greater again when he pleaseth to make it not to flow, to congeal, as it were, and to stand up the mighty waves on a heap. And again,

[5.] If we look a little into another sort of species, what a weighty instance of this power was it to support the manhood of Christ under those sufferings of his, which he, as to satisfaction for the sins of men, and in which capacity only he was capable of suffering; to wit, as he was man, for he could not suffer as he was God. That that man should be able to bear the weight and load of all that guilt, which he undertook to expiate by his blood, which blood was necessary to expiate it, and to lay a foundation for the preaching of the gospel, which saith, "whosoever believeth in him shall not perish, but have everlasting life;" that he did not sink under that weight and load of guilt, and under the power of divine wrath, when all our iniquities did meet on him: that he, one single man should be sustained and borne up, when so vast a load and weight of guilt lay upon him: here was the power of the Godhead sustaining that one man. It was because he was Immanuel, "God with us," God in our nature. That that nature did not fail, did not sink under that mighty load: that that man should stand as the fellow of God, when the sword was drawn to strike that man his fellow: that he should stand against him and not be detroyed, and not be overcome, is a great power. And again hereupon,

[6.] What an instance of the divine power was the resurrection of that man? Smitten he was, and smitten down unto death, into the grave. And yet out from thence he springs up anew, by a divine power, "and was declared to be the Son of God, with power by the Spirit of holiness, by which he was raised from the dead." It was an exceeding greatness of power, as you read, Ephes. 1. 19. which he wrought in him, or exerted, or put forth in him, when he raised him from the dead. And again,

[7.] What an instance is it of the power of God, when he changes the heart of a sinner, when he reneweth and reduceth a lapsed, fallen, apostate, degenerate creature; that is, especially when he changeth his will, the primary, main seat of that mighty change. "Thy people shall be a willing people in the day of thy power." Here is the perfection of divine power to be seen in this: for most plain it is, as I said before about creation, that if all the power of all this world were combined together for this one effect, to alter the will of one single man, it could never be done; you know how to crush, how to tear him into a thousand pieces, but no man knows which way to change the will of a man, not in any instance whatsoever, unless God change it himself. In instances of common concernment, nobody hath power over another man's will; all the power of all this earth is not able to change my will if I have set it this way or that. But his people shall be a willing people in the day of his power: your heavenly Father is perfect, perfect in power in that he knows without doing violence to his creature, without offering any thing that shall be unsuitable or repugnant to its nature, to change its will. He knows how to govern his creatures according to their natures: though he knows how to rule and govern them, yea, to over-rule them contrary to their nature when he will, yet he chooses to govern his rational, intelligent creatures according to their nature, and so agreeably changes the hearts of men, according to that natural way wherein the human faculties are wont to work; a thing that all the powers of the whole world could never do besides. And again,

[8.] What an instance is it of his power to uphold the life of a regenerate soul, during its course through this world! A great instance this is, that their heavenly Father is perfect in power. For most certain it is, as soon as any one production of this kind appears, if there be a child born, a son of God born from above, all the powers of hell and darkness are presently at work, if it might be, to destroy this new, this divine production. But it is enabled to overcome. "He that is born of God keepeth himself, that the evil one toucheth him not:" and "he that is born of God overcometh the world." This is by a divine power annexing itself to, and working in, and with, this new creature. The apostle speaking of one weak in the faith, (Rom. 14. 1.) weary in the faith, as the original signifies, shews that such a one might be received, but not to doubtful disputations: for God (saith he) is able to make him stand. This poor weakling, one that is weak in the faith, receive him (saith he) for God (as despicable a thing as he appears) is able to make him stand. Every new-born child is weak, and we must conceive so concerning every regenerate soul: he is at first weak, and they are always too weak, (God knows) as long as they remain here in this world. They have distempers, weakening distempers always about them. But concerning such a weakling, that it should be said, "God is able to make him stand," makes it to be an instance of a divine, enabling power that ever he should be made to stand. And it is the like case where such are spoken of under the notion of bruised reeds, to make a bruised reed stand against all the shocks of hell, when all the infernal powers are engaged to overthrow it: God shews that he is able to make it stand. And thus it is with such a poor creature all the time of his abode upon earth, hell is engaged in a continual conflict against his precious life, and purposely and with a design to destroy that. But God is able to make it stand, it lives as a spark amidst the raging ocean, and is never extinct but always lives. What an instance of the divine power is this! And again,

[9.] Restraining the wrath of man combined with the power of hell against his church in this world. He hath built this church upon a Rock, and the gates of hell cannot prevail against it. The design hath been always driven, and the attempt continually renewed from age to age. One age hath been industriously at it to root religion out of the world, to extinguish the divine seed, but they could make nothing of it: another age rises up after them, "Come (say they) let us handle the matter far more wisely and take better methods and carry it more secretly, that we may do our business more securely, and see what we can do to extinguish and root out religion:" and so the age after that, and then the next after that, and so from age to age until this age, and yet the thing is not done: yet this church remains, and is still in being, and is yet propagating itself. This is owing to the perfection of divine power. Their Father which is in heaven is perfect, perfect in this power of his, by which he conquers all the powers which are engaged against his poor church in this world, he triumphs over the feeble and impotent attempts of men and devils. "He that sits in the heavens laughs, the Most High has them in derision." The wrath of man shall praise him and the remainder thereof will he restrain. Psalm 76. 10. The wrath of man he turns to his praise; he makes matter of praise and triumph to himself that the wrath of man goes forth; pleasing himself with this, "How shall these wretched creatures see themselves foiled and baffled within a little while!" He raiseth trophies and triumphs to the greatness of his power, from all the wrath of man that goes forth. And that which shall not belong to his praise, all that he will restrain. He can let it go forth as he pleaseth, and restrain the remainder thereof as he pleaseth. What he lets go forth, creates to himself a name upon its going forth, and he suppresseth the rest. And though I might thus multiply instances, I shall add but this one more: and that is,

[10.] The power he shews in forbearing and sparing a sinful world, and (upon his own prescribed terms) here and there, as he pleaseth, pardoning and forgiving particular sinners. This is a power which in some respects surmounts all the rest, or an instance of power that surpasseth all other instances. In other instances, his power shews itself in mastering of a creature, or outdoing all created power, but herein he useth a certain sort of power over himself, restraining his own great wrath, omnipotent wrath, that it break not forth to consume a world, and turn it into flames, as it righteously might have done many ages ago. "Let the power of my Lord be great according as thou hast said. The Lord is gracious and merciful, and of great forbearance, forgiving iniquities, transgression and sin." Let the power of my Lord be great. O! how great is his power over this world! But how much greater is his power over himself, when he withholds his anger, and lets not his fury go forth to consume and make an end of sinners, as he easily could in a moment. But,

(2.) I shall in the next place, after these instances, give you some properties of this divine power. It is,

[1.] Original, as must be said of all divine attributes. All other power is derived, secondary, borrowed, participated from another; but the divine power, God is beholden to none for; it is self-sprung, self-original. "This have I heard," saith the Psalmist, "once and again, that power belongeth unto God." It is in him, as in its native subject. His is the first power, the very beginning of power. It is in him as in the root and fountain: and so he is of himself, the mighty One. "If we speak of strength, he is strong." Job 9. 19. As if it had been said, All other strength is not worth the speaking of. If we speak of strength, meaning a strength fit to be spoken of, or mentioned under that name, that is divine strength. The divine is self-originate, it is in him as in its first original. And again,

[2.] It is irresistible, or invincible, not to be resisted if he pleaseth, and not to be overcome however. He will work and none shall let it. His work shall go on, of whatsoever kind it be; if he have designed it once, resolved it once, it shall be done through all, whatsoever opposition. Saith that man of God Moses, that great man, (Deut. 32. 3. designing there to give an account of God) "Because I will publish the name of the Lord, ascribe ye greatness unto our God: He is the rock, his work is perfect." It is spoken concerning him and his work as a stated, settled character, that whatsoever work he resolves upon, he will make thorough work of it; and so his work shall bear the heavenly image upon it. Your heavenly Father is perfect, and his work is perfect, carried on irresistibly, whatsoever it is, upon which he sets his great heart, against all opposition. And again,

[3.] He is a self-moderating power; a power that can moderate itself. Indeed, the power of all intelligent beings is more or less so. It belongs only to brute agents to act, *ad ultimum*. Intelligent ones can govern their own power. But such is the divine power in perfection, a self-governing power that doth not go forth *ad ultimum*. He can temper it as he pleaseth, and there is a most observable indication of the peculiar excellency of his power in this respect continually, though men observe it not, though men take no notice of it, that it is self-moderating, as was said before, there could be no such thing as motion any where throughout this great creation of God; but through a motive power from him, even his own motive power, he being the first mover; no hand turns, no creature moves but by a participation of a power from him, the great Fountain of all power. But now supposing without the creation, apart from the creation, so vast a power (as the divine appears to be) to go forth without moderation, without restraint, if once there were such a consistent thing and this world, by any means formed and connected together, I say by any means formed and connected together, that divine power, not self-moderated power, must needs shatter this consistent world all in pieces in a moment. If that power were not self-moderated, so that things are guided and moved in a steady, orderly course, it must be so. How easily doth a great wind throw down a house! Then so vast a power going forth from the Creator of this world, supposing it compacted, congested, brought to a consistent thing already, must needs shatter it all in pieces if that power were not self-moderated that goes forth upon it. And again,

[4.] An infinite power; that is a further property of it. How often is the great God, our God, our heavenly Father celebrated as the Almighty. "I know that thou canst do all things," saith humbled, convinced Job, when God puzzled him with so often repeated, "Canst thou? Canst thou do this? and canst thou do that thou seest done? and where wast thou when I did so and so? when I laid the foundations of the earth? where wast thou when the morning stars sang together? who ever thought of thee in that age?" When God had thus argued with him and brought him down to the dust, (chap. 42.) he saith, "I know thou canst do all things and that no thought can be withheld from thee." That is, "Whatsoever thou thinkest to do, nothing can withhold thy thought from proceeding to execution, from coming into fact, if thou wilt do it. Thou hast an unbounded power without limits." But this must be duly understood. It is to be noted here,

First, Concerning the infiniteness of the divine power, its omnipotency, its almightiness, that it can never exemplify itself by an infinite effect. As it doth not follow, because divine power is infinite therefore the world created by that power is, or could be infinite: or, that it was possible for God to make an infinite one; you would think that strange perhaps. Cannot an infinite power produce an infinite effect? Can it produce an effect contrary to itself? No, but yet the other is impossible: and the reason is so plain, that I think when you consider it, every one will understand it. That is, if you should suppose the infinite power of God to have made an infinite effect, this infinite effect can be made no better, no greater than it is; for nothing can be added to what is infinite; and if so, then that infinite power could do nothing more. So that it is a contradiction for an infinite cause to produce an infinite effect, for an infinite cause, would be exhausted by producing an infinite effect: but an infinite cause can never be exhausted, therefore an infinite effect can never be produced by it. That is, it can never be said concerning an infinite cause, that it can do no more. But if it should have produced an infinite effect it could do no more, for nothing can be added to what is infinite. And,

Secondly. This is to be further noted, that this infinite power, omnipotence, almightiness, it cannot do impossible things, neither things naturally impossible, nor things morally impossible.

i. Not things naturally impossible. It can give being to nothing that carries self-repugnance in it, that should imply a contradiction if such a thing should be. Whatsoever implies a contradiction is no object of omnipotency. As for instance, to make that not to be; that is, while it is, to make a thing to be and not to be at the same time; or to make a thing that hath been, not to have been. This implies a contradiction, this is naturally impossible and so, by consequence, is not an object of almightiness. And,

ii. Any thing that carries in it a moral impossibility is no object of divine power. To do an unjust thing, to lie, is impossible with God, impossible to his nature; and therefore, when we speak of the infiniteness of divine power, the perfection, the absolute perfection of it, we are to consider this as it is conjoined with other divine perfections, and so we are not to measure our notion, or conception of the divine power, by what it, abstractly considered, can do, but as it is the power of a Being in all other respects absolutely perfect. It is one thing therefore to inquire and determine what almighty power, considered apart by itself, can do, and another thing to consider what almighty power in conjunction with all other divine perfections can do, as it is in conjunction with holiness, justice, mercy, and wisdom. And it can never work but as it is in conjunction with these, as it is joined with all these together. Though God be almighty, omnipotent, he cannot do any unjust thing, an inept thing, a foolish thing. This were impotency, not omnipotency. It would speak him impotent, not omnipotent: it were an imperfection of power, not a perfection of it. We must consider him as perfect in power, and it would be an imperfection of power to suppose him enabled to do any thing that were unfit to be done. And then,

[5.] In the last place, his is eternal power. His eternal power and Godhead go together, "Trust in the Lord for ever, for in the Lord Jehovah is everlasting strength." A perpetual, never failing spring, he is in this, as he is in all the attributes and excellencies of his being; "I Am that I Am. What I Am, I am without variableness, or without shadow of turning." That continual expense of power that hath been ever since the creation, first arose out of nothing, hath not made that power suffer any diminution, nor can it suffer any. He is still the same, without variableness, without mutation, without so much as the shadow of a turn, of a decay, of any failure.

Let us make some *Use* of this.

1. Labour deeply to apprehend this perfection of the Divine Being: fix the apprehension of it: let all our hearts say within us, "Lord we subscribe, we agree, we yield to the light and evidence of divine truth concerning thy divine power." It is a lamentable case that the clearest notion of divine truth should be with us, as if we held the quite contrary, so as that with reference to effects, and impressions upon our spirits, it were all one to us, to believe that God were omnipotent, and had all power, infinite power, and to believe he had no power. It is a reproach to us, that our notions of truth, when they are never so plain, are so insignificant, so void of effect, and of their proper correspondent impression upon us.

2. Take heed of admitting disputations against the divine power. Let the foundation be once firmly laid with you, that power belongs to him in its highest perfection; and then admit no disputations against it. We are too prone to do so, to misimpute things, to impute things wrong that we take notice of, and that come under our observation, and make that a cause which is not a cause; we think that things do go in this world many times very irregularly, and so as we wish they might not, or they did not do, and secret atheism unobservedly slides in and insinuates itself. "If there be a perfect One, perfect in power as he is in all his other attributes, why are things thus? why do they go thus? why is not what is amiss redressed, and presently redressed?" But, as was said before, we are not to judge of what the divine power *can* do, but to consider it in conjunction with other attributes: consider it in conjunction with perfect wisdom, as we shall have occasion afterwards to speak, consider it in conjunction with perfect liberty and with absolute sovereignty. If we did consider things thus, "We are not to imagine that the divine power is to be exerted according to our will, but according to his will," dispute would cease, the matter would drop: we should presently say, "I yield the cause, he knows better how to use his own power than I can direct him." 'Who hath directed the Spirit of the Lord, and who, being his counsellor, hath instructed him?' And,

3. That it may be so, let us labour to get our spirits into an adoring frame and disposition towards him under this notion, as our heavenly Father who is perfect in power, as the perfection of power is in him. Let him be always great and admirable in our eyes under that notion, and so considered. And further,

4. Let us glory in him upon that account: let our hearts exult in the thoughts that our heavenly Father is perfect in this respect. Walk accordingly in his name, glory in it, make your boast of him all the day long. This hath been the temper and

genius that hath governed among a people related to him heretofore. "Our God is in heaven and he hath done whatsoever pleased him." When all people are wont to walk each one in the name of his god, why should not we walk in the name of the Lord our God? Their gods that are no gods, they please themselves with and take a kind of pride in owning them. O how warrantable a matter of gloriation have we, to go with hearts lifted up in the name of our God! Our God is in the heavens, and doth whatsoever pleaseth him: and can with the greatest facility carry every cause that he is engaged in. He cannot fail, finally to own and right all that are brought to him, and adhere to him, whatsoever their present excuses for awhile may be. Learn hence again,

5. To value an interest in him, and covet it, and labour to make it sure and clear. Who can but think it the most desirable thing in all the world, to have him who is so infinitely perfect in this, as in all other respects, for their God? How secure would it make a man's heart, how quiet and rationally quiet to think, that power, all power, is in the hands of my Father! My Father can do whatsoever he will, he hath all power in his hand. And then,

6. When you have made it your business to secure an interest in him upon this account, and under this notion, then trust in him under the same notion. Exercise a daily, vital trust upon him. "Trust in the Lord for ever, for with the Lord Jehovah is everlasting strength." Isaiah 26. 4. See how things correspond there, "Trust in the Lord:" "Why," might the soul say, "I have need of a God, and a strong one to trust in." In the Lord Jehovah is strength; trust in him. "But I have need of strength for *ever*, being made to live for ever." In him is *everlasting* strength; so that you have as much reason to trust in him to day as you had yesterday, and will have to-morrow as you had to day: for in the Lord Jehovah is everlasting strength, strength that will never fail, and it is trust that must keep you from falling. "He gives power to the faint and to them that have no might he increaseth strength;" and "they that wait on the Lord shall renew their strength." Isaiah 40. 29. 31. And,

7. Lastly, Dread to have him for an enemy. O! consider the fearful case of such as are engaged in a contest with him! Consider their folly, their madness, their misery; and labour to keep at the remotest distance from their state: fly from that sort of men as a dreadful spectacle; you fly from among them by ceasing to be of them. That is, by seeking reconciliation with God, and an interest in him, and striking a covenant with him, then you are delivered from being of them; but think in

the meanwhile with pity and compassion, what mad creatures they are, that are engaged in a contest against omnipotency, "Woe to him that strives with his Maker! Let the potsherds strive with the potsherds of the earth." But what! shall a potsherd of the earth strive with all the powers of heaven? How unequal a match, how mad a choice is this! And from thence take your measure of what is like to become of all the contestations in this world against God, and against his interest. We are not to prescribe to him concerning the times and seasons and methods: but do you see a sort, a generation of men set against God and godliness? It is easy to judge the event; you may easily foresee the effects in the power of their productive cause.

And thus I have gone through those attributes which we call his natural perfections.

LECTURE XXI.*

Secondly. I shall now come to speak of those perfections of God that are to be considered under the head of *intellectual* ones, and there we have these two to consider and speak of, as more eminent perfections, the KNOWLEDGE OF GOD, and his WISDOM. These are great perfections of the Divine Mind, wherein we must understand our heavenly Father to be perfect, as the text stiles him. I shall speak to these both together, they being congenerous, and of one sort and kind, though they are to be conceived of by us, with some distinction. And,

1. For HIS KNOWLEDGE: our heavenly Father is perfect in this respect; or his knowledge is most perfect knowledge. It appears to be so, both in respect of the peculiar nature of it, and in respect of its extent, with reference to the objects about which it is conversant.

(1.) In respect to the peculiarity of its nature: it is knowledge of such a kind as is appropriate to God only: that is, upon this account principally, that it is entirely intuitive not discursive. It is not such a sort of knowledge as that by which we proceed, as we do from the knowledge of plainer and more obvious things to the knowledge of those that are darker and more obscure. But his knowledge of all he knows is simultaneous, that is, he knows all things at once, all at one view. We come to know some things by the knowledge of others which we foreknew, and so are fain to lead on our minds from step to

* Preached October the 9th, 1691.

step, and from point to point. The case is not so with him. All things are at once naked and manifest to his view, so as that, though he doth see the connexion of things and knows them to be connected; yet he doth not know them or any of them because they are so connected; that is, because he knows such things, therefore knows such other things as are connected therewith, as it is with us, while we proceed by rotation from the knowledge of some things to the knowledge of more. His is in this respect most perfect knowledge. And,

(2.) It is so in respect of its extent, in reference to the objects known. And we must,

[1.] Suppose the extent of this knowledge so vast as to reach simply unto all things: that is, not only all things that do exist, but all things that are even possible to do so. In this respect, with reference to the objects of divine knowledge, it is aptly wont to be distinguished into that which they call *Simplicis intelligentia et puræ visionis.* It is no matter for opening to you those terms; but the thing intended to be signified by the one and the other is briefly this—that God doth not only know all those things that shall certainly be, but all those things that are possible to be. And so in that respect the object of his knowledge is equal to his power. There is nothing possible but what he can do, but what he can effect. Every thing is possible to him because he can make it to be. And so vast as that *ambitus, circle* of his omnipotence, so vast also is the object of his knowledge or omniscience; that is, he knows whatsoever he can do, he knows the utmost extent of his own power though he never intends to do actually all he can. But then,

[2.] The perfection of this knowledge, in reference to the object of it, is most especially conspicuous in two things, namely,—that he knows all futurities and—that he knows all the most secret thoughts and purposes of men, or generally of his intelligent creatures.

First. That he knows all contingent futurities. It is needful you should understand me right here, not only bare futurities, that is, things that shall certainly come to pass. There are many men can certainly foretell many future things: that is, natural futurities and such as do depend upon certain and settled causes; as when it is morning, the night will come, when the sun is risen, that it will set, when the sea has ebbed, that it will flow, and the like; but contingent futurities mean quite another thing, that is, such futurities as do depend upon free causes, such as do depend upon the will and pleasure of such creatures as have a certain sort of liberty belonging to their nature. And thence comes that miracle of prophesying; that God should be able to tell so distinctly and with such certainty, for many ages yet to come, that such and such things, men will do. Nor are we to think so debasingly of this knowledge of God as to suppose it depends only upon this his purpose to make a man do whatsoever he knows he will do; which indeed were to debase it into the very dirt, and to make him accessary to all the impurities and wickedness in the creation, by men or devils. And it is to narrow it as much as to debase it: that is, to suppose that he could not know that men would do so and so unless he would make them do the very things that he forbids them, in the very circumstances wherein he forbids them. And this indeed were to subvert the whole entire notion of divine forbearance and permissive providence. As when we are told (Rom. 3. 25) "That God set forth his Son to be a propitiation through faith in his blood, for the remission of sins that are past, through the forbearance of God." To suppose that sin should be past, through the forbearance of God, that is, that he forbearing men, they sin, were a subverting the notion of forbearance, if he made them do (by a positive effective influence) all that they do in a way of sin, though the thing be never so apparently evil in itself most intrinsically evil, as the very act of hating himself. To suppose that he should only so know this or that, that he should be ignorant who should hate him and who should not, among the children of men, unless he should make them hate him, and determine to make them do so that he might know what they would do; this were not only to debase, but infinitely to narrow this knowledge of God. To suppose that he cannot know but upon such and such terms, or in the same way wherein the devil hath some certain foreknowledge of what he intends to his uttermost to make men do, must infinitely debase and narrow his knowledge. He is not an idle or unconcerned supervisor of the affairs of this world, and doth not only foreknow whatsoever one will do, but he knows too how to limit their actions and how to restrain and how to convert and turn to good, what they do with the most evil and mischievous intentions and designs, but upon this it is that he doth demonstrate his Godhead, that he is able to declare future things long before they come to pass, and did so; that he hath given such predictions of what should be, long before it was. In many places of the prophet Isaiah he doth, as it were, magnify his own Deity in opposition to the paganish gods, by this, that he hath declared the end from the beginning, even what shall be in all aftertimes. As in the 41. 44. and 48. chapters of that prophecy we have many passages of that import. And in that 41 chapter, verse 22, 23, he doth, (as it were) provoke and challenge the heathen deities to demonstrate their Godhead this way. "Produce your cause," (saith he) "let them declare things to come, that we may know that they are gods;" as if he had said, "Let them never talk of being gods, or that there is any such thing as deity belonging to such despicable idols unless they can foretell things to come. And this is the true import of that great scripture: Rev. 19. 10. "The testimony of Jesus is the spirit of prophecy:" that is, that which should demonstrate the truth of the Christian religion or prove against all contradiction that Jesus was the Christ, was the spirit of prophecy so long before, that he should come at such a time and in such circumstances into the world as eventually he did. And,

Secondly. This perfection of divine knowledge is most eminently conspicuous in this too, his knowledge of the hearts of men; that he knows the most secret thoughts and purposes of men's hearts, and looks into them with an eye that injects fiery beams. He hath an eye as a flame of fire, that searcheth hearts and tries reins; so as that when there is (as it were) a challenge given to all this world; "Who can know the heart of man?" It "is deceitful above all things and desperately wicked who can know it?" (Jer. 17. 9.) here comes one, that answers the challenge, "I the Lord search the heart and try the reins." And this is one of the great things that both demonstrates and magnifies his Godhead. Amos 4. 13. "He that formed the mountains and created the wind, and that declares to man what is his thought, the Lord, the God of hosts is his name."

I shall not further insist on this, but pass on to the other intellectual perfection, in respect whereof we also ought to conceive our heavenly Father is perfect; that is,

2. HIS WISDOM. He is perfect in being perfectly wise, all-wise as well as all-knowing. I told you we were to speak of these perfections of the Divine Nature, and conceive of them, according to what analogy they have to such things as go under the same names with us, and so wisdom and knowledge are two distinct things. Many know much who are not wise: but so we are to conceive of the perfections of our heavenly Father, that he is not only most perfectly knowing, but most perfectly wise also. Wisdom, you know, is commonly distinguished into speculative and practical: sapience and prudence. Indeed, the former doth not greatly differ from knowledge but somewhat it doth. It is not needful for me to stay to explain to you the distinct notions of intelligence, sapience and science. The first whereof, is the knowledge of principles, the last of conclusions, and the middle comprehends both together.

But besides what hath been said concerning the knowledge of God, it will be of more concernment to us to consider his wisdom, as it corresponds to that which with men is called prudence, as the expression is Prov. 8. 12. for both are most conjunct with him. "I wisdom dwell with prudence." And so this wisdom lies in always proposing to himself the best and most valuable end: and choosing the aptest and most suitable measures and means for computing it. According as any one doth more perfectly both these, he ought to be accounted more perfectly wise. Now his end is known to every one that knows any thing of God, he cannot but be his own end. As he is the Author so he must be the End of all things for himself. He hath made all things for himself, by the clearest and most indisputable right. There could never have been any thing but by him, and it is not to be supposed that he should make a creature to be his own end. It would not consist with the wisdom of a God, that he should do so: it were indeed to make a creature to be a God to itself, or that he should upon such terms make a creature to ungod himself. And whereas, the just display of his own glory is the means to his end, his doing that, is most conspicuous in such things as these, to wit, in the creation of the world, in his providential government of his creatures, in the mighty work of redemption, wherein he hath abounded in all wisdom and prudence; and in the conduct of his redeemed through all the difficulties of time to their eternal state.

These are the means; or his actual displaying or diffusing of the beams of his glory in all these ways, is that by which he doth effect his own glory, make it to shine as that he is thereupon the most worthy and becoming Object unto all eternity, of all the adoration and praise of his intelligent creatures; the most worthy and deserving Object, whatsoever is done, or not done by any of them. My limits will not allow me to insist, at least not largely, on these things.

(1.) The creation of the world. What a display of wisdom was there in that! If we take but the two great and comprehensive parts of it, heaven and earth, "He hath established the earth by his wisdom, and stretched out the heavens by his understanding," or discretion. Jer. 10. 12. And if you should look into the one or the other of these more comprehensive parts, it would not be conviction only, but transport and admiration that we ought to be put into every hour, or as often as we make any such reflection. But I must not go into particulars, as I might. And then,

(2.) For the providence by which he governs this created

world, and all the variety of creatures in it, so as that all things in their own particular places and stations do most directly subserve the purposes for which they were visibly made, they are sustained that they may do so: they are guided and governed and ordered in all their natural tendencies and motions that they may do so. And,

(3.) For that wonderful work of redemption, the apostle gives us this note about it, that he hath therein abounded in all wisdom and prudence. Ephes. 1. 7, 8. Herein did the perfection of wisdom and prudence shine forth, to reconcile the mighty, amazing difficulties, and seeming contrarieties, real contrarieties indeed, if he had not some way intervened to order the course of things, such as the conflict between justice and mercy; that the one must be satisfied in such a way as the other might be gratified; which could never have had its pleasing, grateful exercise without being reconciled to the former. And that this should be brought about by such an expedient, that there should be no complaint on the one hand nor on the other, herein hath the wisdom of a crucified Redeemer, that is, whereof the crucified Redeemer or Saviour was the effected Object, triumphed over all the imaginations of men, and all the contrivances, even of devils and hell itself; for they undoubtedly were so secure upon no account as this, that they saw our Lord die. Satan filled the heart of Judas to bring it about that he might die; animated the whole design: this was the devil's contrivance, "If he that is turning the world upside down, doing such wonders every where, all men running after him be but dead, if we can bring him to his end, we shall certainly make an end of his religion, we shall certainly make an end of his design." But even by that death of his, by which the devil contrived the last defeat, the complete destruction of the whole design of his coming into the world, even by that very means it is brought about so as to fill hell with horror, and heaven and earth with wonder. And then,

(4.) The conduct of the redeemed through this world, notwithstanding all the obstacles, discouragements, and difficulties that lie in their way, what a display, a glorious display of the divine wisdom is there in this! I shall not speak to particulars distinctly, but only give some general account. As,

[1.] That it hath never yet made any wrong step; that amidst all these wonderful varieties of actings and dispensations wherein it hath been engaged ever since there was a creation, there should never be any one wrong step made, nothing amiss done, nothing ever done out of time, or otherwise than it should. And,

[2.] That it is never at a stand, never puzzled, hath always its way open to it, every thing forelaid: "Known to God are all his works from the beginning," as that sage speech is of the apostle James, at the famous council of Jerusalem. Acts 15. He can never meet with a difficulty that can put him to a stand; for his way is always plain and open before him. And,

[3.] That he never loses his design, never misseth any end that he proposes to himself: The counsel of the Lord always stands, and the thoughts of his heart take place through all generations. Psalm 33. 11. And,

[4.] That he doth so frequently disappoint and bring to nothing the designs of the wisest and most contriving men, turns their wiles upon their own heads, "takes the wise in their own craftiness," drives their way headlong, precipitates their counsels into confusion and abortion: as the expressions are in that 5th Job 12, 13. and in the 33d psalm, 9, 10. And many more we have in Scripture, of the like import. And then,

[5.] That he frequently surpriseth the most apprehensive and sagacious among men; doth things that it was never thought he would do; wondrous things, terrible things that we looked not for. Isaiah 64. 3. Sometimes they are fearful surprises that he brings upon men, and sometimes grateful ones. Indeed, the same dispensation may be at the same time most terrible and most grateful, most terrible to one sort and most grateful to another, as they must be understood to be that are mentioned in Isaiah 64. 3. "Terrible things that we looked not for, the mountains flowed down at thy presence." That is, the most mountainous oppositions, the loftiest and most aspiring spirits brought down and made to stoop: and all their pride laid in the dust; so it hath often been beyond all expectation, he still shewing his ways to be as much above our ways, and his thoughts above our thoughts, as the heaven is high above the earth, and as the east is far removed from the west. So it hath been when he hath gone beyond any fear or foresight of his enemies, and above all the hopes and desires and prayers of his people, done beyond what they could ask or think. What wonderful conspicuous beamings forth of the divine wisdom, have there been in such ways as these!

I shall not discourse to you further doctrinally, concerning these things. Something I would say by way of *Use*, before I pass from them. Thus our heavenly Father is perfect. Why these are very clear notices of God, which we soon hear; we have heard them now within the compass of a little time; and we as soon assent to them as we hear them. But pray let us look into ourselves and consider, What impressions have they hitherto made upon our hearts? Have our hearts been all this while leaping and springing within us, and saying, "This God is our God; our heavenly Father is thus perfect?" Hath that been the lively sense of our souls within us all this while? And consider, these notices of God are not new to us. Did we never hear before that the living and true God is all-knowing and all-wise? When were we without these apprehensions? Such a conception of God as this we have had ever since we had the use of our understanding, and heard or knew any thing of God at all. But pray consider, What suitable, permanent and abiding impression have we borne about the world with us hitherto? and what is he so far manifested and made known to us for? Is it not that our spirits might be formed by the discovery, and our minds thereby governed agreeably thereunto? How comes it to pass that such things as these should have had all this while no more influence to beget a correspondent heart and spirit in us towards God? Is it that these things are of little weight, that they sink no more into our hearts and souls? Or is it a matter of small concernment to us, what a one he is whom we take for our God, or profess to have so taken? Is that a matter of small concernment to us? Do we know what the name of God imports? To be a God to us, is to be our "All in all," to be such a one to us every way, in point of good to be enjoyed, in point of power and authority to be obeyed and submitted to. Can it be a little matter in our eyes, what a one our God is, he that we have to do with continually as our God? And by how much the more easily we assent to such things concerning him when we hear them, it argues that they are so much the plainer, and therefore that the guilt must be unspeakably the greater and unspeakably the heavier, if our hearts and spirits be not in some measure proportionably framed and steered and conducted according to the import and tendency of so plain things. These are not dark things that need much explication to us, nor doubtful things that need proof or demonstration. We are satisfied already, that he could not be God, who is not infinitely knowing, and infinitely wise, and perfectly both. So that we have nothing at all to do but to comport in the frame and temper of our spirits, and in the course of our walking with these most evident things. And by how much the greater they are, and the more sacred they are, (and things that we profess to believe and apprehend concerning God must be such, for a greater one could not be concerned than he,) the greater profaneness must it be to abuse such notices as these are, or not to use them, not to improve them to their proper purpose and end. We know such things concerning God: and have we nothing to do with the things of God, but to trifle with them or to let them lie by as neglected, useless things, when they are to run through our lives and to have a continual influence upon us through our whole course from day to day? Are these things right in our minds and understandings, and our hearts in the mean time only as a *rasa tabula, a mere blank?* There are such notices in our minds, but look into our hearts and see what corresponds there. Alas! there is nothing, a mere vacuity: what a sad case is this! and yet the discovery of these things breathes no other design but only to form our hearts and spirits and that our lives may be proportionably governed. It is a dreadful thing to have the knowledge of God lie dead in our souls, as if that were to go for nothing. Here I might shew you what impressions this discovery of the divine perfections should make upon our hearts, and might thence proceed to shew you in many instances that it doth not make that impression which it should. But I must not take that course. I will briefly hint a little at the former, the latter you will recollect yourselves: *rectum est index sui et obliqui*: If it doth appear once what we should be and do, correspondently to the apprehension of the divine perfection in these respects, it will be easy to us to animadvert on ourselves and see wherein we are not what we should be, and do not what we should do correspondently hereunto. It is plain,

1. That such a discovery of God, in these perfections of his, should conduce greatly to the forming and composing of our spirits to adoration, to make adoration of him to be very much the business of our lives. How grateful should it be to us to think we have such an Object for worship and adoration, the all-knowing and the all-wise God! How vastly different in this respect is our case from theirs that worship stocks and stones for deities, senseless and inanimate things! That worship woods and trees and rivers and fountains and beasts and creeping things and the like. What hath God done for us that he hath made himself known to us in these great perfections, as the Object of our worship! that when we pray we know we pray to an intelligent Being that knows all things, and an all-wise God that judgeth what is best and most suitable to be done in reference to what we supplicate him about, and when and how to do all that he judgeth fit to be done. There ought not only to be an adoring frame in solemn worship hereupon, but an adoring frame we should carry about with us through this world, often looking up to him, and considering that we have always an eye to meet our eye, and are to apply mind to mind, (what a satisfaction is that!) understanding to understanding, our im-

perfect understanding to his perfect one. With what adoring souls should we go through this world every day upon this account! But do we do so? Consider how far short we come in so plain a case as this is. And again,

2. Should it not make us stand much in awe? The matter is plain: great knowledge and wisdom in a man, great prudence creates great reverence, especially if it be in conjunction with things that we know are in the highest conjunction here, if in conjunction with authority, power and dignity. But even apart they do much in this kind; when a man hath the repute of a wise man, of a knowing person, it would strike us with so much awe as not to trifle, not to play the fool in the presence of such a one. Is there any thing proportionable with us in our frame and deportment towards the all-knowing God? Our heavenly Father is perfectly knowing, perfectly wise; in what awe should we stand of him continually upon these accounts! And again,

3. It should fill us with shame to think what he knows by us. He is all eye as one said truly of him. With what confusion should it fill us to think he should know so much by us every day? Every vain thought, every light motion of our mind, all our fooleries, all our triflings, all our impurities that lodge and lurk in our hearts are known to him. This thought made a great impression upon a heathen; (Seneca, as he testifieth himself,) *omnia sic ago, tanguam in conspectie, I do every thing as in sight,* as having an eye that doth *rimari, pry* into my breast. O! what a shame is it that we should need a heathen instructor in such a matter as this! and how confounded should we be before the Lord to think what he knows by us continually, that we should be ashamed that men should know such things concerning us, as we are not ashamed he should know. The ingenuity of grace is wanting, it works not, shews not itself. It hath wrought like itself heretofore, "I blush, I am ashamed to lift up mine eyes to heaven," saith good Ezra, and that, when he speaks not so much neither concerning his own sins as the sins of the people.

4. How should it make us study to be sincere. Nothing in us so answers perfect wisdom and knowledge in God, as sincerity. Every thought of my heart thou hast known long before; and it follows in the same Psalm, 139. "Search me O Lord and try me, and shew me if there be any evil way" (any painful way as the hebrew admits to be read) " in me, and lead me in the way everlasting." Again,

5. It should possess us with great complacency, (those that can reflect upon their own sincerity,) that they are continually in view to God. It should be a complacential thought, to think

that he who is so perfectly knowing, and so perfectly wise, knows their sincerity, and knows too, all their infirmities. That he knows their sincerity, "Thou knowest all things, thou knowest that I love thee." John 21. 17. And that he knows their infirmities, and will consider them with indulgence and compassion. "He knows our frame and remembers that we are but dust." Psalm 103. 14. And,

6. It ought to possess us with trust, habitual trust that should run through our lives. Is not such a one fit to be trusted? doth it not highly recommend him to us as the Object of our trust, that we know him to be perfectly knowing and perfectly wise? You can easily apprehend, an ignorant fool is not to be trusted. One that is ignorant and a fool is no fit object of trust. Is not he therefore that is perfectly knowing and perfectly wise, a fit Object? How cheerfully therefore should you trust him with all your concernments, how cheerfully should you intrust him with the concerns of this world, and your part and share therein? considering in what hand your affairs and all affairs do lie, even in his who will make, "all things work together for good." So he hath engaged to do, and he is most knowing and most wise that hath so engaged. Imprudent persons promise rashly what is not in their power, but he that is perfectly knowing and wise can never do so. Though I might mention divers other things I will shut up all with this,

7. It should make us study conformity to him in these respects. Have we this discovery of the perfections of our heavenly Father, that he is perfectly knowing and perfectly wise? It should make us endeavour after conformity to him in knowledge and wisdom: for these are some of his communicable excellencies: that is, his imitable ones. We should think with ourselves, "Is it for me to pretend to him as a child, to call him Father, to say, my Father which is in heaven is perfectly knowing and perfectly wise, when I am nothing else but an ignorant fool?" Wisdom expects to be justified of her children. Are we the children of wisdom, are we the children of him that is perfectly wise and perfectly knowing? Certainly it concerns us to be like our Father in these respects: this is a great part of his image, even of his image to be renewed in us. "Put on (saith the apostle) the new man which is renewed in knowledge after the image of him that created him." Col. 3. 10. Is it for the glory of the all-wise and all-knowing God to have a company of fools for his children, ignorant creatures that know nothing, and labour not to know much of the things that most concerns them to know, in reference to him, and what lies between him and them? We should, upon these accounts,

labour to value and covet, most of all, mental excellencies, such as these. But such is not the common guise of this world. And it is an amazing thing, to think so many intelligent creatures' minds and spirits (though lodged in flesh) should be so lost as to all apprehension of true excellency, or of what is truly valuable, as to value a little glitter, a little exterior pomp and splendour before these mental excellencies of knowledge and wisdom, that are most peculiar to God, and wherein we, if we are possessed of them shall most resemble him. What fools are the men of this world! They esteem men according as they have most of worldly pelf, as they have collected together most of thick clay, but they never think of valuing themselves or any one else by the mental excellencies of knowledge and wisdom in which they resemble God. What base erroneous thoughts must these be supposed to have of God! What do such make of God? As the apostle speaks to these Athenians, but speaks as knowing and understanding them and himself to be of a mind as to this, he argues with them from a principle and *ex concessis* " What! do you think the Godhead is like silver and gold or corruptible things?" As if he had said, " I cannot but know as well as if I were within you that you are of my mind perfectly in this matter, that is, that the Godhead is not like to silver or gold or corruptible things, but he is a Spirit, and you, as you are spiritual beings, or as you have such in you, are his offspring." Certainly it is to be governed by the judgment of a fool in my choice, in my desires, in my estimation of things, to think that earthly things are the most valuable things, that carnal things (as the apostle calls them) are the most honourable things. No, without doubt those are the most honourable and most valuable things that are most Godlike, and by which I shall most resemble God. How was he taken with Solomon for his judgment and choice when he bids him ask what he would have! He was not such a fool as to go and ask riches, honour, long life, or the necks of his enemies, but begs for wisdom and understanding. This was most Godlike: and you see how God was pleased with his choice, how high an approbation he gives of it in that 1 Kings 3. 10, 11. And we should labour to govern our own judgment in these matters accordingly.

And pray consider this with yourselves, and labour to feel the weight of it in your own spirits, if we do not covet and desire that God should create us according to his image and likeness, we shall certainly be apt to create to ourselves a god after our own image and likeness. That is, if we do not make it our business to have ourselves made like unto him, we shall be industrious to make him like to ourselves. As it is in the Psalmist, "Thou thoughtest that I was altogether such a one as thyself." A thing that will lead and plunge us into the deplorable estate of all sin and misery unavoidably.

LECTURE XXII.*

Thirdly. It remains now that we go on to the third head of the communicable perfections of God, to wit, those of the divine will, or which we may otherwise call his *moral perfections*, and the most principal of them which I shall (but briefly too) speak of, are these four, to wit, his holiness, his justice, his faithfulness and his goodness. And before I speak to them severally, I shall give you some general considerations concerning them, and which will also partly respect some of those that have been spoken to already under the former heads. As,

·1. That when we distinguish the divine perfections into natural, intellectual and moral, the meaning is not as if those that were intellectual and moral were not also natural. But the first member in this distinction is larger and more comprehensive than the rest. All that are intellectual and moral are also natural perfections in the divine nature, but all that are natural are not intellectual and moral. And,

2. We are to consider this concerning them, that the divine perfections which are spoken of under the notion of attributes, they do suppose their subject to be such, as to which they can and they must agree: we speak now only of a subject of denomination not of a subject of inhæsion in a proper sense. But they do all suppose their subject, that is of predication, to be a spiritual Being, or they do suppose God to be a Spirit, and might, all of them, be brought as proofs and demonstrations (if it were needful) that he is so. He could not be intelligent if he were not a spirit, nor righteous, nor holy, nor just, nor true, for all these do suppose such a subject of predication as to which such attributes or attributed perfections can and must agree. And therefore (as hath been intimated formerly) when we speak of the attributes and perfections of God, this doth not come among them, but is presupposed and necessarily presupposed. Those that are properly called attributes are spoken of in *quale quid*, not in *quid* as schoolmen do fitly enough say, though

* Preached October the 16th. 1691.

I do not need to trouble you with the explication of those terms.

3. You are to note this concerning them, that as they do suppose their suitable subject, so several of them do suppose others of them. As wisdom doth suppose knowledge, and holiness doth suppose wisdom; and justice, holiness, and faithfulness, justice, and so on. And again,

4. We are to consider that our conception of God and his nature and the properties belonging thereunto, cannot possibly take up things otherwise than by parts: and so all our conceptions of him must be inadequate, and when we have taken up as much as is possible it is but a small portion that we have taken up, or can admit into our minds. And therefore, we are to conceive concerning all these perfections of God that though it be unavoidable to us to apprehend diversly, yet we must apprehend them as all falling into one most simple nature and being: whence it is not to be thought strange that we find a coincidence in very great part indiversive of these perfections, that do (as it were) fall and run into one another. As there will be more occasion to take notice in those particulars that are mentioned. And,

5. You are to consider further that our notices of God must needs be in a great measure by reflection on ourselves. He hath been pleased to let us know that he created man at first after his own image. That is, after his natural image with the addition of his moral or holy image. And that he doth again regenerate and renew men after his own image, that is, his holy image, supposing the natural one, that being still supposed remaining, as the subject both of the corruption and of the restitution. This being so, we have the advantage of discerning much concerning the excellencies and perfections of the Divine Nature by reflecting upon ourselves. What we see by that reflection, we see as in a glass darkly, and indeed, when we are the glass we are a very dark one. But some resemblance, some image there is to be found, even with all there is the natural image of God, and with the regenerate there is the holy image renewed, though very imperfectly renewed, whereupon when we are to conceive of holiness, faithfulness, justice and goodness in God, our conception is much to be helped by these notions that we cannot but have of such things among men, these being, (as you have heard) of his communicable attributes that have the same name in him and in men, and the image and likeness of the same things. And,

6. Though there be somewhat of the divine image or likeness in men, yet this similitude is not to be considered without very

great dissimilitude. It is true indeed, *omne simile est dissimile*, every like is also unlike, but there must be most of all when we are to compare things in God and in us. Though there be some similitude, the dissimilitude must be vastly great which we are to take along with us in speaking of each of those mentioned perfections of the divine will, and so we come to the particulars. And,

1. As to the HOLINESS OF GOD. That very term as it is applied to God, is of various significancy. And indeed, it is so as the term comes thence transferred unto creatures. Sometimes it signifies august, venerable, great, majestic. And the reason of the use of that phrase to such a purpose, that is, holy to signify august and venerable, is obvious : for as things that were holy were not to be violated, were not to be touched (as it were) by impure hands, not to be arrogated, not to be meddled with by any but those to whom they were appropriate, (in which respect, majesty hath been wont to be accounted a sacred thing that was not to be meddled with by any other, and the person a sacred person that was clothed therewith, not by any means in the world to be violated,) so with no very remote translation, holy or holiness being spoken of God doth signify the awfulness, the venerableness, of the Divine Nature. But yet, this is somewhat alien from holiness as it is a moral perfection : or as it is a perfection of the divine will. And therefore, as such we must consider it under its own proper and peculiar notion. It sometimes also, signifies firm, sure, unalterable. The *sure* mercies of David, (Isaiah 55.) the Septuagint renders it sacred, holy. But if we speak of holiness in the proper sense, as it is a perfection of the divine will, so it must needs, in the general notion, signify the rectitude of that will in all things, and so it must have two parts, a negative, and a positive part.

(1.) A negative; and so the divine holiness stands in purity, in being most perfectly free from any taint or defilement, from any thing of moral turpitude, in any kind or any degree. And that purity, the negative rectitude of the divine will which is carried in his holiness, comprehends two things, first, an enmity from all irrectitude, any taint, any turpitude: and secondly, an abhorrence and detestation thereof. Not only that the nature and will of God hath nothing impure, or that is not right adhering to it ; but doth also detest and abhor to have. It signifies the aversion of the divine will, its perpetual, inflexible aversion from every thing that is evil, unworthy of it, unbecoming to it. And so whereas, holiness is spoken of in Scripture under the notion of light, that light is said to be without darkness, in the first place, (1 John 1. 5.) " God is light, and with him is no darkness at all." This is made the matter of solemn message to the sons of men: "And this is the message that we have from him and which we declare to you:" God hath sent this message to the world, this account of himself, that he is light and without any darkness at all, without the least mixture of any thing that is impure, or foul or unworthy of him. But then, as it is said in that place, speaking of the divine holiness under the notion of light, that it is without darkness: so it is, secondly, elsewhere, represented under the same notion as expulsive of it, declining it, hating it, as having with it a most inflexible and eternal aversion from every thing that is signified under the notion of darkness, unholiness being there signified by it. "What communion hath light with darkness?" It is drawn down to signify that there can be no communion between God and unholiness, the temple of God and idols. 2 Cor. 6. 16. And,

(2.) This holiness hath also its positive part which must comprehend two, the like things that have been mentioned concerning the negative part. That is, first the actual, perpetual rectitude of all his volitions, and all the works and actions that are consequent hereupon; and, secondly, an eternal propension thereunto, a love thereof, by which it is altogether impossible to that will, that it should ever vary from itself in this, as it cannot in any other respect. That the determinations of that will are right in themselves, is out of question; and that, his word (and he best understands his own nature) testifies over and over. And then his propension, his eternal, unalterable propension of will to that which is right and good, that we find spoken of as a thing we must conceive too, as belonging to his holiness also; "The righteous Lord loveth righteousness, his countenance doth behold the upright." Psalm 11. 7. And so you have his hatred of all iniquity, and his love of universal rectitude, both mentioned together in one and the same breath; as it were; "Because thou lovest righteousness and hatest iniquity," (it is spoken of Christ it is true, but spoken of him as God, (Psalm 45. 7.) having said immediately before, "Thy throne O God, is for ever and ever") therefore God, even thy God hath anointed thee." He is the image of God, the brightness of his glory, the express image of his person. But here it may be said, when we place (as we cannot but do) the notion of holiness generally in rectitude, every thing of rectitude must have some measure or another, or some rule to which it is to be referred, and which it is to be judged by. What is then the measure and will of divine rectitude wherein holiness stands?

This is the thing that hath been very variously discussed, and with a great deal more perplexity than there was cause for. These things you may take about it, that are all plain in themselves, and will be as much as will need to be, or can, in sum and substance, be said to it. As,

First. That the divine rectitude cannot be measured by any law, that refers to him properly so taken. A law properly taken, is the signification of the will of a superior concerning an inferior. But it is out of question, God can have no superior, and so nothing can in a proper sense be a law to him. And a measure, it is prior to the thing measured, must be before it, but there can be nothing prior to God. Yet,

Secondly. In the borrowed sense, very plain it is that God is a law to himself; and it is the only conception concerning this matter, that it can admit of: nor is that to be thought at all strange, when those parcels and fragments of right notion that are left in the ruined nature of man, do yet leave him a law to himself, where he hath no other law, no written law extant before him: much more, when the notions of rectitude are most perfect, they may supply the place of a rule or measure by which the divine rectitude is to be measured. But,

Thirdly. His mere will, abstractly considered, cannot be this measure, as if the divine will might have made that which is right to be wrong, or that which is wrong to be right: this is altogether unconceivable and impossible, that that will, abstractly considered, should be to him the measure of right or wrong, or of good and evil. That is, as if one could suppose that an act of the will might alter the obligation that is upon an intelligent creature to love the best good; or could make it lawful or a duty to hate the highest and most perfect pulchritude and beauty. This cannot be: as we are told, it is impossible for God to lie. He cannot lie, as it is impossible to him to be unholy, as it is to be untrue. And therefore, that there are eternal reasons of moral good and evil is a most indubitable thing; that that which is right could not in its own nature, in the greatest instances but be so; and that thereupon, that the distinction must be admitted necessarily, of things that are good because God wills them, and of things that he wills because they are good. And so natural laws and positive, they come to have their distinction and diverse consideration. And then in the last place,

Fourthly. That it is equally absurd to suppose, that the ideas of right and wrong, or of moral good and evil, as they are a measure to God should have place any where but in him; that is, in his will, not abstractly considered, but in his will as it is everlastingly conformed to a wise mind. There cannot but be an everlasting conformity between the rectitude of the divine will and the divine word. And whatsoever he doth, he doth all things not because he will, but according to the counsel of his will. Ephes. 1. 11. And indeed, the contrary apprehension, were to resolve all the divine perfections into nothing but sovereignty. It is the divine will that is the measure of good and evil, yet not abstractly considered, but as it doth agree with most perfect wisdom, and that unalterably thereupon, it is as impossible to him ever to will that which is not wise, as it is impossible to him ever to speak that which is not true. And so far, having given some account of the divine holiness, wherein it lies, you may collect in great part from what hath been said, this double property of it, not to mention more:

i. That his holiness is primary, all other holiness is but derivative, imparted. This is the fountain-holiness, the primary holiness. And,

ii. His holiness is essential. It agrees to him, not primarily only, but essentially too, as being altogether inseparable from his nature. Holiness in any creature was always to it an extra-essential thing. We have had instances of it even in the higher orders of God's creatures. Man was created holy, and fell. Among the angels that were universally holy, many fell. So the holiness of the best of creatures is a thing in itself separable from its essence. But the divine holiness is most perfectly inseparable. I shall say no more upon this, (the course that I am upon did oblige me to great brevity in speaking to this head,) but only by way of *Use*.

1. To recommend it to you, that we may live in the adoration of God, considered under this notion: "Who is like thee among the gods, glorious in holiness?" Exod. 15. 11. "There is none holy as the Lord," as Hannah speaks in that admirable song of hers, 1 Sam. 2. 2. How should we rejoice in the thoughts of this, that we have such an Object of worship, so perfectly, unexceptionably holy. And,

2. We ought to study the imitation of him herein, as the adoration of him upon this account, understanding the text as saying that to you, "Be ye perfect as your heavenly Father is perfect" in holiness: "Be ye holy, for I am holy," 1 Pet. 1. 15, 16, referred (for so it is written, as the apostle speaks) to that Levit. 11. 44. and in divers other places.

3. Consider with what great gratitude the condescending goodness ought to be owned, that he should have a design to make such as we, like himself in this respect: we ought to acknowledge great kindness even in such a commandment, "Be

ye holy for I am holy. I would fain have you like myself." It speaks great love and good will to us, that he would have us imitate him. And,

4. It should make us willingly submit to any methods that he thinks fit to use, to bring us to that conformity to him in this respect; that we be gradually perfected herein, as he is most perfect. The state of our case requires that his methods should be sometimes rough and severe for this purpose. We have a great deal of dross about us. The fathers of our flesh, indeed, they correct (saith the apostle, Heb. 12. 9) "after their own pleasure; but he for our profit, that we might be partakers of his holiness." A great word and work, (and which we ought to consider accordingly) that we might be partakers of his holiness! that is, that he might transform us into his image and likeness. What difficulties, what furnaces, what fires, what deaths would we not go through for this, that we might be made partakers of his holiness, to be in this respect, as he is, perfect.

2. The next that I have mentioned of these four perfections of the divine will, is his JUSTICE. And justice is wont to be distinguished into universal and particular. But then,

(1.) As universal righteousness or justice doth comprehend particular justice in it, so it superadds somewhat distinguishing, as you shall see by and by. Therefore,

(2.) For particular justice, that is twofold. It is either commutative or distributive; for commutative justice, with God it can have no place, because he hath no equal: or there are none of the same order with him, that can make exchanges with him or that can transfer rights to him for any rights transferred from him: he can be debtor to none of his creatures. "Who hath given him any thing, and it shall be recompensed to him again?" as Rom. 11. 35. It is a challenge to all the world. But it is that part of particular justice, which is wont to be called distributive justice that properly agrees to him, that is, rectoral justice, magistratical justice, the justice of a governor, ruler, of a superior towards an inferior. And that useth to be divided into these two parts, præmiative and puniative: præmiative, that confers rewards, and puniative, that dispenseth punishments. For the former of these, whatsoever rewards God dispenseth must be all of grace, not at all of debt. He cannot be antecedently a debtor to his creatures, otherwise than by promise, and so his justice runs into his faithfulness, as you will see by and by. And supposing him to have bound himself by promise, then it is a piece of justice with him to make good his promise, and thereupon, the notion of righteousness doth obtain and take place, even in conferring benefits. "God is not unrighteous to forget your work and labour of love." Heb. 6. 10. And "it is a righteous thing with God," not only to "recompense tribulation" to the troublers of his people, but also, those that are troubled rest with him. 2 Thess. 1. 6, 7. And "if we confess our sins, he is faithful and just to forgive us our sins." There is a piece of justice in it. It is, upon one account, the highest act of mercy imaginable, considering with what liberty and freedom the course and method were settled, wherein sins come to be pardoned: and it is an act of justice also, inasmuch as it is the observation of a method to which he had tied himself, and from which afterwards therefore, he cannot depart, cannot vary.

And then for punitive justice, this is most distinguishing of the justice of God, from his holiness abstractly considered. By his holiness he hates sin, and by justice he punisheth it. The one makes him hate it, the other obligeth him to animadvert upon it in a way of punishment, or inclines him to do so. And this he doth as a debtor to himself. Justice among creatures is conversant about the rights of other men; but in God it must be conversant about his own rights; because he is himself the Fountain of all rights. And there could be no such thing as right throughout the whole universe, if it had not its first fountain in God himself: and therefore, his justice must be the faithful guardian of the rights of his sovereignty and government. And thereupon, this justice doth not only allow him but oblige him to award to every transgression a just recompense of reward, as the Scripture speaks.

But of this, I shall say no more, save only, this word or two by way of *Use*, that is,

1. Let us have our souls so possessed with this apprehension of the divine justice as to dread it, and stand in great awe of it, knowing that we have to do with a God that will not be mocked, or trifled with by any; and who never confers favours upon any, so as to forget his just right; nor doth so exercise his mercy towards any as to depress and lose his sovereignty; of which sovereignty of his, as hath been said, his justice must always be a faithful guardian, and therefore, those that are nearest to him must know that if they transgress, his justice must have an exercise about them, even as punitive. There is such a thing as economical, punitive, family justice, by which, even where God is pleased to be related as a Father, he animadverts upon, and chastises and punishes the faults and follies of his own children, even those that are of his own household. Though you must distinguish of punishments, between those that are corrective and those that are vindictive. Vindic-

tive punishments shall not have place there upon those that are, and have, a stated being in the family, that are of it and in it. But corrective punishment shall have place even there. And then,

2. Not only dread divine justice, but labour to engage it to be on your side. What a great blessing is that, to have even justice itself plead for us, and the state of our case brought to that pass that it may. If we confess our sins, that is, with a truly evangelical frame of spirit, he is faithful and just to forgive us our sins: and the blood of Jesus Christ his Son, cleanseth us from all sin. But I pass on,

3. To say somewhat of his FAITHFULNESS. And that also doth in great part run into justice, as justice doth in some part run into holiness. But so far as to superadd somewhat peculiar and distinguishing. The faithfulness of God is his veracity or his truth as it relates to his word, the conformity that is between his word and his mind. And whereas, his word, as his faithfulness that refers to it is twofold, assertory and promissory; so accordingly, must his faithfulness be understood. It stands either in declaring to us truly how things are, or how they shall be. It relates to his *assertory* word; that is, that he doth make a true representation to us of all things that are to be received by us as doctrines. Whereas, he is in no possibility of being deceived himself herein, so neither can he deceive us; God cannot lie. It is impossible to God to lie. So much, the light of a pagan could discern of God, even Balaam; " God is not a man that he should lie, nor the son of man that he should repent." All the declarations that he hath made to us by way of assertion of things that we are to conceive are so and so, we are to look upon his truth and faithfulness as engaged herein. That is, he doth make a representation to us of things just as they are, and no otherwise, in what he saith to us of himself, in what he saith to us of Christ, in what he saith to us of his Spirit, and in what he saith to us of the way and course of duty wherein we are to walk, and the like. And, whereas, our Lord Jesus Christ is the Revealer, the first Revealer of God and his mind to men, he is thereupon, called the faithful witness, as representing and testifying things just to be as they are, and no otherwise. It comes in among his glorious titles, " Jesus Christ, the first begotten from the dead, the Prince of the kings of the earth, the faithful witness:" that falls in among the rest. Rev. 1. 5. God's name is in him, that is, the same nature is in him whereof the divine name is expressive. And therefore, in the whole gospel revelation we must conceive the highest faithfulness to be engaged. That which sums it up, " Jesus Christ came

into the world to save sinners," the apostle calls it "a faithful saying, and worthy of all acceptation," (1 Tim. 1. 15) most worthy to be received and believed. And then,

The word of God, to which this faithfulness hath reference is not only assertory but *promissory;* not only declaratory how things are, but how also they shall be. It is true, we may take in his threatenings too, unto which his faithfulness hath reference as well as his promises. But chiefly and principally, his faithfulness hath reference to his covenant. "He is the faithful God, that keepeth covenant and mercy for ever." Deut. 7. 9. And "he will not alter the covenant that is gone out of his mouth, nor suffer his faithfulness to fail." Psalm 89. 33. 34.

And therefore, concerning this also, take so much of present *Use.* Is God perfect in this respect, most perfectly true and faithful, true to his word, his mind always agreeing most accurately with it? Then,

1. Trust this faithfulness of his. The object of trust is faithfulness most properly, the most immediate object. That which answers to faithfulness is faith. If he be faithful, he is to be believed, trusted in, and relied upon. In that passage of the apostle's prayer that he might be delivered from wicked and unreasonable men, for all men have not faith; the most probable meaning of that, is, that have not faithfulness, (faith being there taken objectively,) that are not fit to be trusted; wicked and unreasonable men, upon whom we can place no trust, that are not fit to be believed. But we are never to admit a thought so diminishing or debasing concerning him whom we have taken to be our God, as if he were not fit to be trusted, as if his faithfulness could fail any whit. Our heavenly Father is perfect in this respect; therefore trust him perfectly, without vacillation, without wavering or suspenseful hearts. He cannot deny himself, he abides most faithful and therefore most securely to be relied upon by those that are, through his grace, enabled to give up themselves to him. He desires no more: give up yourselves to him, and you are safe on his part: rely upon him, for he is faithful; he will keep what you commit to him. And,

2. Imitate his faithfulness as well as trust it. Do you labour to be perfect herein? I pray let us all labour to be perfect in this as our heavenly Father is perfect, to wit, in faithfulness, both towards him and towards men.

(1.) Towards him, O! how can we think it tolerable to break with him who is never apt to break with us! His faithfulness can never fail, why should ours so often fail? When we promise, when we engage, when we vow to live in his love, in his fear, in his communion; what shame should it cover our faces with, to be unfaithful towards him, who is constantly faithful towards us. And,

(2.) Towards men; imitate him there too: this would be the glory of our religion. It is the intolerable reproach of it, that there is so much falsehood among men, and even among them that profess the Christian name, among them who pretend to God as their God: saying he is their God who is the faithful God, most perfectly faithful. This makes a most deplorable state of things. "Help Lord" (saith the Psalmist) " for the faithful man faileth." Psalm 12. 1. It makes the state of things so very dismal that all who understand themselves, think they have reason to cry to heaven, "Help, help, in such a sad case as this." Help, Lord, the godly man fails, there is no faithfulness left in the world. We are undone in this case if God do not help, if we have not help from heaven. But what an ornament is it to the Christian name and profession, when the very words of such and such as do profess it, are reckoned stable as a pillar of brass. " I would no more distrust such a man's word, than I would fear the falling of the heavens over me, or the sinking of the earth under me:" this would be the glory of our religion. O! then let us labour to be perfect in this respect as our heavenly Father is perfect.

LECTURE XXIII.*

Having discoursed from this text, of many of the divine perfections, under the distinct heads of the perfections of the Divine Nature, of the Divine Mind, and of the Divine Will: and as for those of this last rank, having discoursed to you of several others, it remains to say something yet,

4. Of the DIVINE GOODNESS; where, by goodness I do not mean the goodness of being merely, or the goodness of this or that thing in its own particular kind; nor moral goodness in the utmost extent and latitude of it, for that would comprehend the several other perfections of the divine will, that have been spoken to already; but one branch thereof only, which commonly goes under the name of benignity; a benign inclination of will, which we are to consider, both with respect of what it excludes, and in respect of what it includes.

(1.) In respect of what it excludes: it excludes what is oppo-

* Preached November 20, 1691.

site to it, whether it be contrarily opposite, or contradictory. That which is contrarily opposite is an aptness to do hurt, a mischievous disposition to have a mind or will prone to the doing of mischief; which it most certainly excludes: and then, that which is contradictorily opposite is, not to be willing to do good, an unaptness to do good.

(2.) And so, accordingly, it doth include a general propensity to benefaction, to acts of beneficence, and so we are to consider the goodness of God anologically to what we can find of any like specimen among men; for indeed, much of our way of knowing God is by reflection, there being somewhat of God yet left and remaining in man, fragments, broken relics of that image first instamped upon the soul of man in his creation. And by them it is, that we form the general notion, even of those perfections which we do ascribe to God. We see the several features of that image, by reflection, as in a glass, on which we bestow such and such names. Though in the mean time we must know, (as hath been told you upon other occasions over and over,) that whatsoever there is that goes under the same name with God and with us, (as all his communicable attributes do,) yet the things must be infinitely diverse, as his being and ours cannot but be. It is but some shadow, some faint resemblance, of the divine perfections that are discernible in us. But upon those things we bestow these names, still apprehending, that under the same name somewhat infinitely more perfect hath its place and being in God.

And now, as to this perfection, (the divine benignity,) I purposely reserved that to the last place, because it is most in the eye and design of this text, as is very manifest if you look back but to the two more immediate paragraphs, which do more directly refer hither, the former of them more expressly signifying that vacancy that should be in us, (in conformity to the divine pattern and example,) of all inclination to do evil, and the latter, positively expressing and holding forth the inclination that should be in us, after the same example, to do good. Of the former of these paragraphs you may look downwards from ver. 38, and see how the design of that, runs against a mischievous temper and disposition of spirit, an aptness to do evil, yea, though provoked; that there must be no disposition to retaliate, to requite evil with evil, wrong with wrong, injury with injury: but rather than do so, suffer oneself to be injured more, as the several expressions in that paragraph do signify, which it is not needful here to consider.

And then for the latter paragraph, concerning the disposition to do good, the discourse of that, runs from ver. 43 to this conclusion and close of the chapter; all under the name of love; so extensive and large in reference to its object, as not to exclude enemies themselves; those that do with the most bitter hate pursue and persecute us. "You have heard it hath been said, Thou shalt love thy neighbour and hate thine enemy;" such undue limits have been wont to be put and assigned to your love; that you acquit yourselves well enough if you do love them that love you, and if you do good turns to them that do such to you, if you carry it courteously and affably in your salutations to such as will salute you. But this is a mean and narrow spirit, unworthy of a christian, and unworthy of the name and design of Christianity, that being intended to restore man to man, to restore man to himself, to make man what he was, and what he should be. There are no such limitations as those to be made to our love; it must reach enemies, enemies themselves. "I say unto you, love your enemies, bless them that curse you, do good to them that hate you, and pray for them that despitefully use and persecute you:" and all this, that you may be perfect, as your heavenly Father is perfect; (for so he doth,) "that you may be the children of your Father which is in heaven; for he maketh his sun to rise upon the evil and upon the good, and sends his rain upon the just and upon the unjust;" animadverting upon it as a mean thing, and an argument of a base and narrow spirit, to have our love and kindness confined to those wonted limits, wherein men, otherwise taught by their own corrupt inclinations, are wont to confine theirs. This is, therefore, the main and more principal design of this text, as it refers to the context, to commend to us the divine benignity, to represent that, and to set it before us as a pattern to which we are to be conformed. Be in this respect perfect as your heavenly Father is perfect.

And indeed, it is the fittest to consider this divine perfection in the last place; for it is (as it were) the perfecting perfection; it crowns and consummates all the rest. All the excellencies of the Divine Being, they are to be considered not abstractly, each by itself, but as they refer to one another, and as all together they do make one admirable temperament; as with reverence we may speak. Indeed, of those that are abstractly considered, that are wont to go under the notion with us of very great exercise, should be all separated from this, they lose themselves, lose their very name; wisdom, apart from goodness, it were only an ability to contrive, power, apart from goodness were only an ability to execute ill purposes and designs. But divine wisdom, that is in conjunction with most perfect goodness: and divine power, that is in conjunction with the most perfect goodness: and so this is, (as I may say,) the perfecting perfection, consummating of all the rest. How admirable a thing is that wisdom that is continually prompted by goodness! and that power that is continually set on work by goodness, in all the efforts and exertions of it!

And now, in speaking to this, the divine benignity and goodness, I shall briefly point out unto you the various diversifications of it, and then lay before you some of the more observable exemplifications of it. I shall shew you how it is diversified, and wherein it is exemplified.

[1.] How it is diversified. It admits, in sundry respects, (which I shall mention to you,) of sundry considerations and notions that may be put upon it, which yet do all run into this one thing, goodness. First, as it imports a propension unto any thing of suitableness, according as the estimate of divine wisdom and liberty doth determine it, and so it goes under the name of love. Love, is nothing else but a propension towards this or that object. The objects towards which divine goodness is propense, they are estimated by his wisdom and liberty, or sovereignty in conjunction, in respect of their capacities to receive these his propensions, or to be the passive subjects thereof: secondly, as it refers to offenders, guilty creatures, so this goodness is his clemency: thirdly, as it refers to repeated offences, so it is patience: fourthly, as it refers to long continued and often repeated provocations, so it is long suffering, forbearance: fifthly, as it refers to a miserable object, so it is pity and compassion: sixthly, as it refers to an amiable object, so it is complacency and delight: seventhly, as it refers to an indigent object, and speaks large benefactions towards it, so it is bounty: and lastly, as it refers to the principle of liberty and spontaneity from whence it proceeds, so it is called grace, ευδοκια, the very expression that is used to signify the goodness of the will, when, without any kind of inducement, good is done for goodness' sake. "Thou art good and doest good." When there is nothing to oblige, nothing to requite, nothing to remunerate, nothing to invite, this is the graciousness of goodness. These are sundry diversifications, (as they may fitly enough be called) and one and the same excellency, divine goodness and benignity, raised according as such and such respects (as have been mentioned) do clothe it. But then,

[2.] We come to give you exemplifications of it, in instances and evidences that do recommend and shew it forth unto us. And,

First. The most obvious and most comprehensive one is, this very creation itself which we behold, and whereof we ourselves are a little, inconsiderable part. What else can be supposed to have been the inducement to an infinite, self-sufficient, all-sufficient Being to make such a creation as this stand forth out of nothing, but an immense goodness, a benignity not to be prescribed unto, and was only its own reason to itself, of what it would design and do? The creation could add nothing to him; for it being produced out of nothing, it could have nothing in it, but what was of him and from him; and so there is nothing of being in it; nothing of excellency and perfection in it, but what was originally and eminently in himself before; for nothing could give that which it had not: and all that is in this world, is given out from God himself, and therefore, it is resolvable into nothing else but mere goodness that we are, or that any thing else besides is. As in Rev. 4. 11. "For thy pleasure all things are and were created." For thy pleasure; it was a pleasure to him to have that immense and boundless goodness of his, issue and flow forth in such a creation: and among the rest of creatures, in giving being to such as might be capable of knowing who made them, and of contemplating the glorious excellencies of their Maker, and of partaking a felicity in him, as well as a being from him. Indeed, that there should be so vast a creation, (though all that is nothing compared with him, vast as it is,) that is owing to his power; that there should so ornate and amiable and orderly a frame of things be created, that is owing to his wisdom. But that there should be any creation at all, that is owing to nothing else but his mere goodness. He would have creatures that should be capable of knowing and enjoying the excellencies and perfections that make up his being to himself, according to their measure and capacities; and he would have other creatures of inferior ranks and orders to minister unto them. And though this be an obvious thing, and we hear of it often, it is often in our minds, yet I am afraid it is not often enough in our hearts. It doth not sink and pierce deep into our souls, to think what we, by mere nature, are, by more untainted uncorrupt nature; all that we are by divine benignity, that it did eternally depend upon his mere pleasure whether I should be something or nothing. And what a rebuke would this carry in it to a vain mind, if it might be seriously and often thought of! "Was I created to indulge and pursue vanity, to indulge a vain mind, and pursue vain things?" how great an awe would it hold our spirits under! It would teach us to fear the Lord and his goodness, to think, "I only am, and have a place in this world, because he thought it good, and he saw it good to have it so." But,

Secondly. The universal sustentation that he affords to all

created beings, generally considered: this is all nothing but mere goodness; for as he had no need of a creation at first, he hath still no need of it, and he that hath raised it up into being out of nothing one moment, might have suffered all to slip and lapse into nothing the next moment again, without injury to what he had made, or without loss to himself. His tender mercy is over all his works. He lets all this great variety of creatures that replenish this world, continually draw from him. The eyes of all things look towards him. Nature hath (as it were) set an eye in every thing that is made, only to look up with craving looks to the great Author of all things, and all are sustained suitably as their indigent states require, when all are still useless to him, and advantage him nothing. But,

Thirdly. His continual sparing offending creatures; how constant a testimony and evidence is this of the immense goodness of God! That when he hath those that offend him continually, in his power and at his mercy, and he may right himself for what hath been done, in a moment, or prevent doing any thing more to his displeasure, and to his dishonour, yet he spares: how admirable goodness is this! It is not oscitancy and neglect, as if he took no notice of what men did. On purpose to obviate such an expression, Moses useth that emphatical expression, (interceding for offending Israel,) "Let the power of my God be great, according as thou hast spoken, saying, The Lord is long-suffering and slow to anger." Let the power of my God be great. It is not from oscitancy but power, that guilty creatures are spared, that an offending world is not turned into flames and ashes long ago; that a vindictive fire hath not been preying on it, and vindicating the wrong done to the offended Maker and Lord of all. It is not oscitancy but power, that is, power over himself, the greatest of all powers. Creating power is less, the sustentative power, by which the world is borne up, is less. By the exertion of his power towards his creatures he can easily conquer them; but by this exercise of his power he doth, (as it were,) conquer himself; withholding himself from those more sudden eruptions of displeasure and wrath which would argue that these were a predominant thing with him. But he will let the world know it is not so. There is the power of goodness that doth predominate and is governing. It is admirable in itself, and ought to be so in our estimate, that this world which hath for so many thousand years been inhabited and possessed by rebels against the crown and throne and dignity of the Eternal King, is yet spared, and they let propagate their kind, and transmit their nature, though they do, with it, transmit the poison and malignity of an inveterate hate and enmity against the Author of their being. How admirable is the divine goodness, that shews itself in this patience and long-suffering towards a guilty world! We are taught so to account; "Despisest thou the riches of his forbearance and long-suffering, not knowing that the goodness of God leadeth thee to repentance? Rom. 2. 4. And again,

Fourthly. We are to consider as a further instance and evidence of this immense goodness of God, that he is pleased to take such care of the children of men, in their several successive ages and generations, as we find he continually doth; not only sparing them but providing for them; which is a plain and most constantly positive instance and exemplification of this goodness whereof we speak. Two ways he doth more especially take care of the offending creatures that do possess and inhabit this earth of ours; partly by laws, and partly by providence.

i. By laws. How much of the goodness of God is seen by those very laws which he hath taken care shall have place in this world, and by which any thing of common order is preserved? How admirable is it that he should so concern himself for the tranquillity and peace and welfare of those that are in a confederacy and combination against him, and have been so from one generation to another! How wonderful is it! It is owing, partly, to the impressions he hath made and left upon the minds and nature of man, that there are any such laws as go under the name of the laws of nature, which have this tendency and design, to keep the world in a peaceful and quiet state; and do so, as far as they obtain and prevail. And indeed, there is none that do any thing to the disturbance and disquiet of the world, but they abandon the law of their nature in what they do, and offer violence to themselves. But any such law of nature we must understand to have proceeded from the Author of nature, and we must understand it to have been preserved and kept alive among men, by him that doth preserve the nature of man, and doth take care that there should be successions of such creatures in this world. Consider how tender he is of the life of man, that he hath provided, that there should be such a law, even in man's nature, against murder, of which the municipal laws of several countries are all transcripts, and all owing to the general Legislator. Whatsoever laws of this or that country do agree with the natural law, they are all from the supreme Legislator, and are but discoveries of the care and concern that the common Ruler of this world hath to preserve such a creature as man on earth, from violence and wrong. And so likewise, the laws that do obtain anywhere for the preservation of property and for the preservation of chastity, and for the preservation of fame and reputation among men, and the like; that men may not be injured in such respects: they are all so many instances and exemplifications of the great and general benignity of the common Lord and Author of all things, towards his poor creatures in this world, though he beheld his nature poisoned with enmity and malignity against himself, and though that creature takes no notice of him in all this. And then,

ii. The case is seen, not only in the provision he hath made by laws, but which he continually makes by providence, for the sustentation of these, his offending creatures. So you see the text refers us to these very instances, "Love your enemies, do good to them that hate you, pray for them that despitefully use you and persecute you, that you may be the children of your Father which is in heaven:" that you may represent and shew forth the Divine Nature in yourselves, that you may shew yourselves born of God, with such a nature as God hath; give some proofs and discoveries of the Divine Nature in you, because he doth thus; loves his enemies, doth good to them that hate him, feeds them with breath, with bread, with all the necessary supports of life, in a continual course from day to day. And again,

Fifthly. It doth further evidence and exemplify divine goodness, and how perfect he is therein, that there is any derivation hereof to be found any where among men, that there is any such thing among men as goodness towards one another, in any degree of it. Wheresoever there is to be found more or less of that which we call good nature, if there be any thing of humanity, of an aptness to do good to others, or an unaptness to do them hurt, or to take pleasure in their infelicities or miseries, these are so many specimens of goodness that are derived, and their very derivation speaks a fountain from whence they come. These can be no borrowed or participated goodness but must suppose, and imply, a first goodness whence it proceeds. If there be any, the least goodness in any creature, this refers us to God, prompts us to look towards him with adoring eyes. This is a little rivulet from an immense ocean, a beam, a ray from that Sun of love and goodness, from that Nature that is all goodness and all love itself, in the very essence of it. This we ought to consider, if we meet with any kindness in this world, if we see any efforts, any discoveries of pity, of compassion and mercifulness in one towards another, this is all goodness from the First Goodness. All this, shews there is one Immense Goodness, whence all such little parcels of goodness do proceed and come. Even in this apostate and fallen world we see some such appearances of the divine image, (as was said) yet left. We see man hath love in his nature, something of goodness in his nature, a proneness to do acts of goodness and beneficence to some or other, as they come in his way: this should presently make us fall adoring the Supreme Goodness in all this. But then,

Sixthly. The design of recovering apostate, fallen man, is beyond all things, a most admirable discovery of divine goodness; that ever he should have formed such a design. Here is such a creature, such an order of creatures, such a sort of creatures, fallen, sunk, lost, become miserable, and miserable by their own delinquency, by their own apostasy, that is, by their own choice: they have chosen the way that leads down to the chambers of death and eternal ruin. Now, that in this case he should form a design with himself, " I will yet settle a course wherein such creatures as these may be recovered and saved, even from a self-procured ruin." If there were not, I say, a goodness whereof no other account could be given, but that it is divine, but that it is of itself, as the Deity is, as the Godhead is; who would ever have imagined but that such creatures having offended, and by their offensive nature and course, put themselves into a way of perishing, must have been let perish. Nothing more was needful than to let them perish. Why should they not be let perish, when they chose it, when they loved it, and affected the way to it? " They that hate me love death." They that hated wisdom, the Supreme Wisdom, they loved death. And why might they not be left to their own choice, to take the things they love? No, this was Godlike, this speaks the goodness of a God, that he will prevent the perishing of self-destroying creatures. " Their destruction is of themselves, but they shall find that in me is their help;" as by the prophet he speaks his own mind and heart. Partly, the design itself, of saving and recovering such creatures, and partly, the strange and most surprising methods for bringing about such a design, may not only beget conviction, but the highest admiration also, of the goodness of God. We should not only acknowledge it, but fall a wondering, and even lose ourselves in wonder. How unaccountable a goodness was this, that rather than such creatures as we, should finally and remedilessly perish, God should put on man, become man: that man, a man of sorrows; that man of sorrows, at last a sacrifice on a cross, to bring about a reconciliation between an offended Majesty and offending creatures? What manner of love was this! what a transporting discovery of divine goodness! "God so loved the world, that he gave his only begotten Son, that whosoever believeth in him should not perish, but have everlasting life." John 3. 16. But then, if we add in the next place, to all this,

Seventhly. The various means that he useth to draw and gather in souls, to comply with the terms upon which pardon and reconciliation, and eternal salvation are offered to us. There are his ensigns displayed, there is a gospel published, there is an office set on foot, which is to last through all ages to the end of time, on purpose to draw and gather in souls; and all these to be looked upon still under the notion of enemies, they whose hearts were full of enmity and hate against him. For whom indeed he hath been doing good, in common kinds, long before: but they never thanked him for all the actings of his patience and sparing mercy. But such things are continually done towards the unthankful and the evil; yea, these he is so intent upon saving from a deserved ruin, and bringing them to partake, even in a blessedness with himself, to unite them with his Son, make them one with him, to possess them with his Spirit; and to one of the greatest wonders of the divine goodness that can be thought of. When he hath given his Son to be a sacrifice for poor sinners, then to give his Spirit to enter into them, and to inhabit and possess them, and dwell in them; that holy, pure Spirit, that Spirit of all goodness and purity, that Spirit of holiness, as he is called, that he should make his entrance into unholy souls, souls that are so many cells of impurity and filthiness, of every thing that is hateful and noisome and loathsome, how admirable a discovery is this of the divine goodness!

LECTURE XXIV.*

And having thus *demonstrated* the divine goodness, my design is to *vindicate* it. And that is, indeed, of so great importance, that I cannot think it fit to leave off from this subject without placing some endeavour that way. It is of the greatest consequence to us, in all the world, to have our souls habitually possessed with a believing, admiring sense of the goodness of God. We should therefore watch with greater jealousy over

* Preached December the 11th, 1691.

our souls, in no one point more than this, lest any thought should arise, or lest any injection should fix and have place in our souls, that should any way tend to infer with us a diminution of the goodness of God, that the glory of it should be sullied in our eyes, or that it should be obscured or darkened in any kind: for how much may a thought do of prejudice to that genuine, holy, spiritual affection that should be working back again in ourselves towards a good God? How may that affection be stifled by a thought, if it be not duly and seasonably obviated!

And indeed, there are but these two great objections that can, with any plausibleness, offer themselves against the goodness of God; partly, the eternal miseries that do befal the greater part of mankind; and partly, the temporal calamities that do befal the better part. These two ways, men may object to themselves against the divine goodness, wherein God is here represented as so perfect, that the most should miserably perish, and the best should undergo many hard and grievous things, even in this world. Both these, we shall take into consideration, that so, this most necessary part of the idea of the divine perfections may obtain, without any kind of obstruction or objection lying against it in our minds or hearts; so as we may yield ourselves to be entirely swallowed up of the divine goodness.

The former of these is more frequent. And to shew how little pretence there can be from thence, how little colour of objection against the divine goodness, I shall lay before you these many considerations:

1. That no such goodness can be as a perfection in God, that shall exclude or diminish any of his other perfections. No such goodness can belong to the nature of God, as any perfection due to it, that shall be exclusive or diminishing of any other perfection. You should not praise a man, but reproach him, if you should give this of him as his character, that he is so very goodnatured, as never to make any difference between civilities and affronts.

2. Punitive justice is most certainly a perfection belonging to the nature of God, both as he is a Being universally perfect, and as he is the Ruler of the world, to be exercised in such cases, wherein there is occasion it should have place. This is plain in itself, punitive justice to be exercised where it ought to have place, it is a perfection belonging to the nature of God as he is a Being of universal perfection, and the Ruler of the world: as indeed, the Original Being, the First of beings must include all perfection eminently in itself. For there is

no perfection that is not somewhat, and there is no something that can come from nothing, and therefore, the First Being must have all perfection in it. And if this be a perfection, (as every man's judgment will tell him it is,) that is, punitive justive, to be exercised upon proper occasions, it cannot but have place in the Divine Nature, as he is a Being of universal perfection, and as it necessarily belongs to him, supposing a world, to be the Governor of it. It could be from no other but him; and therefore, can be under no government but his.

3. There can be no place for the exercise of punitive justice, but in reference to creatures governable by a law. Punitive justice can never have place, but towards such creatures as do admit of being governed by a law. Punishment is, properly, nothing else but due animadversion upon an offender against the law to which he is obliged, and which he is put under. This also is plain in itself, and only leads to what I add further,

4. That no creature can be capable of government by a law, but such a one as is endowed with the natural faculties of an understanding and a will. There is no place for a legal government, and so nor, consequently, for the exercise of punitive justice, but toward a creature that is endowed with the natural faculties of an understanding and will, supposing that such a creature be guilty of violating the laws by which he ought to be governed.

5. It can be no reflection upon the nature of God to have made such a creature as man. For that which is the very first instance of divine goodness, it would be very strange that that should be a reflection upon it, cloud it, or obscure it. It evidenceth it most highly, that when it was in the choice of God, and a thing merely depending upon his pleasure, to make such a sort and order of creatures stand up out of nothing into being. This is, I say, the first evidence of his goodness, and speaks nothing to the disparagement of it: "for thy pleasure all things are and were created." And that which ought, from the very reason of the thing, to be matter of highest and most grateful acknowledgment and adoration, must thereupon, necessarily, be an instance of goodness in him to whom such grateful acknowledgments are due, and by whom they are claimed. And it is a saying that carries its own light and reason in it, of that ancient, that "If I were capable (saith he) of making an intelligent creature stand up out of nothing, with a present power of using and understanding, the first thing I should expect from him should be, that he fall down and worship me, and

make acknowledgment to me, for having been the author of being, and of such a being to him." And then, for the kind of this being which divine goodness hath allotted to it, it makes it a high instance of his goodness itself. So far is it from being a diminution to it, that is, that he hath given us such a sort of being that is merely imitative and resembling of his own, wherein could there have been a greater signification of kindness and goodness, than to form a creature after his own image, with a spiritual, intelligent nature like his own? And,

6. The things that render any creature capable of felicity, do also render it capable of government by a law: that is, reason and will, an intellective and elective faculty; these make a people capable of government by a law, and make them capable of felicity too. As hath been told you, if man had not had a nature endowed with an understanding and a will, he could have been no capable subject of being governed by a law: but then, if he had been destitute of such faculties as these, he could not have been capable of felicity neither. If he had not understanding to apprehend wherein it lies, and a will to unite with it, choose it, and take solace in it, he would be incapable of being a happy creature. And what! Can it be any argument against the divine goodness that he hath made man with such a nature as renders him capable of felicity? If he were not capable of government, he could not be capable of felicity; the same things making him capable of the one, and of the other.

7. It must have been a very great blemish upon the divine government, if creatures capable of government by law, should generally offend against the most righteous and equal ones, (as his laws cannot but be,) and there should be no course taken for the punishing of such transgressors. This must be a manifest blemish upon a government. Suppose we, in any government whatsoever that there should be any such edict and proclamation published, that let the subjects under such a government do what they please, no man shall be animadverted upon, all shall do what is good in their own eyes, and no one be ever called to any account; would this be a commendation of a government? Such a thing is altogether insupposable in the administration of the best and most excellent government that ever was, or ever can be. Consider it in the whole course of it, not the temporal administration abstractly, from the future state of things, but the course and the end of it altogether; and it must finally appear the best and most perfect and excellent government that ever was, or ever can be. But how insupposable is it, (I say) that the best and most perfect government,

should ever be liable to such a blemish as this, that let men be never so wicked, it shall fare as well with them as if they were never so dutiful and obedient. The thing speaks itself, and Scripture speaks it, but it speaks not as a notion which it suggests anew, but only that which it takes up and observes, as a thing common to men before. "Shall not the Judge of all the world do right?" And see, what immediately precedes, "Wilt thou destroy the righteous with the wicked? That be far from thee; Shall not the Judge of all the world do right?" Gen. 18. 23, 25. Supposing this as a great fundamental, a principle that did always shine with its own light, and that did evidence itself, that it must belong to the Judge of all the earth to do right: and so put a difference between the righteous and the wicked, that they are not to fare all alike. And again,

8. The very nature of the law, that was original and natural to man, is itself a high evidence and instance of divine goodness. The law of nature, that law (I say) which was original and natural to man, and so inwrought into himself at first, that he was even constituted as a law to himself, because that that was enjoined in it summarily, did carry his own reason in it, had in itself, recommending evidence to that conscience wherewith he was created, that God did rule upon those terms that he was to rule himself upon; and so must judge him upon such terms, as upon which he must judge himself. For do but consider, how this law is afterwards summed up, all in one word, love. This was the fulfilling of the law, the loving of God above all: the most equal thing in all the world, that the highest and best love should be placed upon the highest and best good. This was that which his law required, that we should love the Lord our God, with all our heart; and with all our soul, and with all our might. Our Saviour gives this, as the summary and principal part of the law that was natural and original to man: and then, the second part is like the former, loving our neighbour as ourselves. How greatly evidential was this divine goodness, that when he had made a creature capable of government by a law, he should give him such a law as this, and impress it upon his mind, so as it might be said, God was not more to govern him by it, than he was to govern himself: and so finally was to judge him by it, as he must needs judge himself! "He hath shewn thee, O man, what is good; and what doth the Lord require of thee, but to do justly, and to love mercy, and to walk humbly with thy God?" Micah 6. 8. Walk in that dutiful subjection to God, which must be the necessary and easy product of supreme and sovereign love to him: and then, carry it justly and

mercifully towards men. And, certainly, that must needs be an instance and evidence of the greatest goodness in God, that should be the cause of the greatest good in man. Now, do but suppose the world conformed to this law of God, in these two most noble and constituent parts of it; that is, that all the inhabitants of this world did live in the continual love of God, adoring him most gratefully as the great Author of their being, and in a universal and mutual love to one another, each man seeking another's felicity as his own, and having no more design of hurt or mischief against another than he hath against his own life, his own heart; what a happy world were this! And that which tends to happiness, must be from goodness: nothing is plainer. Now, when so admirable a law as this, every part agreeing with the whole, no branch but what is naturally included in this summary, this compendium; I say, when such a law as this was given to men, it is most natural to add, that the same goodness that did enjoin upon man such a law, must also adjoin a penalty to it, a threatening or due punishment for the violation of it; otherwise, the divine government had been ludicrous, if there should have been such a law which is without annexing any penalty. And the better the law, and more unexceptionable, the more clearly righteous and equal is a very severe penalty to be annexed to it: and the annexing it thereunto, is not only what divine goodness must allow, and doth allow, but what it did require. This was a thing not only consistent with divine goodness, but the effect of it, that there should be such intermination added unto such a law. For, if the adding of that sanction to the law, was the aptest means to procure the continual obedience of it, and the law itself had a tendency to the good of the community for whom it was made, then the very addition of the sanction or threatening to the precept of the law, must not only consist with the goodness of it, but proceed from it. Any prince that doth really study the welfare of the governed community, must be understood to adjoin due and proper penalties to good laws, for the good of the people to be governed by them: that the awe of the adjoined threatening may procure obedience, and that obedience, felicity to them that are so governed; so as that such a law being once made, goodness did not only admit of it, but did require that there should be a penalty annexed to it, to enforce obedience. And again,

9. It was never to be expected, that when God made such a creature, he should create him in that which was to be his final state. It could never be looked for from the divine goodness, that making such a creature as man, he should settle him in

a final, good and happy estate the first day he made him. It can be no way inconsistent with the goodness of God, that having made such a creature as man, he should order him a state of trial, of probation, through which he was to pass into that state which was to be final, and perpetually felicitating. For a final state is a state of retribution, a state of reward. The Scripture so speaks of it, frequently, as you cannot but know. Now I beseech you, what was it to be the reward of? It must be the reward of a foregoing obedience. And therefore, it could never have been expected from the divine goodness, that when God first made man, he should have made it impossible for him ever to have offended: or when he made any intelligent creature that he should have made it so. Those two great orders of intelligent creatures, angels and men, it is plain enough God made neither of them incapable of offending. And it was not reasonable to expect that he should. But as to ourselves, (for we are more obliged to mind our own concernments,) this is the account we have given us, (Eccles. 7. 29.) "God made man upright; but he hath sought out many inventions." God made him upright, put him into a good state, if he would have liked it, but he must needs fall to his own inventions, to mend it, and try if he could not make to himself a better state than God had made for him. It was never to be expected from the divine goodness, that he should, by almighty, extraordinary power, have prevented this. For the creature that was designed to be rewarded with eternal felicity, for a present temporal obedience, he must be left to the trial of his ingenuity and dutifulness towards his bountiful Creator. Otherwise, there would have been no place, no room for reward. And if there had been no place for punishment, in case of disobedience, there could have been no place of reward, in case of obedience and duty. Therefore, I add hereupon,

10. That inasmuch as it was necessary there should be such a law, and the threatening annexed to it, or punishment proportionable to any offence committed against it, the execution, according to the tenour of the threatening, became accordingly and consequently necessary, supposing once the violation of such a law. I speak of that law which was natural and original to man; for that little instance of obedience wherein God did put man at first upon, there could not have been transgression in that, without it had been a violating of the most natural law, in the most noble and essential part of it. Now, if a threatening were necessary to be annexed to a law, the execution of it, in case of a violation of that law, was consequently necessary; yea, and if the threatening did immediately pro-

ceed from divine goodness, the execution of the threatening must immediately proceed from it; but not without the intervention of the divine veracity. The goodness of God did lead him to add a due and proportionable threatening to his law: and this law being violated and broken, so as that the threatened punishment became due, it must be executed. That which was ordained from the divine goodness, it comes to be the immediate effects of divine justice, which is not contrary to goodness: it is only in our conception diverse, but far from being contrary. If there had not been such a constitution, the divine goodness had not shone forth with that lustre and evidence that now it doth. And there being such a constitution, his truth and legal justice oblige him, in some way or other, to keep to it, either in kind or equivalency: he must do himself and his own law that right, as to preserve the honour, reputation and dignity of it, and of his own government concerned therein. Therefore, the execution of such a law, by inflicting the incurred penalty one way or other was necessarily and unavoidably consequent: so necessary, that one attribute could not in this case have had its sole exercise without injury to some other, which our first consideration was directed against. But then I yet further add,

11. That whatsoever penalty comes to be inflicted upon unreconcilable sinners, in the final and eternal estate, it must be acknowledged that much of divine goodness was exercised and demonstrated towards them before. Suppose an offending creature whose heart was implacable towards God, and so violently addicted to sensual lusts, that he had the authority of his Maker in continual contempt; and his whole life was a defiance to the authority of his justice and government, and the goodness and kindness of the offers he hath made to him; suppose (I say) such a creature incurs never so severe a penalty, he cannot but acknowledge that much of the divine goodness had its exercise and demonstration towards him before. For otherwise, what room or place were there for that expostulation of the apostle, even with them whom he supposeth finally to fall under wrath in the day of God's wrath, and revelation of his righteous judgment; "Despisest thou the riches of his goodness, and long-suffering, and forbearance? not knowing that the goodness of God should lead thee to repentance?" Despisest thou his goodness! This same despising had no object, if there had been no exercise of goodness towards such a one before: and it would suppose this expostulation to be a great impertinency. Despise goodness; it were to despise nothing, if there had been no goodness, and so there could have been

no such thing as despising: the thing the apostle chargeth upon such a one; for there can be no act where there is no object. There could be no goodness to be despised, if there had not been the exercise of goodness towards such a one in a former state. Therefore, I add,

12. That the general and special goodness of God are things no way inconsistent with one another. These two things do very fairly accord, God's general goodness towards all, and his special goodness towards some. And it argues a very great debility of mind, and shortness of discourse, when any do set these against one another, as if special goodness must destroy the notion of general goodness, or as if general goodness must destroy the notion of special. The matter would be more easily apprehensible, if we would bring it to a case relating to a human government, and suppose the best that is supposable in this world. Would you suppose that the clemency, kindness and goodness of the best prince that ever was (or of whom you can form any idea in your own minds) must oblige him to deal alike with all his subjects, that is, that all persons that are of equal parts, of equal understandings, must be equally preferred, equally dignified? Would the goodness of any prince oblige him to this, that if he find a necessity to have some persons of good parts and understanding to be of a privy council to him, that he must have all to be of that privy council that are of as good parts as they? And shall such a prince not be thought to be good, or his government not to be equal, unless it were so? The best idea that we can form of any government is, that things be equally carried towards all, and yet special favour be towards objects that are not altogether incompetent, at the choice of the ruler. This is the best idea we can form. Bring then the matter to the divine government; we must distinguish between matters of right and matters of favour. For matters of right, we are to expect from it, that God do right to all men universally without exception; but for matters of mere favour, in reference whereunto he is not so much as a debtor by promise; (and he can be a debtor to none by nature) he can owe nothing to his creature. It is possible for a subject in a human government to oblige his ruler, but no creature can oblige God. A subject in a human government may really deserve favour and kindness at the hands of his rulers, for he can benefit them, it is in his power to profit them, they can really be the better for him; but God can be the better for none of us; therefore, he can be a debtor to none but by promise; we are therefore only to expect from the divine goodness, that where he hath promised, there he will be as

good as his word; but for unpromised favour, to which the creature can have no title, that there he do dispense arbitrarily as seemeth good to him. And therefore, upon this ground his general goodness towards all, and special goodness towards some, are no inconsistencies one with another. And if he do generally shew that goodness in the course of his dispensations, to all his creatures, and especially to all the children of men, that every one that considers must acknowledge, then it is no detraction from the goodness that he doth shew to all, that he doth somewhat more of mere special favour for others, yea, though it be never so much, or though it be never so greatly more. There is no cause or pretence why any man's eye should be evil because his is good. For free and unpromised favours, (and all are unmerited, but such as are not only unmerited but unpromised too,) that he dispense out these arbitrarily, is certainly no repugnancy to the highest and most perfect goodness. I further add,

13. That instances of the general goodness of God towards men are most numerous and undeniable. For besides, that he hath given them being, (when it was in his choice and pleasure whether he would or no,) here he entertains them in a world, to the making whereof, none of them did ever contribute any thing; he watches over them by an indulgent providence, supplies them with breath every moment; keeps off, for an appointed time, destructive evils, affords them out of that common bounty of his, the good things that are necessary for the continuance and comfort of life. How rich is this earth in its productions for offending creatures! I cannot but think of it, many times, with wonder, that considering that this inferior part of God's creation so soon after it was made, fell under his just displeasure and righteous curse, there yet should be so great variety of productions, every where in this earth, for the entertainment of rebels, or those that for the most part never give thanks for what they enjoy, never look up, although they have a capacity and disposition in their nature (originally) so to do, to adore, to pay reverence to the first and eternal Being. That which some think to be more the difference of a man from a brute than reason is, a natural religion, which some take a great deal of pains with themselves to erase and tear by the roots out of their own souls. Let us consider that which the text refers to, "Love your enemies, bless them that curse you, do good to them that despitefully use you, and persecute you, that you may be the children of your Father, who doth good to the evil and the good, makes his sun to shine and his rain to fall on one and the other;" do so, that you may represent your Father;

herein lies his perfection. This whole earth that men fill with their wickedness, he fills with his goodness, "The whole earth is full of the goodness of the Lord," Psalm 33. 5. "The Lord is good to all; and his tender mercies are over all his works." Psalm 145. 9. "He hath not left himself without witness, in that he doeth good, and gives fruitful seasons, and fills men's hearts with food and gladness." Acts 14. 17. And I further add,

14. That even those instances of divine goodness that are of an inferior kind, have a tendency and aptitude in them to make way for the exercise of his goodness to them, in a higher and nobler kind. The goodness which God exerciseth towards men in the concernments of this natural life of theirs, they have a tendency and aptitude to affect their minds, and to beget good impressions there, and to make them consider and bethink themselves, "Whence is all this? and how comes it to pass that such provision should be made for one, and for creatures generally, of that order to which I belong?" This is the tendency, even of external mercies. Whereupon, it is spoken of with such resentment, "They say unto God, Depart from us, we desire not the knowledge of thy ways—yet he filled their houses with good things: but the counsel of the wicked be far from me." Job 21. 14, 15. And the same, you have resumed afterwards, in the next chapter, implying that the tendency of things did run quite otherwise; that is, to allure and draw the minds and hearts of men towards God; and make them consider and bethink themselves, and say, Why should we not covet to know our great Benefactor, and him from whom all our good comes? But they say unto him "Depart from us, we desire not the knowledge of thy ways:"—"though he filled their houses with good things;" and therefore, is there such a resentment afterwards expressed: "but the counsel of the wicked be far from me;" representing them as a monstrous sort of creatures, a sort of prodigies in the world, that there should be such a disaffection in rebellious and obdurate hearts against the Author of all goodness and kindness and mercy, that is in so continued a course exercised towards them. The counsel of the wicked be far from me; as if any serious and considering man must, and ought to be startled and affrighted at beholding such a spectacle as this, a reasonable, intelligent soul shunning and fleeing away from him who is daily loading it with his benefits, and seeking, by kindness and goodness, to insinuate himself into it, and so make room and place for himself, in the love and kindness of such a one. But that these dispensations have this tendency in them, the Scripture is full

of it; "Knowest thou not that the goodness of God leadeth thee to repentance?" hath a leadingness thereto, in that mentioned Rom. 2. 4. "And count, (saith the apostle Peter in his 2 Epis. ch. 3. 15.) that the long-suffering of the Lord is salvation:" (he would not have us make a false count, I hope:) reckon that he is aiming at the saving of your souls, while he is doing good to you in external respects. If he feed you with bread, if he feed you with breath day by day, and moment by moment, what is it for? Is it only to support such a despicable thing as this frail body of yours is, which must shortly become a carcass? Is that the utmost of his design? No, he is leading thee to repentance, and would have thee account that both his bounty and his patience towards thee have salvation in design. Count the long-suffering of the Lord is salvation, that is, it is the design of the thing; it is that which the thing itself doth naturally aim at, and lead unto. And hereupon, we are told, in that, Acts 14. 16, 17, 18. that God aimed at the turning men from the vanities that their hearts did doat on as the objects of their worship, to the living God; he did aim at this in giving them fruitful seasons, as you may see, if you take notice of the connexion between the 15 and 17 verses of that chapter. So, Acts 17, he gives them being, breath and all things, that they might seek after him who is not far from every one of us; in whom we live and move and have our being. And then,

15. Lastly; The terms upon which he offers peace and pardon and eternal life to offending creatures are the highest proofs and evidences imaginable, of the wonderful goodness of God, notwithstanding that so great multitudes do, finally, refuse them and perish. And to this purpose, it should be considered, that the apostle speaks of this as matter of transport more than doubt, and that it did need more to be admired than evinced. "God so loved the world that he gave his only begotten Son, that whosoever believeth in him, should not perish but have everlasting life." John 3. 16. The silence that is there used is more speaking than any speech could be. He so loved the world, at so stupendous a rate. It is a very speaking silence that he doth not tell us how great that love is; he leaves us to understand it to be altogether inexpressible, that he should give his only Son, that whosoever believeth in him should not perish—and whereas, men have an impotency to the exercise of that faith that is requisite to their attaining salvation, what is that impotency? It stands only in an affected blindness and obduracy of will; that which they call moral impotency. Now moral impotency doth not excuse, but ag-

gravate the faultiness. No man takes moral impotency to be an excuse, but a high aggravation. As if a man is guilty of murder, and he bring this to excuse him,—"I could not but kill that man because I hated him, I did so violently hate him that I could not but do this unto him." That moral impotency (his extreme hatred) aggravates the crime, that that made it to be done, made it so highly faulty, and so much the more heinous, that it is done. He is not less guilty, but the more, by how much the more his hatred was predominant and prevalent in the case. Why, so this disaffection to God and to Christ and to holiness, (which is impotency) is an impotency seated in the will, and the ignorance hath its root, it ariseth and proceeds from thence, that is, that men are "alienated from the life of God, through the ignorance that is in them, and because of the blindness of their hearts." A blindness which they love, a blindness which they choose, as it is, Ephes. 4. 18. Whereupon, all their misery is self-created. The miseries wherein men are involved in this world, which make it another hell to them, (a hell on this side hell,) and the miseries of the final and eternal state, they are all self-created: that is, they do arise from a fixed, inveterate malignity against the Author of their being, and that very nature itself, whereof their own, at first, was an imitation. An amazing thing, but it were impossible, if men did love God, to be miserable. Loving him is enjoying him, and enjoying him is felicity, if any thing be, or can be. The image of men's future miseries, you have in their present state. What is it that makes the world such a hell as it is, but men's hatred of God and of one another? For (as was said) if there were no contention at all, among men on earth, but who should love God best, and one another best, and who should do most for him, and for one another, what a heavenly life should we live here, a heaven on this side heaven: but the hell on this side hell, is only this, that men's hearts are filled with enmity against God, and one another: and from this malignity proceeds their infidelity, that they do not unite to God in Christ when they are called to it; which is no excuse, but an aggravation. But, in the mean time, that is the most wonderful goodness that can be thought, that such overtures should be made to men, God having given his only begotten Son, that whosoever believeth in him should not perish, but have everlasting life.

LECTURE XXV.*

And this may suffice to be said, in answer to that first objection against the divine goodness, the eternal miseries of the most. And, indeed, the sum of all that can be said upon that account, doth amount to this, as if it were a thing inconsistent with the goodness of God, that he hath made such a creature as man, given him so excellent a being, made him after his own image, that is, endowed him with a reason and a will, in his very creation: and, that having made him such, he did not unalterably fix him in a good and happy state the first day, but that he thought fit to pass him through a state of probation into his final state; and upon this lapse and degeneracy, he did not do for every one in order to their recovery as he hath done for some. In answer whereto, you have these considerations laid before you.

But we pass on to the other objection; the temporal afflictions of good men. Some may be prone to impeach the divine goodness upon this account, and object against what hath been said on that subject. But here, such as find themselves disposed so to object, should reflect upon themselves and consider, what they themselves are. Are they good men that do thus object? Or are they such as are afraid to be so on this account, and are thereupon so very officious as to object this on the behalf of others, while they themselves are loth thereupon to become good, apprehending they shall not serve a good master, and are therefore willing to wave and decline his service? If they be men of this latter stamp and character, that do so object, it seems that their sense must be this, that they will never be good themselves, unless God will hire them to it by temporal rewards and emoluments, by indulging them to live a life of ease and pleasure and opulency in the world. And for them whose sense this is, I have but these things briefly to say to them:

1. That true goodness can never be so mercenary. They are never like to become good upon these terms; if God should give them their own terms.

2. I would have them consider what other choice they can have. If they will not serve God, and devote themselves to him, and admit to be such as he requires, (that is, truly good,) but upon these terms, what else will they do? What other master, or service, or way have they to make choice of? Can they, by

---

* Preached December the 18th, 1691.

their not being willingly subject to the governing power of God, exempt themselves from an unwilling subjection to his vindictive power? Whither will they betake themselves? will they leave God's dominions? will they go beyond the bounds of his territories? whither will they fly? Neither earth, nor heaven, nor hell, can keep them out of his reach; as the Psalmist, at large, speaks it in that 139 psalm, and the prophet Jeremiah in the 23 chap. of his prophecy. "Am I a God at hand, and not a God afar off? Do not I fill heaven and earth? saith the Lord." Is it to be a disputed thing between him and you, whether you shall serve him and comply with his good and acceptable will? And,

3. If God should give such men their terms, whereas they appear to be in the temper of their spirits bad enough already, they have a great deal of reason to think that would make them a great deal worse. It needs abundance of previous and preventing grace not to be the worse for a good condition, here in this world, as all experience shews. And,

4. Lastly, I would appeal to such, whether God is not, in such respects, abundantly good to them already. Hath he not given you breath and being and all things that you enjoy? How great are the favours that you partake of, in common with the rest of men! To instance in what the context mentions: "He makes his sun to rise on the evil and on the good, and sends his rain on the just and on the unjust." What a case were you in, if God should put out the sun, and if he should turn the fruitful land in which you dwell, into universal barrenness, by continual withholding his rain? If he should turn your present health into continual sickly languishings, and your ease into tormenting pains, and your plenty into pinching wants, and straits? And more than all this, if he should turn his invitations to you to pray and supplicate for higher, and those that may tend to eternal mercies, into prohibitions; and say to you, "Never pray, never supplicate, never look up, I will receive no addresses from you?" If his invitations to you to surrender yourselves, and become his, and take him for yours, should be turned into protestations against it, "I will never be your God, and you shall never be my people?" Think while this is not the case, if God be not abundantly good to you already, so that upon your own account you have very little reason to contest the matter with him.

But, if good men do object this, as possibly against their more habitual frame, under the power of some temptation they may be apt to do, as we find it was with the Psalmist in the 73 psalm: and the like offence and scandal, good men are represented as, sometimes, apt to take at their own afflicted condition, compared with the prosperous state of worse men, against which, much of that 37th psalm is directed, and that 21st of Job; and the beginning of the 12th. chap. of Jeremiah's prophecy: let such but go into the sanctuary, as the Psalmist did, (in that 73d. psalm) retire themselves, consider the thing in the secret divine presence, and commune with God about the matter, and not with their own souls, nor consult with flesh and blood, and let them but consider such things as these, briefly,

(1.) Whether this matter of fact be ordinarily and generally true, that the case of good men is worse than that of wicked men in external respects. It is a matter that deserves to be considered and inquired wisely about; and certainly, upon inquiry, it will rather be found otherwise: that is, except in the paroxysm of persecution against instituted religion; (for it is very rare that men should be persecuted for natural but,) "if any man will live godly in Christ Jesus," he must expect to "suffer persecution." I say, except in some such paroxysm of persecution upon such an account, for Christianity itself, as to those that live among pagans, or for this or that institution of them that live among christians, that case being excepted which is not constant; ordinarily, it appears evident that the better men are, the better their state and condition are in this world. Their religion obligeth them to that temperance, sobriety and diligence in their callings, prudent and discreet management of their affairs, that in ordinary cases it is most plain and manifest, that there are much fewer who are ruined by their religion, than that are ruined by their wickedness, by their riot, and by their debauchery; more persons, more estates, and more families are ruined that way, if there be but a survey taken of the state of things in this world: and the apostle offers this very consideration, (in that 1 Cor. 10. 13. even to the very suffering christians of that time) "There hath no temptation," (that is tentative affliction) "befallen you but what is common to men," but what is human. It is true, the account is not common, but the matter of the affliction or the afflictions materially considered, are common to men. Are good men thrown into jails, and sometimes put to death for their religion? Truly, so are bad men for their wickedness, as frequently, and, if we should make a general computation, much more frequently. They suffer the same things very commonly, upon a less comfortable account. And,

(2.) Where this is really the very case, that the condition of good and holy men is, in this world, much worse than that of the worst men, as many times it is so; they are to consider the vastly different value of spiritual and temporal good things, and this is the great business of a christian, to labour to have that spiritual sense in exercise, by which to be able to discern between good and evil, and to prefer the things that are more excellent: as those two scriptures compared together speak; Heb. 5. 14. and Phil. 3. 8. They ought to have their naked, unvitiated senses by which to discern between good and evil, and to abound in that judgment and sense, in all sense, by which they may distinguish the things that differ, and prefer (as that expression admits to be read) the things that are more excellent. And then, how much greater is the value of a sound and well tempered mind and spirit, above that of all earthly and worldly accommodations and enjoyments imaginable, which are but the gratifications of our flesh and external sense, at best. And,

(3.) Such are to consider what is the experience of christians of all times, concerning the aptitude and useful subserviency of external afflictions to inward and spiritual advantage: they say, when they are in their calmer, and more considering frames that it is good for them, that they were afflicted, and, that God hath done it in very faithfulness to them. And,

(4.) Lastly. It is God's own declared end, in the temporal afflictions, he lets befal his, and therefore, would have them count it all joy, when they fall into divers temptations, that is, tentative afflictions. James 1. 2. Count it all joy, because it made greatly for their perfection. The trial of your faith worketh patience, therefore, count it all joy; implying, there is more of real good in that one single excellency of patience, than can be of evil in all the external afflictions, absolutely resigned and submitted to the divine pleasure. Here is so much of an inchoate heaven, such a heaven as our present state admits of, this one thing hath, as is not only enough to make us patient, but joyful under the various temptations and trials of this kind, that we are apt to fall into, or lie under. And hereupon, where this sense hath been impressed upon the hearts of good men, they have thought the sufferings of the present time, were not worthy to be compared with the end of them, which was to be wrought out thereby, as in that, Rom. 8. 18. " I reckon that the sufferings of the present time, are not worthy to be compared with the glory which shall be revealed in us." This is my arithmetic, so I account, or this is my logic, so I reason: the word may be rendered either way, this is the rational estimate I make of this case, having turned it round, and viewed it on every side, and balanced things with things, that the sufferings of the present time, this *now* of time, this very point of time, are not worthy to be compared (alas, it is not to be named the same day,) to the glory that is to be revealed. It is as nothing in the account, as if we should weigh a feather against a mountain. This is my rational estimate and judgment in this case. And, that God doth design the afflictions of this present state, as a preparation for the future, and eternal state, we have most expressly laid down in that, 2 Cor. 4. 17. " The light afflictions which are but for a moment, work for us a far more exceeding and eternal weight of glory." It is a *metathesis* which is not usual in Scripture; do work for us, that is, indeed, do work us for it. And it is to be understood, principally, of subjective glory, not objective; for that can never be more or less to any: it is essentially the same in itself with divine glory, but subjective glory, not objective. It is essentially the same in itself with divine glory; but subjective glory to be impressed, that is, more or less, according to the capacity and disposition of the subject. And we grow more capable, and are larger vessels, receptive of greater glory, as our temper is: and our temper is better, and made more receptive of larger and more glorious communications, even by the sufferings of this present time. By the light afflictions which are but for a moment, we are so much the more apt for the eternal weight of glory, which is to ensue; which we are not barely to be told, but to bear, answerable to the notion of weight. We are not only to be mere spectators of the glory there spoken of, but the subjects of it. And then, if this be all that God doth design by the afflictions that he lets befal good men here in this world, to refine them, to make them more partakers of his own holiness, and consequently of fuller glory, greater and higher measures of glory, is this any ground of taking up diminishing thoughts concerning his goodness? Yea, I might add,

It is that which his very relation doth oblige him to, even as he is our Father: your heavenly Father is perfect. For what a Father is he to us? Or in what sense is he Father to his own? He is the Father of their spirits; so his word speaks contradistinguishly of him, to the fathers of our flesh. Of the flesh we have other fathers. Heb. 12. 9. He is not the Father of our flesh; he is the Creator of it: but of our spirits he is the Father. He is the Father of them, both upon a natural and supernatural account, as they have his natural image, being intelligent and spiritual beings like his own: and, as his regenerate children, have his holy image renewed in them. Now the very relation doth oblige him (if he be a Father to us, that is, to our spirits,) more principally to mind the advantage of our spirits. That very relation doth not only admit, but require that he should let us suffer in our flesh, if it may be for the advantage of our spirits: and that this outward man should be beaten and shattered day by day, even unto perishing, if, while this is a doing and suffering, the inward man may be renewed day by day. He must take the principal care about that to which he is a Father. Affection must follow the relation; the relation is to our spirits, and the affection must be, principally, to our spirits.

But I shall insist no further on that part. It remains only to make somewhat of *Use* of what hath been said, especially touching this divine perfection of the goodness of God. And,

1. Be hereupon encouraged to cherish this apprehension concerning God, take heed that nothing ever shake your fixed belief and apprehension of this. And whatsoever reasonings do arise in your minds at any time, forelay this always, let it be always a thing forelaid in you. Yet God is good to Israel, as the Psalmist begins that 73 psalm. Nothing can be of greater importance, either to the liveliness and vigour, or even to the very substance and being of religion, than a fixed, stable apprehension of the divine goodness: that religion is nothing, the soul whereof is not love. If love be not the very soul of your religion, your religion is a carcass, an empty nothing. But that love may be the soul of it, there must be a constant apprehension of the loveliness of the object. Labour then to have your souls possessed always with a deep and fixed apprehension of the divine goodness. Contemplate it in every thing that you behold, in every thing that you enjoy, yea, even in the lessening and qualifying of those evils that you suffer. Go up and down this world with hearts full of this thought; "the whole earth is full of his goodness." Collect all the instances you can of the goodness of God, and keep by that means, such an apprehension alive and in vigour concerning him. What a mighty spring would this be, of cheerful and joyful and pleasant religion. Let no thought arise, but let it meet with a seasonable check, if it tend to any diminution of divine goodness. And,

2. Preserve a worshipping, adoring frame of spirit Godward upon this very account, having your hearts full of this apprehension and sense; labour always to be in a posture of adoration, apt and ready always to look up, carrying that as a motto engraven on your hearts, "I am less than the least of all thy mercies." And again,

3. Endeavour as much as in you is, accordingly to look upon that immediate promanation of the divine goodness, his law; that which issues, which proceeds so directly from the goodness of God. Esteem it to be what really it is, the product and image of the divine goodness. Look upon him

as absolutely, universally perfect, and consider the reasonableness of what is said concerning this law, in correspondency thereunto. "The law of the Lord is perfect." Psalm 19. 7. And considering this one single perfection of the Divine Being, his goodness, make a proportionable judgment concerning his law, in reference to that; that is, that it is an expression of his good and acceptable will: and labour, more and more, to prove that by a vital sense, by an experimental relish in your own spirits. O! how good is it to be what he would have me to be! what that most perfect rule of his doth require and oblige me to be. And,

4. Accordingly judge concerning the course of his providential dispensations. His law precribes to us the way in which we are to walk; his providences make the way in which he walks; labour to apprehend goodness therein too. All his ways are mercy and truth. That is, you are to judge according to the series of his providences complexly taken, and as together they do make up one entire frame. And so, indeed, we are to make up our judgment concerning his law. Not by this or that particular precept, for it would be a very hard imposition upon the mind of a man, to judge and pronounce concerning the goodness of that command to pluck out the right eye, or cut off the right hand, or the right foot, abstractly taken, without reference to the conjunct precepts, and without reference to the end, to which, altogether, they refer. And so, if you look upon providence, you are not to pronounce concerning this or that, separately and apart, considered by itself. As you would not make a judgment of the goodness of a piece of arras by looking on it folded up, where you can only discern a piece of a leg, or a piece of an arm, it may be, or the limb of a tree, but look upon it unfolded, and there see the entire frame of it all at once. So consider the providences of God, in reference one to another, and in reference to their end in which all things shall finally issue, and into which they shall result, and you must say as the Psalmist doth, "All the ways of the Lord are mercy and truth." And as Moses, in that triumphant song of his, in the 32 Deut. where he tells us, in the beginning, his design was to publish the name of the Lord, that is, to represent the glory of his attributes; "Because (saith he) I will publish the name of the Lord, ascribe ye greatness to our God: He is the rock, his work is perfect." Take all together, you will see it will be perfect work at length, entire, all of a piece; and that nothing could have been spared out of that series and chain of providence that compose and make up the whole course. And then,

5. Endeavour that your knowledge of God may be practical, vital, unitive and transforming, as touching this very thing, the divine goodness. O! how much to be lamented is it, that we should have such a notion of God in our minds to no purpose? the notion of so great a thing, a Being absolutely perfect and infinite, even in this perfection, goodness itself, immense goodness lying in our minds, idle, dead, useless and in vain; so that our hearts are in reference hereunto but a mere *rasa tabula*. There is a notion in our minds, but nothing correspondent impressed upon our hearts, such an apprehension of God as this, if it were vital, lively and operative, would transform us, make us aim continually to be such as he is, which I shall further press by and by. It would powerfully attract and draw us into union with him. What! shall I live at a distance from the Fountain of all goodness, immense goodness, goodness itself, love itself! God is love. He that believes the love of God, is hereupon drawn to dwell in God as he is love, considered under that notion, and so to have God to dwell in him; as the apostle expresseth it, 1 John 4. 16. What mighty influence would this have upon our whole course, if we did go with lively, operative, apprehensions up and down the world of the divine goodness! How should we disburden our souls of care! With what cheerfulness should we serve him! How little doubt should we have concerning the issue of things! of that glorious reward which a course of obedience, service, and fidelity to him, a little will be followed with at last. But that our knowledge of God, as to so great a thing as this, should be like no knowledge, as if we knew nothing, or as if we thought the quite contrary concerning him; methinks, this we should look upon as an insufferable thing, as a thing not to be endured, and so take up resolutions, dependant upon his grace, never to be at rest till our hearts were like this apprehension of God, that he is perfect in goodness. And hereupon further,

6. Make sure of your relation to him as your God, as your Father; and consider and contemplate his goodness with that very design, that you may be indeed stirred up to aim at coming, without more ado, into that relation. We do not much concern ourselves so seriously to inquire touching the character of a person with whom we are never to have to do, with whom we have no concern nor ever expect to have any. If we hear of any such as an excellent person, we hear such a thing of him with more indifferency of mind, "I do not know him, and I am like never to know him; and be as good and as excellent as he will, I am never like to be the better for him." But

when I receive an account of one, as a most excellent person, who designs to adopt me at the same time for his son, and overtures are made to me for that purpose, I think myself highly concerned to inquire into the character of a person to whom I am to be related. And so should we consider the characters that we meet with of God; for we must either have him as our Father, or we must be children of a worse father, or of the worst of fathers. Therefore, this should be hearkened unto, your heavenly Father is perfect, perfectly good, perfect in goodness, upon this account, that overtures are made to me in order to my becoming one of his children: I am to come into his family; this is the thing that is proposed to me. And should not I labour to know what a one he is, and to contemplate the representation that is made to me of him, upon this account? And,

7. Consider with highest admiration and gratitude, the greatness, the privilege, that you are, or may be so related. As the case is stated, if this be not, there is nothing wanting but your own willing and joyous acceptance of the overture, falling in with it, resigning and giving up yourselves most absolutely and entirely to him; and taking his Christ for yours; with him goes the sonship, that is, with the acceptance of his own eternal Son. John 1. 12. "To as many as received him, to them gave he power to become the sons of God, even to as many as believed in his name." And then, consider the greatness of the privilege, that you are, or may be thus related to the Most High God as a Father, to the best, most perfect, and most excellent of beings. You may have him for your Father, and perhaps you have him so already. How great a privilege is this! To have him for your Father is to have all. He that overcometh, shall inherit all things, and I will be his God, and he shall be my son. Rev. 21. 7. "And if children, then heirs, heirs of God, and joint heirs with Jesus Christ." God is to be your portion and inheritance, that if we suffer together with him (which is but a trifle, not to be compared with the glory that is to be revealed) we may be also glorified together. Rom. 8. 17, 18. Methinks, this should run in our minds every day; we are either related to this blessed One, as our Father, or we may be; we are invited and called by the gospel, (and it is the great design of this gospel) into this blessed state. Methinks, it should run in our minds all the day long, that that glorious and most excellent One, should look down from heaven upon such an abject worm as I, and say to me, "Call me Father, take me for thy Father." A heart that were full of the sense of this, would soon grow too big for all this world. What a trifle

would this world be to that soul which were full of that sense; "God is become my Father, I have a Father in heaven, that doth whatsoever he will in heaven and in earth, and there is no withstanding him." He can do what he will, and he will do nothing but what is kind and good to them that willingly consent to come into this comfortable relation to him. You see how distinguishingly such a case is spoken of in the next chapter, Mat. 6. in the latter end. Do not you so and so, like the gentiles. Do not torture yourselves with cares and thoughts, "what ye shall eat, and what ye shall drink, and what you shall put on," and what shall become of your affairs and concerns in the world, and the like: the gentiles do so: after these things do the gentiles seek; but your heavenly Father knows what you need; you have a Father in heaven that knows all your concernments, and that minds all of them, with all wisdom, and all the tenderness and kindness imaginable, I would not have you be as if you had no Father, to put yourselves into the same condition with pagans and outcasts, and those that are without God in the world. And then,

8. Lastly; Imitate God in his imitable perfections, and especially in this his goodness. I say, imitate him with all the goodness that is possible, in all his perfections: "Be ye perfect, for your heavenly Father is perfect." So I would shut up, bringing the exhortation in the text, and inferring reason together. And pray drive it to this one particular thing, to which the context draws and claims it, that is, unto love: and even unto such love as shall reach enemies themselves. You very well know, that God could have shewn no love at all to any in all this world, but he must shew it to an enemy: all were in enmity and rebellion against him. "The carnal mind is enmity against God." And this world was only possessed with such inhabitants, all sunk in carnality and earthliness, and deep oblivion of God, and full of anger and displeasure, upon being put in mind that there is One that claims a right over them, and that would have all their thoughts and their love: this they cannot endure; this carnalized race of creatures cannot bear this. "For the carnal mind is enmity against God." And he could never have been kind to men but he must be kind to enemies. For all were become his enemies, affected liberty, and could not endure the thought that there should be a power and a Lord to prescribe to them. I pray, let us labour to imitate this great perfection of the divine goodness, even in this very application of it to enemies. This is the beauty and the glory of the Christian religion, the thing wherein it excels the precepts of the most refined paganism, and of

that which was higher, (as it was grown,) Judaism itself. "You have heard that it was said of old time, "Thou shalt love thy neighbour and hate thy enemy:" (as it is in the context) "But I say unto you, Love your enemies, bless them that curse you, pray for them that despitefully use you and persecute you; that you may be the children of your Father which is in heaven." I never expect the Christian religion to flourish much in this world, till this appear and be exercised as the common temper of christians. They are to be such a sort of men, as that all the world may be the better for. If you express never so much of unkindness towards them, if you use them hardly, they will bless you, they will pray for you, they will do you all the good they can, all the good and kind offices in their power. When this spirit comes to be revived among men, it will make the Christian religion (as I may say) *grassari*, mightily to prevail and grow upon the world. The world must fall before such a sort of men as this. But that it will never do while, in this respect, christians are just like other men, as wrathful, as vindictive, as full of rage, and as full of revenge as any body else. Christian religion must grow upon the world, by things that will strike the sense, that incur the most sensible observation of men. Every one can tell and sees it when one is kind to them, and when they have good returned for evil. But there are two things most directly opposite to this temper, which christians are wont too frequently to overlook, never to animadvert upon: the one is,

(1.) When they let their hearts tumultuate with too great fervour and anger against men, upon account of their profaneness and irreligiousness; and they think themselves warranted so to do: such a one is a wicked man, an open, visible enemy against God and Christ, a rebel against heaven. And so they allow themselves to let wrath have its vent and liberty towards such men, and upon such occasions. It was a great deal of zeal for Christ, that the disciples discovered, when they would have had fire to fall down from heaven to vindicate his cause upon those Samaritans that would not receive him into their town. But, saith Christ, "Ye know not what spirit ye are of." This is quite another thing from that spirit which I intend to introduce into the world, and which must breathe in, and animate, the religion that I am setting on foot among men. The other is,

(2.) Their confining their kindness and respects to men of such and such a character, to this or that party. It is a temper more grossly remote, more vastly different from what is enjoined upon us here; and the thing that our Saviour animadverts upon in this context, as that wherein we do not only not exceed the pharisees as such, but even publicans themselves. ver. 20. We are told, that except our righteousness exceed the righteousness of the scribes and pharisees, we shall in no case enter into the kingdom of God: not even into the initial kingdom. As if he had said, " Ye are not fit for the Christian state, you do not come within the confines of Christianity, real Christianity, if your righteousness do not exceed the righteousness of the scribes and pharisees. But when men do confine their respects and the kindness of their hearts to a party, this is not only to outdo the pharisees, but even publicans and sinners, for they do so; if you love and salute them that love and salute you, if you are kind to them that are kind to you, what do you more than others? do not even the publicans and sinners the same? But " be ye perfect;"—(that is the contexture of this discourse) " even as your Father which is in heaven is perfect."

And so I have done with what I designed upon this subject, of the divine perfections or attributes; the next we come in course to, will be that of the divine decrees and purposes of God: and more especially concerning men, and with reference to them.

THE PRINCIPLES

OF

THE ORACLES OF GOD,

In Two Parts,

NEVER BEFORE PUBLISHED.

PART II.

CONTAINING

I. The Decrees, or Counsels of God, in eight lectures, on Ephes. 1. 11.

II. God's Work of Creation, in seven lectures, on Heb. 11. 3.

III. God's Creation of Man, in five lectures, on Genesis 1. 27.

IV. The Fall of the First Man, and the Fallen State of Man, with the Death and Misery consequent on each of them, in fourteen lectures on Romans 5. 12.

V. The Justice and Righteousness of God vindicated, as to all men's coming into the world with depraved natures, in eight lectures, on Psalm 51. 4. 5.

VI. The General and Special Grace of God, in order to the recovery of apostate souls, in three lectures, on Luke 2. 14.

LECTURE I.*

Ephes. 1. 11.

In whom also we have obtained an inheritance, being predestinated according to the purpose of him who worketh all things after the counsel of his own will.

HAVING discoursed to you, what I thought requisite, concerning the attributes and perfections of the Divine Being, we now come, according to the order of discourse, to speak to you of the DIVINE DECREES. I choose to call them by that name, because, by divines, they are usually so called; though according to the more ordinary use of that word in Scripture, it more frequently signifies public laws or edicts, whether human or divine, than private and secret purposes. And so in common speech too, and other writings, nothing is more usual than to call the constitutions of states and princes, *decreta*. But however, the word being so explained, to signify a secret purpose, antecedent to any manifestation, it may then fitly enough be so used; and in that sense, it is generally understood by divines, treating on the head of religion.

And upon this subject, my design is not to speak to every thing that is disputed in the schools about it; but only what may be requisite, and sufficient unto the common faith and practice of christians. Nor shall I need to lay down any other doctrine, than the very words of the text, that—God "work-

* Preached December 25, 1691.

eth all things, according to the counsel of his own will,"—wherein you do see, there are several particulars to be considered. There is,

1. The final term of all God's works, that wherein they do directly terminate, *All things*.

2. There is his working itself, tending towards that term, he *worketh* all things.

3. There is his purpose and volition of all that he worketh, called his *will*. And

4. There is the supreme measure of all those volitions or acts of his will, and so of his subsequent actions, and that of his counsel. He worketh all things according to the *counsel* of his own will.

I shall speak briefly to each of these, but most largely to that which is our most proper subject, with reference to the purpose for which we have chosen to insist upon these words, that is, the will of God; not merely the faculty, but the acts of his will. But we shall briefly go over the several particulars already mentioned.

1. For the things wherein the acts willed by him, do finally terminate, which we are told are *all things*, and that universality may be understood two ways, either relatively, in reference to those works that do terminate in these things; as if he said, all things that he works, he works according to the counsel of his will. Or else, also, it may be understood absolutely and simply, there being simply nothing at all, unto which his agency, one way or other, extends not : though not to every thing in the same way; as there will be occasion to shew hereafter.

2. For his working that terminates in these things, that is, in all things; it is emphatically expressed in the text: the word is ενεργουντος, in-acting, or in-working all things. It shews the peculiar kind of the divine agency, such as nothing can exclude, and nothing can disappoint. And then,

3. There is his will itself, which must be looked upon as the immediate source of all these operations of his. And that we shall consider, not only as it is the measure of all his actings, but as it is self-measured by that counsel, that lies in his eternal and all-comprehending mind, which is the fourth particular in order, that we have briefly to consider. And touching that,

4. We must know, that it cannot be understood in the same sense with God, and with men, as indeed nothing can that comes under the same name with him and with us; for nothing can be absolutely common between God and the creature; or have precisely the same common notion : there cannot but be infinite difference, always, between whatsoever is finite, and that

which is infinite. Counsel with men imports imperfection; it signifies that we have not suddenly a perspection of the reason, and aptitudes of things, what it is fit for us to resolve, and not to resolve! and do, or not to do. And thereupon, we deliberate, and arrive more slowly and by degrees from a more indistinct perception of the reason of things, to a clearer and more distinct perception of them. With God, it cannot be so, before whose all-seeing eye, all things lie in their aptitudes and correspondencies at one view; so as he doth not see things because they are connected with one another, so as to proceed from the knowledge of things that are more clear, to the knowledge of things that are more obscure; all things being equally clear and equally present, to his eye and to his view. But by way of analogy, that which is effected by counsel among men in the way of consultation, debate of things with themselves, continued discourse, reasonings and arguings of matters in their own minds to and fro, that, which with men hereupon is called judgment, counsel, hath the same name given it with him also. Not that it signifies the same, but that most perfect judgment of things, which is indeed the highest and most exquisite wisdom, which he hath eternally and all at once, when we do arrive to the like by steps. And so according to that perfect perception, that he hath of the reason of things, and their aptitudes and correspondencies to one another, and to his creatures, and to him, so accordingly he wills, and accordingly he doth.

And this counsel of his, it may be taken two ways, either 1st. As it is internal, lying only in his own mind: or else 2nd. As it hath an after manifestation, as many of those things which lay from eternity, and through many successions of ages of time, secret in his own mind have, and do come to be revealed and made manifest more or less, and in such degrees as to him hath seemed fit. In that latter sense, counsel is taken frequently in Scripture, even when it is spoken of God, as these phrases do plainly signify, " If they had stood in my counsel. They despised all my counsel, and set at nought my reproofs. I have declared to you the whole counsel of God." Jer. 23. 22. Pro. 1. 30. Acts 20. 27.

But here, it must be understood to signify counsel as it is secret, as lying in his own eternal mind, and as it is, thereupon, the measure of all the purposes of his will, and of all he subsequently doth, and hath done, in the creation and continual government of this world. In that latter sense, counsel is, even among men, correspondently in that acceptation of it with God, put for certain, established laws, and constitutions, and even as decrees are. Thus, with the Romans, many constitutions of theirs are known to go under the name of *senatus consulta*, that is, *things consulted of*, and agreed upon, by the governing power among them. But this is not the sense that it is to be taken in here, for notwithstanding much of the counsel of God be manifested, we are to consider it now as antecedent to any such manifestations: and thereupon, to return to that which is our more principal subject, *his will*, according to such counsel, " He works all things after the counsel of his own will;" according to that counsel which doth (as it were) guide and measure all the determinations and purposes of his just and holy will. We are not to understand, that the divine will here signifies the faculty of will, abstractly and precisely, but as comprehending the acts, the volitions, the determinations and purposes of the divine will, that which is commonly meant by the word decrees. And so, concerning the will of God and the purposes thereof, I shall first give you some *distinctions*, and then, secondly, lay down what I conceive necessary to be said concerning this subject in certain *propositions*.

First. There are sundry *distinctions* of the divine will, which it may be fit to take some notice of: and some of them will be of great use to us.

1. There are, who distinguish the will of God into antecedent and consequent. But I know no ground for that distinction, there being no first or last with him, or former or latter, as we shall have occasion further to shew.

2. Again, some distinguish it into absolute and conditional; but certainly, it is over bold to feign any such distinction as that, of the divine will, properly so called; it is indeed agreed on all hands that there are conditions of the things willed, but there can be none of the will itself concerning those things; the faculty and act of the will not being distinguishable in God, as they are in us; for he is a pure act: and to suppose there can be a condition of the will itself in God, is to suppose a conditional Deity and so, consequently, a contingent one, and so, consequently, none at all.

3. Again, some do more truly distinguish the divine will into that which is *bene placite*, and that which is *signi*. And for the former member of that distinction, it is most unexceptionable and scriptural: good pleasure, and the *good pleasure of his will*, we read of again and again in this very context, as well as many times besides in Scripture. But for the other member of the description, it is too obscure for common use; and will require more explication than is proper for this place.

4. It is again distinguishable into his objective and active

will, or his will objectively taken and actively taken, so the thing willed is often called the will of God: as when we pray, " Thy will be done," that is, the thing that thou hast willed. And so that of the apostle, in the Acts, " The will of the Lord be done," and that of our Saviour, "he that doth the will of my Father," and the like. This is the will of God taken objectively, or for the thing willed. But then, it is taken also actively, as it signifies his volition itself, the purpose and determination of his will; and so it must be taken here.

5. It is again distinguishable into secret and revealed; a very useful and necessary distinction. His will, as it lies concealed within himself, and the same will, in many things made at length known and extant to the world, subjected to the common notice of men; that is, in such things as it concerns them to know and be acquainted with.

6. Others distinguish it into decretive and legislative, which is a very proper distinction too, if we take decretive in the fore-explained sense; otherwise, it falls in with the legislative, and is the same thing.

7. Others distinguish it into the will of purpose and the will of precept, which is a true distinction too. Only, that latter member is not extensive enough; for there are many things which, in the compass of God's revealed will, are necessary for us to know; and even within the compass of his legislative will, besides bare precept; but not in all respects. His will concerns what he will do himself, and it also concerns what he will have us to do. But it is his will concerning his own actions, concerning his own works, of which the text speaks: " He worketh all things," that is, his own works, "after the counsel of his own will." And as it doth concern his own works, it may concern them diversely: that is, either such works of his as he designs to do immediately, and apart from us, or such works of his as have a reference to works of ours, wherein he is to work with us, or wherein he is to work, (as in some instances) after us; that is, in those great instances of rewarding and punishing. These works of his come after ours, though the will of them is eternal before. Again,

8. His will is to be distinguished into effective and permissive: his will to effect whatsoever he thinks fit for him to effect; and his will to permit whatsoever he thinks fit to permit, or not to hinder, while what he so wills, or determines so to permit, he intends also to regulate, and not to behold as an idle unconcerned spectator, but to dispose all those *permissa* unto wise and great ends of his own.

These useful distinctions (as there are divers of them) being given, I shall now proceed,

Secondly. To lay down, in divers *propositions*, what is requisite for us to understand and believe, concerning this matter, of God's purpose, by his counsel, in reference to the things which he works among his creatures, and some of these propositions will be more *general*, and fundamental unto some others, which shall be (God willing) more *particular.* But for the more *general propositions* you may take such as these:

1. That all the purposes of the divine will are co-eternal. There can be no such thing as a new will in God; for there is nothing in God, that is not God; and nothing of God can begin *de novo*: for that were to suppose a new Deity. And hereupon, there can be no place for dispute about the priority or posteriority of this or that purpose of God; they must be all simultaneous, all at once, in one and the same eternal view, according to that clear and distinct and all-comprehending prospect that he hath of all things, eternally before his eyes. And though it be true, indeed, that we are constrained to conceive of things; (because we cannot conceive them all at once as he doth,) by first and second, former and latter, and to consider of a natural priority and posteriority, where there is no such thing in real existence; I say, though we are constrained so to do, (which is a thing owing to the imperfection of our minds,) yet, we must take heed of building upon our own foundation, schemes and models of the divine decrees, as a great many have perplexed themselves in doing: and wherein we can determine nothing, but with the greatest uncertainty imaginable, nor, indeed, without too great presumption, bringing down the Deity to our human measures and models, and forms of conception. Again,

2. We must take this proposition concerning the will and purposes of God, that they do always connect together means and ends: that is, supposing he hath willed and determined such an end, we must, accordingly, suppose he hath determined with himself the way or means, by which he will bring that end about; supposing it to be a thing to be done immediately: as those things are to be done, and in the same way wherein they are to be brought about, in the same way we must understand he hath determined to bring them about. As when he did intend to preserve David at Keilah, he did also determine he should not stay there, knowing that if he did, the inhabitants would have given him up to Saul, as you may read it was determined, upon David's inquiry, 1 Sam. 23. So when he determined to save the life of Paul, and all his companions, and fellow passengers in the ship, where they were in so much jeopardy and danger, he did also determine that the mariners should not go away, for the apostle saith expressly, "If these

go away we cannot be saved," after he had expressly, from God, told them, that not a hair of any of their heads should fall to the ground. And therefore, we are not to suppose that he doth determine an end to be brought about by means, but he doth also determine and ascertain the means by which it shall be brought about: so that if he intend any of us to live to such a term of time, he never intends that, and intends at the same time to let us, several years before, starve ourselves, poison or stab ourselves. But determining the end, he also determines those means by which he intends to bring about that end: he intends to bring it about in such a way; that is, in a mediate way.

3. The purposes of God, and his foreknowledge are in some sort commensurate: taking foreknowledge in the proper sense, foreknowledge doth refer to futurity, as knowledge more abstractly taken, doth to all beings actual and possible; all possibilities come within the compass of divine knowledge: but of his foreknowledge, only futurities, or what shall be. And as to these, his purpose and foreknowledge are some way commensurate, that is, whatsoever he foreknows shall be, he either purposeth to effect, or he purposeth not to hinder it. And again,

4. Whatsoever God doth actually bring to pass, that we may conclude he did purpose to bring to pass. Whatsoever he doth, he did purpose to do; for he doth nothing against his will, or without his will: and he can have no new will, as was told you before, and as it is plain in itself. Therefore, whatsoever he actually doth, he did always eternally purpose to do.

5. Whatsoever he actually permits, he did never purpose to hinder. There must be a correspondency between his purpose as to *permissa*, things that are permitted by him, and the things permitted, as there is with reference to *effecta*; between his purpose, and the thing that he effects. Again further.

6. Whatsoever God might, righteously and consistently with all the other attributes and perfections of his being, effect and do, or permit and suffer, that he might righteously resolve and purpose to do, and resolve and purpose to permit and not to hinder. Whatsoever it is that is consistent with his wisdom, holiness and goodness, actually to do, it is equally consistent with his wisdom, and with his righteousness, and with his goodness, to purpose to do, even from eternity. And whatsoever was consistent with his wisdom, and righteousness, and goodness to permit it and not to hinder, it is equally consistent with his wisdom, righteousness and goodness, to purpose not

to hinder it; and so, to have a permissive decree concerning it, if he saw meet and fit to do it. And,

7. Whatsoever, in respect to God's actions and purposes, would imply any thing of imperfection, we must sever and remove from him; whatsoever would imply perfection, we must assert and ascribe to him. Hereupon, if it would be a plain, manifest imperfection to act incogitantly, unadvisedly, or to do unintended things, as it were casually and at random, without a foregoing intention or purpose; if that, I say, would be an imperfection, we ought most carefully to sever it from God, and never think it possible for him to act so; that is, incogitantly, unadvisedly, without any foregoing intention or purpose; and if it be a perfection, to act according to wisdom, and counsel, and judgment, and steady purpose, we must by all means assert it concerning God, and ascribe it to him in reference to all his purposes and actions.

These are general propositions that do lay some foundation for more particular ones, which are to follow. And herein, though it is very true, that God hath his purposes and decrees concerning all things: "He worketh all things according to the counsel of his own will," yet, we shall more especially consider his purposes concerning men. You know, that must be our business: and therein too, though he hath purposes and decrees concerning all the actions of men, whether personally considered, or considered as members of a community, lesser or larger, civil or ecclesiastical, concerning churches, concerning states and kingdoms, their successions, their rises, their continuance, their periods; though he have, I say, purposes concerning all these, and all within the compass of the text, "He worketh all things after the counsel of his own will," yet, I shall chiefly keep my discourse to those purposes that concern our spiritual and eternal state. And so shall lay down briefly the other and *particular* propositions. As,

1. That God did, undoubtedly, purpose to make such a world as this, for we find he hath made it; and he doth nothing that he did not purpose to do.

2. He did purpose to make such a creature as man, and place him here; for we also find, so he hath done.

3. He did purpose to create man in an innocent state, and proportionably good and happy unto the innocency and purity in which he did create him. For his word tells us, that he did create him so. He "made man upright." And it gives us an account of the circumstances of his condition when he made him, though briefly, yet as far as was necessary. And,

4. He did not purpose to confirm him at first in that good state wherein he made him, so as to make it impossible for him to fall; for we find he did fall, and is in a lapsed state: therefore, it was purposed that his fall should not be prevented, that it should not be hindered: though none doubt, but that he that made man, could have made him as well impeccable, without any possibility of sinning, as he did make him sinless at present, without any thing of depravedness by sin.

5. It is evident, God did not purpose to leave fallen man to perish universally in his apostate, fallen state: for we hear of, and know, the methods and appointed means for the recovery and salvation of fallen creatures, of fallen men, which are offered to our view in the word of God.

6. He did decree or purpose to send his own Son to be a Redeemer and Saviour unto lost and perishing creatures, to be born, to live in this world, to die in pursuance of that reconciling design, and to overcome death; and in his resurrection and conquest over death, to erect a kingdom into which he would collect, as the voluntary subjects of it, all those that should resign and yield themselves to him, put themselves under his governing power, and submit themselves to his saving mercy, at once. And the substance of this we have given us as the matter of a divine decree, in that psalm 2. 7. "I will declare the decree. The Lord hath said unto me, Thou art my Son, this day have I begotten thee." Very true it is, that that is not directly meant of the nativity of our Lord: we find the apostle expounds it otherwise, (Acts 13. 33.) "We declare to you glad tidings, how that the promise which was made to our fathers, God hath fulfilled the same unto us their children, in that he hath raised up Jesus again; as it is also written in the 2d psalm," (the most express quotation in the New Testament out of the Old) "Thou art my Son, this day have I begotten thee: and as concerning that he raised him from the dead *now* no more to return to corruption, he said on this wise, I will give you the sure mercies of David." It was in pursuance of a divine, eternal purpose and decree, that this was said, "Thou art my Son, this day have I begotten thee:" that is, when he raised him from the dead, when he begot him again out of the grave, and by that glorious regeneration, he did then put upon him that high and excellent title (that was fundamental to the other glorious one that did ensue thereupon) "The first-begotten from the dead: the Prince of the kings of the earth." Rev. 1. 5. But yet, though that be not the thing directly there spoken of, as the matter of the divine decree, God's first bringing him into this world, yet, that being

the matter of a divine decree, (to wit) his dying, and his conquering death, and being begotten (as it were) a second time, or I may say a third time out of the grave, out of the womb, as his goings forth from eternity in respect of his Deity, and as he was, as man, at first brought out of the womb of the virgin, yet, even that earlier parturition must be supposed here, to have been the matter of a divine purpose and decree too. And so other scriptures do speak of the whole complex of this matter, as falling under a divine purpose. "That he verily was foreordained," (as Acts 2. 23.—1 Pet. 1. 20. and onwards) foreordained to every thing he did, and foreordained to every thing he suffered, in pursuance of that great saving design and errand upon which it was determined he should come into this world. And this is that which the context here doth more specially lead us to insist upon. For when the apostle speaks of God doing all things according to the counsel of his own will, he tells us more distinctly what that counsel of his will did concern, and that is in the foregoing verse: "That, in the dispensation of the fulness of time, he might gather together in one, all things in Christ, both which are in heaven, and which are in earth, even in him." This was the great thing that lay, as the substratum in the divine counsel, to collect and gather all things in Christ, to constitute him as supreme and universal Head to this creation. And whereas, all things were shattered and broken in the apostasy, there was now to be a recapitulation, and gathering all things under one head again, as you see in the close of the chapter. "And hath put all things under his feet, and gave him to be the head over all things to the church, which is his body, the fulness of him that filleth all in all." And this, that was primarily here designed in this context, is that which God hath done according to the counsel of his will. "He doth all things after the counsel of his own will;" but this peculiarly, the sending of his Son into this world and the establishing of him as the Prince of those reduced from the state of apostasy. As the great destroyer of souls was the prince of the apostasy, the head of the apostate world, upon which account he is called "the God of this world." (2 Cor. 4. 4.) and "the spirit that worketh in the children of disobedience," so was our blessed Lord to be the head of that community that should be collected and gathered out of this world. And this was the great mystery of his will, which he purposed in himself, as the foregoing context is, "In the dispensation of the fulness of time" (by the Christian economy, that is the word there used for dispensation) to collect and gather, all under this one glorious head, to recover a people, and raise up a glorious structure, a church, out of a ruining and perishing world, by the Son and eternal God, who was made, in pursuance of this design, the universal Head, also Head over all things, but with special reference to his church. And so was this the matter of divine pleasure; to do this thing in the fulness of time, according as we find in Gal. 4. 4. "In the fulness of time, God sent his Son, born of a woman, made under the law, to redeem them that are under the law: that we might receive the adoption of sons." And as this is the most undoubted matter of divine purpose and decree, so it ought to be the matter of the highest joy and rejoicing; greater than can be expressed by an annual solemnity; such as should run through our lives, and be the matter of every day's rejoicing with us, according to what the first report of this glorious work was, when the womb of divine counsel did teem, and bring forth this glorious birth; when he brought forth the first begotten, into the world, he saith, "Let all the angels of God worship him:" and they did publish the joyful proclamation of it from heaven, " Glory to God in the highest, and on earth peace good will towards men:" the greatest indication of divine good will, and the most significant that ever was known, or ever could be thought, that is, that when men had severed themselves from God, cut themselves off from him; and the world was sunk into a universal oblivion of him, destitute of all inclination towards him, and all interest in him, unapt to make any inquiries after him, or to say "Where is our God, our Maker?" that they should be so surprisingly told of Emmanuel, God with us: that God should so strangely descend, put on man, be manifested in the flesh, there was the greatest mystery of Godliness, that ought to fill heaven and earth with joy and with wonder. For when something like this was apprehended, but upon mistake, in what transports were these pagans! "The gods are come down to us in the likeness of men." Acts 14. 11. And presently they offer at sacrificing. What matter of joy and wonder then, that the glorious, eternal Son of God, should make that descent, that kind descent, into this world of ours! Because we were partakers of flesh and blood, he himself likewise, takes part with us of the same: (Heb. 2. 14.) and because we dwelt in fleshly tabernacles, he himself resolved to erect a tabernacle like one of ours: " The word was made flesh, and dwelt among us:" (John 1. 14.) did tabernacle among us is the expression: this being, as it were, his very sense in this vouchsafement and undertaking: "There is a company of poor creatures that dwell in flesh, or buried in it, rather than do dwell in it, and their flesh is more their grave than their mansion; well! because they are partakers of flesh and blood, and have tabernacles made of flesh, "I will go and set my tabernacle by theirs, they dwell in fleshly tents, and I will go and dwell in such a tent among them." The Son of God was made flesh, did dwell and tabernacle among us in such flesh as we inhabit, excepting the impurity and sinfulness of it. O! what matter of glory and exultation is this! How full of triumph should it fill the souls of men, that such a hope should arise to them, even as a resurrection from the dead! Now we see that God's kindness towards the children of men, is not shut up in everlasting oblivion; it is not suspended from any further exercise for ever; what a glorious instance of it is here!

But as this is matter of highest joy, it ought to be matter of purest joy too. And there is not a little caution requisite in this case. The numerous appearance here this day signifies to me, that there is a great propension to keep on foot an annual solemnity upon this account: and as this is expressive of a disposition to rejoice, or to somewhat of rejoicing, I pray take these cautions in reference to it,—that it be not ignorant rejoicing, that it be not carnal rejoicing, and above all, that it be not wicked rejoicing, more grossly and more sensually wicked.

(1.) Let it not be ignorant rejoicing. Rejoice we may, and must, in such a thing, that according to divine purpose and decree, Christ came into the world, and the Son of God became man, that he might become a sacrifice, and that thereupon he might become a glorious King. To rejoice in this abstractly, that Christ was once born into this world, without understanding or ever desiring to understand what he was thus born for; what was the end of this manifestation and appearance of him in human flesh; this doth unbecome men, and much more doth it unbecome christians, it being to rejoice for they know not what. For what is it to us, if we abstract from the ends of the incarnation of the Son of God? if we subject not to the proper ends of it? What is it to us that Christ lived here on earth, somewhat above sixteen hundred years ago, and to rejoice in that he did so, without considering and understanding what it was for, upon what account it was, and with what design? This, I say, is but the joy of a fool: to rejoice in that, the true reason whereof, our own gross and voluntary ignorance hides from us; to rejoice when we hear that he came as a Saviour, without considering what he was to save us from, (though we are told at the same time,) when we hear of his being called Emmanuel, God with us, of his being called Jesus (Matt. 1. latter end) because he should save his people from their sins; to rejoice in Christ, even as an incarnate Saviour, without any thoughts of this, that I am to be saved by him, from that which made the distance, and continues the distance between God and me: I am to be saved by him from the impurities of my own heart and nature; I am to be saved by him from the vile carnality that hath depressed and sunk my soul so as never to mind God, never to desire after him, never to delight in him, to have inclinations to pray to him: I say, to rejoice ignorantly in these respects, is to rejoice presumptuously, for we know not what, and over confidently, against the direction and instruction given to us in that second psalm. Because God hath declared the decree concerning him, "Thou art my Son," and hath set him as his King upon his holy hill of Zion; and hath resolved to subdue the nations under him, and give him the heathen for his inheritance, and the uttermost parts of the earth for his possession, therefore to serve this mighty King with fear, and rejoice before him with trembling, that is the instruction that is given us. There is a pure and holy Deity hath become incarnate, the Son of God became, here, a God amongst us, with that resolution, not to bear with the wickedness of the world, and let men run on in their old and wonted course; but to revive God's memorial and the awe and fear of him in the hearts of men; and not to let men live prayerless lives, as they did, and without God in the world as they did; here was his great design. But now to rejoice in Christ's having been born into the world, without ever considering the design of it: this is not only mean and brutish, but insolent and presumptuous, to rejoice in the thoughts of so sacred and great a thing as this, without having hearts touched and impressed with the apprehension of the pure and holy end of it. And,

(2.) Take heed of rejoicing carnally, with such a kind of joy as shall be exclusive of, or that shall exclude, that spiritual sense we ought to have of so high and mighty an undertaking and intendment as this. How vain and how grossly incongruous and absurd is it to say, that because the Son of God came into this world upon such a design as you have heard, "Therefore, let us eat and drink and be merry, therefore, let us pamper and adorn this flesh;" forgetting that it is inhabited (even this mortal flesh) by an immortal spirit, and forgetting that even this flesh of ours is claimed and challenged to be a temple for the Holy Ghost, and therein made conformed to the flesh of Christ, which is itself such a Temple, and the model according to which, all Christian temples, that is, a temple in a temple, in every christian, ought to be formed. "Know ye not," saith the apostle, "that your bodies are the temples of the Holy Ghost?" (1 Cor. 6. 19.) and they are to be indulged and cared for accordingly. Christ speaks it of his own body, "Destroy this temple, and I will raise it up in three days!" As he was, even in his human nature, and in his body, a Temple of the living God, so is every christian to be; and therefore, are these bodies of ours to be cared for in subserviency to this design. This body of mine, it is to be the living, animated temple of the Divine, Living Spirit. And what! is it then to be indulged, to be pampered, to be adorned with a fine dress, and is this all that I am to design concerning it? I am to design in it conformity to the great Original Temple, the Son of God. But to rejoice with such a sort of festivity as is only grateful to carnal and fleshly inclination, without any thought of being recovered and brought back to God by this Christ, of having my soul refined, and body and soul made meet to glorify the great God whose they both are: to joy without any thought of this, (I say) looks more like a pagan than a christian; and is much more suitable to the paganish than the Christian state. It ought to be considered, Christ took our flesh to make us partakers of his Spirit; he took our nature to make us partakers of his divine nature, escaping the corruptions that are in this world through lust: and to please ourselves in the thoughts of Christ having been born, without any thought of this, is such a carnality as affronts the very pretence that we make of rejoicing in the thoughts of it, that the Son of God did descend and come down to associate himself, and dwell among the sons of men in this world, and to suffer for them, and so to prepare them to dwell with God in the other world.

(3.) But lastly, Take heed of such a kind of rejoicing as is more grossly and sensually wicked, even in itself and in its own nature: that is, to make the season when we, uncertainly, apprehend Christ to have been born into this world, the season of letting loose to all manner of looseness and debauchery, in direct contradiction to, and defiance of, the design of his coming: that is, when we know the Son of God was manifest to take away sin, and to destroy the works of the devil; as the expressions are, (1 John 3. 5. 8.) that we should make it our business to indulge and fulfil those very lusts which he came to destroy and dissolve and make cease out of the world; what an affront is this to him whose memorial we pretend to celebrate! That is to make that which we imagine to be the day of his birth, to be the day of his most ignominious death, by crucifying afresh to ourselves the Son of God, and putting him to open shame, as if we would proclaim to the world, that the design of the Son of God's descent into it, was to give men the liberty of being safely wicked, that they might throw off all restraint, and without any fear or dread of what should follow, abandon themselves to all manner of wickedness, to fulfil the impure lusts of a corrupt, depraved nature, till sin, being finished, should end in eternal death : and so make the Christian religion an inconsistency with itself, and to represent the matter, as if Christ came into the world, not to make men christians, but to exempt them from being so; and not to destroy sin out of the world, but to exclude and shut out Christianity. As if he came into the world that there might never be any such thing as Christianity in it, that he might bring it about, that men might, with safety and impunity, live in the highest rebellion against the very laws of that Christ by whom they pretend to expect salvation.

But this is one great thing which we see lies under divine purpose and decree, according to the counsel of his will, the sending of his Son into the world to be a Redeemer and Saviour of sinners, by living among them, dying for them, conquering death, ascending to heaven, and erecting that kingdom by which he is to govern the redeemed community unto everlasting life. And by how much the more apparently this was matter of divine purpose according to eternal counsel, so much the higher and more dreadful wickedness must it needs be, to indulge in ourselves such a disposition of spirit, or so to shape our course that both shall lie counter to the divine counsels in all this. That is, when Christ did not come into the world by accident, but by design and by purpose, according to the wisest counsel, and eternal and most stable counsel, we should set ourselves, as much as in us is, to overturn the whole frame of that divine and eternal counsel of heaven; that is, that it shall never take place with me, "I will never be subject to him, I will never know him, never come into union with him, never resign up myself unto him; I will be mine own still, and live still at the utmost distance from God and defiance of him." By how much the more apparent this was the product of the divine will according to counsel, so more fearful and horrid must be the wickedness that stands in direct opposition thereto.

LECTURE II.*

But now to go on with other particular propositions about the decrees of God.

7. That those terms of life and death for sinners, which God hath actually settled and published in his gospel, those we may be sure he did intend and purpose should be the terms of life and death unto us. Whatsoever, (as you have heard in the general propositions,) God actually doth, we may be sure he intended and purposed to do. What he doth, he doth willingly when he doth it. No force can be put upon him; he never doth any thing against his will, and what he once willed he doth always will, for there can be with him no new will. Therefore, whereas, he hath enacted and published such things as these to the world, as the terms of life and death to sinners; that whosoever believes shall be saved, but whosoever believeth not shall be damned: that he gave his only begotten Son with that design, that they who believe in him should not perish, but have everlasting life; that they that believed not, are condemned already: they that believe, have everlasting life; they that believe not, shall not see life; but the wrath of God abideth on them: that sinners are to repent, that their sins may be blotted out; that they that repent shall not all alike perish: (Luke 13. 3.) that the things that eye hath not seen, that the ear hath not heard, and which have not entered the heart of man to conceive, are all prepared for them that love God: (1 Cor. 2. 9.) but, they that love him not, that love not the Lord Jesus, are so many *anathema, accursed*, till he come: (1 Cor. 16. 22.) that Christ shall be the Author of eternal salvation to all them that obey him: (Heb. 5. 9.) but, that he shall come in flaming fire to take vengeance on them that know not God, and obey not the gospel of his Son; (2 Thess. 1. 8.) these, I say, being the declared terms of life and death to sinners, enacted and actually published to the world as such, these you may be sure God did intend and purpose should be such. His purpose was eternal, and a decree, as that word was explained. This is out of all question, that such terms of life or death to sinners, as have been mentioned, are the matter of divine, eternal decree; he did always intend they should be so. Whence it is obvious to collect, that he can have no contrary decree, no contrary purpose. That is, wheresoever his pleasure is published and made known, so as to be capable to be understood about these matters, God will

---

* Preached January the 8th, 1692.

never deal with men upon other terms. There can be no repugnant purpose to any such purpose as this; that is to say, that he will save any whether they believe or no, or though they finally persist in obstinate infidelity and impenitency and rebellion against him to the last. It is never to be supposed, that he will do such a thing without decreeing it, so that he should have ever decreed it against such a decree as this. And so, on the other hand, that he will ever finally condemn, or hath ever decreed or purposed finally to condemn any that shall believe, that shall repent, that shall love him above all, and finally subject themselves to his government, whensoever they are brought to do so in Christ: therefore, it is vain and unscriptural, without foundation any way, for men to embolden themselves on the one hand, "Let me be never so wicked, or never so careless, I may be saved at last for all that; I do not know but God hath decreed to save me." Or, that any should torment themselves on the other hand with afflicting thoughts, "Let me do what I will, if I never so earnestly set myself, and seek help from heaven, that I may believe, that I may repent, that I may have my heart changed, renewed, and brought to love God, and subject myself to him in Christ, yet, there may be a decree against me and I may perish for all this." There is no reason, no foundation on the one hand or on the other, for any such imagined decree of God, against these plain declared decrees of his: they are (as to what is compendious and comprehensive of all) final believers who lie under the decree or purpose of salvation; and final infidels who lie under the decree or purpose of condemnation.

So much, in general, is most certainly decreed, that they who believe shall be saved, and they that believe not, shall perish. But I further add,

8. God hath not purposed this in the general, that he will save such as are wrought up to a compliance with his declared known terms of salvation; but whensoever he doth actually enable any to believe and repent, we may conclude that he did eternally intend so to do. And whosoever he doth actually conserve in a safe state, that is, enables them continually to believe, (it is enough to instance in this one thing, with which the rest are so essentially connected, that they are all implied, if this one be actually to be found, and even in the very mention of this one,) if he actually enable any to believe to the saving of their souls unto their final salvation, he did always from eternity, intend so to enable them. And so, he hath not only decreed, or intended certain indefinite and undeterminate species to life and salvation, but particular persons as is most evident many ways.

(1.) Scripture is most express in it: if you look to the foregoing verses, divers of them in this same chapter, you will find it. In what a transport, towards the beginning, do you find the apostle blessing God. "Blessed be the God and Father of our Lord Jesus Christ, who hath blessed *us* with all spiritual blessings, in heavenly places, (or things) in Christ. According as he hath chosen *us* in him, before the foundation of the world, that we should be holy and unblamable before him in love: having predestinated *us*, to the adoption of children by Jesus Christ unto himself; according to the good pleasure of his will. to the praise of the glory of his grace, wherein he hath made *us* accepted in the beloved." And in this same 11th. verse, where the text lies, "in whom also *we* have obtained an inheritance, being predestinated, according to the purpose of him who worketh all things after the counsel of his own will." And nothing, again, can be plainer than that known and famous text, Rom. 8. 30. "Moreover whom he did predestinate, them he also called: and whom he called, them he also justified: and whom he justified, them he also glorified." This is a chain that can never be broken; and equally expresseth that in the 2 Thes. 2. 13. where the apostle gives solemn thanks, even for them, that God had chosen *them* unto salvation, through sanctification of the Spirit and belief of the truth. And in that, 1. Peter 1. 2. "Elect according to the foreknowledge of God, through sanctification of the Spirit, and sprinkling of the blood of Jesus." These (as it is observable, and was told you before, in those more general propositions,) do manifestly connect means and end together. But they do ascertain both, concerning some, and not leave the matter indefinite and undetermined, as if he did in the dark, make and form purposes with himself, without discerning, at the same time, who should comply with his pleasure, as to such terms of life, and who should not. And besides so express scriptures, the matter is,

(2.) Evident in itself, that whomsoever he doth actually enable to comply with such terms of life and salvation, he did purpose and decree to enable. For when he doth so, when he gives a man faith, when he gives him repentance, which are most expressly said to be the gift of God: to you it is given to believe and suffer; (Phil. 1. 29.) and Christ is exalted to be a Prince and a Saviour, to give repentance and remission of sins. Acts 5. 31. I say, when he doth actually give these gifts, doth he give them with his will, or against his will? Is it to be supposed, that he should give them, and not will to give them? What could so impose upon him that he should give what he was not willing to give? But, if once he was willing, and if then he was willing to give such a gift, he was always willing; for there cannot be with him a new will, and therefore, he was from eternity willing. And again,

(3.) That matter might be further argued, from what Scripture speaketh most expressly too, that as to that great and most comprehensive instance of faith in the Son of God; whosoever do receive Christ and believe in his name, when God enables them so to do, he regenerates them; "To as many as received him, to them gave he power to become the sons of God, even to as many as believed on his name." John 1. 12. And then, it is immediately subjoined in the 13th. ver. "Who were born not of flesh nor of blood, nor of the will of man, but of God." But if he do regenerate any, he doth it most willingly: "Of his own will begat he us, by the word of truth." James 1. 18. Agreeable to the expression in the text, "He doth all things according to the counsel of his own will." He did with counsel, will to regenerate whomsoever he regenerates. And,

(4.) It is altogether unimaginable, that God should do a thing so far exceeding all expectation, and even all wonder, as the sending of his own Son; he that was the brightness of his own glory, and the express image of his person, the Heir of all things, by whom he made the worlds; to be incarnate, to put on man, and to die upon a tree, so ignominiously, a spectacle to angels and men, and to leave it an undetermined thing whether any should be the better for it, yea, or no; or rather to leave it certain that none ever should be the better for it. For most certain it is, that as to those great terms, of life and salvation, none can ever be the better, if he do not, by his overpowering grace, influence minds and hearts, and work them up to a compliance with those terms, and work and effect them in them. The case is vastly different in respect to spiritual good, and in reference to the opposite evil; where, as to wicked actions, and a continued course of them, or any particular act in such and such circumstances, men will always determine themselves; they are apt and prone enough to do so. If they can, in such and such circumstances, they will do wickedly: but in reference to any spiritual action that is good and holy, and of a saving tendency, there is not so much of an indifferency, but a most fixed aversion, which nothing but the power of divine grace can conquer and overcome. Nothing but the almighty power of grace can make an enemy-heart become friendly towards God, and towards his Christ, can vanquish the malignity of an obstinate infidelity, can mollify an obdurate, hard heart, and make it dissolve and melt as in repentance it must. This is, therefore, altogether an unimaginable thing, that God should do what did so far exceed all expectation, and even all wonder, as to send his own eternal Son, to die upon a cross, and leave it uncertain, whether any should ever be the better for it: or rather certain that none ever should. And it is again,

(5.) Very unreasonable to think that the great God should have among men no objects of special favour; and it were foolish to suppose that it should be a reflection upon him to have it so. As it was formerly told you, it belongs only to a good governor, and even to the best that can be supposed, to deal equally with all; and kindly and favourably where he pleaseth. We are to distinguish matters of right, and matters of peculiar favour. Matters of right will be dispensed and administered with an equal hand, matters of special favour according to good pleasure, as it is expressed again and again, in the context. And plain it is, that there can be no natural right, which any creature can claim at the hand of God. Whatsoever becomes matter of right, from him to them, must only be by grace, by promise. He cannot be a debtor to his creature, till he makes himself so; and the promises by which he makes himself so, they " are all yea and amen in Christ;" (2. Cor. 1. 20.) only upon his account, only for his sake. Whatsoever there is that comes within the compass of a promise, for the encouragement of sinners to return and come to God, it will all be made good to a tittle upon his account that is worthy, all promises being " yea and amen" in him. But whatsoever is above promise, more than promise, is all from mere ευδοκια, the *good pleasure* of his goodness. It can be resolved into nothing else, turn we the matter in our thoughts never so long. He will make good all that was promised to every one to a tittle; all unpromised, peculiar favour, that is dispensed according to the good pleasure of his goodness; even as his promises themselves at first were. And,

(6) Lastly: It is very evident that as to communications of grace and favour, God doth dispense very differently; and therefore, must be understood to intend so to do, and to have always intended it. As in the parable of the talents, (though parabolical scriptures do not give ground of argument as to every thing in them, yet they do as to their main scope,) he gives to one ten talents, to another five, to another one, as he pleaseth; he dispenseth as he pleaseth, wherein he hath not particularly obliged himself. But further,

9. If yet he do actually, in a way of common grace, superadd more, wheresoever he hath given any thing of it, upon the due improvement of that, then we may conclude he hath al-

ways intended so to do; this was his pleasure, and his eternal purpose. If that be actually his rule, " to him that hath shall be given;" (you know how *hath* is to be taken here, that hath so as to improve what he hath,) he shall still have more: if this be actually the rule and measure of his proceedings, it was always his purpose it should be so. And so it must be understood to have been his purpose, even in them that do finally perish, yet still to give them more of gracious communications in the way of common grace, upon the improvement of what they had; and they perish as not improving what was vouchsafed and afforded them, according to the tenour of that rule. They do not finally perish, as never having received any thing from the hands of God, in a way of grace, that had a tendency and leadingness in it to their better state, but they finally perish as neglecting and resisting such overtures as have been made to them. What the case was with the old world, before the flood, we must still suppose to be the common case among men. " My Spirit shall not always strive with man." Gen. 6. 3. It had been striving, and it is generally striving more or less; and especially where God doth afford the more peculiar manifestations of himself, as he did to that people whom he severed from the rest of the world, to be more appropriate to him. We have many passages that speak of the presence, and of the operations of the Divine Spirit, among that people. The Spirit of the Lord caused them to rest: He gave his Spirit to instruct them. Isaiah 63. 14. They rebelled and vexed his Holy Spirit: therefore, he turned to be their enemy, and fought against them: ver. 10. and that of dying Stephen, " Ye stiff-necked and uncircumcised in heart and life, ye do always resist the Holy Spirit, as your fathers did, so do ye." Acts 7. 51. Now, there cannot be a resistance where there is no striving, and there can be no striving where there is not a counter-striving. When the Spirit, in its more common operations, is resisted, it retires in displeasure, often and most righteously, and gives to men, yields to them that victory that shall be in the end fatal to them, undoing to them; many such victories undo them at last, and they perish by them. If he be actually working in men to will and to do of his own good pleasure, when he is ever so at work in any, he injects thoughts into their hearts, smites their minds with convictions, and their hearts many times with terrors; or if there be any more placid affections raised in them in any degree towards himself, or towards any divine thing, and the matter go no further than a loseable taste, that may vanish and pass away, it is plain he so far went of good pleasure; and if he did that which he did of good pleasure, then it was before his good pleasure, and always his good pleasure, and eternally his good pleasure, to proceed so far with such and such: so as in this case there can be no pretence to say, if he go no higher, that wrong is done to them with whom he went no higher. It must be justly said, "Friend I do thee no wrong," even to the most careless neglector, and the most contemptuous abuser of the grace of God, "Friend I do thee no wrong." If he do proceed higher, and to less vincible workings with some, there is no cause any man's eye should be evil, because his eye is good. He is Lord of his own grace, he may do what he will with his own. What he hath to dispense, and dispose of, is his, and they to whom he is to dispose so and so are his, and there is no pretence of wrong to any, that more is not done for them; for whom more was done than they could lay any original claim to; for it was all of mercy that there was any offer or overture made at all, or that the case was so stated before, as that it might have been possible, if it had not been through their own wicked neglect, that they that perish might have advanced in the way of salvation, according to his method, still further and further, so as not to make their own final salvation a thing impossible upon any other terms, than their own wilful neglect and final refusal. But I again further add,

10. That such as live quite without the sound of the gospel, and to whom every thing of supernatural revelation hath never been vouchsafed or any thing of it, how God hath determined to deal with them, and the infants of such, he hath not yet declared further his pleasure to us expressly, than it was needful for us to know and understand. And therefore, it would be either vain or overbold curiosity to determine positively in their case, and it is very unreasonable and foolish, oversolicitously to inquire about it. It is enough for us to understand and know upon what terms God will deal with us, according to those circumstances wherein he hath placed and set us: he hath placed us under the dispensation of his gospel, wherein all things are made plain and evident to us, that concern us in reference to our present and eternal state, and will deal with us according to those known and published terms, which stand in so clear a light, before our eyes; and with all others according to those measures they have had. It is enough for us to understand and know what we may, as our case is stated, expect from God, and what God doth expect from us. And, it would be very unreasonable, and uncharitable, for us to trouble ourselves with further inquiries, and it would be very bold to venture on rash determinations, in those more obscure things, and

wherein we are so little concerned. These are to pass among the arcana, that secret things belong to God, when revealed things belong to us, and our children after us, as they shall come to be revealed to them. Deut. 29. 29. A passage placed, as it were, on purpose to caution, and warn too busy and bold inquirers, and that, even in matters of unspeakably less concernment than the eternal salvation of souls. As suppose, that the people, for that is the case there supposed and referred to, who had been so peculiar to God, taken nigh to him, above, and from, all other people and nations under heaven, should apostatise and revolt from him, and draw down vindictive judgments, and destructive ones upon themselves, and inquiry be made how it comes to pass, that such a people, so near to God, should be so treated and dealt withal, their land laid waste and made a wilderness, and nothing to be found but marks of divine vengeance, where such a people, so favoured by heaven did dwell, what is the meaning of all this? Why, they forsook the Lord their God! But that might have been prevented: Why did he not hold them to him? "Secret things belong unto God, but revealed things to us and our children." So is that sad and dismal state concluded and shut up at last, with that seal upon it! That, therefore, I would leave with you, as all I think needful to say, with reference to their case who lie without the compass of superadded divine revelation. Again, I further add,

11. That whereas faith and its concomitants are ever to be found in that, which appears to be at length the subject of God's purpose of saving souls; and final infidelity, with its concomitants, are the characters of the subjects of the contrary purpose, a purpose to condemn with everlasting destruction; these must very differently be understood to be so. Faith, for instance, and so of the rest of its concomitants, are never looked upon by God as any causes, or conditions, or inducements, any way, of his purpose to save any. These are by his grace to be found in the subjects, in those that he will save; but they are no inducements to pass any such determination concerning them. It is honourable to him to save such: and, even in the nature of the thing, they only are capable of final salvation and blessedness, in whom such characters are to be found: for they can never be happy in union with the eternal truth and goodness, who are habitually averse in their temper, and opposite to the one and the other. If happiness result from such a union, then they, in whom there is a prevailing final aversion to eternal truth and goodness, are uncapable of any such felicity, as is to result from a union with these.

But it is no motive or inducement to God, to intend to save such a one, because he will be a believer, or he will be a penitent person. That he is a believer, that he is a penitent person, that he is a lover of him, and that he is obedient to his Son, these are the effects of his grace, and of his good pleasure, and so he is moved in this case by nothing without himself. But the case must be understood to be otherwise, as to those that he intends finally to punish, and to punish with everlasting destruction. That is, he doth resolve to deal with them suitably to the state of things between him and them, and with himself. If any inquire, why there should be a difference, why he should be moved to purpose so and so, in reference to them that perish, (which purpose we are not to consider abstractly as it lies in God alone, for so it is not a distinct thing from his own essence of which there can be no cause; but we are to consider it with a reference to the effects and to the objects, and of that relation there is really a cause, and so there is a just cause for the condemnation of them that perish, even from the creature: but there can be no cause from the creature, of them that are saved) I say, if you will have the reasons assigned of the difference, they are obvious and plain, especially these two.

(1.) That there is no natural connection between the imperfect faith and holiness of the saints, and their eternal felicity; no natural connection, I say, at all between them. But there is a most natural connection between the infidelity, enmity against God, and reigning wickedness, and eternal ruin and everlasting misery. No man can say that these two are naturally connected, an imperfect faith in God, through Christ, and imperfect holiness, and final felicity and blessedness. These are not so naturally connected that the one must arrive to the other. But there is a most plain, natural connection between infidelity and disbelief of divine truth, enmity against divine goodness, repudiation and refusal of the offers and tenders thereof, and eternal misery: so as that the one of them cannot but be the other. Wickedness must be misery, sin persisted in to the last must be destruction, it cannot be otherwise; sin when it is finished can be nothing but death. "To be carnally minded is death:" it is indeed said, "to be spiritually minded is life and peace:" but that is by an intervening divine constitution. And though there be a constitution in the other case too, yet there is a most natural connection between total prevailing wickedness, reigning iniquity, and misery; to which the supervening constitution is added to an indication of the righteous judgment of God, that he doth but let the thing be with such as it is. They love death; and he only lets them have what they love, and what they choose: he doth only not interpose in their case to break the connection. And,

(2.) There is this manifest difference too; that as there is a natural connection between wickedness and misery, whereas there is none between imperfect faith and holiness and eternal felicity, otherwise than what God hath graciously made; so there is in final, reigning, persevering wickedness, the highest desert of eternal misery: whereas, there is in imperfect faith and holiness no desert of eternal life and blessedness. And none that consider, will think this strange, that when a man can never deserve (much less by what is merely gratuitously wrought in him) life and blessedness; yet, by continuing, persevering wickedness he may deserve to perish. That imperfect good that is wrought in him and which he owes not to himself, can never deserve life and blessedness for him. But total wickedness, yea, or any wickedness can deserve death, can deserve for a man's being left to be finally miserable and his falling under divine *vindicta, vengeance:* this is a divine nemesis, what is fit and righteous, what is fit the righteous Judge of all the earth should do; even animadvert upon wickedness, and testify his own just abhorrence and detestation of it, so that there is a vast difference between these two: that though faith and holiness be in those that shall be saved; and so are ever to be found in the subject of God's purpose to save, as characteristical of the subject, but are not inducements, or causes or motives thereof unto God: yet, wheresoever God hath purposed to condemn, their wickedness is a just motive of that purpose, so terminated, so related to the creature, that is, to suffer, and to the suffering that he is to undergo. There is something justly causative in this; and there is nothing more strange in all this, than what God hath himself, in his word, so plainly told us, that men's destruction is of themselves, but their help in order to salvation should be found in him alone. Hos. 13. 9. It is no unsuitable or strange thing, that God should be eyed as the Author of all life, and all grace, and all blessedness, and of life and of felicity for ever. And, that sinners should be looked upon as the fountains of all evil and all darkness and all impurity and all misery to themselves only. God must determine men only to that good by which they are to be led on gradually to a blessed, safe, and happy state. But to that evil that tends to ruin and final destruction, men have it in themselves to determine themselves. More is yet to be added to illustrate this.

LECTURE III.*

But before I proceed further, I think fit to premonish thus much, and declare to you, that I would not, as to these matters, be understood to deny every thing that I do not assert about them, nor to assert whatsoever I do not deny: for my design is only to propose to you what is plain, and what is useable and may be improved unto the common purposes of Christianity. There are a great many things besides, that many have concerned themselves to dispute to and fro, which I think it not at all needful or useful to be brought into such discourse.

But now, that the matter last insisted on, may yet be clearer and more plain. If we speak of this natural bodily life, you can very easily understand that that is in any man's power, it is within the compass of human power that ordinarily men have, for a man to give himself a mortal wound, but, having done so, it is not within the compass of human power to heal him again; and that, in reference to the natural connection between the one of those forementioned things and the other, and in reference to the moral and legal connection that is asserted between them; we may again illustrate it by a resemblance of it to the concernments of this natural bodily life. It is in the power of any one that dares venture to be so far criminal, to deserve death at the hands of the prince and the law, whereas, it may be no way in his power, when he hath done so, to deserve the prince's pardon and to have his forfeited life given him again. These are things, in themselves plain to any understanding. And now, whereas the text hath plainly told us, that God works all things after the counsel of his own will, this doth manifestly imply, that the determinations must be correspondent to the aptitudes of things, and most especially to the apt agreement which they shall hold with the universal perfection of his own nature. Now it is no blemish to the perfection of the Divine Nature, when things are so and so connected in themselves, naturally and morally, to let things in many instances stand just as in themselves they are. This is no reflection on the divine perfection; that is, where there is a real connection between wickedness and misery, both natural and moral or legal, it is no reflection upon the perfection of the Divine Nature, in many instances to let that connection

* Preached January the 15th, 1693.

be as it is. And whereas, there is no connection between imperfect faith and holiness, and perfect felicity and blessedness, (there is, in reality, no connection between these) it is no blemish to the divine perfection (if there be really, and if there be in nature, and as yet any other way between these two, no connection) to make one by grace, in what instances he pleaseth; that being done (as the gospel tells us) upon the Redeemer's account, who it was predetermined should so order the course of his management, even to dying itself, and in dying, that no divine perfection should reluctate or reclaim against such a connection as this; a connection to be made by grace when before it was not, when really it was not, between that imperfect faith and holiness that some should be enabled to in this world and their future felicity and blessedness in the other world. All comes to this sum, that is, that we can both effect and deserve our own death and misery; but we can neither effect nor deserve life and blessedness: that must be owing to divine favour and grace. And the case (as hath been often said) is vastly different in dispensing of punishments and free favours. It being no reflection upon the best government that can be supposed either to inflict deserved punishments, or to dispense undeserved favours. Neither of these can reflect on the best and most perfect government that can be thought. I now go on and add further,

12. That the assertion of a decree of reprobation, antecedent to a decree of condemnation for infidelity and wickedness persisted in to the last, is that which may seem agreeable to the imperfect mind of man; but we cannot be so sure that it will be any way agreeable unto the most perfect mind of God, in which there can be no such thing as first and second, and unto which all things lie open at once, even unto one entire and eternal view. We are very plainly told in Scripture, of some men's being ordained of old unto condemnation: in that 4th verse of the epistle of Jude, and in the same place we have the characters given us of them that are so: " ungodly men, turning the grace of God into lasciviousness, denying the only Lord God and our Saviour Jesus Christ." We are sure of such a decree as doth doom such, continuing such unto the last, unto condemnation and eternal perdition: but that there should be any decree concerning such, prior to this, that must suppose priority and posteriority in *Eternum*. But *Eternum non patitur novum*, there can be no such thing as novity, newness, in eternity. And therefore, being sure there is such a decree as this, and that this decree is eternal, we may be equally sure there can be no decree pre-existent to it; because

every thing in God is co-eternal to him, and so this decree must be co-eternal unto God himself; and there can be nothing before God. And though it be very true, indeed, that many have taken much pains and given great exercise to their thoughts to assign and fix some certain order of former and latter, to the divine decrees, yet that doth only proceed from the imperfection of their minds; but we are sure it is impossible there can be any such thing as priority and posteriority in the Divine Mind; all things lying open to him at one eternal and entire view at once: so that whensoever he beholds and looks upon the subjects of final misery, he sees their character at the same time, and it cannot be otherwise. And again, I add,

13. That will or decree, or purpose of God by which he doth determine the salvation of any, it is, in the proper time and season, effective of whatsoever is pre-requisite thereunto: that is, if he have decreed he will save such and such, that same will of his is, in the proper season, effective of that faith, of that repentance, of that holiness and of that perseverance which is requisite to their final salvation. But, on the other hand, God's will to punish any with future misery is not effective of what concurs to that, neither as naturally causing or deserving it. That is sin that doth both, as you have heard; it doth both naturally cause it and deserve it too. And, if you ask here, "What is the reason of the difference; or is there not a parity of reason in both cases, that if his will doth effect what is necessary to the salvation of the one, his will should also effect what is necessary or doth any ways previously concur to the destruction of the other? The reason of the difference is most manifest upon these two accounts.

(1.) That sin is properly, as such, no effect but a defect, and therefore, it doth not need an effective cause but a defective only. But we will impute nothing of defectiveness to God: that can be found no where but in the creature. And,

(2.) That we can (sure any one may) apprehend it a great deal more congruous and suitable, to the nature and honour of God to make men believing and holy than to make them unbelieving and wicked. We can easily apprehend how well it agrees to the nature of God, and how subservient it is to the glory of God, to make men believing and holy; but no man can ever apprehend it agreeable to his nature, or subservient to his honour, to make men disbelieving and wicked. And therefore, as we make the difference, I cannot but apprehend you see reason enough why we should. And then further, take this,

14. That for these distinct states of blessedness and misery, unto which the will of God doth determine some, and leave others, they are the only states of men hereafter, and there is not a middle state between these two, though there be great intermediate degrees between the highest pitch of felicity and the lowest of misery. There are, I say, very great intermediate degrees, but not a middle state. This proposition hath two parts:—that there is no middle state, and yet—that there are great intermediate degrees, both of blessedness and misery.

(1.) As to the former part, that there is no intermediate or middle state between these two: it cannot, without very great absurdity, be so much as conceived there should be; besides that it is against the most express tenour of Scripture. I need not go about to quote texts to you. Look to the judgment of the great day. Matt. 25. Men are judged but to two distinct states; all go one of these two ways. And it is unconceivable in itself that there should be a distinct intermediate state: for it would be to suppose that there can be such a thing as an intelligent, reasonable creature, having the use of his faculties, (which death, we have a great deal more reason to apprehend, doth promote rather than hinder,) and neither happy nor miserable. This is an unconceivable thing, equally unconceivable as it would be, that there should be such a creature under a law, under government, (as reasonable creatures even as such, either positive or natural at least,) that should be neither good nor bad, that should neither be obedient nor disobedient, holy nor wicked, and this you know to be an impossible thing. And that is enough as to the former part of the proposition. But then,

(2.) As to the latter part, that there are great intermediate degrees both of happiness and misery, that is plain from most express scriptures. It is less needful to insist upon the degrees of blessedness in the other state, about which the Scripture is plain enough. There will be such a difference as there appears to be of one star differing from another star in glory. 1 Cor. 15. 41. But chiefly as to the differing degrees of misery; nothing is plainer from such passages in Scripture :—"They that know their master's will, and do it not, shall be beaten with many stripes; they that do it not, not knowing it, with fewer." Luke 12. 47, 48. "It will be more tolerable for Sodom and Gomorrah, for Tyre and Sidon, in the day of judgment, than for Capernaum and Bethsaida, where so much gospel light shone; and where so glorious works were done, to evidence and demonstrate the truth of the gospel." Matt. 11. 22.

And there is a sort among them that do perish, which do perish more dreadfully. Such and such, it is said, shall have their portion with hypocrites, (Matt 24. 51.) which must be supposed the most fiery, in the worst and hottest hell. God will not lay upon men more than is right, that any should enter into judgment with him, as the expression in Job is. And therefore, we must suppose the case to be vastly different between them that live under the gospel and them that do not. "They that sin without law, shall perish without law;" (Rom. 2. 12.) but with a gentler kind of perdition. But they that sin under the law, that is, under the divine Revelation, for that is the meaning of the law there, supernatural, divine Revelation, they shall be judged by it: not by that light which they have not, or those means of light which they never had, but by those which they have. But whereas, there will be very great degrees of difference in the states of the miserable hereafter, how great that difference will be, that we know not. It is enough that we know it will be very great; and therefore, among them that are miserable, none will be punished unsuitably to the demerit of their own sins. And this ought to have its weight with us, in order to the repressing of undue and hard thoughts concerning the divine proceedings with men in the final judgment: and so, concerning his purposes and determinations before, and from, eternity.

But I think it not necessary to say more to you by way of position; yet, there are sundry things that I shall add by way of *caution*. As,

1. That we should take heed of being too positive about any of these things, beyond the measure of divine Revelation, or too curious in inquiring, or too contentious in disputing about such matters. Let us labour to lay a restraint upon our spirits as to these things. The matter requires it, and the divine word requires it.

2. Never depart from, nor doubt of, what God hath expressly revealed: in reference to what he hath expressly revealed, let us neither deviate nor doubt; but take heed lest we do. And,

3. Take heed that we do not oppose the secret and revealed will of God to one another, or allow ourselves so much as to imagine an opposition, or contrariety between them. And that ground being once firmly laid and stuck to, as it is impossible that there can be a will against a will in God, or that he can be divided from himself, or against himself, or that he should reveal any thing to us as his will, that is not his will, (it being a thing inconsistent with his nature, and impossible to him to

lie,) that being, I say, firmly laid, (as nothing can be firmer or surer than that,) then measure all your conceptions of the secret will of God, by his revealed will, about which you may be sure. But never measure your conceptions of his revealed will by his secret will; that is, by what you may imagine concerning that. For you can but imagine, while it is secret, and so far as it is unrevealed.

4. Take heed of exalting any one divine perfection to the depressing of another, which men are too prone to do in their more fervent disputes about these matters. Great heat and zeal appear to vindicate such a particular divine perfection without attending, that at the same time they intrench upon some other. It were very easy to give instances. Some on the one hand are so much for the magnifying of the goodness of God, his love and his justice, (as they think,) that they quite overlook his sovereignty, make nothing of that, but guide their thoughts by such measures, as if they thought, that God was obliged by his goodness, or even by his justice, to do so with his own creatures, whom he hath so freely produced and brought forth into being out of nothing, as they may do with their fellow creatures. As if God were bound to observe the same measures as they do, and had no more power and dominion over the works of his own hands, than they have over one another, who cannot give one another so much as a moment's breath. And on the other hand, some are so over apt to exalt and magnify the divine sovereignty, that they quite forget to consider him as a wise and righteous and holy and good God; in all these, the best and most perfect of beings. This is quite forgot, and scarce any other notion doth actually obtain; though otherwise these are not denied, are only not denied; but in the mean time they are overlooked; and so hardly any other notion is brought in view, or upon the stage concerning God, than as of an almighty will, quite against the manifest scope and current of the Scripture every where, which makes all excellencies to be in him, and magnifies his wisdom, and his righteousness, and his love and goodness, at so high a rate, as you know. But to suppose the Divine Nature to consist but in an omnipotent will, not guided by wisdom and counsel, as the text speaks, "He doth all things according to the counsel of his own will:" is the strangest and most unshapen notion of God; and, in the tendency of it, most destructive to religion that can be conceived. It tends, indeed, to engenerate in the minds of men, a certain dread and horror: but is that the affection that is to influence religion, and to animate our worship? There can be no worship that doth not proceed

from a dutiful reverential love: and agreeable hereunto, must be still our notions of God. Heathens themselves that speak at so high a rate (some of them) of the divine excellencies, and particularly of his goodness, exalting that far above his power, and above his knowledge, and above his wisdom; yet they, at the same time, say of him, "He is an impartial law;" and they comprehend in that, both goodness and righteousness, according to the strict measures whereof he manageth the whole course of his dispensations towards his creatures, and cannot but do so. He is a law that equally inclines every way, an impartial law he is to himself in all his dispensations. And indeed, such love and goodness in a ruler, as should include in it an insensibleness of injuries and indignities, and affronts, it were stupidity; it were inconsistent with the proper governing qualifications which are requisite in any ruler whatsoever. And again,

5. Take this further by way of caution: Let us take very great heed that we do not, in reference to these things, so magnify human perfection as to depress divine; for that, in this affair, too many are apt to do; that is, to ascribe so much to the reason and will of man, as to detract most injuriously from the counsel of the will of God. Some think they know not how to solve the difficulties in these affairs, without ascribing greatly and highly to the reason and will of man. And all ought to be ascribed thereunto that is due; that is, so much as doth render a man a governable creature, capable of being bound by a law, and of being dealt with in the way of moral government. So much must be ascribed and ought to be so. It would be otherwise, as fit and congruous to have given laws, and assigned rewards and punishments to beasts and trees, as men, if we do not preserve the apprehension of man's capacity to be the subject of government, by reason and will, wherewith God hath endowed his nature. But to think that the reason and will of man are, of themselves, enough to enable him to all that is requisite to his future felicity, is to make a god of him, instead of a man, and to put him into his Maker's throne, to give him a self-sufficiency, as if he had enough in himself to do all things. And this, indeed, is so to magnify the reason and will of man, as upon the matter to nullify the counsel of the divine will in reference unto him; by which we find the methods are described and set, in which he is to expect continual aids and assistances, as being of himself, without them, able to do nothing. And,

6. Take heed, hereupon, of being tempted to take up with a spiritless religion, that shall be only a human product, the ef-

fect only of a man's own power. Take heed of taking up such a repentance, and such a faith, and such an obedience as the power of man is sufficient for: that will certainly lurch men at last. That repentance, and that faith, and that holiness, (if any other were to have the names,) which is not produced by the Divine Spirit, but is short of that, must needs leave men short of heaven and eternal glory; unless you would suppose it possible to a man to be his own Saviour out of such a gulf of sin and misery as men are sunk into.

7, Take heed of admitting any distrustful thoughts, that God will not be always ready to afford his communicated, superadded light and influence to those that see and acknowledge their own impotency and nothingness. Such as see themselves lost, and unable to help themselves, and that, from a sense of indigency and want, cry for his Spirit (even as for bread) to enlighten them and empower them, and enable them to do his will, to comply with his call, and come up to his terms of life and blessedness: take heed of ever admitting a distrustful thought concerning his readiness to impart and communicate to such. He will give his Spirit to them that ask him; when he is considerately asked and sought to: not formally, not slightly, not in words of course; but as feeling our own blindness and darkness and deadness and impotency: or where there is not, as yet, the light of a saint, there is that of a man, and that is to be improved and made use of, in order to our higher light, and if there be that self-reflection to which God hath given to every man a natural ability, much more may be known than usually is. It belongs to the nature of man to turn his eyes inwards. The mind of a man (like the sun can only project its beams and cast them about this way and that, and every way,) the mind of a man, I say, as an intellectual sun, can turn its beams inward upon itself and take cognizance of what is done within him; and what dispositions and indispositions are within. Men can reflect and consider this with themselves: "Have not I an aversion towards God? have not worldly concernments and affairs, by the natural inclination of my own mind, a greater room and place there than heaven and the things of heaven? are not other thoughts more grateful? and have they not a more pleasant relish with me than the thoughts of God?" Men, I say, are capable of using such reflections as these. And thereupon, of considering, "This can never be well with me: if there remain with me an habitual aversion to God, who must be my best and eternal good, I cannot but be eternally miserable: if I cannot think of him, and converse with him with inclination and pleasure, I am lost. If my blessedness lie above, in another world, and my mind is carried continually downward towards this world, I must have a heart attempered to heaven, or I can never come there. Well then let me try if I can change the habit of my own mind, make the attempt, make the trial." The more you attempt and try, the more you will find that of yourselves you cannot; you can do nothing of yourselves, you do but lift at a heavy log, you attempt to move a mountain upwards, when you would lift at your own terrene hearts. Then, is this consideration obvious, " I must have help from heaven, or I shall never come there." Therefore, fall a seeking, fall a supplicating, as one that apprehends himself in danger to perish and be lost, if he have not another heart, a believing heart, a holy heart, a heavenly heart. God will in this case give his Spirit; and of that, you are not to despair by any means. Take heed therefore, of setting the imagination of a secret will of God not to give his Spirit, against his plain and most expressly revealed will, that he will give his Spirit to them that ask it, that is, that do considerately ask it, as apprehending the state of their case; not ask it slightly and in mockery, so as that the manner of their asking to have the Divine Spirit given should imply a contempt of the gift at the same time.

LECTURE IV.*

And I will add, further, to this caution, that we take very great heed that we do not remit either our diligence, or our hope, in reference to the affairs of our salvation, upon the supposition of any divine counsel or purpose lying against us; and to enforce this, (than which nothing is more necessary to be enforced,) I might reason two ways, partly *ad hominem*, partly, *ad rem.*

(1.) *Ad hominem.* That is, from the common apprehension and practice of men in reference to other cases. It is very plain that all the other concernments of men, are as much determined by divine counsel and decree, as the affairs and concerns of their souls and future estate. But it is as plain that men are not wont to suspend their actions, in common cases, upon mere supposition of such purposes and counsels of God, that may, for ought they know, lie against them in such cases. It would make very strange work in the world if they should; if men should suspend their actions in reference to

* Preached January 22, 1692.

common affairs of human life merely upon the supposition that a decree may be against them. What a condition would it reduce things to among men on earth! The whole world would be at a stand, or would be sitting still, and would sit still in very uneasy postures too. The husbandman must never plough nor sow, for he might say, "I do not know but there is a decree against me, that all will come to nothing, I shall have no crop, I shall lose all my labour and expence." The merchant should never send or go to sea; no man should ever make a meal, because he doth not know but that it may be determined that it shall poison and not nourish him, choke him and not refresh him. Men should not walk the streets, for they do not know but that there may be some decree or other that a tile shall fall and strike them dead, or they may meet with a stab in their walk: nor should they sit still in the house neither, for they do not know but that there may be such a decree that the house may fall and bury them in the ruins. Plain it is, men do not in common cases suspend their actions upon such suppositions; but then it argues very great insincerity, and a very ill temper of mind, that men should only pick out their weightiest and most important concerns, and do nothing in reference to them, merely upon such an imagination that there may be some purpose, or something in the divine counsel lying against them. It argues, I say, a very ill mind; that there is some peculiar disaffection to God, and to the way of holiness and to religion as such, that men should only lay themselves under restraint in reference to those great concernments of religion, when they have as much cause, and the same pretence in reference to all things as they have in reference to this. And again,

(2.) We may argue *Ad rem*, or from the true, real state of the case itself; that is, that there is no supposable divine purpose but what is guided by counsel, and that no one hath any reason to fear that the divine counsel can be any way prejudicial to him, even to an honest affair or undertaking, that belongs to the human life itself. For they are always to be considered as the counsels of an absolutely, infinitely perfect Being, whose nature is uncapable of any thing of malignity towards his creatures; (for it is the most perfect benignity and goodness itself, "God is love;") and therefore, that any supposable counsel of the divine will, in reference to our common affairs themselves, are a great deal more encouraging than they can be discouraging; yea, unspeakably more, in reference to these affairs, supposing we will but take up due thoughts of God about them, and have correspondent, due dispositions of heart and spirit towards him: for we are pre-assured by his own express word, that all things shall work together for good to those that love God; which love, will be the evidence of a man's being called according to his purpose, as these things lie connected in that Rom. 8. 28. There is no son or servant of common understanding and ingenuity, but it will be a very great encouragement and satisfaction to him to act in all things under the conduct and direction of a parent or master, that he knows to be a man of counsel, as well as of the greatest goodness; it will certainly be most satisfying and encouraging to any such one. And how unspeakably more will it be to any, to think, that whatsoever affairs that lie within the compass of human life, I have to manage, I am to manage and order them all under the conduct and direction of the wise counsel of a good, and gracious, and holy God; whence I may be sure he will never hinder me in any such enterprize and undertaking of mine, unless it appear to his infinite wisdom, that it will be to my hurt, that it will turn to my prejudice. If it shall be for the best for me, it shall succeed, if it shall not succeed, it would be to my disadvantage if it should. The tendency of all this is to compose men's spirits to the greatest quietude and tranquillity imaginable, in reference even to the common affairs of human life. This word is firmer and more stable than the foundations of heaven and earth, that all things shall work together for good to them that love God: nothing can come amiss to a lover of God, to one, who by the Divine Spirit working in him, is contempered in the habitual frame of his spirit to the divine pleasure. And the disposition of all things cannot but work together for good to such a one.

But, whereas, it may be said, "What if I do not love God? what if I find not that disposition in my heart and soul to him, what shall I do then?" Why,

[1.] I would appeal to such a one, How perverse a notion must you needs have of God, if you think him to be such a one that he should equally take care, that all things should work together for good to men, whether they love him or love him not? that he should as much gratify them that hate him, as them that love him! You must suppose, in this case, somewhat in its own nature impossible: for it is simply impossible that any thing can succeed well with a man that loves not God. He must be the son of peace, or good cannot come to him: it can take no place in him. But what I have further to say is this, which in the second place I designed to say in arguing this matter *ad rem*. That is,

[2.] That supposing a man be not a lover of God, an habitual lover of him, so as he can discern this to be the predominant governing principle in him; yet he hath greater encouragement in reference to the affairs of his soul, (supposing them to lie in this state,) than he can have in reference to his external estate here in this world. For do we ever find any such promises in the word of God, that whosoever labours to be rich shall be rich? or that he that takes care of his health shall be always healthy; as we have, that he that labours to be saved shall have help from heaven in order thereunto? "Work out your own salvation with fear and trembling, for God worketh in you to will and to do of his own good pleasure." Phil. 2. 12, 13. He is working: (so the word signifies:) what he doth herein, he doth according to good pleasure, and he is still doing and working in you. Therefore, there can be no purpose or counsel in the divine will, lying against this plain word of his. So that none can have any pretence to be less laborious, less diligent in reference to the affairs of their souls, than they have in reference to their common affairs. Yea, there is a great deal of reason why they should be much more, and that they should conjoin hope with their diligence in reference thereunto; which I mention in this conjunction, because we find them so conjoined in Scripture; and they are conjoined in the nature of the thing. We find them conjoined, Heb. 6. 11. "That ye shew the same diligence unto the full assurance of hope unto the end: that ye be not slothful, but followers of them who through faith and patience have inherited the promises." And in the nature of the thing, there can be no diligence where there is no hope; where there is much of hope, there will be much of diligence. There is no reason that either should languish: there is the greatest reason why both should be lively and vigorous, and make each other so, even upon the supposition of what lies in the mind and purpose of God, in reference to the affairs of souls. And then, I further add by way of caution,

8. That we do not overlook the advantages that may be made of agreements among them that do controvert this same thing. That is, the purposes and counsels of God touching the salvation of men, or touching the punishment of them who shall be found the fit subjects of his punitive justice in another state. Let us not overlook the advantage that may be made of what is in this matter agreed on all hands; that is, it is on all hands agreed, that no good man shall ever perish. This is a thing wherein all do consent and agree. And truly, what there is of difference, it is so very notional and little, in comparison of this, that here we have what should quiet our minds, yea, and it is fur-

ther agreed, that for them that are wicked, they have always still means for making them better, more than ever they improve or make use of; and that God doth afford no such means to any unwillingly; therefore, always according to his will, and the counsel of his will; and consequently, that this must be found the case at last, that none do finally perish but such as have refused and rejected the overtures, or misimproved, or not improved the means that they had in order to their being saved. Though they had not all at once what was necessary to the saving of them, they had always reason to apprehend, that if they had used what they had, they should have had still more. And such agreements as these are by no means to be overlooked. We should labour to make the greatest advantage of them that the matter admits of. Yea, and it is further agreed, that this world is very wicked; and it cannot but be agreed, that God could make it generally better if he would, and therefore, it ought to be as generally agreed, that he hath something in his wise counsel whence it doth appear to him less fit to exert his almightiness to this purpose. Or, if any should expect he should do so, or wonder he doth not so, they have as much reason to wonder why he did not, by almightiness, shut sin out of the world at first, and why he did not, by his almighty power, (as he might,) prevent the apostasy or fall, either of the angels that fell, or of the universality of men that fell all at once, and are all in a fallen state ever since.

I shall not further insist as to matter of useful caution which in these several particulars hath been given you. But I shall add to these, some *alleviating considerations*, that may help to make things sit more easily on our minds, relating to this great and important subject. As,

1. Consider this, that all the purposes or determinations of the divine will, they are the products of counsel. That the text assures us, that whatsoever he doth, he doth according to the counsel of his own will, whereupon, as to the secret purposes and determinations of the divine will which therefore we know not, because they are secret, we have all the reason imaginable to think, that they must be most unexceptionable from that we do know, that they are all purposes guided by most unerring counsel, and which, whilst we know not in particular what they are, we have nothing to do but reverentially to adore, as the apostle doth in Rom. 11. 33. "O! the depth both of the wisdom and knowledge of God! how unsearchable are his judgments, and his ways past finding out." That part remains, to adore, with a dutiful adoration, what we do not distinctly and particularly understand, and, indeed, cannot understand. There

is no government but hath its arcana; and it would be very inept and foolish for us to imagine, that there should be no secrets belonging to the divine government. But admit that there be, inasmuch as they do belong to the divine government, the government of God; that name is a name that comprehends all perfection, and excludes all imperfection; contains nothing in it but what is most excellent and perfect in all respects; and therefore, of this, in the general, we may rest most assured, that there can be nothing exceptionable in those purposes of his will which we do not particularly know. And,

2. Let us but consider, that for his known and public counsels, they carry their own recommendableness in them to every mind, understanding and conscience of man, that shall consider. Do but bethink yourselves, what is given us as the summary of the whole counsel of God which is published and declared to apostate, fallen man. The apostle tells the Ephesians, (Acts 20. 21.) that he had made it his business to testify to them, "repentance towards God and faith in our Lord Jesus Christ." And in having done so, he tells them (ver. 27.) that he had made known to them the whole counsel of God. Now, I beseech you, what could have been more suitable to the state of apostate, fallen creatures than to say, it is the counsel of God, they should repent, that they should turn to him. And since it was impossible they should return and be accepted, but upon the account of a Mediator and Redeemer who was to bring them to God, and reconcile them to him, what could be more suitable, than that this should be stood upon, wheresoever he is revealed and made known, that men should believe in him; that is, absolutely resign and subject themselves to his saving mercy, and to his governing power? Here is the whole counsel of God, here it is summed up. And what hath any man to say to this? why, being an apostate creature, he should not turn and repent? and why, not being able to satisfy divine justice by himself, but having one revealed to him that hath fully done it, (so as to leave that none of his part) why he should not entrust his soul with him, and cast it upon him, and subject it to his conduct and government; by known and prescribed and most unexceptionable rules? And whereas, men cannot turn of themselves, (it is true,) they have not at present sufficient power in their own hand, it is all one, whether they have it, or may have it; if they do apply themselves. This is a part of the counsel of God too, that he is always ready to assist a returning soul: "Turn ye at my reproof, I will pour out my Spirit upon you." Prov. 1. 21. This is part of his counsel : for they that do not so, are, in the next

verse, said to have set at nought his counsel: "But they have set at nought my counsel and despised all my reproof." How unexceptionable are the counsels that are made known, and that are published and declared to us! And,

3. Consider, that if this be the declared, published counsel of God, which you have heard, that he would have apostate creatures return, and is intent upon it that they should do so, "Turn ye, turn ye, why will ye die O house of Israel?" (Ezek. 18.) and is always assisting to their return,—" turn ye at my reproof, apply yourselves, set about it, I will pour out my Spirit upon you, I will make known my words unto you:" I say, if this be his declared, published counsel, we are sure there can be no repugnant, contrary secret counsel. There can be no contrariety between his declared and his secret counsel. It were monstrous idolatry, that we should form in our own minds, instead of a Deity, an apprehension that he is made up of repugnancies and inconsistencies with himself. And again,

4. Let us but consider, how things would lie under God's present view, supposing that we did not recur and run back into a foregoing eternity, supposing things to lie as they are in their present state, under the present and immediate view of God, only, without conceiving an eternal counsel and an eternal purpose concerning any such thing: and consider with yourselves how matters should lie then; that is, but thus, that whereas, God hath such an order of creatures, intelligent creatures, inhabiting this world, who have all apostatized, fallen, and gone off from him, and by the natural tendency of their course, are universally running themselves into misery, and sinking lower and lower, ready to be ingulfed of endless and eternal misery: he beholds these from the throne of his glory above; he sends forth plain, general significations of the pity and compassion he hath towards his creatures; directs his invitations to all the ends of the earth to look to him that they may be saved: if the express revelation do not reach all, it is they themselves, through their own wickedness, that do obstruct and hinder the diffusion of it, otherwise the gospel had spread and flown like lightning from one quarter and end of the world to another, many an age ago, and still from age to age; but yet, plain significations that God is not irreconcileable to his fallen creatures, are more or less afforded every where; he doth not leave himself without witness in that he doth men good: he is kind to them; doth not treat them as an implacable God; makes his sun to shine, and his rain to fall upon the evil and the good, as in that context we so lately discoursed of to you. He

is secretly striving with them, as his Spirit strove with the old world before the flood. "My Spirit (saith God) shall not always strive with man;" implying, that it had been striving, even with that wicked world before. And after the same rate he is dealing with men still. They despise the riches of his patience and goodness and long-suffering, many of them: suppose they do so more generally, he yet, by a merciful and more powerful hand takes hold of some, and saith (as it were) "Though you are inclined and disposed all to perish alike, I will have a relict from among you out of the hand and power of the destroyer:" and he hath finally a numerous remnant; more than any tongue can number, as we find the matter represented how it will be in the close and period of things; we do not know how vastly numerous they may yet be, or have been in former ages and successions of time. But they that perish, perish by their own wilful refusal of offered mercy, whether more expressly, or whether by more tacit, yet intelligible inclinations. Let but things be considered now as lying before God, obvious to one present view, Who hath any thing to say against God's method of procedure in this case? Who hath not cause to adore his grace and goodness and clemency in all this, though so great numbers finally perish? and then, how easy is the step further, if things to one present view do lie so very unexceptionably, what is there more of exception, supposing this view to have been eternal? If things be very fair thus, under one present view, will they lie worse, if it were a day earlier, or a month or a year earlier, or an age or from eternity? What is itself right and well, is eternally so, and was eternally so, and can never have been otherwise. And therefore, it is very vain and foolish for men to amuse their minds, and affright themselves with the thoughts of future and eternal counsels, that may have lain this way or that: if things look well to a present view, how can they look worse to an eternal one. And again, consider,

5. That things should lie thus open to the eternal view of God, all at once, in all their dependencies and connections and references to one another, certainly, it is owing only to his perfections, that they should do so, and that they do so. Is it not a greater perfection to foresee and to foreknow all things, and to have forelaid all one's designs, than to foreknow nothing before hand? and to do nothing without foregoing, previous design? How unreasonable is it for us to think the worse of God for that he is more perfect! It is very unreasonable to suppose that he should not foreknow what will become of you and me in our eternal state; that he should not foreknow what the condition of that creature he hath made shall be to eterni-

ty. And whatsoever he doth actually make it to be, in point of felicity, by his own grace, or whatsoever he lets it be, in point of misery, by its own demerit, and the depraved inclination of its own nature, it is certainly his perfection to know the one and the other; and to do whatsoever he doth, willingly and with design, not unwillingly, or as if he could be imposed upon, or forced in any thing. Do but seriously consider how unreasonable it is to think the worse, or have the blacker thoughts of God, for that which is nothing else but his perfection. It would certainly be an imperfection to be nescient, and not to know what will become of things, and what will become of men: and so, to act incogitantly and without previous design, were a great imperfection. Is he then less fit to govern us, and to dispose of us and his creatures, for his being more perfect? And again,

6. Consider how things will lie in the judgment of the great day. We know the rule of his final procedure in that day, which is called "the day of the revelation of the righteous judgment of God," that he will give "eternal life to them that by patient continuance in well-doing seek for honour and glory and immortality: and indignation and wrath, tribulation and anguish to those that obey not the truth, but obey unrighteousness." Rom. 2. 5, 6. To none but perverse and persevering evil doers, none but such as refused to obey the truth and were contentious against it, and did obey unrighteousness, did give themselves up to the judgment of an unrighteous spirit and principle, ruling and working in them, to none else but these, "indignation and wrath, tribulation and anguish." If things will be very unexceptionable in the judgment of the great day, (as who can have any thing to say against this rule or this method of procedure) he will then, in the judgment of the great day, both do as he purposed before; and his purpose will no way be found to have differed from the measure of his final procedure. And again consider,

7. That there cannot but a conviction go with the final issue of things, in the very souls and consciences of them that perish. They do foreknow the righteous judgment of God, that they that do such and such things are worthy of death; are worthy of misery. Pagans themselves do so, for to them the apostle speaks and refers in that 1 Romans, in the close of the chapter. And what convictions will be upon the consciences of men in the final issue of things, is sufficiently intimated in that, their principal sting is plainly enough and sufficiently intimated to be from their own consciences. There is the worm that never dies. And it were impossible this hold could be

taken on the consciences of men, if it did not appear to them that they were finally guilty of their own ruin. All such imaginations must vanish and fly away of course, that it was impossible things should ever be otherwise with them than they are; that they were doomed unavoidably into that state into which they are come. Whatsoever might be a fence to keep off the stroke from their consciences, you must be sure will all vanish and be gone, and therefore, can have no place. And then lastly,

8. Consider the high and everlasting approbation that all God's methods will have with the most clarified, refined minds of angels and saints, in all that vast general assembly made up of " the innumerable company of angels and the spirits of just men made perfect;" all agreeing in admiring and applauding the most unexceptionable righteousness of all God's dispensations; whereof the counsel of his will were the measure : "Just and true are thy ways, marvellous are thy works Lord God Almighty." And here will be no dark mind, no clouded understanding, no erroneous thought, no vitiating prejudice. If therefore, we are sure all things will to eternity lie well and right to the most perfect minds and understandings, then they are righteous in themselves : and being in themselves right, they ought to be so estimated and judged of by us. Certainly, these things cannot be mistaken, cannot be misunderstood and misapprehended by those pure and glorious creatures in the other state; those bright and unclouded minds that will see nothing but loveliness and beauty, and what is most highly praiseworthy and admirable in the eternal view that they shall have of them. Therefore, to shut up all for the present, let me but leave these two words of direction.

(1.) Labour to cherish the love of God in your souls. That will commend to you all his counsels and all his methods. Love will never think amiss. And,

(2.) Form your apprehensions concerning him, agreeably, that so you may have nothing in your minds to damp your love; nothing may disaffect you unto him. The understanding and the will (such is the constitution of the human nature) do interchangeably work upon one another: the more we love God, the better we shall think of him, and the better we think of him, the better we shall love him. These things circulate between one another. And nothing can be of higher and greater consequence : for if we do otherwise we shall cramp religion in ourselves; and so far as we propagate the ill sentiment, we shall hinder the propagating and diffusing of religion among others. And do but take this deeply to heart, (perhaps I may have more reason to speak to it hereafter,) that in the latter days wherein, it is said, religion must flourish in the world, (Hosea 3. 5.) men are to "fear the Lord and his goodness." Most certain it is, in those days, (if there are such days yet to come better than we have seen,) thus it must be, there must be a universal diffusion of good thoughts concerning God. This is that knowledge of God that must replenish the world, and fill the earth, and transform the minds of men, and overcome their fierce, savage humours and dispositions, their disaffection towards God, and their barbarities towards one another; make them "beat their swords into ploughshares and their spears into pruning hooks." The revealed and acknowledged will of God, and goodness of God prevailing against the evil of the mind and hearts of men. "They shall fear the Lord and his goodness in the latter days." Their thoughts and apprehensions of God will be so persuasive to their own hearts, and they will look upon him according to that kind and amiable and lovely representation of himself that shall captivate all minds and hearts; and make men hate nothing but themselves, and that they have not sooner and more loved God.

LECTURE V.*

Thus we have fully spoken to these words as they concern the spiritual and eternal state of men, which is the apostle's principal scope as you may see, in the foregoing part of the chapter, and of the same verse; "having predestinated us to the adoption of children by Jesus Christ to himself, according to the good pleasure of his will." verse 5. And here, "according to the purpose of him that worketh all things according to the counsel of his own will." But you see, that from that special consideration of the counsel or purpose of his own will, or the good pleasure thereof, the apostle makes a very easy, natural transition unto this more general proposition which comprehends all that could be said, including the former in it, and much more. And therefore, having spoken to the more limited object already, of the counsel of the divine will, I shall proceed to speak somewhat of the counsel of God's will concerning the other affairs of men, besides those of their souls or of their eternal state.

And though it be very true that God's agency about all

* Preached January 29, 1692.

these outward concernments of men, do belong to another head of theology, that is, his providence; yet, the counsel of his will, according whereunto that agency is directed about these affairs, as well as those others that we have already spoken to, comes properly under our consideration here. And therefore, to that I shall speak somewhat briefly; to wit, the counsel of the divine will respecting the present concernments of men in the world, so far as it may be needful and useful to us; that so we may detract nothing from God, that doth truly and rightfully belong to him, and that we may not lose the advantage of the pleasant sentiments and relishes which we may have ourselves, and in our own spirits from the right stating of this matter, which we shall, therefore, endeavour as much as in us is. And shall in speaking of it do these four things—speak of the extent of the object about which the counsel of the divine will is said to be conversant—of the counsel of the divine will itself, its nature and significancy in reference to that object or sort of objects that we are now to consider—give you briefly the reasons why we are to ascribe such a thing to God as counsel and purpose touching these affairs of ours, and—labour to shew you, that no ill consequence can reasonably and justly, be drawn from hence.

1. The extent of the object: sure we are not otherwise to circumscribe it than the letter of the text; WHO WORKETH ALL THINGS. For that special sort of object, the souls of men, and their spiritual and eternal state, we have spoken to already, which falls within the compass and comprehension, you plainly enough see, in the general expression in the text. And having spoken to that, even all other concernments besides we must understand to be within the compass of the object too: and therefore, that the counsel of the divine will is conversant about them; that is, whatsoever he hath any agency about, about that also, the counsel of his will hath place, for "he worketh *all* things according to the counsel of his will." He doth nothing unwillingly, he wills nothing unadvisedly: therefore, whereas all things lie under his agency, all things lie under the counsel of his will.

More especially, whatsoever he hath made any law about; in reference to whatsoever he hath given us rules and precepts, these are called counsels often, and often in Scripture: they are the counsels and mandates of his will. These all lie under the counsel of his will.

There is no state or condition that men can be in, in this world, but there are regulations, and precepts given in reference thereto. Whatsoever is matter of threatening or of promise, the sanctions annexed to his precepts, (as there are many things of threatening and promise that are of temporal concernments,) these still must be considered as being within the same compass. Whatsoever may be matter of affliction or of comfort, whatsoever may have in it any thing of blessing, or any thing of cursing, (as there are temporal blessings and temporal curses besides the eternal ones,) all these, we must understand to be consulted of, in the sense we formerly opened unto you, excluding all the imperfections, and including all the perfection that can be any way conceived or signified by it.

Moreover, all the private concernments of men, personal and domestic; the concernments of the world, of kingdoms and nations, political concernments: the concernments of the church of God in the world, which may be considered under the measure of time; they are all to be considered within the object of divine purpose and counsel.

The more private, personal or domestic concernments of men; they belong to this object, and cannot be excluded. The time of every one's coming into this world, and the time of his going out of it: the "time to be born, and the time to die;" they lie under the determination of the divine counsel, directive of his will: even touching them, there is a time for every purpose under the sun. These, among the rest, "a time to be born and a time to die." Eccles. 3. 2. Skipping over (as it were) the intervening time, as if that were little worth the notice: yet only not noting it there, but in the mean time not excluding it neither, as is evincible enough from many other texts. But it is to be observed, (if you compare that with another passage in the same book: chap. 8. 6.) as to every purpose, there belongs a season, so to every season there belongs judgment; to every purpose there is time and judgment. That must, undoubtedly, primarily, mean divine judgment, which is the perfection of counsel; that which with men is the result of counsel, and which therefore, must signify somewhat analogous with God: there is the judgment of wisdom and counsel, that is determinative of every season, every time, for whatsoever purpose, or occurrence that falls out to any of the sons of men. And the time between these two times, the time of their being born, and the time when they are to die; that lies under the same determination. His days and months and years are all set and appointed; as it is fully expressed in Job 14. 6.

And so the conditions of men, while they are here in this world, whether they shall be high or low; whether they shall be rich or poor; every one hath his dimension, his allowance ordered for him; and no doubt therefore, pre-ordained. Whatsoever portion any man hath of the things of this life, whether it be more, or whether it be less, it is all given. Even what the ravens have, the fowls of the air and the beasts of the field, it is all given: and much more what every man hath, is by the divine allowance and vouchsafement.. To every living thing he gives what is convenient and suitable for the support of that life which he had given it before. But what he gives, he gives willingly, not against his will. And what he did once will, (as you formerly heard,) he could not but ever will, and there can be no new one with him.

And how particular persons do branch into families; this all lies under the particular direction even of divine counsel and purpose. And so, what allotments such and such families shall have; and those as they multiply and do increase, "even unto nations and kingdoms," as you see, Acts 17. 26. As God. hath made of one blood all nations of men to dwell on all the face of the earth; so he hath determined the times of all, and appointed the very bounds of their habitations; assigned to every one his place where he shall be. It hath been the matter of the counsel of the divine will, even concerning us, that our lot should fall in such and such a part of the world: that we should dwell so much of our time in such a place; that our lot should be cast in England, or for so long a time in London; and in what circumstances and with what advantages one way or other. All these things, as they have been ordered by the great Lord of all, so they are not ordered by him incogitantly, but according to the eternal counsel and purpose that are understood to have passed concerning us. The very meanest things that can any way belong to us, or belong to this world, being expressly mentioned to come under the divine cognizance and care; it is plain such concernments as these cannot be excluded. As when we are told, all the hairs of our heads are numbered; and that a sparrow cannot fall to the ground without our heavenly Father. And that is our Saviour's reasoning from hence, "Are not ye of more value than they, than many sparrows?" Now, if these things be the matter of the very care and agency of providence, they must have been the matter of an eternal purpose and counsel, for the reason again and again repeated before, that nothing can be new with God; no new thought, no new counsel or purpose.

And to consider, to what particularities the divine eye and purpose do reach; what we find recorded and comes under our notice by way of history, that therefore, must suppose there hath been an eternal view, even of the same things, and a purpose concerning them. As for instance, that which appears to be the most barren part of the Bible, that large account that we have of genealogy in Scripture; How should Moses possibly come to know through the successions of so many hundreds of years, even two thousand years before him, what children such and such men had, all those that are reckoned up, and how many years they lived? And it was thought fit that should be put down: and how such families were ranked, and what nations sprang from them; all these must needs have been matter of divine Revelation, and therefore, were matter of divine knowledge, and therefore, were eternally so: all things being in the same order, under the divine eye, wherein they actually come to pass in the world.

So all the removes of men to and fro, here upon earth. "Thou tellest my wanderings," saith David; there is not a step taken this way or that, but all is under the divine direction and provision and purpose, that so and so it shall be.

And if you enlarge your thoughts further, to the concernments of formed nations and kingdoms, collective bodies, they must be understood also, to be within the compass of this object. The alterations in kingdoms; the seasons and intervals of rests and disturbances; of peace and of war, of plenty and of scarcity; of a prosperous and of an adverse posture of affairs, in respect of any, whatsoever, favourable providences or judgments that come upon these; these all lie under the counsel of the divine will. The revolutions of governments, when they are past, when they pass from form to form; God hath been pleased to give some more extraordinary proof and demonstration of his regency in these kingdoms, on purpose that it may be known (as Nebuchadnezzar, that great prince was forced to confess) that God rules over the kingdoms of men, and gives them to whom he pleaseth. Dan. 4. 32. The Most High rules in the kingdom of men. It is not said kingdoms, importing this whole world to be one kingdom to him, one great monarchy, all lying under his imperial power. And all this must be understood to be according to counsel, and according to purposes that were with him eternally. For (as hath been said before) his being is so; *Et eternum non patitur novum; no new thing can fall out in eternity.*

And so, for the state of his church in general, or of particular churches upon earth; all their concernments, as they are such, they fall under the counsel of the divine will which orders all their circumstances in reference to them; sometimes making their condition more prosperous and favourable, and sometimes, more adverse, for trial and needful exercise of their graces, in these kinds wherein it is requisite such graces should have their exercises, which he hath adapted to such special purposes. So large (and for our thoughts, let them go as large, and far as they will or can) is the object about which the counsel of the divine will is conversant. But,

2. Something is to be said concerning the nature of such counsel and will, as it respects such an object; or this more special sort of object which I most intend in the present discourse. Why,

(1.) This is always to be held concerning the counsel of the divine will, that it is most perfectly wise; all things being in view to him at once, open to one eternal view in all their connections, references and dependancies; he having a thorough and everlasting perspection, even of all at once, of the things themselves and of their connection with one another, even as they are connected, not because they are so, so as to pass from one connected thing to another, as we in our more imperfect way of knowing things are constrained to do. And,

(2.) The counsel of his will must therefore, hereupon, be immutable: being most perfectly wise, there can be no imaginable reason of any change. He never needs alter his measures: " Known to him are all his works from the beginning of the world," was that grave saying of the apostle James, in that synod at Jerusalem. Acts 15. 18. Whatsoever he hath to do, or doth do, that he designed to do ; for he acts nothing casually: and what he did design to do, he did consult about, so far as consulting can have place with him: we explained the sense of it before, that is, that he hath perfect perspection of all that is requisite and fit to be done, and so did purpose according thereto, and then doth according to that purpose. And therefore, to consider, besides the nature of such a divine purpose and counsel, its reference and significancy to human affairs. I say,

(3.) This same counsel of the divine will, it is a measure to himself of all his own agency, what he will do, and what he will not do; how far he will exert his influence, and wherein he will suspend it: how he will direct it this way and that, and how he will limit it. And,

(4.) By consequence, it must needs be a measure of all events; because nothing can eventually fall out, but according to his will, either effecting or permitting; and there being no determination of his will which is not still under the direction of divine counsel. And all this, we must understand to be constantly transacting with him, with the greatest clearness, and with the greatest facility imaginable. You do observe among men, vastly different tempers and complexions of mind; some seem to be almost constantly calm and sedate, composed and serene, there appears nothing torpid or unequal in their frame or habit. Now, if we can conceive among human minds what is more perfect, and what is less, sure it should not be difficult to us to take our assent, and conceive concerning the Divine Mind, that it must be most absolutely perfect, never liable to any cloud, to any discomposure, all things lying in a most perfect clearness, and having their eternal formation or form there, with the greatest imaginable facility: and infinitely more than we can imagine. So as there is no cause for any thought concerning a *plenus negotii Deus*, as the epicurean objecteth, concerning such a Deity as should be engaged and taken up about making, and about governing such a world as this, that this must give too much business to such a Being, as we are not to conceive of otherwise than as perfectly happy, it not consisting (as they foolishly imagine) with the felicity and happiness of such a Being. But when we can conceive in some men, with how very great composure of mind they go through a great variety of business, their minds being always clear and serene, can we not consider concerning God, that his understanding is infinite, as reason and Scripture do most plainly speak; and so that nothing could ever be excluded it, or lie without it? as the various images of things are represented in a clear glass, detected there, without giving any toil or labour to the glass, or inferring upon it any change. And so the schools have been wont to speak of God's eternal knowledge of things, that he beholds them all as in an everlasting and eternal *speculum*, there being that perpetual and eternal clearness in the Divine Mind, that things lie there without any discomposure to him, without any disorder, in the same state and frame, wherein they do actually fall out; so as when they do actually fall out, whatsoever disturbance there is of one thing with another, and among the things themselves variously interfering, yet all these things are beheld without disturbance to him: as the various motions and agitations of many persons in a room, all represented in a clear glass, make no disturbance or discomposure in it at all, whatsoever there is in the things represented. Therefore, I pass,

3. To the reasons why we are to ascribe to God such a concern about human affairs, so as to employ the counsel of his will, even from eternity about them. I will shortly name to you these two plain and obvious things, as the reasons thereof, besides what Scripture doth, in many more places than those that I'

have named, expressly assert about it: 1st. The most absolute perfection of his nature cannot but infer it: and 2d. the supremacy, the universality and accurateness of his government.

(1.) The perfection of his nature, that cannot but infer it. He being every way perfect, absolutely perfect, (which he must be, if he be God, we have no other notion of a Deity but of a being absolutely and universally perfect,) he must be omniscient, and must know all things; and if so, he must always have known them; for if ever he did not know them, there will be some addition to his knowledge when he comes to do so. But that knowledge to which there can be an addition is imperfect; and therefore, the divine knowledge could never admit of any addition, but all things, (as was said before) must have lain open everlastingly with him to one eternal view. And,

(2.) The supremacy, universality, and exactness of his government, doth necessarily infer it. Inasmuch as he is Lord over all, and is Most High, there can be none above him that should be director of such affairs. And inasmuch as he is universal Governor, if any affairs lie not under his government, they can lie under none. It is not a supposable thing, that one part of the creation should be governed, and another ungoverned; part under a ruler and the other part under no rule at all. And then, the exactness of his government, not considered absolutely, but respectively, that is, with respect to the state of the governed creatures, the governed communities that lie under the management and dominion of his kingdom. We are to consider this world as in a state of apostasy; and we are not to expect that he should deal with this world, as if men were in a perfect state, for their frame and temper are far from perfect. He deals with them as suitable to the state of apostates, as those that have been, and are, in rebellion against him generally. And admirable it is that the methods of his government should be so mild and propitious; and that so much of common order should be preserved among them thereby, as we find there is, this being considered. But to such government, eternal provision and purpose are always necessary, and could not but be necessary. There must be eternal foresight of all that was to be done, and eternal purpose and counsel thereupon. We thence come,

4. To consider, that there can be nothing of ill consequence, justly and reasonably, drawn from hence. What is most supposable in this case, and of this kind, that is, which may present itself to a first view under the notion of an ill, or incon-

venient consequence, which chiefly lies under one of these two heads, 1st. That this hypothesis will preclude the use of human prudence; and 2d. that it will shut out prayer. These are two things that carry a first and more obvious appearance of an ill consequence, upon the supposition of what we have been hitherto asserting. But I shall labour to evince, that neither of these consequences can, with any reasonable colour, be thought to ensue. As,

(1.) That here, there should be no place nor use for human prudence. Thus some may too hastily think and pronounce, If there be a divine counsel and purpose about every thing that a man can do, or about every thing that shall occur to him, that he may either enjoy or suffer, to what purpose is it for men to consult and determine, or contrive this way or that? as not knowing but that they may, in the very thing they design and go about, run counter to the counsels of the divine will; and so all will be in vain, and to no purpose. We shall give you some considerations to shew the in-consequence, that it follows not, that there is no pretence that the use of human prudence should hereby be excluded. As,

[1.] That all things are determined by God to fall out in the way wherein they do fall out. I told you at first, when I entered upon this subject, we are not to conceive any such thing concerning him, as that he doth decree and determine things abstractly, without reference to the *media* by which they are to be brought about. We are to impute no such thing to God, with reference to the eternal states of men, as we spake then; that whatsoever a man doth he shall be damned, be he never so good, never so strict, never so pious; or that whatsoever such a man doth, he shall be saved, let him be never so wicked, never so irreligious or profane; never so strongly persist and persevere in such a course. We are to impute no such thing, no such counsel to the wise and holy God. Neither his word, nor the reason of the thing leads us to any such thought concerning him. And so, in reference to these lower affairs, we are never to think any such thing concerning him, as if he laid down purposes and decrees concerning this or that end, without connecting in his own eternal mind and view, the whole scheme of all the ways and methods and means by which such ends are to be compassed and brought about. And therefore,

[2.] Those things which, according to the counsel of his will, are to be brought about by the intervention and exercise of human prudence; these things are actually so brought about:

whatsoever is effected, whatsoever is done by the exercise of the prudence of a man, it lay in the divine mind and counsel, as a thing not only to be brought about, but to be brought about so, and in that way, by that very means, by the deliberation, and by the prudent contrivances of such and such of his creatures, that should serve his purpose in such a way. And therefore,

[3.] In this case, and in reference to all such events, the very objection is an argument. The objection, the possible use, or advantageous use, of human prudence is a proof and demonstration of it: for, according to divine counsel and purpose, such a thing as doth actually occur and come to pass by human prudence, was determined so to come to pass, by the intervention of human prudence. And again,

[4.] It is the much more common course, in the way of God's dispensation towards his creatures, to let things go on according to the posture and aptitude of the second causes by which they are effected and brought about; it is much the more common and usual course. He who is the supreme Ruler and Lord of all, is not to be supposed but he may at pleasure lay on a restrictive or regulating hand, as he sees meet to alter the natural course and tendency of things. But ordinarily he doth not so, but things do run on according to the aptitude and disposition and posture of the second causes, by the ministry whereof they are effected and brought about. And even as to voluntary and rational agents, whereas, the men of this world, (who are such agents,) are generally wicked, God generally, and for the most part, doth not hinder the ill purposes that they have formed and contrived and set themselves to execute. That, the Psalmist supposeth to be the common case when, in that psal. 37. 7. he gives so weighty counsel in reference to that case, not fretting, nor letting our hearts tumultuate and arise and swell within us, because of evil men that bring their wicked devices to pass, implying this to be the more ordinary case, that wicked men do bring their wicked devices to pass, God doth not lay that restraint, for great and holy ends and reasons, which will appear in their lustre and glory one day; but lets things run on in their own course according as the inclinations and aptitudes of other second causes do lead. And this being observably so, it is the most unreasonable thing in the world, to suppose that in rarer instances wherein the purposes of men are disappointed and frustrated by some signal hand from God, therefore the natural operations that do belong to men should be concluded to be generally or universally useless, or to be precluded: or that the principles were useless which were suited to such operations or ends as those. But,

[5.] We are further to consider, that if God doth more extraordinarily interpose, so as to disappoint the evil purposes of men, contrived by their subtilty and craft, (which they are apt enough themselves to misname prudence,) he doth it in no such way as offers violence to the rational nature. He doth it by letting men befool themselves, or by letting them befool one another, or sometimes by letting the devil befool them. He sometimes lets one man befool another: as when that counsel of Hushai, proved to be the means by which God turned (as David prayed he would,) Ahitophel's counsel into foolishness. Sometimes, he lets the devil befool men, acting according to his own inclinations which he restrains not. He lets him loose as he did to deceive Ahab, being a lying spirit in the mouth of his prophets, unto Ahab's destruction. He would not, himself, infuse a lie into the mind of Ahab, (which was a thing his nature was most abhorrent from, being the God of truth,) neither would he let a good angel go and tell a lie to him, as unbeseeming and, indeed, impossible to one that had the divine image in perfection in his nature. But there being a proneness in the wicked spirit (as the matter is parabolically and dramatically represented) to go and deceive Ahab, in his prophets, to his destruction, he lets him go. But there is no violence offered to the rational nature of man in all this. He acts by judgment, (such as it is) that is, by a mistaken judgment; not by none, or against judgment, against a practical judgment, which indeed to the nature of man were impossible. And those that are under such deceptions as these, when they do indeed play the fool: as Ahitophel's counsel was turned into foolishness and they all became fools that followed it, yet they thought themselves wise in so doing: and so, those that were reckoned or did reckon themselves wise, were taken in their own craftiness, and their counsels driven headlong, as in Job 5. 13. the expression is. And what they do in such kinds, under such deception, they do freely and with complacency, pleasing themselves in their own way; so as there is no violence offered to the nature of man, considering him as a rational, and as a voluntary agent in what he doth, even then, when his purposes are inverted and disappointed. But then,

[6.] If men do take up such purposes as it seems meet to the great and holy God to frustrate and disappoint, (which by extraordinary interposition, as hath been said, he doth very rarely: he is sparing in instances of that kind,) yet, that, men are to blame themselves for; either, that they did propose to themselves unlawful designs; or, that they did pursue and prosecute lawful ones unlawfully; whence it hath seemed meet to that wisdom which governs the world, either to cross and defeat their designs, or to check and rebuke them, that they may reflect on and understand their own folly in so mishaping in their own course, as they are often wont to do when they take up wicked purposes, and form wicked designs which prove abortive. And how should it be otherwise, if they take counsel against the Lord and his anointed one, his Christ? Do you think it strange that that should be in vain? " Wherefore doth the heathen rage, and the people imagine a vain thing ?" Why is it a vain thing that they imagine and devise? It is counsel against the Lord and his Messiah. And if there be an inverture of the counsel and purposes of men which do lie cross to the divine counsel and purpose, and that they clash with one another, what wonder is that? Nay, whose will is it fit should rule and oversway in such a case? Is God to quit the sovereignty and yield up his throne and sceptre, and say unto vain creatures, "Be it according to your mind, and according to your will," when they will nothing but mischief, wrong to him, and ruin to all that are better than themselves? And sometimes, they pursue the most lawful things unlawfully: and then it is meet that God should some way or other give a check to them. As in such an instance as the apostle James mentioneth, (chap. 4. 13.) of such as say, in the power of their own self-conceit and self-will and self-confidence, "We will go to such and such a city, and will tarry there a year, and we will buy and sell and get gain :" and forget all this while that they live under the divine dominion and government; that they ought to say, " If the Lord will, we will do so and so." It is very fit, that in such cases, God should put them in mind they have a Lord over them, and that he should give a check to such insolencies. And if they meet with rebukes because they will not carry themselves like those that live under the dominion and government of a Ruler who is superior to them, they will not walk in that light which before hath been made to shine in their minds and consciences, and God takes a severe method with them, to make them know themselves and him; there is nothing unfit done in the case. He doth but what he owes to himself to do, that he may do himself right, that he may not lose the honour and acknowledgment that are due to him, as he is Lord of all. But now, upon such a supposition as this, it is no more reasonable to say, that the understanding, or reason, or wisdom, or prudence which any man hath, is given him in vain, than it would be to say, that because such and such a man is a very prudent, wise man, it is altogether in vain that he should have a prudent servant. And yet, there is no man so wise, but if he have occasion for a servant, he will have an understanding man to be his servant, and not a fool; a prudent one, and not one that is rash and foolish, and would do things precipitately and to disadvantage. But how unreasonable would it be to say, that because such a wise master will not let even this wise servant do his business his own way, but will check and control him and exercise the authority of a master over him, therefore, such a man hath a prudent servant in vain? Who would be so foolish as to say, the prudence of such a servant is to no purpose unless he may be master, and carry every thing his own way, according to his own mind and fancy? Or suppose a man had a watch that ordinarily goes well as he would have it, but sometimes he finds it to err, and then he rectifies it with his finger; would the owner of this watch, taking upon him to rectify it with his finger, say, "To what purpose are all the contrivances of this watch, and to what purpose are the several wheels and movements in it, if a man shall move it with his finger?" There is as little reason to pretend, that prudence and wisdom are given to any man in vain, because God will over-rule him and shew himself to be supreme in sundry such instances as may occur. I say, there is as little reason to say and allege this, as there would be to say, that all the articles in a watch are in vain, because it may need sometimes to be rectified and corrected by a wise finger.

LECTURE VI.*

I shall only add to all that hath been said on this head, that the counsels of the divine will do very well admit of the use of human prudence, in subordination thereto, and it hath its great significancy in such subordination, but in opposition thereunto, it can signify nothing. And nobody is to think this strange, in subordination to the counsels of the divine will. Human prudence signifies much, all that it is covetable that it should signify. Many times God designs to bring about such and such events by the ministry of human prudence, and then the counsel of the divine will is so far from excluding it, that it doth necessarily include it, and take it in; cannot but do so. But most plain it is, that human prudence can signify nothing

* Preached April 19, 1692.

in opposition to the divine will. And would you have it? would any one wish it should? That human prudence should take place against the divine will, is that a thing to be wished? Or are we to be fond of human prudence in opposition to the divine counsel, as if we thought the world would be better governed by men than by God? That, sure, is never to be regretted, that there is no wisdom, no counsel, no understanding against the Lord. Sure, that should trouble none of us, but please all. And to think, hereupon, that human prudence must needs be a useless thing, because God doth not put all into the hands of men, and leave them to do in the world, whatsoever they please as so many ungoverned creatures, (as was formerly hinted,) it might as well be said, To what purpose is it for a man to have a prudent servant, unless the servant's will and pleasure may take place in every thing against his master's.

(2.) But I come in the second place to that other supposed ill consequence, to wit, that the assertion of such a counsel of the divine will, must exclude the great duty of prayer. And I think it is very material and of great importance to discourse to you somewhat largely upon this head; because, I know how commonly it lies in the minds of many men, as an objection against that great duty; or else, they make use of the objection of that great duty, as an objection against the divine counsel and purpose, and the hand which they are to have in all human affairs. Now, that this seeming difficulty may be cleared, I will give you sundry considerations. As,

[1.] That the primary or more principal notion that we are to have of prayer, is to conceive of it as an act of worship, that is, as an homage due and claimed to be paid to the great sovereign Lord of all. That is the principal and prime notion that we are to have of prayer; that is, that it is such an act of duty as wherein we are to own and acknowledge God: it is due to him, as he is God, to be supplicated, sought to: that there be a dependance upon him, professed and avowed by his reasonable creatures. Now this being the first and primary notion of prayer, an acknowledging of God, and avowing our dependance upon him, and of his superiority over us, as that adjunct expression of it, bowing the knee before him, doth import, I would fain know whether he be the less adorable, for that he is infinitely wise? And if he be infinitely wise, then his wisdom and counsel must extend to all things. But doth his infinite wisdom render him a less adorable Object? Doth he less deserve to be worshipped, or have his due homage paid him by his creatures, for that he is infinitely wise? The counsel of his own will extending to all things doth import so much; he is wise without limit, so as that the exercise of his wisdom cannot be excluded or shut out in any case. If it could be excluded in any case, it were not infinite: but because it is infinite, is it therefore, a less excellency for being infinite? And so, Doth he less deserve to be adored and honoured, and to have homage paid unto him as such? And,

[2.] Whereas, when we do pray, we do also express inclinations and desires of our own, that we would have this or that brought about, when we foreknow the event to be determined by the divine will: prayer is so far from being excluded by that, that we pray with so much the more vigour and cheerfulness and alacrity; and our hearts and souls are so much the more enlarged and engaged and drawn forth in prayer, even when we know the things we pray about are determined by the counsel of the divine will. As in that memorable case of Daniel's foreknowing by books, by Jeremiah's prophecies, that the approaching period and end of the seventy years, determined for the continued captivity of his people; when he understood this book, and discerned the approach of the time, he sets himself with so much the more vigour to pray: (as you see Daniel 9. 1, 2.) finding out that the matter was near, and towards a period, he doth not therefore think prayer excluded, but sets himself to pray with so much the more earnestness and vigour hereupon. As, indeed, if any do consider the nature of man's constitution, and the frame of the human soul, it is evident that desire and hope do influence one another. It is a mighty damp to all rational desire to have no hope. And if the thing be looked upon as desirable in itself; so much the more of hope, so much more of desire: and by how much the more hope doth rise towards confidence, desires grow so much the more fervent. As simple despair of any thing which we have an inclination to desire, damps desire; when we see that the thing is altogether to be despaired of, reason itself dictates to us to withdraw our minds, and turn them another way. Daniel understood the time drew on, when this sad calamitous state of his people was to find its period and be determined; then he sets himself with mighty vigour and fervour of spirit to prayer. And,

[3.] When we do not foreknow the event, as not having any discovery made to us what the counsels of the divine will concerning it are, yet, even then, the business of prayer is to refer ourselves, with reference to any such concernments, to the divine disposal. A thing most suitable to him and to us; to him as he is the wise and sovereign Lord of all; and to us, as we are depending creatures, subject to his government, and are disposed of, in reference to all our concernments, or whatsoever we have any concern about, as he sees good. And therefore,

[4.] In reference to such things, wherein we are ignorant of the event and what God will do, the proper design of prayer is, to endeavour to obtain at his hands a disposition of spirit complying with his pleasure, so as there may be no contest between him and us; that whenever the event falls out, if it do prove agreeable to our inclinations, we may rejoice in it with so much the more raised and sincere gratitude: if it do not, that we may submit to him, without engaging in a contest with one who giveth no account of any of his matters; and with whom, none can contend and prosper. They must always have the worst of it, they must be worsted in it if they engage in a contest with him. Therefore, the business we must design in such prayer, or in prayer about such things, (the issue whereof we do not foreknow,) is not to bring the divine will to ours, but to bring our will to his. As the matter is aptly enough illustrated by some, suppose one comes down a rapid stream in a boat, and hath the opportunity to throw an anchor or hook on the shore, there he pulls, as though he would draw the shore to the boat, and yet, all that he can be rationally supposed to intend, is to draw the boat to the shore. So are we to design in prayer, that plucking ourselves unto God, the drawing of our souls to a compliance with him, that our wills may be brought to unite with his; not that we can imagine to change his will by any thing we can say, more than in the narrative of our prayer we do suppose to ourselves the informing him of any thing whereof we suppose him before ignorant. "He is of one mind, and who can turn him?" Job 23. 13. And therefore,

[5.] The availableness of prayer, considered in reference to the counsels of the divine will, is to be estimated by the tenour of our prayers: according as our prayer is modelled, so it will be available or unavailable. This is the confidence we ought to have in prayer, "that if we ask any thing according to his will he heareth us." 1 John 5. 14. And therefore, further,

[6.] We must make it our great business, in all our addresses to him in prayer, and especially in reference to temporal concernments, (about which we have no express signification of his will, as we have about spiritual and eternal ones) to have our prayers so formed as that they may agree with the court of heaven, (as I may speak,) whither they are to be addressed. As if any man on earth, is to petition a human judicature, he must endeavour to know the stile and phrase of the court, and that his petition may be right in point of form; and especially so are we concerned to do in this case, when we are to address the great God. There must be a becomingness of God observed, that we address to him, as God is to be addressed to, and one that is absolutely supreme, and perfectly wise and good, who (according to that observable saying which I remember in the great Jew Philo, who gives us this notion of himself) hath given us that discovery, that we have always a ground of so fixed and formed an apprehension of him as one that can do all things, and will do that which is best. Such a conception of God, if our prayers do but carry with them a conformity to that conception, that is, that we have this fixed confidence concerning him, that he can do what he will, and that he will always do what is best, we can never think that such prayers can ever be unavailable. But this doth so highly agree with this apprehension that he doth all that he doth do, according to the counsel of his own will, that it not only is not prejudiced thereby, but we are greatly confirmed in it, that if he doth all things according to the counsel of his own will, he will never do any thing that is wrong, he will never do any thing that we ought to have so much as a wish, that it be otherwise than as he will do it: for as he can do whatsoever he will, so he will always do whatsoever is best. And,

[7.] Therefore, we ought to form our addresses and petitions to God, according as his word hath given us direction. As there are rules, some way or other, to be known in any prince's court, or in any court of judicature, how they are to be addressed to: some way or other, it is to be understood. And we may understand by his plain word, how he is to be addressed to. As to all those things that are of principal concernment and necessity to us, we find directions in his word to pray for such things, with promises they shall be granted upon serious and sincere prayer. We know his will so far about our principal concernments, as that they who repent shall be forgiven, they who ask his Spirit shall have it, to them that improve what they have, he will give more, that if we set ourselves to work out our own salvation with fear and trembling, he will work in us to will and to do of his own good pleasure. About these, our greatest concernments, we are at a certainty. He hath told us in his most plain and express word, what he will always do in such cases. But we are always left uncertain about such things as are less considerable, and about things too, that are of a mutable goodness, that is, that are sometimes good and sometimes evil. The things of the mind are invariably good, always good; what is the goodness of the mind is always so. That the mind be knowing, intelligent; that it be holy, pure, subject unto God; these are things always good, invariably good. But it cannot be said so concerning the *bona corporis, the good things of the body,* or the *bona fortunæ, the good things of fortune,* that they are always good, for their goodness is to be measured according to their suitableness and conformity or subserviency to some greater good. For we are to consider that as we have bodies so we have minds too; and that which would be good for my body, if hurtful to my mind, it loseth the nature of goodness; and therefore, is that goodness mutable, according as circumstances will render such and such things more and more subservient to a higher good, to a nobler kind of good that we are more to be concerned about. And therefore, for those things which are of a mutable goodness they cannot be the matter of an absolute promise, that shall be concluding and determinative concerning them universally, and at all times; because at some times that which would be a good, it may at another time degenerate into evil, by the variation of circumstances. But an evil cannot be the matter of a promise; it would be the matter of a threatening at such a time when it ceaseth to be good. If it should stand in the promise under the notion of a good, but by this and that circumstance loseth its aptitude and suitableness to the end wherein this goodness lies, then doth that good turn into an evil, and so cannot be the matter of a promise. You cannot say, you promise any one that which is evil, or which would be a hurt to him; therefore, the promises of God, in reference to things of this nature, are always suitable to the nature of the things. We have as express promises concerning temporal good things as the nature of the things will bear, or our circumstances admit, and therefore, God hath done more suitably to himself and us, in reference to such things, in telling us "all things shall work together for good to them that love God and that are the called according to his purpose." Rom. 8. 28. Indeed, a person that is a sincere lover of God, cannot but be the better by whatsoever event occurs to him in external respects; for that love is an active principle in him, that co-operates to the making good of the promise. It thinks no evil, it makes a man construe well, all the divine dispensations, it forms his spirit to a compliance with the divine pleasure, and so, good will come out of it to such a one, to a so qualified subject, whatsoever the event be. And therefore, all the business of prayer that it may be significant and available, is to have it formed and modelled according to the tenour of the divine will as God hath expressed that will to us in his word, and to pray for things agreeably to the discovery we have thereof: that is, with a peremptory confidence, in reference to those things that are expressly promised; and with submission, in reference to all other things : satisfying ourselves, with this, that he who is the most perfectly absolute, supreme God, nothing of evil can proceed from him, but as an ill affected subject turns things into evil to itself. And so the gospel becomes "the savour of death unto death," to an ill disposed mind; not from what it hath in itself, or as it proceeds from God, but only from the disaffected state and condition of the subject. And then again,

(8.) We are to consider this, that the interests of men in this world, in reference to their temporal concernments, do so generally interfere and cross with one another and oppose one another, that it is impossible all prayers should be granted. For there are many times prayers against prayers. One man or this sort of men prays for this event, and another sort, for the quite contrary event. Therefore, it is most absolutely necessary that the divine counsel should moderate, and have its agency, not only in bringing about events, but even in forming the spirits of men. When interests do so clash, and desires and prayers so contradict one another, (as they many times do,) with what confusion would it fill the world, if every irregular desire should be granted? And indeed, if the wills of men were to regulate the will of God, and their prayers were to prescribe, it would make fearful work in the world: if we had such a kind of *fatuum numen, a silly deity*, to be the object of our addresses and prayers, that were to use no counsel, no wisdom in judging what is fit to be done, and what is not, but every human desire should engage the divine power, and employ the divine hand, with what ruin and desolation would men's prayers fill the world! And so this world would be made a desolate wilderness, at that rate, if the prayers of men, without the interposition of the counsel of the divine will, were to prescribe finally what were to be done for them. And therefore, again,

(9.) It ought to be considered, that wherever there is any such thing as right prayer, there is a divine Agent to be employed, in reference to the whole business of prayer. As we have an Advocate and Intercessor without us at the right hand of God above, so, all that do belong to God have an Advocate and Intercessor within them. All the children of God, because they are such, because they are sons, God sends the Spirit of his Son into their hearts to teach them to cry, Abba Father; as Gal. 4. 6. compared with Rom. 8. 15. And it is therefore, called the Spirit of adoption, because it belongs to the adopted ones, to those that are taken into that state and condition of sons; because they are sons, the Spirit is given. It is an intolerable injury, and absurdity, that among us who are called christians, with whom it is an article of our creed, that we believe in the Holy Ghost, we should so little consider what hand and part, he is to have in this matter. It is an idle vanity to think, that he is to dictate words to us, and that there ought not to be prayer, but what the Spirit ought to indite the very words of. No, that is not the business of his office; but to possess the soul with such a living, internal sense to which words will correspond; that soul that is filled with such a sense, will not want suitable words, (at least between God and itself) in which to utter that sense to him. And so is the work of the Holy Ghost, in this matter, expressed in that Rom. 8. 27. That when we know not what to pray for of ourselves, that Spirit makes intercession in us according to the will of God; (so we read it and do interpose in the translation more than is in the text,) it makes intercession according to God, (so it is in the original,) not barely according to his will, but in subserviency to his interest; and to his great one, which (it is true) his will must always respect too, as we cannot doubt. And therefore, if he is to be applied unto, and relied upon, that great Agent of God: and we are to refer it to him (as it were) to mind our petitions, that they may be right in form, this is the great business of that Spirit; he is thus far (as it were) the Master of requests, and we are to resign ourselves to him, to put our spirits under his formation, under the dominion of the Divine Spirit. "I do not know whether my mind may agree with the divine mind yea or no, but O! do thou make it agree, and conform it thereunto." And lastly,

(10.) We have, upon the whole, this to consider, that all prayers once so rectified and put into the right form and tenour, they do ever obtain their principal answer. According to the great platform and model of prayer that is given us, we pray with principal reference to the divine honour, if we pray aright, that the name of God may be hallowed; we pray that the governing power of his kingdom may obtain and take place all the world over: we pray that his will may be done on earth, as it is done in heaven. We have particular inclinations and desires of our own; these we are never to express but with this reserve, "Lord, if these desires of mine, agree with thy will; if they agree not with that, I renounce them, I disclaim them." So every good man is then answered, if he be denied: if he be denied in one respect, he is answered and his petition granted in higher and more principal respects; for the principal thing he aims at is, that God may be glorified, "Hallowed be thy name;" and that in order and subserviency thereunto the governing power of his kingdom may take place, and that his will may be done. These are the great and principal petitions: and all things else are to be petitioned for but as they subserve these.

And therefore, now to sum up all. Prayer, it may be from two sorts of persons, either from a devoted or from an apostate creature. Prayer, proceeding from a devoted soul can never fail of its principal answer: for every such prayer is influenced by supreme love to God; his interests comprehend all our true interests: so that all doth but come to this, whether I love God more than myself, then that love will always dictate such prayers as can never miss of their answer. That is, if I pray as a devoted creature, and to be a devoted creature is to pray, is to love God more than myself. But, if I pray as an apostate creature, that is, as one that is gone off from God and keeps off from God and hath a separate interest from God, and will not come to him and return to him again; then my prayers always run after this tenour, "Lord I pray that my will may be done, that my interest may take place and be served, whatsoever becomes of all, or any concernments besides." But what! would we have the counsels of the divine will to give place to such insolent requests as these? that were, in effect, to pray, "Lord do thou descend and come down from thy throne and resign it to me, and let me set up for myself; I would be a god to myself, and I desire to make no other use of divine power, (finding my own impotency in many things,) but only to serve my own purposes and ends."

Therefore, there is all imaginable encouragement to sincere prayer, from this doctrine, that God doth all things according to the counsel of his own will. And this, surely, we are greatly concerned to consider in such a juncture of time as we are now cast upon: nothing can be more opportune. We have a dubious prospect before us; we know not how things may issue. Now to pray with hearts possessed with the sense that God doth all things after the counsel of his own will, is the best preparation for prayer, in reference to the present concernments of this season, that can be thought. That is, it is such a disposition of spirit that will, in this duty of prayer, be both most honourable to God, and most comfortable to ourselves.

Most honourable to God; nothing could reflect on him more than to pray with a contrary notion concerning him; that is, that he doth not do things after the counsel of his own will, but as poor foolish creatures here in this world, shall prescribe and dictate to him: they make him do any thing, draw him to this or that by the importunity of their requests and desires. You cannot give a notion of God more injurious to him, or more repugnant to his very nature. For then we must suppose him a Being of mere power, absolute, almighty power, which any fool may command when he pleaseth. What a strange sort of Deity do we worship! particularly if we pray with such a notion of God as this. But nothing can be more comfortable to ourselves, than to supplicate him, according to this true notion of him, that he doth all things after the counsel of his own will. With what quiet minds may we pray; and acquiesce in all the issues of things! Things lie in the best hands they can lie. We have this to satisfy our hearts in: and though we pray as men, we are to expect he should answer as God. We can pray but with the wisdom and foresight of poor fallible creatures: but then we are to expect him to answer according to the wisdom of an all-comprehending Deity. And as this is most highly honourable to him; so it will be most highly satisfying and comfortable to ourselves, and upon the best terms from which a reasonable mind can receive any satisfaction.

LECTURE VII.*

It only remains to make some *Use* of all that hath hitherto been spoken. And so comprehensive a truth, as this, you will apprehend to be of very large and copious usefulness. I shall contract as much as the matter admits. It serves,

1. To shew us, how we are to *form our notion of God*. And if any have a mistaken one, how they may rectify and reform it. It lets us see we are to conceive of God to be a Being of infinite wisdom, for according to our notion of counsel, it is the immediate product of wisdom. Only, when we apply it to God we must do it so as to sever all that it imports of imperfection, and to include all that it imports of highest perfection. We find it needful with us, to consult and advise with our friends sometimes; however, with ourselves, and our more deliberate thoughts; but no such thing can be said of God, with whom all things lie open, in one infinite, eternal and all-comprehending view at once. That is not the meaning of counsel with him, as it is with us, as though being uncertain and doubtful, we did need to be counselled and advised: but

* Preached May 27, 1692.

that of perfection, which we mean by counsel and most perfect judgment of things, that we are to ascribe to him: and so, as that is the result of wisdom, it is with him in the highest perfection without consideration, so, that we can have no notion of wisdom, that doth not imply counsel; nor of divine counsel, that doth not imply the most perfect, most exact, and most accurate wisdom. We see he doth all things according to the counsel of his will, so as never to err in any thing; never to make one wrong step. For how often is he celebrated by expressions, that do import so much, God who is wise. What glorious ascriptions are there to him as such. " To God only wise, be honour and glory." Rom. 16. 27. And so that of 1 Tim. 1. 17. You have the same kind of doxology even in the same terms. And so in the epistle of Jude, the concluding words of that epistle : " To God only wise, be honour, and glory, and dominion, for ever and ever." This appropriate term, *only*, only wise, speaks that there is no wisdom, that is not from him, nor in him, that he is primary wisdom, the original seat of wisdom. If any man lack wisdom, let him ask it of God, who giveth to all liberally. He can do so, he hath it in all its fulness, in its most absolute plenitude in himself. James 1. 5. And therefore, is he said to be the Father of lights, from whom cometh every good and perfect gift, every congenerous gift; we must understand it agreeable to so exuberant a Fountain: and hereby, we are to rectify our thoughts of God, if we have taken up wrong ones; for we must conceive of the several attributes of the Divine Being, agreeably to this, as they are complicated with this most perfect wisdom, as that is most especially conjunct therewith. If any should think of God's power, as only an act of boisterous omnipotency, working at random, not guided by wisdom and counsel: if they should conceive of his will, as if it were a stiff, inflexible resolvedness of doing things without judgment or wisdom, if they should conceive of his wrath, as an all-consuming flame, burning up all before it, without distinction, without discrimination: if any should think of his love as a fond inclination to this or that person, or thing, without being directed by wisdom or counsel: all this is infinitely to wrong God; it is indeed to create to ourselves a God like ourselves. But this is infinitely injurious to represent him by ourselves, as a being of mere power, and of mere will, without considering, that he is a Being of infinite wisdom, and so doth all things according to the counsel of his own will. And again,

2. We are further to learn, how we are to conceive of God's works; for every thing works as it is: and as he is a Being of

wisdom, we are to reckon, that there must be characters of wisdom and counsel upon all that he doth. There is eminently so, upon the works of his creation. He hath established the world by his wisdom, and stretched out the heavens by his discretion. Jer. 10. 12 Wisdom is the parent of order, wheresoever there is any thing of order, that surely must be attributed to wisdom as the directive cause of it; it must be found, if not in second causes, yet in the First. The stable ordinances of day and night, the certain returns of summer and winter, the regular motions of sun, moon, and stars, and the like: in all these we are to behold the wisdom of God, who hath settled things by so accurate counsel, according whereunto he doth all that he doth. And so we are to conceive concerning the works of his providence too, that there are counsel and wisdom, which conduct them all, which regulate human affairs wherein men have themselves but a subordinate agency, under the supreme and sovereign Ruler of all. We are to reckon nothing falls out casually, nothing undetermined, either to be wrought or effected by him, or at least to be permitted, for greater and more preponderating reasons, against the restraints that might have been laid upon the second causes, by which they are wrought. And again,

3. We are further to learn hence, the extensiveness and universality of God's powerful and governing influence. He worketh all things, he hath an agency about all that is done. It is true, the words are capable of being thus understood, He worketh whatsoever he worketh according to the counsel of his own will. But there cannot a hand be lift up, nor a foot stir, not a power or faculty of any creature be exerted, but he hath a working agency one way or other in reference thereto: not so much as a sparrow falls to the ground, but it is within the compass of that agency of his, which doth all things after the counsel of his own will. Not so much as a hair drops from any head without him: all things, as they refer to him, are done with number, weight and measure: and so, wisdom and counsel, have a universal exercise, in reference to all things that are done under the sun, even the meaner concernments of men in this world. If you go to the business of agriculture or husbandry in the general; the several methods of husbandmen in ploughing, sowing, threshing and the like, are all said to be from the Lord, who is wonderful in counsel, and excellent in working. Isaiah 28. 29. And therefore, we are hereupon to acknowledge, and own with adoration, the universal extensiveness of his governing influence; as was formerly noted in the opening of the words, in working all things; that is the ex-

pression, an energy that is most intrinsic, intimate, inward to every inferior agent, still exerting and putting forth itself, in whatsoever is wrought or done under the sun. And he is even more intimate to us, (as paganish light itself, doth more anciently observe) than we are to ourselves. That phrase is fetched from more refined paganism, into the schools of christians, that he is more inward to us, than we are to ourselves, so as that there is a divine energy working and stirring in every created agent whatsoever. And,

4. We may next learn hence, the reasonableness and congruity of all his public constitutions and laws, which he hath made for the government of his reasonable creatures. Legislation is a great act of sovereignty, indeed the prime and most principal. If God do all things according to the counsel of his own will, it is according to the counsel of his will that he hath made laws for those who are capable of government by law, as only the reasonable creature is. Laws are frequently spoken of under the name of counsels. Your human laws are commonly called *consulta*, as among the Romans, those that went under the name of *senatus consulta;* such things as were advised upon, and, as it were, weighed in balances. Are they fit, or are they not? Will this be a useful constitution, yea or no? And so is the frame of divine laws spoken of, under the name of the counsel of God. The pharisees and lawyers rejected the counsel of God against themselves. Luke 7. 30. It is spoken in opposition to Christ and his teachings. Those that were doctors of the law among the Jews, they rejected the counsel of God against themselves. Indeed, the whole revelation of God's mind, about the salvation of men, it bears that name, which included the perceptive as a very noble part of it. I have not shunned, saith the apostle, to declare unto you the whole counsel of God. Acts 20. 27. In all this, therefore, we ought to acknowledge and adore a divine wisdom, and especially in that, which is the standing constitution, for the governing of men, in reference to their salvation and final blessedness, since the apostasy, and you find God most highly celebrated and magnified, upon that account, in that Rom. 16. latter end: the apostle there speaking of the gospel constitution, under the name of a mystery, concludes all thus, " Now to him that is of power to establish you, according to my gospel, and the preaching of Jesus Christ," (ver. 25.) according to the revelation of the mystery, which was kept secret since the world began, but now is made manifest, and by the Scriptures of the prophets, according to the commandment of the everlasting God, made known to all nations, for the obedience of

faith, "To God only wise, be glory, through Jesus Christ, for ever." His wisdom is conspicuous in this established constitution of his, which is to last through all the ages of time, and which is the constitution of that kingdom, which is never to be shaken. That is called the kingdom not to be taken down: Heb. 12. latter end. The compages whereof are so firm and strong, as to suit a designed perpetuity. Whereupon, they that live under the gospel, are warned concerning their deportment under it. Now that we have received a "kingdom, that cannot be shaken, let us have grace to serve God acceptably, with reverence and godly fear." He will not now be dallied with by men, whom he hath put under the dispensations of the gospel; as that epistle to the Hebrews begins. There were some temporary constitutions wherein God did deal with men, and speak to them in various and variable methods. But now, he hath spoken to us by his Son: and this is such a state of things as shall last as long as the world lasts, and those that do not comport with this method, or law of grace, in order to being saved, shall never be saved! Therefore, let us seek grace to serve him acceptably. The last efforts of divine wisdom are seen in this constitution.

5. It thereupon, therefore, further lets us see, the impudence of sinners, who confront their own imaginations, and their own lusts, to the wisdom and counsel of the divine constitutions; for that is indeed the case, and the very state of the controversy between God and a guilty creature that hath been in an apostasy from him, and doth yet refuse to return. This is the very sum of the controversy between God and them, Who is wiser, who is best capable of prescribing and giving laws? for wisdom is the most conspicuous thing, (as was said) in legislation. Authority is supposed, it is true, but if there be never so unquestionable authority, if there be not wisdom to use it, it would be strange work that one destitute of wisdom would make of governing authority: strange laws, strange edicts there would be, where there was uncontroulable power without wisdom. But (as was told you) when laws are to be made, here is the great exercise of governing wisdom, such as doth befit the state of a ruler, to consider how the exigency of the case may be answered, what laws will be more suitable for such and such, or for a people in such circumstances. Now, when the counsels of heaven are opened, (as it were) into a result, in such a constitution; here is the law of that kingdom that is erected and set up for them that are to be saved. And here comes an insolent creature and contends against the Lawgiver, and disputes the matter with him that gave him breath; what impudency is here! That law of grace,

it saith, wheresoever it is promulgated, to them that come under this government of grace, or will be the disciples of grace, grace doth teach them that live under it, " to deny ungodliness and worldly lusts, and to live soberly, godly and righteously in the world." But here, is an impure, obstinate sinner, to whom notices are given of the good and acceptable will of God to this purpose, that the gospel that is preached to him, the law of the Redeemer's kingdom, it saith at the very first, Repent, now that kingdom is come among you, repent, turn. The divine wisdom saith to the sinner, " Turn, turn or die, turn or thou art lost." But he saith, It is wiser to go on, to persist in my own course; it is a wiser thing to live a stranger from God still, and as without God in the world. Divine wisdom saith to men, " God hath a mind and design to save you, deny you all ungodliness and worldly lusts, and subject yourselves to God," " No, it is wiser (saith the sinner,) to live an ungodly life still, it is a wiser thing to lay the reins on my own lusts, and do whatsoever is good in mine own eyes, it is wiser to please my own flesh than the God that made me; it is wiser to indulge sensual inclination and follow the imagination of my own heart." For men, I say, to confront their own imaginations and lusts to the divine counsel, it speaks the height of impudency in sinners, that they do not turn, that they will not be brought back to God. And,

6. It further lets us see how sad and forlorn the case of unreconciled and impenitent sinners is. God hath done all things according to the counsel of his own will, therefore, the constitution that he hath made and settled, is uncapable of change. There is an immutability stamped upon the divine counsel, and what is likely, then, to become of such men as run counter to all the wisdom and counsel, that is conspicuous in the divine constitutions? Because of their perfection they cannot be changed, and because of the sinner's wickedness, he will not. God cannot change, and men will not. What is then like to become of things between him and them? But,

7. We may further learn hence, how hopeful and comfortable their state is, whose minds and hearts are brought to a liking of the methods of God, for the saving of sinners, to a compliance and agreement with them. O! happy man! The unerring, and therefore unalterable counsels of heaven, have determined well concerning thee, and concerning thy state. You see in this same chapter where the text lies, that the gospel constitution carries, (as it were) this inscription upon it, " To the praise of the glory of his grace." Look upon the whole frame of divine constitutions, that refer to the saving of sin-

ners, and you may see (as it were) in golden letters written upon this noble fabric, "To the praise of the glory of his grace." Thus the gospel constitutions stand, (as it were) dedicated, "To the praise and glory of divine grace, wherein he hath made us accepted in the beloved." And observe then, what follows in the next verse, "In whom we have redemption, through his blood, even the forgiveness of sins, according to the riches of his grace, wherein he hath abounded towards us in all wisdom and prudence." This is the mystery of God; he hath made known to us the mystery of his will; it is a most mysterious thing that ever he should have such a will towards me. But he doth all things according to the counsel of his own will; and thereupon, there is an immutability and unchangeableness upon the determination of it, as you see in that Heb. 6. 17. Wherein, God willing more abundantly to shew unto the heirs of promise, the immutability of his counsel; He hath confirmed it by his oath, added to his word, that by two immutable things in which it was impossible for God to lie, the heirs of promise might receive that strong, that steady, that unshaken consolation. It is to be attributed to want and deficiency of wisdom and foresight, that the constitutions and determinations of men, need so often to be altered. Such and such an inconvenience was not foreseen; such a law was made, and it may be, a little trial and experience, shew it to be very inconvenient, and so, it is fain to be reversed, repealed, or needs some explanatory additions, or the like; it is reckoned a piece of meanness, and disparagement, to be put to alter edicts; and because the Medes and Persians were a proud and haughty nation, therefore, were their laws and statutes irreversible, never to be changed; so that they did assume to themselves infallibility, and beyond what could agree to the condition and capacity of creatures, of men, in an imperfect state. But the divine counsel being all upon foresight, all the determinations thereof, being made and settled upon one comprehensive view, here is no place for the supposition of a change. And therefore, is this most highly consolatory to all that feel their hearts comply with the gospel terms, with the evangelical constitutions: "I find my heart is wrought to a closure with that, and I am never to fear a change." It is the effect of his counsel, his immutable counsel which he hath shewn, that such as we might have strong consolation who fall in with, and comply with his terms.

8. It further serves to let us see the vanity of their confidence, who have any separate interest, and drive any opposite design from, and to, this of the great God himself. His coun-

sels must stand, and the thoughts of his heart to all generations; whereas, the counsels of the froward are turned headlong: as the expression is, Job. 5. 13. How unequal is the contest, when there comes to be a competition between the design of a mortal man, though never so insolent, and that of the immortal God? Some of themselves have thought it insolent for creatures so to assume. Rabshakeh thought it were an imaginary thing, and very wrongly charged upon Hezekiah, yet seems to look upon it as a great piece of pride, "Thou sayest, I have counsel and strength for war," thinking it to be an unbecoming thing: yet, though he only speaks of the counsel and might of Hezekiah as opposed to his own, or that of his master Sennacherib; but he never thought how insolent it was to oppose that, his counsel to that of heaven. "I have counsel and strength for war," but how soon are all those counsels and strength blown upon, blasted and brought to nothing when God hath any work of his to do, whereunto, that counsel and might are opposed. And to conclude, I add,

9. That since God doth all things according to the counsel of his own will, the times and seasons for doing any great work that he intends, are always chosen by him, with most accurate wisdom. They are most fitly chosen; therefore, whereas, we are apt to blame the divine methods because he doth not take our time and our way, how unreasonable is it, since it is plain, that all the things he hath to do are affixed to particular seasons, which lie under divine determinations? "Unto every thing there is a season and a time, to every purpose under the sun. Eccles. 3. 1. And if you will look a little further in that book, you will see there, that as there is a time for every purpose, every event, so there is also judgment for every time, there is judgment, which is the effect of counsel, or that whereunto counsel results. For every thing there is a time and judgment. And so thereupon, there comes to be a critical nick of time into which such and such things must fall, and into no other. And therefore, it is said, that "the misery of man is great upon the earth." Eccles. 8. 6. Because there is time and judgment to every purpose, therefore, that is, because time and judgment are not considered, are not understood by men, therefore, their misery is great. And so they are taken, many times, in an evil time, without foresight; they do not know the time; not because they are ignorant of the time, but because they are unready, unprepared, for what is to be done and suffered in such or such a juncture of time. And so you see their case is represented still, upon that account, miserable. But the wise, they do consider time and judgment:

Happy men! therefore, happy men! as those two verses fall in together: Eccles. 8. 5, 6. This ought to be considered, and it makes a man a happy man that considers it. Therefore, how quiet and calm may all men's minds be; and the minds of the wise will be that do equally consider things. We find things were determined most punctually, relating to the great concernments of that people, God had in the world heretofore, when they were yet an unconformed people. Four hundred and thirty years must pass, just so many from the time of his capitulating with their head, Abraham, striking a covenant with him. And so much time there must be, because the sins of the Amorites were not yet full, and Canaan could not be ready for the reception of them, and there did four hundred and thirty years pass upon this account. When they were in captivity in Babylon, seventy years was determined for that. When the woman is in the wilderness, there is a set time; forty and two months, or twelve hundred and sixty days. And we are not to think that the determinations of divine wisdom and counsel are less certain because they are less known to us, and we only see by the event what was determined. Twenty years have elapsed since the haughty French tyrant hath been the terror and scourge of Europe, and especially of reformed Christendom; for it is so long, (in the year 1672) that he first attempted on our neighbours and brethren of Holland. Many might have been apt to think, why hath not God animadverted on him sooner, put upon him an earlier rebuke? Why was it not the last year? Why was not his fleet scattered, and his army broken then, as they have been, in several parts, this year? Or why was it not the year before that? Why, it is a foolish thing for us to contend and dispute with the counsel of heaven, and we are to refer it to the determination of divine counsel, to choose the fittest time to begin to animadvert on so insolent an enemy, and the aptest means how first to let him know that he is a mortal, and that they in whom he trusts, have a mortality upon them; that they are liable to defeatments, to disappointments; that their strength is not brass or iron, or such as cannot be broken when he will. He can make so weak and mutable a thing as the wind to serve his purpose against so haughty a one. We are to consider that these things fall out according to the counsel of the divine will: he is not to give us a reason why no such thing was, so many years ago, why he did not raise up such and such, who might have abated his pride, and brought a blast upon him long before now.

Hitherto, we have by way of use, from the doctrine of this text, let you see so many *inferences*, and recommended so many *truths* from it, which, according to the aptitude that it hath in it, may help to rectify and regulate our thoughts, apprehensions, and notions in many things.

LECTURE VIII*.

The further use which remains, is to direct *our practice;* for in many respects, it hath in it a great aptitude, and suitableness too. In order to this, it is requisite,

1. That we take up the several sorts of the considerations which may be had of the counsels of the divine will. And then,

2. That we reflect upon our own distemper, and the faultiness of our spirits and practice, in reference hereunto. And accommodately, then, to consider both of the counsels of the divine will, and of our own miscarriages, and so recommend to you sundry heads of instruction, in reference to our future practice. We are,

1. Variously to consider the counsels of the divine will. They may be either considered indefinitely; or else, they may be considered with some distinction, according to the various references they may bear towards us, and our concernments and affairs, whether they may be eternal or temporal; and these, whether they be private or public.

And again, whether they be known to us, or unknown; so variously may the counsels of the divine will be considered. And then, for his precepts, which are the result too, of the counsel of his will. They expressly declare what it is the counsel of his will we should do, though therein also, we are to expect his co-operation; he working and in-working also therein, according to the counsel of his will. And many times, the counsels of his will are known to us only by the event. We never know what God would do in this or that instance, till the event shews us. And so in such and such things, because the event hath not shewn the counsels of the divine will in many things, they are yet altogether unknown to us.

2. Now, according to these various considerations of the counsels of the divine will, we shall find ourselves, many ways, to be faulty in reference thereunto.

As in reference to the counsels of God indefinitely considered, that either we ourselves do not firmly enough believe the great doctrine of this text, that he really doth all things

* Preached June 3, 1692.

according to the counsel of his own will; or that we deeply enough consider it not, and carry not an habitual sense in our souls correspondent thereunto: that we have not high and great thoughts as we ought hereupon: that we are so prone to dispute matters with him: that there is no more of dutiful compliance with the counsels of his will, even then, when they are known: that many are so apt to cherish in themselves a perpetual dread about their eternal concernments, which lie most certainly under the disposition of his own eternal will: that they are so distrustful of so wise and mighty an Agent, that doth all things according to the counsel of his own will: that there is no more of quietude, tranquillity and rest of spirit in him, so considered, as one that doth what he pleaseth, and always according to wise counsel.

Now, according to these various considerations, which we ought to have, both of God and ourselves, of his counsels, and of our own miscarriages and distempers, are these *instructions* to be, which I am now to recommend to you. And,

(1.) I pray, Let us charge this upon ourselves, more thoroughly to establish the belief of this truth in our own souls, that God, in very deed, doth work all things after the counsel of his own will. Let not our minds waver and hover, in reference hereunto, as if this were a doubtful matter, as if possibly, it might be otherwise, as if either he were ignorant or oscitant, and unconcerned about the affairs of his creature, as if any thing might possibly fall out without his advertency. For we should consider with ourselves, being once at a certainty about the existence of God, about which if we be not at a certainty, we can be certain of nothing; if (I say) we be at a certainty concerning this, and we may be as sure of it as that we are, and that this world is, and that there is any such thing as wisdom and power and goodness, any where to be observed and taken notice of in the world; we and this world, and whatsoever there is of excellency and perfection in it, must all have some original; they are not nothing, and therefore could not come out of nothing. If we be (I say again) at a certainty about this, that is, in short, that there is a God, we may be at equal certainty about this, that he worketh all things after the counsel of his own will. For I beseech you, reflect and consider how well would it agree with your own minds, and with the natural notions and conceptions that are placed and fixed there, to conceive of an ignorant God, or of an impotent God, or of an oscitant, neglectful God. Do but consider, how well any such conception or apprehension can agree with the natural notices you have in your minds already, and may take notice of, if you reflect. And thereupon, let disputes be at an end with you, and fix and establish the belief of it in your own souls, that in very deed he worketh all things according to the counsel of his own will. And,

(2.) That hereupon (this being once thoroughly believed) it may be more deeply considered: and that we would labour to carry an habitual sense of it about us, from day to day, through this world. For to any one that considers, these things are very distinguishable; dead notions, and living sense, even in reference to the same truth. I have such a truth in my mind, but how have I it? If I have it as a dead notion, then it is all one to me as if I had it not. Let it not, therefore, satisfy us to have so mighty, important a truth as this lie in our minds as a dead notion; but let us labour to have it there as living sense, that we may resort to upon all occasions, and draw forth into present use as the matter shall, from time to time, require. And,

(3.) Labour to live adoring lives towards the glorious God, so considered, as one that worketh all things after the counsel of his own will. How should we, hereupon, be composed of adoration towards the blessed God, so as that wherever any actual present instance occurs and appears to us, wherein that agency of his shews itself, we be always in a disposition to bow our heads and worship! Here is a manifest effort of Deity, as the power and wisdom of God, that doth all things after the counsel of his own will. We should especially labour to maintain an adoring frame and disposition of spirit, with reference to these two great excellencies of the Divine Being which appear and shine forth in view, in this truth held forth to us in this text: "who worketh all things after the counsel of his own will:" that is, almighty power and infinite wisdom. Two things, than which nothing can be supposed to make an object more adorable, to make any thing a fitter object of adoration. Almightiness—he worketh all things. Is not he almighty that can do all things? and infinite wisdom—for he doth all things after the counsel of his own will. So, that wheresoever there is an exertion of his power, there is an exertion of his wisdom too, guiding that efficacious exertion of his will, that he doth not act in any thing by a boisterous and extravagant exertion of power, without judgment or without wisdom or without counsel, that all things that are done, are done by him: one way or other he hath an agency in every thing; and that nothing is done by him but by the direction of that wisdom that can mistake in nothing: all things consulted, and done after the counsels of his own will. A man of great might and of great celebrated wisdom too, how venerable a person is he in the account of all? But to have these two things in conjunction, to wit, almighty power, with infinite, unlimited wisdom, sets a very adorable Object before our eyes. And it is a reproach to us, if we, thereupon, do not carry an adoring frame of spirit, every day, about this world with us.

(4.) Another instruction, hereupon, will be, that we never contend against him. What! Against him that worketh all things after the counsel of his own will? Is he a fit Object for our contention? Will we undertake to dispute matters with him? Think with yourselves, both how foolish and how wicked that must be. He that can do all things, whatsoever he will, it must be a very foolish thing to contend with him. What shall we get by it? He that contends with God, can he hope to be a gainer? He that strives with his Maker, woe to him: all that we can gain by it is but to infer a woe upon ourselves. Isaiah 45. 9. Therefore, it is a very foolish thing to enter into a contest which we are to despair beforehand of ever getting any thing by. And then, How wicked a thing is it! For certainly, the sovereignty must belong to him who worketh all things, and that after the counsel of his own will. It must, upon all accounts, belong to him. He will certainly carry the matter, and have the sovereignty. He worketh all things: almighty and resistless power is lodged in him; and he ought to have the sovereignty. For to whom should it so fitly appertain, as to him that doth all things according to counsel, never any thing rashly, nothing unfit in itself, nothing unseasonable, whensoever it is done? Therefore, (as the expression is there) he that contends with God, let him answer it; let him try if he can; for to be sure he never can, he never will be able to answer it, to enter into a contest with God, who is One that so wisely, and according to so stable, and so steady counsel and judgment doth all things. Again,

(5.) Labour dutifully to comport with him as he is such a One that "worketh all things after the counsel of his own will," and according to such considerations, (as hath been hinted to you,) as we may severally have of these counsels of the will of God. There are counsels of his will that are made known and signified by his express precepts. As was told you, the last time, legislation, making of laws, is one of the prime acts of wisdom, wherein above all things that excellency is to be conspicuous and shew forth itself. Now we shall dutifully comport with the counsels of his will, made known by his precepts and laws, when we do obey them. That when once we find that charge laid upon us to do so and so, by express divine precept, we immediately labour to get our spirits formed to an obedient compliance, saying within ourselves, "I have nothing to do, in reference to such and such a thing, but to obey." "Mortify such a lust," saith the command, "Lord I yield and will endeavour to obey." "Love me with all the heart and soul and mind and strength:" "Lord, I will to my uttermost." It is a law founded in counsel; there could never have been a wiser law, nor a more merciful one, from a good God, towards an indigent, depending creature, than that I should place my love, my desire, my delight on himself. If, considering me as a wandering creature, I find his word saith to me, "Repent;" a wise counsel is spoken to me according to the counsel of his will. I will persist in sin no longer; I will turn that I may live. If he have made known his counsels concerning such and such things that he will do, that he will put an end to this world, that the wickedness of the wicked shall come to an end; that his Son shall appear in the end of time, and shall be the final Judge; it is then dutiful to comply with such counsels of the divine will, to be always in an expecting posture: to say, "O let the wickedness of the wicked come to an end, according as thou hast determined; we approve of the counsel of the divine will, and will patiently wait till it come. And as for that appearance and coming of our Lord, we will wait and long for it; looking for it as the reviving, heart gladdening hope of our souls." Whereinsoever the divine will is made known to us, or which way soever the counsels of it are known, let them be dutifully comported with. Such things as are only known to us by the event, let us dutifully own and acknowledge them. I know it was the divine will, according to counsel, that such and such things should be either effected by himself, or permitted to be effected by those in whom he saw such a disposition, or from whom he did not withhold power to effect it. Again,

(6.) Take heed of slavish dread, in reference to your own eternal concernments. Most certain it is, that there are counsels of the divine will conversant about the eternal concernments of every one of us; but take we heed of slavish dread in reference hereto. There is no cause for it. It is an ungospel-like spirit to live in a slavish dread, even about our eternal concernments, under a gospel of grace which deals with us principally about them, and whose special, particular, and great design is to advise and direct us, even touching them.

But it may be here said, How is it possible for one in an uncertainty, not to be in a dread about his everlasting concernments, about those concernments of his, which however they lie, will never alter, will always be the same? One that finds himself to have been, hitherto, under the power of some reigning lust or other, have not I reason to be in a continual dread, what shall become of me for ever?

That was a thing we find represented as not suitable to the state of a very Cain. Suppose thy state to be as bad, suppose thyself a very Cain for wickedness, you see how God bespeaks him, when there was some present token that he was not so acceptable as Abel was. Cain might perceive it, hereupon his countenance falls, and God reasons the matter with him, "Why is thy countenance fallen? If thou dost well, shalt thou not be accepted? If thou persist still to do evil, it is true, sin, that is, vengeance, the consequent of sin, lies at the door. But if thou dost well, shalt not thou be accepted?" So he bespeaks even a Cain; so you must understand him to bespeak you. In the worst that you can suppose of your case, this is the counsel of the divine will, even concerning thee. Hereupon, then, God ought to be the Object of thy reverence; not the Object of thy dread. Thou oughtest to reverence him, not to dread him, as one that doth all things after the counsel of his own will. But you will say again, "Where lies the difference?"

The difference is great, and most manifest, between reverence and dread. Reverence carries love in it: dread carries hatred. And am I now to dispute the matter with you, whether any man ought to hate God? Ought you to hate him, think you? Ought he to be the Object of your hate? No, place all your reverence upon him, which certainly carries love in it. For reverence hath goodness for its object; the most excellent good is the object of my reverence. By how much the more there is of goodness in any one, by so much the more is he the object of my reverence. But it is evil, destructive, pernicious evil, that is the object of my hate, and consequently of my dread. But you are no more to think that God can be the Object of a man's dread, than you can think that a fit notion, or a self-consistent notion, an evil God. Can there be any such thing as an evil God? There can be no such thing as the affection of dread (involving essentially hatred in it) duly placed upon God, unless you would suppose an evil God, which is a contradiction even in the very notion. Therefore, turn all your hate (let the case be the worst that can be supposed) upon yourself, and all your love upon God. Think of him with reverence that carries love in it. And think of yourselves with that dread (as you are yet wicked creatures) which carries hate in it. And this is a true gospel frame, to hate one's self, loathe one's self, fall out with one's self, judge one's self, condemn one's self; but all the while to reverence God: let him be ever amiable in your eyes.

Aye, but you will say, "How can this be but matter of dread to me, when I find myself a wicked creature, and whom, therefore, the wrath of God must pursue? for his wrath is revealed from heaven against the ungodliness and unrighteousness of men: and I find myself such a one, a wicked creature, an ungodly, an unrighteous creature."

Do but consider here, the objection carries its own answer in it. "The wrath of God is revealed from heaven." Against what? Against ungodliness, against unrighteousness: and you are such a one. But what, is it necessary always to continue such? The wrath of God can never be directed against any creature but as he is wicked. But then his word saith, "Let the wicked forsake his way, and the unrighteous man his thoughts: and let him return unto the Lord, and he will have mercy upon him, and to our God, for he will abundantly pardon." Isaiah 55. 7.

But you may perhaps say, "I am a wicked creature, and this is the thing I dread, that I shall be always so, I cannot alter the state of my own case, I cannot mend myself; this is that therefore, which makes me stand in dread."

Why, to that I shall shortly say, either you desire to be other than you are, or you do not; either you desire, of a wicked creature, to be made holy, godly and righteous, or you do not desire this. If you do desire it, and you say, this is the object of your dread, that you shall never be other than a wicked creature, because you cannot mend yourself; why dread, (as I told you,) carries hatred in the nature of it, and hatred of wickedness. If you dread this continuance in wickedness, you hate it. But I would fain know, if it be possible to desire and hate the same thing. Do you desire and choose to be always wicked, and yet hate and dread to be so? These are inconsistent: what you say now, overthrows itself. It is impossible for you to desire to be always what you are, if you really dread, that is, hate that state of wickedness wherein you are. If that be the matter of your dread, (as it ought to be) then you do hate to be what you are, and you desire to be what you are not. Then pursue this apprehension further, a little, "I am a wicked creature, and I desire to be otherwise than I am, I dread myself, I hate myself as I am such: then I do desire to be such as God would have me to be, that is, a holy creature, and one conformed to his holy nature and will;" and if this be the posture of your soul in reference to yourself, and your own state Godward, you very well know what he hath declared of his readiness to accept such. When we confess our sins, with self-loathing, self-indignation, self-judging, "He is faithful and just to forgive us our sins : and the blood of Jesus Christ his Son cleanseth us from all sin." And when we judge ourselves, we shall not be judged. He never condemns that man that condemns himself, not notionally, but inwardly, with a concomitant hatred and loathing, which is somewhat else than the notion of the state and frame wherein you find yourself. But now, if you suppose that God will have no mercy upon such a one, that is to make a supposition to yourself of somewhat in the notion of God that is repugnant to the known notions of him : that is, as he is the God of all grace; as he is love itself, and as he hath told us this to be his name, "The Lord, the Lord God, gracious and merciful, forgiving iniquity, transgression and sin." But if you have such notions of him, that he will abandon and throw away a self-loathing and self-judging creature, and one that desires nothing in all this world so much as to please him, this is to create to yourself a formidable idol, instead of the true and living God : there is no such God as you imagine to yourselves. As an idol is nothing in the world, so is this nothing but your own idol, which is a nullity. There is no such God; but you create to yourselves such a formidable idol, and then hate him. You call that God, which is but of your own making, your own creature. But take God as he is in himself, and as he hath revealed and reported himself to be, the God of all grace, whose name this is, (and his name doth express his nature,) the name that he hath made himself known by, " The Lord, the Lord God, gracious :" take this true notion of God, and set it before your eyes, and consider, " though I be an object of hate, sure I have now before mine eyes an Object of the highest love." Is not this an Object of love, a fit Object, the most deserving Object, the most amiable Object that can be thought? Conceive of him so; and let that be your apprehensions of him, till you find his love gradually work itself into your souls, and transforming and changing you. And if you come once to this perceiving and believing this love, you have a love begotten and wrought in you, then God and you are happily met. Love and love, cannot but unite and dwell together, and will everlastingly cohabit and dwell together. But if you say, you are a wicked creature, and you desire to be always what you are; if wickedness and you are inseparable, as they can only be by the union of your will with wickedness, then are misery and you united too, and can only be so by your adherence in heart and will to wickedness; and so you will be your own hell, and an everlasting fountain of misery to yourself; but God and his throne will be guiltless for ever, for he never hates a creature as a creature; his wrath can never reach you, but as you are one that continues in a will to be wicked.

But if you can truly say, "I would be otherwise, only I fear, God will not help me." Why! hath he not said, he will give his Spirit to them that ask him? You are to take heed of forming a notion of God against his word; for he can have no will against his word: it is impossible he should. There can be no counsel of the divine will that contradicts his plain word. Therefore, take heed of imagining any such thing to yourselves.

And so, upon the whole matter, there is place for that counsel, as what we are to resolve to live and die by, that is, never to entertain a slavish dread concerning our own eternal concernments. But consider how the distinguishing characters are given in Scripture, between them that are saved, and them that finally perish. And if you find the present characters upon you that mark you out for hell and damnation, only say, " I am such and such now, but it is not necessary that I should always be what I am." Sin is not you, and you are not sin; they are separable, these are partable things: and only implore that grace and help of the Divine Spirit that is offered, suitable to the estate of lost and apostate creatures. And never entertain any despairing thought but that that Spirit shall be given when it is seriously asked and sought after, and desired by you: the state of no man's case can exclude such considerations as these, for while there is any thing of sense about a man's eternal concernments, though it be from common grace, it is from the Spirit of grace, for all grace is from that Spirit, and that common grace may be gradually leading on to special grace, if it be duly complied with.

So that there is still no cause for a slavish dread: that soul is not quite abandoned and given up by God, in which remains any concern about its future state, and about its case Godward. You are not, indeed, to ascribe it to your own nature, if you are so solicitous about the divine favour, if you are not so swallowed up in this world, and immersed in sensuality, as to have all thoughts excluded about your soul-affairs, and your everlasting concernments. You are not to arrogate this to yourself; for we are not sufficient of ourselves to think a good thought: and there is a good tendency in those thoughts; and therefore, all this ought to be ascribed to the Divine Spirit that is now, some way or other, at work with you; and those workings of his, have a leadingness and tendency in them to move to further and higher workings, which accordingly you are to expect with hope, and so to lay aside a slavish dread accompanied with despair, with utter despair that ever things shall be better with you.

(7.) And then, as to all your other concernments, intrust them freely and cheerfully to this God. He that worketh all things after the counsel of his own will; how complete an Object of trust is he! Whose heart would misgive him, who trusteth him that worketh all things after the counsel of his own will? Can the counsel of his own will, can the counsel of that will which is guided by unerring wisdom, ever hurt any body? Will any body be the worse for lying under the determination of that will, which is guided by unerring counsel? Never fear to trust him, in all things, who bears this character; a cheerful trust, a delightful trust, is most suitable to this representation of God. Never fret, never tumultuate, never admit of any distrustful thought; but at the same time, (as the direction is, Psalm 37, beginning.) "Trust in the Lord and do good," and place your delight in the Lord, and not fret at any thing we see fall out in the world, never fret but trust, never fret but do good, never fret, but delight thyself in the Lord. And therefore,

(8.) Lastly; The direction that is most suitable to this apprehension of God, is to preserve a continual quietude and tranquillity in our own spirits. The proper effect of such trust is quietness: "His heart is fixed, trusting in the Lord." And, "Thou wilt keep him in perfect peace, whose mind is staid on thee: because he trusteth in thee." Isaiah 26. 3. There is no room, nor place for rational disquiet hereupon, in reference to any thing he hath done, or in reference to any thing we may apprehend he will do. Let there be such a constant calmness and tranquillity of spirit maintained, in opposition to vexation, about past events; and to solicitude about future events: for these two things, we are apt to disquiet ourselves: about past events, with vexation; and future events, with solicitude: and so we live uncomfortable lives. But there will be no place left, either for the one or the other, if we will but carry this apprehension about us, that God worketh all things after the counsel of his own will. What cause then, can there be for solicitude? God will not change his nature, he will be still the same. He will as much govern the world by counsel in all future times, and all the particular concernments of his creatures, and especially our own concernments, in respect of which we are apt to be solicitous. He will do as much as ever he did. For this is his essential character, and therefore, can never cease to be so, that he doth all things after the counsels of his own will.

But you may say, "He may permit wicked men to do so and so, injuriously."

If he do so, he wisely permits it, and according to the counsel of his own will. And who would be afraid of the counsel of such a will? If he permit ill things to be done and fall out in the world, it is either for the exercise of their graces who belong to him in the world, and who are the called according to his purpose; it is that their faith, and their love to him, and their patience, and their subjection, and their heavenly mindedness, and the raisedness of their spirits above the world, may be more tried, and may further appear: or, it may be, for the correction and chastisement of his own offending people. And then, there is no place for fretting and inquietude of spirit, but calmly to accept the punishment of sin, lying down under it with a calm and submissive patience. Or, it may be in reference to the future, more illustrious display of his own glory, that he lets wicked men prosper and triumph for a time, and flourish like the green grass, when it is that they may be destroyed for ever. And never doubt but that he doth all things after the counsel of his own will, he will make all things finally to result into such an end as shall be suitable to so glorious an Agent, worthy of himself, so that angels and saints shall confess to all eternity, that all his ways and works were marvellous, just, righteous and great; and worthy of himself, taken altogether. It cannot but be so, that the issue of things must be such as is most agreeable to him "who worketh all things after the counsel of his own will."

LECTURE IX.*

Heb. 11, 3.

Through faith we understand that the worlds were framed by the word of God, so that things which are seen, were not made of things which do appear.

IN that order of discourse, (wherein we have made some progress,) of treating of the several more principal heads of that religion which we all profess, we have spoken at large (as the last subject we insisted upon in this course) of the counsels of the divine will, or (which is all one) his purposes and decrees, according to which he is said to work all things, in that, Ephes. 1. 11.

And now, the next thing that comes in order to be spoken of, is that great WORK OF CREATION, which is part, and the first part, the beginning of the execution of his external counsels or purposes of his will. This is the first of his external acts that terminate upon somewhat without himself. His decrees, though they have their term within him, and so come into the account, not of his transient, but of his eminent acts, and yet do differ, too, from all these internal acts of the divine Hypostasis towards one another; for they have their very objects in the Divine Being. But the decrees of God, though they have their term within the Divine Being, that is, they do, while they are but decrees, effect nothing *extra Deum, without God*, yet they have their object without him; that is, they refer, some way or other, to the creature. Now, in contradistinction to those internal acts of God that have reference to the creature, we consider his exter-

* Preached Jan. 17, 1698.

nal acts, whereof this of creation is the first, and is leading and fundamental to all other subsequent and external acts of his, towards, or upon, the creature, as now existing, till some act or other hath preceded, by which it might exist.

This is, therefore, such an act as makes its object, and doth not suppose it; as all following acts of God towards the creature do suppose the object, and not make it; suppose it preexistent, and then are concerned and conversant about it, as already existent; to wit, to sustain it, to regulate it, improve it, perfect it; or any ways alter it as he sees good.

And whereas, this is the first step that God takes in executing the counsels of his will; that is, that being ascribed to him, to do all things according to the counsel of his will, he doth this great work of creation, according to that counsel of his will. This will put an end to the great dispute about the original of all things; whether this world, and all that it contains came, of itself, or by fate, or by chance; or whether it were all entirely owing to some wise and designing intelligent Agent. If, I say, the authority of divine Revelation may decide the matter, and so far obtain in the minds of men, there is an end of that dispute; that is, that since whatsoever is done by that great and almighty Agent, was done according to the counsels of his own will; then this world came not into being of itself, or by any fatality or casualty; but by wise counsel designing the thing, and the time, and whatsoever circumstances might refer thereunto.

And, indeed, those that have not a divine Revelation to guide their apprehension in this matter, and have but allowed themselves (as many have) a liberty of thought, have discerned those characters of divine wisdom and design, in the whole frame and contrivance of things in this great creation, as not only to acknowledge, but to adore the wise Creator that hath given being to all. Every thing of order, being the product of wisdom; wisdom and order have most certain relation to one another, as the productive principle, and the object produced. If there be such a thing as order produced, wisdom and counsel must have been the productive principle.

We, formerly, in the beginning of this series of discourse, had occasion to speak of the creation, from Romans 1. 20. The invisible things of God, even his eternal power and Godhead, are clearly seen in the things that he hath made. It was upon another account that we discoursed of the creation then; not making that the terminative subject of our discourse; but considered it only as evidential of the Deity; we are now to consider it as effected by that almighty, divine power: we now consider it as a matter of faith. "By faith we understand that the worlds were framed by the word of God." And it was of absolute necessity that there should be that rational consideration of the creation, first, in order to the evincing of an object of faith, before we came to speak any thing of faith, or what was to be matter of faith; for no one can believe any thing, by the proper assent of faith, till he understands who he is to believe, and why. And it is the formal object of faith that we were to evince to you, in order to our shewing the ground why we were to believe any material object that comes within the compass of divine Revelation.

Therefore, having first evinced to you the existence and being of God; and then, evidenced to you, that that Revelation which we have in the Book of Scripture is from God; and thence having more distinctly considered the nature and perfections of God, as they are held forth in that Revelation, together with the distinct Hypostasis which that Revelation assures us are in the Deity; we now come to consider the creation too, as a matter of faith also.

And it ought not to seem strange to us, that when we have heard the creation spoken of, as tending to evince to us the being of God, we should come now to discourse of it as a matter of faith; for most plain it is, that the same conclusion may be assented to on different grounds, and the one doth strengthen the other, and not detract from it. It is no prejudice at all to our receiving the doctrine of the creation, as a matter of faith, that it is also demonstrable in a rational way, any more than it doth detract from, or lessen the credit of, a human testimony that many do concur and say the same thing; which detracts nothing from the validity of that person's testimony, but instead of that, adds thereto.

And we are to reckon it a great discovery of the divine favour and indulgence to us, when one and the same thing may be the matter, both of a fiducial assent upon a divine testimony, and of rational demonstration also. God condescends to us, and is so much the more favourable, that he is pleased to make the same thing evident more ways than one, according as the occurrence of several *media* for the evidencing of any thing, doth beget a stronger and firmer impression of the thing itself, upon our minds. This is referred unto, allusively, to set forth the great assurance wherewith the gospel Revelation was given, 1 John 1. 1, 3. "That which we have heard, which we have seen with our eyes, which we have looked upon, and our hands have handled of the word of life—that which we have seen and heard declare we unto you."

It is very true, indeed, that the creation, generally considered, and more abstractly, is very demonstrable by reason; not only to be rendered probable, or a likely thing, but certain and more demonstrable. That is, as I said, when we have in view so many sorts of things that we are sure were not always; and therefore, could not be of themselves; (for whatsoever is of itself must be always, must be from eternity;) then we are sure every such thing must have had some maker or other. And so, nothing can be more demonstrable, than that there hath been, and must be, a creation, even unto reason, and by reason.

But though reason may clearly apprehend and evince, in general, that there hath been a creation, it can never evince the way and manner, the method and order, wherein things have been created. All this must be owing to divine Revelation, and to faith thereupon, if we understand, (as here it is said,) "through faith, the worlds were framed, by the word of God." By reason, we may know that the world or worlds were some time or other made: but we can only know by faith that they were made in six days, and that such and such was the order of making them, as the divine history doth report the matter to us. And therefore, doth this text inform us, not only of this as an apprehensible thing, that the worlds were made, but it lets us see how we are to apprehend it. We are not only to understand this, but we are to understand it by faith, that the worlds were framed by the word of God.

We have, in the text, two distinct propositions, which are of two divers kinds; the first is dogmatical, or more expressly assertory, and the second is explicatory of the former.

The former, I say, is mere dogmatical. "By faith we understand that the worlds were framed by the word of God." It is a thing to be understood by faith, that the worlds were framed by the word of God. And this, I shall make the main subject of my discourse which I intend upon this scripture.

The latter is explicatory of the former, so that things which are seen, were not made of things that do appear, or were made, (which is the truer reading of the text,) of things which do not appear, or were made of not appearing things, not pre-existing things, that had stood forth into being before.

First. And for the first of these: you see it contains two parts—what it is we are to understand; and—how we are to understand it.—The thing to be understood, that the worlds were framed by the word of God, and—how we are to understand it, by faith: or through faith. It is faith that lets in the notion the more distinctly into our minds. We have this notion by faith, as the word in the greek signifies, the forming of a notion, begetting it in our minds. We have the notion begot in our minds by faith, that the worlds were so framed by the word of God.

1. We have first, and more principally, to consider the former of these, the thing to be understood. We shall consider the manner afterwards. And for the thing to be understood, that the worlds were framed by the word of God, we have here three heads of discourse more distinctly to be considered and spoken to—the object of this act, the worlds—the Agent whose this act or work is, that is, God, exerting his power by his word, and—the act of creation itself, what kind of act that is. It is here rendered, "framed." We shall speak to the emphasis of that expression hereafter, in its proper place, when we come to give you an account of the nature of the act, creating, which though that word doth not primarily and directly signify, yet supposeth, as we shall in a proper time come to shew you.

(1.) We are to consider the object of creation, as it is here expressed by this comprehensive term, the worlds, "The worlds were framed by the word of God." The word, here, so rendered, doth signify sometimes eternity, especially being plurally used. But sometimes also it signifies time, and sometimes an age, and in the plural, ages. But it doth also signify, in the narrower sense, time: not only time, in itself, abstractly and nakedly considered, but the things that lie within time: not the *mensura* but the *mensurata*, not only that duration, which is the measure of such and such things, but the things themselves that are measured thereby. And that is the sense wherein it must be taken here. Therefore, it is not the naked thing, time, that is spoken of here, (though the word, sometimes, hath that signification as the object of this creative act,) but all things that come under temporary mensuration, all that are measured by time, which is fitly enough expressed in our translation by this term, "the worlds."

And whereas, it is not said, world, but worlds, that shews, that the *continens* is more than one: and if the propriety of the greek be considered, it also signifies them to be more than two; for the word is not a dual but a plural, and so it is more than one, and more than two worlds that are signified by this expression. And indeed, the matter is less indefinite; and it being impossible to us to know how many are the several circles of things that are above us, that are all made things, things altogether without our knowledge or comprehension, (as we have had occasion to tell you on another account, of our Lord's being ascended, and gone up far above all heavens,) we are left in a just uncertainty, (which belongs to us, and is proper to our state,) how many those heavens are, or those orbs of things which are replenished with creatures, (parts of the universe,) that altogether make the entire object of this creation, and this great creative act.

And taking that phrase, "the worlds," to signify whatsoever lies under the measure of time, so we are not barely to consider such orbs, but we are to take in all the *contenta*, as well as the *continens*, all the things contained, as well as the things containing. And so, it is the whole universe of created beings that comes under our present consideration: which, therefore, in speaking to us of the object of the creation, or what it is that is created, it is not to be imagined that we should speak of it in the singular, nor of all the particular kinds; but only under some general heads, into which the universe of created things may be distributed.

[1.] The first, and most general and obvious distribution of the created universe, is into the more substantial things, and the modifications thereof; what is in itself a substantial thing, and what doth only some way or other modify such a being. And it is the former of these, that is the proper object; creation more strictly and properly taken. Creation is, in the strictest sense, *suppositorium* of *supposita*, of things that do subsist not of themselves, in reference to any efficient cause: for so no created thing doth exist, by itself, in opposition to what doth inhere, so as to be a subject of things that do reside in it. And so, the modification of things are not properly created in the strictest sense of creation; but are educed and brought forth out of those substantial beings that were themselves created, or made out of nothing; and so they, that is, substantial things, are the most proper objects of creation, that have a proper subsistence of their own, though with dependance on the efficient Cause that gave them being. And after this distribution, comes,

[2.] The distribution of such created things, that is, substantial beings, in which all the diversifying *modi* do reside and have their place. And we are to consider what may be the more general distribution of substantial things, that are themselves created. And we can consider none more general, than this one, to wit, of all those created substances, into these two heads, matter and mind. If the inquiry be, What doth this universe of created beings contain? Or what are the great spheres of being that lie within the compass of the created universe? Why, speaking of substantial things themselves, that are the subjects of divers distinct *modi* or modifications, they can be but these two, all will fall under these two heads, to wit, matter and mind. And this is that distribution of created things which the Scripture gives us a ground express enough for: Col. 1. 16. "By him were all things made that are in heaven or that are in earth, visible and invisible." We may well enough suppose all matter to be, some way or other, visible, though, there be indeed a finer sort of matter than is visible to us. But then, there is the other head of things, in that Col. 1. 16. things that are simply invisible, altogether invisible, as it is altogether impossible that any sense, any external sense, can perceive a mind, or a thought, which is the immediate product of that mind. So, that every distribution of created things into visible and invisible, I take it, sufficiently corresponds with this that I now mention, that is, matter and mind.

And otherwise, we have the creation distinguished as to the object of it, or creation, passively taken, into heaven and earth, as we find in that history of the beginning of the creation, Gen. 1. 1. "In the beginning God created the heavens and the earth." Some, indeed, that go to the cabalistical way, will have by heavens, all intellectual beings that are created, to be comprehended and meant: and by earth, all matter whatsoever. We shall not dispute the propriety of that conjecture, or what probably it hath, or hath not; but take what is more obvious to ourselves in common understanding. And if we take that as a distribution of created things, heaven and earth, as was intimated before, we must comprehend together both the *continens* and the *contenta*. And so, by heaven, must be understood and meant, not only all the several superior orbs, but all their inhabitants that do reside and dwell in them, and wherewith they are replenished, and unto which, our very minds and spirits, (though now they are clothed with terrestrial vehicles and dwell in flesh,) do originally appertain and belong, as being nearer of kin, and more allied to the world of spirits than they are allied to this world of flesh and earth, this terrestrial world. For, if we take the mind and spirit in us, to be the nobler and more excellent part of ourselves, taking our denomination from that which is more noble and excellent, we have greater affinity, according to our primitive and original state, with heaven, than we have with earth, which affinity is not to be judged by the place of residence, but by the nature of the thing. Mind and spirit are more akin to heavenly inhabitants, than they are to any thing that is made merely of earth.

And so, taking the things contained, with all the heavenly orbs, you have great diversifications, in that mentioned place,

Col. 1. 16. And there indeed, the Spirit of God runs out more than it doth in the distribution of things that fall under that other head, that is, the visible things of this earth. For we are told, under the head of invisible things, (and which also in very great part, indeed, are the things which do belong to the heavens,) of thrones and dominions, and principalities and powers; which are very reasonably thought to mean so many several orders of celestial creatures that do inhabit the other world or worlds, for how many of them there are, we do not know, nor can know; as we formerly told you.

And then, if we speak of the things contained in this lower orb, signified here by earth, they do more generally fall under a common notice, and are more obvious to every one's apprehension. This world, you know, is replenished with very numerous sorts of creatures that live one way or other, or with one or another sort of lives; either, that do live an intellectual life, or live from an intelligent soul, as we do all live; or else, that live a merely sensitive life, as all the brute creatures do, of that next order below, or else, things that do live a merely vegetative life; as all the several sorts of plants that have some kind of life, though it be of a meaner and lower kind.

And then, there are all your inanimate things that have no proper life at all; that is, have no self-moving or self-acting principle within them, or peculiar to them, from whence they do act or order themselves, or are capable of being moved, as from any internal *vis* in this kind or that.

Of such extent is this created universe: it takes in all these several sorts of things. And to descend to the enumeration of more particular kinds would be an endless work, and not proper for us. But, in the mean time, we have very great amplitude in the object of our present thought and consideration, when we are to look upon the universe of created beings, that is, of created substances, look upon all those that come under the notion of matter, and that, as such, is inanimate: matter, as matter, has no self-moving principle in it. Look upon all those things that live some kind of life or another; whether they be things of this earth of ours, or whether they be things of the superior or refined orbs and parts of the universe: these come in all the orders of angelical creatures of which we have only that general and more indistinct account which that Colossians 1. and some other passages of Scripture give us. What their diversifications are, we know not; but some or other they are, and such as do import superiority and inferiority among themselves. And then, go to that other head, of things destitute of life, and that more properly come under the notion of matter beforementioned: and so, descending downwards from the more noble and excellent creatures, to the meaner and lesser ones, what a vast scale of created being is this! descending from the highest to the lowest, or ascending from the lowest to the highest, and all within the compass of the created universe, and all this signified by that one expression in the text "the worlds."

Indeed, all this being summed up into this one expression, of the universe or the world, taken singularly and in the largest sense of which it doth admit, we have, even within the compass of created beings, that which far exceeds any of our thoughts. And it hath been a question, much agitated, amongst philosophical men, whether the created universe have any created limits at all, yea or no. It hath been agitated by some with a very ill design: and some have made it their business, in moving the controversy, to hide their design. And with a strange mixture of fraud and folly, in discussing that question, Whether the created universe were infinite or no? they have gone about to disguise the matter, and told us, they would not, indeed, say it was infinite, but it was indefinite; to wit, the extent of the created universe: and by the extent of it, the meaning could not be the mere local extent, but the real; not barely what space it took it up, but what of essence and real being it did comprehend and contain; and that, some of them have told us, was not infinite, but indefinite only.

But there hath been a very great mixture (as I say) of fraud and of folly: of fraud, that they have disguised their meaning, and laboured to hide it: and of folly, that in their very attempt of hiding it, they have unawares discovered a very ill meaning. And it could not but be so; for when the terms are distinguished of infinite and indefinite, I would fain know what they mean by the latter. If, by indefinite, they mean that which hath in itself no certain limits, then they plainly say, it is infinite, the created universe is infinite, because it hath no certain limits. But if they mean by it only, that it hath no known limits to us, that every one readily acknowledgeth: we can never know the limits of it; and so that is but to say it is finite, if they mean only so. And indeed, it is a very dubitable thing, whether any finite understanding can measure the created universe, or is capable of comprehending the extent of it. Very willing I am to aggrandize that as much as I can, in consistency, still, with owning it to be but a created thing; because still, the more we magnify that, the more we magnify the Creator. But to pretend it to be an indefinite thing in that sense, that is, that it hath no certain limits in itself, that is to make it an infinite thing.

And if it here be inquired, What is the inconvenience of that, to make it to be so, or how can we prove it not to be so? Why truly, to the former of the questions, there would be this to say, that to say it were infinite, or could be infinite, were to say that it were not a creation: for most certain it is, whatsoever is infinite is God. Infinity is the proper predicate or attribute of Deity. And so, the inconvenience would be, the taking away all the foundations of religion; for it would be the confounding of God and the creature, the taking away the difference between them. And it would be equally impossible, that there should be any room or place for religion, if you take away the subject of it, as much as if you take away the Object of it. If the creature were infinite, there could be no subject of religion: and there can be no place for religion, if there be no subject of it, any more than if there were no Object of it.

And as to the question, How can it be proved that the created universe is not infinite, and cannot be infinite? It is very clearly to be proved by what hath been said, in very great part: that is, whatsoever is infinite is God. Therefore, to say that the created universe is infinite, is to say, that it is not created. But besides, it may be easily evinced, that not only this universe of created beings is not infinite, but that it is impossible that it ever should be, or could be. And as the plain reason of the thing doth lie against that imagination; so, the most pernicious and destructive tendency of that philosophy that would impose upon us the imagination of an infinite universe, is most studiously to be disclaimed and abhorred, as taking away all place and room for religion. For it would confound created being and uncreated, and deify the creature, and so, leave no subject of worship, as the more avowed atheism leaves no Object of it.

I shall not say more to you about the object of this said act. We are further to consider the great Agent, the Creator: and the nature of the act of creation. But let us make some stand and pause here, and consider what improvement is to be made of what hath been thus far discoursed to you. It is of very vast extent, what we are to consider under the notion of the created universe. But when all this is done, it is still but a creation; make it as great a thing as you will, magnify it as much as possible, consistently with its being a creation, and when all this is done, then say within yourselves, "All this is but as a drop, a drop of a bucket, a dust in a balance, a mere nothing, yea, lighter than nothing and vanity, compared with that Being which is of itself; that Being which owes itself to none; that Being to which it was impossible not to be; for all this vast creation doth but depend on will and pleasure; "For thy pleasure they are and were created." It was determinable, merely upon good pleasure, whether there should be any creation, or no creation: so that one *nutus*, one *nod* (as I may speak) of the Divine Mind, either makes this vast thing, the whole created universe, to be something or nothing. "If I please, it shall be something, if I please, it shall be nothing."

It should lead us into adoration of the great self-subsisting Being, that owes it to none that he is, is beholden to none, but is by the excellency of his own eternal nature, to which it was repugnant not to be, and which comprehends all plenitude and fulness of being in itself, even an infinitude of being.

Consider this then, and when it hath prompted and led you into admiration and adoration, looking up to the great Creator, it should prompt and lead us into the greatest detestation of the insolency of creatures, even such creatures as (if they would use their minds) are capable of apprehending this, and yet take upon them as if they were absolute. They started up out of being but the other day, and at the fiat, and by the pleasure, of the great Creator; and now, they look upon themselves in this world as if it were all theirs, and as if they might do in it what they pleased. He that is the Creator of heaven and earth is also, we know, in Scripture, stiled the Possessor of heaven and earth. And for a company of upstart creatures sprung up into being but the other day, to take upon them, as if they were possessors (as much as is possible for them to grasp) of this creation, and to do in it what they will; what a detestable insolency is this! It is but a dependant, borrowed right that any one hath in whatsoever he calls his own. And yet, men are apt to hug themselves in conceit of propriety, saying, "This is my own land, these are my own goods, this is my own house; and it is so by the best title a man can have." Now suppose a stranger enter your door and come into your house and take no notice of any thing as yours, but useth all things as he pleaseth, and saith he will do what he lists in this house of yours; or (without saying so) doth what he lists, takes and uses what he will, and as he will, would you not take yourself to be highly injured, and would you not right yourself, if it lay in your power, upon so injurious an intruder as this? Why, at this rate is the great God treated and dealt with, by his apostate, revolted creatures, inhabiting this lower world, though it be even the meaner and baser parts of his creation? Creatures sprung up into being here by indulgence of divine favour, take upon them as if they were their own lords and owners, and as if every thing they lay their hands on were their own, without ever taking notice of God; He that gave them breath and being and all things, that they might seek after him, and consider, "Whence come I? and all things that I use and enjoy, whence are they?" No such thing enters into their minds, from day to day, but a life's time is run out in these bodies, wherein they should love, and serve, and adore, their great Creator, without taking notice of him.

But a more copious use of this yet remains, when we shall have opened other things that yet are to be doctrinally opened unto you.

LECTURE X.*

(2.) We are now, in the second place, to consider the Agent in this great and mighty work, and that is, (as the text expresseth it,) God himself, that great, all-comprehending Name. There will be occasion to take notice of the way of his agency, (by his word,) by and by. The Creator of all things, of heaven and earth, can be no other than he who comprehends and contains all things, virtually, in his own power. But whereas, we have heretofore shewn to you at large, that there is in the Deity a threefold subsistence, the Father, the Son and the Holy Ghost, they are each of them to be comprehended under the notion of Creator here. It is a plain and self-evident truth, commonly given us as a maxim, *Opera Trinitatis, ad extra, sunt indivisa, vel communicabla;* that the works of the three persons in the Godhead towards the creature are undivided, and communicable to each of the persons: so as that we must understand them to be conjunct, in every such act as they do exert without themselves or towards any thing that is not God. Their distinguishing actions are towards one another; but the actings that they exert towards any thing without them, these are common to them all. So that the Father creates, the Son creates, and the Holy Ghost creates. This action which, as we have told you, makes its object, and doth not suppose it, as other acts, *ad extra*, do, it is the common act of each of these. And so you find that the creation is usually ascribed to God, under that name of God (that name, being essentially taken) which compre-

* Preached January 24, 1693.

hends all the three persons. And so we must understand that, in the beginning of Genesis, where God is said to have created the heavens and the earth. And that observation is not to be slighted, that Elohim, a plural noun is conjoined with a verb of the singular number; Barah Elohim. As if it were said, Gods created the heaven and the earth; that is, it is an expression to note that there is a plurality in the Deity; that is, of persons, each of which is God. But it being conjoined with a verb in the singular number, it shews that these three were but one; did agree in Deity, as well as in this creative act. And this is that which that learned man Zanchy, in his treatise, "De tribus Elohim," doth prove profitably and at large. But more particularly, when the name of God is taken,

[1.] Personally, as divers times also it is, then it signifies, eminently, God the Father: and that very term doth sufficiently express him to be the Original of all things, of all beings, both created and uncreated. He is usually, and fitly enough, said to be *Fons Deitatis et fons Trinitatis*. The Deity is first in the Father, and all created beings first and originally from him, as the matter is plainly expressed in the 1 Cor, 8. 6. To us there is but one God the Father, of whom are all things. Him we are taught to adore as the great Original, from whom all being hath its rise. And yet,

[2.] We have the creation, very frequently, ascribed to the Son, speaking him conjunct with the Father in this great creative act. And even in that last mentioned place, (1 Cor. 8.) where it is said, "To us there is but one God the Father, of whom are all things and we in him," it is added, "and one Lord Jesus Christ by whom are all things, and we by him." And so, in that Col. 1. 15, 16. his agency in the creation is most expressly asserted. He who is there said to be "the image of the invisible God, and the first-born," (as we read it, but it may as properly be read, according to grammar, with only the alteration of an accent, the first-begotten of every creature,) "by him were all things created that are in heaven, and that are in earth, visible and invisible; whether they be thrones or dominions or principalities or powers, all things were created by him and for him." There is his concurrence and conjunction with the Father, both as the efficient and final Cause of all things. So that Heb. 1. 2. "God hath in these last days spoken unto us by his Son, whom he hath appointed the heir of all things, by whom also he made the worlds." He that is "the brightness of his Father's glory and the express image of his person," by him the worlds were made. And so we have it, most expressly, in the beginning of John's gospel;

" In the beginning was the Word, and the Word was with God, (a known name and title of Christ, God's eternal Son and consubstantial Word) that Word was in the beginning with God, and that Word was God. The same was in the beginning with God. All things were made by him, and without him was not any thing made that was made." He is spoken of under a title of like import, frequently, in other scriptures, and most expressly in Proverbs 8. That is, by the name of the wisdom of God, and, under that name, is asserted to be with him, even throughout the whole work of this creation. Not with him in an idle concomitancy; which no man can understand, either according to the reason of the thing, or the plain import of the other scriptures that have been named, and many more that are to be named. He was with him, when the Lord laid the foundations of the earth, when he stretched out the heavens, when he did all that was done in the work of creation. And then,

[3.] The creation is ascribed to the Eternal Spirit, to the Holy Ghost, as you find expressly in that Gen. 1. when we had been told, " In the beginning God created the heavens and the earth, and that the earth was without form and void; the Spirit of God is said to have moved upon the face of the waters:" that is, upon the fluid matter of the yet unformed chaos, that profound abyss; that Tohu and Bohu, as it is expressed; upon that fluid and yet unformed matter that was fluctuating, even as waters do: upon that, the Spirit of God did move to collect and form things out of it, according to divine pleasure.

Thus, it is plain, each person in the Godhead hath his hand and part in this great work of creation. What hand and part each hath, some are very curious in describing. But so far as the Scriptures expressly do lead us, so far we may allow our conceptions to be formed concerning their distinct agency. And it is plain,

First: That the name Father doth signify him to be the Original of all things, the first Fountain Being, the Fountain of all being, created and uncreated. The Divine Being itself is first and originally in Him, as the name Father signifies: and that comprehends the fulness of all being in itself, all excellency, all perfection whether conceivable by us, or unconceivable. So from him, the creation must have taken its rise as the Head of all things. And then,'

Secondly: The Scripture speaks of the Son under the name of the eternal consubstantial word of God, or his essential wisdom, which must needs be understood to contain in itself the first idea of all things. All being originally contained and comprehended in God the Father as such, he is now said to be the image of the invisible God, and in him do all the glories of the Deity shine, as in their first image. All things being to be created and produced into actual being according to that image which lay in the Divine Mind, which he is. As there is no one goes about to make any thing, but hath the image and idea in his own mind, first, of what he intends to make. He that intends to make a book, or to make a house, or a garment, hath the idea in his own mind, first, of what he intends to make, and according to that idea all things are made. All things that were to be created, the eternal wisdom of the Father comprehending them all in himself, he is the rule or *norma*, according to which, the creation is at last produced into actual being. And then,

Thirdly: The agency of the Holy Ghost may be conceived according to that light the Scripture gives concerning the distinguishing characters of that person. From the actuous love, between the Father and the Son, for an eternal production of the divine image by the Father in the Son, there cannot but be an everlasting spiration of love between the Father and this, his consubstantial Image: an actuous love, and that image, containing in itself the ideas of all the things that were to be produced. This mighty power of actuous love, it goes forth to produce all things, according to this image, with the highest delectation and complacency, according to which, God pronounced concerning all things which he had made—that it was very good, and so a derivative object of divine love; all things being produced according to that excellency of his own image that was the Original Root of all things. And hereupon, do other scriptures speak of the agency of the Holy Ghost in this matter; that is, that by his Spirit he garnished the heavens; one part of the creation there spoken of. "Thou sendest forth thy Spirit and they are created." Psalm 104. 30. And so you see, that Father, Son, and Spirit have their parts and agencies in this great work of creation. But then,

(3.) We have here to consider the act itself. You have seen the object the worlds; and you have seen the Agent, God himself, Father, Son, and Spirit. We are now next, according to the order proposed, to consider the act that is expressed here in the text by a word, which is, fitly enough, rendered, "framed;" but we must note unto you, that, that word doth *express* one sort of act, and *supposeth* another. It expresseth one sort of act, that is, the framing of things; framing (as it is fitly enough translated here) when there was somewhat now brought into being, out of which, they should be so and so diversly framed, especially as to the material part of the world. That is the act here expressed. But then, it supposeth a former act, a foregoing act, and that is, the making all out of nothing, out of which any thing was after framed. We shall speak of the act the word expresseth, first; and then shall speak of the act that word supposeth.

[1.] The word in the text is very fitly expressive of the former act, that the worlds are said to be framed. It comes of a word that signifies perfect and entire, and it seems to come from that we commonly denote by art; or, as some would have, the relation of this word to *artus* which signifies our limbs, the limbs of any creature that is endued with life. And so they would borrow the illustration of this word from chirurgick art, that doth aptly place the bones which have been dislocated, and puts them into joint again. So the worlds were framed (as it were) by the most curious and exquisite chirurgick art: or else, that which is precedent to that, the locking and joining things into one another throughout the whole creation.

And in this respect, the framing of the worlds was more immediately the work of the divine wisdom, which may be meant by the expression here, that they were created by the word of God, which I told you we should take notice of in its proper place. Which may be meant not of the word spoken out, but of the internal word, agreeable to what we are wont to call *verbum mentis:* as there is no one that speaks, (if he speak sense,) but he hath in his own mind first, that which he afterwards expresseth and speaks out. But herein was the wisdom of the Creator principally conspicuous; in that beautiful order and frame of things that appeared every where throughout this great universe; that there is that order that we behold daily among the heavenly bodies, in reference to one another and in reference to us; that which, in the 8th psalm, you find the Psalmist in so high and holy an adoration of: "When I consider the heavens, the work of thy fingers, the moon and the stars, which thou hast ordained." It is a great argument of a holy heart, to be much in contemplating the divine wisdom that hath settled every thing of that order which is any where to be found in the whole creation.

If you look into this lower world, and consider that, as to what falls under our notice, there is every where that correspondency of actives to passives, of faculties to objects, as every one that will use thoughts may easily discern, the wisdom of the Creator is greatly to be adored in it. For think we with ourselves, how great a piece of vanity this creation had been, if it had not been so; if there had been objects upon which there had been no faculties to exercise: or, if there were, faculties to be exercised that had no objects; as if there were visible things, and no eye to see them; if there were audible things, and no ear to hear them. And so, back again, if there were eyes, and nothing to be seen; and a faculty of hearing, and no such thing as sound. But herein is the admirable contrivance of the divine wisdom in this creation manifest, that there is such a correspondency throughout, of objects to faculties, of active powers and principles to passives.

And then, in that order that is settled amongst things, therein we have the great display of the divine wisdom, there being (as hath been often said) that relation between wisdom and order, as between cause and effect. Wheresoever there is any of stated, settled order, we may be sure there was wisdom to contrive and design it. Stated and settled order cannot be a casualty. When we see the contrivance and order that are in such a thing as a watch or a clock, and the like, we are presently sure that such a thing was not made by chance. And to think that such a mighty agency, a mighty power of motion, as was once exerted in this creation, should produce things in that orderly frame wherein we behold them, without design, without wisdom, is as absurd an imagination, as if we should imagine a thousand men, by violent strokes with axes and hammers, upon brass or iron, or the like, without any design, should produce so many watches, clocks, or any such like engines; meaning no such thing.

Therefore, nothing is more to be wondered at, nor a greater argument of the degeneracy of man, or how low his mind is sunk, than that there should be any who should go into the account of the more thinking sort of men, that yet should make it their business to exclude the power of final causes out of the world: as if there were no such thing as a final cause, or an end designed, that had any influence at all upon this great creation. Whereas, if we consider the several orders and sorts of being, how useful the meanest creature, even the inanimate part of the creation is, to very great and necessary purposes and ends; and when we consider, among those things that have life, how aptly they serve for their own purposes, and how aptly every thing in them serves their own purpose, that is, to beget and maintain that life, we cannot but see the absurdity of that conceit. To look upon the lowest sort of living creatures, the mere vegetable creatures; Why are they made with roots? but to take hold of the earth from whence by them their nutriment is drawn; that those little fibres, without which a leaf could not be nourished, should be dispersed every where throughout the whole, with so fine a texture as they are? Very well doth Cicero, a heathen, speak of nature under the name of the divine art, the art of God. And whereas, "*Boni artificis est celare artem;*" *it is the part of a good artist to conceal his art,* truly, if the divine art were not, in great part, concealed, one would think all the actions of intelligent creatures, should be swallowed up in wonder, to behold the divine agency running through all things, and so variously exerting itself for the production of things as we find them; and contriving the several kinds of things in the same rank and station in the creation, into which at first they were set.

If we should look to that admirable, rare contrivance, that appears in the forming of our own bodies, upon which you find the Psalmist in that transport, "Marvellous are thy works, fearfully I am made," that is, wonderfully; "and that my soul knoweth right well." Psalm 139. 14. That is, "This is a beaten subject to me, a thing that my thoughts are much used to, it is a thing about which my mind is accustomed, I know it right well :" as we know the path that we have often trod.

And not only is the divine wisdom conspicuous in this framing of things, but his goodness too. How adorable is the goodness of God, even in that frame and disposure of things that we find in the creation; that things are so framed and adapted, as to answer and correspond to one another. Here is a great appearance of the divine goodness, that whereas he hath put into such sorts and orders of his creatures, a desiring faculty, there is still somewhat in that creation to answer that faculty of desire. Every thing is, by natural instinct, taught to desire that which is good for it; that is, that which is convenient and suitable to it. So we have the Psalmist (psalm 145. 15.) admiring God upon this account, that the eyes of all things were up unto him, and that he gave them their meat in due season: a continual argument and testimony of the divine goodness. He hath not left himself, in this, without witness; the whole earth is full of his goodness, even that which the inhabitants of it replenish and fill with their wickedness and malignity against him. He doth good to all, even to the evil and the good. He hears the ravens when they cry, and they seek their meat from God: psalm 104. which psalm is full of expressions to this purpose. This is the munificence of the great Creator, that when he did design to replenish such and such parts of the created universe, with such and such inhabitants, creatures able to receive and entertain some correspondent and suitable good, he hath also stored the world with that good which shall answer every appetite throughout all this creation of God: so that none can be miserable, amongst even those that are rendered, by their own natures, capable of government by a law, but such as make themselves so by aversion and disaffection to their proper and suitable good. They only have it not, because they refuse it, because they are disaffected thereunto.

But then, we should come, in the next place, to speak of the second act which this expression in the text doth suppose. That which the word in the text is most expressive of, is only that sort of act by which things are adapted and suited to one another: but this supposeth a former act, by which those things, out of which things are thus framed, were themselves at first produced and brought forth out of nothing; which is creation in the strictest and most proper sense; though, indeed, there is not a word that doth exclusively signify that act in any of the learned languages. But the nature of the thing, doth plainly evidence that there must be such an act. That is, look upon all uncreated being, the being of God himself, and then that which is created and made being, must have been made out of nothing; which they that will not apprehend, run into various and most manifest absurdities; one sort, thinking there must be such a thing as eternal, necessary matter; another sort, thinking that things must be made out of God as so many parts of the Deity. But I shall, on the next occasion, labour to evince to you the absurdity of any such imaginations as these.

And in the mean time, pray let us make so much of present reflection upon this great work of God's creation; that is, that he who hath made such a world as this, cannot but have both right and ability to rule it, and all things in it, to the best and most valuable purposes. And truly, I fear we do not, on this account, enough study the creation, and the attributes of the Divine Being that are exerted and put forth in that creation. There is his wisdom and his goodness to be seen in that first sort of act already spoken to.

And his power is most visible, and especially to be seen in the latter sort of act, as we shall shew when we come to speak to it. But to any that would give themselves liberty of their own thoughts, one would think, they should not part, for all the world, with the consolation, that this one thing should afford us: that is, that all this vast frame of things should be produced by divine wisdom, goodness, and power, into that exquisite order, in which we now behold them: and that, hereupon, he that could tell how to make such a world as this, replenished with such variety of inhabitants, knows how to govern, and dispose every thing he hath made. And, as there hath been that display of these glorious excellencies, in the Divine Nature, in the frame and contexture of this whole creation, we ought, hereupon, always to expect, that he will, with the same wisdom, power, and goodness, regulate, govern, and dispose of what he hath so made. All these things will appear, and shew themselves in the most proper seasons, without our distracting and self-tormenting cares. Let us be desirous, principally and finally, of nothing but that he who made such a world as this, for himself, and for his own glory, may, in his own way and time, have that glory out of it which he seeks and designs for himself. Yea, let us be content, that he should have it in such a way as may possibly be conjunct with our suffering many inconveniencies; things that may be grievous to us, to our flesh and blood, and external sense. Should not he have his glory out of his own creation, his own way? This world was not made for us, but it was made for him, by whom it was made.

LECTURE XI.*

[2.] But then, as I have told you, in the second place, we are now to consider, that as the expression, here in the text, doth more directly signify that one act, of putting things into order, which is the native import of the word; so there is another act necessarily supposed; and that is, the bringing of things out of nothing, which are the proper, the truly proper matter of production, or whatsoever is *extra Deum*, whatsoever is a diverse thing from the being of the Deity itself. This word, "frame," doth not signify directly this act, but it doth necessarily suppose it. Order, doth suppose a subject, the things in being that are brought into that order. And as the two great attributes before mentioned, divine wisdom and goodness, do shine forth in that former act, the putting of things into order; so his power doth most eminently appear in this latter act, the bringing of the things which he so puts into order, out of nothing.

As we do not pretend to assert this act, from the import of this word that is used in the text, abstractly considered, so neither do we pretend to assert, from the native, proper force and significancy of any one word at all, that we must think appropriate to this purpose, as only to signify this act and nothing else. We do readily grant, the hebrew and the greek words thus rendered, are frequently used with more latitude than barely to signify the bringing of things out of nothing. And so, this act is not to be concluded from the force and import of such words, abstractly considered by themselves. Words that

* Preached July 1, 1693.

are of a more indefinite signification, that may signify more things than one, they are always determined to some one particular sense or other, by the circumstances of the place where they are used. There is not any one word at all, that is to be confined and limited to one certain sense by its own native import: or, at least, there are very few words that are capable of that confinement and restriction by constant and unvaried use. But what they mean in this or that saying, is to be judged by the circumstances of the discourses wherein they lie.

What of the creation is *de fide*, a matter of faith merely, we have hinted to you already, and shall further have occasion to shew you, when we come to speak of that second head, how we are to come to this understanding. But, in the mean time, it is very evident, when it is said, that we are to understand this by faith, that the worlds were so and so framed, we are not to understand it exclusively, as if the meaning of the text were to shut out every thing of argument, or ratiocination in the matter. One and the same thing may be assented to, from divers different premises, as was hinted to you before. It is enough for our purpose, and even to make this which I am now speaking of, a matter of faith, to wit, the producing of created things out of nothing, if it shall evidently appear, that in some texts of Scripture, this must be ultimately intended and meant; and that no other thing can be, so as to exclude the necessary pre-supposition of this: and there are, undoubtedly, some texts that must be so understood, that there hath been somewhat produced out of nothing, out of which other things at length were made to arise.

As to that first text of Scripture, "In the beginning God created the heaven and the earth." Created, must necessarily have this sense, at least, by an unavoidable necessity; for this making heaven and earth, being said to be in the beginning, when things took their beginning, had their first rise, it must suppose that heaven and earth were not only brought into order, but that of which they were made, was made of itself to exist, not having existed before. Otherwise, how was that the beginning of things? How was that the head of things? as the hebrew word Resch, from whence the word Bershith, in the beginning, signifies. Otherwise, this word must assert a contradiction, that things were begun, and not begun, at that time when God created heaven and earth.

And so, if you go forward to that first of John's gospel, ver. 2, 3. "In the beginning was the Word, and the Word was with God, and the Word was God. All things were created by him, (that is, God) and without him was nothing made that was made :" every thing that was not God, was then made : all things. And, therefore, to suppose that all these made things were made out of pre-existent matter, is to suppose, that that pre-existent matter was not a thing, for all things were said to be made by him. All things beside himself were then made; therefore, matter itself was then made, out of which other things were made; unless it shall be said that matter is nothing, and, if so, we have what we seek, that is, that there are some things made out of nothing; but if it were a thing, and were not the Divine Being, as it is impossible to be, it was a self-made thing, and then made out of nothing.

And to this purpose must the explicatory proposition in the text be necessarily adapted, so that the things that are seen, were not made of things that did appear. The phœnomena, (that is the word there) things not then appearing, when the worlds were thus framed by the word of God; that is, things not before existing, for there is nothing at all that can be supposed to exist, but doth appear to some faculty or other, either divine or created. But they were things simply not appearing at all, and, therefore, not existing at all, out of which these worlds were made.

And lexicographers do take notice of that among the other senses of the word φαινομενων, that it signifies to exist. And, therefore, the worlds are said to be framed out of that which once did not exist, till it was made to exist by the divine creative power. And therefore, they foolishly think who would put a difficulty upon God in this case, such as was put upon the Israelites in Egypt, to make brick without straw: as if omnipotency could be posed, or meet with any obstruction to its designed acts, for want of matter to work upon. It was all one to him, (who calls things that are not, and makes them be as if they were, as the expression Rom. 4. 17.) whether there were the pre-existent matter to work upon or no: and the non pre-existence can never nonplus omnipotency.

And therewith should we obviate the vain and idle question, when we hear of the worlds being framed by the word of God: "Aye, but of what were they made? made they were, but what did he make them of?" They must have, originally, been made out of what before was not, seeing it was his pleasure that they should be; for, for his pleasure all things are and were created. Rev. 5. 9. And so, (as was said before,) if you take matter within the compass of being, it must itself be a made thing.

Now, concerning this act, the bringing of all things out of nothing, take this twofold assertion, which we shall evince to you, and according whereunto we are to conceive of it—that it is possible to no created agent: and—that it is possible to God.

First: To all created agents, it was impossible to bring something out of nothing. It is impossible to all the power of nature, unto the power of whatsoever creature, or unto all the creatures uniting their power. I shall not trouble you with the reasonings of the schools to this purpose, by which they plainly enough demonstrate creation (that is, bringing something out of nothing) to be impossible to any creature. It is, indeed, a much disputed thing among them, whether God cannot impart his power, whether it cannot be communicated to a creature, so as that he may not make use of a creature in creation; but it is little material how that goes.

But that a creature cannot, by all its own strength, be able to bring any thing out of nothing, nor all created power put together, needs no other conviction, but an appeal even to common understanding. Nor can you conceive it any way possible for you. And if you say, "No, I cannot do it alone; but if I take in the advice, or superadded helps of such and such things, possibly we may together." Why, suppose all the power and force of all men in the world, and of all created agents besides, were to be united in one act, you cannot so much as conceive that they could produce so much as one single atom into being out of nothing. As it is equally impossible to all created power to annihilate, as to create, to reduce something back again into nothing, as to produce something out of nothing. So also is it equally possible for the divine, uncreated power to bring all things out of nothing. And, then, therefore,

Secondly: We are to conceive concerning this act, as it is impossible to any created agent, so it is possible to God, and to the divine agency. For it is plain, it implies nothing of contradiction in the thing itself; that that which did not exist, should exist, as it is evident that many things do exist which did not exist. Therefore, there is no contradiction in that, what did not exist, should exist, as it is evident that many things do exist. And, therefore, to suppose it impossible to God to make that exist, which did not exist, is itself to assert a contradiction. For the notion of God doth carry infiniteness in it: you cannot form a notion of God, but it must include infiniteness. But to say that he is infinite, infinite in being, in his perfections, in his power too, and yet, that he cannot do that which implies no contradiction to be done, is to deny God to be God. It is to say, God is but a finite being, or of finite power; to say, that which you call God is not God, which is a contradiction, when you say that he cannot do that which implies no contradiction that it should be done: that is, that that which did not exist, should exist.

But admit this, perhaps you will object, that it is possible to divine agency to make something out of nothing, that doth not, however, prove, that God hath now done so. There are many things possible to be done, which are not actually done. And it is no argument, from the affirmation of the power to assert the act.

To this, I only say, It is not alleged to that purpose; we do not assert the possibility of creating something out of nothing, to prove that something hath been created out of nothing; but only by way of answer to them, that would thereby prove, that something was never created out of nothing, because it is an *enunciatio* affirmation, that which is impossible to be done is never actually done, though it doth not follow, that because the thing is possible to be done, therefore it is actually done. And, therefore, this is alleged only in answer to them, that do say it is simply impossible. But we prove it not to be impossible, for many things exist that did not always do so.

But we otherwise prove, that it hath actually been so, that is, that he hath made something out of nothing; that is, that we have proved it from those plain texts, that cannot but be understood in that sense. And we shall now prove it, from the gross and manifold absurdities, that they are unavoidably cast upon, who disallow something to be made out of nothing. That is, such absurdities as these; first, they must suppose this world to have been eternally, of itself, as it is; or, secondly, they must affirm there hath been necessarily self-subsisting matter from eternity; or, thirdly, they must assert, that God hath made all things out of himself, that whatsoever is made, is part of himself. But these are all of them the most manifest and gross absurdities that can be thought.

i. That this world should have been eternally as it is, without beginning. They that will pretend to say so, must first throw away all divine revelation about this matter, which manifestly asserts it never to have been eternal, but hath begun to be. But besides that, they do assert, here, repugnancies in the very nature of the thing, for they must assert the world to be as new now, as it was several thousands of years ago; that it was as old, the first year, as now it is; that is, the first year in our account. Besides what is wont to be alleged by them who are for that second horrid opinion, that matter was necessarily self-subsisting from eternity; they think themselves concerned to prove the world's being from eternity, as it is; and they do so from that consideration, that then it is most unconceivably strange, that we should have no records of things, (as one of those Epicureans speaks) elder or of a more ancient date than the times of the Trojan war, and the like. But,

ii. That which is more plausibly, and more usually, taken up in these latter times, (though it was an ancient by-gone absurdity too,) is, that there must be such a thing as eternal matter, out of which many things were brought into this frame, in which now they are: and some that will not pretend to atheism do think, that only that matter did pre-exist, and things could not have been produced into that order and state wherein they do now appear, but by a divine agency; that is, by a divine power and wisdom running through all things, and modelling them into that form in which we do find they do now appear, and are now cast; but nothing is more obvious to them that do consider, than the gross absurdity of that opinion, that there must be such a thing as eternal, self-subsisting matter, out of which God made the worlds. For,

(i.) That would ascribe to the matter, the most fundamental attributes of the Divine Being; that is, self-subsisting or necessary existence. Nothing can be imagined more grossly absurd, than, that the highest and most radical, and most fundamental attribute of the Deity should be ascribed to dull and senseless matter, that is, to exist of itself, and that it should be possible to him, if he would, to reduce it to nothing: and that this prerogative should belong to every particle of matter, and that all matter being reduced into minute particles, even in our conception, then each minute particle must be in itself, an independent thing, existing of itself without dependance on any thing else. Which, if it be acknowledged, then shall you have as many deities as there are minute particles of matter throughout the universe.

(ii.) This will further confute that gross conceit, that there must be any self-subsisting matter from eternity. And if there were such, it were altogether impossible that this world should be made out of it. And so it is asserted, not only impiously, but vainly: impiously, as it doth intrench upon a peculiar and most fundamental attribute of the Divine Being, to wit, self-subsistence: and vainly, because it were impossible this world should be made of such matter, if there were any such: for whatsoever is necessarily self-subsisting is unchangeable; that which is necessarily what it is,—can never be other than it is. And it is altogether impossible that a world could be made of it, without its undergoing various changes. If it be necessarily such, of, and from, itself which now it is; that which is necessarily what it is, is eternally what it is. And therefore, can never be liable to any change, not so much as that intrinsic change of motion. For suppose any minute particle of matter to be of itself necessarily, it must be somewhere; and if it be necessarily any where, it can by no succeeding change be any where else: and so must be simply unmoveable. And then, this world could never be made of it, that is, of unmoving matter: and it must be unmoving matter, and uncapable of motion, if it be of itself what it is. For if it be of itself, it must be necessarily somewhere; and if it be somewhere necessarily, it must be somewhere eternally, and can never change its place. And again,

(iii.) That opinion of eternal, necessary, self-subsisting matter, the absurdity of it is enough to be evinced from hence, that is, that the ground upon which it is asserted, equally serves for the asserting of a manifest falsehood; that is, that nothing else is made out of nothing. We may as well suppose matter to be made out of nothing, as any thing else to be made out of nothing; but something else must be acknowledged to be made out of nothing. We told you, at first, speaking of the object of creation, that the universal distinction that created things are capable of, is into two heads, of mind and matter. Now, they must acknowledge minds to be made of nothing, that they are not eternally self-subsisting. And if a mind can be made out of nothing, why may not matter as well as mind? and it is plain, that (speaking of the mind of a creature) that must be made out of nothing: for it could never be made out of matter, matter being uncapable of thought; and thought is the most essential thing we can conceive of in the notion of a mind. This can never, upon any terms, agree to matter; that is a material thing: as such it is impossible that that should be capable of thought, or of the power of thinking.

There is no part of matter to which that can agree, for you can conceive nothing of matter, or of the several particles of matter, but either its size, that is, being bigger or lesser, or its figure, that is, being so shaped; or its situation, that is, being in this place or that, in reference to other parts or particles of matter: or its motion to one part or another. Now, none of these can make the power of thought to be any way at all compatible to matter: for it must be grossly absurd to imagine, that if matter be of such a size, such a bigness, now it is true, being of such a size, it cannot think; but if it were a little bigger, or a little less, it could think. And then, again, if you speak of the figure of it, if it be round, it cannot think; but if it were square, or triangular, it would; how absurd is such a conception or imagination as this! So likewise, to think that motion should endow it with a power of thought is most absurd; that, being here, it could not think, but carry it there, and then it can think. Or to think that situation could give it that capacity. And you cannot think or conceive any thing of matter but one of these. Now if any of these cannot contribute to make it have a power of thought, to make a mind of it, I say, since there were minds that were not of themselves from all eternity, and could not be made out of matter, then those minds were made out of nothing. And if minds were made out of nothing, why not matter as well as minds? And that is a third consideration to evince the absurdity of that imagination of self-subsisting matter, from eternity, out of which the world must be supposed to be made. And,

(iv.) It will be further proved from hence, not only to be absurd, but blasphemous; that is, that it would make God to be a finite being. That was intimated another way before, but it will also appear this way that is now offered to your consideration. That is the only reason that is pretended, why there must be self-subsisting matter, because God cannot make something out of nothing; and so that he had not power in himself of creating matter: and then he cannot be understood to have in himself infinite power, or to be himself, virtually, the all-comprehending Being. But most certain it is, that the name God, doth comprehend all;—as even the significancy of that title Pan, given to the god among the pagans did import, that he was virtually all things; that is, that there is virtually, nothing which is not comprehended in the most perfect excellency of his being. And therefore, if matter be something, if it be a real something, then it must be comprehended within the virtual power of the divine power: otherwise, that is not all-comprehending, and that it should not be so, is repugnant to the very notion of God, a Being of infinite perfection in himself. If he be such, then he comprehends this perfection in himself, the power of making matter, as it is a greater perfection, sure, to be able to do this, than to be, as to this, impotent. And then,

iii. A third absurdity which is conjunct with no less blasphemy too, which they are cast upon who deny the creation, at first, to have been out of nothing; and that is the conceit of many of the stoics of old, and which hath been taken up by some more lately is, that God made things out of himself. Not meaning, nor referring as the efficient, as the agent, (as we all do) but to himself as the *subjectum ex quo, the subject out of which* things were made. So that all the creation, and the greatest sorts of creatures, they are several parts of God, so and so diversified. But to this, nothing more needs to be said than,

(i.) That the Divine Being is simple, impartable, uncapable of division into parts: it is inconsistent with the perfection of God, that it should be otherwise: and,

(ii.) The Divine Being is the most perfectly spiritual Being, the most purely and perfectly spiritual; and therefore material things were never made out of it. For it is altogether as impossible to turn a spirit into matter, as it is to turn matter into spirit.

Something I would say by way of *Use*, before I go off from this head, and proceed to the other, the manner, here, as ascertained how we come by this notion of the creation; that is, faith. Pray make this reflection, upon what hath been already said: If this creation could originally come out of nothing, then let no doubt, I beseech you, trouble your minds about a new creation. Did God, at first, make heaven and earth, or make the worlds out of nothing? Sure he can as easily make a new world out of that ill state of things in which we now behold them, as he did the whole world, as now it is, out of nothing. If you will say, There are no appearances looking that way: if there shall be a new heaven, and a new earth, how can we admit that thought; when there are no appearances tending thereunto? Why, this world was first made out of things that did not appear. There were no appearances as to the creation of this world before it was made: what if there be no appearance, nay if there be contrary appearances, if things look quite another way, and with a quite contrary face and aspect? What is all that to Him who, at first, made heaven and earth with a word? It would greatly facilitate our faith, if we did this, if we did but consider these two things: first of all, the greatness, and secondly, the facility of this work of God. The greatness of it, so vast a thing and so great a thing as this world is; and the facility of his doing: he spake and it was done; as the Psalmist expresses it; *Dictum factum*, As soon as it could be spoken, Let such a thing be! and it was, "Let there be light, and there was light;" Let there be heaven and earth, and they were. So to make a new heaven, and a new earth, when the season thereof comes, is equally easy, as all things are equally easy to Him that can do all things.

LECTURE XII.*

Before we proceed to the next head, it remains only to consider somewhat that is wont to be *objected*, by such as too much indulge a litigious temper and disposition of spirit, against the one and the other of these acts; the putting things into this order wherein we find them, and the bringing of things into being that were nothing before.

1. There are that do *object* against that act, which is here expressed in our English, by the name of framing of worlds, the putting things in them into the order which we now behold. That is, It is objected, that if this order which we see in the universe, were the effect of divine wisdom and design, it would be certainly much more accurate than we find it; things would be done with more exactness, there would not be so many defects as we see in the universe. It seems not to be congruous (such do imagine) to the wisdom of God, that he should undertake the settling of an order in this creation, and that it should, in such respects as have been mentioned, and many other, be liable to so much exception. And to this, there are several things to be said. As,

(1.) That it is very true, indeed, the order of things would be more exact, and accurate than it is, if it had been God's design to make every creature, and the whole frame of things as perfect as he could have made it. But we have no reason to imagine that that was any thing of his design. He did not make it to answer our purpose, but his own, all being to run into an eternal state of things at last, and this temporary state to be of short continuance. And therefore, let such as do think, there should have been greater exactness and accuracy in this frame of things, (if this will not satisfy them) sit down and wonder, that when it was intended, one time or another, such creatures as they, should be raised up into being in the world, that God did not put things into better order for their entertainment, that he did not make every thing more exactly to answer their fancies, appetites, and humours. But,

(2.) It is enough to the purpose here asserted, that the worlds were framed by the Word of God, by the Eternal Logos, that did predetermine the order of things, and by a powerfully exerted word, in the time and season, when things were to exist and come forth into being. I say, it sufficiently answers what

* Preached July 8, 1693.

is here asserted, if it doth appear that all things were done with design, and so as that they could not be done by any wisdom or power less than divine. This is enough for our purpose, that there are characters of design upon the whole frame of things: but that such a design as this could never have been laid, nor could ever have been effected by any created wisdom or power whatsoever, for the wisdom we see in the contexture of the things which we behold, is no where, in the creature, accompanied with power capable of doing such things. Not to speak of things in particular, if you do but consider these two properties of things that are framed and made, either first, the magnitude of some, or the parvitude of others; (only to instance in those two,) as it is manifest there was a design, so it is equally manifest that no created agent could have done any thing like either of these. Either,

[1.] As to magnitude: the magnitude of the universe, what created agent could have made so vast a fabric as heaven and earth, as "the worlds?" which is the expression in the text. All created agency must confess itself outdone. Nothing is left us upon that account to consider, when we ask the question, How came there to be such worlds? It is resolvable by nothing else, but that the worlds were framed by the word of God. And then,

[2.] On the other hand, if you do but consider the parvitude of things, the many multitudes of things that have life: no created agent can contrive or do any such thing. Multitudes of little creatures, in the kinds of them, too little to be seen by our naked eye, but that by instruments may be seen to have their respective motive powers. And those that are capable of dissection, that there should be as many parts observable, for the several functions of life, in some of the minutest insects as are to be found in an elephant. It is plain, that a wise design there was in the framing of things as they are made, and that it is altogether impossible it should be done by any other but a Divine Agent: whether you consider the magnitude or the parvitude of things that are made. And again,

(3.) There is this further to be considered as to this objection, that in looking upon, and taking notice of, the works of God, we are not to consider them abstractly and severally, but we are to consider them as parts of one entire whole, and in their reference to that. As a heathen philopher, among the Greeks, tells us, "If we should make a judgment of the whole work of creation by this or that less comely part of it, it were the same thing as if one would give an account what sort of creature man is, and take for instance and example, such a one as Thersites, or one of the most deformed of all men, and so give an account of the structure of the human body by such a one, that there would be as little cause of cavil, as he would have with a picture drawer, who should find great fault with him that he put not bright colours every where, that there are, any where, dark shadows to be found." This, and much more to this purpose, is discoursed by a heathen, for the vindication of God as to this thing, that there should be any thing of defect, or not the most absolute perfection to be found in every creature that we can look upon. And again,

(4.) It is further to be considered to this purpose, That we are to consider the time and texture of things in this universe, not barely as now it is, but as at first it was, and to consider what this inferior part of the creation, which was made for the use and service of man, was in its original state, when he was in his original state: that man for whom all this lower world appears to have been made, is become a degenerate creature, an apostate creature. And that, as he is gone very far from his original, things are very far gone from their original, in which they were made for him. The frame of this world is not like what it was. What changes there were in it for the sin of man, before the flood, we know not. But that must have inferred a universal change in all this earth. And we find, as to the point of longevity, things have altered apace and did gradually alter in that respect. So as in a short compass of time, in comparison, lives of seven or eight hundred years, or more, were come to sixty or eighty years, a very great, and hardly a tolerable age, all labour and sorrow. That sickness and mortality are come into this world, it is true: but who brought them in? They were sinners that introduced them. It is sin that hath so slurred the creation of God, as to that noble creature, and as to the subservient creature, proportionally. And,

(5.) It is further to be considered too, that God hath, since the first creation of things, settled an ordinary course of nature in the world, which ordinarily he doth not invert or alter, but for some very great purposes. As when, now and then, a miracle is to be wrought; otherwise, usually, he doth not interpose to change the course of nature, but lets things run on according to the tendency and current of second causes.

(6.) In the last place, as to this objection, this is further to be considered, that this is more an argument, that the order we find in things should proceed from God, that there is not such an accuracy in every punctilio to be beheld, than if it were so: that is, it is more suitable to the divine greatness. There is this, among men, to be observed, that according as they are of greater minds and spirits, they do less concern themselves about light and trivial matters. And they reckon a kind of rational neglect to be greater, to have more in it of majesty, more that doth beseem a great man and a great mind. They are little minds that do minutely concern themselves about trifles and small matters.

2. But again, there lies matter of *objection*, with some, against the other of these acts. The former, his putting things into order, the latter, his putting things into being. And with this, the objection that lies with divers, and hath done, in latter and former ages, is the authority of that maxim, *Ex nihilo, nihil fit*, that nothing can come out of nothing, and therefore, there can have been no such thing as a mere creation; which (as I told you) the act supposed, the act of framing of things: the order of things doth suppose the being of them. But this, say they, could never be, that that which was nothing should become something; for common reason doth allege, that out of nothing, nothing can be made, nothing will be nothing still, everlastingly.

But to them, I have only two things to *answer*—that herein they do mistake the maxim that they rely upon, and—that they contradict themselves.

(1.) That they mistake the maxim, upon the authority whereof they pretend to rely, that nothing can come out of nothing: for it can only imply these two things—that it is impossible for any thing to come out of nothing by itself, and—that it is impossible that any thing should come out of nothing by a created agent. In both these senses, the maxim is most certainly true.

[1.] That it is impossible, that any thing should come out of nothing of itself: that is evident to every understanding that reflects and considers. If we should but, in our own supposition, imagine, that there were nothing now at all in being of one kind or another, it is certain that to all eternity there would never be any thing in being: as we have had occasion to argue to you heretofore. We find that somewhat now is, and therefore, we are sure that something hath always been: for if there were any time when there was nothing, to all eternity there would be nothing. Because it is impossible that something should ever itself arise out of nothing. In that sense, the maxim is most indubitable; that it is impossible that something should arise out of nothing. And,

[2.] It is equally indubitable in this sense too, that a created agency, or all created agency put together, if it were all to be-exerted into one act, could never raise something out of nothing. But to bring the authority of this maxim against the omnipotent agency of the supreme and sovereign Cause, is the most absurd collection that can be thought. As if we could measure the Divine Agency by that of the creatures. It might every whit as well be said, that because a child newly born, cannot build a house or a city, that therefore, it can never be done, no agency could ever do it: and the difference is infinitely greater between God's agency and any creature's, than between that of the meanest and weakest creature, and that of the mightiest that can be supposed. This is to circumscribe omnipotency, and to deny omnipotency to be omnipotent, which is a contradiction. What greater contradiction can there be, than to deny a thing of itself, to say there is any thing that is not what it is? But it is no contradiction, that that which was not, should be made to be, that that which did not exist, should exist, and so to bring something out of nothing; for that is within the compass of the object of almighty power. And then, I *answer*,

(2.) As they that do so object, do most manifestly contradict the truth, so it is equally evident that they contradict themselves, in giving the account they do give of the original of things, such as it is. There are two sorts of them.

[1.] There are some; first, that will have all substance to be one, (such as Spinosa and his followers) and so to be uncreated, and that there is nothing created but the modifications of things. But as to them, I inquire whether these modifications were in that substance before, yea or no? If they were before, then they were not produced, and so nothing is produced. But if they were not in that substance before, (which they imagine) and yet be something, (as they cannot pretend them to be nothing) then this something is throughout of nothing: and they cannot but be compelled to own so much. And we find it actually to be, for we find things are modified so and so. And then,

[2.] There is a second sort, who do not make all substance to be self-existent and eternal, but only matter, as the passive subject, which the eternal, unmade Mind doth work upon.

But even they also, must be constrained to contradict themselves. And it will appear most evident, that they do so, the matter being pursued: for a mind is not made of matter; there is no kind of cognation between a particle of matter and a thought, and so between the whole of matter and of mind. A mind can never be made of matter, or out of matter. But there are minds that are made; our own, theirs, if there were any that were not always; and then, they must be made out of nothing, for out of matter they cannot be made. And so, as to that objection, the objectors are manifestly found, both to contradict the truth, and to contradict themselves; and we need concern ourselves no further with them.†

LECTURE XIII.*

Secondly. The second general head we now come to is, how or by what principle we are to understand all this. And for that, the text tells us, it is by "faith" that we are to understand it. How come we to know that this vast universe, these worlds, (which how many they are we cannot tell,) did all spring up into being by the word of God? How come we to be informed, or how are we informed of all this? Why it is by faith. Here, it is requisite to shew how this is to be taken, that we are by faith to understand the worlds to have been created by the word of God. Why,

It is not to be taken exclusively, as if it were to be understood no way, but by faith. It is plain, and hath been made plain, that it may be understood by reason too. And there is no prejudice at all in it, that the same conclusion should be capable of being proved by more arguments than one; and by more sorts of arguments than by one sort. Nothing is more ordinary, than to bring many arguments of one sort, of those we call artificial arguments, to prove the same conclusion: many such arguments may be useful to serve one and the same purpose: and it is no more inconvenient, and incongruous, that there should be arguments of more sorts than one, to prove the same thing, than that there should be many arguments used of one sort. Therefore, this is not to be understood exclusively, that we are to have the notice of the worlds being made by the word of God no way at all but by faith; or that we are to understand this by faith only: that the text doth not say, and we are not to take it so. But,

We are to take it thus, that is, that we are to understand this by faith more advantageously; not exclusively, but with

† Several things, by way of use, were at this time inferred: but the enlargement thereof, being on the entire use made on this act of God; what was now said, is to be found in the Lecture preached December 9, 1693. vide page 266.

* Preached November 25, 1693.

much more advantage than by any other way alone. My meaning is, that having plain, rational evidence of the creation, (as indeed we have such as is irrefragable, and as no mind which considers, can withstand) then, it is a great superadded advantage, to understand the same thing by divine Revelation too. It adds a great deal, to have the matter so stated, that I may also understand this by faith, that the worlds were made by the word of God.

And, I shall now shew wherein this great superadded advantage lies; and wherein, if we compare the two ways of understanding this by reason, and of understanding it by faith, this latter way hath the advantage, even of the other. For, first, we understand more of it by faith, than we can by reason; and, secondly, what we understand by faith, we understand better.

1. We understand more of it by faith, than by mere rational indagation or search, we could understand. We have a more circumstantial account of very important, considerable circumstances of this creation, as faith represents the matter to us, out of God's own Revelation, than by rational disquisition we could have had. We understand within what limits of time; and we understand in what order this work of creation was performed, by faith. Reason could never have informed us of either of these,

(1.) We understand within what limits of time this work was done, that is, that all was absolved within the space of six days: no reason could ever have informed us of that. But it signifies much towards the liveliness of any representation, that the matter be represented in its circumstances. Reason, in the gross, could only have informed us generally, that all these things which do appear, are not of themselves, and were, some time or other, raised up out of nothing, by an almighty, creative power; but it could never have informed us within what limits of time such a mighty work as this was done. But our faith in the divine Revelation informs us of that too. And then,

(2.) It informs us of the order in which things were produced, which no reason could ever have informed us of, or found out; that is, that on the first day, there being nothing at all but a disorderly chaos, (which must have been supposed first raised out of its primitive nothing) that God causeth a glorious light to spring out of that horrid darkness, that had every where spread itself over this chaos, this vast confused heap. He did but say the word, " Let there be light, and it was so."

And then, it informs us, that on the second day, God ordereth a firmament, dividing the waters, or the fluid matter that was superior, made up of finer particles, from that which was inferior and more gross: the one, being designed for a nobler kind of use, and the other, for meaner services and purposes.

And then, we are informed, again, that on the third day, God made, in this inferior world of ours, dry land and sea to appear, severally divided, and separate one from another, and distinct. And, that, as to the dry land, God doth implant in it the seminal principles of all sorts of vegetation, to make it capable of serving its after uses and purposes.

And then, on the fourth day, all these glorious lights are made to appear, and shine forth in the firmament, that are ever since observable and conspicuous in the world.

And then, on the fifth day, he replenisheth this earth with all those sorts of sensible animals that we find it inhabited with, and by which they are so much the more to be fitted for the habitation and use of man.

And then, on the sixth day, he makes man, and brings him forth into this orderly and so well prepared world; all things being fitted and accommodated to his use and purpose, as was most suitable and congruous; and gives him dominion over all; as the matter is so copiously, and with admiration of God, represented to us in that 8th psalm.

And then, that having thus, in six days, absolved and finished all this great and glorious work, he now sanctifies, and hallows, and blesses, the seventh day. The Lord himself, (as it were) resting with complacency in the view of his own work, finding it to be good, and answering to the complete, eternal idea which lay in his own all-comprehending Mind. He beholds, with complacency, all that he had done, and so takes up that satisfying rest that was suitable to a God, in the contemplation of his own work. He did it with delight and pleasure; and now beholds it with delight and pleasure done. And so, takes man (the creature, here in this lower world, which he had made capable thereof) into communion and participation with him, in this blessed rest of his: upon which is founded the law of the sabbath.

Now, all these things that could not otherwise have been known to us, but by divine Revelation, and our faith therein, God, telling us that things were so and so, and we believing him, and relying on the truth of his word therein, He did graciously provide that those things should be made manifest; that they should be made known to the children of men, in succeeding times, by casting all into sacred records. Though, that, indeed, were not done till a considerable time after this beginning of all things; yet, till it was done, the knowledge of these things was more easily transmitted or conveyed; three or four men, having seen all from the beginning of the world, and so were capable of telling one another, until the time when these things were capable of being transmitted into sacred records; these records themselves giving an account of those particulars that were transmitted, from hand to hand, by three or four of those that lived, successively, nearest to the beginning of time, who seeing and knowing, might tell one another.

And we have these notices, all of us, from God, that thus these worlds began. And, indeed, if such a notification of these things, did but now first arrive to us; if there were but one such manuscript in being, that should give this account of the first rise and production of all things, and it were sufficiently attested and proved to be divine, of how great value and account would it be! Your great antiquaries, that have been so highly pleased in searching into the ancientest original of things, what would not one of them have given for such a monument of antiquity as this, informing us distinctly, from point to point, how all things came into being, and in that order wherein they now lie to our notice and view? The price thereof, would be above that of rubies, and all that could be desired, would not be compared therewith.

That is one thing, whereby this understanding, by faith, the creation of the world, hath its advantage over any other way of coming to the knowledge or notice of it: that is, that we know more of it, by faith, than we could do any other way. And,

2. What we do know, we know better. It is a better way of knowledge, or we may know better this way, to speak of the one and the other, comparatively, in several respects. As,

(1.) It is an easier way of knowledge, than that of rational search and disquisition. There must, in order to that, to know things so, be usually a laborious inquiry into the reference of one thing to another. There must be an adaption of a frame and series of consequences and deductions; some whereof may be more obscure, but leads us gradually into clearer light; step by step. This is a more painful way of understanding things: it requires a very great exercise of mind to know many things by the deduction of a long series of consequences, one following upon another; and which the minds of men, generally, are less apt for, in this low and lapsed state of man.

But how easy a thing is it, to have such a matter told us, by One who, we are sure, will not deceive us, and cannot deceive us? and then, to believe it, and take his word that so it is? This brings us to a satisfaction about this matter presently, and with the greatest facility. It is true, indeed, that as to this particular point of the creation, the matter is most plainly demonstrable; and very soon, to any capable and apprehensive mind: but if men were left to themselves, though they may be capable of discerning things represented to them in their dependencies, one upon another, they would not so easily find it out of themselves; and, therefore, as this is far the more easy way of knowing, so,

(2.) It is a way, too, by which the thing may be more commonly known: so far as the divine Revelation doth obtain and extend, it may be more commonly known. Very true, as I told you, it may be demonstrable, most plainly, to an intelligent, apprehensive, unprejudiced person, that this world was raised up out of nothing, by divine power. But as there are few that have ever made it their business, so far to cultivate their minds, as to be capable of demonstrating this to themselves; so there are few, that have opportunity of consulting with those, who will take the pains, (having acquired so much knowledge themselves) as to make such a demonstration to them; so as that, with the most, it goes but as a matter of opinion. But few, if they were put to it, are able to prove that this world had its rise thus, at first. But now, if it be to be believed, as a matter of divine Revelation, so far as that divine Revelation doth obtain, every one may presently be informed; and so this knowledge would become as much more common, as it is much more easy:—every one can read, or hear this read, to wit, the account that Scripture gives concerning the original of things: and so this knowledge, by this means, shall not be confined to a few, as it would be confined to a few, if none could come to the knowledge but those whose minds are sufficiently cultivated, so as to be capable of demonstrating this to themselves, or of apprehending well the demonstration made of it by others. And again,

(3.) It is a much clearer and more satisfying way, as well as it is more easy and more common. When the understanding of this matter is grounded this way, it is more satisfying to the mind; it makes things much more clear. They are but dark, and confused, and indistinct notices that we could have had in a rational way, of the beginning of things. But to be told this, from point to point; how all things were produced at first, and brought forth into that being, and order, wherein we behold them; what a satisfaction is it to an inquiring mind, to have such notices of these things!

How much hath the matter been otherwise, with those that have been destitute of divine Revelation, in this matter, and who could not discern the state of this affair by faith. How conjectural have their apprehensions been; and how wild and exorbitant their conjectures, even concerning their own beginning. Man is nearest to himself: and if one would inquire concerning the beginning of things, one would inquire first of all, and chiefly, How did we begin? How came it first to be, that there should be such a creature as man here in this world? Those that have not had the help of divine Revelation, so as to be capable of understanding the matter by faith, as their apprehensions have been conjectural, so their conjectures have been the most strangely disorderly, inordinate, that could be thought; some imagining, that men were thrust out, at first, in little bags out of this earth, having been formed there: others have apprehended, that they were begotten in the bellies of fishes; (these were the conjectures of the great philosophers in the former ages of the world,) and by those fishes exposed and thrown out upon the earth. But to have an account given us, by the word of God, so plainly, how satisfying it is to the mind of an inquiring man! All dubious hallucinations about this matter, come now to be decisively and plainly represented, so as here is no more place left for dubious, and uncertain conjecture in the case. But this was the determination of heaven; and according to the determination of heaven, the thing was done. "Let us now make man:" and so God made man: "In his own image male and female created he them." Here is an expedite, clear, and satisfying account how we had our beginning. And then,

(4.) This way of understanding, by faith, the beginning of things, the creation of all things, is much more impressive; which is the greatest, and most important thing of all the rest. It is more easy; it is more common; (where divine Revelation obtains,) it is more satisfying; and, lastly, more impressive; more apt to make deep, and suitable, and useful impressions upon our mind and heart. By faith, we understand, that is, to make the thing enter into our souls. That notice of such a thing, of so great importance to us, which is by faith, transforms the subject; moulds it into a suitable frame towards the Creator, towards itself, and towards its fellow-creatures, especially, those of the same order and kind. Here will be corresponding impressions made by faith: whereas, mere rational knowledge of the same things, makes very little, or that, that is, at best, but faint and languid.

And the matter is very plain, that till faith comes, it is but an empty, notional knowledge, which people have of God's Creator-ship; and of their own creature-ship: of God, as their Creator, and of themselves as his creatures. It is but a slight, superficial knowledge that any have of these things, till faith comes: that carries a transforming power with it, so as to work the truth revealed, and believed, into the very inwards of our souls. And it is more impressive, the knowledge and understanding even of this matter, which comes by faith, upon several accounts.

[1.] Because the ground of this my faith, is distinctly and immediately divine. I believe such a thing, as God reveals it, because it is reported to me upon the authority of God, which carries a mighty awe with it, upon the soul, and so makes the thing revealed and believed, the more impressive. I attend to God in the matter, the authority of God. If I believe such a thing, with a divine faith, it strikes my soul, and carries the matter to my heart. And again,

[2.] The notice that I have by faith, of these things, is very agreeable to an apprehensive mind; and so it enters in the more. Look to the matter really, as it is revealed, and the substance of the divine Revelation, concerning this matter, is congruous, and suitable to the mind and spirit of a man. There lie no unanswerable exceptions against it. The knowledge that comes by rational inquiry, and search, admits of objections: when the matter is to be wrought out by mere ratiocination, there will be reasons *pro* and *con*; arguments on the one hand, and arguments on the other hand: and many things that may seem reasonable to one, will not seem reasonable to another. But, as to what we are here required to believe about this matter, or what is matter of faith in this case, there is nothing in it but what is very congenerous to an apprehensive and unprejudiced mind, that is willing to know the truth of things. It may be, there is what should never have been found out, or known, if it had not been told: but to a considering mind, the thing appears to be just as it is told it is. I should not have thought of it before; but now I am told of it, it is very agreeable it should be so. And things do impress the more, accordingly as they are more suitable to them, they are the more easily received, there is less of obstruction lies against them. And,

[3.] The notice we have of such things by faith, is the more impressive, for that this very faith itself is a divine principle, immediately divine, implanted, inwrought into the heart by the Divine Spirit. We find faith reckoned among the fruits of the Spirit. Gal. 5. 22. And we read of such a thing as the spirit of faith. 2 Cor. 4. 13. The Divine Spirit, when it comes to new-create, to raise the new creation, amongst all the necessary principles of the divine life that are now to be implanted in this new creature of God, there is faith, that great receptive principle, by which it is to take in all light and gracious influences from him. The very principle itself, is from God; and therefore, the discoveries that are made by it, must needs be so much the more deeply impressive upon the soul, because, that faith by which the impression is made, is immediately a divine thing. And, then,

[4.] If you look to the act of faith, or its more immediate and connatural effect, it must be more impressive: faith, being described by its most appropriate act, or by its immediate effect, is called, "the substance of things hoped for, and the evidence of things not seen:" expressions that represent faith to us as looking forward and backward, as what goes so immediately before the text in this same chapter. Hope, that always refers to somewhat future, is that by which we have the prospect of futurities; faith is the substance of those hoped for things, those futurities; that is one expression of the work of faith, to substantiate future things that we do but hope for. And, then, there is another work of it, or its work is otherwise expressed: it is, "the evidence of things not seen:" and that is larger and more extensive, and represents faith to us as a principle that can look backward as well as forward. We do not see how this world was raised out of nothing: no matter for that, we can believe it; faith will be to us the evidence of that we never saw, or have not seen: faith will (as it were) place us upon the verge of this world: and let us see, as if we had stood by, when God did, in this orderly way, raise up this creation, part by part, out of a disorderly chaos, and heap of confusion, wherein all things lay. If we have that obediential subjection to the divine authority, revealing things, (which subjection, faith doth involve and carry in it,) this faith serves us instead of eyes; doth the same thing (being the evidence to us of things not seen, or of what we never saw) as if we had been by as spectators, when God was doing this great and mighty and noble work; one thing raising up after another into view before our eyes. Faith shews all this with evidence, and, therefore, is much the more impressive: so that, after the hearing of such a discourse as this, if it be entertained by faith, we should go away with hearts deeply impressed, having God in all the glorious excellencies of a Creator in view before our eyes; and our own spirits formed as dutiful, loyal, dependant, subject creatures, all full of adoration and praise; so as continually to behold him, and his fulness, filling all in all, which way soever we look or cast our eye: and that is the general use indeed which is to be made of all this.

LECTURE XIV.*

And now, it is the particular *Use* of the whole which we are next to come to. And you see the heads of discourse, hitherto, have been two; and so we shall have two things to improve by way of use, that is, first, that we are to understand the worlds to have been made by the word of God: and, secondly, that we are to have this understanding by faith. Each of these do claim their distinct improvement. And,

1. For the former. This is a matter to be understood, that these worlds were made, created; that this great universe which comprehends all the worlds, (we do not know how many the text means; but we noted to you, that it is not the dual number that is used here, but the plural,) is, most undoubtedly, a made thing. That the worlds were made, this we do understand. And we learn from thence,

(1.) That the world was not eternal, that it had a beginning. This hath, on the by, been hinted before, and we have formerly proved this to you in itself; and, I think, sufficiently. We now consider it as an inference, that, because it hath been created, therefore, it was not eternal; therefore, it some time began. Indeed, this inference hath been doubted, and disputed by philosophers, whether it were good and strong, yea or no, that, because the world hath been created, therefore, it cannot have been eternal, but must have begun. Some have imagined, that it might be dependently eternal, notwithstanding its being a created thing. Some such as grant it to be a creature, have yet imagined also, that it might be, in a way of dependance, eternal. But in truth, the question would only need to be distinguished, and then it would be soon and easily answered: for that supposed dependance upon a cause, must be understood to be, either upon a necessary cause, necessarily acting and producing such an effect, or upon an arbitrary cause. If we should suppose this world to have been from God, as the necessary Producer of it, that would make this world itself to be a necessary being, and would be simply inconsistent with its being a creature. All necessary being must be divine, must be God; whatsoever is necessarily, can be no

* Preached December 9, 1693,

other than God. But if it be meant of dependance on God as an arbitrary cause, considering an act of the divine will to intervene; that is, that it was his perfect choice whether the world should be, or not be, so it is impossible it can have been eternal, dependantly eternal, if the matter were determinable by divine pleasure. Shall this be, or not be? that supposeth it some time not to have been. It supposeth a *transitus* from not being to being; but that it is impossible it should be eternal; for there can be no change in eternity. That of which eternity is spoken, must have been always what it is, and as it is. Therefore, nothing can be more manifest, than that this world began: its being, depended upon the divine word, upon his pleasure: for that is the notion that the Scripture gives of the creation: "for thy pleasure all things are and were created." Rev. 4. 11.

And that should be a measure to us, how we are to conceive of this universe of things. Be it, or they, (the things contained in it) as great as we can imagine; let our thoughts be enlarged and raised as much as is fit, or they are capable of, upon such a subject,—the greatness and vastness of this universe: yet presently think, once this was all nothing, raised up out of nothing, sprang from nothing. It is a mighty disgrace upon created being, once to have been nothing. This is a disgrace upon created being, which it is fit it should bear; all shrinking into nothing before him who is the *All*. Magnify it to yourselves as much as you will or can, yet presently think it back into nothing: great it is indeed; but once it was nothing, mere nothing. It began to be, and therefore, there was a vast, immense duration wherein it was not, wherein there was no such thing.

And, moreover, the worlds, in that frame wherein we behold them, cannot have been eternal: for it would be the most absurd contradiction, and nonsense, imaginable, to say, that in this changeable state, wherein things are, they could be from eternity. It is a manifest contradiction to the understanding of any body, that would use his thoughts, that there should be eternal changes. And pray consider it. It may seem a little dark and obscure to you at first hearing, but stay a little upon it in your thoughts, and there is not any here of so mean capacity, but if they would use their thoughts a little, they may easily apprehend it impossible that there can be such a thing as an eternal change. Now there is in this world a continual succession, and a succession of changes. As to things that have life, to instance, there we see a continual succession of living and dying amongst all things that have life, and come under our view from day to day. But it is altogether impossible that there can have been such changes from eternity; for there can be no death; but there must have been life before: nothing can be said to die, that did not live. But to suppose any such change from eternity, an eternal change from life to death, it is a contradiction in itself; one must be first in its place; life must be first; and if life were eternal, it could never die; what lies under the measure of eternity must be always as it is. *Eternum non patitur novum*, there can be nothing new in eternity. And, again,

(2.) As it is manifest, that this universe, these worlds, were not eternal, but began to be; so it is also manifest, that it did not begin to be by any kind of chance or fate. Some, who have admitted this world not to have been always what it is, in that order we behold it, yet thought, that it came, by a sort of casualty into this state we now see it. That matter having always been of itself, (as they absurdly imagine) they have thought that the eternal motion of this matter, the various rollings to and fro, of it, have at last produced this strange and orderly frame of things which we behold. But nothing is more plain, than as this world is a late thing, in comparison; for there was a vast, immense duration wherein it was not; and in comparison of which it is but lately come into being; so that, when it did come into being, it was brought forth, into that being, by a designing cause.

The word, in the text, is emphatically enough expressive of that; it was brought into that exact and accurate order, wherein we see things lie, designedly, as the greek word here used, implies; as the several parts and limbs of a body are joined together, so as to consummate and make up one orderly frame. Order is the effect of design; wisdom is the parent of order. To behold that orderly frame of things which is observable to every eye in this universe of created beings, doth sufficiently shew, that it was not chance, but most profound wisdom, that hath brought things into this state wherein they are.

That is most plain; that is, if the worlds were made, they are not eternal, but did begin; so that they did not begin without design. The wisdom of him that did design this orderly frame of things, ought to be discerned, acknowledged, and adored; and a continual disposition of heart to adore it, ought to be habitual to us, and often going forth into actual exercise. It hath been the constant frame of holy ones of old, and we should take heed of letting it be an alien thing to us. "Lift up thine eyes on high, and consider; Who hath made all these things," that we behold, in so much lustre, and beauty, and glory, over our heads? who hath made them, and produced all the hosts of heaven, and called them by name? " When I consider the heavens, the work of thy hands," (saith the psalmist) when I do, (it implies he did it often, that it was his wont,) then, I say, "What is man that thou art mindful of him?" Look to such places as I relate to, that Isaiah 40, 26 and psalm 8. throughout, and many more. It should be more our business to contemplate and admire the unsearchable wisdom of God, in the creation of this world. The great exercise and argument it is of a holy heart, that wherein it doth exercise itself, and by which it discovers itself to be such. Again,

(3.) We may learn hence, the meanness and poverty of all creature-being, even upon the account of its being such; created and made. The worlds were made. As that doth argue them all, once, not to have been, so it argues them still to be next to nothing, continually depending. What was not of itself, cannot continue to be by itself: that which was drawn forth out of nothing, by an almighty power, still needs the continual exercise of the same power, to keep it from a relapsing, and sliding back into nothing again; which otherwise it must soon do. Sin being come into the creation, there needed a mediator, for this purpose, that all might not be thrown back into nothing again: "By him all things consist." Col. 1. 17. It is he that upholds and bears up the pillars of a tottering world; even where it was not obnoxious to justice, to a divine *nemesis;* yet, as being created, the mere liability, its dependableness, (which is proper to all created beings as such,) must have rendered it continually liable to relapse into nothing, if not continually upheld.

You see hence, therefore, by the way, what an ungodly creature hath to trust in; what he hath, for the final object of his trust, to wit, that which is every moment ready to *mutare*, to drop into nothing, to go out of being, that is only sustained momentarily by him that made it. This is all that a wretched soul, that is off from God, hath to rely upon, to trust in; nothing but creature; nothing but that which itself is next to nothing: all such a one's dependance is upon that which doth itself, too, depend. He that hath not a God to trust, to rely upon, what doth he depend upon? Let him but name it to you; be it what it will, God it is not. Alas! mistaken man! thou dependest upon that which depends, itself: and how miserable a case art thou in? Indeed, the vanity of creature dependance, is obvious to every man's thoughts, that will but allow himself to think. But the wickedness of it, is but a little thought of: few think of that. Any man may apprehend how vain a thing it is to place confidence in a creature that is next to nothing: but it enters into the minds of but few to consider how wicked a thing it is. You must know, that to be the final Object, is the divine peculiarity of the Deity; and one of the highest, and most appropriate: a glory that he will not impart. As to he prayed to, to be invocated, that is but secondary to this of his being trusted in: we trust first, and then invocate. This is a glory that he will not give to another. It is a homage due to Deity, which belongs to God alone, to be, I say, the final Object of trust; he, into whom my trust doth ultimately resolve. I know there may be a subordination; you may trust in a friend, in a relation: but for the final, supreme Object of trust, it is the highest, supreme worship of the Deity, to be placed only upon him.

And therefore, it doth not only infer misery by disappointment, when a man trusts in a creature; but it infers a curse by revenge. It is not only an infelicity, that doth befal a man in such a case, when he doth expect that which is not to be had, from that which affords it not; but it is a wickedness, that is followed with a divine curse, with a just *vindicta*, for a wrong and injury done to him; that is, that I place upon a creature, that which is peculiar and belongs to him alone; and so, I do not only punish myself as a foolish, mistaken creature; but God punisheth me as a sinful, guilty creature, upon this account: " Cursed be the man that trusteth in man, and maketh flesh his arm." Jer. 17. 5. But, alas! how many do place their trust in ignobler creatures than man is, in things beneath man? So much the meaner and baser is the temper of their spirits herein, to place a reliance upon that which is meaner than themselves. To neglect and forsake, to avert and turn off from God: and then sink beneath themselves, creep to an inferior creature, this calls for the blast of heaven upon such a one that hath "forsaken God, the Fountain of living waters, to dig to himself broken cisterns, that can hold no water." For which the prophet (Jer. 2. 12, 13.) doth call heaven and earth to behold, with astonishment, as witnesses of such folly and wickedness as this; especially as being found in a people pretending to God. " My people, they that call themselves my people, have committed these two evils, to forsake me the Fountain of living waters, and dig unto themselves broken cisterns that can hold no water." When a man lets his heart unite, by trust, in that which hath nothing in it, forsaking the All for that which is of itself nothing; and which in itself cannot be a moment, what folly and wickedness is this!

This is the snare that carnal, worldly-minded men run themselves into, and do not consider it as a deadly one; it is a snare of death: " Charge them that are rich in this world, that they trust not in uncertain riches, (the lubrious things, the uncertain things of riches, as the words admit to be read, (1 Tim. 6. 17.) but in the living God, who gives us all things richly to enjoy." That trust which is not reposed on the living God, it is not only the greatest folly, but the highest iniquity: folly lies in it, that they place Deity upon a nullity, a mere nullity. That which thou makest the final object of thy trust, is thy god; and, then, likewise, that trust is idolatry. God will be jealous in this case, when his rival is set up in his place; when a creature is made his rival; and the little minute things in this creation are made to fill up his room, and to be to thee instead of God.

Naturally, every one affects to be happy, and when this is the natural tendency of a man's spirit, that it is now quiet, in some measure quiet, either in the possession of what he hath got, or in the probable hope of getting more; and of having within one's compass, that which one doth desire and covet, and reckon most suitable: here is my felicity, and I am so far quiet, because, I think here I have enough. As he is brought in, in the parable of the wicked fool, saying, " Soul take thy rest, thou hast goods laid up for many years." That which he had in his barns, that was his god; and now he thought his soul should rest, as thinking to have enough no where but there. Alas! thou fool, thy soul will be gone from thee this night, and then what will become of thee, and all these? What folly it is to set a man's heart upon such things: as the heart is set by trusting upon any thing. Trust fixeth it, as in its own place, as is spoken concerning trust in God; " His heart is fixed, trusting in the Lord." Trust, is that which fixeth a man's heart. But thou dost fix thy heart like a fool, who fixeth it upon any thing unfixed itself: for then what becomes of thee and thy trust, when that is gone? So do they who trust in uncertain riches; for " riches make themselves wings and fly away, as an eagle to heaven."—A strangely emphatical expression! It may be the soul would say to itself, " Shall my wealth, and my riches be gone? why, I intend they shall have no wings." Alas! they make themselves wings: they will not be beholden to you for wings; they will be gone of themselves, though you would never so fain they would stay. And there is an expression that is likewise strangely emphatical, and which is very proper to our present purpose, of setting the heart upon that which is not. All created being is so poor a dependant being, that it is next to nothing, and is rather fit to be called a mere nullity, a mere nothing; and that so despicable a thing should be put into the place of God! should supply the room of Deity: O! what an indignity is this to the Majesty of heaven; and how severely to be reproved! Because there is nothing else stable besides God; when the soul is once off from him, it offers to fix, but cannot be fixed; because its object is not fixed. Therefore, heathen light hath seen this, and a most significant expression was it of a heathen. "That a soul off from God, is like a cylinder upon a plain, that moves necessarily and perpetually, cannot be fixed, but continually rolls and moves this way and that; and cannot be otherwise, for it hath nothing to fix upon." And, again,

This lets us see the absolute independency of the Divine Being; for what is there without himself for him to depend upon? These worlds are all that can be thought of *extra Deum*, without God; and they were all made by him. Can he depend upon that which he himself made? The worlds were created by the word of God; therefore, his being must be absolutely independent. And herein we should give our thoughts scope, it is pity we do not do it oftener, and more designedly, to consider the difference between that which is of itself, and which is not of itself. We might even lose ourselves and be swallowed up in the contemplation, to think of a Being, that, by its own peculiar excellency, could never not be, to which it was impossible not to be; which was not beholden to any thing; for all things were beholden to it.

How is the great God magnified before our eyes, upon this account, in that 40 chap. of Isaiah, in several verses of it together, from the twelfth verse and onwards. "Who hath measured the waters in the hollow of his hands, and meted out the heavens with a span, and comprehended the dust of the earth in a measure, and weighed the mountains in scales, and the hills in a balance." Who is he that hath done all this? The "who is he?" there, is not an expression of doubt; but of admiration and wonder. O! what a One is he! How glorious a One that hath done so! "Who hath directed the Spirit of the Lord, or being his counsellor, hath taught him? With whom took he counsel, and who instructed him, and taught him, in the path of judgment?" Who had he to commune with, besides what was himself, in going about this mighty work of creation? Who prompted him, who suggested it to him? "Come now make a world, give being to a creation." No! all was *proprio motu*. Who instructed this Spirit of God, as to this great affair of the creation, or any thing else that he doth? "Who doth all things after the counsel of his own will! Behold the nations are as the drop of a bucket, and are accounted as the small dust of the balance; behold he taketh up the isles as a very little thing, and Lebanon is not sufficient to burn, nor the beasts thereof sufficient for a burnt-offering. All nations before him are as nothing, and they are accounted to him less than nothing and vanity. To whom then will you liken God? or what likeness will ye compare unto him?"

So should we, upon this account, greaten to ourselves the Divine Being, and heighten and raise our own thoughts and apprehensions concerning him: that when all things else, of this vast universe of beings, are so absolutely and purely dependant every moment upon him, he, in the mean time, depends upon nothing. All that he is, he is in, of, and by, and for, himself. He can have no dependance upon the creature, either for the support of his being, or for any other addition to his felicity: but is his own All. And how convictively doth the apostle reason with those philosophers at Athens, to this purpose, Acts 17. 24. 25. "God dwelleth not in temples made with hands, nor is he worshipped with men's hands as though he needed any thing, inasmuch as he hath given to all, life and breath and all things." And what can you add to this? What support can he have from you? what improvement of his felicity any way from you, or from any thing else, since all things are his own creatures? And further,

(5.) You may learn, hence, the divine all-sufficiency; and how vast an amplitude of being there is in him, when all this great creation sprang from him; and yet, nothing could be detracted from him by it neither. How vast an amplitude of being must that be, when all this great creation is gone out from him, sprung from him, and yet his being not diminished, nothing the less! O! consider this, and think how great and desirable a thing it is, to have him for a portion; the All; he that comprehends in himself the all of the creature, and who formally possesseth his own All still: that is, is simply All. What can he want that hath him for his portion, who is All? All his own creation, it was virtually in him before, and is still virtually in him, depending still upon that power of his, for its sustentation, that gave it being at first. And there is his own infinite All too. O! happy that soul that can say, "The Lord is my portion." How rich, how full, how satisfying a portion! And,

(6.) We may, further learn hence, the absoluteness of God's dominion over all his creatures. Will you not allow him to do whatsoever he will in heaven and earth, who made both by his own word? Shall he not do what he will with his own? We are apt, most unreasonably and peevishly, to regret it when there is a disposal of creatures; or any little minute part of this creation of God, this way or that, any otherwise than we would. But how absurd it is to repine at God's disposition of his own! He gives more of this world to such a one, and less of it to me. What then? What he gives to me, and what he gives to the other, was it not all made by himself? And may he not dispose, as he pleaseth, with what he had made?

How doth he plead the matter with Job, to exalt his own dominion upon the ground of his creation? Job thought it hard that he who was so rich a man, so healthy a man, should be bereaved of all so suddenly, and of his health, and comforts of his life besides: "Why," says God to him, "Where wast thou when I laid the foundations of the earth? declare if thou hast understanding. Did I consult thee when I made this and that, and the other creature? And may I not dispose of the creatures I have made, my own way, and as I will?" And,

(7.) We may further learn, that if these worlds thus began, that is, were thus framed by the word of God; if they had such a beginning, even at his pleasure, then at his pleasure, too, we must reckon they will have an end. That which began to be at some time or other, it began to be what it is. Such and such things began to be at the pleasure of the great Creator: and at the pleasure of the great Creator they must cease to be what they are. And we ought not to think it strange, that there should be such an end determined for this world, as the Scripture informs us there is: that is, a time will come, at length, when, the purposes of the great Creator having been sufficiently served upon it, these visible heavens, which we behold, "shall be rolled up as a scroll; pass away with a great noise; and the elements melt with fervent heat; and the earth, and all things therein, be consumed and burnt up," as 2 Peter 3. 10. and we are not to think it strange. And it is only upon this ground, that it hath been thought strange, that this should be the end of this world, because the beginning of it was not understood, as we may see, looking in the same chapter, at the 3d and 4th verses: "Knowing this first, that there shall come in the last days, scoffers, walking after their own lusts; and saying, Where is the promise of his coming?" "It is talked of that he will come, and then an end will be put to time, and all the successions of time. But all things continue as they were from the beginning of the creation to this day. And therefore, we cannot imagine that there should be any such end." But (saith the apostle) "this they willingly are ignorant of, that by the word of the Lord the heavens were of old;" and because they are willingly ignorant of this, therefore, they are wilfully ignorant of that end which is determined concerning this world. They will not believe it, because they believe not its framing at first: "that by the word of God the heavens were of old, and the earth standing in the water, and out of the water." Because they do not believe the beginning of things, therefore, they will not believe that which is told them expressly, too, concerning the end of them.

There are a great many things more, that we might learn hence, but they will more immediately belong to the consideration of our own creatorship, than of the world: they do not so immediately result from the consideration of God's having made the world, as the consideration, more particularly, of his having made us; and therefore, I shall not insist on them till I come more particularly to speak to the creation of man from another text.

LECTURE XV.*

2. I shall, therefore, now proceed to make application of that second general head of discourse; that the more principal and advantageous way of our coming to understand the creation, is by faith. And it is a very manifold use that may be made of this. As,

(1.) We may learn from it, the excellency of faith; how soul-enabling a thing it is. It hath a certain power, with very great light, to help a man's understanding, and to clear his intellectuals. By faith we understand. It hath, in great part, its seat in the understanding: there it is originally, though it is not finally there; thence it descends, too, into the heart. But it hath a great work in the minds of men. Faith doth supply minds with notions; so it is if we would read the words literally to you. It doth furnish us with notions, which we should otherwise never have. It is true, if it be faith indeed, it will not let them always remain mere notions; it will inspirit them; it will make them vital, and powerful, and operative. But notions they must be first, and faith makes them so. By faith we have notions of things, that otherwise we never should have had. But this, I say, speaks faith to be

* Preached December 16, 1693.

a soul-enabling thing. It nobilitates the mind and spirit of a man; acquaints it with things from God, (for that is the business of faith,) unto which it would otherwise be a stranger.

This should raise and heighten our apprehensions of faith, that despised thing; that little understood thing. That by which we are to understand; men do not understand.

Whatsoever it is that divine Revelation doth, in order to the informing us of needful and useful things, that faith doth. And take we the compass of divine Revelation, and consider all the great and glorious things that are contained and brought to light in it, and by it, and thence you are to collect the excellencies of faith. Because, without that, the divine Revelation signifies nothing to us; no more than light doth to a blind man. The divine Revelation and faith, must both concur to the same effect, to wit, our understanding of things; as light and the eye do both concur to the same effect, our seeing of a thing. We cannot see by light without an eye; nor will an eye enable us to see without light, but both together. The divine Revelation, that is light to us; faith is the thing by which we discern things in that light. And so, if we do apprehend an excellency in the divine Revelation, which brings so many great and important things into view before us, we are proportionally to apprehend the excellency of faith too; without which all that divine Revelation could signify nothing to us. And,

(2.) We may further learn, hence, how wonderfully kind and gracious God's condescension is to us, that he should make such a discovery, and offer it to our faith, of things, in reference to which we should be at so great a loss, and understand so very little of: as for instance, this creation of God: what we do owe to the bounty of heaven for this, that it should condescend, so distinctly, to tell us how things came at first to begin. Faith, in that discovery which God makes to us of this matter, supplies the room and place of sight; and so it is the same thing in effect, as if he had let us see him making the world; for faith is the evidence, to us, of things we have not seen. We were not present, we were not by, when this mighty glorious work was done. "Where wast thou when I laid the foundations of the earth?" Where wast thou? saith God to Job: chap. 38. 4. But now, God having vouchsafed to us, such a Revelation and discovery of this mighty work of his; if he also gives us faith by which we believe this discovery, it is as if he had set us by him while all this was doing; so, we have (as it were) the idea, the representation, the landscape of the rising creation; as if God should before that time have created one of us, and have taken us, and set us up, spectators of his whole work.

Whereas, yet, there was nothing but horrid darkness spread every where, then for God to have taken one of us, made us stand up out of nothing, and said to such a one—"Come, cast about thine eye, there is nothing but vacuity, emptiness and darkness every where; come see me make light out of this darkness." He that calls things where they were not, and makes them be, or as if they were, saying, "Light, where art thou? come out of that dark, profound abyss;" and immediately it springs forth, what an amazing light were that! Why, faith in God's discovery gives you this light: by faith we come to be so intelligible, to have so much understanding about us, as to know how this world did rise out of nothing, eternal nothing, into that state in which now it is. And what vouchsafement is this to such as we, to do, in effect, the same thing, as if he had set us by him at making of the world. "Come see me collect a mass of grosser matter; see me (as it were) spin out of it that fine texture of the vast and spacious firmament, those heavens that do encircle this little habitable world in which we dwell; see me adorn it with sun, moon and stars; see arising on this earth, plants, and trees, and woods, and springs, and rivers: all lately nothing, and now begin to be: see me replenishing this world with living creatures, in their several varieties and kinds." O! what condescension is this, that God should vouchsafe to tell us all this over again, and give us the representation so distinctly, of what, in so many successive days, he did and wrought in this kind. But, again,

(3.) We may further learn, hence, how inexcusable it is, that they who pretend to faith in this matter, should use it so little. If we falsely pretend, it is a most unjust usurpation of a name, to call ourselves believers; and that, of such things, when we are not. But if we pretend truly and justly to the faith of these things, then we are most inexcusable to use that faith no more hereabouts; to live so long, in such a world as this, and so seldom to consider how it began. A strange and inexcusable stupidity. That this world should be replenished with intelligent creatures, reasonable creatures; and that it should come into the minds of so few, and into any minds so seldom to consider, How did all things begin? Sure we are there, where multitudes of things are existing, that must have had a beginning, that are not self-existent, or unto which existence is not essential, so, as that they could not but be and exist. It is amazing to think that intelligent creatures should not more frequently consider with themselves, how things first began to be, beholding such a world as this, which they are sure was not always, but had a beginning; and not consider how it began. That men can behold such varieties of creatures, and use such varieties, and enjoy such varieties, and never consider whence they are, whence came they, how came there to be such things in the world, and how came there to be such a world? It is most inexcusable and strange stupidity, and dotishness of mind, in any reasonable creature: but most of all in them that do pretend to believe and know by faith, that the worlds were created by the word of God. And,

(4.) We may, again, learn hence, that what is commonly called faith, about this matter, is really and indeed not faith: that is, the apprehension of such a thing as this, is without effect, and that impresseth nothing upon the soul. It hath been very justly and fitly told you, that we have the notions of things by faith, many things which we should otherwise have no notion of. But though faith first begets such notions, yet it will not let them continue mere notions long, if it be faith: that is a mighty, lively, operative principle, powerfully working in the soul, to form that suitably to the thing believed. But while there is so little of suitable impression upon the souls of men, in reference to this thing, what they call faith about it, is not faith, but must be something else.

For the most part, it is not any thing else but a negative faith, which men are wont to call faith in this and many other such cases. It is, I say, but a mere negative faith upon which they place that great name: that is, a not believing the contrary, not having formed explicit belief of the contrary, that they call faith. They have not yet (it may be) laid down in their minds any formed conclusions to this purpose, that the worlds were not made by the word of God; and their not disbelieving it, they call believing it: whereas, faith is a most positive thing, a thing of great reality, and a thing of great efficacy and power, wherever it is. And, therefore, for such as never yet found their souls impressed by their apprehensions of the world's creation, I would admonish them no more to call that apprehension of theirs by the name of faith, but call it something else,—call it by its true name,—call it a floating uncontradicted opinion; and that is the best they can make of it, while it is an apprehension that hath no power; and while it doth not represent God in his excellent glory, as the great Creator and Lord of all, so as to form the soul to adoration and subjection to him thereupon. Never say till then, that you do believe, or that you have faith concerning the creation of the worlds. Alas! how many that have it often in their mouths—"I believe in God the Father, Maker of heaven and earth"—yet do but usurp the words, "I believe," and their heart, and their practice, contradict their tongue, and tell them they believe it not. Believe it! yea, as much as a known romance, while they live in affront of the Creator, and take upon them as if they were lords of the creation; and as if they had made the worlds; and not He.

These things we may, by way of just inference, collect from hence; that it is a thing to be understood by faith, that the worlds were made by the word of God. But we shall thence proceed to some further *Use;* that is, to counsel and exhort those that have faith in this matter, to use it more; to have their faith more in exercise upon this great and noble subject, the creation of the worlds by the word of God. And it is to many great purposes, that faith upon this important subject may be employed and used. As,

1. To engage us in the more frequent and serious meditations on the beginnings of things. To engage us, I say, in the more frequent, more serious, more affectionate, and more fruitful meditation of this matter. If we believe it indeed, let us think of it often. Our faith is an apprehension that it is true: and if it be once owned to be true, it cannot but be deemed to be a very important truth; a very considerable truth; a truth that requires, and challenges, great attention of mind, and application of heart and soul to it. Think and judge it an unreasonable thing, to live from day to day, in this world, and never consider whence it came, and how it began. And let your faith be set on work in frequent and most affectionate meditations of the beginning of the worlds.

2. Let your faith, hereupon, form your souls into adoration of the great Creator. Go up and down this world with adoring souls: let every thing you behold, from time to time, put you in mind of him, and make you bow your head, and worship. Admire that fulness of his, that fills all in all; and those variable displays of his wisdom, and power, and goodness, which are conspicuous every where, more or less, in all sorts of creatures. We are but nominal believers and christians, if there be not many, if there be not much of this about us; and if we are not aiming and endeavouring that there may be more and more.

3. Let our faith instruct us unto the grateful and reverential use of the creatures of God, as remembering they are made things; and that we have the use of them by divine vouchsafement and allowance. There ought to be a mixture, a temperature of reverence and gratitude in the habitual frames of our

spirits hereupon: and if we have a real and true faith in us about this matter, it will make it to be so; it will impress our spirits; it will fill us (as it ought to do) with a wondering gratitude, that such creatures as we, should be so accommodated by such a world as this, so suitably ordered for us. If we use faith in this matter, it will make us sit down and wonder; look upon it as it is, an admirable thing, that the great God should have raised up such a creation, such a world, as this is, out of nothing, by the word of his power. That it being designed, "I, in time, coming to have a place and being in it, should want nothing while I am there; such and such creatures, made out of nothing to supply me, to furnish me. What is it that I eat? What is it that I drink? What is it that I wear? Are they not all the creatures of God? What is it that refreshes me? What is it that delights me? Are they not God's creatures?" How full of reverential gratitude should our hearts continually be, on this account! To think such and such parts of the creation were made on purpose that I might not be in distress, that I might not feel necessity; and to think how this world generally accommodates its inhabitants: and to wonder with all, that their apostasy was foreseen! O! how should it replenish our souls with wondering gratitude, to think that there should be such a provision made with design, and upon foresight, for the entertainment of rebels and apostates! This whole world replenished and filled with the divine goodness, all sorts of creatures made for the unthankful and the evil. A design laid through so many successions of ages, " My goodness shall diffuse itself, and flow in such and such a part of my creation, (as this world is but a little, a very little part of it,) for the supply and support of those that will never give me thanks, (though they have natures capable of doing so,) even for the unthankful and for the evil."

4. Our faith, upon this subject, should instruct and enable us to contend with difficulties in reference to whatsoever God hath encouraged us to expect, or told us he means to do. What can pose that faith which believes the creation of the world? He that could make such worlds as these are, out of nothing, by his word; what cannot he do? what is there to be expected greater than this, that should be the matter of any present solicitude, thoughtfulness, concern and care? If very perplexing thoughts of heart do arise about the ill state of things in this world, he that made heaven and earth, and all the worlds by his word, cannot he make new heavens and a new earth when he will, and when the time and season of it comes? How frequently may we observe it to be, in Scripture, for the

people of God, to animate and raise their own hearts unto the belief and expectation of great things from God, upon this ground, that he hath made heaven and earth, that he is the Creator of all things. "Our God hath made the heavens." When those vain creatures that dislike the divine government, and oppose themselves to it, taking counsel against the Lord, and against his Anointed, when, I say, they have nothing to trust to, in the designs of this kind, they are forming and driving continually; nothing but stocks and stones, the work of men's hands; "Our God hath made the heavens;" (so you have it expressed, Psalm 115. 3, 4.) made the worlds; given being to all these worlds: and what cannot he do, when his time and season for it are come? And things will come to their full issue in the fittest time. Our God it is, who hath power enough to do the things we expect, and wisdom enough to order the times and seasons for them. Again,

5. Our faith ought to have exercise with us, upon this subject, in order to the keeping of our minds quiet and composed, amidst the various expressions and instances that we behold of the divine dominion and sovereignty, doing what he will in the disposal of affairs in this world. It may be, some we find him exalting, and it pleaseth us; we find him depressing, and it displeaseth us; we have a little share and portion in this world, and we regret it: others have a great and large portion of it, and that we envy. But we should consider whose this world is, who made it. May not he dispose of what he hath made, as he pleaseth? This (as we noted to you before) is a just inference from the very thing itself, abstractly considered, that is, to form our spirits agreeably, and to make us content, and well pleased, that God does dispose of what he hath made, as seemeth good to him.

6. We should further learn, hence, to behold, with great complacency, what appearances there are of divine glory in this world, which he hath made by his word. And to behold, with just regret, the dishonours that he meets with in it; or that these appearances of his are so little taken notice of; and that such glory shines unregarded as to the most. These are but dutiful dispositions and affections towards the Creator and Maker of these worlds: and faith should furnish our souls with such dutiful affections; otherwise it is a fruitless faith, a lifeless faith, if it doth not do this. Do I believe that God made these worlds, by his word? how can it then but please me to behold his glory shining in such and such aspects and appearances of God? and how can it but fill my soul with such dutiful wishes? "O! may thy glory, more and more, be exalted

above the heavens, and shine through all the earth." And how can it but fill our souls with resentments, that there should be such glory shining, and not regarded? The great Maker and Lord of this world, excluded out of his own creation, as if the All in all did signify nothing! men taking upon them, every where, as if they were absolute, as if they had been self-created, and using the creatures of God at their own pleasure, and in affront to him that made them. If faith would do the part in our souls which belongs to it, it could not but fill them with regret, and with a dutiful concern, that the great Lord and Maker of this world, should be so little acknowledged, and taken notice of in it. Again,

7. The faith of the creation of the worlds, should engage our hearts in an earnest desire and endeavour to have a sure and clear interest in Him who created and made all. What doth this world signify to me, to behold it, to be in it, to be of it, a part of it, but to have nothing to do with him that made it? The faith of this, would make a soul restless till it can say, "The Lord of heaven and earth is my Lord." Were these worlds created by the word of God? then he shall be my God. He that could make such worlds as these, by his word, is it not a covetable thing to have an interest in him? Is it not desirable? Can I satisfy myself till I have it? especially, when I find it is matter of hope, a thing not to be despaired of; when there are such notifications of his pleasure, (that he is inviting and teaching men to take him, and choose him) published and proclaimed in his gospel to the world, declaring now the terms by which he offers himself to be our God, and invites us to take and accept him for ours? The serious belief of this thing, that these worlds were made by the word of God, would certainly put us upon a most industrious inquiry. "How shall I do to know him, and to be acquainted with him, and to be interested in him, by whose word these worlds were made? And, I cannot satisfy myself not to know him that made them, and not to have him for mine, since I find there is a possibility of the thing; that it is a thing not to be despaired of, and it is no unjust, or presumptuous aspiring, for me to seek an interest in him." My faith of the thing ought to make my soul restless in this case.

And if one consider, cast one's eye round about, and behold this world in the extent of it, (as far as our dim and short-sighted eyes can go,) and behold the great variety of creatures in it, methinks the thought should presently arise, "Amongst all these things, there is nothing suitable to me, to my spirit; nothing in which I can be satisfied, and in which I could take rest, unless I could find out him that made these worlds by the power of his own word:" till then, methinks one should always look very wisely about one, and behold the amplitude of this world; and then, presently to think, likewise, "Sure it is a sad, melancholy thing, to be in this world, as without God in the world, what an empty cipher is it, if God be out of my sight, if I cannot find out the Maker of all, so as to know him, and have him as mine." And then,

8. If one can do so, how should our faith fill our souls with high gloriations in that God? I have him, that made the worlds, for my God. "All people will walk every one in the name of their God." And we should say, And we will walk in the name of our God: and see, where there is such another God to be found that hath made these worlds, (how many soever they be, and how great soever they be,) and all by his word: I have him for my God. And again,

9. It should, by a little further recollection, make us apprehend too, the greatness of our Lord Jesus Christ, upon whom the business lay of redeeming and saving lost creatures in this world; and must lie of making a new world; of repairing a ruined and languishing creation. For you had to consider, that he had his part, he concurred, he was Creator even of this world. Look to the 1 chapter of the epistle to the Hebrews: He is styled "the brightness of the Father's glory, the express image of his person;" he that upholds all things by the word of his power—the heir of all things, and by whom he made the worlds. "By him he made all things, visible and invisible," Col. 1. 16. and John 1. 1, 3. "In the beginning was the Word, and the Word was with God, and the Word was God. By him were all things made: and without him was not any thing made that was made." And I will not undertake to exclude that from the signification and meaning of the text, "By faith we understand that the worlds were framed by the word of God," the essential Word, the divine Logos. Though, I would not lay a stress upon a thing that is not plainly and manifestly intended: yet, to take it in, is very suitable to the current of other texts of Scripture. The eternal Word had its hand and part in the creation; and it was by it, that these worlds were made. And thereupon, by a right of creation as natural, as well as by the acquired right of a Redeemer of a lost world, by the effusion of his blood, and the sacrifice of himself, he comes to have a governing power over all this world: being ascended and gone up far above all heavens, he hath all power given into his hands, both in heaven and in earth.

I would only improve the consideration hereof, to this purpose, to greaten your thoughts concerning your Redeemer. We are fain in very important cases, from time to time, to be beholden to our senses, even in the most important cases that can be thought. Our sense tells us something of the greatness and amplitude of the world; though it cannot tell us much, yet it tells us something: and by that, make your estimate (for we need such helps) how great a Redeemer we have; him that made these worlds. They were made by the word of God: he was the eternal Word; and as such, we are sure, having the eternal idea in him, according to which the worlds were to be made; by him, at length, they came to stand forth into being. Think this with yourself, "This is my Redeemer; he that had so mighty a hand in the formation of all these worlds; and in whose hand the government of them now lies. It is with him I am to trust my soul. It is to him that I am to subject and devote my soul. Have I not reason to do so? Have I not encouragement enough to trust him, that made this soul, and all these worlds, and to obey him who hath so great and universal a power over these worlds?"

10. Our faith in this matter should, more and more, release our spirits from mean and vile confinement to this one world only; for by faith we understand that there were more: therefore, our faith should release our spirits from a base confinement to one world, when it tells us of more. It tells us, there were worlds created by the word of God: therefore, it speaks an abject mind, a mean and base spirit, and so much the more if we have faith, (as we pretend to have,) to be confined in our thoughts, in our desires, in our designs, in our expectations and hopes, to this one world. Tell a believer, "Your all lies in this one world;" "No, (he will say,) my faith hath got ken of more, notice of more." By faith I understand that there were worlds, framed by the word of God; therefore, it is a base thing to be tied to the present: "Demas hath forsaken us, having loved this present world." A believing soul would look upon that with disdain, (there is such a generosity in faith) and would say, "I scorn so base a confinement as that, to be limited to one world, when I know there were worlds created by the word of God." Though we are not told how many there were, yet we are sure they are more than one; and we have a very distinct account of one more, in which our principal concerns do lie, and are signified to be. And blessed be God for that, that we know so much, that there is one more, with which we have more to do than we have with this world, or can have, even where our principal interest lies, and where our Lord and our Head is. O! how should we bless God for this! that

since there are more worlds, he hath told us so, and hath let us know it. To be limited, in our spirits, to this one world, this present world, is to run counter to the design of our Lord's dying; "He gave himself for our sins, to deliver us from this present evil world." He gave himself for our sins: what doth that signify, in conjunction with the latter words? but that they are our sins that chain us in our present dungeon. And by how much the more we can be released from these chains of our sins, so much the more shall we get out of this confinement, and get above this present evil world. O! if we have many things that we dislike in this world, let us bless God that we know of more worlds. And in the last place,

11. We may further learn, that our faith concerning the creation and being of this world, should very much facilitate our faith concerning the end of it. If we can believe, that these worlds were made by the word of God, we may easily believe what he hath told us concerning the unmaking of them. And particularly, the unmaking of this, the dissolution of it as to its present frame. We may argue from the one to the other, that since the one hath been, the other is not harder to be: if one be a thing to be believed, the other is as believable as that, when we are told it will be so.

It is very true, indeed, that believing is not formally arguing; but as faith doth rest upon the strongest argument in all the world, so it may supply matter of further arguing, though it be not in itself formal arguing, it rests upon the strongest argument that ever was; that is, that because there is a Being infinitely perfect, therefore, he cannot but be true, therefore, it is impossible for him to lie; therefore, it is inconsistent with his nature to impose upon his creatures: heaven and earth cannot have a surer foundation than this which my faith hath upon this matter, and upon this ground. And then, resting upon the strongest argument imaginable, it can easily supply matter of further argument; that is, if my faith hath once believed this, that these worlds were made by the word of God, because God hath told us so, if also, he hath told us he will put an end to the present world, and how he will put an end to it, as he hath told us how it began; if I can believe the one, I can believe the other, too, with the same faith: and so am to live in the suitable expectation of such a time, when these visible heavens "shall be rolled up as a scroll, and pass away with a great noise, and the elements melt with fervent heat, and the earth and all that is therein, be consumed and burnt up."

And, if I believe this, then how entertaining must the belief be! How pleasant the belief of the other world (as was said before) that is to come afterwards, that pure, and peaceful, and orderly, and blissful world! that lasting, permanent, and everlasting world! that when this world and all the lusts thereof are past away and gone, shall abide for ever, and all they that do the will of God: as that expression is 1 John 2. 17. "The world passeth away and all the lusts thereof." Love it not, nor the things of it. If you love it, the love of the Father is not in you: and it is passing away. God is not so unkind to you as to place your love upon vanishing things, upon shadows. This world, I tell you, and all the lusts thereof, are vanishing, passing away; will shortly be gone; the shew will be over: but he that doth the will of God abideth for ever in that blissful world, which it is his will and pleasure shall abide for ever.

LECTURE XVI.*

Gen. 1. 27.

So God created man in his own image; in the image of God created he him.

WE have discoursed to you, more generally, concerning the creation. We now come, (as we are more especially concerned,) to consider the creation of man. It is true, that there is a nobler order of creatures, that were before him in dignity and excellency (at least) in the creation. But because that, of their creation we have not so particular an account; and because our concernment lies less there, I shall immediately fall upon the consideration of what this text puts under our notice, to wit, our own creation, the creation of that creature, called man.

The connexed particle here, that refers these words to what goes before. "So God created man," invites us to call back our eye a little. It is said in the 26 verse, "And God said, Let us make man in our own image, after our likeness, and let them have dominion over the fish of the sea, and over the fowl of the air, and over the cattle, and over all the earth, and over every creeping thing that creepeth upon the earth." And then, the text tells us, "So God created man in his own image." This connexion shews us, that (as you have heard at large,) God worketh all things after the counsel of his own will. So

* Preached December 23, 1693.

he did particularly this great work according to forelaid counsels. "Let us do so; let us make man, and make him such a one, even like God." And so accordingly he did. This may be understood as an allusion to human methods; that is, that men, intending this or that work, they do use somewhat of self-excitation; in order thereunto, they do *accingere se,* they do apply themselves to the action which they intend, and, as it were, recollect their strength, that is now to be exerted and put forth. So is God introduced speaking—" Come now let us go to work afresh, and make that creature man, even the resemblance of ourselves."

And it may also be understood to carry with it, an intimation of that great mysterious doctrine of the Trinity. "Let us make man;" that conjunction of the pronoun of the plural number, with a verb singular, (as we have formerly noted to you,) being probably enough to give some intimation of the glorious subsistencies of the Deity: and who (as you have formerly had noted to you) are to be considered jointly under the notion of Creator.

And it speaks the perfect spontaniety of this work, or (if that may import any thing higher) the perfect intellective liberty wherewith it was done. "Let us make man;" there being no foreign inducement before the creation, there could be nothing *extra Deum,* nothing without God himself, but *proprio motu,* from the inward propension of his own mind, and that vast and boundless abyss of goodness, the fulness whereof was in him, now flowing forth, by free choice and consent, into a creation; and into the creation of such a creature as this. "Let us now make man; it is our mere pleasure to do so:" according to that in Rev. 4. 11. "For his pleasure all things are and were created." He only pleased himself and took a delight in such an effusion of his own glorious power and goodness, breaking forth into such a creation.

In the words themselves, we have two things distinctly to be considered,—the work itself, of God's making man—" God made man;" and—the *norma* or the pattern according to which he made him—" he made him after his own image," made him the designed representation of himself: we shall consider these severally.

I. Consider the work itself, or the making of man—" God made man." And therein, we are yet more distinctly to consider—the product—man; and—the productive act—God made him.

1. For the former of these, the creature now made, and signified by that name of " Man," that we are to consider and con-

template awhile; that is, that we are to turn our eyes inward, and contemplate ourselves, and consider what sort of creatures we are. We hear it often, that man is a microcosm, this whole world in little, an epitome of the universe; the two great classes of being meeting in him; viz. mind and matter, the invisible world, and the visible, touching one another, and having (as it were) a *nexus* with one another in his nature. He hath a mind belonging to the invisible world; and a matter belonging to the visible, in his composition and frame. And so is set a middle creature between the angels and brutes, having the intelligent nature with the one, and the sensitive and inferior nature with the other.

We need to be put in mind of what is so obvious to us; for of all things in the world that we are so prone to overlook and forget, we are most of all apt to forget ourselves: though it were a precept of so high and great importance, and so obvious to a reasonable mind, that it did proceed from the mouth of a Pagan: *Nosce teipsum, first know thyself*, yet it was reckoned too great and important a thing, to be primarily attributed to such a one. And therefore, it was said of it, *e caelo descendit;* surely *it came down from heaven:* no mortal could assume to himself the honour to be the author of so great a saying as this. But though it be a matter of so great an importance, and the obligation thereunto, men perpetual lie, and do lie under; and though it be so obvious to a reasonable mind, yet, generally, look upon all the world, and you may say, "Men are the least part or study to themselves, they least of all consider themselves, to know their own natures, and what sort of creatures they are."

But that we may a little more distinctly consider this subject, plain it is, that man is a twofold creature; he hath a double nature in him; he is a man and a man: or there belongs to his constitution and frame, an inner and an outward man: as the apostle elegantly enough distinguishes them, in 2 Cor. 4. 16. "An outward man," that is a perishable and perishing thing; and "an inward man," which, while that outward man is perishing, is yet capable of being "renewed day by day," as he there speaks.

Indeed, while we turn our eyes upon ourselves, we are least of all apt to consider what is most considerable in our own frame. A people related to God of old, and even the strictest sort, or sect of them, (the pharisees themselves) our Saviour justly upbraids them with this stupidity, this piece of inconsideration: he speaks to them as a company of besotted fools: "Ye fools, hath not he that made the outward, made the inward too," in that Luke 11. 40. "He that made that which is without, did not he make that which is within also?" But both of these parts of man, or each of this twofold man, we are distinctly and severally to consider, for both have that in them which claim and challenge the deepest intention of our thoughts. There is the outward man which the Scripture speaks of, but under the notion of a tabernacle, the outward case or frame of man, (as I may so speak,) a thing whereof he is capable of being divested, and which may be laid aside. "I must shortly put off this tabernacle," saith the apostle 2 Peter 1. 14. He speaks of a going forth, an exodus, as out of his house, out of his dwelling—"the earthly house of this tabernacle." So it is called 2 Cor. 5. 1. "For we know that if the earthly house of this tabernacle were dissolved, we have a building of God, a house not made with hands, eternal in the heavens:" therefore, called a tabernacle, because it is designed but for a temporary and very short abode and residence that we are to have in it; in comparison whereof, the future residence of holy and good souls, is spoken of under the name of a "mansion," in John 14. and in Luke 16. "everlasting habitations;" these are but very temporary ones. But though they are so, yet their present frame and structure doth challenge a very serious, and reverend, and adoring contemplation; whether we look upon the grosser, or more bulky part of this structure or frame; or whether we consider that which is more latent, less obvious unto common notice. If we consider the grosser part of this structure, or tabernacle, either in the whole of it, or by parts, how admirable a thing is the composition of a man, even of the outward man, this exterior part of man! Such, as claims to have such things said of it, as we find, Job 10. 10, 11. "Hast thou not poured me out like milk, and curdled me like cheese? Thou hast clothed me with skin and flesh, and hast fenced me with bones and sinews. Thou hast granted me life and favour, and thy visitation hath preserved my spirit." All being prefaced with this, "Thy hands have made me, and fashioned me together round about, yet thou dost destroy me;" he then seeming, as if he were all of a sudden about to ruin, and throw back into dust again, his own excellent and so curious work: and of how great excellency is it, according to the account that these words give us, and according to that too which we have Psalm 139. 13, 14. "Thou hast possessed my reins; and covered me in my mother's womb. I will praise thee; for I am fearfully and wonderfully made: marvellous are thy works; and that my soul knoweth right well. My substance was not hid from thee, when I was made in secret, and curiously wrought in the lowest parts of the earth. Thine eyes did see my substance, yet being imperfect, when all lay yet in a rough creation; and in thy book were all my members written, (or in the idea of the Divine Mind) which in continuance were fashioned, when as yet there was none of them." They were all fixedly formed in the mind of God, while as yet there was nothing brought forth into actual being, so that, this was the effect of the wisdom of a God, this exterior frame of man, so contrived with so exquisite order, every thing belonging to it, in so apt subserviency to the several uses and purposes for which it was originally designed. Here is that which a pagan calls *ars Dei, a divine art*, the art of God himself, in this structure or frame, a fabric composed and made up all of miracles; if we consider the elegancy and curiosity of the whole, and if we consider how the several parts were equally made to serve, both for use and comeliness: so that of all the wonders in the world, I know no greater wonder than this, that man himself, a creature so capable of consideration and thought, should ever have thought it possible, any of them, that there should be such a production as this without design; as if it were a casual, an unintended thing, that there should be so many severals in this composition and frame of man, but never intended for the uses and purposes for which they so manifestly and peculiarly serve. How stupid a creature is man become, that he is willing to admit even the greatest absurdity, rather than to admit God into his thoughts.

If we look into this frame; (though I can but touch upon things, and it is hard to know where to touch upon so great a multitude of things both observable and admirable at once,) if we should consider the aptness of the several parts that are in common use for the several offices and functions which they perform; if we consider what is external; if we consider what is internal; if we consider what is ornamental in our frame; how full of the highest and clearest judications of the greatest wisdom that can be conceived! There are, belonging to this frame of ours, the organs of the several senses, which do give so many advantages to such a creature as man is: every sense, or sort of sense, it hath its censorium inlaid in this frame; the things that are necessary unto feeling, and necessary unto touch, and necessary unto smell, and necessary unto hearing, and necessary unto sight. All these organs do belong to the outward man; though the sentient be somewhat diverse and distinct, from this outward and external frame: for it is not the eye itself that sees, but the soul in the eye; nor the ear itself that hears, but the same soul in the ear; and so as to all the rest of the senses too; which we all know, if that soul were dislodged, and retired, and gone, could no more see, or hear, or touch or taste, than a stone: but the aptness of these several organs for their several uses and purposes, such a curious contrivance as that of the eye for the sight, and that of the ear for the hearing, it would require volumes to unfold and open these to you.

And then, if we consider that which is more latent, even in the outward man itself, not obvious to the notice of any of our senses, and that is the more spirituous part, in this frame of man, or the several sorts of spirits. I do not now speak of his purposes, and without which it were impossible that any of these operations could be performed, which do belong to the nature of man in this present state. There are the elementary spirits that are to be found in it, and that are common to it, with the inanimate part of the world. As there is no sort of body conceivable, in which we may not also conceive somewhat or other of that which they call elementary spirit. And then, there is a higher sort of spirit, which serves for vegetation; and a higher than that, which serves for sensation; and all these, no doubt, some way or other distinguished, though we are not capable of assigning their differences, otherwise than from their effects; but all meeting in the frame of a living man: one sort of these spirits finer than another; another, again, finer than that; but undistinguishable by us by any other way, than only by such indications as the things effected do speak and hold forth to us. All these things we use continually; and we could do nothing without them; nor be what we are without them, in this present state. But seldom or rarely doth it occur to any thought, what they are, or that there are such things belonging to us, when without them there could be no motion: they are not things that are self-moving, (as no matter can,) yet they are things by which that which hath the power of motion in itself, doth perform such and such kinds of motions as are necessary in this frame of ours.

If we should consider the several things which are thus used: as all the muscles in the body of a man, reckoned to be about four hundred and thirty, without which, and without the spirits that do move them, the man were a mere trunk, a dead trunk; so many several sorts of muscles to turn that one member of ours, the eye, this way and that way, and the several agitations of spirits that must be the continual spring of all these motions. How quickly do we turn our eye this way, that way, upward, downward, and never consider what turns it about us, without which no such motion could be performed.

If we think of all this, what cause have we to break out often into those same raptures, that we find the Psalmist, herein, in that last-mentioned place: "How fearfully and wonderfully am I made: Thy works are marvellous, and that my soul knoweth right well." And it is a mighty emphasis that these words carry in them: "and that my soul knoweth right well:" that is, it signifies this to have been with him a wonted study, that his mind used to be fixed on the contemplation of it—"my soul knows it right well;" these are with me beaten tracks, they are not uncouth or unusual thoughts; these are things that I think of, over and over again, from day to day." Indeed, when any one comes to consider the works of God, and particularly, this work of composing this fabric of our outward man, they are wondrous; and we must consider them so. If we do but glance but one single thought upon this work of God, we cannot but say, "they are wondrous." But how few of us can say, "and this my soul knoweth right well:" that it is a thing to which my thoughts are used, and which is my continual work; I do, from day to day, employ them and keep them in exercise upon such a thing and subject as this.

But time, and my own design of speaking as succinctly as is possible unto the several heads which I am to discourse of, allow me not further to insist on this same outward man.

We are to look yet further: and when we have taken some view of the habitation, to consider the inhabitant, that thing in man called mind and spirit; spirit in a higher and nobler sense than we used that application before. According to the exterior part of man, that you have heard of, he is called Adam, a composition of earth, of red earth, as that word signifies, or out of the dust of the ground; that earth pulverized, reduced to the finest particles, according as more or less, so they were capable of being wrought into that curious contexture which their great Maker did design: hereupon man is said to be thus made. He hath the denomination there, first from his outward, more visible and observable part; this is the creature which appeared first to come under notice and view, upon this stage of this lower world. There was nothing perceivable of him, but this exterior frame that was called man: he hath that denomination *Quoad apparentiam*; in respect to what he did appear, and was obvious to common notice, or that might be in such creatures obvious to the notice of one another, the first notice. It could only, in that respect, be said, that God made man of the clay or dust of the ground; that is, what of man was capable of being made out of matter, was made out of such, or out of that matter.

But you have afterwards, a further account of this creature, in the 2nd chap. of Genesis and at the 7th verse; that " God did breathe into him the breath of life, and he became a living soul." The outward man carried the name of man before; but now we are given to understand there was a nobler thing belonging to this frame and composition of man, which admits that he should be called "a living soul," from that breath of life, which it is said God breathed into him, that breath of life. It is as significant an expression as we could have in words, or that words could furnish us with, of vital spirit, a living spirit, that is the principal thing in man. And so, now, he hath the denomination, *Quoad rem* as he had it *Quoad apparentiam* before. Before, he was denominated according to his appearance: so man was said to be made of the dust of the ground: now he hath his denomination according to what he is in reality; a living soul being breathed into him, as vital breath, from God himself, most immediately.

And here we are to stay our thoughts a little, and consider what this is. It is to be known, (as all essences are,) but by certain properties that do speak themselves in such and such peculiar effects, and so tell us what the cause must be from whence such effects do proceed. It is plain, that this same soul of man must be a substantial being; otherwise, it were never capable of such actions and effects as we manifestly find do belong to us, and are wrought by us. Now if we do consider them severally,

1. That which is fundamental of all other, is, that it manifestly appears to be a vital thing; the spirit of man is distinguished by vitality, by being essentially vital. It is very true, indeed, that these bodies of ours, as long as the soul inhabits them, live too, have life in them: but I pray consider, what is so very obvious, the difference of that life, from what we must understand and conceive to be the life of our spirits. We know the body of man so lives, as that it doth not constantly live, it doth not always live; and so life doth not belong to it essentially; life is separable from it. The body of man, it can be killed; it is capable of losing its life, and so its life is but a derived and a borrowed thing from somewhat else. Spirit hath life radically in itself. For we must conceive the spirit of a man, this breath of life (as the learned languages, hebrew, greek, and latin, have no word for spirit but that which signifies breath,) I say this spirit, or breath of life, is, in itself, vital, so as that unto it, to be, and to live, is all one. The body may be, and not live; (as I told you) life is separable from it; but the spirit, the soul, while it is, it always lives, its being and its life are not capable of being parted from one another, as it is in the

life of the body. And so it is from that life, that the life which is in the outward man is derived, and transmitted in all the several parts of that body that do partake of life. And then,

2. Next to life, (which is fundamental and indeed of larger extent, and not so distinguishing,) there is intellect; there is a power of understanding that belongs to the spirit of a man, by which his spirit is a thing capable of thought, or doth consist in a thinking power, a continual source or spring of thoughts; so that if we never so continually attend ourselves, we cannot find ourselves not thinking: there is a perpetual forge of thoughts, from whence they fly and spring up, as sparks from this or that fiery substance, and never cease to do so. And within that compass of intellect, lies not only power of forming thoughts, but of connecting thoughts; of affirming one thing that we think, of another thing that we think; and the power of deducing thoughts from other thoughts, of inferring some thoughts from former thoughts; that is, that because I think so and so, therefore, I consequently think so and so too; some thoughts having a dependance upon other foregoing thoughts: and a power of ranging thoughts, of methodizing thoughts, of putting thoughts into a frame and order, according to that relation which they mutually bear to one another.

And this, shews this same thing called spirit or mind in man to be, not only a substance, but a substance quite of another kind from this outward man of ours, that is made up of matter, though there be things belonging to this frame, never so fine, and did require never so high purity of matter; yet plain it is, that the spirit, that is in man, must be somewhat of a quite different nature; inasmuch as there is nothing of matter, whether gross or never so fine, that is capable of a thinking power: for you can no more discern a tendency of a power of thinking in a flame of fire, than you do in a piece of clay; a flame of fire is nothing more rational, nothing more capable of understanding, than a log or a stone; and therefore, whatsoever hath the power of thought belonging to it, must be a being of quite another nature and kind, from any thing of matter, be it never so fine, never so pure; there being no property at all belonging to matter, that hath any possibility of contributing to such a thing as thought—neither figure, nor the size, nor the motion, nor the connexion of parts one to another. It is altogether an unimaginable thing, that a piece of matter, be it never so small, should be more capable of thought for being of such a figure, or less capable of thought for being of such a one: that if it be square it cannot think; if it be round, then, it cannot think:

if it be of a less particle, then, it can think; if it be a greater, then it cannot think: if such and such particles be separated one from another, then they cannot think; if they be put together they can. No reasonable understanding can imagine any contribution in these things unto the act of thinking. And the motion of so many parts can contribute as little and no more than so. A heap of sand lying still, can be capable of no thought; and if it be agitated, never so much, it will be as little capable: therefore, nothing is plainer than, that this property of the mind or spirit of man; that is, intellect or the power of thought, or thinking, doth speak this spirit, or mind of man, to be quite a diverse thing from all the matter that belongs to the outward man; even from every thing of the outward man; that the inward and the outward man must be quite diverse or different things. And then,

3. There is the power of will or choice, belonging to this inward man, the mind and spirit within us, by which we are capable of determining concerning our own actions; of choosing or refusing, of resolving to do so and so; of resolving not to do so; or resolving to do the contrary: a strange power, and of vast extent, that doth distinguish and belong to the spirit of man, and through which this soul and spirit of man come to have that double capacity, to wit, of duty and felicity. I were capable of neither of these, if it were not for that elective power, and consequently upon the intellective, by which I am capable of choosing my own actions, and the objects upon which they are to be employed. I speak now of the original capacity belonging to the spirit and mind of man, not considering, at present, the impairment or diminution thereof, by the apostasy: of which there may be occasion to speak in the proper place, and season, when it may come in our way. But it is the same faculty or property of the mind or spirit of man, to wit, the power of election and choice, that makes him the subject both of duty and felicity. He were never capable of duty, if it were not for this; nor capable of felicity, otherwise than by this; as he is a creature obliged by the law of duty, and capable of being rewarded and remunerated by felicity. This is the thing inferred by the power and faculty in man, the power of volition, depending upon that understanding or cogitative power, which you have heard of before; though some take that term of cogitation to extend so far as to take this in too. But we are not considering of words now. And then,

4. There is the executive power, by which we reduce into act, these purposes and intendments of ours; a strange sort of

power; that is, being directly under the dominion and government of that former power, the power of choosing; that is, because we will do so and so; and so choose we to go to such a place; or we stay and move not: we move this and that member, or we restrain that motion. If we will, we can move our whole frame with very great facility; or else if we will not, it is very difficult to move it. That I can by the notice, by the command of my will, make my whole bodily frame so easily move to this or that place, which without that empire or commanding act of my will, it would give so much difficulty and trouble to others to do. And I move it myself *nullo conatu, nullo negotio*, upon the matter, I make nothing of it, I do it with ease. This is a power that we continually use; but we very seldom reflect upon it, that we have such an ability belonging to our natures, and even to the very nature of our spirits, the soul within, by which to move to and fro, these members of our body, as from time to time we do. And,

5. There is belonging, as very peculiar, (and some think it is most of all peculiar,) to the mind and spirit of man, the capacity of religion, of which the brute creature is altogether uncapable: some think this more differencing of man than reason itself. It is a very dubitable and disputable matter, whether there be not that very thing in many creatures, that are reckoned brutes only, that we call reason. But concerning this, religion, the matter is out of all question and doubt, that it belongs, most peculiarly, to the mind and spirit of man; that is, the capacity of acknowledging a Divine Being, the Author of our being, and of reverencing and adoring that Being accordingly; that power by which I do *suspicere numen*, by which I consider a Being above me, the Author of my being, and of all beings, and of any disposition in me to pay a reverence and adoration to that sovereign and supreme Being thereupon. And,

6. Lastly, there is belonging to this spirit of man, (as peculiar and distinguishing too,) the power of governing the inferior faculties; the power of governing sensitive appetites and passions; and even, in very great part, the acts of the exterior senses: I say, in very great part—there will be some involuntary actions; but how far the natural power of man did herein originally extend, we are not in this state of our apostasy capable of knowing now. But undoubtedly, when man was himself in his innocent and instituted state, and where the inferior nature was held in direct subordination to the superior, as there were then no undue thoughts, so neither were there any undue motions of an inferior nature itself, but what were certainly

commandable and kept within due limits. And this empire did belong to the mind and spirit of man, to govern and conduct all the inferior appetites and affections, and all the external actions, so as they should move or not move, be done or not be done, as to that governing wisdom seated on the throne, in the mind of man, did seem meet.

Of this there will be more occasion to speak when we come to the latter particular in the text; to wit, "that in the image of God made he man:" when we come to treat of the *norma* and pattern of this great divine work. But upon what hath been said, thus far, concerning the product, the thing produced, man: surely our thoughts cannot but reproach us that they are so seldom employed upon so important a subject, and that lies so very near us: for what can be so near us as ourselves? That we can have our eyes round about us, like the eyes of the fool in the end of the earth, and so seldom find time and room for any such thing as self-contemplation.

LECTURE XVII.*

Whereas, in the former discourse, we told you, that it is impossible that the spirit of a man, this inward man, can have been made of matter, so neither can it be made of spirit, for spirit is not a partible thing. If any should suppose it to be made of created spirit, it is as good to suppose it made immediately out of nothing, as any former created spirit; for the necessity will recur of referring this production, at length, to that special kind; to wit, of making a thing out of nothing. But for its being made of the uncreated spirit, God himself, that would be to make the Divine Essence a divisible thing, a partible thing, as if there were parts capable of being severed from parts belonging to the same essence of God. And therefore, though among some of your heathens, (your stoics particularly) there have been those high hyperbolical expressions of men's being parts and members of the Godhead, *Des partes sumus et membra*, as Seneca's expression is: and that celebrated stoic speaks softly enough indeed of the soul's being *divinæ particula auræ*, the soul should be a *particle of divine breath;* these are expressions allowable enough as high rhetorical strains, but not as expressions of rigid truth, by any means. If, therefore, the spirit of man were neither made of matter, nor of spirit, it must have been made out of nothing. And so

* Preached January 6, 1694.

in reference to this part of the product, the effect, the thing produced, man, that must needs be by most immediate creation in the strictest and most proper sense.

As for the question, "Whether that these souls were made at once, or whether made successively just then, when put into a state of union with these bodies?" is a thing altogether unfit for us to concern ourselves about; it being, indeed, such a thing as divine Revelation hath given no determination to; and such a thing as no human investigation can ever be able to make a determination of, one way or other; we must be content to be ignorant where God hath drawn a veil over things, and not brought them into any kind of light that we can discern them by.

And then, for the completing of this production or productive act, we are to consider, (as comprehended in it) the union that is brought about between these two parts, the outward man and the inward man, without which there could not be one product considerable in the case: for when we speak of God's making man, (as this text doth,) the meaning cannot be barely, that he made a body for him out of the earth, and that he made a soul for him out of nothing; the production of these two parts will not amount to the making of a man, unless these two parts be united and brought together, so that of both to compass and make one thing: a man is not created till then, not made till then. And most plain it is, that this union, it was made, at first, by God himself immediately, without the co-operation of any second cause. But it is in the after productions, brought about in a settled way and course of nature, in which, yet, we cannot say that man's being produced, doth consist in the making of his body, or the making of his soul; but in the union of the one with the other. There is not a man produced till then; till these two parts, being produced, are brought together. But they are not brought together in union in the same way as they were at first: for at first it was by God's own immediate operation; but he hath now settled the course of nature wherein all following productions are brought about. But yet, still it is his work; otherwise, man which was God's creature at first, would cease to be God's creature, if he were not still the Maker. Now concerning this union we have this to say:

1. That it doth not confound the parts united, one with another; for the body is a body still, and not a spirit; and the spirit is a spirit still, and not a body. These parts do remain distinct in the union: there is no confusion of them in the case, nor identification; as if the nature of the one were

lost and swallowed up, in the nature of the other. But the body continues to have all the properties of a body; and the spirit continues to have all the properties of a spirit; the properties of the one are not communicated to the other. It is not the body that thinks, nor the spirit that grows; or the like, but these particular distinguishing actions proceed, that are proper to the one and the other, they remain unto each. But,

2. We have further to say, concerning this union, that, though under it the parts remain distinct, and are not confounded one with another, yet they are most intimately united; though it does not identify them, nor confound them, yet is this union a most close union, a most inward union, so as not to be ordinarily separable by any means that shall not discompose the recipient herein, that it shall be no longer naturally capable of being; so the soul cannot but stay there: and when it ceaseth to be capable of being the apt recipient of the soul, the soul can no longer stay; it is, therefore, a most intimate union; and a most marvellous one; and one of the greatest mysteries in all the creation of God; considering the vast difference that there is between these two natures, a piece of clay, and a mind; that these two should be so united together, that so long as the one remains naturally susceptible of the other, they can by no means be parted, they cannot be separated, while the crasis of the body remains entire. It is one of the greatest miracles in all the great creation of God; that is, that when this mind of mine, this spirit, is loose from all matter besides, I can move myself from this place, or that, as I will; I cannot yet, by any means, from this body of mine: to this piece of matter I am tied and fixed: and though this soul of mine be an elective and voluntary agent, and I do things electively, and at choice, I cannot at my own choice take myself out of this body of mine, to separate it from my soul; but whither ever I have a mind to go, it follows me, and goes with me, and cleaves with me; I cannot shake it off while the crasis lasts. This is a thing whereon the wisdom of the Creator hath infinitely outwitted us, and gone beyond us. We know not what hath tied this knot, this knot of man, made of these two parts, that are so little of kin, as dust and spirit are to one another, yet so to adhere to one another, as that they cannot be severed by any art, or any power, as long as the crasis, or whole constitution lasts, so as this mind or spirit can go out and come in at pleasure. Let it be considered, for it is one of the deepest mysteries of divine wisdom in all the creation of God. A great wonder it is in itself; and really, it is not a less wonder

that it should be so little considered, that man, that hath such a thing as this belonging to his nature, a union of two such, so disagreeable parts, should so seldom reflect upon it, so seldom allow himself to contemplate and look into the mystery of his own composition.

But now, to go on to the *Use* of this former part—God made man: here are but a few words. But it is a vast improvement that they are capable of, if we would give our thoughts scope; and if it might please the Divine Spirit to concur and fall in with his own word. Here lies before us the foundation, laid bare and open to view, of the whole law of nature: that which we call the law of nature herein, it hath its foundation even in this—God made man. It results but from the nature of God, and the nature of man compared together, or with one another; the nature of the Creator and the nature of the creature, this creature, such a creature. Inferior creatures are not governable by a law; it is an intelligent, voluntary subject that alone is capable of being so governed. And inasmuch as God is the most perfect intellectual Being, and our Creator, and we are intellectual beings too, and his creatures, hence results upon us the obligation of that law which is called "the law of nature;" and may justly be so called, or which otherwise may be called "the law of our creation." Take that in the general. But to be here a little more particular, there are these several things to be learned even from hence—that God made man. As,

1. Is God indeed our Maker? Then certainly there ought to be in us a most thirsty, longing desire to know him, as far as our minds are capable of knowing him. For what! Can I be content to be ignorant who it is that made me? Indeed, there cannot be a higher and more notorious violation of the law of our nature, or creation, to be willingly ignorant of that God that made me, and gave me being. But how dismal a thing is it, that we should so generally need to be taught how to answer the very first question that we are wont to ask our children: "Who made you?" I hope you are wont to do it; God knows how it is; but I hope it is your wont and use to ask your children, "Who made you?" But pray let us consider, Do we not need to be taught ourselves, what we pretend to teach our children, "who made us?" When you would teach your children so much, do you mean that they should repeat the words and no more? Is it not your meaning, that you would have them understand who made them? Is it not your meaning that they should have some notion in their minds of him that made them? If we had so, and a true, right, correspondent notion, O! how mightily

impressive would that very thought be upon our souls; how would it strike through all our powers, for ourselves to answer that question, "Who made us?" He that is infinitely beyond all thought, beyond all conception, declare his name, or his Son's name, if thou canst tell: as it is said unto Ithiel and Ucal, Prov. 30. 4. Into what an amazement should it put us to consider, what answer we should put to this question, "Who made us?" Into how profound thinking should it cast our minds? Into how deep thoughts? Out of how vast and immense a fulness and plenitude of life, and being, and power, we did spring? That vast plenitude, that abyss of being, that answers the question, "Who made me?" He made me, that is the infinite fulness of all being, and of all life, and of all excellency, and of all perfection: and shall not I covet to know him? At the same time that I acknowledge him incomprehensible, I must look upon the knowledge of him as most desirable, the most desirable of all knowledge.

And therefore, it speaks a most horrid degeneracy (as there will be occasion more directly to take notice of hereafter) of this thinking part of man, his mind and spirit, that it can think of so many thousands of things, and covet to know them, affect to know them, but not affect to know the Author of its own being, of its own life, and of all those great powers and faculties that he hath furnished the reasonable, intelligent nature with; "They liked not to retain God in their knowledge." Rom. 1. 28. They did not approve of it: that is the import of the word: a strange thing that this matter being proposed to God's own creature, and a creature capable of thought and understanding. Hast thou a mind to know God, to understand him that gave thee being? No, I do not approve of it. They approved not to retain God in their knowledge; there was a secret dislike and disaffection; "an alienation from the life of God," as it is expressed, Ephes. 4. 18. "and this they are willingly ignorant of," (saith the apostle Peter 2 epis. 3. 5.) "that the world was made at first by the word of God, the earth standing out of the waters and in the waters. Of this they were willingly ignorant." This matter, it lay hid from them, being very willing that it should: that is the import of the expression the Spirit of God makes use of there. It lies hid from them, being willing of it. What lies hid? That this world had a creation; of this they are willing to be ignorant; and so, consequently, that they had a creation. They desire not the knowledge of it; they say to God, "Depart from us, we desire not the knowledge of thee." Job 21. 14. Here is divine light and glory shining every where through this world; but we choose rather to dwell in the dark as to this thing. "The light shineth in darkness, but the darkness comprehendeth it not;" receives it not, would exclude and shut out that light: a voluntary darkness; as if that darkness should entertain thoughts and communings with itself; as if there should be an agreement among the several clouds of that darkness; "Come, let us collect and gather together thick about such and such minds, to fence them against the beams of such light;" this mind is self-collecting, and gathering these clouds, drawing them in, inwrapping itself in them; "O! let us not know God, though he made us; God made me and yet I will not know him." O! unnatural thing; most monstrously unnatural.

Even so it is with men in their distresses, when nature itself would dictate to them, "O cry to him to give thee help who hath given thee being." Do but observe that, Job 35. 10. "They cry by reason of oppression of the mighty; but none saith, Where is God my Maker." An amazing thing that men in their distress will many times cry to rocks and stones but not say, "Where is God my Maker?" Cry to rocks and mountains, (as they will at last) but lift up no cry to heaven, "Lord I would fain know thee, manifest thyself to me in this my distress." No, men will perish under their burdens rather than do it: such is the disaffected temper of men's minds towards God. Indeed, for ease and relief they will cry, but not for God, or say, "I want to know God;" that is none of their sense. "My soul thirsteth for God, for the living God, when shall I come and appear before God?" Nothing more remote from the minds and hearts of men than this sense. And yet, it is not understood, what they are incurring of guilt and misery, by this neglect of getting their minds furnished and enriched with the knowledge of him that made them. It is not considered what lies upon it. "It is eternal life to know thee the only true God and Jesus Christ whom thou hast sent." And if these two be necessary (as we find in that John 17. 3.) If both these, I say, be necessary, how fearful a case is it, if we cannot get men over the first, or to the first, which is more natural. But the knowledge of the true God, that lies within the compass of the sphere of nature, that belongs to natural religion. And a compliance with the divine pleasure in this, to wit, seeking to know him, belongs to the law of nature, by the first and primary obligation of that law upon us. At what a distance are their souls then, from blessedness and eternal life, that when it is "eternal life to know the only true God and Jesus Christ, whom he hath sent," we cannot get man to the first. No, they are content to be all their days ignorant of God; yea, though he be a Father to them.

O! strange prodigy of unnaturalness! So you would account it, if that were the temper of any child, that he did disaffect to converse with, or take any knowledge of, his own father. But this is the peculiar relation between God and men. He is a Father to them, a Father upon a natural account; as he hath been the immediate Creator of their spirits. And therefore, when Christ's line is run up to the highest, you find it run up to Adam—"Who was the Son of Adam:" and then by Adam it is run up to God—"Who was the Son of God," Luke 3. 38. and upon that account it is that we are said to be "his offspring," in that Acts 17. 28. An expression that the apostle borrows from a celebrated poet of their own, a certain astronomical poet, who was highly in vogue with that people, or with the philosophers of that place; that university at that time. One of your own poets tells us "we are his offspring." Man is the creature of God: but with very great peculiarity. He hath many creatures besides. All the inferior universe are his creatures too: but among all, man only is the son; that is, there is none below him to whom that title is ever given of being his son. "And shall we not be subject to the Father of spirits and live?"

Besides this supernatural ground of this relation of Father and Son between God and the spirits of men: I say, besides the supernatural ground of it in regeneration, it hath its natural ground. And you will see more of it when we come to consider the Second Part—Man's being created after God's image: for if we speak of human productions, a man makes many things himself, yet what things he makes they are of a different nature from himself; but whatsoever he begets is of the same nature, of a like nature with his own. Human nature can make many things, make houses, make garments, but they have nothing of a similitude or agreement of nature with the maker. But it is this peculiar sort of production that gives foundation to the relation of father and son, even that which makes the product to be of the same nature and kind, or of an agreeable nature to the productive cause. If man be the son of God, then he must be an intelligent being, as He is. And this is the state of things between God and men; and yet they do not know it, and choose not to know it, are willingly ignorant of it. The matter is upon account plain, that their ignorance of God is voluntary; for that it is evident, it is not necessary; that is, they do not live ignorant of God because he cannot be known: for his glory shines every where. There is not the meanest creature but proclaims Deity to every one who will attend: there is not the most despicable pile of grass, or grain of sand, or any such thing, that will not make an argument to us of Deity, that cannot fail but be most cogent and unanswerable. For take but one single pile of grass, one single grain of sand, and here is a real something; that is plain. But is it a thing that came into being of itself? Is this pile of grass, or grain of sand, a self-subsisting thing? No, by no means; no reasonable thought can imagine that, that it can be a self-subsisting thing: for then it would have more perfection in it than all the world hath besides, that did not make itself, or come into being of itself: then it owes itself to a maker, and so we are unavoidably led to God. If you but so much as set yourself to contemplate a grain of sand, or a pile of grass, follow the train of your own thoughts but a little way and you are led to God, whether you will or no: this is either something or nothing; I find it to be a real something: well, but what is it? a thing that subsisted of itself? No, by no means; for then it would have all the perfections, all the excellencies of the universe in it; and infinitely more; this grain of sand, and pile of grass, would have more excellency in it than all the world: for it is plain, that this world did not make itself; why then we must refer it to the Maker; and so you are led to God, whether you will or no, by so mean a thing.

Therefore, I say, men's ignorance of God is not necessary; because they cannot know him: it must, therefore, be voluntary, because they are willingly ignorant of him. And the more plainly so, because, whereas they have a sufficient demonstration of the being of a God, even in the meanest creature, they have a more abundant demonstration in themselves, and from themselves. If a grain of sand, or pile of grass, will prove a creature and a Deity to me, how much more must I myself who know I did not make myself. I know I came into being so many years ago: so that this work of giving an answer to this question "Who made you?" doth not lie remote: I do not need to fly up into heaven, or go down into the depth of the earth, or to cross the seas, for an answer to it; but only look into myself. The word is nigh me, in my mind, and in my mouth; if I will allow that to speak my mind: I have in me these powers, these faculties, that nature, that most expressly represent God to me. I find myself a creature that can use thoughts; I find I have a power in me of laying designs, of forming projects, of foreseeing things, of comparing thought with thought, of inferring and deducing one thought from another. How manifestly doth all this lead me to God, the perfectly intellectual Being!

Therefore, it is the most amazing thing, that our thoughts can reflect upon, that there should be such an indisposition and averseness in us to know him that made us. God made man; but man will not know God, though he be not a Creator, at large, only to him, but a Father; and man, in respect of his soul and spirit, his very offspring, he being the Father of spirits: upon the account whereof, pagans themselves have been wont to speak of God, as the paternal Mind, Father of all minds, and of all spirits, as some of them by the light that shone, even to them, could not avoid to see and say.

There is but one thing that leads to many more parts of the law of nature, and our condition which results in all the several parts of it, from the collation and putting together these two things—God and man: man being considered as the thing made, and God as his Maker; God made man. Sure, I say, in the first place, nothing can be more reasonable, and suitable to this state of the case, than that man should have a mighty thirst to know God, to know him that made him. One would think it should be an uneasy state of the spirit of man, to be in any such ignorance of God as should proceed from neglect: to be ignorant of God by neglect, by not caring to know him, by not concerning one's self to have that knowledge, that should be the uneasiest thing in all the world to the spirit, to be capable to have that said to him, "So many years thou hast lived in the world, lived in the flesh, a tabernacle, that thy Creator and Maker hath framed for thee, and put thee into it, and all this while thou hast not cared to know him, nor concerned thyself to get any acquaintance with him." It very much becomes and concerns us to covet to know him. It is a very unnatural thing to be content to be ignorant of him that made us; but not to be willing to know him, that is much worse. But now,

LECTURE XVIII.*

2. We may hence collect, that our constant, grateful adoration of God, is a most reasonable duty incumbent upon all of us. Nothing is more deeply fundamental in the law of our creation, than the law of worship. "Let us come and bow down, and kneel before the Lord our Maker." It is a joyful homage

* Preached January 13, 1694.

that is claimed unto him on this account, the most complacential adoration. "Let us come before him with thanksgiving: it is he that hath made us, and not we ourselves." Indeed, nothing can be more reasonable hereupon, than those two great parts of natural worship, to wit, supplication and thanksgiving. Supplication; Should not a people seek unto their God? Did he make us? did he give us being? from whom else are we to expect all the good we need? He that hath given us being; all the accessories of being are to be looked for only from him. And thanksgiving; these two parts of natural worship, are complicated in one another; in the institution of them, as they are in the reason of them, and root of them. "Let your requests and supplications be always made to him, with thanksgiving," as in divers texts of Scripture, which I might refer you to, and even upon that account, that he hath given us our very being itself, which is the fundamental unto all other good that we are any way capable of, that he hath given us being of such a kind. So God made man.

We should consider what is involved in the nature of man, and so bethink ourselves what we have to bless God for: that is, the primitive nature which God gave man at first, or wherewith he made him, every thing that he made was good, and so was that more excellently good. It is storied concerning Plato, a heathen, that dying, he gave God solemn thanks for three things: "That he made him a man, and not a brute; that he had made him a Grecian and not a barbarian, (there being much more light among them in his time, than with the rest of the world, to wit, the light of philosophy and cultivated reason;) and the third was, because he had ordered it so that he should live in Socrates' days, who was reckoned so great a luminary in that part of the world among them, while yet they were overspread with paganism." O! how awfully should we adore God that he hath given us a being; that he hath given us rational, intelligent natures, capable of knowing and enjoying so great things! that he hath assigned us our station in such a part of the world, and where we have opportunity to know a greater One than Socrates was! that he hath ordered our creation in such circumstances as he hath done, in such a time and such a part of the world! Nothing is a more equal law that can be upon us, than that we should have an habitual, adoring gratitude, possessing our souls upon such accounts.

And, upon the whole, Adoration! how correspondent a thing is it to creation; adoration on our part, unto creation on his part? How convictive a saying was that celebrated one of Austen? "If I (saith he) were capable of making a reasonable creature to stand forth out of nothing, endowed with the power of reason and understanding, the first thing sure that I should expect from him would be, that he should fall down and worship me." In what an unnatural state, then, is this world upon this account, that being inhabited by so many reasonable creatures, it is inhabited by so few worshippers! Again,

8. Another practical deduction from hence, is, that we ought to live in a continual dependance on him that made us. So God made man. Hath he made us, and will not we depend upon him? trust in him? This is most essential homage due to our Maker, to place upon him, and exercise toward him, a continual, vital trust. This is a glory which he will not impart; but concerning which he is jealous. And, indeed, as to purely internal worship, this is the first, and most radical of it, trust in God: and so very natural to an intelligent creature, that I remember Philo Indæus hath this expression concerning it: "That he is not fit to be called a man, that hath not in him hope towards God." He seems to mean it of what is most natural to man, that he is not to be reckoned a man, that doth not trust in God, and doth not place a hope in him.

Natural dependance is reckoned, consequentively, essential to a creature; and it is so. A creature is naturally a depending thing; an explicit dependance, that doth as properly belong to an intelligent creature, as natural dependance doth to all other creatures. A creature, as such, taken at large, is a mere dependant upon him that made it. This whole creation is nothing else but a thing dependant upon God, upon divine power and upon divine pleasure; according to which it was determinable, whether it should be, or not be; and according to which, it is continually determinable, whether it should continue to be another moment, yea or no. And so suitable as natural dependance is to a creature, as a creature, so suitable is intellectual dependance to a reasonable creature, as such: that is, that it should consider its dependant state, and often recount with itself, How came I to be what I am from moment to moment, when I cannot promise myself a moment's breath or being? This is so appropriate a glory to the Deity, that when trust is supremely placed any where else, there is a curse pronounced upon it; "Cursed be the man that trusteth in man;" Jer. 17. 5. for this is to rob God of his peculiarity; to place a homage on the creature, that is most appropriate and peculiar to the Creator.

But it may be said, In our state of apostasy from God, what room or place is there left for trust in him?

To that I answer, very certain it is, men are in an apostasy from God. But are they, therefore, always to continue so? especially when he is so intent upon a design for their recovery and reducement; and he insists still upon the right that he hath in his own creature. Because his creature is revolted and apostatized, and run away from him, hath he, therefore, lost his right in it? If there be an obligation upon an apostate creature to return, (and if it were a wicked thing to apostatize at first, it must needs be an increase of the wickedness, to continue in that state of apostasy and not to return,) then, wherein stood our revolt, therein must stand our return. The revolt of a creature from God in his apostasy, lay in departing from him through " an evil heart of unbelief;" that it could not trust in him, did not trust in him; trusted the tempter and destroyer of souls, against him, and in opposition to him. And to come out of a state of apostasy must be by trust, if the going into the state of apostasy was by distrust. But this must be in God's own prescribed and appointed way and method. When once it hath pleased him to signify the way in which he is pleased to admit of sinners' return unto him, wherein he hath made the constitution of a Redeemer known, there must be a return in and through him, and trust in God through him: " Ye believe in God, believe also in me." John 14. 1. Where this way of returning to God, so as to make him the supreme Object of our trust, is not known, there the state of a sinner is less capable of remedy. But where it is known, it admits of so much the greater and deeper guilt, if yet there be no thoughts of returning, and returning in this very act, by placing again our supreme and vital trust upon him who was the first great and commanding Object of it; that did most rightfully command it, and challenge it, for himself; Shall I have a creature that shall not trust in me? not make me its all in all? Therefore, to have our interest in God restored by Jesus Christ, that must be our great business, who live under the gospel of Christ.

And then, we are to trust in God under that very notion of the Author of our being, knowing, that because we are apostate creatures, therefore, that he will never, for our sakes, but he will, for Christ's sake, do the part of a kind, benign Creator to us. Our interest in him as Creator being now renewed; not lost and swallowed up, but renewed and restored: and therefore, is the charge laid upon christians (1 Peter 4 19.) to " commit themselves to him in well-doing, as unto a faithful Creator." His interest in us, as our Creator, was never lost; our interest in him, as such, was; but being now restored, upon this restitution, we are continually to trust in him, and commit ourselves unto him under the same notion of Creator, still. To commit ourselves unto him as a faithful Creator, that is, he did put himself, at first, under obligation (implicitly at least) to his reasonable creatures: "Obey and thou shalt live," shalt be happy, he freely putting himself under this obligation. But the creature, upon his revolt, forfeited all his interest in him, and all right to that promised felicity, which, as an obedient creature, he might have expected: by Christ this right is restored; and so God is to be considered now, by such as through Christ have returned to him, not merely according to the benignity of a Creator, but according to his fidelity also: "commit yourselves to him as a faithful Creator," he having resumed the obligation upon himself to treat such kindly; and he doth it, not merely from unobliged goodness, but obliged, which the notion of faithfulness doth imply. He will be to you a faithful Creator, if you commit yourselves to him accordingly as such. And again,

4. Another piece of practice that we may induce, and should learn, hence, is a constant and most profound humility. What! am I a creature? So God made man: there had never been any such a thing as man if God had not freely made him. O! then how deep an impression of humility should this fix upon our souls! What am I? A creature depending upon will and pleasure; it was lately in the power of another, whether I should be, or not be. A proud creature is a monster in the creation of God; the most horrid monster in the creation. What have I to be proud of, who am of myself nothing, and should never have been any thing, but by vouchsafement, by the good-will of another? It is to that only that I owe it, that I am any thing.

If one creature have more, or do think he hath more, of real excellency than another, that, with the whole of his being is all but a made thing. Thy whole being, whatsoever excellencies belong to it, either as common to that sort of creatures to which thou art annumerated, or more special and peculiar to itself; if it be any thing, (if it be not merely a concealed thing,) it is a made thing, as thou art: thou wast made, and it was made, and it was made to be thine; but all depending upon will and pleasure, therefore is pride a most monstrous thing in the creation of God: The continual sense of all creatures, of any intellectual sense, should be this, "We are all nothing but what it pleased our Creator we should be. We have nothing but by his pleasure; our being is a borrowed being: and the additions, and all the ornaments that have occurred to it, are all made things, all borrowed things." Should any one be proud of that which he hath borrowed? To wear ornaments that every one knows were borrowed, and to be proud of them, what a madness is that? Our very being is a borrowed thing, and all that belongs to it.

When God would humble a creature down into nothing, thereby to make it the capable receptacle of a Deity, a cohabiting Deity, that with such a one he might dwell, how doth he magnify himself the higher; "Heaven is my throne, and earth is my footstool. Isa. 66. 1. All these things have I made, they are all the works of my own hands. Now, if I can find a creature sensible of this, to such a one will I look, that is of a poor and contrite spirit, that humbles himself into the dust before so mighty and glorious a Creator; with such a one will I dwell; he shall be my temple the habitation of a Deity;" for the Deity will suffer no diminution in uniting with such a one; because that will still be looked upon as the All in all, while he still looks upon himself as nothing. And,

5. We further learn, hence, the great equity of the law of self-denial; it is a most deeply natural law; and when it is made fundamental in Christianity, that is but the revival and re-inforcement of a natural law: "Except a man deny himself he cannot be Christ's disciple." Why so, why cannot he be Christ's disciple? Pray consider what was Christ's business, when he was to collect to himself disciples. His business, as a Redeemer, was to recover apostates back again to God; and their discipleship to him, was only to put themselves under his conduct; that under the direction thereof, and through his mediation, they might return to God and be accepted. The very design for which a mediator was appointed, shews the necessity of his insisting upon this law as fundamental to the whole frame of Christianity. As if he had said, "My business as a Redeemer, as Mediator, is to recover and bring back apostate souls to their God again. Wherein were they apostates? In that they did set up themselves apart from God, and in opposition unto God. None can come to me and own me for their Head, and for their Lord, and Intercessor, and Mediator with God, but it must be under this notion; that is, that they look upon me as the only One by whom they are to be restored, and brought back into their primitive state, reduced to God, the great Author, and consequently the end of all things. And therefore, did Christ, in dying, "redeem us to God by his blood." Rev. 5. 9.

We are not to think, that we were, ourselves, the principal end of Christ's redemption: that would be an injurious and absurd imagination; to think that the creature was Christ's chief end, it were a horrid conception. God must be the chief end of all things; therefore, the design of Christ's dying was to redeem us to God; to restore back such and such creatures to God, that the end for which they were made, might be served upon them. Our interest in him is a secondary thing; but his interest and right in us was the primary thing. Therefore, it was impossible to be otherwise, but that Christ's designing the redemption and reduction of sinners to God back again, must lay this law as fundamental, at the bottom of all that religion he was to set up in the world; that is, self-denial. "You have lived in a separate state apart from God. If you are weary of that life, and will come off from yourselves, then you are for me; then you come under my conduct; I will make your peace; I will buy it out for you, (and he hath bought it out,) and procure your acceptance with God, upon your return." But this can never be, if you have a mind to live separate still, to stand upon your own bottom, and make self your first and last. No, God must be your first and last; and he really is the first and the last. And therefore, "unless any one be willing to deny himself, he cannot be my disciple," saith Christ; he cannot be a christian under any other notion than as one that is now willing that God in all his authority, and greatness, and excellency, and glory, shall entirely fill up that room which, before, self had usurped. And therefore,

6. We further learn, hence, how reasonable and necessary a thing it is to man, as he is a creature, a created thing, to seek an interest in, and union with, God, as his highest and best good; for of himself he is nothing. That he is any thing (as hath been said) did depend upon divine pleasure. Such a one, if he do recollect and use thoughts, must needs state his case thus: "Not only am I uncapable of doing any thing towards my own felicity, but I cannot preserve myself in being one moment. What good have I then, but what I must expect from him that made me? I have been severed from God, cut off from God, the great Author of my life and being; I have not, in this my separate state, my good in my own hand; I have not enough in me to make me a happy creature; a creature I am; but I still need to be a happy creature. And when my very being is not my own, what shall I be able to command for myself, or procure for myself, or raise up to myself, within me, that shall be able to be a felicity or satisfaction to me?" He that is nothing of himself, it is the most reasonable and necessary thing to such a one to seek a union with him who is All. I am in myself nothing; there ought, therefore, to be in me a propension towards him who is my All. My soul ought to in-

cline towards him, to adhere to him, as its supreme and best good; "Whom have I in heaven but thee? who can I desire on earth in comparison of thee?" And,

7. A life of the most absolute devotedness to God, is the only righteous way of living; no man lives a righteous life that doth not live a devoted life. And what are we to deny ourselves for, as neither being able to procure a felicitating good to ourselves, nor as being allowed to design a supply for ourselves by any interest of our own? And why are we to deny ourselves in these respects, but that what we take off from ourselves, may be immediately placed upon God who is our All? As we are to seek a union with God for our real, present support, and for our final satisfaction, so are we to devote and addict ourselves to him in order to this service. When we adhere to him, (according to what was expressed in the foregoing head,) that refers to our support and satisfaction; when we devote ourselves to him, that refers to his service; that we may serve and glorify him: for that we are to devote ourselves to him.

And that hath its reason in this too, that we are his creatures, he hath made us: and what did he make us for? Did he ever make a creature to be its own end? He hath made all things for himself: "Of him, and to him, and through him, are all things, that he alone might have the glory. Therefore, is our own created being, (as it is such) our very being itself, a perpetual, standing testimony against us as long as it lasts: if we live not devoted lives; if he who hath been the Author of our being, be not the end of it, this very being of mine is a testimony against me; for what sort of being is it? Not a self-sprung being, but a created being: So God made man. I am a made being; therefore, is my being a testimony against me, (the kind and nature of it being considered.) I am a continual testimony against myself, as I stand a created thing, depending upon will and pleasure, if I live not a devoted life, so as my own heart can bear me record, in the sight of God, that I do live to God. Being to ask myself the question, (and it is a shame to us if we do not often ask ourselves the question,) "What do I live for?" what is my business here in this world? If I cannot answer it with a sincere conscience, "Lord, thou that knowest all things, thou knowest that I principally design to live to thee, and that I reckon my life, and my being, a vain and a lost thing, otherwise than as it is sacred unto thee: I continually testify against myself; I should think it living in vain, to please myself, and to serve an interest of mine own, when I have not a moment to command, but depend upon the pleasure of another for every moment's sustentation in the being that I have." Who can answer it to himself, to live that sacrilegious and ungodly life? that is, not to live devoted to him by whom we live?

8. We may again learn, hence, what reason there is why we should love God more than ourselves: you cannot but know, this is a thing most strictly charged upon us, and wherein we are upon no terms to be dispensed with; namely, that we are to love him above all. We owe unspeakably more to him than we can do to ourselves. We do not owe to ourselves that we are any thing. "He made us, and not we ourselves." If there be any thing of real goodness in the being that we have, there is infinitely more in the Author of that being: and if goodness, as such, be the object of love, the greatest goodness must be the object of the greatest love, and the highest goodness, of the highest love. And therefore, do not think that we are hardly imposed upon, when the law of our creation doth require and claim this from us, that we love God more than ourselves. And therefore, when our Lord Jesus Christ takes upon him the great business of our redemption, and reconciliation unto God, (which it was impossible for him ever to have effected, if he had not been God as well as man, upon the account of the Deity that was united in the same person with his humanity,) he claims so much for himself from us, that is, he doth tell us, that, if any man do love father, or mother, or wife, or child, or his own life, more than him, he cannot be his disciple. We are to consider that there is Deity in his person, the fulness of the Godhead; and so that he is, as such, the supreme Object of our love, to wit, the Deity which is in him, common to the Father and Spirit, must be the supreme Object of our love. It is as if he should have said, "I come, in kindness, to redeem and save you as lost creatures: you are not to think in doing so, I have laid aside my Deity; for then I could not have been a Redeemer and a Saviour to you: and therefore, having that Godhead united with my humanity, in my own person, I require this of you, that is, that you love me more than your very being: and you cannot be my disciples upon any other terms." He was Creator, in conjunction with the Father, and the Spirit; for "by him were all things made, visible and invisible; and without him, nothing was made that was made." And therefore, we are not to think it a hard or an unreasonable imposition upon us, that we are to love God, and to love Christ, more than ourselves; more than this natural life or being of ours, so as that all must be a sacrifice to his pleasure, if he once say the word, or signify his will to that purpose.

And that is the way, having lost ourselves, to find ourselves again, by loving him above ourselves. "If any man love his life," (that is, supremely,) "he shall lose it; but if he will lose his life for my sake,' he shall find it." We find life, and all, in God through Christ, when we are lovers so as to make him the supreme Object of our love, as in that, John 12. 25. No man can really be a loser by so abandoning himself, as to place that love which he unjustly placed upon himself before, (that is, his supreme love,) now upon God, and upon Christ. No man can be a loser, but he finds himself again in this case. He had lost himself before; but now he is restored to himself and to his God both at once. Then,

9. We may further learn, hence, how reasonable a thing it is, that man should be under government: Is he a creature? then he ought to be a governed thing. The most reasonable thing in all the world it is, that he that hath given us being, should give us law. Hath he been the Author of being to us? and shall he not rule his own creature? Shall that be allowed to have a will against his will? To have been raised up out of the dust, but the other day, out of nothing, and now to dispute whose will shall be superior, mine or his that made me, what an insolency is it! We may again learn,

10. How foolish a thing is self-designing, when men lay their designs apart from God; forming their projects, as the apostle James speaks, chap. 4. 15, 16. "I will go to such a city, and buy and sell and get gain. And I will reside there for such a time." This all proceeds from our forgetting that we are creatures, made things. God hath made us; so that our breath is in his hands. How great an absurdity is it, as well as an injury, that I should talk of forming projects, and laying designs, when I am but a made thing, and there is an arbitrary hand underneath me, which sustains me; but that may let me drop and sink, in the next moment, if it be withdrawn. We ought to say, "If God will, we will do so and so." If your being depend upon his will, certainly your actions and affairs depend upon his will too. But for men to design so and so, without consulting God, or referring themselves to God, is to take upon them as if they were not creatures. And,

11. We may hence learn, further, (as that which is fundamental to all the rest,) how indispensable an obligation there lies upon us to preserve a continual, awful remembrance of God upon our minds and hearts, from time to time, all the day long. "Remember thy Creator in the days of thy youth." I pray, let us but use our own understanding in considering this. When it is said, "Remember thy Creator in the days of thy

youth." (Eccles. 12. 1.) Is the meaning of it, that we are only when we are young to remember him, and forget him all our days afterwards? No, the meaning is, that those days of our youth are not to be exempted, we are not at liberty to forget him even then, but that he claims an early and first interest in our time and thoughts, and in the truth and vigour of our spirits, and that we are to begin then, when we are young, as we are to continue all our days afterwards. And how is he to be remembered? Why under the very notion of Creator: that suggests to us the very reason why we are to remember him; because he is our Creator, and our breath is continually in his hands. What! do we think a man can subsist without God, any better when he is grown up, or when he is grown old, than he could when he was young? No, the reason upon which the obligation rests, is still the same upon us all our days; that, therefore, it is a most monstrous thing, to consider how men come to dispense with themselves in this fundamental duty, that virtually comprehends all the rest. All is lost and gone, if we do not so much as remember God. How can we dispense with ourselves to rise up in the morning, without a serious thought of God, and run after our common affairs all the day long, and still forget him? And lie down at night (it may be) without any serious remembrance of him? and yet lie down with the apprehension that we are innocent in all this; we have passed over this day well if we have succeeded in our business, if there hath been no disaster that hath befallen us, all hath been well; though there hath been no serious thought of God; no minding of God at all; that is to live in a downright rebellion against God, through a whole day; and also from day to day, through a whole life's time hitherto: for it must be entire and universal rebellion, inasmuch as all duty towards him depends upon remembering him: we can do nothing besides if we do not do that. Therefore, is that given us as the character and diagnostic of wicked men, of men that are designed for hell, and allotted to hell for their final and eternal inheritance and residence. "The wicked shall be turned into hell, and all the people that forget God." Psalm 9. 17. And they, accordingly, are characterised as such, who more peculiarly belong to God, and as those whom he owns for his own, and counts his jewels; "In the day that I make up my jewels, saith God, they shall be mine:" Who? why "They that feared the Lord, and thought upon his name." Mal. 3. 16, 17. "And the desire of our soul is to thy name, and to the remembrance of thee." This is the profession of his holy ones. Isa. 26. 8. And, again we may add,

12. Since God made man, you see how easy it is for him to prevent all the evil designs of ill men, if he see good: for they are all his creatures: and hath he made a creature that he cannot govern? If then we see wicked men, at any time, bring their wicked devices to pass, it is not because God cannot rule them; but because he hath deeper designs that they understand not, and we understand not. And therefore, their insolency, and good men's despondency, upon that account, are equally unreasonable. They triumph; and good men are dejected; their hearts sink, and they hang down their heads; and why? because wicked men prevail, and prosper in their way, many times, ages together; and, it may be, in many parts of the world. But,

(1.) Their confidence, on the one hand, is so unreasonable as to be even ridiculous. "He that sitteth in the heavens, laughs, the Most High hath them in derision." 'A company of bubbles of being, that I can let drop into nothing in a moment, if I please: and yet they please themselves in the hopes and imaginations of succeeding in such and such designs as they have laid.' "He that sitteth in the heavens shall laugh" at them. He knows how soon he can let such bubbles drop into nothing; and he sees that their day is coming. And,

(2.) Good men's despondency is, upon this account, equally unreasonable. "Hast thou not known, hast thou not heard, that the everlasting God, the Lord, the Creator of the ends of the earth, fainteth not, neither is weary? There is no searching of his understanding." Isai. 40. 28. Thou dost not know the counsels of God, what that all-comprehending mind and understanding of his doth design, in letting creatures awhile run such a course. But we are to be assured, he hath his own creatures in his own hand and power, both men and devils, and can govern them as he pleaseth. He hath a hook in their nostrils, that they themselves are unapprehensible of. He knows their coming in, and their going out, (as he said of that proud Assyrian,) and even all the rage which they have against him. But, I say, he hath a hook in their nostrils, and can turn them as he pleaseth, and when he will: we shall have done a great thing towards the whole business of our religion if we can but get this truth impressed upon, and deeply wrought into our souls; *So God made man;* if we will but learn to look upon ourselves as made things, and look upon all men as made things, continually in the hands, and at the command of their great Creator.

LECTURE XIX.

Gen. 1. 27.

So God created Man in his own Image.

WE have treated of the first thing, to wit, this creation itself. So God made, or created man. And now,

II. We come to speak of the *norma* or pattern of this work of his; or the estate wherein man was created; in his own image; which is mentioned with a reduplication; " in the image of God created he him;" and this we shall speak to briefly, by way of explication and application.

1. In the explication, our great business must be, to inquire, and shew, wherein stood this image of God, wherein man was created. Theirs was a strange and absurd dream, (that of the anthropomophites,) that is, they who did ascribe to God a corporeal shape, and supposed man to be made like to God in that respect. We know, indeed, that in tract of time, our Lord Jesus Christ did assume a human body; but that gives no pretence at all to this imagination: for therein he was made like unto us, man being the pre-existent pattern, and not we like to him, man being made long before. And to ascribe to Deity itself a corporeal shape, must needs speak very mean and base thoughts of God, founded in gross ignorance, and rising up into a mental blasphemy; and indeed, very vile thoughts even of

* Preached January 20, 1694.

ourselves, as if we were but to imitate God in somewhat corporeal.

Some of the more refined pagans have disclaimed, and declaimed against such gross thoughts of God, warning us to take heed of ascribing any thing corporeal to him; as one, inquiring how we are to conceive of God, according to the doctrine of Plato, (I mean Maximus Tyrius,) he tells us, "we must be very shy, and it ought to be most remote from us, to ascribe any thing at all corporeal to him, neither shape, nor colour, nor magnitude, nor any kind of figure whatsoever: but somewhat of that high excellency as neither to be seen with eyes, nor felt with hands, nor expressed by any words." In some such things we are to understand the excellency of the Divine Nature and Being to consist. And accordingly, the apostle, discoursing to those Athenian philosophers, (Acts 17.) supposeth them very capable of understanding so much as this; he quotes one of their own poets for it, that "we are God's offspring." "And forasmuch," saith he, "as we are the offspring of God, we cannot conceive the Godhead to be like any corporeal thing of never so great excellency;" as silver or gold, of which some corporeal shape or resemblance may be made, or stands never so curiously graven by the art or device of man: we must understand our resemblance to him, as we are his offspring, to lie in some higher, more noble, and more excellent thing, of which there can be no figure; as, who can tell how to give the figure or image of a thought, or the mind or thinking power? This image therefore, must principally lie in some mental thing, and is to be only mentally understood: that is, it must have its seat and subject in the soul and spirit of man itself: and so we must know this image of God in man, wherein he was made, to be twofold; natural and moral.

(1.) Natural, standing in such things as wherein the very nature and essence of man's soul and spirit doth consist and lie. As,

[1.] In spirituality: the soul of man is a spirit, as God himself is a spirit. He, the paternal Spirit, (as a heathen very aptly speaks of,) the fatherly Mind; and agreeably to that, we are his offspring, he being the Father of spirits.

[2.] And in life; essential life. We have bodies that live a borrowed life. Our spirits are, themselves, living things in their own nature and essence; so that life is inseparable from them, as it is not inseparable from our bodies; for our bodies can die; but our souls cannot. If it be, it lives: being and life are the self-same thing. As the blessed God is so frequently spoken of in Scripture, "the living God," the original well-spring of life; so making a creature like himself, and in his own image, he makes him to be such as to whom life should be essential, though it be dependant upon him; (as all being must be,) yet life being made so much of the essence of man's soul that it can never be severed from it; therein its life is like the divine life; that is, it is an immortal life. It is true, "he only hath immortality;" that is, he only hath an orignal, independent immortality. But the souls of men, and all created spirits, have a dependant immortality, together with their dependant being, and not separable from it. And,

[3.] In the power of understanding; therein doth the soul of man bear the image of God naturally, as it is an intelligent thing, a thing that hath a power to understand and know the impress of God is upon the spirit of man in this. "He that teacheth men knowledge, shall not he know?" Psalm 94. 10. And he that declareth unto man his thoughts, (as having given him the thinking and the knowing power,) are we not to suppose, he should know his own work? And,

[4.] In liberty, or the power of willing this or that; of acting or suspending its own acts, and of acting this way or that, accordingly as it shall chuse; a dominion it hath over its own act, a self-determining power, or self-dominion; but subordinate to the divine dominion; for he never made a creature that he was not to govern. These are things that I now mention, but which being included in the nature and essence of man, when I gave you an account of this creature man, which God is said to have made.

I shall only add two things more generally concerning this natural image of God in man.

First. That it is permanent and lasts always, as long as man lasts, as it cannot but do, it being essential to him, or his very nature: for his very nature did resemble the divine, "the image and glory of God," as he is called 1 Cor. 11. 7. It must, therefore, be permanent, and can never be severed from man; this is an image that could not be lost. Man could not lose this image; his soul must be a spirit still; a living thing still; and an understanding thing still; a spontaneous, free thing still, subject only to the divine government. And therefore, considering man, even in his estate of apostasy, we find this image of God, still remaining, as the perpetual reason of that law of preserving the life of man in this body, as in the 9. Gen. 6. "Whosoever sheddeth man's blood, by man shall his blood be shed; for in the image of God made he man." If the reason of the law were lost, the law were lost, and would cease: but plain it is, the law was made with reference to man, already fallen: fallen man, apostate man, still bears, in that respect, the image of God; therefore, he will not have his life to be touched. He is a Godlike creature, and he that strikes at the life of man, strikes at the image of God! A very awful thought, to consider that man, even as he is man, while he was in innocency, or in apostasy, is still the image of God, and, therefore, must be inviolable, not to be touched beyond his rules, who reserves to himself still, the dominion over lives, as being the God of our lives, so as to kill or to make alive, either immediately, or mediately, by his own authority in men, but not otherwise. And,

Secondly. There is this to be said in general, too, concerning the natural image of God in man; as it is permanent, so it is fundamental unto the other image, and the contraries thereunto; that is, if man had not the natural image of God upon him, he were never capable of having a moral image, could never be a holy creature, nor unholy, if he were not naturally such a creature. And he could never be happy or miserable, if he were not such a creature: that is, if he had not a soul that were a spirit, and that were a living thing, and that were intelligent, and that were capable of acting voluntarily and by choice. And therefore, this image must still be presupposed unto the other.

(2.) Which other we now go on to speak of, that is, the moral image of God in man, founded on the former. And so man doth bear, and did originally bear, the image of God, in the moral sense, in these two respects—first, in purity—secondly, in felicity. He did at first resemble God as a holy, and as a happy Being. In reference to both these, the natural image of God was fundamental to the moral; this was the very foundation in him of all duty, and of all felicity; and of the contraries thereunto, that is, of sins and of misery; as contraries must always have the same subject in which they take place, successively, or in a remiss degree.

[1.] This image of God in man, which we call *moral*, superadded to his natural image, stood in this, to wit, in the sanctity and holiness of this creature in his original state; the rectitude of his natural powers and faculties with reference to his rule and end. But this is to be understood with *caution*. We are to take heed of asserting either too much, or too little, concerning the holiness of man's original state. We must take heed of asserting too much concerning it, to wit, so much as would not consist with the possibility of his falling; or too little, to wit, what would not consist with the possibility of his standing. But, in general, this sanctity or holiness wherewith man was made, and wherein he did originally resemble God, it stood in these two things;

First. In innocency; that is, that he was made perfectly innocent, and it was impossible that it should not be so: for it could not consist with the holiness, and the other perfections of the Divine Being, to make him a sinner. He could not come out of the hand of God at first, an impure and unholy thing. Wherein stood the image of God, but in that he was originally holy, as God is holy? to wit, in some similitude to the holiness of God: he was created in this, as part of the image of him that created him, as that Col. 3. 10. and Ephes. 4. 24. do plainly imply: for the image of God restored and renewed must be the image that was lost. It could not be a specifically different thing: therefore, when the soul is renewed after this image, it is plain, that he was created in it; that is, was created an innocent and sinless creature: not barely in the negative sense; for so is a stone or a brute innocent. I say, not in that sense only; but as being free from all taint and impurity, when he was a capable subject of being both pure and impure; which a stone or other unintelligent creature was not. And then,

Secondly. This holiness, wherein man was created, as it did include innocency, freedom from any taint of sin; so it did include a possibility of continuing so; that is, that there was no depraved inclination in his nature, as it was made or created by God, to determine him unto sin; unto any sinful thought, or to any sinful act. It is true, he was not made impeccable, or with an impossibility of sinning, yet he was made with a possibility of not sinning; that is, with an intrinsical possibility thereof: for we must distinguish here, between possibility and futurity. It is true, that his fall was future; but his standing, for all that, was possible; we mean only by it, a simple possibility, not compounded with any consideration of God's foreknowledge. It is true, God did foreknow what would become of man; but that did not infer a necessity upon his nature; that could have no influence to make him fall; that is, that God foresaw, that being left to himself he would fall; but he saw at the same time, that though he would fall, yet that he had done that for him by which it was possible for him to have stood, if he had followed the law of his own nature. And therefore, though we call this image moral, in contradistinction to natural, yet we are not to think that it was in no sense natural; for it was con-natural. It was not natural, as that signifies essential; for then it could not have been lost: but as it signifies somewhat agreeable to the nature of man; and nothing could be more agreeable to his nature, than to have continued still an obedient creature to God, and consequently happy in him: so that it was not at all to be ascribed to man's nature that he fell; for that were to resolve the cause of his fall into the Author of his nature; and so, to cast all upon God at length; whereas, man's destruction is only of himself, he is the fountain of whatsoever is evil, and God the only fountain of all good.

But then, we are to consider the holiness wherewith man was created, more particularly. And so, it stood in the confirmation, or the conforming of the faculties of his soul unto the rule and order wherein God did at first set them; that is, as for the mind and understanding, it did agree with the Divine Mind; and for his will, it did agree with the Divine Will; and so, the faculties of the human soul, those two great leading faculties, the mind and the will, did each of them bear the stamp and impress of God upon them. And therefore, whereas, we find God spoken of under that twofold notion in Scripture, and by one and the same penman of the holy Scripture, the evangelist John, in his 1st epistle, that "God is light," and that "God is love;" the one in the 1st chap. verse 5, and the other in the 4th chap. the 8th and 16th verses. Such a creature was man in his mind, and in his will, conformed to the Divine Mind and Will.

i. "God is light," saith the apostle, "and with him is no darkness at all; and he that walks in darkness, and saith, he hath fellowship with God, lies:" there can be no fellowship between light and darkness. We are not to understand light, there, to mean merely speculative knowledge: but we are to understand it as signifying practical principles, lodged in the mind, and which are most con-natural to holiness in the will and heart. They are the ideas contained in the one, which are exemplified in the other. So, "God is light," essential light itself; and so was the spirit of man, "the inspiration of the Almighty having given it understanding;" that is, that it was,

(i.) A knowing thing; not only had a power to know, but did actually know all that concerned him to know, or that it was his duty to know. And as such, this part of the divine image is referred to morality; for there are some things which it is our duty to know; and to be ignorant of them is a sin. But we are not to suppose man to be destitute of any knowledge, that he ought to have had, in the state of his primitive innocency; though it must be far from us to think that he had universal knowledge, that he knew all things: for that would still be proper to God as an incommunicable attribute of the Divine Nature. And therefore, his knowledge must have been a growing thing in that state wherein he was made. But he did know all that did belong to him to know, for the state wherein he was.

And so are we to conceive of that knowledge, as the moral additament to the faculty or power of knowing, which is natural. And then,

ii. Besides his actual knowledge, we must understand, in his mind, a docility, or an aptitude to learn, or know more; and still more, according as the Creator should vouchsafe to reveal more to him, or as he should give him opportunity (as he had given him a natural ability) to reason himself from the knowledge of some things into the knowledge of more.

(ii.) For his will, that must have been the seat too, of the holiness wherein the image of God stood, and wherein he did resemble God; and there is the seat of God's law impressed: for we must know, that man was made at first with the law of God written in his heart. Besides the positive precept which he transgressed, there was the whole frame of that whole law in him, which was to be the permanent rule of his practice and obedience: for the apostle, speaking of man in his fallen state, (Rom. 2. 15.) tells us, " that even pagans themselves," (where there are the greatest ruins of the human nature to be seen,) " even they have the law written on their hearts." And if it be so with fallen man, what an entire impression must there have been of the divine law upon the mind of man yet in his integrity. A law written in his heart, of which some pagans speak, calling it the *non scripta, sed nata Lex*, not a law written, (that is, in any external scripture,) but an engraven law, an innate law, that was impressed on man on his creation, or that he was made with.

And so, as this law which, is in itself, of universal and everlasting obligation, is all summed up in *love*, which is the fulfilling of the law; why, therein we must understand this creature to have at first resembled God; that is, as God is said to be "light," so he was in respect of his mind : and as God is said to be "love," so he was in respect of his will or heart : a creature made up of love, which sums up all duty; for " love is the fulfilling of the law." And therefore, when men are renewed and brought back to God, and his image restored in them, they are created after God in this respect, so as to be capable of dwelling in *love*, as in a proper element and region con-natural to them. This was the great principle that did conform men to both parts of the law; that part which was to respect God himself; and that part which was to respect men towards one another : for these were the two great natural and moral precepts; " Thou shalt love the Lord thy God with all thy heart, and with all thy soul, and with all thy might; and thou shalt love thy neighbour as thyself." O! what an excellent state was this! when the impression of this law, whereof this was the summary, was entire and perfect; not the least inclination to violate it in any part, or in any point, either towards God, or towards a fellow creature.

And we may yet further, and more distinctly, consider this rectitude of the faculties of man's soul to stand in this—first, that the superior faculties of his mind and will, were more directly and exactly conformed to the divine mind and will—and secondly, that the inferior faculties were subject to the superior; this being the law of man's nature at first; that is, that though he had inferior faculties, as well as superior, suitable to his compounded nature, (being made up of an inward man, and of an outward man, or of an intellectual, and of a sensitive nature,) yet, these inferior faculties belonging to the sensitive nature, they were made so as to be obedient and subject to the superior; that is, to an enlightened mind, and to a holy will: so as to have no appetitions that were irregular or disorderly, of an inferior kind, or belonging to the sphere of sense, but what reason, governing the will, could prescribe to: no violent passions or appetitions in one kind or other, so as to love or desire, or fear, or hope, or joy, or sorrow, or be angry inordinately, but according as a right mind should dictate, and as a right mind should command. And then,

[2.] As this moral image, superadded to the natural, and founded thereon, stood in holiness, (which we have thus far explained,) so it stood in happiness too, in sanctity and felicity; that is, as God is the blessed God for ever, so did this creature imitate him in his blessedness; bear the image of that upon him too. We must understand that he had a present inchoate blessedness; a present blessedness begun in a satisfaction to all his faculties, in having what was proportionable and accommodate to all the powers of his nature.

First. As to his superior faculties: herein stood the blessedness of this creature, that he had a mind capable of knowing God, and a will capable of enjoying him; and which did know God, and which did actually enjoy him: and it could not but be so; for here was no culpable darkness or cloud upon this mind; there was no corrupt or depraved inclination in this will: and God was pleased to exhibit himself, and manifest himself, to make himself known, and to offer himself to be his portion and God, according to the tenour of that covenant, that law of works, and that law of his creation, under which he was made. Therefore, there was nothing to hinder his present happiness: there was no aversion from God, no disinclination to him; but, a steady propension towards him. There was no guilt upon him, to make him afraid of approaching God; as it was with him soon after he fell, when he ran and hid himself. Vain creature! thinking there would be some darkness wherein he could hide himself from the Divine Majesty. But while he remained yet in his integrity, as there was no faulty darkness in his mind, so there was no depraved inclination in his will: but knowing God to be the best and highest Good, most absolutely perfect, all-comprehending and every way suitable to him, his will could not but be a propense towards him accordingly, so as then it must have been his sense in perfection, (though not unalterably,) which comes to be the sense again of the renewed soul: " Whom have I in heaven but thee, and whom can I desire on earth besides thee? When he had the beauties of a new-made creation all in view, a heaven that was then new, and an earth that was then new; yet, " Whom have I in heaven but thee, and what is there upon earth that I desire besides thee?"

As to his inferior faculties, there was what was most grateful to them too. Man was created in a paradise, full of pleasantness, and of pleasant good things, which it was then lawful for him to enjoy without restraint, except that one forbidden tree. And he not only had the perception of all, all grateful, sensible good, but an interest in, and a power over, all. And you see, that God estates him in a dominion, sets him over all the works of his hands, in this inferior, lower world, and doth so, immediately upon his having created him. " God blessed them, and said unto them, Be fruitful and multiply, and replenish the earth, and subdue it, and have dominion over the fish of the sea, and over the fowl of the air, and over every thing that moveth upon the earth."

What a glorious prince was man then! and into how great a principality did God put him as soon as he made him! Whatsoever was most suitable, and most delectable, for his enjoyment, in that kind of inferior and sensible good, was all put into his power; so as what innocent, well-tempered nature would choose, as most grateful to it, that he might choose, one thing excepted; which very exception, (as all exceptions do *firmare regulas,*) was but a confirmation of his dominion over all the rest; and did but more fully speak his right and title to enjoy what he would beside. All this as to his inchoate happiness. But,

Secondly. Besides this, we must understand him to have had a title to continuing and increasing and, at length, perfect felicity. We are not to suppose him made in that state, which, if it had stood, should have been eternal, without change or alteration. But most rational it was, that God having newly created an intelligent creature, should create him in a state of probation, upon which was to follow a state of retribution; as it is most natural, that duty go before felicity: that there must be obedience before recompence. His full and final recompence was yet to come.

And the reason of the thing plainly speaks it. We cannot suppose, that God made man in a better condition than he made the angels: (a superior sort of creatures:) but it is plain, that he created them in a state of probation; otherwise it had been impossible that some of them should have fallen, and left their first station, forsaken it, and thereupon, to be " bound in chains of darkness, and reserved to the judgment of the great day." And it is plain, further, upon this account too; as to this earth, supposing man to have stood, (though God foresaw that he would not; that he would fall,) yet we must suppose his constitution to be such, as agree with the supposition of his standing too. It had been altogether impossible that, in the succession of many ages, this world would have contained all the men, if they had been innocent; and so, consequently, all immortal. But we must necessarily suppose, though not death, (for that was only introduced by sin,) yet some such kind of translation unto higher and more glorious regions; as from perfect arbitrary, good pleasure, Enoch and Elijah found at the hand of God.

And so, besides the actual felicity he had, there was a title to future felicity, supposing he had stood. For when the divine constitution runs in this tenour, " Cursed is he that continueth not in all things that are written in the book of the law to do them," do but consider what the reverse of that must be: " Blessed is he that continueth in all things written in the book of the law to do them." If not continuing in all things written in God's law, to do them, must infer a curse, then to have continued must infer a blessing: and as that curse did put him into a worse estate, that blessing must have put him into a better estate; otherwise, it had not been a state of retribution suitable to a foregoing state of probation.

Thus far, you have now the explication of this state, wherein God is said at first to have made man; that is, made him in his own image, the image that was natural and essential to man; and that image that was moral and superadded. And can we look upon this as a useless doctrine? Of what importance is it to us to look back, and consider the original of this creature! what it was; and what it is! What man was in that perfect rectitude, of which we have had some account; and what he is in that forlorn and abject state into which he is now sunk and fallen. It is this that must make redeeming mercy, and our recovery by a mediator grateful. It was a noble expression of a heathen; *Nemo improbe conatur unde descenderat ascendere:* (speaking to this very case, the depraved condition of man as he now generally is, and what his state before was, of which they had hallucinations, though not distinct conceptions;) *no man blameably endeavours to ascend from whence he did descend. Capax est noster animus dei, atque eo fertur, nisi vitia deprimant: we have minds capable of God; and towards him they would be carried if vice did not depress and sink them.* But nobody doth unwarrantably aim to ascend thither, whence he did descend; if he did descend, sink from so excellent a state, there must be some aim upwards, some aspiring to get up to that state again, or to somewhat agreeable thereto, by which the natural appetite in man to blessedness and felicity should be excited and stirred and put into action, and kept in action, even by the very law of his own nature.

LECTURE XX.*

The more distinct *Use* and *application* of this subject, and such as may most aptly and properly be made, we shall now proceed to. And it will afford us a very various, and a very copious use, if we seriously apply our minds to consider it. God created man in his own Image. Why there are,

1. Sundry inferences of truth that we may collect and deduce. As, that man was, at first, a creature of great excellency, (whatsoever he is now become,) a noble and a glorious creature; the image of God being intire could not, sure, but be a very glorious thing. As it is blurred and defaced in a great measure, yet in respect of that remainder, or that mere ground of it, man is now said to be "the image and glory of God." 1 Cor. 11, 7. The image and glory of God, he is still, notwithstanding he hath diminished and disguised himself, as an intelligent being, a living thing: he hath a soul that is essentially life, or to which life is essential; that cannot cease to live; that hath a self-determining power belonging to its nature; that acts not under the laws of a fatal necessity, but according to reason and liberty, in the common affairs and actions of life.

Take man as he was at first, when those powers that belonged

* Preached February 10, 1694.

to his nature were unvitiated and pure, what a glorious creature was this creature! Dei-formed, made after the likeness of God. The world replenished with such creatures, what a delectable habitation had it been! to have so many Godlike creatures inhabiting this world of ours, all representing God to one another, so many visible representations of divine knowledge, and divine light, and divine love and divine purity! O! what an excellent creature was man in his original state!

(2.) We may further be informed, hence, of the more peculiar excellency of our souls: for we must consider them as the primary seat of the divine image: "So God made man after his own image." Wherein stood that? Where lay this image, or where was it seated? What! in our bodily frame and structure? (as the anthropomorphites did formerly dream.) Was it a piece of clay that was made so like God in us? And therefore, if man be to be looked upon as an excellent sort of creature, we must understand wherein his true value lies, and whereupon men are to value themselves.

A great many are apt to value themselves because they have laden themselves with a great deal of thick clay; because they have a sort of propriety in much of this earth. Some highly value themselves upon an airy title: "I am such and such a dignified thing, among those with whom I dwell." Some are more vain to value themselves upon gay apparel, or because they have so and so trimmed and adorned those carcasses: but it is in respect of our mind and spirit, that we are the offspring of God, and bear the image of God: and if ever we have any thing truly valuable, or excellent about us, there it must lie; a mind and spirit must be the seat and subject of it. Again,

(3.) We may learn, hence, that there is much of God to be understood by ourselves; for we were made after God's own image; and we may discern much of another thing by that which is really like it. Indeed, to direct the intention of our minds immediately towards God, is that which we are not so well capable of in this present state. The intuition of his glory, our weak minds cannot admit of: "No man can see my face and live," saith God to Moses. But we can see our own faces; that is, the face of our own souls: we can take a view of them, and consider what naturally, and in themselves, they are: that is, according to what there remains of true primitive nature in us; and so may discern and understand much of God, as his glory is reflected on ourselves.

Though we know not how to face the sun when it shines in its strength and glory, yet we can sustain it to behold its image in the water, and look upon it there. So we cannot bear it, to behold the immediate radiations of divine glory directly shining forth, but reflected; and as it hath produced its image in ourselves, so we may be capable of beholding it. And by what we see in ourselves, when we understand that we are made after God's image, that there is a thing called mind in ourselves, then God must be a mind; there is a spirit in man, and we are his offspring: then he, sure, must be a spirit too; but an infinite, purer, and more perfect Spirit. If we find such a thing as love in our own natures, we may be sure that it is infinitely higher, and greater, and larger, and more perfect, every way, in God. But again,

(4.) We may further learn hence, that upon the account of our being made after God's image, we have much the less reason to hesitate at the receiving of that most mysterious doctrine of the Trinity in the Godhead: for if we seriously consider, we may discern the image and impress thereof in ourselves: and we find that we are made after God's image. There is none that doth so seriously contemplate himself, his own soul, but he may and must discern and acknowledge a trinity there; those primary principles which, considered in their conjunction, do carry a most manifest and express representation of God in this respect; to wit, active power, intellect, and love, those three great primalities in God, his word (who best knows his own nature) doth, upon all occasions, repeatedly express and inculcate to us. And the very like hereof we find in ourselves, considering these things in ourselves; not severed but conjunct: that is, a power to act, and to act according to understanding; and so act towards things that we love; and towards which there is a propension from a suitableness in ourselves to the things that we act towards.

Any one that will make himself his own study, must discern and acknowledge such things in himself as do make a real trinity; one and the same soul having active power belonging to it, understanding belonging to it, and love belonging to it, which, though all meet and unite in one and the same soul, are yet diverse and distinct from one another; for my power is not my understanding, and my understanding is not love; but all these do meet together in one and the same soul. So that considering man made after the image of God, the doctrine of the Trinity claims to be received with so much the more facility and agreeableness; we finding, so manifestly, the impress thereof upon our own souls. And so we may, upon many things in the created universe besides; yea, and we may find running through all things; but most manifestly and discernably in ourselves, concerning whom it is most eminently said, that "we were made after God's image." Again,

(5.) We may further learn, hence, that since man was made after the image of God, (so excellent and noble a creature as this image impressed upon him, must speak him and make him,) then sure, God did, in making this creature, design him for higher and greater things than can be compassed within this temporary state. He never did design, in making such a creature as' man, to confine him to time and to this lower world. For as he is a creature made after the image of God, he is made with capacities of far higher and greater things than this world can contain, or than time can measure.

If we look upon the present inhabitants of this world, so many minds and spirits inhabiting flesh, and cast about our eyes this way and that way, how thick is this same material world? how thick is it set with minds, with spirits, as so many diamonds sparkling in mud? Any one would say, "This is not their proper place: here are so many diamonds scattered here and there in dirt; surely they are not always to be there! Spiritual and immortal minds inhabiting flesh, and only casting their present rays upon low and sensible things; surely it will not always be thus." Did God make such creatures, did he make man, after his own likeness, for so mean and so low ends and purposes, as they are every where intent upon in this their present state? Did he make man after his own image, only to support and animate a little portion of breathing clay? Did he make him only to take this flesh to keep it awhile from turning into a putrid, stinking carcass. Was this all that a spiritual, immortal mind was made for?

Men should understand, by reflecting upon their original state, what the capacity of their nature was; and that they must be made for some other state, and for higher and greater things, than they commonly apply themselves to mind while they are here. You have so many minds dwelling in flesh; and many, but for a very little while. But suppose it, as long as men do more ordinarily live upon earth, why to have a mind, a spirit, created and put into flesh to inhabit that, suppose twenty, or thirty, or forty, or fifty, or sixty years, or to the utmost pitch that the lives of men do commonly reach to; and then that creature disappears and is gone. That flesh which that mind inhabiteth, turns to dust; the soul is fled and gone: here is no more appearance of this creature, this particular creature, upon this particular stage: what are we to conclude upon this then?

But that sure these have their parts to act in another state, upon an eternal stage, that shall never be taken down. Here are so many Godlike creatures brought into this world, and put in flesh, only to abide here such a certain number of years, and there is an end of them. This can never be thought, that God did make so many creatures after his own image, for so mean and ungodlike ends and purposes. And again,

(6.) We may further learn, hence, that an abode in the flesh, is not inconsistent with a very excellent state of life; for God did at first make man after his own image, of whose creation, as to the outward man, (of which I spake to you distinctly,) we are told, he was only made (as his name Adam doth import) out of the earth; but God breathed into him the breath of life, that intellectual vital life: he placed that spirit in him, by the inspiration whereof he came to be an understanding creature; and therein to resemble him that made him. Though this mind and spirit was to dwell in flesh, yet a very excellent state of life might be transacted here in this state: for admit that a mind and spirit be united with such flesh as we now inhabit and dwell in, yet here it hath the image of God entire and undepraved in it: not only a capacity of understanding, and of willing, and of acting, this way and that, but of doing all these aright, with a due rectitude adhering to each faculty; not remotely, not inseparably, as the sad events have shewn; but really and truly, so as that they might have remained in the state wherein they were made. O! then, how excellent a life might have been lived here, on these terms, in this world.

Though our likeness to God did not consist in this fleshly part of ours, or had not that for its seat and subject, yet it might very well consist with our having such a fleshly part about us, when there was pure and incorrupt integrity in all the powers and faculties of the soul of man: to have his soul replenished with the knowledge of God; possessed with a holy and adoring disposition, in a continual aptitude to look to, and a continual inclination to delight in, God, and in his converse; together with a universal love to one another, under that notion of being made after the image of God, as they should behold God's resemblance in one another. And O! what a happy world were this, and how pleasantly, and with what delight, might time have been transacted here: a very pleasant, happy, excellent state of life might consist with dwelling in flesh.

Such, in whom the image of God, to wit, his moral image, hath been (though less perfectly) restored, yet how pleasantly have they lived here in this world, amidst all the abounding wickedness of it: such a man as Noah; such a one as Enoch, who walked with God so many hundred years in this world. This is not to live an unhappy life, to walk with God every day, to live in his fear, and live in his communion. Is this to live unhappily?

Men are apt to transfer all the causes of their complaint to other things, and set them at a remote distance from themselves. Some, when they do evil, or evil befal them, accuse their stars or external circumstances. But we have nothing to accuse but our own ill inclinations. If we live evil lives, bad and sinful lives, or miserable lives, in this world, it is our own fault: for mere dwelling in flesh imposeth no necessity upon us, of being either sinful or miserable creatures. And that we might be convinced of this, we have the exemplification of such a life in our blessed Lord living in flesh (after all flesh had corrupted their ways) without taint. Therefore, being in flesh, as such, doth necessitate none, either to live wicked or miserable lives in this world: the mind and spirit of man being stamped with the image of God.

(7.) If man were at first made after God's own image, he must now, sure, be a very degenerate creature; the degeneracy of man must needs be exceeding great: how ungodlike a creature is he become! How unlike to God do men generally live and act, here in this world. This ought to be considered with deep and bitter regret. It is true that the natural likeness still remains, as it cannot but do, because it is natural, because it is the very nature of man himself. As his mind and spirit (being the immediate seal of the divine image) is a living thing, an understanding thing, a voluntary, active thing, this way and that, the natural image cannot but remain as long as man is man. But the degeneracy is with reference to the moral, superadded image; for that was at first superadded; and is *still due;* a thing concerning which we must say, it is a *Debitum esse;* and which, in reference to the natural image, is as the more curious lines of a picture are to the first rude draught. It is true, that first rude draught, consisting of maimed strokes, doth shew the true symmetry and proportion of the parts, in such a picture, to one another; but while every thing is yet wanting that tends to make up the comeliness and beauty, it is a very ungrateful spectacle that a man hath before his eyes in looking upon such a thing.

The natural powers that do belong to the soul of a man, shew his original capacity, what he was capable of; then all these capacities are to be filled up, as the rude draught of a picture should be, with what would add beauty, and the appearance of comeliness and vigour to it, as far as the pencil can express that. Here is a capacity in the very nature of man, of knowing much; but look upon that understanding power divested and destitute of all true knowledge. Here is a will capable of choosing, and of enjoying with highest complacency, the best and most delectable good; but totally divested of any such propension and inclination. And, here is a soul that is a spiritually active being; but it is active now any way but towards God, by whom it was made. Why in these very ruins of human nature, you may discern what originally it was.

Take the walls of some noble palace, yet standing: we will suppose all rooms to remain distinct from one another as they were, but it is totally unfurnished. It was inhabited, it may be, by some excellent person; but he is gone and hath left it: there was an honourable family that lived in splendor there; but they are removed, and now there is nothing to be beheld but bare walls: there be the rooms, the several apartments, as they were; but inhabited by nothing but owls and vultures: a habitation of dragons and serpents. And such is the soul of man, destitute of the divine, moral image, and of that holy rectitude which was the furniture and ornament of each several faculty and power.

We may here see what man was in his original state; and hence see and collect how great his present degeneracy is. O! how art thou fallen! what art thou fallen to, thou Lucifer, son of the morning! A Godlike creature, one made after God's image, a little lower than the angels, that did so perfectly resemble him; and now sunk into so low a degree of darkness, and impurity, and misery, and death: of which also we were not capable, if the natural image did not remain, if he had not an understanding still, and a will still, and an active power still. And then,

(8.) You may further learn, hence, what the work of regeneration is to perform in the souls of men; and of how absolute necessity such a work is to be effected and brought about there. So God made man after his own image. That plainly tells us what regeneration hath to do; that is, to restore that image wherein it was defective and lost. That must be the business of regeneration, considering together what the original state of man was, made after God's image: and considering what his present state is, his degenerate state, it is easy to collect what his regenerate state must be; a renovation, a state of renovation after the same image that man was impressed with at first, consisting of knowledge, (not only in a capacity to know, but in knowledge,) and in righteousness and true holiness. Not only in having the faculties that are capable of these, but in having these things themselves impressed into these faculties: this, regeneration must do: or the restoring us to ourselves, or repairing the image of God that was lost; that must be the business of regeneration. As man was made after the image of God at first, in his first creation; in his second creation, when he is made a new creature, he must be created again after God. The new man must be put on, "which after God is created in righteousness and true holiness." And this image is renewed in knowledge, as those two texts speak, Ephes. 4. 24. and Col. 3. 10. compared. Thus, is this part of the doctrine of the text improvable to the learning of several truths that do depend upon it, and that lie in connexion with it. Again,

2. It may be improved too, and very largely, in representing, and reprehending, several sinful evils that this wretched world abounds with; by which it appears how much men, by sin, have fallen short of the glory of God; such characters of his glory having been impressed at first upon them. Why, to consider such things as these that too evidently, and too commonly appear in the temper of men's minds, and in the course of their practice, here in this world: For instance,

To consider how low designs men do generally drive. What! Is this Godlike? Is this becoming a Godlike sort of creatures, such as man was at first, when they wear out their days here in this world, and make it their business to serve divers lusts and pleasures? What a base kind of servitude is this? Is this the creature made after God's image? Men to spend their days in the pursuit of shadows and trifles? Is there any resemblance of God in this? Is this like a creature that had in his own original and primitive state, a representation of divine in it, which was to conduct his whole course? And again, consider not only what men do pursue, that their minds and hearts are set upon; but (which carries more of horror in it) what they decline, and what their minds and hearts are set against. Men made after the image of God, and yet transacting their course in continual ungodliness. What! Thou made after the image of God, and yet an ungodly creature, and yet live an ungodly life in this world, when thou hast a soul about thee that can know God, that hath a capacity of knowing God, and of choosing him, and of loving him, and of delighting in him! That there should be in such a creature, stamped at first with the divine image and likeness, a disaffection to God; not only no inclination, but disinclination. What! disinclination to thine own true Pattern? disaffection to thine own Original? Thou wast made like God; why dost thou shun him? Why dost thou fly from him? Thou carriest the natural characters of his image upon thee whithersoever thou goest. And what! art thou running away from God with his image on thee, in the remainders of it? The remainders of it thou hast upon thy soul: a mind that can understand, a spirit that can and must live; and thou art running away from God with his own image upon thee. What a monstrous thing is that! And again,

3. It might, in the third place, instruct us in several duties that are also very congruous and con-natural to this part of the doctrine of this text. As,

(1.) More frequently to look back to our original estate. Such a truth as this made known, published to us, standing upon record in the sacred volumes, doth continually and repeatedly call upon us to look back, to consider and bethink ourselves what we were in our original state, made after God's own image, a God-like sort of creatures.

(2.) It will be our duty, hence, to be now ashamed of ourselves in our present degenerate state. It is no shame to a mean creature that was always so, to be now so; no shame to a worm that it is a worm; to a toad that it is a toad. But that man should become an impure, and a poisonous worm, part of the serpent's seed, this is a most shameful thing, and ought to be considered with the most confounding shame. We should even be startled at ourselves to think what, from such a conformity to God, we are now come to. And,

(3.) It should put us upon inquiring and listening after any means or ways of recovery. It would become a thinking creature, (as man naturally is,) apprehending as even the pagans, (the more refined of them generally have,) that men are not now what they were at first. And it would put such upon considering, "Is there no way of recovery?" And it hath put even pagans themselves (destitute of all revealed light) upon many considerations of that kind, insomuch as that we find several of them to have written treatises concerning the purgative and ornative virtues. It shews us to have a great deal more of stupidity among us, than was among pagans themselves, if we have no thoughts about restitution, about being restored, about being recovered out of so low a state as we find ourselves lapsed into, compared with that which we know was original to us. It should make our minds full of thoughts from day to day. "Is there no way to become again what once we were?" to have minds, and wills, and inclinations, and affections, so rectified as we find, and must apprehend to have been, in our first state? Is there no way to get into that conformity to God, and acquaintance with him, as to be able to lead my life with God, which was the thing most agreeable to my first state? And one that would use the understanding of a man, when he hears of a better state, that was original to him, would certainly be upon his inquiries—"Is there no way of recovering, no way of getting back into such an estate again?" And again,

(4.) It should render the gospel very dear to us, that doth so expressly reveal to us such a way, wherein the image of God is recoverable: and thereupon, converse with him, and a continual intercourse with him, are become possible to us. At present, where there is no likeness, there can be no converse, no disposition, no agreeableness or suitableness. How dear then should that gospel be, that is not only God's revelation, but his way and method to bring this about. To this end he hath revealed his Christ to us, his first Image, his primary Image. He that is said to be "the Image of the invisible God, the first-born before all the creation;" in whom his glory shines as "the glory of the only begotten of the Father;" the archetypal Image, according to which, the Image is to be renewed again in us. That gospel that reveals this to us, and which is designed to be God's instrument for the making of the impression afresh on our souls, how precious should it be to us! For his glory shines through it, as through a glass; that, "beholding this glory of the Lord, we may be changed into the same image, from glory to glory, as by the Spirit of the Lord:" since this, I say, is the design of that very gospel under which we live, O! how dear should that gospel be to us! By this, the image of God may be restored, which hath, in so great a measure, been defaced and lost out of our souls. And it again shews it to be our duty,

(5.) To aspire to the highest pitch of that perfection, in conformity to God, that these souls of ours are any way capable of; especially, that we should be continually aspiring unto the perfection of that state from whence we are fallen. Take the forementioned instruction of a pagan to that purpose. Whereas some might be apt to imagine, and their thoughts might suggest to them, "It is a presumptuous thing for me to think of being made like God, to be holy as God is holy, and to be blessed as God is blessed," and the like; we should consider what we are, that as that heathen said; "It is no fault, no blameable thing in any one to endeavour to ascend to that state or pitch, from which he did descend; we have a mind capable of God; and it would be carried towards him if vice did not depress and sink it. It is therefore matter of duty, from the consideration that we are to aim and aspire after such a state. I do not aim to be what I was, and what I ought to be, in duty towards him that made me, as well as consulting any interest of my own, in the first place: for I am first his, before I can consider myself as my own: and therefore, in duty towards him, the Author of my being, I ought to be aspiring and aiming at this, to have his image renewed in me, and to be restored in this respect, to what I was.

LECTURE XXI.*

Rom. 5. 12.

Wherefore, as by one man sin entered into the world, and death by sin; and so death passed upon all men, for that all have sinned.

YOU know we have, of late, been treating at large of the creation, and particularly and more especially, of the creation of man, and his original state, as he was created after God's image; not only his natural, but his moral image, so as to resemble him, both in holiness and blessedness. We come now, from these words, to consider the lapsed, degenerate state of man, now grown most unlike to God in both these respects; to wit, of purity, and of felicity; sunk into a state of sin, and into a state of misery; become a most deplorable, forlorn creature.

An amazing change! And indeed, it might amaze us, that it doth amaze us no more; that we can consider so astonishing a thing as this, with so little concern; when it is not a thing remote from us, but incurs our observation and sense, unavoidably, every day; whether we look about us, or whether we look into ourselves. And it doth so much the more need that such a subject should be insisted upon, the lapse of man, and the lapsed state into which he is come, and in which he is.

It is true, indeed, that usually, immediately upon considering that subject of the creation, providence useth and is wont to be treated in the next place. And that is a method rational

* Preached February 17, 1694.

enough in some respects. But it being my design to speak of the heads of religion as practically as God shall enable me; and the providence of God, (when we shall come to consider that) being for this purpose, is chiefly to be considered as it doth respect man: and the course of his providence towards man, having been for almost six thousand years backward, conversant about fallen man, lapsed man, whereas it was conversant about innocent man but a very little while; it seems to me more reasonable, with reference to the design in hand, to consider God's providence (especially when we are to consider it in reference to man) rather, first, as conversant about fallen man. And so, first, to consider his fall, and that state into which he was fallen, rather than to bring in the whole head of a discourse about providence, with reference to the very little inch of time wherein he stood in innocency.

And further, too, because the lapsed world of mankind is, as such, thereupon, manifestly put into the hands, and under the government of the Redeemer, who died, and revived, and rose again, that he might be Lord of the living and dead: yea, and not only the lapsed world of mankind, but even the whole creation, as a surplusage of remunerative dignity and glory, for that free and voluntary susception and undertaking of his, it will be, thereupon, most suitable to my design, to bring in the consideration of providence, under the mediatory kingdom of our Lord, and as it belongs to that vicegerency of his which he holds now, not only over this lapsed world, but over the whole creation, as by whom all things consist and are held together. And so, the discourse of the fall, in reference to this design of mine, very fitly intervening, I have chosen to pitch it on this place, from this text of Scripture now read.

In which we may take notice, that there is that which is called a *protasis*, the former part of a sentence, without an *apodosis*, or latter part in form, answering thereunto. Through that rich abundance of divine sense wherewith the apostle's mind and understanding did abound, and was replenished, it was not so well capable of being comprehended and limited by rules of art, or within artificial limits. But yet we may take notice too, that in the following verses there is that *apodosis*, the latter part of the intended sentence in substance, most fully and most copiously represented; the design of the whole paragraph being, in short, this only, to shew that as Adam, the first man, was to be a root and fountain of sin and death unto all his seed; so the second Adam would be, of righteousness and life to all his seed, there being a resemblance in the former of the latter, according to what is elsewhere said, that "the first

Adam was a figure of him that was to come," of the second that was to follow: though, there is not, it is true, an absolute and exact parallel or parity, as is never to be expected, in such cases, throughout.

My business will only be with what we call the *protasis*, the former of these parts, and that abstractly and by itself considered, without present reference to what follows in the succeeding verses. And so we are to shew you, that whereas, according to the tenour of the last discourse, man was created after God's image, not only his natural, but his moral image, made like him in respect of sanctity and felicity; he is now fallen into a state wherein he is most unlike God in these two things; to wit, into a state of sin, and into a state of misery. Both these, the text expressly represents and lays before us: " By one man sin entered into the world, and death by sin."

Here was the state of the one, the first apostate; he sins first, and thereby becomes miserable. He did represent and resemble God in holiness, purity and sanctity; now he is become a sinner. He did represent and resemble God in felicity and blessedness, in perfection and fulness of life; (not absolute perfection, it is true, not consummate perfection, but a perfection suitable to his present state;) and now he is become a creature lost in death: death immediately pursued the sin into which he lapsed and fell.

And thus it was, not only with the first sinner personally considered, but with all that were virtually comprehended in him; the whole offspring, the whole progeny: and the same two things have ensued upon them all; that is, sin, by that one being introduced, hath spread itself over all: and death, that way introduced, hath also diffused itself, and equally spread over all: all lost in death, inasmuch as all have sinned.

Very plain it is, that general notices of these things have obtained in the pagan world: and some of the more instructed and refined pagans have spoken strangely about this; magnifying the original and primitive state of man at first; as that it was a state wh in they did partake of a divine portion; and wherein they lived in that converse with God; and there was among them that righteousness, and that mutual love towards one another, as made this world a pleasant region, and most delectable habitation. We have large discourses in Plato to this purpose; and divers do speak as largely concerning the degenerate state of man;—that he is not the creature that he at first was. And they speak it with a great and most affectionate lamentation, that there should be such a change,

But yet, they having nothing in reference to these matters to guide them, but either dark or dubious conjectures, or false traditions, they could not but remain very ignorant of much: that is, how long that innocent state did continue; and, wanting divine revelation to guide them herein, some have drawn forth that state to a vast tract of time, speaking of it under the term of the "golden age:" and though it be generally acknowledged among them that there is a degeneracy in man, yet, how he came to fall, and wherein his fall at first stood, and how the dismal effects came to ensue so generally upon mankind; in reference to these things, they speak (as it could not but be) as men quite in the dark.

But here we have a most express and punctual account, and as comprehensive as we can have, in one text of Scripture, in these words of this text; that is, both of the fall of the first man; and then of the fallen state of all men: and both these in the mentioned respects, sin and death, transgression and the consequent doom.

And here are, in reference hereto, these three general heads that require to be distinctly spoken to—the fall of the first transgressor, this one that first sinned; and—the sinful and miserable state of all the whole race of men hereupon; and—the consecution of the latter of these upon the former, that by one that sinned there should be such a diffusion of sin, and consequently of death upon the whole race of men: how from the one man's sin whereby it first entered into the world, and by which death entered with it, there should be such a transfusion with it of sin and death too, through the world. These are the three general heads of discourse to be insisted upon. We begin with the first,

I. The fall of the first man. And in reference thereto, we have these four things more distinctly to be spoken to—wherein his sin stood by which he fell—how it came to pass that he (an innocent creature, made upright, as in that Eccl. 7. 29) should thus transgress—what the death was that was threatened and did ensue hereupon; and the dueness of this death upon his having once so sinned.

1. We are to consider his sin in itself, wherein that stood: and it is plain,

(1.) That it stood in the breach of a positive precept, which had said to him, that he must by all means abstain from the fruit of such a tree; as you see Gen. 2. 16, 17. "Of all the trees of the garden," wherein God had placed and set him, he might freely eat; but of that one, the tree of knowledge of good and evil, he must by no means eat: in the day wherein he did eat of it he must die, fall under death, become mortal.

There are here, some, that would fain imagine another way of understanding this whole history of man's fall, whom I shall meet with upon a more particular occasion by and by. But this is the first step by which man departed from God; to wit, his making bold in an interdict, in reference whereto, he had a positive expression of the divine pleasure in that signification which God gave him by his mind relating to that matter. He having both a liberty given him, and a limitation: a liberty—"thou mayest freely eat of all the trees of the garden;" and a limitation—"of this one thou mayest not eat:" and that interdict enforced by that tremendous sanction, "Eat and die; if thou eatest, it will be mortal to thee:" it was a breach of this positive law. Take that, (as we shall have occasion to note to you, more distinctly anon,) I say, take that act of eating in conjunction with all the concurrents, whatsoever it did lead to, or whatsoever was concomitant of that transgressive act. Herein, I say, it first stood, the breach of a positive law. But,

(2.) It did not stand in that alone, but in the violation of the whole law of nature too. This positive law, would never have been understood or known, if it had not been, some way or other, expressly signified. But we must understand a law of nature, besides, to have been given to Adam: to wit, by impression upon his heart; for the remains of such a law are still to be found in the nature of man, as the apostle in that 2. Rom. takes notice: "Men do shew the work of the law written in their hearts, their consciences either accusing *or excusing*," or accusing *and* excusing, *alternatim*, by turns; sometimes accusing, and sometimes excusing, as they did comport or not comport, with the dictates of their own conscience, which is appointed to be the conservatory of the precepts of that law.

And of this, there are divers celebrated passages among heathens themselves, who have called it not a written but a "born law," the *non scripta, sed nata lex;* so Cicero, and divers others, speak much to the same purpose. This same law of nature was transgressed in the transgression of this positive law, this particular interdictive precept, or negative command. For that particular precept had its foundation in the universal natural law; that is, this one comprehensive law must contain in it all the laws that could be supposed; that whatsoever our great Creator should signify to be his mind and pleasure, that, his intelligent, reasonable creature should be obliged to comply with him in. This sums up the whole law of nature, and so cannot but virtually comprehend all positive laws too; when once, by any such law, there is a signification given of the divine pleasure, and mind, and will, of him that made me: I ought to obey, when I know his mind; I ought to be ruled and governed by that expression thereof, which he is pleased to afford. This law of nature, (comprehensive of all laws) was broken in this transgression; and sundry great breaches of it, which strike deep into the very foundation, must be contained in this transgression. As for instance,

Here was contempt of the highest and most indisputable authority. God said, "Do not this thing:" the creature saith, "Aye but I will do it." God saith, "If thou doest it thou diest:" he saith, "I will do it though I die for it." Here was no fearfulness of his displeasure, and of his punitive justice, the very sword whereof was drawn, and did glitter before his eyes, in the commination and threatening wherewith God fenced his law. Here was disbelief of the first eternal truth. Here was believing of a creature against the Creator. Whether that were an innocent creature, or a fallen creature, though he could not tell, yet he could tell it was a creature that spake to him and tempted him: and yet, this creature is believed against God; and here was an interpretative, constructive saying, "God is a liar; this creature speaks more truly than he." Here was vain curiosity, an affectation of knowing more than God yet thought fit for his estate. Here was impatiency of waiting for God's further most seasonable and opportune discovery. Here was discontent with that excellent state in which God had set him. Here was pride and ambition; he must be some greater thing than God had made him; "Ye shall be as gods." This is contained in it. So that we are not to think that the bare act of eating the forbidden fruit did constitute all the sin of man. But there are all these horrid things complicated and meeting together in it, which made it a sin most exceedingly sinful; especially for him that was hitherto in a right mind; upon whom clear light shone; no cloud upon his understanding; no perverseness hitherto in his will; a power to master the appetite, and keep under the otherwise mutinous inclinations of sensitive nature. Take all together, and we find, here was not only a transgression of the positive precept, but here was also a most manifest breach of the natural law, in the greatest and deepest foundations thereof. Now, herein stood this sin; which was the first thing to be spoken to about that first more general head. But,

2. We are to consider, next, how this should come to pass, that a creature perfectly intelligent, and perfectly holy, yet in his integrity should come to be guilty of so horrid a violation of the divine law as this. It is an astonishing thing, to think

of, or speak to; but an account is to be given of it so far as God hath been pleased to give it us. And so, to the inquiry, "How came this sin into the world by this one man?" we must answer, "It came so as the divine history doth inform us." The law given him, you have in the 2 chapter of Gen. 16, 17. verses: the violation of it, in the 3 chapter, at large, as distinctly as the divine wisdom did think needful for us. And so you find several things to concur, and must be understood so to have done to the bringing of this matter about, or that there should be such a thing as sin thus entering into the world. As,

(1.) We are to consider herein the divine permission. Most certain it is, that God did permit, or otherwise it could not have been. And it is easy and obvious to us all to apprehend, that if he had pleased, he could easily have hindered it. The event shews that he did permit; for it did evince, it did come to pass, and he could easily have prevented so dismal an issue, if he had thought fit. But concerning that permission; it is true we are to refer it to the divine permission, in very great part, to whom it did belong to prescribe, but not to be prescribed unto; that he might do what he pleased with his own; give more or less of a gracious influence as he saw fit. But we are not to ascribe it to his sovereignty alone, or to the absoluteness of his power, but to that power of his, guided by the supreme wisdom, that discerns all the reasons of things.

We have, you know, discoursed largely upon that text, "Who worketh all things after the counsel of his own will." All things that he doth and permits; all things that he suffers and lets his people do: all do fall under the determination of the wisest, and deepest, and most righteous counsels: nothing is done rashly; nothing incogitantly done, or permitted to be done. That, therefore, is to be considered in the first place, how it came to pass, that there should be such a transgression of the divine law, both positive and natural together—God permitted it. And,

(2.) This is further to be considered, that the apostate angels (who made a defection from God) were manifestly apostatized, and had made that defection before. They were gone off from God, had made a schism in heaven, and forsook their first station. And,

(3.) Nothing was, hereupon, more obvious, than that they should affect to draw this now made creature (man) into a combination and confederacy with them, against the rightful, sovereign Lord of all. And,

(4.) It is plain, that as they were inclined to it, (and easy it was to suppose that they would be inclined to it,)so we find that they did actually attempt it. It is likely, one of their number and, most probably, their prince, the arch-devil; it was he that made this attempt. The matter is put into his hands to make trial, whether he can draw off this new-made creature from his loyalty, and involve him in the same guilt and misery with himself and his companions; and bring him under the displeasure and curse of his and their Maker, as they were.

It is very plain, that it was the devil that tempted in, and by, the serpent. The Scripture doth expressly call him "the old serpent, the devil, and satan," as you see, Rev. 12. 9. That puts the matter out of all doubt. And that he might not fright Adam, (who possibly might hitherto be ignorant of a superior order of creatures,) by appearing to him (as it were) in some angelic form: and Adam very well knowing, that there were not any other men besides himself: therefore, the devil slides into the body of the serpent to tempt. I know no reason we have to suppose or imagine that the devil did form of condensed air, another body like that of the serpent, (though that might be no impossible thing to do, as there are frequent instances in following times and ages,)but there being such a creature already formed, it is a great deal more probable, that he should insinuate and slide into the body of that: and how often hath he possessed human bodies, even when they have been alive, and sometimes when they have been dead! Histories give us many instances of it: and it is, therefore, not at all strange that he should possess the body of the serpent for such a purpose as this, and some way or other speak in, or by it. He hath spoken in the bodies of men, many times, (the stories themselves that we have of that sort importing plainly so much,) not making use of their organs of speech, but speaking more deeply in them than their organs of speech did lie. And so it is not strange, that though such a creature was not naturally furnished with the power of speech, yet that he might speak in it, and by it.

And now here it is true, there are those who are so over wise above, and beyond, what is written, that they think it a mean thing to understand the history of the creation; and then, of the fall of man, according to the true literal meaning and import of the words wherein it is given. And as they are too wise (I hope) to be our instructors in such a case, so I hope we shall not be foolish enough to be instructed and taught by them. The apostle himself, if it were mean and low to understand that history in the literal sense, was content to be of that low form, when he told us "the serpent beguiled Eve," and "he was afraid lest they should be beguiled, as the serpent by his subtilty beguiled Eve," 2 Cor. 11. 3. Pray let us content ourselves to be of that lower form with the apostle; that is, modestly understand this history just as it lies.

For the history of the creation, some are sick of it, because they cannot tell how to reconcile the literal account thereof, in the beginning of Genesis, with the philosophy of their Descartes: as if his reputation were a thing more studiously to be preserved than that of Moses; though, yet, more might be said than hath been, to reconcile with rational principles, even the whole history of the creation: and it might be discerned even by themselves, if there were not more ill will, and an affectation to slur Scripture in the case, than the love of reason. Most plain it is, that it is a very ill compliment which they put upon Moses, when they would have him to have written the story of the creation, and of the fall of man, in that form wherein we find it, only to amuse the people over whom he was set: some account or other must be given; and such a one as this, would serve their turn, and help to awe them, and render them more governable.

This is the account that some presume to give of this part of the divine Revelation: and therein, they express a great deal less reverence for, and esteem of, Moses, than some heathens have done: Diodorus Siculus, in particular, who magnifies him as one of the wisest men that the world hath had. But certainly, as these persons do take off all that can be imagined, from the integrity of any honest historian, so they did it without any respect to the reputation of his wisdom too. For if it were to be supposed that the fidelity of an historiographer were to be dispensed and laid aside: and if Moses could have obtained of himself to have done that, surely he might easily have contrived a more plausible romance than this that is supposed to be feigned by him: so as that no man can imagine what should induce him to give such a narrative, but only the known revealed truth of the things themselves. If one would have deviated from that, it might have been with a great deal more speciousness than this hath been.

And it is, likewise, a very ill compliment that such, too, put upon the people of the Jews; yea, and upon all mankind, to suppose that they would be capable of being so imposed upon, if there be not evidence in the things themselves related to them and reported.

But it is the greatest slur of all the rest, which they put upon divine Revelation, that when that appears and is so manifestly allowed to have been written for the instructing of men, it should yet be supposed to be written for the cheating of them. It is, therefore, plain and out of question, that the devil did tempt this new made creature man, in the serpent, into which he insinuated himself to this purpose, unto this transgression. And that is the fourth thing we are to consider about the manner of this sin coming to pass.

(5.) And that the devil applied himself to Eve apart (as it is apparent) from her husband, when there was not an opportunity of consulting with him, she being, though (it may be) not of less clear, yet of less strong intellectuals; and in that respect the weaker vessel; her, he attempts: for Adam was not deceived, but Eve; that is, not first, but she first; and so was made use of as an instrument to deceive him, as the apostle tells us: 1 Tim. 2. 14.

And because time doth allow me to go no further now, let me only close what hath been now said, with a caution to that sex: and especially those that are in the conjugal relation. Let them consider what God hath appointed that relation for. He gave Eve to Adam as a help meet. We see what a help she proved; a help to destroy him; a help to undo him, and his whole race and progeny; perverting the very end for which God appointed that relation. O! let such consider and look to it, that are apt to tempt their husbands into sin, because of their relation; because of the affection that they bear to them; because of the constant opportunity they have to insinuate into them, when their pride, and their vanity, and their vindictiveness, very often, must be all employed and set on work to draw their relative into sinful combinations with them against God, when he appointed them to be helps in the relation and capacity wherein they are set. They should be helps to duty; helps Godward; helps heavenward; joint helps, walking in the way to life. It lies in my way to note this; and let it be seriously considered and noted, according to the import and concernment of it.

LECTURE XXII.*

But we are to consider in the next place, and that as the main thing more immediately to be considered in this case,

(6.) The primitive state of human nature, in respect of the morality which was founded there, and wherein, or wherewith, man was at first created. You may remember, that speaking

* Preached February 24, 1694.

of that former great head, the state of man by creation, from that text which tells us of "God's having made him after his own image," and in speaking of the moral image of God upon man in his creation, comprehending both sanctity and felicity, that there we told you we were neither to lay the matter too low, nor too high; not so low as to make it thence apprehensible, that the sin of man was intrinsically necessary, however it might be extrinsically, with reference to divine foresight; that it should be thought intrinsically necessary would be of horrid consequence to admit; for that would be to make the Author of his being the Author of his sin. Therefore, great care was to be taken, not to lay the matter so low as to exclude the intrinsic possibility of man's standing: nor again, was it to be laid so high as to exclude the possibility of his falling; which the sad event doth shew.

The matter, therefore, of his fall, is principally to be resolved into the estate wherein, upon the account of his morals, he was created; that is, that he was made innocent, but not impeccable; he was made a sinless creature, but not with an impossibility of sinning: and in particular, his mind, it was made apprehensive, very capable of true and right notions of things, but not incapable of wrong: it was made without error, but not indeceptible, under no present deception as it was made, and yet, not under an impossibility of being deceived and imposed upon by false representations and colours. And so as to his will, it was created without any determination to good; it was made in that state of liberty as to be in a certain sort of equipoise, according as things should be truly or falsely represented, by the leading faculty, to the mind and understanding. And so hereupon, according to this original state of human nature, there was a possibility remaining of what, no doubt, did ensue. As,

[1.] Faulty omission in several respects. As,

First. Of prayer, in the instant and article of temptation. It had been a creaturely part in that instant, presently to have looked up; "Lord I am thy creature, the work of thine hands, leave me not to err in such a critical season as this." And again,

Secondly. Of dependance. The creature, as such, was by the law of his creation obliged to depend; that is, a reasonable creature capable of being governed by a law, was obliged to an intelligent, voluntary dependance, as all creatures, as creatures, have a natural dependance: and it cannot be otherwise with any of them. There should, by such a dependance, have been a derivation and drawing in a sustaining, strengthening influence, *de novo*, as the exigency of such a case did require.

Thirdly. And of consideration. There was, no doubt, an omission of that; that he did not use the understanding power and faculty that God had endued his nature with, to ponder, and weigh, and balance things in that juncture of time. He being essentially, as to his mind and spirit, a thinking creature, should have used thoughts with more equity; that is, have balanced things on the one hand and the other. And this, it is plain, was not done. And there was no doubt,

Fourthly. An omission of the exercise of the great principle of love, which could not but be most connatural to such a creature: love to God, love to himself, love to his posterity. This principle was not excited and drawn forth into act and exercise, as it ought, in such an exigency, to have been. And this, as easily made way for,

[2.] Faulty commissions even in the inward man, mental and cordial ones in the mind, and in the heart. As,

First. The allowing himself to aim at greater measures of knowledge, than God had yet thought fit for him: whereas, he should have been content with a state in which God had set him in this respect, and have waited for his further manifestations to him, of what it was fit and convenient for him to know. It is plain, the temptation was specious unto the cognitive power of man: " Ye shall be as gods, knowing good and evil;" a very plausible temptation to a creature made capable of knowing much, and therefore, could not but have a desire (suitable to such a capacity) of knowing more than he yet did. He might easily apprehend that this his state, in this respect, was not so perfect, though it was not sinfully imperfect. He was guilty of no culpable and blameable ignorance before; but not endued with so much knowledge, but that he could easily apprehend it might grow. But it was to have grown in a regular way; partly by his own improvement of his reasoning power; and partly by a patient expectation of God's further manifestations and discoveries to him. But he complies with the temptation that thus is given to his cognitive faculty, catching at a sudden power of knowing, beyond what belonged to his compass, and was within his reach, by ordinary and allowable methods and means. And then there was no doubt,

Secondly. A sinful cherishing of sensitive appetite, which it belongs to a reasonable creature to have governed, and kept within limits. He was of a compound nature; intellectual, and sensible; and the sensitive nature is permitted to aspire and set up for the government, and it is yielded. A great violation of the law of his nature, and that order that God had settled, at first, of superiority and inferiority between his natural powers. The object, no doubt, was very tempting, fair to the eye, and it is likely might carry a fragrancy and odoriferousness with it to the smell; and, in conjunction with the other methods of temptation, this might signify much. But, in the mean time, the cherishing and indulging sensitive appetite against the law of the mind and rational nature, could not but be a very faulty commission in this respect.

And so, altogether comes to discover the difference between paradise and heaven, the paradisiacal state and the heavenly state. There was at first, in paradise, sinlessness; thus far, there was a *posse non peccare*, a *possibility of not sinning:* but in the heavenly state a *non posse peccare, an impossibility of sinning*. This difference was soon to be understood; that is, it is now to be collected from what did soon and early appear in view. Man was not made in a state of *comprehensor*, in that which was to be his ultimate and consummate state; but in a state of probation, made a probationer, in order to some further state, which upon his approving himself he was to be introduced into. And such a defectibility, a possibility of understanding things wrong, and choosing wrong, it was most suitable to the primitive state of man. According to all that we can apprehend of the wisdom of God, there must be a state of probation, before a state of retribution; before punishment or reward, there must be an obediential state, wherein a man shall, as he acquits himself, be capable of, or liable to, the one or to the other. Nothing could be more congruous unto the perfection of that Supreme Being who was the Author of our being, than, that this should be the state of things between him and man, at the first.

And now, before we pass from this head, there are sundry instructive corollaries or inferences, that we may take up from it.

1. One we have mentioned already, (as it the last time came in our way), that is, of what concernment it is to the female sex, to take heed of comporting duly with, or lest they should violate or pervert the intent of, their being made what they are: and that they, coming into the conjugal estate, should be helpers to them with whom they are conjoined in that state. "Let us make for man a help meet for him:" we see how the design of that very institution was perverted and lost at first. A help! such a help as helped to destroy him, and ruin the world with him. It was not he that was deceived; (as the apostle to Timothy notes;) that is, not first deceived,

but she, a woman that God had given him. And it is not without apparent need, but most agreeable to the ducture of Scripture in this case, that such a remark as this should be made; and that they whom it concerns, should receive instruction by it: for history is full of many dreadful instances, what tragedies, feminine subtilties, and pride, and lust, and envy, and vindictiveness, hath brought about in this wretched world. But,

2. We may further learn from the whole, that it is of equal concern to that sex to which God hath given the priority, that they keep up to the law of their state; which is to be leaders and guiders in the state of marriage when they come thereinto; and that they dwell with the other relative, according to knowledge; (as the apostle Peter's expression is, 1 Pet. 3. 7.) that they comport with the obligation that the original institution hath laid upon them as to this. For we are not to think that Adam could, therefore, be excused because Eve solicited him, having offended first: no more than afterwards, Ahab was excused for being a wicked man above all others, (upon the matter there was none like him for wickedness,) because that Jezebel his wife stirred him up, as it is, 1 Kings 21. 25. He was not, therefore, a more innocent person; no, he was wicked, even beyond parallel, though Jezebel his wife stirred him up: for Adam ought to have done the business of his station. He that is first in such a relation and that hath the higher dignity, ought to comport with the obligation of the law of his state, and to exercise that more confirmed judgment which is supposed did belong to him. That he did not so, this made him guilty before the Supreme Judge. "Because thou hast hearkened to the voice of thy wife:" (Gen. 3. 17.) therefore, the malediction of the doom comes upon him, which hath been so generally transmitted as we know. Again,

3. We learn, hence, that the grace of God, not as it is eminent in himself, but as it is transient, doth issue forth, and is communicated and imparted here and there, doth admit of degrees: there may be more, or there may be less, given forth, according to the mere pleasure of the Free-giver. A contemplation that tends highly and justly to exalt and magnify the grace of God, and the God of all grace, in the absoluteness of that liberty which maketh it what it is, that is, "grace." It could not be grace if it were not most free. And being so, then he might dispense more, or he might dispense less, as to him seemeth good. We are not to think there was nothing of grace, nothing of dignation, nothing of vouchsafement, in God's first treatment of Adam; that he would make him such a creature,

that he would give him such endowments as he did, it was all of good pleasure. But so absolute liberty, as doth belong to grace, might issue forth in higher or in lower degrees, as should seem meet to the Free-giver: he might give so much of his own influence, as by which it was intrinsically possible (as was said before) not to have sinned; while he was under no obligation to give forth so much as to make it impossible to sin. Again,

4. We may further learn, hence, that by the same steps and degrees by which man did at first depart from God, God did depart from man; forsook not, but being forsaken: so that the measure which he gave long after, was at first observed strictly; (as it still is every where in the world;) God is with you while you are with him: so it ever was, so it ever will be, between him and his intelligent creatures. As the creature goes off from him, he righteously recedes and goes from the creature. Not, that on the part of favour he puts himself under any negative tie, that is not to be thought or imagined, but he is pleased to put himself under a positive one; that is, he hath put himself under no obligation to do more than according to this rule. For that he most frequently doth: and (in the state of apostasy) without it, who could be saved? None could, if God did not draw nigh to men; or took up a thought so to do. That rule is no negative tie upon God: but he hath been pleased to put himself under a positive tie; that is, such as are in the state of grace now, God will be with them while they are with him. As to Adam, who was in a state of grace of another kind at first, God would most certainly be with him as long as he was with God. And so it is still, with any that are in a state of grace, any that God takes to be his peculiar people: " I will be with you while you are with me;" he will never do less than that. He may, many times, do more, incomparably more, unspeakably more: he may prevent, and be beforehand; or he may follow men in their wanderings, even as he did Adam himself when he was wandered and gone off. But he would never go off from Adam first; he only did go off and depart from him by such steps as by which Adam did depart from God: and not being tied to the contrary, he might do so, and for wise and holy ends did. But again,

5. We may further learn, hence, that such a liberty of will as stands in a mere indifferency to good or evil, is no perfection unalterably and immutably belonging to the nature of man: nothing can be more apparent, such a liberty as that, is most unfit to be magnified and made such an idol of as it hath, by many

within the Christian world. For it is plain, and nothing can be plainer, that it did not belong as a perfection, immutably, to the nature of man. It was very suitable to that less perfect state in which man was created and made. But it is not to be found agreeing to it immutably, and without variation, at any time since, or ever will again. It just served for that state wherein he was at first made, such a liberty as stood with an indifferency to good and evil, (whether that good or evil should lie in doing or not doing, or whether it should lie in doing this or doing that,) it never belonged to man, but only in that first juncture, as being very suitable to the state in which man, as a probationer, was made and set at first. But it is not found to be with man ever since, or is ever like to be again: for in the unregenerate state, there is a liberty only unto evil, so as " all the imaginations of men's hearts are only evil, and that continually." There is no liberty as to any spiritual good, saving good. And again, even the regenerate state, though there be a liberty to good through grace, yet it is very imperfect. And then, look to the consummate state of saints in glory, and there is only liberty to good; no liberty of sinning: nay, no liberty to good or evil, (consider the matter morally,) not at all. So that so magnified an idol of liberty of will, as if it were an inseparable perfection of the nature of man, was never known to agree to it, but in its first state: and no more was ever found belonging to it since, nor ever will be.

It may be said, it is only the moral good and evil, which is superadded to the nature of man, that alters the case with him; and that doth not change his nature; but that his nature will still be the same. And it is very true, his nature is the same that at first it was: otherwise, he could not be the same creature that did offend, and comes to be punished; or that shall, by grace, be made to comply with the terms of God's gracious covenant; and that shall afterwards come to be, through grace, rewarded. He would not be the same creature, if there were a change, quite, of his nature, and the essentials of his being: man would not be man, he would be another thing. But then, as moral good superadded hereunto, the one or the other of them may be without making his nature another thing. It cannot, therefore, be said, that this liberty of will is altogether inseparable from his nature. And if, in the heavenly state, (which is most plain and evident,) confirmation in good, doth nothing spoil a man's liberty, then, the efficacy of his grace in his present state, doth not spoil a man's liberty neither: nay, it doth much less; for if it should be supposed to do so, then, a man would be less a man for being a glorified man; it would be a diminution to the dignity of man, and he would be the worse for going to heaven; because there, his liberty ceaseth, a liberty to good or evil. What an unimaginable thing is that, that it should be a depression, a diminution, to a man, to glorify him! that that should be a maim of his nature! But if the glory of heaven do not diminish a man, or be a maim to him, because it takes away the possibility of sinning in the heavenly state; then, the efficacy of grace, in the present state, is no diminution, nor blemish, nor maim to the nature of man now neither. Again,

6. We may further learn, hence, what cause we have to apprehend and dread the destructive designs of the devil. For what! do we apprehend that he is less an enemy to God, or less an enemy to man, now, than he was at first? Do you think the devil is grown kinder, more good natured, less intent upon the destruction of souls, and less malicious against heaven? It is a most intolerable, most inexcusable thing, that we who pretend to believe the Revelation of God about these things, and do hereby know the devil to have been a "murderer from the beginning," and may collect, that he is still going about, that he may destroy and devour as a roaring lion; I say, the Lord have mercy upon us, that notwithstanding we pretend to know and believe all this, we should live so secure as we do, without any thought of any such thing. And,

7. It may give us to understand the madness of self-confidence, that we should be so little afraid of sin; that we should be so little afraid of temptation; that we should be so apt to trust our own strength: and when that perfect state wherein Adam was made in paradise, was not enough to secure him, that we should live such independent lives, so seldom look up, that we have not the sense of that petition more deeply wrought into our souls, "that we may not be led into temptation." Divers other things there are that might be hinted, but I shall only add this, for the present,

8. We may further learn, that there is no need that there should be any new invented account of the first apostasy of man, so as therein to depart from the plainness and simplicity of the letter of that history, which God hath given us of it; there is no need of any such thing. The matter, as Scripture represents it, and as we have (though less perfectly) represented it from Scripture, as it lies, is rational and congruous enough; and such as we need not be ashamed to own and avow to the world. There are those that are so over-officious

in these matters, as to trouble the world with their fine notions and accounts thereof, altogether alien from the letter of the history, that so they may (as is pretended) make things look a little more plausibly than the letter of history doth represent them; when indeed, if the matter be searched into, the design seems to be, not to make them look plausible, but ridiculous: and their business is not to expound Scripture, but to expose it, and the whole of our religion. But I shall say no more to them now neither.

LECTURE XXIII.*

SO far we have gone in our course of treating, in some order, of the several heads of religion, as to enter upon this doctrine of the apostasy, which we proposed to consider and speak to from this text, *Sin entered into the world, and death by sin,* and therein to treat of these three general heads.

I. Of the fall of the first man.

II. Of the fallen state of man. And,

III. Of the consecution of the latter of these upon the former.

And for the First of these generals, the Fall of the First Man, we proposed, therein, to consider and speak to these four more special heads: 1. the sin by which he fell; 2. the way how he fell into, and by this sin; 3. the death that did ensue; and, 4. the dueness of that death upon this sin: and we have spoken to the two first of these.

3. We come now to the third, the death that did ensue as to this first man. And here the inquiry may be, whether that the death contained in the commination or threatening, be principally meant, or the death that is in other-terms expressed in the consequent sentence? The first of these, you read Gen. 2. 17. and the latter you read, Gen. 3. from the 17. to the 19.

* Preached March 10, 1694.

ver. I say, whether the death expressed in the commination—"In the day that thou eatest thereof, thou shalt surely die:" or that which is in other words expressed (not by the word death) in the sentence, " dust thou art and unto dust thou shalt return," be the same, yea or no; it is plain, that there is a real difference betwixt the commination (formally considered) that contains the one, and the sentence that expresses the other.

By the former, the commination or threatening, is established (as far as the comminatory sanction could go) that law, or covenant of works, which was to concern all mankind. By the latter, to wit, the sentence, there was a particular application of this law, now transgressed, unto this particular case of transgressing Adam; as that is the proper business of a sentence, to apply the law according to which it must be understood to pass to the particular case of offenders, when they come to be judged by that law.

But it is here more distinctly to be considered, whether that the sentence do not carry with it some moderation as to the evil or penalty contained in the threatening of commination: in reference whereto, these particulars are worthy your consideration.

(1.) That the terms, wherein the one and the other are to be delivered, are not the same; for the terms of the commination, by which the law or covenant of works, that was to concern all mankind is established, as by a solemn sanction, goes in these express terms: " In case thou eatest, thou shalt (as we read it) surely die:" thou shalt die the death, or, dying, thou shalt die. But the sentence hath not the word "death" in it; but it speaks of sundry miseries that should attend this life, and that should end, at length, in the dissolution of the compound, and especially, of the earthly part : " Dust thou art, and unto dust shalt thou return." Having worn out a sad life amidst many sorrows here on earth, thou shalt go to the dust at last, as thou art dust. And,

(2.) It is to be considered, that these different terms are not apt, fully, to express the same thing: for whereas, it is said in the commination, " In the day thou eatest thereof, thou shalt die the death," these are expressions very fitly accommodated to signify death in the utmost extent, in all the latitude of it, "thou shalt die the death:" all the fulness of death seems to be comprised therein without limitation. But in the sentence, when the great day comes to pass judgment upon the delinquents, (the law being now violated and broken,) you have not, in his application to either of the human offenders, any so terrible expressions as this, only they are doomed to manifest sorrows and miseries: and it is told to Adam, (in whom the woman must be comprehended as being taken out of the man) that "dust they are, and unto dust they shall return;" therefore, there seems to be much less in the sentence than in the commination. And,

(3.) It is to be considered, that between these two, the gospel did intervene; that is, between the commination and the sentence: the commination was given with the law to man yet innocent: when he was now fallen and had transgressed, then cometh the sentence; but it so comes as that the gospel steps in between, being tacitly insinuated in reference to them, in what was directly said to the serpent; that which was a curse to him, was a blessing to them: "I will put enmity between seed and seed, between thy seed and the woman's seed; and that seed shall break thy head, though thou shalt bruise his heel." And this, the grace of God might, for ought we know, apply and bring home to the case of Adam, as it was applied to all the more special seed of the woman, that should come to be united with him who was most eminently the woman's seed. And therefore, it might very well be, that though all the fulness and horrors of death, taken in its utmost latitude and comprehension, were included in the commination, there might, in pronouncing the sentence upon Adam, be as great a mitigation, as the variation of the terms doth import.

But our inquiry here, must be concerning the death contained in the commination, where we have the term of " death," double death, or dying the death, most expressly made use of. And it is by that, that the dying of this death is to be measured; to wit, by the commination, as it did concern Adam, and it must concern Adam's posterity. And admit, that there was a real mitigation upon the intervening of the gospel, and the exercise of the grace of God, applying it in Adam's case, yet we are still to consider the death that was contained in the commination, as due to Adam; due, to wit, in a former instance, before there could be a mitigation in a latter, in a following instance: for supposing there were then so quick and speedy a remission in so great part, yet, the penalty remitted must be due, before it could be remitted. It must be a debt, before it could be a remitted debt. And so concerning the death that was due, which offending Adam and his posterity became subject and liable to; I say, concerning that, it is, we have to inquire, as this dueness is measured by the commination; though indeed, we are not yet, according to the series and order of discourse, to consider this death in the extensiveness of it to Adam's posterity; for that comes in, under the next general head, the fallen state of man; whereas, we have only now to consider the fall of the first man, and what did concern the case of Adam himself. And so, our inquiry is, What death it was that was threatened to him, upon the supposition that he should transgress? And of this matter, I shall give you an account in several particulars.

[1.] Most plain it is, that corporeal death was included in the meaning of the commination; for that he did actually incur. You read, in the short history that we have of him, that death, at length, finished his course. He lived so long, and he died. And it could not be, that he should incur that which was not due. And if it were due, it must be so upon the commination; as the dueness of any such punishment, upon any delinquent, is first measured by the law; the sentence is to proceed according to law; that is, so far as not to go beyond it: it is possible there may be mitigations, but the extent of the law cannot be exceeded. That is therefore plain, that corporeal death was included. And,

[2.] It is very evident too, that much more was included than corporeal death: for Adam did actually suffer more (as is manifest) than mere corporeal death; as the labours, and hardships, and sorrows of life, and whatsoever else besides, about which we shall further inquire anon. And,

[3.] That more beyond corporeal death could not mean annihilation, or an extinction of his being. For,

First. We do not find that either he, or any one else, was ever annihilated, or that any creature ever was. No such thing appears that either he, or any man, or any thing, was actually reduced to nothing. Nor again,

Secondly. Could death be a proper expression of annihilation: for annihilation is not adequately opposite to life. There is no adequate opposition between life and annihilation: if there were, then life and non-annihilation, or continuing such a thing in being, must be equivalent terms, if the other be adequately opposite terms. But it is plain, they are not so; because it is manifest, there are many things in being, and which are somewhat, and yet do not live. Therefore, to suppose that annihilation should be the thing meant by death, here, as is threatened to Adam, and so to offending man in him, is a dream, without a pretence or ground, neither to be found, or any shadows of it, in Scripture; nor at all agreeing to the reason of the thing.

To reduce a thing to nothing, is no apt kind of punishment. There is no other thing, indeed, but a reasonable creature, that is capable of punishment, properly so called. But the reduction of any thing to nothing, is to put it absolutely out of any capacity of apprehending itself under divine displeasure; or, that it is self-fallen, under the animadversion of justice: and therefore, is a most unsuitable thing to be designed for the punishment of a reasonable creature, if it were to be called a creature. But the very notion is most unsuitable to it. And therefore,

[4.] There is no doubt, but spiritual death is included. "Thou shalt surely die," thou shalt die the death: here must be included spiritual death; the death of the soul; not naturally understood, but morally: for naturally, the soul is immortal, and can never die. But death, in reference to the soul, being taken morally, that is, as inclusive both of sin and misery, so the soul was liable to death, and became no doubt the subject of it, in this very case, antecedently to the restitution, and recovery, and the actual supervention of the divine grace. And when we say that death, in this sense, that is, the moral sense, doth include both sin and misery, it must do so, even by the same reason, by which life, in the moral sense, doth include both sanctity and felicity. And it is manifest, it doth include both.

But then, we must further know, that sin being included in this death, it must be in a twofold notion, which we must understand in our minds concerning sin; that is, sin is to be considered, either as it is an evil against God; or it is to be considered, also, as an evil to ourselves. As an evil against God, so it could be a wrong to him, though it cannot be a hurt. And in that sense, or according to that notion, we are not to take sin here, for so we considered it under the former head. Very true it is, we must add,

[5.] That there is a necessary complication of sin and misery with one another, as there is of sanctity and felicity with one another: they are complicated, and cannot but be so, even in their own natures. But though they cannot be severed, they may be considered distinctly. Severed they cannot be, neither of these two pairs—neither sin and misery, nor holiness and blessedness. Neither of the pairs can be disjoined or severed; the love of God, that comprehends in it all our duty, and all our felicity, virtually, as being the great active principle, and the great fruitive; that principle, from whence I am to do all the good I do; and that principle by which I am to enjoy all the good that I enjoy, or am capable of enjoying. Both of these two things, summed up together in one virtual principle of love, can never be disjoined or severed, any more than a thing can be torn and severed from itself. And so the case is, as to the opposite pair; sin and misery, they can never be disjoined or severed, for they are virtually comprehended in one and the same principle; to wit, enmity to God; upon the account whereof, while it prevails, it is impossible either to obey God or enjoy him. These two, therefore, cannot but be inseparable. But while they are inseparable, yet they are distinct too. As to this latter pair, wherein we are now concerned, to wit, sin and misery; "To be carnally minded is death." And as it is misery, and so a hurt and ruin to us, so it is to be considered here as it comes under the notion of the threatened death, and so doth make a part of the threatened penalty; that is, sin carrying a self-punitive malignancy in it. God having been once offended, he leaves the sinner (till grace doth work the reparation) under that self-punishment. "Thine own wickedness shall correct thee." And so, in this sense it is, that spiritual death must be comprehended in that death contained in the commination: "In the day thou eatest thereof thou shalt die the death." It must comprehend spiritual death: and that spiritual death doth also comprehend in it several things, of which I shall give you a very brief account. As,

First. The retraction of God's Spirit. That it contains, as the first and most fundamental thing, in this threatened spiritual death, the retraction of God's Spirit. When Adam had abused, or not duly used, the power which his Creator gave him, of obeying and complying with the divine pleasure, the Spirit retired; and now, we must consider the difference (as hath been intimated before) between the spiritual influence which was vouchsafed to Adam, while he yet remained innocent, and that which is afforded to the regenerate, in their present state, to preserve that state; that is, as to Adam in innocence, that influence was enabling, but not determining. It was such as by which (as hath been told you) he had a possibility of not falling, but not an impossibility of falling; he had a possibility of standing, not an impossibility not to stand; that he had not, that influence of the Spirit which he had, being suitable to his state of probation wherein he was made, that is now justly withheld, the Spirit retires, leaves him to himself.

This we do not say *gratis dictum;* for do but consider that plain text: (Gal. 3. 13.) "Christ hath redeemed us from the curse of the law, being made a curse for us: for cursed is every one that hangeth on a tree: that the blessing of Abraham might come upon us Gentiles, the promise of the Spirit, (or the promised Spirit) through faith." If the remission of the curse do carry with it the conferring of the grace of the Spirit, then the curse, while it did continue, could not but include, carry in it, the privation and suspension of the Spirit. This was part of the curse upon apostate *Adam*, the loss of God's Spirit. For that which the *grace of Christ* and redemption by him, removing, inferred *the communication* of the Spirit, that must include the *suspension* and withholding of the Spirit. And,

Secondly. Hereupon, it could not but ensue, (which is a further thing contained in this spiritual death,) that the holy image of God must be erased, vanished; and, antecedently to the restitution, it could not but be so. And,

Thirdly. There must be included in this spiritual death, an aversion from God, the turning off of the apostate soul from God; that whereas it minded him before, with a complacential adoration, now it is quite alienated: here is no inclination in him towards God. The thing speaks itself; and it was apparent in Adam's case. As soon as he becomes guilty, he hides himself, vainly attempts to hide himself from the doom. That which was before the most grateful thing of all things, to have God nigh him, is now quite otherwise; he cannot endure that God should approach him. If it were possible to keep himself from God, (but that he vainly attempts,) his sense would be, "Let me have no more to do with God." And,

Fourthly. There must be further contained in it, hereupon, a cessation of that intercourse and communion that was between God and him. For the Spirit of God was retired on his part, and man was become averse and disaffected to God on his own part. The image of God, that rendered him propense towards God, and meet for his communion, being vanished and gone, nothing can ensue more necessarily and certainly than a cessation of communion: God refuseth to converse with him, and he refuseth to converse with God. And,

Fifthly. There could not also but be included as consequent hereupon, regrets of conscience: not penitential but tormenting; not penitential as yet, or not penitential first; but first tormenting, before they could be penitential, while grace was not yet applied. How soon it might be we know not. It is very likely it might be very soon, by the account that short history gives us. But in the mean time, there could be only tormenting regrets of conscience: "Very lately I was an innocent creature; now I am a fallen creature: I then stood right in the acceptance and favour of God; now there is war between him and me." Penitential regrets, indeed, could not be a part of the penalty; they are a part and degree of the sinner's restoration and recovery; but the preceding tormenting regrets, they are included in the death. It is a deadly thing to be stung with the sense of one's having offended him whom we can never propitiate to ourselves again. And hereupon, also,

Sixthly. Very black and gloomy thoughts must ensue; amazing thoughts! He that was in the eye of the innocent, unoffending soul, his highest delight, now he is all inwrapt in a cloud; or the mind is inwrapt in a cloud that it cannot behold him; such a cloud as it can by no means penetrate. God could be conceived of under no other notion than that of an enemy and avenger. And,

Seventhly. There must be, hereupon, most astonishing fears; for it is obvious that a reasonable, intelligent mind would consider, "He who did so lately fetch me and all this creation out of nothing, is almighty, and it is impossible for me to fence against his power. That power that could create a world so easily, what can I do to protect myself against it, when it is set on work by just displeasure?" And then,

Eighthly. It must include despair: for the first covenant gave no hope of forgiveness, and therefore, gave no room or place for repentance till grace came, till an inspired gospel came to be actually applied and brought home in this case. And therefore, there must be the epitome and sum of hell, in the state of this case; God offended and never to be reconciled, and against whose displeasure, armed with power, I can have no defence, no protection. All this more, all this surplusage, must be contained in this death; that is, spiritual death, the present death of the soul in the moral sense, in all this latitude and extensiveness of it. And then, further,

[6.] There is in this surplusage, too, these many external miseries of life that we find to be contained, also, in the very sentence: for though the sentence may contain less than the commination, yet it could not contain more. Therefore, all these being found in the sentence, must be in the commination too: all the external miseries of life that a delinquent creature could be liable to. And then, in the last place,

[7.] This death must carry in it, too, death eternal, as the sum of the penalty, or the consummation thereof, as the evil threatened and contained in that. And though many would speak very distinguishingly of this matter, and labour to do so when they can, yet let but plain Scripture be considered in the case, and you will see how it speaks. Do but follow this very context unto the shutting up of this chapter, and you will see what kind of reign it is that sin hath in the world. It now began its reign, even in this first apostasy, or in the apostasy of the first man. Sin, we are told, it reigns unto death, verse 21. "As sin hath reigned unto death, so grace might reign through righteousness unto life." What life? "Unto eternal life through Jesus Christ our Lord." You see how these two stand in their antithesis, in their opposition to one another. Here is death set in opposition to eternal life. What death is that that stands in opposition to eternal life? Surely, it must be eternal death. So in the conclusion of the next chapter: "The wages of sin is death; but the gift of God is eternal life, through Jesus Christ our Lord." "The wages of sin is death." It is not said of this or that sin, some greater sin; but, "The wages of sin," as sin, "is death." And what death, the opposition shews us: it is put in opposition to eternal life; therefore, it must be eternal death that is the wages of sin, of sin as sin: and therefore, if Adam's transgression was sin, such a death must be the wages of it.

And that is the *third* particular, belonging to this first general head, that we were to treat of, to wit, to shew what the death was that did ensue, and was designed to ensue, by force of the divine law; or the commination added thereto, upon this first sin of the first man. Now,

4. The fourth of these heads is the dueness of this death upon this sin; and upon that I shall not insist, it being enough to touch it, things being obvious of themselves. The heinousness of the sin, and the too naturalness of the punishment taken together, will evince the dueness of this event upon this sin.

(1.) Consider the heinousness of the sin. We have opened that unto you in many particulars formerly, to which I shall only add the consideration of these four circumstances. As that,

[1.] The first man should so soon transgress. But just now made; (upon the matter it being generally thought to be but a little time: most think the same day;) just now made by God, a reasonable, immortal creature, and so soon made by himself, a sinner, transgressor, and a rebel.

[2.] Consider that he sinned with open eyes, having, before, no cloud upon his mind, but all things in clear light before him.

[3.] And while his nature was antecedently untainted, no vicious inclination in him. And,

[4.] That there was nothing which could be matter of complaint in his state, his condition so entirely good, and yet did not please him. Think, I say, of the heinousness of the sin, in these and other respects, and then the incurred death cannot be thought unproportionable, or undue, though you take it in the extent that hath been mentioned. But,

(2.) Consider, too, the con-naturalness of the punishment to the sin, this death to his transgression. He turns from God to the creature: God turns away (in just displeasure, upon being offended,) from him. Hence, all these things ensue and follow of themselves. And there was no preventing it by any ordinary methods, unless God would annihilate him, unless he would throw his creature back again into nothing. But that became not the wisdom and greatness of God to do. It had been too much trifling to raise his creature into being, and put him under such an equitable, and so righteous a law, and, he offending, presently to nullify his own work. That had not been becoming God, not suitable to the divine wisdom and greatness.

And therefore, now to give some brief notes of *Use* upon the two last mentioned heads.

1. You may learn, hence, that the act of eating the forbidden fruit, is not to be considered too abstractly, as the first sin of man; that is the thing wherein the most do foolishly impose upon themselves, and so speak and think diminishingly of this whole matter. What! was it so great a matter? was it so great a thing to eat the fruit of a tree that was forbidden? This, abstractly considered, was not the first sin. Not abstractly considered; take it comprehensively, and take it in all that was belonging to it, and it was the first sin. But the act of eating alone, considered by itself, was not the first; there were a great many mental evils (as we have shewn in opening the sin) which did precede the act of eating, and that altogether, make it a most horrid wickedness; distrust of the truth of God's word, and trusting a creature that he might easily apprehend to be an apostate, fallen creature, by opposing the word of God; trusting him against him that made him, and gave him breath. He trusted against God, one, he knew not whom: but he might suppose it one that was not in his original integrity, that was fallen and gone off from God; otherwise he could never have counselled against God. There was great ingratitude for goodness, shewn and exhibited; for mercy received: mercy, indeed, as yet it could not properly be called, he not being as yet a miserable creature, or in a miserable state. There was opposing his will to the Supreme Will. There was exalting the sensitive nature against the rational, against the law of the mind; and so confounding the order of things, in that part of God's creation; to wit, himself breaking the order and dependance of the faculties in reference to one another, with many more.

2. And you may further learn, hence, how nearly sin and misery, sin and death, do border upon one another. They are things very near to each other. These two spheres of life and death; that lightsome, glorious sphere, all full of vitality,

pleasure and bliss; and that sphere of darkness and death, that comprehended every thing of horror in it, you see how nearly they do touch, and how nearly they did touch; so that we might suppose, but even a moment between the one and the other. This moment, an innocent creature, standing in delight, and favour, and acceptance; and the next moment, an accomplice of hell, associated with apostate spirits against God. How nearly do the spheres of light, and life, and bliss; and of death, and horror, and hell, touch! How near did they touch one another! How immediate was the *transitus*, the passage from the one to the other! And,

3. You see, not only the nearness in point of time; but the natural connexion that is between sin and misery; that the one doth in so great a measure involve the other, as I have shewn they do. Sin carries death in it; "To be carnally minded is death." And we may further see,

4. What occasion we should take, hence, to admire the grace of the gospel, that it should so soon intervene; and when it so doth, here is place for repentance by the constitution of a new covenant, the evangelical one, which the covenant and law of works could not give upon any terms: for it could represent God no otherwise than as an unappeasable enemy. "Cursed is every one that continueth not in all things that are written in the book of the law to do them."

LECTURE XXIV.*

Rom. 5. 12.

And so death passed upon all men, for that all have sinned.

FROM the former part of this scripture, we have insisted upon the fall of the first man; "By one man sin entered into the world, and death by sin;" his fall, by sin, into death. And so you have seen the entrance of both these, sin and death, into the world, in the fall of that one man. Now we come in the next place;

II. To speak, from the latter words, of the fallen state of man, generally considered. And you see the ground of that, too, lies as fully in the latter words of the text, that "death passed upon all men, for that all have sinned." I read the words according to our translation, though some would have them to be otherwise read, and the letter of the text doth admit of another reading: instead of "for that," they read "in whom," all have sinned. But of that there will be more occasion to speak hereafter.

In the mean while we are to consider the fallen state of men in general, according as these expressions do represent and hold forth to us. And they do represent his state to be a state of sin and death; these two complicated with one another. "Death hath passed upon all, for that all have sinned." And,

* Preached March 17, 1694.

according to that reading of the words, and the nature of the thing, that which is here last mentioned, requires to be considered first, though these are complicated with one-another; sin and death run into one another, are most inseparably conjunct; yet, they are all some way distinct. And so far as they do admit of being distinguished, we shall consider and speak to them distinctly. And so,

1. Of the sinful state of men in general. Now, in speaking to this, as the letter of the text leads us, we shall—consider the nature, and—the universality, chiefly, of this sin that is thus spread through the world. We are,

(1.) To consider the nature of it. The general nature of sin is plainly expressed 1 John 3. 4. " Sin is the transgression of the law." And therefore, that we may shew you more distinctly the nature of that sin which hath so generally diffused itself among men, (as we shall afterwards shew,) it will be needful to inquire, What it is that we must take for the measure of such sin? inasmuch as the following words here do plainly tell us, in the latter part of the 13th verse, that " sin is not imputed where there is no law:" wherever any sin is, some law must be supposed to be. And what is that law, against which it can be understood that men might so generally sin?

You have heard, by what law the first sin of man was to be measured: that was partly a positive law, a particular precept, a law made by a spiritual revelation to him: but much more principally a natural law, which was violated in the violation of that positive one, inasmuch as that positive law had its immediate root and foundation in the natural one: nothing being more apparently natural, than that the reasonable creature ought to comply with the will of his Maker being once known. But though it were very apparent what law that first sin did transgress, yet it is not so apparent what law it is that the common sin of mankind doth now transgress. And so that needs to be inquired into.

In the general, it may be said, that the law that doth obtain in the world now, and from age to age, doth consist of two parts, as the law at first did which was given to Adam, even in his innocency; to wit, that it is partly natural, and partly by superadded Revelation. So it was at first, so it is still; but with great and remarkable difference. That whereas, at first, the natural law was full, perfect, intire, most comprehensive, and large, even in the discernible impressions of it; and the superadded law by special Revelation narrow, lying in a very little compass (one particular interdict only with its penalty esta-

The Fall of Man considered generally.

blishing it) that we read or are informed of. But now the case is very diverse and opposite: that is, the natural is diminished, not in the obligation of it, but in the impression, the discernible or discerned impression, that frame in the heart or mind of man broken into fragments, many parts very obscure and illegible, and divers, with many of the inhabitants of this earth, (as it were,) lost through inadvertency, and their not reflecting upon themselves so as to discern and find out the sculpture of what remains engraven upon their hearts. And the revealed law, (where that obtains,) that is so much the more large, and comprehensive, and full, and perfect, so as to discover every false way; and every true and right way: one and the same rule being the same measure, *recti et obliqui*, of that which is right and that which is wrong too.

And the exigency of the case did require that it should be so: that is, by how much the more that the natural law was erased, broken into fragments and parcels, and many of them (as to their discernibleness) lost with many; so much the more requisite was it, that the superadded law (which was to be by revelation) should be entire and complete, that there should be another impression of that original law, that should collect and gather up all that was lost of it, and rendered it obscure, from the prevailing corruption of the world. And so thus, in short, did these two cases stand in opposition to one another. At first, the natural law was most entire and full and large and comprehensive: and the revealed law narrow, and lying within a very little compass. But now the natural law, to wit, in the discernibleness of its impression, is greatly diminished; and the law that is by revelation so much the more large, comprehensive, entire, and full.

At first, that revealed law after the apostasy, must, for several successive ages, be easily transmitted (by reason of the great longevity that remained before and after the flood) from hand to hand by a certain tradition. But afterwards, God provided that it should be collected and gathered up into Sacred Records, though not all written at once, but successively, according as supreme wisdom had determined concerning the different states in the future church, in point of light. And so, what we have of it now, lies entirely and fully in the sacred volumes, of which we have discoursed to you largely heretofore; but that doth actually obtain but in a small part of the world in comparison: but a very small part. That it doth obtain no further, is owing to the wickedness of the world itself, which obstructs the diffusion of it. God, in his holy wisdom not obtruding, not by extraordinary means and methods making way for it, as it were easy for him to do, if it were so agreeable to the counsel of his own wisdom, the results wherereof we now see, in fact; and the reasons whereof may be better understood in the appointed season. But we are not to think this wicked world innocent in its having no more of revealed light than it hath; that light shines in darkness, but the darkness doth not comprehend it, strives against it, otherwise there must have been a diffusion, even of most evangelical knowledge many an age ago. Men fence against it and keep it off, and will not let it spread; and God doth not exert the greatness of his power as yet (for ends and purposes best known to himself) for the gaining of a victory over that contumacious darkness.

Yet, in the meantime, where there are no notices of that revealed law, or that law by Revelation, we are not to think that the world is without law: do but observe to this purpose what follows the text: "Until the law (verse 13.) sin was in the world;" until the law. Until what law? It is certain, here, "law" must be taken in a restrained and limited sense, otherwise the expressions in the following part of that verse would contradict those in the former: "Sin is not imputed where there is no law:" then there could have been no such thing as sin, from Adam to Moses, if there had been no law at all in all that interval. When therefore, it is said, "Until the law sin was in the world;" that is, until the written law, or until the law that was given on mount Sinai, it is not the law simply, but respectively only, that is there meant; not in an absolute and general, but in a particular and limited sense.

It is true, there was a time (that time that is there mentioned, from Adam to Moses) when there was no such law as came afterwards to be in the time of Moses. Not that there was then no law at all; for then there could be no sin; but it is expressly told us, that "sin was in the world" for all that time; and therefore, there was some law; there was a law by which men might be reckoned sinners: for there was such a law according to which they were punished, as the following words shew; "Nevertheless, death reigned from Adam to Moses;" there was such a law as made men still liable to death; and therefore, such a law against which men might still sin, even in the long interval from Adam to Moses. "Death reigned from Adam to Moses, even over them that had not sinned after the similitude of Adam's transgression."

I pray consider that expression, "that had not sinned after the similitude of Adam's transgression." How was that? That is, that did not sin against a particular and express law, with its annexed sanction, as Adam did. Some would understand that of infants; and, it is true, it must include them. But I see no cause at all for such a restriction; but most manifestly the contrary: for infants were not the only ones that did die; death reigned over all, in that interval from Adam to Moses; and so, the sin must be as general as the death. But herein was the great dissimilitude, that, whereas Adam did sin against a framed, express precept, with its annexed penalty in the commination, the generality of men from Adam to Moses, did not so sin; but they sinned against such a law as they had; that is, the relics and fragments of the law of nature, first impressed upon the heart of man, or put into his very nature.

This is agreeable to what we have in this same epistle, chap. 2. 12. " As many as have sinned without the law," (that is, without a written law,) "shall perish without law;" to wit, without that written law. Some law or other they were still under; they must be supposed to sin against some law; otherwise they could perish by none. But a written law they had not. " As they that are under the law, (as it there follows,) they are to be judged by the law." And afterwards, in the 14. and 15. verses of the same chapter: " When the Gentiles who have not the law, do by nature the things contained in the law, they are a law unto themselves, which shew the works of the law written in their hearts, their consciences also bearing witness, and their thoughts in the mean while accusing or else excusing one another" So we read it, and I think very defectively, " accusing and excusing:" it is in the greek, "by turns;" not " one another;" but, " sometimes accusing, and sometimes excusing." Not as if their thoughts did accuse one another, or excuse one another; but the expression may admit to be read, I say, " sometimes accusing, and sometimes excusing," according to the discernible evidence of the case.

And so you may now easily collect, how, in this general sinful state of the apostate world, men do every where transgress against a law. Those that have a written law, or might more easily have it, they sin against that; to wit, the Revelation that God hath given of his own mind concerning their duty, and in order to their felicity. They that have it, or might more easily have it, I say, sin against it. They that have it not, or from whom it lies more remote, they yet, sin against the dictates of the law which they have in themselves, or which they are to themselves. They that have no other law, being a law to themselves, they having some measures, though broken and imperfect ones, of right and wrong in their own minds and natural consciences.

And now, the measure being stated by which this general sinfulness of the world is to be estimated, the natural law and, generally, that law that is by Revelation in the word of God, so far as it doth obtain, or might more easily obtain; it will be our further business, in the next place, to open to you the sinfulness of men in reference to this law, of which you have this account. And it is, in the general, the sinfulness of their inclination, or of their nature, that we are obliged, by the design of our present subject, to consider and speak to: "For that all have sinned."

Here is not, it is true, actual sin: that the expression doth literally signify. But that must be understood as supposing a sinful nature, which is more principally to be considered; or it is to be considered in the first place; that which is the *peccatum peccans*, as it is significantly enough called by some. That evil heart, that nature, not as it is nature, but as it is depraved, it is now transmitted every where from age to age, and from generation to generation, among men: the fountain from whence all those streams of wickedness flow that have deluged the world, and made a raging ocean, "the waves whereof continually cast forth mire and dirt," as the prophet expresseth it. Isa. 57. 20. That nature of man, which as it is degenerate and corrupt, is become a seminary, a seed-plot of all kinds of wickedness.

This is for *peccatum originale originatum*; as we formerly discoursed to you of the *peccatum originale originans*, as some do choose to express those things. It is, in the general, a sinful inclination which lies opposite to the law of God, natural or revealed: for we are not to suppose that the love of God doth only provide against sinful acts, or sinful omissions, no, this is the very peculiar excellency of the Divine Government, in contradistinction to any other; that it determines first, what men ought to be, and then, consequently and dependantly, what they ought to do. Human laws and governments do not respect the former of these, otherwise than consequentially. They only take notice of actions, and those, external ones too. But internal inclinations they make little provision about, and do not otherwise take notice of (as indeed the nature of the thing doth not admit they should) but by consequence, as a man's habit and internal inclination may be collected and gathered from the series and course of his actions. But it is quite contrary as to the Divine Government, and the laws that belong thereunto; that is, that God having an immediate inspection into the minds of men, and his government, laying its first obligation there; its laws do first provide what men should be; and then consequentially, what they should do. They should be so and so; be holy, be righteous; and then, all is to correspond hereunto.

Therefore, we must understand that an evil inclination, or a depraved or corrupted nature, is that which doth first violate the law of God, lies first against it: and so, that it is not infelicity only, to be ill inclined, but it is sin—sin in the highest and most eminent sense thereof. It is the habitual frame and bent of the soul, that the law of God doth in the first place direct: and then, it doth direct that men should act correspondently thereunto. So that now that empoisoned nature of man, the malignity of the heart and soul, or inner man, is that which makes the first and principal breach upon the law of God, which is in its own nature holy, just, and good: whatsoever there is of this law left, it is all holy, just and good, even as it doth obtain to be called "the law of nature." What is truly such, is holy, just, and good, still, as much as ever it was, and as expressive of the mind of God.

Now concerning that corrupt inclination in the minds and souls of men, that doth first violate the law, it is to be understood agreeably to the law itself. The law itself, is partly preceptive, and partly prohibitive. It consists of these two parts. And these two things are accordingly to be considered in the corrupted state of human nature: to wit, first, that there is a disinclination to all that is truly good; and, secondly, that there is a propensity, a perverse inclination, to all that is sinful and wicked.

[1.] The first of these, that is, which is signified by the want of original righteousness, that rectitude which did first belong to the nature of man, the absence, and not the mere absence; but the want and privation of that, is the first thing we have to consider in the corruption of man's nature; that now it wants the inclination that there ought to be in it according to its primitive state, and the first obligation of the divine law upon man. This is the loss of God's image; not by his taking it away, which we must carefully abstain from thinking, even so much as one thought to that purpose; that is, that God took away his image from man, to wit, his image in respect whereof, man was to resemble him in point of holiness; that would be, to devolve the sinfulness of man's nature upon God himself. But God did righteously, upon the first apostasy, withhold his Spirit, whereupon his image, being a created thing, and not capable of self-subsistence, must vanish: and so, as that in effect to erase the holy image of God out of his soul. He (man) hath expunged and blotted it out; provoked the Spirit of God to retire; cherished and indulged corrupt inclinations against it, and in opposition to it. And, God finally still retiring, that image falleth and vanisheth: not being withdrawn by him, (speaking of the effect,) but being expelled; not withdrawn, but drawn away; not by violence (as it were) obliterated out of the soul. That which was, indeed, God's workmanship at first, is defaced by our wicked workmanship: the work of our hands hath so far destroyed the work of his.

There is, therefore, in the corrupt nature of man, a disinclination to all that which it ought to be inclined to; that is, both to objects and acts, that it ought to be inclined to. We are principally to consider the objects; the acts will of course most obviously ensue. The objects wherewith man was to have to do, were God himself, his fellow creatures, (those especially of his own order,) and himself.

There was, upon God's having made man, the direct relation first between Creator and creature; and then, hereupon, (there being divers such of the same order,) there follows, of course, a collateral relation between one such creature and another. In the first respect, man being a reasonable creature by his nature, a creature and a reasonable one, he comes under obligation to God most directly: and then, collaterally, (from God still,) he comes to be under obligation to his fellow-creatures of his own order: and inasmuch as he is capable of bearing a relation to himself, so he comes to owe duty to himself also.

To God in the first place. There is an aversion from God, to be considered in this fallen state of man, not of one single faculty of the soul alone, but even of the whole soul, and of all the faculties of it. But according to the natural order wherein they lie towards one another, the whole soul is gone off from God; mind, and will, and affections, and executive powers, altogether turned off from God. So is the account given of the fallen state of man in that 14. and 53. Psalm, from which texts and from others, you have so many quotations taken in the 3d. chapter of his epistle to the Romans, all summed in this, that " All have sinned and fallen short of the glory of God." This, then, is the great thing that, in the first place, is held forth in this text; to wit, that the state of man is a state of apostasy and recess from God; he hath withdrawn himself, and stands now in his whole soul in a quite averse posture from God; towards whom he was originally and naturally most propense.

But then, whereas God, the Object of this aversion, is to be considered two ways; as our Supreme and Sovereign Lord, and as our Supreme and Sovereign Good, the soul of man is averse to him under both these notions; refuseth to take him as his Supreme Lord; or, for his Supreme Good; that is, it will neither obey him, nor be happy in him. And whereas, under this twofold notion, we are to consider God the Object of this aversion, it is under the former of these notions that we are to consider it now, while we are speaking of the sinful state of man, or the sin of man. It will be under the latter of these notions that we are to consider it, when we speak of the death that hath passed over all men, as that whereunto it doth more peculiarly and properly belong.

But consider God as the Supreme Lord, and the sinfulness of man's nature, in this respect, lies in this, that he is, under this notion, averse to, and turned off, from him, and declines obedience to him. And the whole is, under this notion, averse; that is, the mind is averse, not only doth not know him, but declines knowing him, labours under, not a mere nescience of God, but an affected and chosen ignorance, desires not to know him. So is the representation made to us of the opposite state and condition of man in those mentioned psalms, the 53, most fully, 2, 3 verses; that is, "That God looking down from heaven upon the children of men to see who would inquire, who would seek after God, he finds them all gone back;" (the Hebrew word signifies a perverse retrocision, waywardly gone back;) no, here is no inclination to inquire after God; according to that, Job 21. 14. "They say unto God, Depart from us, we desire not the knowledge of thy ways," of thy concerns, and of thy methods. Those ways of intercourse that thou wouldst have to be between thee and us; these ways of thine we do not desire to know; we do not desire there should be any intermeddling, any intercourse between thee and us. And according to that Rom. 1. 28. "They liked not to retain God in their knowledge." They did not only, or barely, not know him, but disliked to know, refused to know him. "Through deceit they refused to know me," saith the Lord, Jer. 9. 6. The same corrupt nature remaining, even under a professed relation to him, with the generality of that wicked people.

And so, in this respect, the state of man is a state of darkness: to wit, of affected darkness. "There is no darkness or shadow of death where the workers of iniquity can hide themselves." It speaks the inclination of men's minds that they would fain hide themselves in some darkness or shadow of death if they could; but they can find none, none that hides them from him, though they can easily so inwrap themselves in darkness, as not to behold him. Their darkness is a fence against themselves; but not against him. They make it so thick that they cannot penetrate it; but he most easily can. They would fain have such a darkness as that he might not see them; but there is none, they cannot find any: "There is no darkness or shadow of death where the workers of iniquity can hide themselves." But, in the mean time, that speaks the inclinations of their minds: "O! that we could be hid from God, and that there might be nothing at all to do between him and us." "Ye were darkness," (here is the common state of the unconverted, unregenerate world,) Ephes. 5. 8. "Ye were darkness," not merely in the dark, but darkness itself. "The light that is in them is darkness," as our Saviour speaks, Mat. 6. 23. "If the light that is in thee be darkness, how great is that darkness." This, I say, speaks an aversion of mind from God; they care not to know him; they desire not to know him.

And hereupon, it becomes so unaccustomed a thing to think of him. Thence is the character of a wicked, unregenerate man, "A forgetter of God." It is his usual paraphrase in Scripture; "A wicked man," and that lies, as such, under doom, is under such a character as this, one that is "A forgetter of God:" "The wicked shall be turned into hell, and all the nations that forget God" Psalm 9. And in opposition hereunto, a regenerate man, a holy man, a renewed man, is characterized by one that remembers God, that thinks of God: "A book of remembrance was written for them that feared the Lord, and thought upon his name." Whereas, it is said of the wicked man; "God is not in all his thoughts." Compare these two places together, Psalm 10. 4. Mal. 3. 16. A good man is such a one as thinks much of the name of God, hath God's name impressed on his mind: so as every actual thought of God, it is only reading the letters that do (as it were) compose that name, and that are impressed on his own mind; to wit, his actual thinking of God. Now a book of remembrance was written for them that feared the Lord, and thought of his name. As if it had been said; "Well, is there so much kindness towards me yet to be found in this revolted world, that they will remember me? I will have a book of remembrance for them; there shall be remembrance for remembrance. Do they think of me? I will think of them too: have they kind thoughts of me? I will have much kinder thoughts of them: I will book it up. Every kind thought that is taken up concerning me, in this general apostasy and revoltedness of the world from me, I will set it down, I will have a book of remembrance for every one that has any thoughts of me, in this forlorn state of things."

And then, as this aversion hath place in the minds of men, it hath so, more formally, in their wills: they will not have this Lord to be their God; he shall not reign over them; they refuse his empire; throw off the reins: "Let us cast away his cords, and break his bands off from us." So, in the apostate world, do the princes and people combine together against the divine government: and those that lead others consent to be led themselves in this case. "Let us break their bands asunder, and cast away their cords from us:" (Psalm 2.) those of God, and of his Anointed, the Redeemer, the Messiah, as that word signifies.

And then, likewise, there is a consequent averse or transverse posture in the affections of the soul, whereof, indeed, the will is the seat and subject; desires, fears, hopes, delights, anger, sorrow, all transversed in a quite contrary course and being, to what they should be: and so it is proportionably towards men, so far as men are concerned with men; and so it is towards ourselves. We should have discoursed of these distinctly, but cannot now.

It is, in the mean time, strange, (and let us consider that with ourselves,) that this being so apparently the common case, it should be so little considered; that men take such complacency in themselves; that it comes so seldom into the thoughts of any to think, "I either am, or have been, an apostate creature, quite turned off from God." It is to be admired, that men's own thoughts are not painful to them upon this account. Certain it is, that I, and the rest of the world, have been all in an apostasy from God. This hath been my state; it is my present state. I am either an apostate creature, or a returned creature: either still apostate, or renewed towards him, altered in my habitual frame and inclination. How is it with me? am I one of the *reduces?* one that the mighty hand and power of the Redeemer (he that died, "the just for the unjust to bring us to God") hath reduced and fetched back to God.

Or is this the case of none of us? That whereas we were all off from God, in an averse posture to him, are we not striving against the design of the merciful Redeemer, who is still striving to bring us back, and who strove herein unto blood, resisting against the wicked inclinations of degenerate, apostate men? "He resisted to blood striving against sin." That is the thing plainly implied in that of the apostle to the Hebrews, chap. 12. 4. "Ye have not yet resisted unto blood, striving against sin;" whereas, he had been, immediately before, bespeaking them to "run with patience the race that was set before them, looking unto Jesus the author and finisher of the faith: who, for the joy that was set before him, endured the cross, despising the shame." But why did he endure that cross and shame which we find him to have despised? The following words shew, he had been striving against sin. But that is none of your case: it was his. He suffered that cross, and fell under all that opprobium, ignominy and shame, in this striving against sin even unto blood; that sin by which men are held off from God, continued in a state of apostasy from him.

Now let us bethink ourselves what the Son of God hath been striving unto blood against; to wit, "sin;" which hath turned us off from God, and kept us off from God: and are we striving against him, will not be reduced, will not be brought back? Strangers to God we have been, and so we will be still: go from day to day, from morning to night, and will have no concern with God; we will not pray to him; we will not think of his name; we will entertain no converse with him.

But the further *Use* is referred to be spoken to, after a further explication of the sinful state of mankind.

LECTURE XXV.*

It hath been shewed, that the ill inclination of men towards God, affects the whole soul. The mind knows him not, thinks not of him, is habitually forgetful of him: and, more formally, this aversion is in the will: that doth not choose the Lord for his God; wills him not, even where a people do profess his name. If yet the work of renovation have not taken place, his own Israel will have none of him; "Israel," saith God, "would have none of me." Corrupt nature is the same, even in such a people, whatsoever the external profession and garb, and appearance, and shew, may be. A corrupt heart is still the same thing, indisposed, disaffected to God; "alienated from the life of God." And conscience is stupified, doth not do its office or, sometimes, is outrageous and over-does it, the affections and passions are all as so many furies; original rectitude being gone, and the soul destitute of that holy image which originally it bore.

But there is, also, an evil inclination towards fellow-creatures of their own order. That love is wanting which is "the

* Preached March 24, 1694

fulfilling of the law;" and that sums up all that rectitude of heart and soul towards fellow-creatures of our own order. All is summed up in this; "Thou shalt love thy neighbour as thyself;" and therefore, is love the fulfilling of the law.

And then, also, towards ourselves. Our love to our neighbour, is to be measured by that to ourselves: as that great fundamental precept which our Saviour calls the "second," next to that; "Thou shalt love the Lord thy God with all thy heart, and with all thy might'; and thou shalt love thy neighbour as thyself;" in opposition whereunto, stands that aversion to God, in the first part. And as to the second great commandment, it is a measured thing; and the measure is love to ourselves.

But now, in this state of apostasy, men want even that, they do not love themselves: to wit, if they did know themselves; and that they do not affect, to gain a true knowledge of themselves; and therefore, do not love themselves; their more noble self, their more excellent self. The soul, which is the man, that they do not love; they care not for it; care not how they prostitute it; how they enslave, how they hazard it from day to day. Yea, and,

[2.] In all these respects, there is not only an aversion, an ill inclination, to that which is good, a want of original righteousness, or of the holy image of God as such; but there is, likewise, propensions to all manner of evil; there are violent propensions towards forbidden objects. God being forsaken and left, and the soul of man being conscious to itself that it is not enough for itself, it must adjoin itself to somewhat else, when it is off from God: and so, by the same steps by which it recedes from him, it turns to the creature, to this vain and impure world, which is God's rival and competitor for the minds and hearts of men.

But here, it is to be considered, that when the soul is off from God, and therefore, must seek for somewhat else to supply his room, it finds itself under a necessity to make a false and ascititious deity, a divided thing, as if it were under a secret consciousness that no one thing could fill up the room of God. And therefore, the new deity is divided between these two; to wit, between this world and a man's own self: that is, his meaner or baser self; his ignoble self. And all of you know (if you recollect a little) what God is to be to us, namely, our Sovereign Lord, our Sovereign Good: him we are to serve; and him we are to enjoy.

The soul being off from him, and being now to fill up his room as it can, it doth (as it can) attempt to fill it up by these two things—self and the world: self supplies the room of God, as he is to be served by us; and the world supplies the room of God, as God is to be enjoyed by us. And here are the propensions, now, of the apostate soul, continuing so, and yet unrenewed towards self, as the only one to be served, obeyed, and pleased, instead of serving, obeying, and pleasing God. And this is one of the greatest idols that is set up in the apostate world, even—a man's self.

But then, remember it is his baser, meaner, and more ignoble self; when it is become the vilest thing that it was possible a reasonable, immortal soul could become; when it is besotted, carnalized, brutified; when it is, in short, become a brute, when it would be a god. While it was itself, it must abhor any such thought, with the highest measures and greatest pitch of indignation. But now it is brutified into the vilest and most degenerate thing, become even as the beasts that perish; now it must be a god. "I will have none to serve but this self."

But then, finding (as that is obvious to every one) that it hath not its own good in its own hand, (as, alas! what have I in me to make me happier; and though that is more to be considered under the other head of death, yet there is sin in it too, as it underwent a direct interdict,) it finds it must forage, it must go abroad; it finds it hath not enough in itself to satisfy it. And therefore, now in this kind, and under this notion, the world is the other idol that is to supply the room of God. "Love not the world nor the things of the world; for if any man love the world, the love of the Father is not in him." That shews, however, in the unrenewed state, the propensions of the soul are, by love, carried towards this vain and wretched world. All the good that it designs for itself, it seeks from it. And so, these are the two idols that are set up in this apostate world against the living and true God: self, as the God that is to be served, and the world as the God that is to be enjoyed.

But then, we must observe, by the way, that as there is towards these two substituted objects a violent propension; so it is forbidden, only under that notion wherein it is excessive. It is no unlawful thing for a man to love himself, and even his meaner self: but to love himself with that love wherewith he should love God, that is sinful. It is no unlawful thing to love inferior creatures, things of this world, which God made all very good; but to love them with that love wherewith we should love God, as our supreme and highest Good, herein stands the sinfulness of this propension. These are to be in the room of God; not to serve ourselves under God, but above him and against him: not to enjoy and please ourselves, in this world, in subserviency and obedience to God, but in direct opposition.

And so, there is, upon this account, not only no inclination towards God, (which was considered under the former head,) but there is direct enmity. Not only, in this case, doth the soul not love him with all the heart, mind, and might; but it hates him. And this is the character of the apostate world. Look to that Rom. 1. 28. "They liked not to retain God in their knowledge." And a little lower, they are called "God-haters." The word signifies, they hate him with a stygian hatred, they hate him as one would hate hell; that is the signification of the word "God-haters," which sums up the malignity of this corrupted nature of man, that is made out in so many particulars in all that latter part of that 1 chapter to the Romans.

So likewise, in reference to their fellow-creatures, when this love is wanting, which they should bear to them, and which is the radical principle that comprehends in it all duty of that kind, (that is, doth virtually comprehend it all,) the want of that due disposition is supplied by a contrary principle, that is, by one contrary thereunto, which is that of "being hateful and hating one another," mentioned Romans 1. 30. 31. and Titus 2. 3. And it is, too, upon this account, that "self" is one of the two substituted idols, as you have heard. And because the interest of this "self" interferes, and there are now as many deities to be served, as there are men; hereupon it is, that jealousy works into hatred. And it partly proceeds, too, from the narrowness and minuteness of this world, which is the other idol that men set up in the room and stead of God. This world is too little for men; (it cannot but be so;) too little for immortal souls. It is a thing in its own nature unsuitable to them; but yet, men being deceived, think to have their all out of it: and so they are all pulling and tearing one from another, every one for himself, to make his own portion out of this world as great and considerable as he can, still imagining he shall repair his loss of God, out of this world. And all being under the power of this delusion, they do not consider, that "there is a lie in their right hand;" that they are seeking that in this world which it can never afford them.

But hereupon, instead of that love which should be "the fulfilling of the law" of the second table, spoken of Rom. 13. there is that enmity, that mutual hatred of one another, that hath for so many ages made this world an *aceldama,* a field of blood;

and comprehends and sums up all those lusts, from whence come wars and fightings among men: among men, I say, who lay under the obligation of so equal a law, and so kind a law of love, which so directly tended to the welfare of mankind; and so would have made this world a heaven upon earth, every one loving one another as himself, and seeking another's good as his own: whereas, all make it now their business to tear this world out of one another's hands as much as they can, and to pluck it in pieces, and so to worry and destroy one another for it.

And in reference to men themselves too. In the room of a right disposition towards themselves, there are substituted, wicked propensions: they do affect themselves wickedly, sinfully, illegally, against the direction of the divine rule: and this is the root of all the insincerity that is to be found, any where in the world, that is, that the superior powers do not govern the inferior, do rebel and disobey. The mind and judgment that should govern the will, and its determinations, and purposes, this way and that, neglect their office; so that in the mind, now, is blindness; not generally a not seeing, but refusing to see, a willing blindness: that which the Scriptures express by " blindness of heart." There is error, self-deception, about the most important and most practical matters; the calling of good, evil, and evil, good. There is somnolency and drowsy slumber upon the minds of men; a supine negligence, that they cannot consider nor care how things go within them, or what is uppermost.

Then again, there is, in the inferior soul, the imaginations, the appetites, the affections or passions, a continual mutiny and disorder, a rebellion against what doth remain of the law in the mind; so that what remains is very imperfect, much obscured, shattered and broken: yet, there is a continual mutiny and insurrection against these reliques of that law. And this, indeed, constitutes a man, within himself, the continual seat of a war; he is in a state of war with himself: for he hath some light in his mind; but there are these mutinous and rebellious appetitions and passions working in continual opposition thereunto; so that he cannot rase out those notions, he hath in his mind: "This I should do, and that I should do so;" nor will his inferior faculties be induced to any kind of compliance therewith. It is not such a war as in the regenerate, to wit, in one and the same faculty, and especially in the heart and will, where there is an imperfect inclination to that which is good, but yet victorious. But the war lies here, between that which should be the governing faculty, the mind, the practical judgment, the conscience, and the mutinous dispositions of a rebellious heart, that are entire, and in their full strength, in the unregenerate; whereas, in the regenerate, they are subdued and brought under; not quite expelled, but yet conquered.

Thus, we have the true state of the case, how it is with men with respect to the sinfulness of their nature, which lies spread through all the several powers and faculties of the soul, and shews itself with reference to the several objects wherewith men can be any way concerned. But we are to consider,

(2.) The universality of this revolt; that is, that all men are in it, they are all gone back; all men, and the all of every man. All men are in it. And it is, therefore, on the whole matter, not strange that this corruption of the nature of man should be represented with such rhetorick as we find in divers passages of Scripture: as in the 14 and 53 psalms, and Romans 3, where you have divers passages quoted out of the Old Testament, especially out of the book of Psalms, of that same import, to signify, how general a consent there is in this matter of man's rebellion; that as men have agreed herein with infernal spirits, so they do generally agree with one another; "Come let us cast off his cords, and throw away his bands from off us." All, from the highest to the lowest, agreeing in such a design as this.

If you would take a brief view of the state of the case, that 3 of the Romans will give it you very shortly and succinctly, and yet with all, very copiously and fully. The apostle tells us, that he had proved, (as indeed he had done in the 1 and 2 chapters of that epistle) that " Jews and Gentiles were under sin." Those two distributing terms, Jew and Gentile, taking up the whole of the world, and was then the known distribution of the world of mankind. And he had not only said it, but proved it, that they were all under sin; even the very Jews themselves, as well as Gentiles, though a select people, a people that had the oracles of God; the peculiar tokens of his presence and favour, (where grace was not victorious,) yet, as great an enmity appears among them, against God, as in the pagan world and nations of the earth.

And if you look into the 1 Romans, and the latter end, you see, that men having expelled and driven God out of their minds and thoughts, as not liking to retain him in their knowledge, what becomes of them hereupon? Why, God gives them up, leaves them to themselves: they become now to be under the dominion and power of exorbitant and unruly affections and passions. "God gave them up to vile affections; and as they liked not to retain God in their knowledge, he gave them over to a reprobate mind:" and hereupon, they are filled with all unrighteousness, fornication, wickedness, covetousness, maliciousness, full of envy, murder, debate, deceit, malignity, whisperers, backbiters: and, (that which is central of all the rest, which was noted before,) haters of God: despiteful, proud, boasters, inventors of evil things, disobedient to parents, without understanding, covenant breakers, without natural affection, implacable, unmerciful.

Here is a representation of the apostate world, of that wickedness which all proceeds from the corrupt fountain which every man hath in himself. And then, in the 3 chapter, he goes on to add, from the Psalmist:, "There is none righteous, no not one; there is none that understandeth, none that seeketh after God, they are all gone out of the way, they are altogether become unprofitable: there is none that doeth good, no not one." "All have sinned and come short of the glory of God, both as it was to be their end, and as it was to be their transforming pattern. Thus it is, as to all men.

And so, the all of every man: which divers expressions in that 3 Romans do most emphatically represent and hold forth to us. "Their throat is an open sepulchre, with their mouths they have used deceit, the poison of asps is under their lips: their mouth is full of cursing and bitterness, their feet are swift to shed blood, destruction and misery are in their ways, and the way of peace have they not known." Even the several parts of the outward man are made use of, as so many engines and machines for wickedness. And for the inward man, the source and fountain of it, we are elsewhere told, that "all the imaginations of the thoughts of the heart are only evil; and continually" so; Gen. 6. 5. So early had that universal contagion spread itself among *all men*, and through the *all of every man*.

And hence it is, that they are so frequently spoken of, (even notwithstanding a profession of God's own name, if they remain in the unrenewed state,) as "a generation of vipers, and as a seed of evil doers;" yea, (as was said before,) as the seed of the devil, that old serpent. "Ye are of your father the devil, and the works of your father ye will do." And hence it is, that all wickedness do proceed, which we have any where seen perpetrated and done, upon the stage of this world. So that when the renewing work comes to take place, there is need that it should pervade, should pass through, the whole man. "The God of peace, sanctify you throughout in your whole spirit, soul and body." You see, every part of man needs a sanctifying influence; and therefore, all is corrupt and impure.

Before we go on, let us make somewhat of present useful reflection to ourselves. And consider, Is it not, hereupon, wonderful that there should be among men so general a self-complacency? How strange is it, that this being the state of the case with men in this world, there should be among them, I say, so general a self-complacency? that they all should seem to be so well pleased with themselves? look with a kind eye upon themselves? that it doth not come into men's minds to think, antecedently to their recovery, to their regeneration, "I am a fallen creature, an apostate creature, one separate and cut off from God, by mine own revolt; one fallen in with the devil against God; that am in league with him to do his will, and to disobey *him* who gave me breath; who is the Father of my spirit, and the Author of my whole being."

Are not these true thoughts that a man might think of himself, being yet unregenerate, unrenewed? And is it not strange, when they are things that lie so much in view, they yet should so seldom come into men's minds? Can we think it possible, if they did come oftener, that they should be so well pleased with themselves? Yet this, they are generally prone to be. It is the character of the wicked man; that is, one that continues yet in a state of apostasy, that "he flatters himself in his own eyes, (Psalm 36. 2.) until his iniquity be found to be hateful." He still looks upon himself with a self-flattering eye. If there be any thing which, abstractly considered, may be looked upon as amiable, this is singly looked upon: but it is seldom, in the mean time, thought, but generally forgot, what is a man's state.

O! how few are there that cry out, "What is the state of my case? If I have strength, if I have wit, if I have any thing of comeliness, I can presently strut, and think, What a fine creature am I? But, in the mean time, that I am a rebel against heaven; I am an accomplice with the devil against God; I am an apostate from my Rightful, Sovereign Lord." This would surely turn all man's self-complacency into horror and consternation, that a man would be afraid of himself, and wish he could run away from himself; and wonder how the earth comes to bear such a creature. O! this monster of an apostate soul that is off from God, and without a disposition or inclination to return to him, carries so much of horror and prodigy with it, that it is strange all are not filled with fright and amazement, till they find some manifest proof of a regenerating, transforming grace upon their spirits: it is strange that, till then, they are not a continual terror to themselves.

LECTURE XXVI.*

But that which doth yet give us a fuller and more dreadful account of this state of the case, is, besides the consideration we are to have, what man is in himself, and in his faculties and powers, precisely considered, which do make up the sinfulness of his state, and which might be mentioned under this head, is,

(3.) The aggravations of man's sinfulness.

[1.] We are to bethink ourselves, therefore, with whom there is a coincidency, and into what society and combination he falls, in this his corrupt state: and so, take the state of the case briefly and summarily thus; that he is, in all this, an accomplice with those apostate, disloyal, infernal spirits, that had revolted, and were fallen from God before: an amazing consideration! In all this, he is in confederation and combination with devils, with the powers of hell and darkness, against his Rightful and Sovereign Lord. And so doth the Scripture most expressly speak in divers places: so far as that the devil comes thereupon, to be stiled, "The god of this world," who "hath blinded the minds of them which believe not." 2 Cor. 4. 4.

And O! that we could consider this, according to what it doth import and carry in it of horror and detestableness. It is a thing that we do not yet believe, that a world inhabited by reasonable creatures, God's own offspring, are universally fallen into a confederacy and combination with another god, with an enemy-god, an adversary-god, against the living and true God. Men have changed their God. And what a fearful choice have they made! fallen into a league with those wicked creatures that were weary of his government before, and that were, thereupon, thrown down into an abyss of darkness, and bound up in the chains thereof, unto the judgment of the great day. But doth the Scripture say this in vain? or hath it not a meaning, when it calls the devil, "The god of this world?" O! with what amazement should it strike our hearts, to think that so it is; that the whole order of creatures is gone off from God, and fallen into a confederacy with the devil and his angels, against their Rightful, Sovereign Lord.

It is not a thing spoken (as it were) once on the bye; but the Scripture doth industriously represent this as the settled state

* Preached April 7, 1694.

of the case with men. Look to the Ephes. 2. 1. "You hath he quickened, who were dead in trespasses and sins:—wherein we all had our conversation in times past, fulfilling the desires of the flesh and of the mind." And under whose regimen is this? Why, "according to the course of this world, according to the prince of the power of the air, the spirit that *now* worketh in the children of disobedience." They live subject to the government of that prince: and that is a long-continued *now*, referring to the whole time and state of the apostasy. It speaks the fixed state of this case, that as long as men do remain dead in trespasses and sins, as it is in the 1 verse of that chapter; and all the while that that death lies upon the world, which, as we are told in the text, "hath passed upon all;" all that time, during that long-continued *now*, all their actions, all their motions, all their designs, are "according to the prince of the power of the air, the spirit that worketh in the children of disobedience." they are led captive by him at his will; 2 Tim. 2. 26. He hath his will of them. "The lusts of your father ye will do." John 8. 44. That "will" is not a sign of the tense, but a distinct word, "you will;" you will to do the lusts of your father; you have a proneness, a propension of will, or it is grateful to your will, to do the lusts of your father: the devil is become even a father and a god to this apostate world: they are the serpent's seed: he hath (as it were) impregnated them with all the principles of malignity and disloyalty, against their Rightful, Sovereign Lord.

Methinks, this should make us afraid of ourselves, and even of one another, till there be some appearance of a change in the state of our case. We look upon it as a very terrible thing, to have the body of a man possessed with the devil: but how much more dreadful is it, to have his soul under that possession; acted upon by satan in all his designs through the whole of his course, led captive by the devil at his will! Waiting if God will give repentance: that is represented as the great business of the gospel ministry, and of a gospel minister, as in 2 Tim. 2. 24, 25. to wait with patience, and endeavour with gentleness, that they may be brought to repentance, and enabled to recover themselves out of the snare of the devil, who are led captive by him at his will. See what his part then is, as a god over this world; he makes them do what he will, he hath his will upon them. "My will is, that you forget God; and they do: that you live in a continual contempt of God; and so they do: that you mind nothing but the affairs of this world, and how to please and gratify your flesh and sense, mind nothing but what shall, or shall not, profit your external part, or ensnare and hurt you, and undo you; and they do just as he would have them do, throughout the whole of their course. So that, in this state of the apostasy, they are in a continual confederation as accomplices with devils, those apostate spirits, that were gone off from God before.

[2.] It is a further aggravating consideration of this sinfulness, that the understandings of men do all this while remain with them: they have their understandings yet about them. Man is still an intelligent creature. "There is a spirit in man, and the inspiration of the Almighty hath given him understanding," (Job 32. 8.) to distinguish him from a brute. It is very true, indeed, if sin had totally unmanned men, it had brought them into an utter incapacity of sinning any more. If the leading faculty were destroyed quite, he were then no more capable of sin than a log. But this makes the matter beyond all imagination wonderful, that a man should have his understanding remaining, and become such a monster as this; and yet apprehend nothing of it: an understanding that he can use about other matters; he can discourse, reason, project, lay designs, form methods in reference to all things that are of an inferior concernment. We find that in that great transformation of that haughty prince Nebuchadnezzar, (whom God turned to graze among the wild beasts of the field,) a transformation, not of his body, (as we have no reason to think that it was,) but of his mind; and we are told, that at the end of so much time, his understanding returned to him. But in this common case, men's understandings do remain with them all the while they are under this monstrous transformation: that is, while a reasonable, immortal spirit disaffects his Maker, the Father of spirits; joins itself with clods, the base things of this earth; yea, joins itself to devils, apostate, impure spirits, and falls into confederacy with them against God: and yet men are not aware of their case.

And this makes that transformation which sin hath wrought in the very nature of man, in the soul of man, his reasonable soul, so horrid a thing. If he had been transformed into any other bodily shape, (though never so monstrous,) it had been incomparably a less monstrous translation than this: to make a reasonable, understanding creature, engage in a contest against him that gave him breath, the Author and Parent of his life and being, nothing could be a more monstrous thing. If all these metamorphoses which poets feign, had generally taken place and effect, every where among men; if they had been transformed into trunks of trees and the like, (as hath been feigned concerning divers,) it had been a less strange, a less fearful transformation than this; a reasonable, intelligent, immortal spirit turned against his Maker; and intent upon razing out every thing of his holy image out of itself.

Now this understanding still remaining, the persisting in a way and course of sin, is a running counter to that light and knowledge which every man hath, in a degree, remaining in him, though it is but a dubious kind of twilight; light that doth rather admit to be called "darkness." "If the light that is in you be darkness, how great is that darkness?" that is, it is ineffectual to answer the proper purposes of a directive, practical light: yet what doth remain thereof, doth serve most highly to aggravate the wickedness of them in whom it is.

This is that which is more than intimated, when men are required to shew themselves men; as it is in Isaiah 46, 8. You have the proper principles of humanity yet about you, and the great distinguishing principle of reason, that exalts you above inferior creatures: you have it in you, but you do not use it; you are men, but you do not shew it: "Shew yourselves men ye transgressors." And again, psalm 53. 4. "Have all the workers of iniquity no knowledge?" It is implied that they have it, but they will not use it: the interrogation is a more forcible affirmation; men have knowledge in them, yet transgress: and so keep up a contest and a war against God, and against themselves. And again,

[3.] It is a further most aggravating consideration, that as, in general, they have understanding about them, and still remaining with them, they have also some natural notions of God, all the while they are thus at war with him, and in this defiance against him. Still they have the natural impress of God upon their minds that they cannot raze out; so that they do not fight against him altogether in the dark; "Light shines in the midst of that darkness which comprehends it not." That light by which God reveals himself, not only round about them, but in them; there is that which might be known of God in every man, as in that Rom. 1. 19. That which might be known of God is manifest in them, for God hath revealed it to them.

And there is, hereupon, such a thing as natural religion: for while they have a notion of God in their minds, it is not as of a Being irrelative to them, but it is as an Object of worship; an Object of trust, so as that commonly men, in their last necessities, untaught and uninstructed, do pray to him. As I remember that ancient, (Minutius Fœlix,) in opposition to paganism, asserting the oneness of the Deity, and that God whom the christians serve, speaks thus: " You yourselves (saith he) when any thing ails you and are in distress, do not you use to lift up your eyes and hands to heaven? *vulgi isti naturalis est sermo*, this is as a natural kind of prayer, which your own nature doth even constrain you to, whether you will or no; there is a natural susceptibleness of religion. Men are instructed by nature itself, to dread a superior Being, and to place some kind of dependance upon it, and to have some kind of expectation from it, of help and relief in their necessities and distresses, and yet remain, all this while, in an apostasy, in war and rebellion.

This makes this monster of an apostate creature to be so much the more monstrous, beyond comparison; even beyond all that can be thought. The case being thus with them, that such sentiments of God as they have about them, they cannot erase, and yet, cannot obey; they can never get them out of them, nor comply with them: this is their case. So monstrous a thing as an unregenerate creature that remains yet in the apostate state. They carry about a notion of God with them in their minds wherever they go: and so have not only reason left them, but somewhat of religion; which some take to be a more distinguishing property in man than reason itself, it being less disputable whether it do peculiarly belong to man; to inferior creatures it manifestly doth not: and in great measure it is evident that it doth belong to all men. For those that have been the most diligent inquirers into the state of the world, in former ages, among the pagans themselves, have taken notice that it was even an impossible thing to hear of a man any where that had not somewhat of religion, or some sense of a Deity in him. As, I remember, Plutarch saith: "It is not impossible to find cities without walls, without government, without coin:" but to find a city without religion, he thought to be altogether impossible. "And it were (saith he) as easy a thing to build a city without a foundation, without ground to set it on, as to form a society of men without religion." This was the apprehension of such knowing men as he and others, even among heathens themselves, in former times.

And this is the general matter of God's controversy with the world, when we are told in that Romans 1. 18. that "the wrath of God is revealed from heaven against the ungodliness and unrighteousness of men who hold the truth in unrighteousness." What that truth is, we are to collect from what follows in the 19 ver. before mentioned: for that which may be known of God is manifest in them; for God hath revealed it to them. He hath so inwrought his name, his own idea, into the spirits of men, that there it remains as an indelible impress, not quite to be razed out. And therefore, they who have been more avowed atheists, have been so, more in endeavour than in fact; endeavouring to extinguish those notions of God out of their minds, which yet they could never rid themselves of. "The fool hath said in his heart, There is no God." He hath said it in his heart: not with his mouth, not in his mind, but in his heart; which implies it rather a wish than an assertion. And so, the hebrew text doth lead us to understand: for there is not the copula to make it an assertion: The fool hath said in his heart, "no God;" not that there is none, that is not in the text, but—"no God;" let there be none: or, O! that there were none: I wish there were none. It is rather a wish than an assertion with these fools. And these fools, they are the generality of the apostate world.

But that men should carry that notion in their minds about them, up and down the world; have (as it were) God so much in view, (if they will but look into themselves and commune with their own minds,) and yet should be continually warring and fighting against him, when they could not but at the same time conceive him to be God, but conceive him too, to be the very Author of their life and being; "He in whom (as the apostle quotes a heathen poet saying) they live and move and have their being;" and another saying, "Whose offspring they are:" his very offspring; and yet in a continual, general rebellion against him; this aggravates the matter beyond all measure. And again,

[4.] They have in them also, the practical principles of right and wrong, in reference to one another. In this state of apostasy from God, they have, I say, practical principles; that is, principles that ought to govern practice, telling them what is right, and what is wrong, in reference to one another, as well as in reference to God: and yet, there is nothing else but aversion, hating of one another, and designing against one another, and every one labouring to tear the world in pieces, that they may grasp into their own hands, what yet lies in other men's. They do so far know what is right and wrong in reference to one another, that they can no sooner hear of the general measures of right and wrong among them, but their minds do inwardly consent to the reasonableness of such a constitution. As that great maxim of our Saviour; "Whatsoever ye would that men should do to you do ye so to them," as being that which sums up the law and the prophets. A saying so taken, even among heathens themselves, that it is known, that the emperor Alexander Severus, caused it to be inscribed on the gates of his palace, as if it were the most suitable, agreeable thing to the minds of men, and to the necessities of human society, that could be thought. And,

[5.] Yet further, they have all this while a most connatural desire of their own felicity. This is a further aggravation, that every man naturally desires to be happy, when yet, he is continually engaged in a way and course of sin, against his Sovereign, Rightful Lord, which so directly tends to involve him in all misery: and so, is doing perpetual violence to himself, and even to the law of his own nature; for there cannot be a more radical principle in any man, or even in the nature of man, generally considered, than to desire to be happy. "Who will shew us any good?" is the common vogue, according to that of the Psalmist in the 4, psalm. All the world is full of craving desires after felicity, after a happy state, and yet running on in a continued course directly counter hereunto; fighting every where against the desire of their own hearts.

[6.] It is a further aggravating consideration too, that, in all this time, they have some apprehension with them generally of a future state in another world, the soul of man having a secret consciousness of its own immortality inwrought into it. So that (as you have heard) mere irreligion hath been a thing very rarely to be known in the world, and never but as men have pretended and endeavoured to erase and root out the principles of religion out of their own souls; but without total effect. So there hath been no sort of religion in the world that hath not proceeded upon the supposition of a future immortality. Not only christians and jews, but mahometans and the grosser pagans, have all agreed in this one sentiment, that "there is a life to come," and a state after this. And yet, they are continually taking the way that takes hold of hell, and leads down to the chambers of death; though that sentiment is not more natural, more common, that there is another state, another world, a life to come, than the sentiment is, of the connexion between goodness and blessedness, and between wickedness and misery. They have generally apprehended so, as the apostle, in the close of the first chapter of this epistle (referring to the gentile world) saith: "They did know the righteous judgment of God, and that they who did those things were worthy of death, and yet, not only did the same, but took pleasure in them." They did apprehend a connexion between wickedness and death, between sin and misery, and yet run the course which corrupt inclination carried them into, without resistance. And again,

[7.] There is in them all this while, a self-reflecting power, by which they are capable of taking knowledge of themselves, of looking in upon their own minds. "The spirit of a man is the candle of the Lord, searching into the innermost parts of the belly;" that is, searching into his most inward *penetralia*, into all the secret recesses of itself, even to the very-centre. It is such a kind of light as can invert its beams, and turn them inward upon itself; being therein a nobler sort of eye, than this external bodily one is. For this exterior bodily eye of ours that sees all other things, cannot see itself; but the mind, the intellectual eye, cannot only see other things, but can see itself too, is capable of contemplating itself. That conscience that is in man, that natural conscience, it is not only the conservatory of natural principles, the seat of them, that shew what men are to do, and what they are not to do, (as was told you before, under the former head,) but it is also a self-reflecting principle, that which is called properly and more strictly, συνείδησις, by which a person is conscious to himself what he is, and what he doth; what his dispositions are, and what the series and tendency of his actions are.

And yet, this principle is rarely used; rarely, in reflecting upon actions, and in reflecting upon their states; scarcely ever in reflecting upon their actions, very rarely; so that, among a people professing the name of God, he may long hearken, and hear none saying, What have I done? "I hearkened and heard: no man spake aright; no man said, What have I done?" Jer. 8, 6. Though they have that self-reflective principle in them, by which they are capable of taking cognizance of their own actions; they never do it, never allow themselves to say, What have I done? in a long continued tract of time. But every following day passeth as former days have done; and seldom, from morning till night, is there a self-reflecting thought.

Indeed, where natural light hath been improved, even among some heathens, they tell us it should be otherwise: *Vir bonus et sapiens*; *a good, a wise man*, will not go to bed at night, will not compose himself to rest, before he hath revolved with himself the actions of the day. So we are taught by a heathen instructor. But, though there have been some such instances, they are very rare, of those that allow themselves to reflect upon their actions; but much more rare, of those that reflect upon their state, that bethink themselves, or say, "In what state am I? How do things stand between God and me, whose creature I am, and under whose government I live?" And yet, again,

[8.] It doth more highly aggravate all this wickedness, to consider, how inflexible men are, and averse to compliance with any means and methods for their reduction, whether they that are without the gospel, or they that live under it. For those that are without it, that have no gospel, no verbal gospel, among them, such an aversion to all the methods of recovery doth very sufficiently appear: for, otherwise, if that were not the common temper of the world, even where the gospel is not yet come, it would soon be among them, and nothing could have hindered it from spreading over all the world many ages ago, but an indisposition and opposition in the minds and spirits of men to the progress and diffusion of it. For there hath been no nation where the gospel was, but they that were hitherto destitute of the gospel, some or other of them, must have lain next to that nation where the gospel was, so that it was impossible for them not to have heard the sound thereof: and, if there were not an indisposition in them, even in the minds of men, and a contrariety and disaffection, they would, at least, have been inquisitive; they would have examined—"Is such a declaration from God, or is it not?" which, if they had, it carries with it such undeniable characters of divinity, that inquiring minds could not long have been ignorant; but prejudice and disaffection have kept off the inquiry; which, if it had taken effect in one country, it would soon have reached another, and so another, till the world had been leavened with the gospel long ago. Therefore, such aversion and disaffection to the gospel appears even where there hath no gospel yet come.

Besides that, even there, though there be no verbal gospel, there is somewhat of a real one, that God shews himself placable, or no implacable, no inflexible, no irreconcilable enemy. He doth not carry it with men generally as one seeking their destruction, leaves not himself without witness, in that he doth good, and gives them rain from heaven, and fruitful seasons, filling their hearts with food and gladness, as in Acts 14 and 17. So the apostle speaks of God, in reference to his dispensations towards the pagan world; and he saith it unto pagans: "He makes his sun to shine on the just and on the unjust:" and requires of us, upon that very ground, to love our enemies, because he shews so very much philanthropy, and good will towards men. "Love your enemies, bless them that curse you, do good to them that hate you, and pray for them that despitefully use you, and persecute you, that you may be the children of your Father, which is in heaven;" (Matt. 5. 44, 45.) that you may appear such, that you may represent herein a Godlike nature; for God doth so, making his goodness diffuse and spread itself through the world: so that, "the whole earth is full of his goodness;"

though it be so full of men's wickedness. And, Romans 2. 4. "Despisest thou the riches of his goodness, and forbearance, and long-suffering, not knowing that the goodness of God leadeth thee to repentance?" As we have copiously shewn from that text, that there is a manifest, discernible leadingness and ducture in the continued exercise of God's goodness, and particularly of his patience and forbearance, unto repentance.

But where the gospel is, there, this disaffection and prejudice doth most apparently and conspicuously shew itself. Not only were the pagans of old accused to be "God-haters," (Rom. 1. 30,) where he speaks of the Gentile world, but the very Jews too, where God's light did shine, and where his grace and saving design did appear, and were most expressly testified; even of them our Saviour saith, "Ye have both seen and hated me and my Father," John 5. 24. And hence came these complaints, even where the gospel is: "I have laboured in vain, and spent my strength for nought and in vain." Isaiah 49. 4. And, "Who hath believed our report, and to whom is the arm of the Lord revealed?" Isaiah 53. 1. quoted by the apostle, Romans 10. 16. "Have they all obeyed the gospel?"—No; far from that; for Isaiah saith, "Who hath believed our report?" And in the close of that chapter, "All the day long have I spread forth my hands to a gainsaying and rebellious people."

The experienced unsuccessfulness of the gospel, which we generally so much see cause to complain of and bemoan, speaks this continually. What representations have we of God, in Christ, intent upon a reconciling design! But how few are won! How few hearts touched! So that men are gone off from God, and there they affect to abide; they have chosen distance from God, and seem resolved to continue it, say we to them what we will or can. We speak to them in the name of the Lord, but they will not hear; and for the sake of their own souls, but they regard it not. And, which is still,

[9.] More aggravating, that is, it is a further addition to the load of aggravations, and adds unspeakably to it; men are all this while certain they must die; they are in no doubt concerning that; they know the things they are fallen in with, in opposition to God, can be enjoyed by them but a little while; they see not only that the fashion of this world passeth away, but they find themselves passing away; changes are upon them. It is a thing concerning which they can be in no doubt; they have no instance of any one that escaped death. And yet here is generally no consideration what shall become of them hereafter. They find they are not happy here, they are still crying and seeking to be happy, but obtain it not: and yet they have no concern to be happy hereafter; though they know they must be gone, and their places on earth will, in a little while, know them no more. They have continual instances before their eyes, of other wicked ones like themselves driven away in their wickedness, torn up by the roots, plucked from their dwelling place and gone: they know it must shortly be so with them too; and yet have chosen a state of distance from God; they never look after him, till (it may be) their last vain dying breath is uttered in some such unreasonable desire as this: "Lord have mercy upon me:" when they can live and sin no longer, then they cry to God for mercy.

These are all most fearful aggravations of this common wickedness that prevails in every one; and serves farther to represent to us the sinfulness of man in his fallen state. I should next come to speak of the death that hereupon passeth over all men, as we have spoken of death as it befel that one, as it stood in the commination, and as it stood in the sentence. It requiring a further, and, somewhat, a distinct consideration, with reference to the universality of man, whose case doth (though not substantially, yet in very great and important circumstances) differ from him who was the first transgressor. But before I come to that, some use of this representation which hath been made of the sinfulness of man's state, should intervene.

LECTURE XXVII.*

And there are many things which it is obvious to us to take notice of, for our instruction and use, from hence. As,

1. We may see, hereupon, how altered a creature man is; how little he is himself; or what that one man, by whom sin and death entered, at first was. You have lately heard in what estate God did at first create man: "So God made man after his own image," a Godlike creature. Such a thing was man at first; thence called the son of God. "Who was the son of Seth, who was the son of Adam, who was the son of God." Luke 3. 38. A glorious pedigree run up backward, in its assent, as high as heaven; "who was the son of God." And it is not supposable that God should raise up a son immediately from himself, unlike himself. Therefore, it was very

* Preached April 21, 1694.

suitable unto the state of things, that it should be so expressly told us, "God made man in his own image," which you have heard was to be understood not only of his natural image, as man hath a spirit in him that was naturally, essentially vital, intelligent, free, and immortal; but it was also, and more principally, to be understood of the moral image, comprehending both sanctity and felicity, and, according to which, man was made a happy, and a holy creature, pure and blessed.

How unlike himself is he now become! Let none of us think that this concerns not us. Are we not also of the posterity of Adam, degenerate creatures, fallen from the original excellency of our own nature, and especially in respect of that conformity and inclination which were in our nature towards God, our great and common Parent? If any of you had a son that was newly gone forth from you, and you met him by and by, and he doth not know you; You tell him, "I am your father;" he replies, "No, it is no such thing, you are no father of mine;" would it not cut your heart? Who would not look upon it as a deplorable case? This is the common case; men are sunk into such deep ignorance and oblivion of God, the Author of their being, that now they retain no knowledge, no remembrance of him, no conformity to him, no inclination toward their ancient Original.

It is an amazing thing that it should be so! It is much more amazing that it should be so little considered, that this earth should be peopled with such inhabitants, every one having in him (that is, all that are of human race,) an intelligent, immortal spirit, a mind capable of thought, capable of just thought, capable of duty, and capable of blessedness. But so miserably sunk into carnality and earthliness, that this body in which it should but dwell, therein it rots, therein it putrifies. And that which (as hath been said) was designed to be its mansion, is become its dormitory, and its grave. A living soul carnalized! A most horrid creature! And, as it is said, Adam was at first a living soul: ("so God breathed into him the breath of life, (that pure, divine, and heavenly breath;) and he became a living soul,") so, then to have asked the question, "What is man?" must have been to receive the answer, "He is a living soul: he is all soul, and that soul all life." But now is this living soul buried in flesh, a lost thing to all the true, and great, and noble ends and purposes of that life which was at first given it.

It is true, indeed, that this is a thing much less than what is said of the second Adam, in that 1 Cor. 15. 45. "The first man Adam was made a living soul; the second man Adam was a quickening spirit." This latter is a great deal more. A living soul signified him to live himself: but a quickening spirit signifies a power to make others live. That, the first Adam could not do: the more excellent kind of life which he had, (for there was a complication of lives in the first creation of this man,) he could not lose; but he could not give. He could not lose it from himself; but he could never have given it by any power or immediate efficiency of his own to another. Here, the second Adam, the constitution of the second Adam, was far above that of the first, in that he could quicken others; a quickening spirit, not only quickened passively, but quickened actively, such a spirit as could give spirit, and diffuse life.

But take this matter as it was—" The first man Adam was a living soul," with all that life in him in all the kinds thereof, which was the highest and most noble that could belong to a reasonable, intelligent soul: such a one he was; and now we have this living soul entombed. It is naturally a living soul, and naturally immortal still; but as unapt to serve and answer the proper purposes of that life which was at first given it, as if it were quite dead, dead towards God. It was principally alive towards him: that holy life which did belong to Adam's soul at first, could have none but God as its highest and noblest term: upon him it was terminated. Therefore, where there is a restitution and recovery, this is the immediate effect, persons do " become dead to sin, but alive to God through Jesus Christ." Rom. 6. 11. And here is now a living soul alive to sin, but dead towards God; dead towards the prime and most glorious Object; and dead to all the noble operations, for which it was originally and first made a living soul. And this is the state of man: like the living God in this respect he was; but now, towards him he is become a dead thing, putrid, and noisome, and offensive, even as a carcass. He is dead in that respect, wherein a soul may be said to be dead, which cannot be in a natural sense, as you have heard, and as is plain in itself; but only in a moral sense. In that sense wherein it can be said to be dead, in that sense, it must be the most fearful alteration which hath passed upon it, that could be passed upon a creature: that is, it was alive towards God; and is become dead towards him, cut off from him by a self-separation. Therein lies the sinfulness of this death that we are considering, and which belongs to the present subject we have in hand to consider. That God hath hereupon retired from him, that is the punitive notion of this death. But the sinful notion of it lies in its severing, retiring, and withdrawing itself from God; plucking itself away from him, as it hath done in the apostasy; and as it every where doth as long as the state of apostasy is continued in.

Now it is become a most unlike creature to God, and most unlike unto its original self, that could be thought. It was a knowing, intelligent creature; and especially knowing God. This image of God, that was at first impressed upon it, stood in knowledge; now it is become ignorant of God, "alienated from the life of God through the ignorance that is in it, and the blindness of the heart." Ephes. 4. 18. It was like him in knowledge; but now it is become most stupidly ignorant of what it is most concerned in. Is this Godlike? It was a holy, pure creature; but now delighting to wallow in the impurest sensualities. Is this like God? It was a most orderly, regular creature; but now all confusion; its powers engaged in war against one another; the whole frame of man disorganized, the whole dependance of will and affections upon, what should lead them, an intelligent mind and judgment; but these shattered all to pieces. The whole frame is discomposed. Is this like the God of order? O! how unlike to God is man now become! And therein unlike himself, and unlike what he at first was. But,

2. We may further learn, hence, that this world cannot, hereupon, but lie under divine displeasure. And it is most just and righteous that it should do so. This, the law gives sufficient intimation of, wheresoever it comes: "That every mouth may be stopped, and all the world may become guilty before God." Romans 3, 19. Impleadable at law, that is the import of the word there used, to signify God's having a just and legal controversy with all this world. He hath in point of law, that to be said against it, which can never be answered; which admits of no apology, no defence. But again,

3. We may yet further learn, hence, that the sinfulness which hath spread itself among men in this world, cannot but be in a true sense natural, such as hath poisoned the very nature of man with an enmity and malignity against God: for you see it is universal. Nothing can be supposed to be common, but what must be understood to have some common cause, a cause that is common. But the text tells us, that "all have sinned." And whereas, (as was noted to you formerly,) it is said in the 3 chapter of this epistle, ver. 9, "We have before proved both Jews and Gentiles to be all under sin;" (which Jews and Gentiles did divide the world;) and "There is

none righteous, no not one," as the same apostle quotes from psalm the 14th and 53. This plainly speaks this contagion to have infected the nature of man, and to run with his propagated nature every where, from age to age, and from generation to generation.

It appears to be so, for that when, upon the general defection and revolt of this world from God, he was pleased yet, (in order to his asserting and preserving some interest therein,) to select to himself one people, one people to be peculiar to him; all the endearing favours of providence, all the peculiar manifestations of light from heaven, all the intercourse that, in a more external way, God vouchsafed to hold with this people, (unless he did here and there powerfully transform their hearts,) still left them evidently as full of malignity, and of the enmity of wickedness against God, as if they had been the merest strangers to him in all the world. And, therefore, is he sometimes represented as calling heaven and earth as astonished witnesses against them: "Hear O heavens, and give ear O earth, I have nourished and brought up children, and they have rebelled against me." Isaiah 1. 2. "My people would not hearken to my voice, Israel would have none of me." Psalm 81, 11. "He came to his own, but they received him not;" John 1, 11. What can this signify, but a deep depravedness of nature? Sin hath inwrought itself even into the very nature of man.

We have the same instances multiplied in the days of the gospel. God hath shewn more peculiar favours, vouchsafed distinguishing privileges of the highest external kind, unto sundry nations into which the light of the gospel hath spread itself. But where is there greater wickedness in all the world, than in the Christian world? where greater, than in reformed Christendom, as it is called? Where is there more avowed atheism? where is there higher insolency against heaven? more direct and open rebellion, tearing all the constitutions and laws, which they themselves pretend to own for divine and christian? A deep depravedness this must argue.

You may see in the continual springing up of one generation after another, that even from infancy, sin still springs up with reason, and the improvements of the natural faculties. So that as soon as any do begin to act rationally, they begin to act wickedly. Heathens have observed it, and speak of it with regret, and take notice how a child neglected, grows monstrously vicious: common experience tells us this. Education, indeed, (which therefore ought to be practised with a great deal more care and diligence than it is,) doth somewhat repress, but it doth not change and alter nature. You see that the corruption of it proceeds, even with the nature itself, from the immediate fountain. "Behold I was shapen in iniquity, and in sin did my mother conceive me;" so the penitent Psalmist confesseth concerning himself; Psalm 51. 5. And it is generally spoken concerning the wicked, (as all the world doth naturally appear to be,) that "they are estranged from the womb, and go astray as soon as they are born." Psalm 58. 3.

This was a notion that did obtain so much among the Jews, that you see with what severity some of the worst of them fall upon the blind man: (John 9. 34.) "Thou wast altogether born in sin, and dost thou teach us?" implying, that he who would take upon him, in an extraordinary way, (not being called,) to be a teacher and instructor to others, must be some very extraordinary person, must be born a sinless man. A testimony that they give against themselves unawares: for they had such a Teacher among them, but regarded him not; a Teacher that came forth from God, and that was not born in sin. "Thou art altogether born in sin, no better than any other man, and dost thou take upon thee to teach us?". And again,

4. We may further learn, hence, how little reason men have to think it strange, that the state of things in the world is not so constantly favourable, or so benign to them, as they could wish, or are apt to expect; that they meet with many things so ungrateful; that men find themselves subject to pain, sicknesses, crosses, in the course of providence; that they meet with disappointments so often; that so many are reduced to straits, and wants, and distresses; pinching poverty and the like; that there is so much of confusion and disorder and violence in the world, the inhabitants of it ready to tear one another and the world in pieces. Why, all have sinned. This gives an easy, ready account. O! how little is it considered when people are so full of complaints of their own particular ails and evils. "Nobody's case is like mine. How am I injured and wronged by some or other that are stronger and mightier than I? My right is withheld from me," and the like. Alas! poor creature, dost thou so little consider how thou hast wronged God, and withheld from him his right in thyself, in thy life and soul, and all thy powers? Saith another, "I have a child sprung up in my family, I have a son that is undutiful and rebellious, a perpetual vexation to me." How little is it considered that thou hast carried it with much more undutifulness towards God, who was the original Author and Parent of thy very life and being. You think, when you are sick, you suffer a very great hardship;

you do not consider what it is to have been a sinner, to have torn the constitutions and laws of heaven, and violated the government of the Supreme and Rightful Lord of all. "Why doth a living man complain, a man for the punishment of his sin?" Lam. 3. 39. "Let us search and try our ways;" let us once but take a clear view of our own ways, and that will stop the complaint. Consider what a vile creature I have been; so many years of my time gone, and I have never minded God; never paid him a duty; never thought of him with any reverence; never designed him any service; never resolved on living to him, but to myself. And yet, now, a little affliction, that grates upon the flesh, makes us cry out "O! how hardly are we dealt with." Again,

5. Have all sinned? Then instead of complaining, wonder at the divine patience, that things are no worse with the inhabitants of this world, than they are; that men are allowed a being in it; that this world is not turned into flames over the offender's ears; that they are not continually pursued with divine terrors; that he is not, with more dreadful severity, exacting his right from his own creatures whom he made, (as their own understandings can tell them,) not for themselves, but for himself: and nobody minds him, when they so generally behave themselves with such insolency in this world, as if they had been the creators of it, as if they had made the heavens and the earth; sun, moon, and stars, and all things, the help and influence whereof they any way enjoy.

How admirable, I say, is the divine patience, that bears with offending creatures, lets them propagate and transmit their like from age to age, and from generation to generation, through that vast tract of time as hath hitherto past, since the apostasy? With what wonderment should we consider this power of divine patience! Who, that hath it in his hands to right himself for such indignities and wrongs, would refrain? When we think how quickly, how easily he can do himself right; can frown or wink such a world as this into distraction in a moment; that as it sprung up by his fiat, "Let it be," how easily could he frown it into nothing! Yet he lets men live, lets them live neglecting him, when they have natures capable of adoration. But again we have,

6. Much more reason to admire the divine bounty towards such creatures: not only that he spares and lets them live, but that he maintains them, and keeps them in life and being, each one for his measured time, and so, provided that there should be a transmission of life from age to age, in so continued a course. How admirable should the divine bounty and munifi-

cence be in our eyes, upon this account! He doth good to the unthankful and evil; to those that never thank him for it. If you did but feed a brute creature, it would be brought by degrees, and in time, to take some kind of notice of you, with gratitude. "The ox knows his owner, and the ass his master's crib, but Israel doth not know, my people will not consider." Men will not know their Owner, though the ox knows his. It is your Owner that cares for you; as who provides for the ox and the ass, but the owner? So God, as the Owner of you and of all the inhabitants of this world, all the children of men, (for I speak of these inhabitants,) he doth his part towards you and them. He provides for them, he maintains them, and affords them all that is suitable and needful for their support; but they will not take that notice of their Owner, which an ox or an ass takes of his. How wonderful a thing is this on God's part! how horrid a thing on man's!

I have thought of it many times, and it would be a thing not unworthy of your thoughts and serious contemplations, that we should, in so continued a course, find the earth so productive as it is of all things, not only necessary for the support of the life of man, but so grateful too; such pleasant, delicious fruits in their season: and for whom is all this entertainment? For a world of rebels, offending creatures; those that never look up; we enjoy all, as if it were our own, and never consider, we have a Lord over us, the free Donor of all. Again,

7. Since there are so many sinners in this world, (all have sinned,) it is very strange there are so few self-accusers; when the same light, and the same rational powers, by which men are capable of sinning, they are also capable of understanding themselves to be sinners. There is, indeed, a natural conscience in men, and it hath its exercise sometimes, and a very impartial exercise, in reference to some cases, but how little is there of conscience towards God! "Herein," saith the apostle, "do I exercise myself to have always a conscience void of offence towards God, and towards man." So it is, where once regenerating grace comes to restore an entire divine Image in the soul again, to do an entire work, to produce a general rectitude in the soul, there will be conscience towards God, as well as towards men. Towards men: there is among men some conscience, though too often violated when interest sways: many do not care whom they injure, to advantage themselves; but yet, while they do wrong, they cannot be altogether without reflection that they do wrong: and upon such accounts, chiefly, they have consciences "accusing, or excusing by turns." Rom. 2. 15. But towards God, generally, no conscience at all; they live in the world as

without him, and their hearts never smite them; spend days, and months, and years in vanity; throw away their lifetime, so as they are useful for nothing, they were made for; and never say—" God have mercy upon us;" never think a serious, reflecting thought. So it is with the most; they live at that rate, till in a moment they go down into the grave, and never consider what they have thrown away; a lifetime in the world, without ever minding the proper business of life. But,

8. We may also learn, hence, to take notice, with wonder, that there is so much self-complacency in the world, as one of the most incongruous things, the most monstrous incongruity in all the world, that men should generally be so well pleased with themselves. If things, in external respects especially, be well with them; if they find themselves to be in health; if they have any thing of natural strength and vigour about them; especially if they can take notice, they have wit above the common rate: if they have wealth; if they have reputation and esteem among men; if they have any thing of human dignity or grandeur; O! how well pleased are they with themselves, what self-admirers are men generally upon such accounts, without even considering, (and what a dash would one such thought be to all this,) " I am a fallen creature, an apostate creature, a sinner, one with whom heaven hath a controversy, a rebel still, if not yet reconciled." Strange! that men should be pleased with themselves, and their little external circumstances, and forget this, " I am a lapsed creature, and under the displeasure of heaven." But again,

9. We may take notice, hence, of the reason, whence it is, that there is so much displeasure and wrath against any, in this world, who look towards God and heaven. All have sinned, all are generally in a state of sin. It is by wonderful and peculiar grace if there be so much as an inclining thought Godward, a thought of returning, if any frame their doings (as the prophet's expression is) " to turn to the Lord," this presently comes under observation: if men's doings be framed that way, if a man's way and course be shaped, so as to look Godward and heavenward again, then all that behold it, (and with whom there is not the same disposition of mind and spirit,) they are under a judgment, under a doom. Noah condemned the world. And as the righteous soul of Lot was vexed with the filthy conversation of the wicked, among whom he lived; so, no doubt, he also vexed them only by their observation of his better ways. And yet, further,

10. We have great reason, hereupon, to admire a divine hand and power in it, that there hath been any thing of

religion preserved and kept alive in the world, through the several successions of time, unto this day. A world where all have sinned, all have been in apostasy and revolt from God, and war against heaven; it is from a mighty divine hand that there is any such thing as serious religion. Natural religion there is, and an ineffectual thing it is, every where, almost. But for serious religion, vital religion, such as shall speak itself to be such by a self-demonstrative evidence, that such religion hath been kept alive in such a world as this, from age to age, is one of the greatest miracles that hath been wrought in the world since there was one! And further,

11. This serves to let us see how mighty a work regeneration is, or which the regenerating grace and Spirit, the Spirit of repentance, have to effect and work upon the soul. It cannot be a slight, superficial change that is to be made, where the depravation is so universal, and so total. The corruption of human nature, it hath not reached so little a way as the surface of the man only; it hath gone deep into the *penetralia*, into the inmost centre, into the very spirit of the mind: even that needs a renovation too. "Be not conformed to this world, but be ye transformed by the renewing of your mind." Rom. 12. 2. And the like expression in Ephes. 4. 22, 23. "Put off the old man that is corrupt through deceitful lusts, and be ye renewed in the spirit of your minds." O! do not think slightly of regeneration and repentance! think that they must have a mighty work to do; and that it must be a very deep change which is to be effected thereby, which must reach through a man, into the very inwards of his soul, and go as deep as corrupt nature hath done. And, in the last place,

12. How solicitous, hereupon, should we be, whether any such change hath been wrought in us, yea or no? Thus stating our case to ourselves: "Once, for certain, I was in apostasy from God, an accomplice of hell, with infernal powers, against the Sovereign, Rightful Lord of heaven and earth. Do I feel myself under a recovering influence? Am I upon a return? Is there any thing done, or doing in me, towards a renovation and effectual change?" If I be not changed, I am the same apostate creature still; that is the state wherein I persist, it carries this import with it; as if I should put it into these plain express words: "I have apostatised from God, and I will stand by it." This is the sense of many a soul, and that which words would truly express, if they were used to that effect. But many have the sense in their hearts, and yet do not consider that such horrid words as these would only serve to express that sense of theirs. "I am an apostate creature, and I

will stand by it?" this is your sense while you do not turn, all the while you have no aim at turning, no design of turning. "I have rebelled from God, I have rebelled against him, and this is that which I will abide by; I will live and die by it." O! what a horrid thing is an impenitent soul! especially under a gospel that makes so many overtures to men, of reducing apostates, and of reconciling afresh to God.

LECTURE XXVIII.*

2. Now it remains to speak of what is consequent upon this sinful state, to wit, *death passing upon all;* that which ensues upon this universal diffusion, and is, in great part, (as you will hear by and by,) complicated therewith. Now in speaking to this death that is said "to have passed through all, or over all," it must be in substance the same with that death which we have spoken to in the former part of the verse, that which befel that one first man. I shall, therefore, speak, first, of what is common under this notion of death; and then, secondly, come to consider the gradual differences afterwards.

(1.) For what this death signifies here in common, the larger discourse whereof I referred to this place. Why,

[1.] We must consider in it, that bodily death which (in common experience) all do undergo according to divine appointment. "It is appointed to all men once to die." There is a statute law in the case, that hath not been repealed, and that admits of no repeal; this lies upon the world: in the virtue of that law it is, that death hath reigned. As the strength of sin, so the power of death, even of this death, is in the law; that is, in the sentence of it, or in the commination annexed by way of sanction thereunto. If there were no law first, no man should die. And most plain it is, that this same bodily death, unto which all are subjected, it must be within the meaning of this death. "Death hath passed over all." For,

First. We find it to be, most expressly, in the sentence itself that was laid upon Adam, and as a comment upon the commination, that was at first given. The commination was before his fall: "In the day thou eatest thereof thou shalt surely die," die the death; the sentence was after his fall: and this

* Preached April 28, 1794.

death is fully enough signified by the sentence—"Dust thou art, and unto dust thou shalt return." It cannot but be meant, as being so expresly mentioned, both in the commination and in the sentence. And,

Secondly. The actual execution shews it to be meant, to be meant as one part of the penalty unto which transgressors are adjudged under the name of death. For though it be very true, that, abstractly considered, it may be looked upon only as a misery, or as a physical evil, yet considering, that God hath vouchsafed to govern his reasonable creatures by a law, and according to the tenor of a covenant, he would never lay any thing of afflictive evil upon them, which was not legally due. He will herein not go above the legal constitution, by laying any more than was due by law, though he might go as much below it as he would.

A righteous ruler will never exceed the law in punishing, though he may exceed it, without any injury, in shewing favour. And the difference in these two cases, is manifest, because that these promises of favour, make those, to whom such promises are made, creditors, and make the promiser a debtor. But in the inflicting of punishments, the person to be punished is the debtor, and he that is injured and wronged, being the sovereign ruler, is the creditor *pœnæ*, which also the common phrase signifies, and shews it to be agreeable to the reason of mankind, to look upon the ruler as the creditor *pœnæ*, and the offender as the debtor *pœnæ* ; to wit, that phrase of *Dare pœnæ*. It is the person that is to be punished, who gives satisfaction to law and justice, and so, thereupon, is said to owe it; and it is the government that is the creditor he owes it to.

There would be, then, no such thing as this bodily death in the world, if the violation of the law of God had not made it a debt to divine justice, and to the divine government, as the proper wages of sin. God will not lay upon man more than is right, (more than is just and due according to law,) that he should enter into judgment with God. Job 34. 23. Whereupon, the execution, (of which all the world hath experience from age to age; for we see the world hath been continually and actually under death, and we still daily behold death round about us,) this actual execution, I say, shews that this must be part of the designed penalty signified here by "death."

And unto this head we may very well refer all those corporeal evils and miseries that men in this world are liable to, and lie under, which are so many tendencies unto death, or which we may look upon as death begun; so much of a man's time as is past over with him, so much death hath eaten up: as the heathen moralist expresseth it: *Quicquid nostræ ætatis retro est mors habet; death hath devoured all that of our age which is already past*; so that men may be said to have begun to die as soon as they begin to live, which makes it seem congruous enough, or less strange, that Ecclesiastes the preacher, speaking of the events or purposes for which there is a season, unto every one a time, he speaks of a time to be born; and a time to die, without any mention of the intervening time of life: and fitly enough, or it is not strange, because, indeed, men do begin to die as soon as they begin to live.

Death is wrought with the very *primordia* of our sensitive nature; so that well might that prince say, upon the loss of his son; *Novi me genuisse mortalem; I begot him and mortality in him, both together*. I begot him a mortal thing. Death is working in us, (as the apostle's phrase is,) all our days, all our time, between our birth and the grave, still working in us. And so the longer any man lives in this world, he is but so much the longer a dying. Death did for a great while work more gradually and slowly, where a man's life extended to some hundreds of years. It hath since come to work a quicker dispatch with men; but still they are dying, tending towards the grave, even from their first entrance into the world; and this is part of what is signified by death here. But yet it is, in comparison, but a small part, though it be a real one, a true part. Therefore,

[2.] Spiritual death is, without doubt, more principally intended, as it is in itself a far more principal evil; that is, all those miseries which do now in this present state infest the spirits of men. And this needs a little more to be insisted on. Herein, therefore, I intend (as God shall enable) these two things: first, to shew you that such spiritual evils as these, are very fitly comprehended as part of the penalty under the name of death; and then, secondly, I shall shew you, what this death doth comprehend in it; namely, spiritual death.

First. That the spiritual evils to which the souls of men are generally subject, are very fitly comprehended under the name of death here. That death that is said to "have passed over all," is a real and great part, even the more principal part of the penalty under which they lie: and this doth need some explication, the rather for this, that this spiritual death is in itself a sinful evil, and, therefore, that it should be a punitive one, may seem strange to some. I shall explain the whole matter to you, therefore, in some distinct heads and particulars. As,

i. We are to consider, that though sin be principally an injurious evil against God, yet it is also by consequence, and collaterally, a mischievous evil to the sinner. And thereupon are we said to be " dead in trespasses and sins." Ephes. 2, 1. Death is certainly a horrid and afflicting evil to him that must suffer it. But such a death as this, to wit, to be dead in sin, it is primarily an injurious evil against God. For we are to consider what sin is. It is a trangression of the law; therefore, considered in strict propriety, it must be chiefly and principally against the Law-Maker, a transgression against him that made the law; to wit, as a wrong to him. But yet, for all that, it is a hurt to ourselves. It lies both against the Object and the subject. Against the Object : " Against thee, thee only have I sinned," have I offended. It works upward even against heaven: but that, it cannot reach to do any real hurt there; but a wrong is done against heaven. " I have sinned against heaven and in thy sight." But then it works downward so as to hurt and do mischief; that is, as it works in its subject, corrodes, and envenoms, and poisons that, and so carries a self-punishing malignity in it. " Thine own wickedness shall correct thee." Again,

ii. Consider, for the clearing of this matter, that that life unto which this death is opposite (as it is in us, or as it is in an intelligent subject) is, both a principle of action, and perception. I pray mark this, for it is obvious in the meaning of it to every one's understanding and experience. By that life that we generally live, we are enabled to act what we do act, and we are enabled to enjoy what we do enjoy. It is both a motive and active ; and it is both a perceptive and a fruitive principle. Now consider this life, as it is an active principle, so it makes us the subjects of duty, of all duty which we owe to him who made us, and gave us breath and being : but as it is also a perceptive and fruitive principle, so it makes us capable of enjoying what is good for ourselves. And, again,

iii. This being plain in itself, we are to consider, that both our duty, which we owe to God, and our felicity, which we enjoy in ourselves, they are substantially and radically the same thing, and do only differ in distinguishing respects ; they meet in one and the same root, and which is the principal thing in the moral life, (that life we are now speaking of ; and it is death in the moral sense, and not in the natural sense, that we are now speaking of too ; for in the natural sense, the soul cannot die,) I say, that moral life doth carry, as the principal thing in it, both our duty and our felicity, in the same common root ; to wit, love to God ; that is, both radically and virtually, all our duty, and all our felicity too. And it is the main thing to be considered in moral and spiritual life.

The love of God, I say, comprehends both these in it. It comprehends duty; "If ye love me, keep my commandments." We can never do that which he will interpret obedience, but from a principle of love. It is no obedience to him, if it do not proceed from love. And, again, the same love, our love to God, is that by which we enjoy him, as well as that by which we obey him. We can enjoy what we love; but what we love not, we can never enjoy. And so that life to which this death stands opposed, carries in it that one principle of love, which sums up our duty and our felicity both together, and is radically both of them; upon which account they are in substance the same thing.

But they differ only in the different respects that love hath, as it respects God, the Ruler of all this world, (and so whom we ought to obey and be subject to as our Ruler,) so this love is the principle of duty: but then, as it respects ourselves, so it is the principle of enjoyment; that is, it eyes God, pitches and terminates upon him, but with a reference to ourselves. And,

iv. These acts, proceeding from this principle of love, which have a more direct tendency unto God, do yet involve and carry in them a gainfulness and gratefulness to ourselves, so as that our felicity and duty will still be complicated in those consequential acts. As, for instance, where our felicity is most complete in the heavenly state, the eternal adoration of God, which is the immediate and perpetual product of the highest and most perfect love to him, it cannot but infer perpetual pleasure to them that do so adore. And though that act be carried directly towards God, yet it infers a delight, a pleasure, (as it cannot but do,) to perfectly right minds, to them who are everlastingly so employed and taken up. And I can apprehend nothing higher than that, in the pleasure of the heavenly state; to wit, the felt congruity of everlasting worship, the soul apprehending and feeling within itself, and relishing, with delight, its own act in adoring and worshipping God for ever, and finding how congruous a thing it is, how comely a thing. And so that which is a right to God, is also a satisfaction and delight to the soul itself, that renders it, and is continually paying that homage.

And again, too, in this our present state, wherein felicity can be but begun; and if you look to the very beginning of that, the first turn of the soul towards God by repentance which enters it into a holy and happy state. It is called "repentance towards God," it directly terminates upon him;

but when once it comes to be true, genuine, evangelical, vital, even that itself cannot but carry a sweetness and pleasure in it to the penitent soul. For it is not a forced thing, but an act that flows freely from a vital, connatural principle, the soul pleaseth itself, in abasing itself, in humbling itself, before him; in pouring out itself in free confessions and acknowledgments to him. And then, consider further,

v. That for such acts as do more directly respect ourselves, they do involve and carry still in them, homage and duty to God too, though they do more directly respect ourselves: as trust and joy in God, they have a manifest reference to our own safety, and a direct reference thereunto. By trust in him, it is, that we secure ourselves, and, by which, we become safe from wrath and ruin. Joy, or delight in God, it is that by which we entertain, and receive into our own souls, positive good, by which we are to be happy and satisfied. As by the other, (trust,) we decline and avoid the evil by which we were otherwise, to have been miserable, these have a direct reference to ourselves; but, they have a consequential reference, too, unto God, or, a conjunct reference, as carrying in them, a homage to him, while, at the same time, they carry in them, an advantage to us.

For we cannot render to God higher homage than that trust. It is vital trust, by which the soul unites with him, comes into union, enters into a state of union with him. By that trust, we give him the highest glory creatures are capable of giving him; we, thereupon, acknowledge him to be the First Truth. We give him the glory of that great attribute of his faithfulness; we acknowledge him to be a God that cannot lie, with whose nature it is inconsistent not to be true; we honour him, and advantage ourselves, at once, in that very act. And so, delight and joy in him, there the case is the same: it is we that are satisfied by our delight in God; but it is God that is glorified: for thereby we acknowledge him to be an all-sufficient Good, an all-comprehending Good, when our souls do centre and rest in him as such; which is the true notion of delight; *Quies appetitus in appetibile*, the rest of the desiring faculties in the object desired: it is the rest of our love: that by which our love doth move towards its object, till it attain and possess it. And then,

vi. It is hereupon, most plain, that the death which is opposite to this life, (that I have so far opened to you,) while it is an injury to God, it is also a hurt to ourselves: for the same reason that life doth involve these two things in it, even in all the several acts of it; by the same reason, it must needs be so, on the opposite hand; to wit, that death must comprehend in it, opposite things; and that the same evils that are sinful against God, cannot but be hurtful, and pernicious, and mischievous to ourselves. And,

vii. Those evils, that are so said to be signified by this name, are very fitly signified by it, very aptly: for, though such a death of the soul be not death in the absolute sense; for, if it were death in the absolute sense, then would the soul be said naturally to die, which would not consist with the doctrine of its immortality; but, it is death, in a respective sense only;—yet it is, however, properly, death, inasmuch as that respective sense must needs mean the principal respect, that such a thing is capable, or can any way admit of; to wit, a respect to the end. A respect to the end is always the most principal respect of any thing whatsoever, though it be clothed with various respects besides its own simple nature: its respect that it bears towards its proper adequate end, is always to be reckoned its principal respect. Now, look upon man, principally as to his soul or spirit, (which is the subject of our present discourse, and the subject of this death, which we are now speaking of, spiritual death,) and it is to be considered this is a created being. He that made it, made it for somewhat. What is the end of such a being as the spirit of man? What was it made for? It is a mind, an intellective thing, an intelligent being, unto which belongs the power of thought, and that of vast compass, extending to multitudes, even to all sorts of objects, and to the very highest of all objects; for, God hath made us capable, even of thinking of himself, of having an idea of him, a notion of him, which all have, more or less, in their minds; now it is to be considered, I say, What hath God made such a creature as this for? This mind, or spirit of man? Why, principally to converse with himself. For he hath made all things for himself; and the spirit of man, more immediately for himself, as, he is said, to have fashioned the spirit of man within him. That must be, with design, that it should be employed immediately upon him, as the principal and most noble End for which it was made: but, to this End, it is become useless, the spirit of fallen man, apostate man, unconverted man, yet remaining in the state of apostasy, not regenerate, not renewed in the spirit of his mind, (the great seat and subject of that regenerating work,) it is altogether unapt for the end that it was made for, nothing can be plainer.

Therefore, though it be not simply dead, yet, it is dead *quoad hoc*, it is dead to this purpose, it is dead in this respect; and that is the principal respect that such a thing is capable of: for the principal respect is, the respect it bears to its end, its great and ultimate end, the end that it was made for. Any man that will understand himself to be God's creature, especially that he hath a mind and spirit in him, that God hath, himself, fashioned immediately, he must needs presently apprehend this mind, this spirit, was made for some more principal purpose, than only to mind the things of this earth, than only to serve a brutal flesh for a few days, that must, at last, rot in the dust: no man, that communes with himself, and considers his own nature, that hath such a thing as a mind and spirit about him, but must presently apprehend, "Sure this mind and spirit of mine, which is impressed with the natural image of God, and, which, immediately proceeds from him, (who is, therefore, called the Father of spirits,) must be made principally to converse with him, to employ itself principally upon him, by acts of love, and trust, and adoration, and subjection, and the like."

But, most plain it is, that the spirits of men are become altogether *inhabile*, unapt, to serve this end, for which they are made, and, so, are truly said to be dead in this respect; that is, dead to the principal use and end for which such a being is said to be made. And, therefore, when once the great regenerating turn, and change, comes to be made upon the souls of men, this is the effect of it,—they are "dead to sin, but alive to God, through Jesus Christ," as Rom. 6. 11. intimating, that before, they were only alive to sin, but dead towards God and Christ. And what! Do we think that God ever made an intelligent and immortal mind and spirit, only to live to sin? they are only alive to sin before; but, when this change comes to be made, then, they are alive to God: before, quite dead to God; and, so they are dead, in reference to their principal end, and the proper design of their creation, that they were made for.

And so, it is a death in equivalence, it is an equivalent death; it is the same thing in reference to the end they were made for, as if they were not. As if we speak of a human maker of any thing: if an artist have made such a thing as a clock or watch, he considers the end of it, that which it is to serve for; it is to measure time, to let me know the hour of the day, as it passeth. Why, suppose such an instrument as this made, and elaborated by a curious hand: What hath this in it? it hath in it motion, and the regularity of that motion. Motion alone would not make it serve this end, if that motion had not a regularity belonging to it. There is, in that instrument, (a watch,) such a thing as a balance, wheels that regulate that motion; so as that it shall not move at random: if it move at random, the design is lost, the use of it frustrated, though it should retain motion, and there were still a motive power in it: if its motion were nothing else but an uncertain hurry, you could never know how the time passeth by it. And, therefore, it were all one, though the thing remain, and though the motion remain; it were, I say all one in reference to its end, as if there were no such thing, or as if it had no motion at all.

Take the needle of a compass—it has a mobility, it is put in such a posture as it may be easily moveable; but then, withal, it hath a verticity, that is, an aptness to turn and stand directly towards the north. If it retained never so much its mobility, and loseth its verticity, it serves not its end, it is unuseful so, and useless, as the needle of a compass; and it were all one as if it were not.

Suppose these instruments, that are mechanical, were someway vital; suppose a watch were a vital thing, and its motion vital; as it is but mechanical, when it hath lost all kind of the regularity of the motion, the motion itself remaining, it were all one as if it were dead; if it had been a living thing, it would no more serve its purpose now, than as if it were dead.

And so it is with reference to the spirits of men: if they do not serve the principal design for which they were made, then it is all one as if they were dead. God may say of them, "I have no more service from them than if they were dead, no more of love, no more of adoration, no more of dutiful observance are paid me by them, than as if there were no such things." It is to be considered, therefore, that that which makes the name of death, in this case, proper, is, that that life that doth remain to the spirits of men, that is, by which they live naturally, it no more serves the end and purpose for which such a mind and spirit were created and made, than if such a thing were quite extinct, and there were no such thing. And, thereupon,

viii. Though this, in itself, be a sinful thing, as an offence to God, it is never a whit the less a punishing thing to them that do offend, a punishment upon them, that is, they are left to punish themselves, because that they do injure God by that violation which they have made even of their own frame and natures: and, so the same thing may very well be a sin, and a punishment too. And it is most reasonably so: for, do but consider the parity of the case, to what is obvious to our notice in human governments. If a man be a self-murderer, a *felo de se;* this is the very case, as a man cannot be dead in trespasses and sins, (sin being his own act,) but he must be a self-destroyer. In human governments, he that doth destroy himself, it is very true, he suffers this evil first, immediately, directly; he is the person that is killed, and hath lost his life; but here is, in the mean time, a wrong done to the prince, a wrong done to the community; the prince hath lost a subject, the community hath lost a member; and this is the case with every self-destroying sinner, in reference to God. And, he is liable thus to be impleaded: "Thou hast destroyed my creature." This interest of God, in all, is superior to any interest we have in ourselves: and this the sinner is to be accountable for. "Why hast thou undone my creature? Why hast thou made my creature a miserable creature, that was capable of being a happy one?" Yea, the whole heavenly community have a just plea against any such one that perisheth, and so is eternally cut off from them by his own iniquity. "Duly, and by original right, you ought to have been a partaker with us; you ought to have been of our chorus, in worshipping, adoring; in loving and enjoying God eternally. But, you have cut yourselves off from God, and us." Therefore, it is no strange thing that this same death which carries in it the greatest hurt and mischief that we are capable of suffering in ourselves, should yet be also complicated with sin, as it is an offence against God, and an offence against the rest of his creatures,—especially those of the sinner's own order in the creation. So fitly is all that doth concern us, the whole of man, summed up in the fearing of God, and keeping of his commandments, as in that 12 of Ecclesiastes. This is the whole of man; the fear of God is nothing else but reverential love, carries love in it; that is the principle from whence we keep the commandments of God; these commandments are all summed up in love to God, and love to ourselves, and to our neighbours as ourselves. Where sin, therefore, comes to obtain, and take place, and be in power, there must be, at the same time, an injury done to God, an injury done to ourselves, and an injury done to the whole community to which we belong; so as that death, even spiritual death, is nothing the less capable of being intended here as a penalty and punishment, for that it is also complicated with sin: for, in the very nature of the thing, it cannot but be so, even in the very nature of the things themselves.

More is yet to be said in reference to what we further promised to shew, that this is a real part of the penalty here meant, by the name of death, spiritual death, as it is the hurt and evil that does mischief to ourselves, to our own souls, to shew that it must lie in the compass of that penalty, which, under the name of death is here said to pass over all. And then, for the extent and comprehension of that, the several things that this spiritual death doth involve in it, that we are to speak of afterwards. But, in the mean time, from what hath been hinted of these two things—corporeal death, and spiritual death, it should entertain our thoughts with, and a little fix them upon the prospect we have before our eyes. Now, by way of *Use*,

1. It is a doleful state that this world lies under, as it lies under that which is fitly to be called death; men, in a continual succession, lately sprung up here in this world, swept away presently from it, sooner or later, but soon all; one generation coming, and another going, but the earth abides. For persons that are capable of using thoughts, to behold themselves in this plight, and to look round about them, and to behold this to be the common case; "Here we are, lately sprung up into being in this world, and we know we are to stay but a little while: Dust we are, and unto dust we shall return." A most melancholy theme for a man's thoughts, if he have not somewhat beyond all this, to support his spirit, and to afford light, and lustre, and sweetness, and pleasure, to it; "life and immortality brought to light in the gospel" of Christ.

Alas! it is strange, amazing stupidity that is upon the spirits of men, that this common case is so commonly slighted and made so little of. If death did make quicker dispatches, (though we are certain of it, it can make no surer, for it reaches to every one sooner or later, but if it did make quicker dispatches,) it would set towns and countries presently upon a lament, upon bemoaning themselves, and put them into a panic, dread and fear. If the plague were (as sometimes it hath been in this city, sweeping away thousands in a week) in what a consternation would the minds of men generally be? You cannot have forgot, (many of you,) how it was. But let this matter be rationally considered, and whether it be so many thousands, or so many hundreds, it is the same; persons are still mortal, and must as certainly die; it is, therefore, an irrational stupidity to be so little apprehensive of this.

When the plague came upon the people of Israel, (in that of Numbers, 36.) see what an outcry is raised among them! "Behold we die, we all die. How are we consumed with dying!" What a fright were they in! And yet, this case is no way different at all from the common case of all mortals, more than only this—dying a little sooner, or dying more together, more numerously. It is strange there should be a dying world always in view, and we should find death working in us, and yet we live so unmindful of it from day to day, and are so little apprehensive, that, in this respect, death hath passed, and is passing, over all. We do not speak to one another at such a time as this; we do not hear; we do not look upon one another's faces as so many mortal creatures; sure there is not an apprehension suitable to the state of such a case, in this respect, that we are all subject to corporeal death. And then,

2. For the other part of our prospect, sure we should stay a little upon it, in our deepest reflections; that is, thus, in sum, that the soul of an unregenerate man is a most miserable creature; dead, dead to the principal purposes for which such life was given, any such creature made. It were as good never to have lived; better, (upon many accounts better,) to have been an untimely birth, and never have seen the sun, than not to live to God; than to have a total indisposition in my soul towards him, to think of him, to love him, to delight in him, to make him my life and my all. This is strange, that it should be the common case, and so little understood, and so little considered, so little taken to heart. O! the restless thoughts that would continually possess such a breast, if the matter were but understood, till the regenerating work come to obtain, and take place: " I am one that lives to as little purpose, as if I had never lived; as if no such creature had ever been."

As if we should consider the matter in reference to an inferior thing, belonging to our nature, to wit, the power of speech. Suppose a man should retain the power of speech, but hath quite lost his reason, which should govern his speech, so that he can speak still, but to no purpose; the use of speech were lost; for the design of speech was to convey the sense of one man's mind to another; but, when the reason is gone, which should form that sense in the man's mind, speech serves for nothing. It is just so with the souls of men, in reference to the principal end and purpose for which God hath made such a creature. They can think, they have a power of thought belonging to them, but to no purpose: thought is internal speech, the speech of the mind within itself; there they can speak; that is, they can form thoughts, connect thoughts, but all to no purpose: for religion, that which should govern the motion of the mind, that, is wanting, there is no such thing; this makes the soul of man a most miserable thing: it can move, it hath a principle of motion in it, which is essential to it; but it hath no principle of rest, no inclination towards God, the true rest of the soul. Do but illustrate that to yourselves, by the case of a bodily motion. Suppose your bodies had the power of bodily motion in them, without the power of rest: O! what a miserable thing were man, in respect of his bodily frame and constitution! to be in an everlasting hurry: he can move, and he must move, perpetually; but he cannot *sistere se*, cannot stop his motion, he can never take any rest. It is just so with the unregenerate soul. God is the true rest of the soul. It is in perpetual motion, in continual desires, in everlasting cravings; but hath nothing by which it can satisfy itself. It never comes into its mind, "Return unto thy rest, O my soul." Such a creature, one would think, made for torment, that can everlastingly move, must be perpetually in motion, but can never rest, can never take up any rest in any thing that is agreeable and suitable to it, that can satisfy it.

LECTURE XXIX.[*]

It remains now, in the next place, to shew,

Secondly: What those several evils and miseries are: and, so, what the spiritual death that is now upon the world, and hath passed over all, doth comprehend, and contain in it. It comprehends,

i. The loss of God. A mighty thing! the very thought whereof might set all our souls a trembling; and that, whether we consider it as our present case, or, as having been our case. The loss of God two ways: first, as men have lost all their interest in him; and, secondly, as they have lost all inclinations towards him. A loss, that stands at once in God's aversion from them, and their aversion from God. A mutual aversion between God and them. But, because that, in every thing that belongs to our misery, we are first, as in every thing that belongs to our felicity, God is first, it is more proper to consider,

(i.) Our aversion from God, or, men's having lost God, through their own disinclination towards him: this is represented as the common case of the unconverted, or yet apostate world of men, yet remaining in the state of apostasy, that they are atheists in the world. Ephes. 2. 12. " Without

[*] Preached May 19, 1694.

God in the world;" so we truly enough render it. "Alienated from the life of God:" Ephes. 4. 18. Alienated from the divine life, from a life of commerce with God; they are strangers to God, as men of another country: that is the significancy of the expression; so they carry it to God, (as it is elsewhere expressed,) like foreigners. He is none of our country; we are not of that country of which he is; we have nothing to do with him. At that rate men live, and bear themselves, generally, towards God.

And this aversion of the souls of men from God, is total, of the whole soul; the mind, the judgment, the will, the affections, they are all wholly off from God. So that, when he looks down from heaven upon the children of men, to see who will inquire, who will seek after God; lo! they are all gone back; (all in a revolt, all flying away from him, to the utmost distance that they can;) there is none that doeth good, (not this good, it must be specially meant,) no, not one: as in the 14, and 53 psalms, which are both to the same purpose; as divers passages quoted from them, in the 3 of Romans. They are without God, and very well pleased with themselves that they are so. They know him not, and they all affect not to know him. They are "alienated from the life of God, through the ignorance that is in them, and the blindness of their hearts." That blindness of heart is a voluntary blindness; they are blind towards God, because they will not behold him, nor take notice of his majesty, though his hand be lifted up, though the appearance of him be never so bright and glorious. They forget him, he is not in all their thoughts. It is the usual character of a wicked, unconverted man, that he forgets God: "The wicked shall be turned into hell, and all the people that forget God;" the one expression being exigetical, or expository of the other. Psalm 9. 16. They refuse him, they are unwilling of him. If persons do remain in an unconverted state, though related to him as Israel was, (for yet, of them, it is said, "Israel would none of me." Psalm 81. 11. "My people would not hearken to my voice, Israel would none of me.") they will not God. We will not have him to be our God. It is a disaffecting of him; the affections that should be placed on him are quite off: in the room of pious affections, there is nothing else but enmity: "The carnal mind is enmity against God."

And, touching this aversion from God, it was formerly intimated, that, as love doth comprehend together, (as the radical virtual principle,) all our duty, and all our felicity; so doth this aversion from God, (which stands in opposition thereto,) all sin, and all misery. That this aversion is the radical principle of all sin; we spake to that formerly; and so we, must understand it now, as it is the radical principle of misery, God being to be considered by us, under a two fold notion—as he is to be obeyed, and as he is to be enjoyed; as the Sovereign Authority, and as he is the Sovereign Good. It is the aversion from God, as he is the Sovereign Good, that we are now to consider, having, under the former head, of the sinfulness of man, spoken of it as an aversion to him under the notion of the Supreme Ruler, and, as the Highest Authority. But, yet, we have also told you, that there is a complication of these things with one another: for men do really sin against God in their declining the enjoyment of him, in their declining him as their best and highest Good; the constitution of the divine laws being such, that there are obligations upon us to be happy. So that, a man cannot but be miserable, as he cannot be happy without obeying him, even in his very enjoying of the best and highest Good, because God hath made this our duty, to place our supreme delight in him.

And so, God hath a just ground upon which to implead the ungodly, wicked world; for that, thereby, they make themselves miserable: " Why have you thus used my creatures, the souls that I have made? Why have you cut and torn them off from me, they which are the works of my hands? Why have you used and dealt with them so?" As was told you, he that is *felo de se*, is criminal by human constitution; for though he thereby doth afflict himself, destroy himself, yet he doth also injure the prince, and injure the community to which he belongs: for he destroys a subject and member of the commonwealth. And those who, by the law of their creation, should have joined with the rest of the creatures of their own order, in the eternal adoration and praises of God, have by sin, as much as in them lay, defrauded him, and maimed the community unto which they did originally and naturally appertain. But then, this misery, as it stands in the loss of God, includes, too,

(ii.) His just and righteous aversion from them. " God is not a God that takes pleasure in wickedness, neither can evil dwell with him." There can be no fellowship between light and darkness, between righteousness and unrighteousness. He did owe it to himself, to retire from an apostate, rebellious world: it was but to do himself right, to express a just detestation of the wickedness of a lapsed, degenerate world; to hide himself, to withhold his light and grace, which were shut up from men by the bar of an everlasting curse, till such time as that should be counter-wrought, in reference to any; Christ having been made a curse for us, upon that account, that the blessing might come upon us, even us, Gentiles, as it did before upon the Jews, those of them that did belong to the election of grace; thereupon it is called "the blessing of Abraham;" that that might become a more diffusive thing, to reach the Gentiles too; to wit, receiving the Spirit, the promised Spirit, through faith. Gal. 3. 13, 14. Therefore, where this curse is not removed, it still lies as a bar against all gracious communications of light and influence from God to men. And so he is righteously averse from them, as they were most unrighteously averse to him: and thus they have lost God.

O! the lamentations that this world would be filled with every where, if this case were but understood! What girding with sackcloth would there be all the world over! God is gone! God is departed! This would be the common cry in town and country, in all parts and places—God is departed: that is the amazing thing! Heaven would resound with shrieks and cries from the miserable inhabitants of this earth. But, I say, that is the amazing thing, (as there will be occasion to take notice hereafter,) that such a matter as this is so patiently borne, so little resented; that men can so quietly wear away their days here in this world, without God, and think themselves to stand in no need of him. They can rise in the morning without God; and walk about all the day long without God; and lie down at night without God: and yet, all is well.

ii. This spiritual misery contains in it, too, a wretched conversion of soul to the creature. Where God is lost, they design to repair that loss. And O! the miserable case of the inhabitants of this world upon this account; that they can think or imagine, when they want God, that any thing can fill up his room, and be to them instead of him! that it doth not come into their minds to consider, "How shall we recover God again?" But, "How shall we repair our loss another way?" imagining that some thing or other can be found, and may serve them, and be to them, instead of God! that is, that he, (in comparison of whom the whole creation is but "as the drop of a bucket, and the dust of the balance, lighter than nothing, and vanity itself,") that he can, (I say,) have his equivalent; that there may be somewhat found out of equivalent advantage and use to them. This is the highest reproach to the Deity, as it is the greatest misery to themselves, and both comprehended in one thought; to wit, that there may be an equivalent to make up the loss of God; that very thought, I say, carries in it the highest blasphemy against the Deity, to think that any thing can fill up his room, and be as good as he is; as well as the greatest misery unto wretched souls themselves, that they should be under so fearful and pernicious a mistake.

But this is the common case when God is gone, and men are gone off from him, then they turn themselves to the creature: "Let us make the best of that we can." So is the project laid all the world over. Not, Let us consider how we may regain God; how we may get God back again to us; but, How we may supply his absence out of inferior things: and this is the general posture of mankind. Look on them, and, in reference to God, they are in an averse posture; in reference to the creature, in a propense posture.

And what sort of creatures? That we may understand this to go somewhat towards the consummating of the state of misery man is fallen into, do but consider, I say, what is the kind of that good which they design for themselves, when God is no longer eyed by them as the Good that they should enjoy, and design for. And consider, too, in what circumstances they may expect to have what enjoyments they can have of that substituted good.

For the kind of it, we are to consider in the vast universe of creatures, what it is that the apostate world do seek to repair this loss of God to themselves out of. It is not out of the nobler parts of the creation; they do not look as high as the heavens, they are too remote: they are not the angelic beings, that their thoughts fly upon, with any design of repairing the loss from among them. But the whole bent of their soul is directed towards this lower world, and sensible things, things meaner than themselves, meaner than their own minds. They think an intelligent, immortal mind must have its enjoyments, even unto felicity, in things of so vastly inferior dignity to a mind and spirit; that these minds are to be fed upon earth, upon ashes, upon the basest and most despicable things within the creation of God! What a misery is that! Unto such things it is that all this world is turned, being turned off from God, sensible things, earthly things, things that can please appetite, things common to them with the beasts that perish, only they have ways and arts to refine them, but they are of the same nature. As clay will be but clay still, be it figured never so curiously. "They mind earthly things;" this is the character of the insincere, those that are afar off from God, not turned to him; they mind earthly things; their whole souls are let out upon that which is, in itself, vain, and a lie; that is, which promiseth fair, but never makes good, and so lies to them.

And consider, under what circumstances men apply themselves to enjoy the things by which they would repair to themselves the loss of God: especially consider these two most important circumstances: that is, that they are things that lie, first, under an interdict; and, secondly, under a curse, in reference to them, and, in reference to what they design, and seek to themselves by them; to wit, a felicity; or with respect to the notion under which they do covet and would enjoy them; that is, as their best good, so they lie under an interdict and under a curse.

(i.) Under an interdict: "Love not the world, nor the things of the world; if any man love the world, the love of the Father is not in him." 1 John, 2. 5. What a misery is this, that the poor souls, revolted and gone off from God, are now uninersally seeking a felicity for themselves in things that, under that notion, lie under an interdict, are forbidden to them, and cannot but be forbidden, under that notion; because, under that notion, they are made rivals unto the Deity. In subordination to God, men might comfortably have enjoyed the things of this world; not in competition, nor in opposition: for now this world is made his rival, and, therefore, is the love of it idolatry, and is the setting up of another God, in opposition to the true and living God; and by taking this licence, men think to repair themselves for their having lost God. And,

(ii.) They are things that lie, not only under an interdict, but under a curse, a malediction,—apostate souls, gone from God, they can have no enjoyment of this world, but under a curse, nothing is blest to them; they can have no blessed enjoyment of them, or any thing they enjoy;—for sin turns all into gall and wormwood, bitterness and death. How dismal is the case with fallen man, upon this account! "Cursed in the basket, and cursed in the store; cursed in the city, and cursed in the field; cursed in the coming in, and cursed in the going out;" as the matter is largely and most emphatically represented in the 28th of Deut. A people, though related to God, when they go off from him, and so put themselves into the common state with the rest of the pagan world; a curse lies upon them, in every thing that they do, in every thing that they enjoy, they perpetually live under a curse. It is with strange rhetoric that this matter is represented in the 109 psalm: a curse that they are girt with perpetually, and that is as a garment that they are clothed with, and that flows or insinuates itself as oil into their bones, and as water into their bowels. So, they are under a divine curse, in reference to every thing that they enjoy. And that is a second part of this misery which fallen man lies under, even in reference to his spirit; to wit, that that is *off from* God, and is turned to a vain world, which is to him an interdicted and an accursed thing.

iii. This *misery* further includes in it, a continual unsatisfactoriness with whatsoever they do or can enjoy. And, as the essence of blessedness and felicity doth lie in satisfaction; so, on the other hand, must misery consist in continual unsatisfiedness, which results from these two things together; first, perpetual craving desires, and secondly, the want of any suitable and adequate object by which they may be satisfied.

(i.) In continual craving desires. And that is the common case with all men in the fallen state. Why, they have put themselves into an utter impossibility, whilst things are just with them as they are, to be happy; and yet they have a desire to be happy all this while, nothing being more deeply natural, than these two opposite things; a dread of misery, and a desire of felicity: and by how much the larger men's desires are, so much the greater is their misery in this case. Desires enlarged even as hell, and that could even swallow up a creation and more; for a creation was never to satisfy them. It was not a created, but an uncreated Good, that was the object designed for the satisfaction of the souls of men: " Who will shew us any good ?" There is the character of an unrenewed mind and spirit, in that psalm, 4. 6. But it never comes into their minds to think, what that Good is that could be adequate to them. " Lord lift thou up the light of thy countenance upon us:" they never think of that, but still cry out, " Who will shew us any good ?" Roving, uncertain desires, which, with all, find that they can meet with nothing that is suitable and adequate for the satisfaction of them: these desires must turn to torment, when there is not an object for such desires to feed upon; they prey upon their subject, turn inward; and, so men's desires are their tormentors, and make them miserable, in that they continually desire and crave that which they cannot reach. For,

(ii.) The other thing that concerns, and falls in, to make this a miserable case, or to render it a real misery, is, the want of a correspondent good for so vast and large an appetite; and that, upon a double account: to wit, that what would satisfy them they cannot desire; and, that which they do desire, cannot satisfy them. That which would satisfy, they cannot desire: God would satisfy them, he were an adequate, correspondent Good, to the most enlarged desire of the soul. Aye, but him they care not for; towards him they have no motion: towards him there is nothing but aversion and disinclination and disaffection, as you have heard before: so that, as the carnal mind cannot please him, so it cannot be pleased with him. And, that which they most of all desire, that cannot please them, as you have likewise heard.

And so, in reference thereunto, they lie always in the same restless posture. As, I remember, a heathen saith, concerning a soul loose from God: (it is the saying of Hierocles:) "That such a soul being loose from God, is like a cylinder upon a plain, that can never lie still; it is always in perpetual motion." The state of a soul that is off from God, is just such, circled all within itself, capable of setting upon no basis. There is nothing that can give a firm posture, or a posture of rest to it; for all things, beneath it, and beside it, are unsuitable, inadequate; and, therefore, nothing can ensue but perpetual unsatisfiedness. A miserable case! To have so capacious a thing, as the soul of a man is, capable of so high and great enjoyments, and to be under continual dissatisfaction, because that which would satisfy, it cannot desire; and that which it doth desire, cannot satisfy. And,

iv. This misery hath this further in it, a continual delusion, which the souls of men lie under, in reference to the objects of their enjoyment; a being continually imposed upon by the false and delusive appearances of things, so as, hereupon, they meet with disappointments, both in reference to what they attain, and in reference to what they attain not. Herein stands their perpetual delusion; that is, they are cheated into the expectation of meeting with that rest and satisfaction for themselves, which they can never find, and that, whether they do attain the things they seek, or attain them not.

The case is generally with men, in this respect, as with some weak, half-witted persons, who, looking about them here and there, they see some rising ground, such or such a hill, or mountain, and they think, if they were on the top of that mountain, they should reach heaven, for heaven seems to touch that; when, if they should be at the pains to travel to the top of that mountain, they should find themselves at the same distance they were before. So it is with the men of this world, with reference to what they expect from it, of good and rest to themselves: "O! I should be in a very heaven, if I were in a condition so high." Some men's states and conditions carry their appearance with them of very high lofty mountains, that do even over-top heaven, or touch heaven. "If I were but so high as such a man, or such a man, I were a happy man." Alas! they are deluded and disappointed, both these ways: first, that the most can never reach that which they do expect and design, in point of wordly advantage; and, secondly, that if they do, they are much what they were, as far from felicity as before :—nay, it may be, sunk by that very means, by which they thought to be raised, into deeper misery than before. This is a very dismal, yet, it is the common case! Men spend their days, wear away a wretched life-time, here, in this world, in pursuit of such an outward good state, or condition; and most of them always die short of what they designed, of what they projected in any such kind. And, if any have compassed this, or that great design, or project, for this world; why, they are still, when they have compassed it, nothing the nearer. In a like case with that great prince, of whom we read, who, discoursing with one of his courtiers, about several great designs that he had for this world, told him, He would move his arms, against such a country, and such a country; and take in such a town, and such a city; "Then," saith the courtier, "what will you do after that?" "Why, then I will carry my arms such and such a way." "And what then?" "Why, then I will labour to accomplish such a thing, after that." "And what then, after that?" "Then I will sit still, and be quiet." "Why, sir," saith he, "you may as well do so now." Men might as well now sit still, and be quiet, when God hath given them some tolerable competency. And now, let me be thinking of, and caring for a soul, and providing for an eternal well-being. But, men think not of this, but let their lives run to waste, in a continual pursuit of shadows, and are in a continual delusion, with reference to what they attain, and what they attain not. In reference to what they do not attain; for that it would not satisfy; and, then, with reference to what they do attain; for they thought they should be much better for it, when, it may be, they are much the worse.

LECTURE XXX.*

Our business hath lately been, and still is, to represent the common miseries of man, which are all comprehended under the name of "death," very fitly, and very usually, not only in sacred language, but in other authors; several particulars have been instanced in. And now, the next in order, which I designed to be more largely insisted on, is,

v. This misery stands in slavery, in that base and ignoble

* Preached May 26, 1694.

servitude, which the generality of men, in the state of apostasy, are subject to: a thing which will but slowly enter into the minds of those who have not been instructed, and considered well the matter afresh; that is, that the generality of men, in their state of apostasy from God, are become the meanest, and basest sort of slaves; and, that is fitly enough called—" death;" (as I have told you, death must be taken here, not formally, but, in a large and comprehensive sense,) men of more ingenuous minds, rather choosing death than slavery: as it hath been with all those more noble-spirited men, who thought their lives laudably sacrificed for the liberty of their country, to redeem it from slavery: and, thereby, shewed themselves, that they did scorn to live as slaves, with the rest; they thought death a more eligible thing; and so, could say as he did dying: (though nothing else was effected.) "I have done this one noble thing; that I have chosen to die, rather than live as a slave." It is a misery much worse, than that which goes commonly among us, under the name of death, to be a slave.

But, if the matter be narrowly inspected, and looked into, every one that understands himself, and what the nature of man is, especially as to that part of man, which, more deservedly, bears that name, (the mind is the man,) he cannot, upon reflection, but consider the state of slavery as the common state,—the life, and strength, and faculties, and powers of a reasonable, intelligent mind and spirit, being generally subject to things beneath, and below the dignity of their nature; this is to be very basely servile. But this is that which they will very hardly think to be so, who do consider that they live according to their own wills, which, indeed, is the vulgar notion of liberty. He is a freeman: *Liber est qui vivit vult*—He lives as he affects to live, as he chooseth to live. Why, sure it cannot be that this man chooseth to be a slave.

But, there cannot be a more mistaken notion than this; or, that will more easily (if the matter be considered) prove itself false. For by how much the more the will of a man is inclined and led to choose things that are mean, and base, and unworthy of a man, so much the worse slave he is; when he is cheated into a consent unto that which debaseth him, and makes him mean; when he is fraudulently imposed upon, against all rational dictates and sentiments. And, undoubtedly, it was but that vulgar mistake, (not peculiar to the Jews, but common to sinners, as such, unto the world of mankind, yet in a state of apostasy, or not recovered out of it,) that our Lord animadverts upon, in that 8 John, in several verses, where he is dealing with that people, who were his immediate auditors upon this very topic; that is, he promiseth them liberty: "If the Son make you free, you shall be free indeed." But they tell him, with disdain, "We were never in bondage to any man; we are Abraham's seed." He replies upon them, "Whosoever commits sin, is the servant of sin;" and, being the servant of sin, is the slave of the devil too; and so much more miserably, and so much the worse he is so, by how much the more naturally, and according to inclination, he is so: for, when that is the case, when such appear to be the devil's own seed, his offspring, considering themselves not naturally, but morally, according to their inclination, with reference to the practice of duty, and with reference to consequent or connexed felicity; they are so far acted upon by that impure, apostate spirit, as that they do appear to be his very progeny, begotten of him. And, so is this whole world divided into those two great families—the children of God, and the children of the devil. "Herein are the children of God, and the children of the devil, manifest," as the same apostle, in his 3 chapter of his 1st epistle, tells us. And so, our Saviour speaks correspondently hereunto, to these, his present hearers, in the 44 verse of that 8 John: "Ye are of your father, the devil, and the works of your father ye will do." And, therefore, is that very suitable to this purpose, (which I have taken notice of formerly,) what Austin observed out of a heathen moralist: "That it is a far more miserable thing to will that which is unjust, than not to obtain that which one willeth." It is so in the very reason of the thing. If men could make themselves masters of all that they covet, during their abode in this lower world; if they could have every thing in their possession and power that they cast a fond eye upon, or place an irrational wish upon, they were a great deal more miserable, even in being left so to wish, so to desire, so ineptly, so foolishly. And, therefore, that kind of liberty, which stands only in gratifying inordinate and enormous desires, it is no other kind of liberty than that which God threatens the Jews with; a liberty to perish; a liberty for the sword, and famine, and pestilence: "I thus manumit you; I give you that sort of freedom, to run on in those ways, which shall infer upon you the most miserable end; that shall lead you into tragedies and death, which way so ever you tread your foot, or cast your eyes."

And, therefore, what a noted author among the pagans saith, concerning one particular people, may be said concerning mankind, while they remain in the state of apostasy, and, antecedently to their recovery, that they are such as, *Quos decuit esse servos*, a state of servitude is so suitable to them, that it befits them to be nothing else but slaves. And so much the rather because it is that which they themselves choose. And do not think Scripture speaks ineptly, or unsuitably to the case, when it bids them that are recovered out of the common misery, that lay upon the world, to consider what they were before: "Ye were sometimes foolish, deceived, serving divers lusts and pleasures;" Titus 3. 3. It is that which men, recovered to a right mind, would look upon with the greatest disdain imaginable; to wit, that a reasonable, intelligent spirit should only employ itself, its noble faculties and powers, from day to day, in pursuing a design, how to serve and gratify a thing no better, or no worthier of a high state and station in the creation of God, than a brute creature. Nay, not so worthy; because those creatures, are what they are by no degeneracy. They were never better, never higher: but, if a man be in the condition of a brute, he comes to be so by a lapse, by a fall, by a depravation: he is sunk beneath himself, he hath lost a good that he was capable of, and a perfection belonging to his own nature, that was the glory thereof; and, this he hath exchanged for the basest and vilest sort of slavery. The apostle Peter, 2 Epis. 2. 19. tells us, "That while men promise themselves liberty, they themselves become servants of corruption;" for, of whom a man is overcome, of the same is he brought in bondage: and to be in bondage to corruption, is the vilest kind of servitude that can be thought. We can form no idea in our minds of so base a vassalage as this,—to be servants to brutal and unreasonable appetitions and desires.

Man being by the constitution of his own nature a reasonable creature, to have that very reason of his depressed into a subserviency to what is unreasonable, is, in itself, a real misery, whatever the common estimate concerning it may be; and whatsoever that is now, undoubtedly it will, within a very little while, cease to be what it is. They that glory in their fetters, that please themselves in being such slaves, in being "led captive by satan at his will," they will shortly, very soon, (though not soon enough it may be,) change their minds. It is much to be feared that many may not change soon enough; but it will be very soon however; for how soon is the life of a man run out? and then the vain dream ends in the horror of an awakened soul: then it sees what it feels, and what estate it hath, by its own wilful choice, declined, and what it did addict itself unto, against the common sentiments and dictates which were not alien from them all that while; but only were not attended to. They were not at leisure to commune with themselves, and to consider what their own thoughts would suggest; and their misery is not the less for their having been under mistakes concerning this whole business all this while, when that mistake will be so soon detected, and they cannot be of that false opinion always. Indeed, we might admit, that happiness and misery stood always in opinion, if that opinion would always last: but when we are sure it will not, but that men will quickly alter their minds, as soon as their course is run out, then that will be found to be real misery before, which becomes now to be only misery apprehended. But again,

vi. A further thing wherein this misery lies, even that of men's minds, is the continual infatuation under which man, in his state of apostasy, is every where: and it is this that betrays him into that slavery which we have been now discoursing of. He is a slave, because he is a fool: he is fooled into the slavery which he so patiently undergoes. So you find these things connected in that Titus 3. 3. "We were sometimes foolish, disobedient, deceived, serving divers lusts and pleasures." And (as I have heretofore had occasion to note) that Greek word which we render "foolish," as if it signified only the being without a right mind, it signifies more; it signifies being put out of a right mind. It is not being without a mind, for so is a stock and a stone, which were never capable of any such thing; but that word signifies being disminded, or having lost one's mind in the use of it: "I have a mind, but I have been never the better for it. I have not known how to employ it:" and this comes in immediate connexion with serving divers lusts and pleasures; men having been so mean, and so base servants and slaves, because they were fools before; foolish, deceived, easily suffering themselves to be imposed upon; mocked, shamed into foolish expectations of felicity, where there is no such thing: so that in the very pursuit they still sink themselves lower and lower in miseries and death.

And hence it is, that that language is so usual in Scripture, of signifying a wicked man by the name of "a fool," as nothing is more familiar in the whole book of Proverbs, and sundry texts besides. Nor, indeed, is that sort of expression peculiar to the Scripture. Nothing hath been more usual among some of your more noted pagan moralists, than by the name of *sapiens*, a wise man, to denote a virtuous man, a good man. A good man is dignified with the name of a wise man; then the opposite hereto is obvious, that every evil man; every vicious man, is a fool: for it is not said of this or that person, more signally stupid or wicked, that he hath said in his heart, (as a fool,) "There is no God." But that, (as you see in the 14. and 53. Psalms, which are congenerous, and have almost the same passages in the former verses of the one and the other,) by that name is meant apostate man, in his state of apostasy. And so it is the general character of all men, yet remaining in that estate, and antecedently to their reduction and recovery out of it: "The fool hath said in his heart," not that there is no God, that is not the text, but—"no God," reckoning it to be rather the matter of their wish, than their assertion: it is capable of being understood in the optative, not in the indicative form; not as if they did say, "There is no God;" but " O! that there were none;" the fool hath said in his heart, " Would there were no God."

And who those fools are, you see in what follows: God looks down from heaven on the children of men to see if there were any that did good, any that did seek after God; but they are all gone out of the way, all gone back, all in an universal revolt; none doing this good; to wit, not inquiring, not seeking after God, but all agreeing in the same wish: "O! that there were none: O! that there were no Ruler, no Lord over us; none to concern himself in any of our affairs; none to animadvert on our way and course, and to call us to account." Whereupon, nothing is more manifest than that according to the import of this scripture, the universality of apostate mankind lies under this character of folly. And somewhat it doth suppose, and somewhat it more formally includes. That which it supposeth is ignorance, the want of right notions of things: those, men have in their minds, are generally false: but somewhat it more formally includes, and that is, the inefficacy of those notions which they have. And this is folly more formally, and which stands in an immediate connexion with misery, or rather, more naturally inclusive of it.

In reference to things of principal concernment to men, they are not so generally ignorant as they are foolish; ignorance consisting in the not having of right notions, but folly consisting in the inefficacy of those that are right, in opposition to governing wisdom; that practical wisdom by which a man must steer his course, and walk agreeably and consistently unto that light and knowledge which he hath. And herein lies the common prevailing folly of this world; that in things wherein men have knowledge, they corrupt themselves, and their "foolish heart is darkened," as the expression is, Romans 1. 21. upon account whereof it is that God doth give them up, for their contending against the light and knowledge which they have, unto those brutish sensualites, as that they should do things that are not convenient, things very disagreeable to the nature of man, to the dignity of a human, reasonable creature.

And so, also, the light which men have, is called "darkness" by equivalence; that is, it signifies no more to the proper purpose of light, to steer and conduct a man's way and course, than if it were real darkness. And so, if you will allow our blessed Lord to be a Judge and Master to us of such propriety of speech, you must acknowledge that to be a very proper expression, that the light that is in man's unconverted mind, is darkness. "If the light that is in thee be darkness, how great is that darkness?" Matt. 6. 23. That is, it answers no purpose of light, it serves for no such purpose as light is designed for, to guide a man in his way: they have such and such notions; but they do in their constant course run counter to them: and this is not ignorance, but folly, that they prevaricate with their own light, that they should know they ought to do so and so; and so and so they ought to choose; but they do choose and do quite the contrary.

And hence it is (which is the very *achme* of a man's misery; that is, the misery of his mind and spirit) his misery in this respect, that he is, by this means, made a bundle of contradictions and inconsistencies. And so hath nothing but confusion within him; or is in a continual war with himself: and there is no accord, no agreement, between his most rational sentiments and resolutions, and his consequent way and course: for if a man did sit down and deliberate but in the morning of any day, "How ought I to spend this day? ought I to employ it in following the inclinations of the man, or of the brute?" Certainly, he would think it more worthy of him to act like the man this day, than to employ the day, or his thinking, manly powers, only in pursuing the inclination of the brute. But then, if in fact he do run counter to any such sentiments as these, it is not because he is ignorant, but because he plays the fool. He hath not that wisdom that he ought, to govern his way, and to act suitably unto the clearest and most rational apprehensions of things. And so he is made up of nothing but inconsistencies with himself, or incoherencies, which shew him to be a miserable creature. For what? Do we think, did God make him such, (with such a mind that equals him with the angels of God,) to be employed in serving such desires, and pursuing such designs, as puts him below a brute?

vii. And a further thing in this state of misery, is the ignominy that men are hereby drawing upon themselves. And there is no man that considers, but will acknowledge that just ignominy is a misery, ignominy truly and justly so accounted. "Sin (we are told) is the reproach of any people." And then it must be as much the reproach of any person: as in that

Prov. 14. 24. every one accounts him a miserable man who is universally despised by every one, especially by the wisest and best of men. And suppose all mankind were, without a recovery, in that state of misery together, so that none must be found wiser or better than another, that could not at all mend the matter, with any of the individuals; as if it were not misery, because amongst men, none thought this to be misery, or none thought it to be truly ignominious. For we are to consider that we have other spectators, besides men, that are more capable of judging.

It signifies little to any man, what he thinks of himself, or what others think of him, in comparison of what is thought of him, by him who is wisdom itself, and whose judgment of things never erreth. It is not what man thinks of himself, or commends himself for, but what the Lord commends, that is approved. And our Lord Jesus Christ is peculiarly called by the name of "wisdom;" it is his common style and character. And we must suppose him greatly to concern himself about the affairs of a world, whereof he is the immediate Creator. "All things were made by him, and without him was nothing made that was made." And therefore, that he hath a continual inspection (if he had not taken the Redeemer's part) upon this world. He is said to be "the Image of the invisible God, and the first begetter of all creatures," and that fitly enough (as that title fitly enough admits to be read) for "by him were all things made, visible and invisible, whether they be thrones, or dominions, or principalities, or powers."

And then, we consider ourselves in this lower world under the continual view and inspection of those nobler creatures, that are intended by those names, they cannot but apprehend our apostasy, and much more the continuance of it, to be very ignominious and reproachful unto this whole order of creatures, fallen from their rightful Lord, because accomplices with the other apostate spirits of their own order, who were fallen before. How might it cut and wound a man's heart, to think what the resentments of these wise, holy, and kind, and benign creatures (the glorious angels of God) are, concerning our common state here in this world? we having had the same Author and Parent of our being with them; he being "the Father of spirits." An appellation equally agreeing to them, and to us, and not more to them than to us. To think that a world of such creatures, the progeny and offspring of the same Father, (the Father of spirits,) should be fallen to such a low pitch of misery and wretchedness, as they generally are: why sure they cannot but look upon our state and case to be most miserably ignominious and reproachful.

And therefore, they that continue in the apostasy, and are never recovered in this world, when they come to rise from the dead, they are said to "rise to shame and everlasting contempt;" Dan. 12. 2. One that was an apostate from God, and would never be recovered, he cannot but be had in everlasting contempt. And unto an ingenuous mind, and one that God hath recovered to his wits, in some measure, nothing hath a sharper pungency upon the mind than shame. And then, to be under everlasting shame, everlasting contempt, by those wise and holy creatures that were so full of kindness and benignity in their complexion towards men, and the spirits of men, upon account of their near affinity, being in so great a measure, of one kind and nature with us, must be a great misery.

They that are recovered are called "angels," fellow-associates with God. That they should be the devil's fellows, followers of those wicked angels that were all in rebellion against their Rightful Sovereign Lord; and that, too, when they might have made a better association; overtures being made to them for their recovery and return: overtures being made to them of the most kind reception, though they were prodigals and rebels against their Father; this must leave them under everlasting shame and contempt: and every one looks upon them now (that is, every good angel doth) to be infamous, being sunk to so low a state of shame and misery; and any wise and good man would scorn to keep such a one company, think it a reproach to him to reckon any such among his associates: and this will be the common case of apostate creatures, even eternally, to wit, such as are not recovered, that is, that they are abandoned to shame and everlasting contempt. And their own reflection, hereupon, must needs be the most sharp and tormenting thing that can be thought, to think what they are, and what they might have been, if they had not declined and refused to comply with so apt and suitable methods for their recovery. But further,

viii. It is another ingredient in the misery of the state of man in the apostate world, that they have such continual sharp resentments in their minds of the external evils that befal them here. They live in a world wherein they are continually liable to those evils which do first affect their sense; but not only of external evils, they become internal and fill their minds and spirits with torment. Herein lies much of their misery, they comfort themselves in such and such present enjoyments that are variable, mutable and uncertain, which they have this hour, and are gone the next. They have this hour a delightful and joyful dwelling, and it is of a sudden, turned into flames. They had the other day a rich and plentiful estate; it hath all of a sudden taken wings, and is gone. Health turned into wasting sickness; ease into tormenting pain, all on a sudden. All these are very considerable as they terminate in the external sense; but as they enter into the mind, so they become inward evils, their minds are continually liable to anguish and torment by such events, and upon such accounts. And then,

ix. When it is so, they have no relief from God; for they have not before known the way of addressing to him. Good men, in their external calamities, have this refuge always ready. David, when he had lost his all at Ziklag, yet, comforted himself, in the Lord his God. His wives and family were all led captive by the Amalekites; his goods rifled; his house and city burnt with fire; that place that was left him for retirement, all rendered uninhabitable, on a sudden, by consuming flames: the people themselves, (the companions of his flight,) spake of stoning him; thus was he in the most deplorable case that could be: "But he encouraged himself, (it is said) in the Lord his God." But men, in their apostasy from him, have none of this comfort, none of this relief; they have obstructed and shut up the way of address to God against their own souls; they know not how to apply themselves to him.

Such a case as that you have represented, Hab. 3. 17. 18. It was a very forlorn and distressed state, and a case, he supposeth, that "the fig tree did not blossom; that no fruit was in the vine; the labour of the olive did fail; the field did yield no fruit; and the flocks were cut off from the stall;" nothing but perishings: "yet," saith he, "I will rejoice in the Lord, and joy in the God of my salvation." A most deplorable case it is, when, amidst whatsoever distresses a man hath, he hath no God to betake himself to, nor inclination to betake himself to God. Think of the distresses of Saul, (Sam. 28. 15.) as there he laments his own case: "The Philistines make war against me, and God is departed from me, and giveth me no answer;" he could have no relief from God. It hath been the privilege of souls, that are returned to God, and come back to him, that, when they are cast down under affliction, they could apprehend themselves not cast off: "They were in tribulation, but not in distress, afflicted, but not forsaken;" as 2 Cor. 4. 8. 9. But men, in an apostasy from God, have no relief, they know not where, nor how to betake themselves: "They cry out because of the oppression of the mighty: but none saith, Where is God my Maker?" Job 35. 10. No, instead of that, they count him an enemy; and, there is really too much ground for it, while they persist, and go on in their wickedness.

And, these are heads that might further be insisted on, together with that general stupefaction, fitly called "death," or signified by the name of death, that possesseth the souls of the most in this present state; that, while in the midst of such miseries, they are so ingulphed, they feel them not, apprehend them not, or, at least, the worst, and most formidable part of that by which they are the most miserable:" the anger of the Lord preys upon them, as a consuming fire, and they know it not; it hath burnt them, yet they lay it not to heart," as the prophet expresseth it, Isaiah 42. 25. And that, indeed, is a most calamitous case, and calls for deep lamentation; the inhabitants of this earth, generally, as in the suburbs of hell, (as we have no other notion of this world, than as a portal and introduction into the eternal state of blessedness, or misery,) and, that men should be so near perishing, having wrath to the uttermost coming upon them, and yet, so generally unconcerned. This is a like case to that of a lethargic body, that may be tossed and rolled hither and thither; you may, perhaps, cut it and wound it, but it feels not. As little sensible are the minds or spirits of men of this state of their case, of those miseries, by which they are now wretchedly miserable, and are in danger of being finally and eternally so.

With what lamentations might we bewail the case of apostate men, upon this account, would we but admit the thoughts of the common case to enter and sink into our minds and hearts. Men are so strangely habituated to misery, that it is now become their element, and natural to them: they can see themselves gradually sinking lower and lower into death, and, might apprehend, that consummate death was at hand, but they are not startled and amazed, no amazing thought has place in the minds of men, to awaken them, and make them bethink themselves, while it would be seasonable, and while any thing might be done towards their escape from the wrath which is to come: but, they remain generally, in that dead sleep, which binds up all their powers, and are like so to do, (if wonderful mercy prevent not,) till flames awaken them out of their pleasant dream. And now, I add, further,

LECTURE XXXI.*

1. The consequent discomposure of the whole frame of man, I mean of the inward man, as the apostle distinguisheth of man, making him double, a man, and a man; an outward man, and an inward man; 2 Cor. 4. 16. Now for this inward man, there is a universal discomposure of the whole frame. They that will look upon what we insisted on before, but as a reputative evil; to wit, ignominy, must reckon this a most real one; that is, that that noble piece of workmanship, the inward man, is so marred, and spoiled, and discomposed throughout, and become a far more monstrous thing than any dislocations, or transpositions of the parts of these bodies of ours, can make them, though it would be easy to suppose it possible that men might be, as to the outward man, a most monstrous sort of creature, by the mere transposition of parts, yet, let any, the most horrid metamorphosis of that kind you can think of be supposed, and, it is nothing to that discomposure of the frame of the inward man, that is to be found and observed in every, yet apostate son of Adam, not converted, not returned to God, out of that state of apostasy.

For, as to what we have insisted on already, (that infatuation that is upon the minds of men every where,) consider, what must hereupon be consequent; that conductive governing light, that should lead men in the whole of their course, it is extinct, it is darkness, as our Saviour speaks in Matt. 6. 23. "If the light, that is in thee, be darkness, how great is that darkness." It is not said, concerning an unregenerate man, that he hath darkness in him; but, that he himself is darkness. Eph. 5. 8. "Ye were sometimes darkness:" their governing light was lost and gone, and then, what must become of the man? What is the state and frame of the inward man hereupon? Why you are to consider, (that light being supposed,) what was to be under its direction and government, in man, to wit, the inward man. There was his will, which was to be guided by that directing principle, but it is gone. And, there were all the passions of the soul, that were to have been moderated thereby, but, that being gone, the will is under no such guidance, the passions under no such moderation. What

* Preached June 9, 1694.

a horrid creature is man, hereupon, become, in the complexion of his soul, and inward man?

For his will, that is naturally wont to be called *cæca potentia*, an unseeing faculty; why, admit that it were properly to be so called, according to the natural constitution and frame in man, it was yet to be guided by a faculty that could see, by a seeing mind: but now, when an unseeing will is to be guided also by an unseeing mind, the blind is to lead the blind, (to allude to that of our Saviour,) what will become of this, but a being plunged into the ditch? This is the common case with man: that will of his, which is the commanding faculty in the soul of man, comes to be itself under the conduct of no reason, an unreasonable will: O! what a fearful case is this, when, yet, it is most manifestly the common case.

For, do but ask, What is the object of that faculty, that we call the *will*, in man? It is primarily his end, that is the object of it: that is, good; for good and end are wont to be taken for convertible terms; the means are only good by the goodness of the end. Now, when a man wills his end unreasonably, without the ducture or guidance of any seeing, discerning principle; and, to think of a man acting accordingly, shaping his course accordingly, and, to think of all men doing so, what a monstrous deformity is this of that noble creature; though it be true, indeed, that many are found to act rationally; that is, indeed, wilily and subtilly enough in the pursuit of such and such ends that they do design; but, yet, it is plain, they do, universally, mistake their end itself, and so the whole life of man can be nothing else but a continual error: "They do always err in their hearts, not having known my ways." What doth it signify, that a man can pursue such and such ends, with courage and dexterity; but these ends themselves, either he may gain them, or he may gain them not? Many times he never gains them; but, if he doth gain them, they are worth nothing. Why, here is a life lost, thrown away by the very complexion of the inward man; this he is inclined to do, to take such a course, as by which his whole life is lost, and thrown away.

A thing that that pagan moralist most aptly animadverts upon, when he saith, "Men are very shy of destroying their lives all at once, losing their lives altogether; but they make no difficulty of losing them all by parts:" that is, this day of my life I pursue an end, that is worth nothing; and I do so to-morrow, and the next day, and so from year to year, as long as my life lasts. Here is a life quite thrown away; and a man is led to it by the inward complexion and temper of his soul, as he hath mis-made himself, misshaped himself; for he was made upright, but he would be trying inventions, and this it hath come to. This is plain and evident concerning all the world of apostate, unrenewed men; that whereas, their will is the commanding, governing principle of their lives, it doth command *nulla ratione*, it universally commands without reason, and so must signify as much of misery to a man, as if his eyes were out, and he among pits and precipices, where he cannot do so much as set a foot, without danger of perishing presently.

It is plain, the minds of men, as they lie under the direction of such a misguided will, they are conducted by no rational principle at all, upon this ground, that it is the end which is the principal object of every one's will. But they are universally out as to their end, running a quite counter-course to what they should, through the whole course of their time; so that, in this respect, the apostate, unregenerate man, is *natus ad miseriam*, he is wholly framed unto misery; and to nothing else but to misery. It is true, men have generally some practical notions of truth, that is, notions of truth about practical matters, that should be the principal things. They have generally some apprehensions of God, some apprehensions of a future state, some apprehensions of the immortality of their souls; but these notions are too weak and debile, to do the office of principles. They do not do the office of principles, in that nobody steers his course, (antecedently to regenerating grace,) pursuant to any such principles. And if you would reduce the determination of men's wills to any principles at all, they can agree to no other principles than such as these; (though they should more generally disclaim and disavow them yet they are apt to be governed by them, and no other;) that is, that a man is made for himself; that he is his own end; that he that hath made him, hath no right to rule him; that from him, from whom he hath received his being, he is not to expect blessedness; but that he is to seek it in inferior things, things inferior to himself; that time is far more considerable and valuable than eternity, that mortal flesh is far more valuable than the immortal spirit. The actual resolutions and determinations of men's wills which do govern their course, and according to which they lead their lives, do only square with such principles as these; though, when they are made explicit, they would be ashamed of them, and say they own no such principles; yet they own them most expressly as they can, as emphatically as they can. For a whole course of actions is a far more speaking thing, than words can be; words do only express a man's present sense, the present sense of mind: but a series and course of actions do speak his constant and continued sense.

And, O! what a miserable creature is man, upon this account, when the habitual complexion of his soul leads him through his whole course, all his days, all his lifetime, but to pursue shadows and lying vanities; and at length to lie down in sorrow, hopeless, endless, sorrow.

And as the will is the so misguided thing, so the principle is wanting, too, that should moderate the passions. And what a hell do they create in every man to himself, or make him to himself. Every one, if he would but consider and reflect might be so far a preacher to himself upon this theme, as to save me or any man the labour of representing this case—"What a miserable condition the soul of man must be in, being the seat of so many passions, all left destitute of the conduct and government of any rational principles that should conduct them aright." Unreasonable desires, what a hell must they make! desires either after that which cannot be had, or which is not worth the having; either what is unattainable, or will do me no good; or I shall be never the better if I do attain them. To have any soul the continual seat and subject of such desires, and of no better, what a fearful case is this!

His delights, themselves, (though that may seem a paradox,) they are most fatal to him, and contribute as much (nay it may be more,) to his misery, as his desires; because they detain him, they put a stop to him; they divert his course. Delight is the *quies appetitus in appetibili*, it is that by which the soul takes up its end, and is at a stop: but in what? in the enjoyment of wind and vanity, that is unsatisfying, very unsatisfactory. It is detained and diverted, it is withheld, by these, from pursuing what would do it any good, or contribute to its true felicity: "The woman that liveth in pleasure, is dead while she liveth." Do you think it is not as true in the other sex? whoever lives immersed in sensual delights and pleasures, they are dead while they live. It is but a dying life that they live.

And their very hopes make them miserable: they are miserable by their own hopes, continually reaching out after that they can never compass; or if they do, still they do but fill themselves with the east wind. Hope is the spring of endeavours: for no man will endeavour for what he is hopeless of. But they do but labour for the wind in all that they endeavour, and possess and reap the east wind; that is all that they can reach to.

Their good things will often run cross to them; and then

how doth that passion of anger corrode and tear them! what a rack is there in the soul upon this account, especially when it works up as high as malice against men: men that they do an injury to, if it arise to envy, that most unreasonable passion; that I would rather be miserable because another appears nearer to happiness, in my apprehension, than I; he enjoyeth what is better, or he is better than myself, therefore I will be miserable; that is, I will be envious.

Add to this, the meditation and study of revenge, whether for real or apprehended wrong done to me. It is the most cutting, wounding revenge, that every man takes upon himself. "Such a one I think hath hurt me, done me harm, I will revenge it upon myself:" for it is the person himself that feels it most of all; (if he have any sense left in him;) it makes him a continual hell in himself. It makes him a devil to himself, as he would be to another man. It may be he misseth that; but as to himself he doth not miss it.

And as to his griefs, unreasonable griefs, what a deluge of misery are they! when men lament and mourn about things unreasonably, beyond proportion, (as every unrenewed man is apt to do,) he doth deluge himself with those sorrows: and his fears, by which he is continually prophesying dismal things to himself, what a miserable creature do they make him!

And all now upon this one account, all the things of this kind, do meet in this one juncture, in this one point; to wit, that there is no right mind to lead a man: that principle that was originally to have been conductive of his course, is gone, and it can never be supplied but by the Spirit of wisdom and holiness from above: while that is yet withheld and wanting to him, what is it that doth govern in the man? It is the spirit of this world, as it is called: "we have not received the spirit of the world, but the Spirit that is from God." Every unregenerate man, he is in his spirit under the government of the spirit of this world, one common genius which adapts and attempers men in their habitual frame into this world, unto this lower sphere. "Greater is he that is in you than he that is in the world." The contest lies between spirit and spirit; as to what part God hath in this world, and as to what part the devil hath in this world. If the spirit of this world doth govern in any one, and be the ruling principle in him, that unites him with this world; and upon that, all his appetitions, and all the various motions and passions of his soul, are determined, and confined to this present world, this sensible world; he is linked to that in spirit, he hath a spiritual, vital union only with this world, and so feels all the pangs, all the paroxysms, that, in this lower region, he is subject to: he is always shaken with this shaking world, and tossed and hurried, hither and thither, as that is.

What a miserable creature must apostate man be, upon this account! This world being become such a region of death and of misery, the spirit of this world plungeth and ingulfs him in all that misery, makes him a continual partaker in it, as that wherewith he only hath a vital union. That Spirit that is of God, would unite him with the other world, and attemper him to that which the power of that Spirit (when this world is grievous and troublesome to him,) might ascend and go up, and have his way above, (as the way of the wise is,) to depart from hell beneath; but, the spirit of this world entangles him, ensnares him, fixeth him in that gulf, that he cannot ascend; can be carried out of this world by no thought, no vivid desire, no hopes upwards; his all lies here.

And, that which is yet more tremendous in this case, is, his continual unwillingness, and dread of leaving this world; that fear, to wit, the fear of death. What a miserable creature must that make him, to be under the continual expectation of what he knows is inevitable, and he cannot escape; so that his only remedy in this is not to think of it! His relief must be to unteach himself, his own nature; that is, whereas he is naturally a thinking thing, he is to stifle such thoughts as are proper and suitable to the state of his case. All his care must be to make himself not think of that, than which no thought can be more proper and suitable to him. For, when I do certainly know that I am, as to this present world, this present state, a mortal creature, I should, therefore, bethink myself, with all the seriousness and concern imaginable, What shall come next? I dwell in an earthly tabernacle, which I know must come down, but I do not know, when I shall dislodge, where to have another habitation. I cannot say, "I have a building with God, a house not made with hands, eternal in the heavens,"—no; the spirit that governs me is the spirit of this world, and that confines me only to this world.

A man, in this case, is miserable among all his enjoyments, when he thinks it goes never so well with him: "I have what heart can wish for," as well as that fool in the gospel propounded to himself, to have it with him, "I will say to my soul, Take thine ease, thou hast goods laid up for many years;" upon this account he is pronounced a fool: "Thou fool, this night shall thy soul be taken from thee." And whereas, that is spoken with peculiar reference to a rich man, yet you must not confine it so; for our Saviour saith in the next words, "So it is with every man that layeth up treasure for himself, (designs treasures to himself on earth, as every man doth one way or other,) and is not rich towards God." "This night shall thy soul be required of thee." O! dreadful word, to a man that hath his all here! O the torture that such a man must be subjected to, (if he thinks, if he considers,) that hath his all lying in this world, and yet, he knows he cannot stay here long: "The wicked is driven away in his wickedness."

This is so great a thing, that it is made one part of the design of the mediation of Christ, and his redemption, for which he became a man, and for which he took upon him flesh and blood, that he might be so: "that he might, by death, destroy him that had the power of death, that is, the devil, (undo him as to his design and purpose,) and deliver those who, through fear of death, were all their lifetime subject to bondage." To be under this unreasonable fear, what a dreadful thing is this! In this respect, it is to be called unreasonable, because, when a man finds that the thing is necessary, and unavoidable, that he is afraid of; all wisdom would direct him to reconcile himself to necessity, and never to be at rest in his own spirit, till he finds, that as he is to think of death with certainty, so he may think of it with complacency too: till, I say, he may upon good terms so do. And again,

xi. We are to consider, as to what is contained in this misery of man, that as (which I formerly told you) they have in all this, no relief from God, so God hath a real displeasure towards this wretched creature in his present state: and, if in his favour be life; in his disfavour is death: which way soever he turns, or what way soever he thinks of comforting himself, he is still under a *nemesis*: divine displeasure hangs over his head. "God is angry with the wicked every day. The wrath of God is revealed from heaven against all ungodliness and unrighteousness of men. On the wicked he will rain snares, fire and brimstone, and a horrible tempest, this shall be the portion of their cup." While they continue wicked, and as such, that relates them to the divine wrath, constitutes them the proper subjects of it, upon which it preys as fire doth upon suitable fuel. And,

xii. They are not without some apprehensions hereof: misgivings they have in their own minds: there is a kind of gloominess and a dark shadow, that is cast by guilt over the soul and spirit of a man. He is not without some secret surmises, as men cannot rid themselves of all notions of God. A person that is habitually wicked, under the power of sin as a governing principle in him, cannot but apprehend him as an offended

God, though his apprehensions be not so distinct, so formed, so explicit, yet such secret gnawings and corroding thoughts there will be, conscience accusing as well as excusing by turns; as it ought to be read: self-accusing thoughts do take turns in the soul. The writings of heathens are full of expressions, what the gnawings and tortures are of a guilty, misgiving conscience, of a self-accusing conscience. But, in the last place, which was mentioned the last time,

xiii. That which is the more common case, and is more fitly signified by the name of death, is, the stupefaction that more generally, and more ordinarily, takes place in the minds of men; that they are without feeling. Wrath is upon them, and they do not know it. Some more unformed thoughts they have, but not explicit and distinct ones; such as might affect their hearts, and enter into their very souls: more generally their disease is a lethargy, without sense, and without feeling. And you know how sad the case may be in that respect, with the diseased body of a man. We do not reckon it the better when it can feel no pain, while the matter of the disease is present, and all the morbific matter remains. If it do not only endanger, but stupify, it is so much the more dangerous in common apprehension: and that is the case of the soul of an unrenewed, unregenerate man, that he can be tossed, and hurried, and torn, even by himself, by his own passions within him, this way, and that way, and yet, he doth not reflect and think with himself, "I am a miserable creature;" but misery is become his element: where things do not *gravitate*, they do not lie with pressure, as nothing is pressed by being in its element. And misery is become so connatural to men, in this their present state, that misery is round about them, and they feel it not: the anger of God is preying upon them, consuming their souls, but they lay it not to heart, as in Isaiah 42, latter end, the expression is; divine anger is kindling upon this world, but they know it not; and destroying and consuming it, but they take it not to heart.

This is that death that is passed over all, as to the spiritual import of the expression, or, as it denotes the spiritual evils that do now infest the souls of men. But I would, before I had gone off from this head, have said somewhat by way of *Use* to this particular. And though I am prevented of saying much, yet, plain it is,

That whereas man, in this state of apostasy, is now a miserable creature, it may be gathered, from all that hath been said upon this head; that he generally mistakes the cause of his misery, and so, is as much likely to mistake the way and method of his cure. He little thinks, his misery is a self-sprung thing, and, that he hath the fountain of it in himself. This will not enter into the minds of men. "The backslider in heart shall be filled with his own ways;" Proverbs 14. 14. That word, because it is rendered "backslider," may strike a wrong notion into the minds of many, as if, thereby, were meant an hypocritical pretender to religion, who hath apostatized, and made a defection: but, the word carries no notation at all of any other apostasy, than the common apostasy. And it is plain, that by "the backslider in heart" there, is meant the wicked man, in general, a sinner, in opposition to a righteous and good man, as, generally, the two parts of several verses up and down in this book, do distribute men into good and bad, by one appellation or another. And, that is a proper expression, by which the bad is distinguished from the good man, in that verse: the word signifies perverse, froward; a fit character for a wicked man, an unconverted man; such a one "shall be filled with his own ways," as the good man is so satisfied from himself. The good man is not the first fountain of happiness to himself, but a subordinate one a good man is, and so is satisfied from himself. But the wicked man is the prime and first fountain of all misery to himself: and, therefore, when these wicked ones have any sense at all of their own miseries, they do create to every man a hell within himself.

But this is a thing least of all apprehended: men generally say, "What is the matter with me? what aileth me? I cannot be well, I cannot be quiet;" and, they would have this or that thing rectified, in their external circumstances, and they think that will do their business; but, alas! that will not do. They talk of flying from their misery, but, that they cannot do, unless they could fly from themselves. I remember the moralist saith, "Go whither thou wilt, that intolerable companion, (thyself) will go with thee, wheresoever thou flyest, and layest down thine head." Till thou art new-made, thou art self-made, for misery. God must new-make thee, if ever thou art happy. And, therefore, an amazing wonder it is, that men should so much mind things that are foreign to them, and never cast their eye upon themselves, or think how it is within. They are greatly concerned how affairs go in France, in Flanders, in Germany; but never think how it goes within. O! what a miserable world will it be, (it may be often said by such,) if that side prevail over the other side! What a miserable world will this be then! But men do thus think altogether amiss, and besides the purpose: what good will it do to me if so good men, and never so good a cause, prevail and prosper in the world, when I have my own hell within myself? I shall be a miserable creature still, till all be rectified within. It is not a new world, but being a new man, that can ease me, relieve me, and make me a happy creature.

It doth not lie in the power of all the world to make me a happy or miserable man. You may think, if such and such a party of men prevail, we are all undone, we shall be very miserable. But, I tell you, it will be in their power only to make you miserable, in whose power it is to make you ill men. If it be not in the power of any in all the world to make you ill men, they can never make you miserable men. If it were in the power of men, to pluck you off from God, to disaffect you to him, that you take no complacency in him, that you cannot love him, nor pour out your soul to him, this would make you miserable. But, it is not in the power of all this world to make any man miserable, that doth not make and keep himself wicked.

" And so death passed over all men."

LECTURE XXXII.*

You know our business upon these latter words hath been, more lately, to give an account of that death, which is said to have passed over all. And, therein, we proposed to consider it,

(1.) In its nature, in which respect it is common to all. And,

(2.) In its degrees, in respect whereof it admits of great difference, according to the several circumstances of men's states. We have been hitherto speaking to it upon the former account, and labouring to shew you its ambitus and extent, of how vast a comprehension it is, what a mighty sum of misery it carries in it. That misery, we shewed, must involve,

[1.] Bodily death, with all the tendencies and appurtenances, (as I may say,) thereunto. And then, we have more largely insisted,

[2.] In shewing that here must be included in it, death spiritual, such as the souls of men are liable to, and susceptible of; death, not in the natural, but in the moral sense. In the former sense, souls cannot die, as is an agreed thing, among

* Preached June 23, 1694.

all; and, in the moral sense, because morality doth comprehend both men's duty, and their felicity, we are not, (as was told you,) here, to consider it in opposition to the former of these: for so we spake to this death, as it falls under the head of sin, in that other clause of the verse: but, as it stands in opposition to felicity, and to the real blessedness of the souls of men. Or, (as was told you,) that aversion from God, which sums up all in point of evil; as a right propension towards him, or love to him, sums up all in point of good. That aversion from God, it may be either from him as the Sovereign Authority, and so it stands in opposition to our duty; or, as it is an aversion from him as the Sovereign Good, and, so it stands in opposition to our felicity. And so, we considered spiritual death. And, it is called death, (as hath been noted to you) in an equivalent sense, as that which serves not the end it was designed for, and so is all one as if it were not. When the souls of men will not serve the natural end to which such beings were originally designed, it is all one as if they were not. They are lost as to their proper end, both as they were to be serviceable to God, and as they were capable subjects of felicity for themselves; for, that double end was to be designed by them, though the one in subordination to the other.

Now, I go on in the next place,

[3.] To note further to you, that, under the name of "death," we may also understand that condemnation, which the whole apostate world lies under. This is a thing that, fitly enough, is to be conceived under the notion of this death, that is said to be "passed upon all." Whatsoever there is of present death upon this world, it lies under a doom to more, to that which I may say, is more deadly, and more dreadful.

And I need not insist, in opening to you so obvious and so plain a thing to any one's understanding, how properly a condemned man may be said to be a dead man. A world under a doom unto a future misery, (besides all that is actually incumbent on it,) how properly, in that respect, death may be said to have passed over all. One that is under condemnation is dead in law; he hath no longer a legal title to his life. The law doth not further protect his life, is no longer a guardian to it; yea, and it doth not only withhold its protection, but doth direct its sword against such a one's life, and cut it off.

This is the common state of this world; it lies under a doom: besides all the actual miseries that are upon it, it is doomed to worse; "death hath passed over all;" but that death is in a continual tendency, (as being yet but begun,) to a consummate state of death. Death finished, is approaching; and men are, by the righteous judgment of God, led on, hurried on, towards the consummate state of misery or death, that is most righteously determined upon them. And this, the context can by no means allow us to overlook. It is inculcated again and again, in the 16 and 18 verses of this chapter: "that judgment is come upon all men to condemnation." This whole apostate world stands condemned by the righteous judgment of God. And so, as justification is, in a relative and respective sense, the life of the soul; so is condemnation the death of it. That passage, in the same context—"the justification of life," it carries that manifest import: and condemnation doth as truly carry death in it, as justification doth life.

Antecedently to that change which God makes in the state of men, condemnation is a thing belonging to them, as when such a change is made, in the state of any that are brought into union with Christ: "There is no condemnation to them that are in Christ Jesus;" Romans 8. 1. But that tells us what the common state and case of the rest is; there is no condemnation to them, they lie under a universal condemnation; they are, (as the apostle's most apt and emphatical expression is,) *υπόδικος*, we render it, become guilty; the meaning is impleadable before God, liable to be impleaded by law, in *jus vocari*, to be called to account. And, as the course that men have held, according to natural corrupt inclination, is unaccountable, so they are liable to be brought under judgment before the Lord.

This condemnation is to be understood to be as its opposite justification, either (as some fitly enough express the matter under those terms,) constitutive, or sentential: either they are, by the constitution of the law, condemned, and that is to be condemned virtually, by that sentence which is written in the law, by which they are to be judged; or sententially, which is that condemnation that is to be pronounced upon them at the last by the mouth of their Judge. Justification is taken the same, two ways. A person may be said to be justified, either when the law doth constitute him just, or else there is a final justification, when he is pronounced or declared so, from the judgment seat, by the mouth of the Supreme and Universal Judge.

It is in the former sense that the world lies under condemnation. As a person that hath violated and broken the law, by the commission of some capital crime, though he be not formally condemned, by the mouth of the judge, yet the law condemns him beforehand. And there must be the less difference in this case, *in foro divino*, then would be *in foro humano;* because the judgment of God will always, at last, pass according to the mind and intendment of the law, when many things may prevent its doing so in human judicatures: this is one sense wherein death is further said to have passed over all. All are under a general doom; their lives are actually forfeited; the forfeiture may be taken whenever God will. Men are at mercy, respited from the utmost of death, and by patience, (without promise,) as a condemned person may be executed whenever the prince pleaseth; there is no moment of time given to him; he can claim no addition to his life. Thus it is with all men. "So death hath passed over all." And lastly,

[4.] We are to consider within the compass and extent of this death, that eternal death itself, unto which this doom, this judgment, makes men liable and subject: and that hath actually passed upon as many as have died impenitent, and not reduced, not brought back to God, through the several thousands of years that are revolved and gone over this world already. And as to what remains of human generation, death may be said to have passed in that respect, even over all of them too, it being as sure that they will come into the depth of that death, as if they were plunged into it already,—supposing their continuing not reconciled, not reduced, not recovered, out of the common state of apostasy. Concerning that death, it doth more properly belong to another topic or place in theology; and therefore, I shall not discourse of it here; only hint thus much concerning it, that it cannot differ in kind, and in the main substance, from that spiritual death, which we have spoken of already. As spiritual life doth not differ substantially from eternal life; so, nor doth this spiritual death differ in substance from eternal death, any more than a child newly born, doth differ in nature, or specifically from a grown man. Spiritual life will grow up into eternal life. Spiritual death will grow up into death eternal. It will, hereafter, consist and lie in separation from God, and in subjection to his wrath; even as now it doth; the difference herein is only as to the degrees, and as to duration and continuance. There is now a loss of God, as our best and most satisfying Good: and so there will be to all eternity. There is now a subjection to his displeasure, and various manifold impressions therefrom; there will be higher and fuller degrees hereafter. Both that which is called *pœna damni*, the *punishment of loss*, and that which is called *pœna sensus*, the *punishment of sense*, will have unspeakable, unconceivable additions hereafter. But there is the same thing in reality now, with every ungodly man, every one that is not reconciled to God. Though, by the way, I could never satisfy myself concerning the fulness of these terms, *pœna damni*, and *pœna sensus*, the punishment of loss, and the punisnment of sense; for, undoubtedly, the former, the punishment of loss, is as sensible as the other, every whit; we do not know but that it may be more so. Souls will be eternally stung with their loss, as much as with any positive suffering: as a man may be as sensibly pained by hunger, as he may be by a dagger, that strikes him to the heart. But that only by the by.

These are the great things, that this same *death* in the text, which is said to "have passed over all," must be understood to comprehend and contain within the extent of it. And so far we have considered it, but in its kind, wherein it is common to all. But if,

(2.) We should also consider it in its degrees, so there will be found to be great differences. It will not be in degree the same to all, but differ and vary, according to the very various circumstances of men's states, whether we consider the matter, with reference to the natural tendency of things, or whether we consider it, with reference to the righteous judgment of God: both in nature and divine judgment, there must needs be great differences between the miseries of some, and of others. There is, in this present state, and there will be, no doubt, in the future state too, where all the subjects of wrath are called "vessels of wrath;" but those vessels are not all of the same capacity; some vessels will hold more than others do: and their capacity and measure hereafter, will be much according to what is here in this present state.

And, I shall only here hint, at some of the more obvious things that must difference the state of men, in point of that misery which hath deluged, and will deluge for ever, the apostate world. It hath different degrees of depth, as the ocean hath; which, though in some places we may suppose it a hundred fathom deep, and in other places not above two or three, yet, it is deep enough to drown all. So is this deluge of misery upon fallen mankind; though as to some deeper, than it is as to others, yet, it is deep enough to drown all in misery and destruction. As the apostle's expression is, 1. Tim. 6. 9. But to name to you some things that more obviously do appear to difference the case of men's states, in point of misery, or that death which here is said to have passed over all. As,

[1.] There must needs be some difference, from the better or worse complexion of nature, that is to be found with some and with others; of which some heathens do fitly enough speak. There is such a thing as good nature in this world, obvious enough to the observation of every one, as there is ill nature, observable enough in others. These must make very great differences in the state of men's case, if we consider the matter according to the ducture and tendency of mere nature. So that, whereas the natures of some do render them less propense to vice, it is also possible, that, as they are less vicious, this will be one of the measures, that they will be hereafter less miserable, but miserable still; and, notwithstanding not being reconciled to God, being turned, renewed, changed, never made partakers of the divine nature.

But, if you consider that case morally, then the better natured any are, supposing that they do violence to that nature, they spoil that nature, and make it much worse;—then, I say, the better natured, the more miserable; for they are undoubtedly the more guilty. Many well-tempered persons, of much ingenuity, of good disposition, that are not inclined to do ill things to other men; but they are continually propense to all acts of injustice towards God: him they will not know; from him they are habitually alienated; never look after reconciliation with him. It may be, when they were not naturally inclined, yet, they have taught themselves to be more grossly and sensibly vicious; and so have that way, and in that respect, spoiled a good nature, done, in that respect, continual violence to themselves; learned to be wicked, even beyond what they were inclined: here must be so much the deeper condemnation.

A thing, I am afraid, very little considered by parents, in reference to the children of their womb and loins; branches of themselves, whose tempers they make it their business to cultivate as they grow up. But, many parents have not only neglected this, but have made it their business to instil (as much as in them lay,) vicious inclinations into them: or they have so managed matters towards them, as to make them craspish, peevish, and froward, to embitter their tempers, and to lay foundations betimes, both of present and everlasting misery, in their very tempers, in their spoiled, or not improved tempers. Many parents might more mercifully, with more kindness, pluck out their children's eyes, and cut off their limbs, than indulge the vicious humours which appear in them betimes; and wherein is a foundation laid for their misery in this world, as well as for future and eternal misery, when their tempers are so spoiled, as to be cross, peevish, froward, discontented, quarrelsome. Alas! much of this might have been qualified, and prevented, betimes. But, in the mean time, that there is such a thing as better and worse nature, which may, in different respects, make present and future misery, more or less, is out of all question. But,

[2.] That which is more considerable, is, that they must be plunged deeper into this death, who live in sin to the last, unconverted to God, and unreduced under the gospel, than they that never enjoyed a gospel: this must make a vast difference in the states of men. "This is the condemnation, that light is come into the world, and men love darkness more than light." John 3. 19. When the gospel itself becomes deadly to men, that is a most terrible sort of death:—to die by a gospel-plague, is a most terrible way of dying! Death passed upon all, but it triumphs more, and with greater terror, over that part of the world where gospel light shines, but is wickedly resisted, opposed, sinned against, and the design of it counterwrought; that is, as in that mentioned place, it is expressed, "Men love darkness more than light:" the darknsss better pleaseth them, is more grateful to them, as it gives them opportunity of being wicked still. The light offends men; they cannot endure (as it is in that context) to have their deeds brought to the light; resolved they are upon a course of wickedness. Where there is an honest, sincere mind, he affects light, runs into the light, that it may appear, that his works are wrought in God, that the divine tincture and impress that is upon his works, may show itself, and appear. There is that in them, which is very agreeable and congruous to the light. But, when men have a resolution of being wicked, then they are for a corner. "There is no darkness, or shadow of death, where the workers of iniquity may hide themselves:" that implies what they affect; they would have a shadow of death wherein to hide themselves: that which they covet is, "Where shall we be hid?" It is a night they seek, and a cloud; *nocte peccatur*. When there is a course of dispensation kept on foot towards men all their time, to keep them within the light, to hold them within the region and verge of gospel light; this is that which they could wish extinct: "O! that this light were out." As they are brought speaking in that Isaiah 30. 1. "Cause the holy One of Israel to cease from before us. His bright and glorious appearances, they are ungrateful and unwelcome to us. O! who will take away God, and that divine light, that shines so much to our disturbance and annoyance; we wish it gone."

But more tolerable will it be to Sodom and Gomorrah, to Tyre and Sidon, in the day of judgment, than to Capernaum and Bethsaida, (as our Saviour inculcates in the 11 Matt. 22 and onwards, when he upbraids those cities, where his wonderful works were done,) where there were so bright and glorious appearances of divine power, attesting and bearing witness to that truth which he came to publish to the world. O! woe, woe, to them, among whom there have been such glorious appearances of God, but counter-striven and resisted. Though there will be one common hell to all in time, yet, the hell of Sodom and Gomorrah will be a more tolerable hell, than theirs. And again,

The case must, in point of misery, be worse with them who, living under the gospel, had a better parentage, were born of godly parents, than with others with whom it was not so. And that upon a double account:—Because, that such would certainly devote them to God; and,—as they would be more intent upon educating them for God. Here, come in very great differences in the case of such, from the more common case.

First. I say, they that were born of religious parents, those parents would, by conscience of duty, be obliged and urged to devote them to God; to take care that those great and venerable names, the name of the Father, the name of the Son, and the name of the Holy Ghost, should, according to divine appointment, be early named upon them, to signify whose they were, and to whom they did belong. But they afterwards, when they are grown up, refuse to stand to that covenant, according to the tenour whereof so early a dedication was made of them. "We will not have our parents' God to be our God." Thy friend, and thy father's friend, forsake not. A horrid thing that were: but how horrid to forsake our God, and our father's God. When man's case shall, in this respect, be brought into judgment at the last day—Thou wast born of such and such parents, that recognised God's right of thee betimes; for it is only a recognition of God's right. It is not the creation of any right to him, nothing can be given him, that was not his before, but only a recognizing his right, and this hath been done with solemnity. "But thou, when thou wast grown up, wouldst not stand to the covenant of thy father; thy father's God should not be thy God." How much more dreadful must be the case of such, than that of pagans, in the grossest darkness! And again,

Secondly. Such parents must be supposed to have educated them for God, pursuantly to their having devoted them to him. But, alas! many in our days, have counted it a glory to have broken loose out of the fetters of a pious education; to have thrown them off, torn their bonds, as Samson did his withes and cords; and therein they think they have shewed themselves mighty men; that this was a great piece of fortitude and courage, to outface God and heaven; and to bend themselves to a course of wickedness, in opposition to whatsoever of good principles were endeavoured to be implanted; that is, principles of truth, which were laboured to be infused and inlaid into their minds; and of practical truth, such as might have a tendency to form and govern their practice. Their godly parents did, no doubt, charge their own consciences with duty, in this kind, to teach their children the train of their ways betimes, that "when they were old they might not depart from them." But as for such as have formed their way, and broken loose, undoubtedly the child of a pagan, though it perish, yet perisheth under less guilt than such. And,

[4.] There cannot but be great differences, too, according as among those that live under the gospel; some have lived under a more powerful ministry than others: where the same gospel for substance is preached, it cannot but be acknowledged, that it is preached by some more convictively, with more pungency, and with greater aptitude to do good, than others: many are more closely urged, and dealt withal, from time to time, in the ministry of the word, than others are. And, according as men's case may differ in this respect, so will this death, that passeth on them, have more or less of deadliness in it. And (as was said) when the gospel is "a savour of death," so as that men die of a gospel plague, it is a fearful way of dying. But the savour of the gospel, or the odour, rather, (as that word should be read,) is stronger, as it is diffused by some than by others. But if it prove deadly, by how much the stronger, by how much the more of efficacy, so much the more, may it be said, doth the death that ensueth partake of the horror of death. And again,

[5] There cannot but be great difference, too, according as some do sin against greater convictions of conscience than others. Having more of internal light let into their minds, and which, therefore, they are put to have a closer contest and grapple; the case cannot but be so much the worse, unto how much the more of conviction men do oppose themselves in a wicked course; convinced, but yet go on: convinced that they should turn to God, but never turn; that they should break off such wicked ways, but they persist in them; that they should engage in such and such ways of duty, but they decline them. That conscience which doth not govern, it doth judge, it doth doom, and doom so much the more heavily, by how much the more of resistance its tendency to govern meets with. And,

[6.] There must be deeper degrees of this misery and death, according as there have been stronger strivings of the

Spirit of God; God still resisted and striven against. Where his gospel is, there his Spirit will more or less, and in one kind or other, be at work; but it works at liberty. God works in you "to will and to do of his own good pleasure." And, I doubt the emphasis of that scripture, is not noted as it should be, and the correspondence of part to part in it. Phil. 2. 12, 13. "Work out your own salvation with fear and trembling, for it is God that worketh, (or is working) in you, to will and to do of his good pleasure." Work because he worketh. There is the substance of the precept enforced by that which we are to consider as substantial in the motive. Do you work, because he worketh. But then, there is a circumstance in the precept, unto which a circumstance in the motive doth also correspond; work you with fear and trembling: Why? because God works at will and pleasure, under no obligation, but may desist, may give off, when he will. Now then, he being at perfect liberty, under no bonds or tie, he may strive longer with some, than he doth with others: and, according as he doth longer continue to strive, or as he doth more earnestly plead, (but yet in a way short of victorious, all-conquering grace, which bears all down before it,) so, the guilt cannot but be the greater, that is incurred by continual resistance; and, they must needs sink themselves so much the deeper into misery and death: they that have some taste of the good word of God, and been made partakers of the Holy Ghost, and the powers of the world to come, and, yet sin themselves into such a state, as that their repentance becomes finally impossible. Perhaps, it may admit of a gentler meaning as to some; but that such an expression is used as admits of a latitude, there appears so much the more of divine wisdom in it. But it is plain, that many never do repent. By how much the more of vigorous efforts have been put forth upon them, without effect, so much the more, undoubtedly, must they finally incur of this misery, or sink the deeper into this death.

There is a sorer punishment, that is incurred by sinning against that gospel, wherein that Spirit breathes, than could be by sinning against the law of Moses; as in that Heb. 10. 28 and onward. "If he that despised Moses' law died without mercy under two or three witnesses; of how much sorer punishment, suppose ye shall he be thought worthy, who hath trodden under foot the Son of God, and hath counted the blood of the covenant, wherewith he was sanctified, an unclean thing, and hath done despite unto the Spirit of grace?" There lies the *achme* and height of the wickedness that appears in this case: that is, that Spirit is a Spirit of grace, that they have been contending and striving against; that Spirit of all goodness, and love, and kindness, and benignity: to have striven against that Spirit, to the last breath, of how much sorer punishment shall such be thought worthy? The sinning against one's own conscience, it is doing a violence to one's self, and to what God hath made superior and governing in us, did appoint it to be so. But this is a more immediate and direct affront to heaven, when resistance is made to the Spirit of God himself, who insinuates, slides into the mind, repeats and inculcates from time; and still in vain. It is a fearful thing when men do engage in a continual war with their own consciences,—it is unnatural; and it is a great offence against God too. Heathens have thought so; as particularly Marcus Antoninus: "that warned men, if they would live well, they must live with God, and keep up a conversation with God, and that (saith he) we shall do, if we do not offer violence to, and tear that vicarious God that is in us, which God hath set over every man to be the guide of his life." But when an affront is offered to God himself, the Supreme Good, (as I may say,) not to that vicarious God, but to the very Divine Throne: this is a fearful thing to do so. And so it is when men are continually fighting against that Spirit, that breathes in the gospel. And,

[7.] I might add that, undoubtedly, men's guilt and misery must be greater and deeper, according as they do arrive to great pitches of sin. As such come more explicitly to hate every thing of goodness, to deride and scorn it, according to the gradations that are observable in the beginning of the first psalm, they at length seat themselves in the scorner's chair; they that make it their business to ridicule religion or godliness; or they that sink themselves into deeper degrees of sensuality, why, according as the wickedness in which they wallow is fouler and grosser, so it cannot be but their misery must be the greater in which they involve themselves. And,

[8.] They must needs be in the worst case, in point of misery, that are more instrumental in spreading wickedness in the world; whose wickedness is more diffusive; who are mere partakers of other men's sins. There can be no such thing as supererogation, in point of merit, by good works; but, no doubt, there may be in point of demerit, by wicked works, according as men do draw in more accomplices, and do more join in a conspiracy against God and heaven. So much the more guilt, so much the more miserable must they be. And again,

[9.] Such as are wicked in public stations, they must proportionably be more guilty and more miserable; wicked magistrates and wicked ministers, according to the greater hurt that they do, or the less good that they do, being intrusted with such talents, or having such power, such opportunities improvable for good, put into their hands.

And lastly, *cæteris paribus*—They that live longer in sin, must sink deeper into death, supposing all things concur equally, the longer the worse. The sinner of a hundred years old, he is the more deeply and dreadfully accursed. As in that Isaiah 65. 20. So we see there cannot but be different gradations, or graduate differences in that death, which, in the kind and nature of it, is common to all.

This doth claim somewhat of general use, which, I cannot insist on now: no subject can claim it more than this doth, to which we can apply, or turn ourselves, as you may hear afterwards.

LECTURE XXXIII.*

Use. We therefore come, in the last place, to improve what hath been said of this death, by way of application.

1. And we may learn hence, inasmuch as death is said to have passed over all, for that all have sinned; that God is not unobservant of the ways of men in this world, nor indifferent how they demean themselves. Have all sinned? Death passed over all. They that think God hath forsaken the earth, concerns not himself in human affairs; Why do they think so? It is true, the judgment day, and the state of retribution are not yet come. But, in the mean time, are there no tokens and indications upon men, of divine displeasure? Is there nothing to signify that he is not well pleased with a wicked world? Indeed, because his judgments are not executed with greater terror, therefore, many times, men's hearts are set in them to do evil. And if things run long on with them, after one manner, because they have no changes, they fear not God. But, if they would use their understandings, which can go a greater compass than sense; and, if they would look about, and not consider merely and abstractly what they themselves do now at present feel, but what appearances there may be perceived of divine displeasure towards this world in general, they may see by tokens express enough, that God is not well pleased with the state of things in this world, and with the course,

* Preached Oct. 6, 1694.

and carriage of men in it. They may see that his wrath "is revealed from heaven against all ungodliness and unrighteousness of men; for how constantly is death every where following sin, death passing upon all men, for that all have sinned. When death is making, in a more sensible way, such spoils and havoc in this world, tumbling men into the dust every where, and none escapes—What! have men reason yet to think, that God is indifferent how they carry themselves; that he takes no notice whether men obey him, or disobey him? But again,

2 Since this is the very state of the case, death past upon all, or men are generally in a miserable state; we may collect, hence, that God's deportment towards men, is very becoming of him, and most suitable to the state of their case. " Death hath passed over all, for that all have sinned." Nothing could be more worthy of God, than to let it be as it is with men, in this respect; that is, to let death pass over all; that it should spread its dark and horrid shadow over this world, as we find it every where doth. Nothing could, I say, be more worthy of God, or more suitable to the state and condition wherein sin hath constituted the sons of men. And this will appear yet more distinctly, whether we consider God's dispensation towards men, in this respect, for the present; or, whether you consider, again, his determination concerning them for the future.

(1.) If we consider his dispensation towards them, for the present, nothing could be more becoming, more worthy of God, or more suitable to such a creature as man, now in his lapsed and apostate state. For, as to his present dispensation, you may find a concurrence of two things: first, such a severity, as wherein God doth most becomingly animadvert upon the sinfulness of the world, and shew himself displeased; and secondly, such lenity, as by which he yet signifies himself placable and willing to be reconciled. Nothing could be more suitable, more becoming God, considering the present state of lapsed man, with respect to the tenour of his present dispensation towards him, than that there should be such a mixture as this of God's conduct towards this world: that is, severity, to shew that he is not well pleased; lenity, to signify that he is yet placable. What could be more becoming God? Both these are interwoven in the whole course of God's dealings with men; as hath been told you. There have been tokens of severity, that men might understand and know that God doth not like their ways and manners. Death is every where playing its part, and rolling men into the grave before one another's eyes. And men may every where perceive the effects of a malediction upon themselves, and upon their concernments and affairs in this world. But yet, notwithstanding, there are significations, too, of God's placableness, his willingness to be reconciled, even where there is no gospel, but much more where there is: where there is no gospel, God leaves not himself without witness in that he doth good, giving men rain from heaven, and fruitful seasons, and filling their hearts with food and gladness. And even his patience, and forbearance, and long-suffering, they have a leadingness, (as we have had occasion at large to shew you) unto repentance. And men will have a fearful account one day to make of it, that have not been led thereunto, nor understood that design.

But where the gospel comes, there (you know) God shews himself as he is in Christ, "reconciling the world to himself, that sin might not be imputed." 2 Cor. 5. 19. What can be more suitable than this, to a Being of most absolute perfection, in whom the perfections of wisdom, and justice, and holiness, are in conjunction with the perfections of kindness, goodness, love, and favourable propensions towards his creatures: nor could any be more suitable to men in this their present state, (it being a state of probation,) a state of trial, of leading, and precedaneous to another state.

And, according to all the measures of wisdom and equity, this is always reckoned most suitable where there is guilt that appears chargeable, and that it may be charged; and that, while as yet a public judgment is not given, and hath not had its effect. If we do but consider, (and, indeed, we can but judge as men, of things, and use the best understanding as such, that we have,) we see how men do commonly judge in such and the like cases. That is, suppose one be vehemently suspected of some flagitious crime among men, but the matter is not yet brought to judgment; such a person is neither to be treated as an innocent person, nor as a convicted one. You know that so the wisdom of human governments doth determine every where. And the case speaks itself, that these are apt, and fit, and suitable methods; they carry their own reason in them. Such persons, before the solemn public judgment, and the consequent execution upon that judgment, are neither, I say, treated as innocent, nor as convicted; but there is a mixture in the treatment, which they generally find and meet with: some kind of severity they do undergo, even before their trial and judgment, which may be looked upon as someway penal: and in some degree it is so. Nor is there any thing of severity used towards such, but upon some proof, upon some evidence, as such persons are convened and accused before a magistrate, convicted in some way, though they have not a full conviction: they are brought before them, committed by them, held under restraint, that justice may not be eluded; but that they may be in safe custody. But yet, for all that, there is no formal judgment passed upon them, nor execution consequent unto such judgment, till there have been a very formal trial, and a full conviction.

Much at the same rate, is the state of the case here between God and men, though not for the same reasons, not in all respects for the same; not that the delinquents may be in safe custody, and so finally not escape his justice; for he knows well where to have them at any time, and any where. Nor is any thing of lenity used towards them, upon the acount that they are not convicted, nor fully convicted. For every man's case lies perfectly open to the divine view; but there is severity used towards them, partly for warning to others, and partly for monition and excitation to themselves; because God intends a treaty, and deals with them in order to pardon and forgiveness, which is not the usual design of human governments. And for the same reason is lenity used towards them; not because they are not convicted: for their matter hath, to the divine eye, a thorough perspection, and the whole state of their case at last is seen through and through. But, as was said, that by such gentleness they may be more treatable, and capable of being applied to, in order to their conversion, and final salvation. But, upon the whole, nothing could be more becoming of God, than that there should be such a mixture as we find of severity and lenity, in this present dispensation, antecedent to the future judgment that is to pass upon them. And then,

(2.) Nothing could be more becoming of God, than the determination that he settles concerning man for the future; that is, that this death, in all the fulness of it, shall finally be inflicted upon them that are finally impenitent; those that persevere in enmity and rebellion to the last, and never consort with, never hearken to the terms and overtures of reconciliation; for what else should be done in such a case as this? Do but consider the nature of man. He hath a mortal part about him. It is not reasonable to think, that God should make that mortal part immortal, only that men might continue sinning against him, on earth, uninterruptedly and everlastingly. Was that to be expected that it should be so? And he hath an immortal part, a mind and spirit that is immortal. What should be done in such a case, with such a creature as man?

was he to annihilate that immortal part? That was as little to be expected, that God should have made such a creature with such a nature, and then seem to repent that he had made him such, and so that he should immortalize that which was mortal; or, as I may say, mortalize that which was immortal.

But, I say, that he should do either the one or the other, was for no reason in the world to have been expected from God, the great Lord and Maker of all. He deals with the creatures that he hath made, suitable to the natures that he hath given them. It could not be any blemish to the divine perfections, that he made man at the first with such a nature. If his mortal part always hanged about him, it should have made him capable of no higher felicity than this earth did afford: and sure that had been a diminution of the divine goodness. If he had not made him with an immortal mind and spirit, he had not been capable of felicity, as he had not, it is true, been liable to endless misery. But then, he had not been capable of future felicity. Therefore, consider the matter how you will; look upon all men as having sinned, and consider death hereupon to have passed over all, nothing could, in this case, be more becoming of God, than his deportment towards men; whether you consider his present dispensations towards him, or whether you consider his determinations for the future. But then,

3. We have this further to collect, that men's deportment, in this case, is most unsuitable, most unbecoming of them, and most unanswerable to the state of their own case. Death hath passed over all. Do men carry it suitable hereunto? We might, in many instances, shew you how far they are from doing so, from carrying it suitable to this state of their case; that is, their being under a universal death.

(1.) Very plain it is, that many never think any such thought, —"I am under a doom." It is true, they cannot escape thinking themselves mortal, and that sometime or other they must die; but that this is a doom, a sentence upon them from an offended Creator; how many are there that pass away their days, and never think such a thought? "I am a sinful creature; and God hath been offended; and, therefore, I must die: and, therefore, I am, in many other respects, miserable in the mean time." How many that never think one such thought, that never consider the state of their case as it relates to God. The miseries that befal men here under the sun, they seem to apprehend as if they sprung out of the dust, but apprehend nothing of a *nemesis*, of a *vindicta*, of divine displeasure therein.

Indeed, if there were a correspondency in the temper of men's souls, unto the state of their case, in this respect, wherein soever God testifies his resentment, they would have a resentment. By all these efforts of present divine justice, upon an apostate world, God is expressing this his resentment: "I am ill used by my own creatures;" that is the language of every such providence. "The creatures that I have made, carry it insolently, injuriously, undutifully to me." Providences are vocal and articulate, do not only carry a voice with them many times, but a voice that is expressive of a meaning, which is interpretable; the Lord's voice cries many times to the city, and, in general, it speaks this sense every where; where his providences are afflictive, and reach men's bones, and their flesh, or touch them in any other sensible effect, God is angry, these are the breakings forth of his just displeasure towards a wicked world, against sinful revolted creatures. But with the most, there is nothing of this kind thought of; and therefore, they are full of lamentations for the evils that do befal them, accounting them infelicities; but never look upon them as penalties; which, if they did, that would carry a signification with it of their own guiltiness; that these things befal me as a sinner, and as an offending creature. And,

(2.) Where there are any such thoughts, how rarely do they stay in the minds of men, and how seldom do they dwell upon the contemplation of any such thing? Whereas, if matters were with men as they should be, in these respects, these should be their thoughts lying down and rising up, and from day to day, all the day long, as while men do yet remain in an impenitent and unreconciled state. God speaks his mind in reference to such, that he "is angry with the wicked every day;" so then it should be thought of every day. And it would make men's spirits most restless and uneasy within them. O! what an insupportable thing is it to be under the displeasure of him that made me! and that he should be angry with me every day: that his displeasure should be upon me, even while I am eating, as was said concerning the people in the wilderness: "his wrath came upon them while they were eating, while the meat was yet in their mouths." Sure it would make a man never eat with pleasure, when this should be understood to be the state of his case. And again,

(3.) Men do not meditate an escape. How little is there to be seen of any such thing, in this world, as flying from the wrath to come? as John the Baptist's auditors are said to be doing in a kind of fright—"Who hath warned you to flee from the wrath to come?" How little is it, that looks like this, in this wretched world! There would be consultations, if men were aware of this state of their case, and their spirits were impressed any way suitable to it. There would be counsel held: "We are under divine displeasure; what course shall we take to avert it? to appease that anger which we cannot bear; which will consume and burn up all before it, if it continue unappeased?" And again,

(4.) For the most part, men are taken up about alien things, things most alien and remote from any thing of this kind, or what the exigency of their case requires and calls for; even though they are warned and told of it, and called upon from time to time. This is no new or strange doctrine among us, who live under the gospel; that the state of man is a state of sin and misery: to tell men, you are by nature children of wrath; you are under guilt; you are sinners; and "the wages of sin is death;" this is not strange to the ears of men. You cannot have lived years together under this gospel, but you must have heard of these things often: and surely the generality of them who were wont to hear the gospel, do hear these things frequently inculcated. But what are the workings of their minds and thoughts? Do they bear any correspondency to such things as these, so often urged upon them? "You are a guilty creature," saith the word of God unto them: "you are under death; What will you do in this case? what course will you take?" "Why, I will clothe myself as decently as I can; I will go in a modish dress, I will try the relishes of this, or that, or the other sort of wine." "Why, you are an undone creature; you lie under death: what do you wish in this case?" "I wish I had as neat and as well-furnished a house as my neighbour: I wish that such a commodity would fall, that I might have the better time to buy; or that such a commodity would rise, that I might have the better time to sell." With things so altogether alien from this business, are men taken up in a continual course. What is all this to the state of your case? You are under death, man! do you understand that? You are under guilt; and by being under guilt, lie under death. And,

(5.) They seek relief against the miseries of their present state, by such things as not only do not afford it, but make their case worse, or they have that constant tendency to make them worse. Death that hath passed upon all, hath passed upon you:" they are repeatedly told so. "Well, what do you think of it?" They have the presumptuous appearances of death continually in view: but the inward sense of their heart is such as this: "O, that I were a rich man; that I had a great estate; that I had but opportunity enough to live a voluptuous life!" or, "Such a one hath wronged me; I wish I knew how to be revenged of him!" Men think to relieve themselves against what annoys them, and is a part of the misery of their present state, by things that would not only be no relief, but make their case far worse. For do you think it would mend your case, or would you be happier men, and safer from eternal death, and from divine justice, that threatens you, or presseth you, if you were rich? If you were never so rich, could you thereby redeem your souls, and expiate your guilt, and make satisfaction to the justice of an offended God? If you could live immersed and swallowed up in pleasure and voluptuousness, would that better your case? Would it not make it far worse? If you had the revenges you would seek; if you could gratify the enmity of your own heart, (which is part of your misery, and a great part too,) by making another man miserable also, would that mend your case? Nay, would it not increase the guilt? Would it not strengthen your bonds, and lay you yet more open to divine displeasure? Again, in the last place, though one might multiply instances of this kind much further,

(6.) They are, for the most part, (so far as their external circumstances will admit of it,) jocund and merry, and very well pleased with their state. How little suitable to this apprehension, "Death hath passed over all." We dwell in a world deluged with misery, and through which, men are generally making way, and sinking deeper and deeper into eternal misery, and into that state wherein death is to be consummate, and in its fulness. To have the opportunity (as there are none but have very frequently) to hear discourses of men, in whom there yet never appeared the least sign or token of repentance or reconciliation with God, how jolly and frolicsome they can be, (if, I say, their external circumstances can admit it,) would you think these men considered themselves as under death, as under a doom from the God against whom they have sinned?

Is it not wondered at, if a condemned crew in chains, and only expecting the hour of execution, should be entertaining themselves with music and dancing, and pleasant stories? how amazing a thing is this! would you not say of such "laughter, it is madness?" and of such "mirth, what doeth it?" as the wise man saith, Eccl. 2. 2. Why such deportments as these, are they like men perishing, going down to perdition? To be pleasant and merry, and not to be reconciled, not yet to be at peace with God, to have no security from the wrath to come; to have death hanging over a man's head, not as the way to glory, but as a doom and curse upon him; and to be jovial and frolicsome under all this, would amaze any man that were serious, to consider that it can be so! And,

4. We may further collect, hence, how little it is that principles do signify, generally, with men. Though those principles be never so common, and never so certain, and evident, yet how little do they signify? That the state of man is a sinful and miserable state, is a common principle; it is a principle that doth obtain, not only among christians, but among pagans; their writings and books are full of it. Most pathetical complaints and lamentations, we frequently meet with, in their books, upon this account, speaking of the degenerate state of man, and that he is not the creature that at first he was; and speaking of his miserable state, and even in a way of *nemesis*, and as the effect of his displeasure, who made him, and hath been offended by him. But among christians, it is so common a principle, that every child that hath learned any thing of his catechism, (as I hope you generally do catechise your children,) if you but ask them, What is the state of man by nature? they will answer, It is a state of sin and misery:—just the very meaning of the text: " Death hath passed over all, for that all have sinned."

But how strange is it now, that so common a principle should signify so little? and again, that so evident and so certain a principle should have so little signification and efficacy with it as a principle? that, though the state of man is a miserable state, and that he lies under death, is matter of fact, it should have no more effect? Indeed, as to the most tremendous part of this death, that is out of sight with many; but, for the more sensible part, that lies open to every one's view. It can be a doubt with no man, whether he shall die or no. Death passeth over all. But how wonderful a thing is it, that a principle, a common principle, a most evident principle, and that carries the greatest certainty with it imaginable, (as to what at least doth highly deserve our consideration,) should be so ineffectual!

And as to the other part, it is generally professed, and they who make it their business, as much as they can, to disbelieve that more dreadful part, that remaining and unseen part of this miserable state, yet have not conquered the fear of it; if they have conquered the belief of it, yet, it is plain, they have not conquered the apprehension of it; there is a *formido opposito*, and cannot but be; for at least they know nothing to the contrary; they can never prove the contrary, that there is no hell, no judgment to come. And, in a matter of this nature, men that would but act according to the common reason of men, would think that the matter did need demonstration; that there is no such thing, and not run a mad hazard and adventure; when there is nothing lost in the course, to which the truth, in this case, (supposing it to be truth,) would lead: and when, by following the contrary course, the misery and mischief that must ensue, are both unsupportable; and will shortly be irretrievable.

LECTURE XXXIV.*

The remaining *Use* that I intend, will be only directive.

1. To such as yet abide in this death, that have passed over all: and we have reason to apprehend that to be the case of some: and, 2. To those that have, through the grace of God, in good measure, escaped out of it,

1. To the first sort, I have a few things to recommend by way of direction. I cannot tell how to apply things to persons particularly: that you must do yourselves, as you find it to be with you. But if that be the case of any among you, that they have reason to judge so, that they abide in this death that have passed upon all, then I would have such,

(1.) To apprehend that this is the common case, and may probably be their own, as to that which is most dismal and horrid in this death, that hath hitherto passed over this world. It is (as I told you the last time) one thing to entertain a truth, as a mere notion in the mind, against which we have nothing to say, and to give but a faint negative assent to it; to wit, not to dissent or disagree to it: and another thing to receive it as a vital and practical principle, that influenceth a man's heart, forms his spirit, and governs his course accordingly thereunto. And so is this very little apprehended to be the common case, that "death hath passed over all." But labour you feelingly to apprehend it, as to what is most obvious every way; that is, that we are all subject to bodily distempers and diseases, which, are tendencies to, and will end in, death: why, about this, we can none of us be in any doubt. We are sensibly told it, even in our flesh and bones, from day to day. But the worst part of this death is what our flesh cannot feel; that is, a death

* Preached Oct. 13, 1694.

upon our spirits; that our minds and hearts are disaffected to God, dead towards God, in direct opposition to what the case is with the regenerate, and which they ought to be judged and reckoned, as to themselves. " Reckon yourselves (saith the apostle, Rom. 6. 11.) dead indeed unto sin, but alive unto God." The death that stands in opposition to this life, is the worst and most horrid part of the death that hath passed over this world.

Labour to apprehend this to be the common case; and then consider, whether it be not your own. If the matter do look with a dubious aspect, it ought to be considered with so much the more attentiveness, and with so much the deeper thoughts. And a slight hope that there is an alteration, should not satisfy: and, indeed, you cannot reasonably think this to be a little thing, or that it should not be greatly considerable. For is it a small matter to have passed from death to life? This death passed over all; and an escape out of it, is not so little a thing, when you compare those two expressions, 1 John 3. 14. " Abiding in death;" and, having " passed from death to life:" it must be a most close and pungent question—"Which is my case? Either I have passed from death to life; or I continue still in death." And, therefore, it ought to be considered over and over, "How stands my case towards God? I have a natural life in me, in which I am capable of natural actions: but have I a holy life in me, by which I am capable of the actions that are suitable and proper to that? by which I can act and move towards God, not *simpliciter* or absolute; but *quoad hoc:* to that one end and principle it was made; for there is a deadness, no propension towards God, as regeneration would make it alive towards God. " How is it with me in this respect?" That ought to be deeply considered. "Is not this, the horrid, dismal death that hath passed upon all, still upon me?" And,

(2.) There is this further, that will be suitable by way of direction to that former case, to mind those things principally, that are most pertinent to it; and to be less concerned about lesser things. And pray let such take in this direction: Have you reason to apprehend this to be your case; (and a fearful case it is;) that that death, even the worst of it, that hath passed over all, remains upon you? Why, then think of those things that are most pertinent to that case; and consider less the lesser things. As to whatsoever you have to complain of besides, say with yourselves, " Aye, but all this is nothing to this death that is upon my soul;" and it looks like distraction, when men's minds are wholly engaged and taken up about lesser things: but, about this greater and more important thing, they have no consideration at all. As if one should seem concerned that he hath a scratched finger; when he hath a mortal wound in his breast that he is unconcerned for: or, that he should have lost a pin, when his house is on fire; or, that a man's head should lie easy upon the block, when the fatal stroke is just going to be given. For, do but consider what this will come to at length: this death will be eternal death. The disinclination and deadness of man's spirit towards God, can have no other issue, finally, but "Depart from me," if it continue. You are departing from God; you will be continually departing: why, Depart from me for ever. This sort of death upon the souls of men, it is not a distinct thing from the state of hell; it is the same thing begun: there is no further difference than between death inchoate, and death consummate. And, indeed, every thing that a man doth, and every thing that a man saith, is all idle impertinency, while this great thing is neglected. "Seek first the kingdom of God and his righteousness," is the advice of our Saviour. You are seeking many other things; but have you observed the order, to seek that in the first place? Otherwise you have mistaken the order. What other things you may lawfully seek, you are then to seek, when you have begun duly and regularly, with the first. And, therefore, if another should tell you of such and such things that are not so well in the state of your case externally: such a man hath failed, that owes you money, or the like, you may answer him; "Alas! do not tell me of these things, I am dead towards God, what do you tell me of this or that? I am like to be lost for ever, if grace do not give a speedy help to the sad state of my case." And again,

(3.) Look upon this case of your's as being, though very sad, yet not remediless, yet not incurable; look upon it as a remediable case. For it is, indeed, all one as to any thing of real gain and advantage, not to apprehend your case to be sad, and not to consider it as capable of a remedy. Upon the former supposition, there will be no care at all exercised about it; and upon the latter supposition there will be no hope. But there must be a setting of both these on foot; you must have a care about the state of your souls; and you must have hope about it too; or else nothing will be done in you, or by you, that will be of any value. You should, therefore, consider and bethink yourselves, that there is a way of escape out of so great a death; that many have escaped you know; and they can think of it with pleasure, and take delight in their knowing of God, and conversing with him. Divers that have (it may be) spoken to you of such things of God, as you have not found in yourselves. But that which hath been, may be: that which you see by frequent experience wrought in others, may be wrought in you. God, that hath been so rich in mercy to others, why may he not be God, rich in mercy to you also?

Thus you should consider the matter as capable of a remedy. There is a word of life sent forth; and there is a Divine Spirit breathing in this world; even upon this world that is lost in death: and it hath reached many with mighty influences. This is that which ought to be a mighty spring of hope to such as will not abandon themselves to despair. Do not say concerning yourselves, "There is a death abiding upon my soul, and therefore, it must be always so:" for that is to suppose there is no difference between earth and hell; between the state of men under the gospel, and the state of devils under an eternal doom, in the full execution of it.

I pray consider, our business is not to instruct the inhabitants of hell, but to speak to the living on this side the grave. We are teaching men, and not devils. And none should put themselves into their state and case, as if they had nothing at all to do, but merely to wait till the fulness of death should come upon them, and swallow them up. Our Lord saith, "Look unto me and be ye saved, all ye ends of the earth." And when such a voice as this hath come into this miserable earth, no man ought but to look upon himself as concerned therein, as well as others; and not to say, "God doth not mean me; he intends no such kindness to me:" but rather, on the other hand, to say, "If a vital savour hath been diffused with that voice, with that invitation of grace, in and by the word, and its vital influences have reached many, it may also reach me." There ought to be an expectation raised in us, that it may: and many are ruined for not expecting it, not waiting at the posts of wisdom's door. Prov. 8. 34, 35. "Blessed is the man that heareth me, watching daily at my gates, waiting at the posts of my door. For whoso findeth me, findeth life, and shall obtain favour of the Lord." This, men ought to set before their eyes, in all their attendances upon God, in his ordinances; so that they may be able to give this account, if any should ask them, What are you going for? "Why, I am going to find life; wisdom saith, They that find me, find life. Here I go to seek life for my soul."

The very order of the divine precept in this thing, is, "Hear, and your souls shall live;" which shews with what design men should hear and wait upon ordinances. "Ho! every one that thirsteth, come ye to the waters; come ye buy and eat, yea, come buy wine and milk without money and without price, hear and your souls shall live; and I will make an everlasting covenant with you." "He hath made with me an everlasting covenant, (were David's own dying words) ordered in all things and sure; and although my house be not so with God; as to domestical concernments things are not so well, yet he hath made with me an everlasting covenant; and this is all my salvation, and all my desire." Now saith the prophet, in that Isaiah 55. 3. "Do you but incline your ear, and hear with expectation that your souls may live, and they shall live: and this will tend to bring you into an everlasting covenant, even the sure mercies of David." And yet, again,

(4.) Let me further recommend this to you, to hasten your designed escape, without deliberating and pausing long upon the matter. We are to look upon this world as deluged by death and wrath, which have overspread it, as that sulphureous flood did the valleys wherein Sodom and Gomorrah stood; and when Lot was to be saved out of that ruin, in mercy to him, for this the angel hastens him, and cries out to him, "Escape for thy life." So should you consider the exigency of your case not to be less; nay it is incomparably greater. It is not a little valley, but it is the world, that is deluged with this sulphureous flood. Here is a complication of sin and death overflowing the world; and which hath made the world a far worse region than that plain was. Now it is said to you; God doth by the voice of his word, and of his ministers, say to you, "You are to make haste and escape for your life." How many did the fiery flood of Sodom overtake quite! Therefore, this case doth not admit of any delay: for how soon this flood may overtake you, you know not. It may, so as to overwhelm you quite: and so as to make a hopeful case a desperate one. And, therefore, consider from hence, in the next place,

(5.) Of how great importance it is for you to apply yourselves to, and gain an interest in, the favour of God. Make from hence an estimate of the divine favour, and of the necessity and value of it; for if this be your case—Death hath passed over all; if any man thinks of an escape, from thence it must come: "What can I do for my soul? How can I fetch my soul from that death that is within me; that my soul is ingulphed in?" Why, "in his favour is life." There is no hope of life but in his favour. Look which way you will, and there is death overwhelming of all; and you are no more capable of getting out of this death of yourselves, than of touching the heavens with your hand, or seating yourselves among the stars in the firmament: therefore, it must be an all-favourable, and all-powerful hand, and that too, stretched out from heaven, that must save in so distressed a case as this.

Now how should this recommend to us the favour of God, as that wherein our life doth stand, when death hath thus passed over all. If you should speak to a neighbour, to a father, to any one that hath the dearest affection to you, "O! my soul is in a state of death: how shall I get it out of it?" They must all answer, as Jacob did to his wife, "Am I in the stead of God, to give thee children? Can I inspire life into thy dead soul? No; I cannot do it for thee." This you ought to inculcate to yourselves, over and over; that your life stands in the divine favour. It is he that breathes into you the breath of spiritual life, to make yours become a living soul. They are his kind looks that carry life in them. If he will breathe upon your soul, it shall live. As that hath been his way, when souls have been wallowing in their blood, to look upon them with a kind look, and say unto them—" Live:" his look doth carry life in it. He looks life into the soul that is dead. As in that 16 Ezekiel, in the beginning, and towards the latter end of that chapter, you will find how the matter ends: " I entered into a covenant with thee, and thou becamest mine." He looked upon them in their blood, and said unto them—" Live;" and enclosed them in the happy bonds of that covenant, that are vital bonds; their souls being bound up in the bundle of life. And, therefore,

(6.) That I may shut up what I shall say to this sort of persons concerning that death which hath passed over all, it ought to prepare them for the reception of the gospel, wherein are discoveries of the divine favour, and the way wherein it reveals itself for the saving and renewing of souls lost in death: what a preparative for the gospel should this be! To have this inwrought into my soul, that death hath passed over all, so amongst the rest, it hath passed over me, involved me also. Then how pleasant a sound should the gospel be to lost souls! "The Son of man came to seek and save that which was lost." The forlorn and distressed estate of this world, hath been compassionately considered by the great Lord of heaven and earth; and God hath given him life, that he might give eternal life to as many as he hath given him. And when men are once prevailed upon, to give themselves to him, as the great Prince and Lord of life, who only can deliver them out of death, then, it is without question, that God hath given them unto him, and it is with that design, that he may give them eternal life. But then,

2. As to those who through grace, have in a good measure made an escape out of that death that hath passed over all, it is obvious to yourselves, to understand wherein that death stands, which hath passed over all, and which you have made your escape from. You know, that part of it concerns the outward man; there is no escaping that which is equivalent, and more than equivalent. There is an escaping out of it; not that such shall not die, but they shall rise again: "their corruptible part, (as the apostle saith) shall put on incorruption: and their mortal part shall put on immortality; and their vile bodies shall be changed and transformed into the likeness of Christ's most glorious body." There must be a conformity between the Head and the members, so that by him they escape not from it, but out of it; emerge, get out of that state, that must sooner or later seize upon these mortal bodies.

But then, for that spiritual death that is, in this present state, naturally upon all men's souls, that you have been actually in, that you have escaped, that there must be an escape from eternal death. Now let me ask you, Have you, through grace, been enabled to escape, in good measure, out of the worst of this death that, in the present state, men are liable to; to wit, death towards God? Then, if the matter be so, there are several things I would recommend to you, and so put an end to this discourse.

(1.) Be much in grateful acknowledgment of God's wonderful mercy; make that much the great business of your lives, for it is a great thing God hath done for you, in that he hath delivered you from so great a death! think what the state and posture of your souls once was God-ward. "Why, let me have heard never so much of the most glorious, the most excellent of all Beings, in which all the excellencies of all beings did meet together, infinite love, and light, and life and purity, and holiness; yet, alas! I had no inclination towards him; no desire after him; no complacency in him; my soul was as a stone, or stick, or a log, without sense, without motion. God-ward. I have heard (it may be) of his name often; but it never carried a pleasant sound to me. It was no pleasure to me, to go and shut up myself in a closet, and pour out my soul unto him. As for taking complacency in him as my best Good, so as to account him my exceeding great Joy; Alas! I knew not what this meant. It was a soul that might have been a stone, as well as a soul as to any inclination it had Godward. But, O! blessed be God, that it is otherwise! When

I hear of that very Sacred Name, it transports my soul, to think that All of being, and blessedness, and wisdom, and purity, and light, and love, is mine. And if all the world should frown on me, and he give me but one smile, it is as life to my soul. Now, the very seasons of my converse with him, are as my repasts. What pleasure do I take when the sabbath is come; when the light of that holy day doth dawn upon me! Formerly, I knew not what to design for God. Now my end is the glory of God: if I can but speak a good word for his honour and interest, it falls in with the inclination of my spirit."

Why sure, if this be the case with you, it is the most inexcusable thing in all the world, that there should be no more of gratitude for so great a change wrought in you. Consider that God, in so altering the case, hath done that for you, which all the world could not have done. Lay all the powers of men on earth, and of all the angels in heaven together, they could never have made your hearts to love God, or desire after him, or delight in him. But he hath touched your hearts with a vital touch, and made them love him, and live to him.

When the difference is so vast (as I was saying to you lately) between abiding in death, and having passed from death to life, (and, whereas, every one must be in one of these two states; so that every one must say, either " I do abide in death," or " I have passed from death to life,") if we, by gracious vouchsafement, are passed from death to life, if this be our case, and we are not much in thanksgiving; O! how inexcusable is this! And, christians, I would have you to consider this, that this it is which starves religion, and is the reason why, where it is, it languisheth; for want of this exercise of thanksgiving. And know, that where such praises are ascending to heaven, benedictions will be also descending from heaven. Were there more of these acknowledgments, how would blessings descend! O! we should be more in blessing of God for heavenly things in Christ Jesus; that we should have that opportunity, from day to day, of beholding death spreading abroad its dark shadows over all the intellectual world, to wit, over the minds and spirits of men, and, I was myself a sad instance thereof: but God hath delivered me out of this miserable state; O! not to be much in thanksgiving, is the most inexcusable temper that can be! But again,

(2.) You ought, hereupon, more to pity the miserable world that is yet in death, over which death hath passed, and in which it abides. There is altogether a fault among us upon this account; we want bowels, we have not compassions, as we ought to have within us, towards perishing creatures.

"Blessed are the merciful, for they shall obtain mercy." It is a great evidence of our having obtained mercy, our being merciful in this kind. But to be destitute of compassion for the sad case of dead souls, is a sad symptom. To say, I have a husband, a wife, a child, that are under the power of death, have nothing of the life of God, no favour of God, no fear of God, in them; nothing that looks like the grace of God; why, not to compassionate them, sure, such a frame as this hath in it no indication of divine life springing in us: we see them, and converse with them, but seldom have a regretting thought that toucheth our hearts: this is, sure, altogether a fault, and knows no excuse, admits of none. It argues, at least, a very great languor of the divine life in us, when we have so little a sense of so horrid a death, as lies upon the generality of the world. Those, in whom this divine life doth take place, they are regenerated after God's own image: and that must intimate to them to be like minded with him. God hath shewed mercy unto us, and, therefore, mercy was his nature, it is in the highest perfection in him. If I am transformed after his image, I must imitate him in this. If I have nothing of the divine offspring in me, how am I his child? And, if I have, why should it not operate in me in this kind, in reference to those that were in the same case with me, before I obtained mercy. And again,

(3.) If you have, through the grace of God, in a good degree, escaped out of that fearful state of death, which abides generally upon the world, make little reckoning in comparison of what you suffer in lower kinds, and in lesser respects, whatsoever you have to complain of upon other accounts. Let not the sense of lesser evils enter deep into your souls. He hath saved you from the greater evils: he delivered you out of that so great a death, which overwhelmed you and all the world. It is then, very disingenuous to complain of lesser and smaller things, when, from the greatest evils of all, he hath saved us. As the apostle saith, 2 Tim. 1. 9. "Who hath saved us and called us with a holy calling." Saved already in a degree, and, by saving us in that degree, hath made eternal salvation as sure as if we were in heaven already. And therefore, I say, reckon little of these lesser evils that may befal you in this present state. And, in the last place,

(4.) It is very suitable to such, further to consider, that the rest of the evils of the world ought not to be considered as strange, when it is to be remembered, that a universal death hath passed over all men. That such and such evils should befal in this world, should not be thought strange, since this death hath passed over all. We hear of a great mortality (it may be) in such a country, and of a great many lives cut off in a battle, in another country. There ought to be bowels of compassion upon that account; otherwise we have put off humanity. But it is a great madness that we should make a greater matter of these things, and, at the same time, make nothing of that universal death that hath passed over all. Where are our minds, that we do not weigh the difference of things?*

I have one thing more, before I pass to the doctrine of a Mediator, and God's method of saving souls. And I desire to speak to it from another text. And that is, to vindicate the justice of God as to this sad and calamitous state, that is universal upon mankind, by reason of the fall.

---

* In the commencement of this subject, a III. Head was proposed —the consecution of death upon the fall—(vide page 342 and 356,) which the Author has not discussed separately; but the attentive reader will perceive it is kept in view in the preceding and the following Lecture.

EDITOR.

THE JUSTICE AND RIGHTEOUSNESS OF GOD, VINDICATED,

As to all men's coming into the world with sinful depraved natures from the womb.

LECTURE XXXV.*

Psalm 51, 4. 5.

Against thee, thee only, have I sinned, and done this evil in thy sight: that thou mightest be justified when thou speakest, and be clear when thou judgest. Behold, I was shapen in iniquity; and in sin did my mother conceive me.

HAVING discoursed to you at large from that Rom. 5. 12. concerning the fall of the first man, and the entrance of sin and death into the world, thereupon, I told you in the conclusion of the last discourse on that subject, my further intention was to say something for the clearing of the Divine Justice, in reference hereunto: and it is a debt, a right that we owe to the Supreme Ruler and Lord of all, not only to confess his righteousness, but, as occasion serves and requires, to vindicate it too. We cannot be just ourselves, if we do not, to our utmost, in all things, justify him.

My design is not, from this scripture, to speak absolutely of the corruption and depravedness of the human nature, which I did before, from that mentioned scripture. But to speak of it relatively and comparatively, in reference to the righteousness of God, or so far as that may appear any way concerned in the

* Preached Oct. 20, 1694.

matter. And indeed, it might be thought, there lay before, a very unexceptionable state of the case between God and man, in that scripture that I last, and so long insisted on; which makes death only to have followed sin into the world. And what can be more natural than the connexion of sin and death, or the consecution of the latter upon the former, that death should only be said to have entered into the world, and to have passed over all, inasmuch as all have sinned.

But men's curiosity doth not rest here, while they will not pretend to deny the actual consecution of death upon sin; they make a great deal of difficulty to understand how sin should follow upon innocency. And here the difficulty is not so great neither, concerning the lapse of the first man, and the death following upon that as to him; as also the case hath no appearance of difficulty concerning the angels that fell, when (as the case was with the first man) every one offended in his own person, and so was in his own person to answer for the offence. But that that makes the difficulty is, that men should be generally involved in sin and ruin, upon the lapse and fall of one, (their common parent) when they could not help it that they were his children, or that they were born of such progenitors, that all should be undone by a fault which they could not prevent, and unto which they had no accession.

This difficulty hath cast divers men upon distressing thoughts. Some have thereupon denied the corruption and depravity of human nature; and they might as well deny that there are men upon earth. Some would have the souls of men (the only capable subjects of sin) to be propagated as the bodily part is, which would hazard the doctrine of their immortality. Others have had their other conjectures, which I shall not mention.

But, upon the whole, we ought not only to censure with indulgence, but to commend and praise the spirit and practice of such, in reference to this matter, as have, with sincere and unbiassed minds, set their understandings on work, how best to maintain high and honourable thoughts of God; that have been studious to find out, or apt to entertain any hypothesis that might be more suitable unto that. This (I say) is not only to be censured indulgently, but to be commended very highly, provided that men do not, herein, run counter to express Divine Revelation and unto uncontrolable experience. And that they be not so over-officious as to affix characters upon the blessed God, under the name of perfections belonging to his nature, which do not truly or really so belong, and which he never owned or claimed as such.

It is very plain, that this holy Psalmist had seen through this difficulty, he saw with better eyes than the most; more sincere, less malevolent; and had digested the matter in his thoughts, otherwise he would never have laid down these two things thus together as we find, "That thou mayest be justified when thou speakest, and be clear when thou judgest. Behold, I was shapen in iniquity, and in sin did my mother conceive me." He, at least, thought these things very agreeable with one another, if rather, he did not bring in the latter as a proof and demonstration of the former, which the demonstrative particle prefixed (Behold) would lead one to think.

But let us, first, view the words a little in themselves, and we shall discern the schesis and reference to one another, a little better thereby, afterwards. That which is here, in this place, rendered actively, is in the 3 chapter to the Romans, rendered passively, that thou mightest be justified in thy hen sayings and overcome when thou judgest;" there it is, "w wed thou art judged," as we read it, the septuagint being follo (as (as frequently it is) by the apostle. But I cannot apprehend of some do note) any need of a different reading in the letter either text, as some critics take notice, the Hebrew affix being set as there it is, may indifferently be read, either actively or passively. And so may the Greek word, as is most evident, and so we may render either place, either way; and all will come to one and the same sense; that God may appear just, that his justice may be triumphant and victorious, whether it be when he judgeth; or when men judge and censure him, and his proceedings.

And so the current of this discourse of the Psalmist will be plain and clear: "I acknowledge mine iniquity, and my sin is ever before me; against thee only have I sinned: that thou mayest be justified when thou speakest"—that is, referring to the 3 verse, "I acknowledge," (as here I do,) then the acknowledgment follows, "that thou mayest be justified." "I make my acknowledgments so and so, that thou mayest be justified when thou speakest, or mayest overcome when thou judgest, or when men presume or take upon them to censure thy proceedings towards me; though thou shouldest proceed with all the severity that thou hast threatened by the prophet sent unto me: for not only have I done this particular evil against thee, and in thy sight, but I have been an impure creature, even from my own original: thou hast much against me, not only for this single instance, but as I came a sinful polluted creature into the world: I was shapen in iniquity, formed, turned therein; as soon as I grew warm in the womb, (as the word signifies) so soon sin did insinuate into my very *præ-mordia*, into the very *principles* of my being."

And to the same purpose is this passage quoted by the apostle, in that mentioned Romans 3. 4. for when he had been charging sin, before, upon all the world, on the Gentiles, in the 1 chapter, and on the Jews, in the 2. he only puts a question in the beginning of the 3 chapter, " What advantage then hath the Jew, if all be found equally under sin ?" And he only admits them to have an advantage in order to their recovery, but none at all as to their degeneracy. In reference to their recovery they had a great advantage, inasmuch, as to them were committed the Oracles of God, the discovery of his counsel and way for the reconciling and saving lost sinners. But he considers nothing, in reference to what he had asserted of their part and share in the common depravation and apostasy; they were as bad as the best.

Then he immediately lays down what is quoted from the Psalmist, and makes that his scope and mark in all the rest of the chapter, that is, to justify God; that he might be justified, and overcome in all his pleadings and judgings : or when man should implead or take upon him to censure God, that still his justice might be victorious and triumphant. This is the mark, that he aims at manifestly, in all his following discourse; shewing at large, the universal depravation and corruption of human nature every where; having proved (as he saith at the 9th verse) concerning both Jews and Gentiles (which did then divide the world) that they were all under sin.

Indeed, the immediate subjoining of this unto the mention of the design in this psalm, seems to carry this aspect with it, that the Psalmist intended to speak or introduce the mention of this depravedness and corruption of human nature, (even as it was in himself) as a proof and evidence of the divine justice, as that which might tend to clear it so much the more. But at least, it must be collected from his subjoining the mention of the latter to the former, that he looked upon them as very consistent, and very reconcileable things, as things that carried no repugnancy in them to one another. And even this, will serve my present purpose and design. So that all which I shall observe from this context, and the connexion of these two, herein, shall be this,—

That it is very consistent with the justice of God, and very reconcileable to it, most reconcileable to it, that men, born of human parentage, do universally come into this world impure and polluted creatures, even from the womb.—

The Psalmist did not so much as imagine (you may see) an inconsistency between the corruption of nature in man, and the justice of God, in that he so lays them down by one another. Surely (thinks he) these cannot quarrel, no man can reasonably think they will; they are to be looked upon, and ought to be looked upon, as sociable truths, that can agree well together, even these two, that man from the womb is an impure, sinful creature: and God is everlastingly and immutably a holy and righteous God.

Now, in speaking to this, I shall reduce all that I intend, unto a Four-fold Conclusion. And shall gather up all, under these four; As,

I. There can be no real opposition between truth and truth. And so, that whatsoever we are convinced of is truth, another truth that we are equally as certain of, cannot be opposite thereunto. If there be any such appearance, it is but a false appearance, it is only a seemingness of opposition and contrariety, but really there can be no such thing. And,

II. That we may be most certain, that many things are, when, how they are, or come to be as they are, is by us unexplicable and unaccountable. And,

III That it would be very unreasonable to oppose and object dubious and uncertain things, against what is sure and plain, and most certain. And,

IV. That it will be, especially, most unreasonable to oppose uncertain to certain things, when there are many considerations capable of being alleged that will break the force of such objections. But nothing can be alleged to shake the certainty and firmness of the foresaid truths. Then it will be most of all unreasonable.

Unto these *four conclusions*, I shall reduce what I intend, and what I think reasonable to be said to this matter.

I. That truth can never be opposite to truth: and that therefore, what things we are most certain of as true, they can lie in no opposition to one another. But whatsoever of such appearance there may be, must be a false appearance. I instance, here, in these two things, that we are concerned to reconcile,—the perfection of the Divine Nature (comprehending his justice) and—the sinful imperfection and pravity of the human nature. These are both most certain truths; and, therefore, it is impossible they can be really opposite to one another.

1. The absolute perfection of the Divine Nature, comprehending his justice, which must be one great perfection belonging thereunto. It is that indeed which, by the ducture of the text, we are principally concerned to vindicate, and so we are, indeed, any divine perfection against which the doctrine afterwards asserted may seem to militate. Every one will grant, that acknowledgeth a God, that justice must be a perfection

belonging to his nature. And we may, these two ways, be most absolutely ascertained hereof.

(1.) That whatsoever doth belong to God, belongs to him essentially: his nature can receive no additions nor diminutions, and consequently is immutably so; can no more cease to be so, than he can lie, or do any ill thing; nor this, more than he can cease to be; because all perfection (and that of justice among the rest) belongs unto him essentially. So that he can no more cease to be just, than cease to be God. And,

(2.) Of this we may be ascertained further, thus, that whereas, justice is a virtue inclining a person to give to every one his due, that which is owing to him, rightly belongs to him, God cannot be a debtor to his creature, otherwise than by voluntary obligation that he takes upon himself. No one can be a debtor to another but one of these two ways; either naturally, or by some other sort of contract. He is, indeed, naturally a debtor who is possessed of somewhat that doth belong to another, that was originally his, and to which he retains a right: a man is in this case naturally a debtor to such a one by the immediate law of nature, to give him his own, or a full equivalent that he shall be satisfied is so. But so it is altogether impossible that God can be a debtor to his creature, who, (as the apostle speaks, upon another account, 17 Acts,) hath given to all life and breath, and all things. They can be proprietors of nothing, in opposition to him or against him, that are not masters of themselves, or of their own being. They owe him their all; to them there can be owing nothing; that is, not from him, to whom they themselves owe their very all. It is a just challenge, therefore, that is given to all the world by the apostle; Rom. 11. 35. "Who hath first given to him, and it shall be recompensed unto him again?" Produce me the man that can say, "God is a debtor, that he hath given him this or that, for which he is owing to him, let any man produce his claim, and it shall be recompensed to him again." So that, naturally, God cannot be a debtor to his creatures.

And then, if we speak of the second way of his being a debtor, God hath never obliged himself to keep sin out of the creation, so as that he should break with his creatures, and do them wrong, in not doing all that was possible to omnipotency to make them impenable. Shew the obligation, produce the bond, Where is it? If this were to be alleged, He broke with his reasonable creatures at first, in making them free, in infecting liberty into their natures: why he never laid himself under any obligation against this. And therefore, it is every way most evident, that God must be immutably and unalterably just in all his dispensations; and particularly in this, in not hindering that sin should come into the world, and draw death after it, and spread itself through the world, (as we find it hath done,) still drawing on, and attracting death. And,

2. On the other hand, it is a most clear and certain truth, that as the nature of God is most absolutely and unalterably perfect, including all perfection, and that of justice unalterably among the rest; so, the nature of man is, in this present state, and from the very original of individual persons, sinfully imperfect; and they come into the world impure and polluted creatures from the womb. The justice of God is not to be solved that way, by denying that there is such a corruption and depravity of nature, transmitted even with the nature of man itself from age to age, as therein is comprehended both a negative part, a disinclination to all good; and a positive, an inclination to all evil. And that this also may be in our minds as a certain truth, I shall insist a little, and but a little, upon it. It not being my design (as I said) to do what hath been already done, to insist purposely upon the corruption of human nature absolutely, but only relatively and comparatively, according to what reference this matter may bear to the righteousness of God's dealings with men. And to evince this,

(1.) It is the most plain and express language of the Scripture. And what ought to determine in such a case? what could determine us but that? There is not another tolerable sense to be put on these words, "I was shapen in iniquity, and in sin did my mother conceive me." It is most unreasonable and absurd, to pretend this to be only a particular acknowledgment of David concerning himself: as if he had the most unhappy procreation of all mankind; as if there were more corruption, or another way to convey corruption to him from his parents, than was with all the rest of men. It can carry no meaning, but that he doth involve his own in the common case, that it was only with him, in this respect, as it is with all others, that they are, (as the expression is in John 9. 34,) altogether born in sin, all unclean. And it was, therefore, impossible that any thing clean should come out of them. "Who can bring a clean thing out of an unclean? Not one." And you have the same thing more expressly asserted in general terms, in the 58 psalm; "The wicked are estranged from the womb, they go astray as soon as they are born, speaking lies." And sure, every man is wicked till he is converted, till he be regenerate and turn to God. Therefore, it must be an affirmation concerning all mankind, that they are estranged from the very womb, averse and disaffected to every thing that is good; and propense to that which is evil, as the following words signify: they go astray as soon as they are born, speaking lies; made up of falsehood, even from their original. And,

(2.) The Scripture doth, in multitudes of places, speak of the universal actual sinfulness of the world: and whence should that come? In that 3 chapter of Romans, how often it is inculcated. I have proved (saith the apostle) Jews and Gentiles to be all under sin: and they were all the world. And all have sinned and come short of the glory of God; (afterwards in the same chapter 19.) and, that every mouth may be stopped, and all the world become guilty before God. Now, this being plainly asserted in the word of truth, how should this actual sinfulness begin with every one, so as to be universal? If it were only by imitation and example, it is strange that all should imitate the sin, but none follow the better examples, which, when renewing grace hath done its work, do come to be extant and appear in view, so as that many do carry it (through the grace of God) without visible scandalous enormities. But that which is so universally common, must have some common cause. The reason of the thing speaks itself: when there is not an instance to be found of any one that hath lived without sin, how should this be, but that it hath and must have sprung up with them? must have come with their nature, their very nature itself? for it is as common as their nature. And we may,

(3.) Argue from experience, that such a corruption and pravity as this, doth spring up with men and all human creatures, that come into this world, the ordinary way: that is, we cannot name the time when such are capable of acting electively or rationally, but they are of acting sinfully as soon. Doth not every one's experience tell him so? That there are disinclinations to that which is good, and inclinations to that which is evil, appearing most early; peevishness, crossness, pride, strife, falsehood, a disposition to lie, to be revengeful and vindictive; nothing is plainer; so that to deny the pravity of nature, even from men's *primordia*, is all one, as to say there are not such natures in being. And then,

(4.) We may argue, too, from the manifest subjection and liableness of infants, even in their infancy, unto punitive strokes; sickness, pains, and death itself. Wherein is this, that the infant age is not exempt, if it be innocent, if it hath nothing of impurity and pravity adhering to it? If here it be said by way of reply to this, that " we find the inferior creatures, brute creatures are liable to the same thing; sickness, and pain, and death, but that doth not prove them to be sinful, or that they have any sinfulness adhering to them;" why the case is so manifestly different, that it is an easy matter for the objector, if he please, (whosoever he be,) to answer himself. It is plain, death was never a threatening to them: it is plain that the brute creatures, as they grow up, do not come to sin at last, they never sin, nor are ever capable of it. And if, therefore, it should be said, that such infirmities, ails, maladies and mortality itself, are afflictions only, and not penalties, I would fain know whether that do not equally reflect upon the divine justice, (of which such do seem to be so tender,) and a great deal more, to afflict a creature which is at the same time asserted to be innocent, every way innocent; doth not carry a worse face, a worse aspect with it, than to assert this creature to be nocent? And to say, these things are not punitive, but afflictive, is but a notional difference; and the notion doth neither do them good nor harm; neither makes the affliction less or more. But sure, it is more honourable for God to say, that, observing the impure and depraved state of human nature, even from its very original, he animadverts upon that impurity. As why should not the holy God express a displeasancy with every impurity wherever he finds it? And no man accuseth another of any injustice if he do destroy a creature as soon as it begins to live, that is known to be noxious, hurtful and mischievous; as the crushing of serpents in the very egg; when this is so apparent, that there are so noxious qualities, which there is nothing but want of opportunity and time that hinders their exertion in noxious and hurtful acts. To express a displeasancy towards the innate disposition, can be no way unworthy of God. But that we shall have occasion to speak of more hereafter.

In the mean time, this is the First Head proposed—that truth cannot be opposite to truth.—And therefore, we being ascertained of this twofold truth, that God is most perfectly and unalterably just, and that man is sinfully imperfect and impure, from his original, that is, the original of the individuals, these two cannot be opposite to one another: one truth cannot destroy another truth, or impart any repugnancy thereunto. And therefore, if there be any appearance of contrariety between these two, it must be but a false appearance. For of these things we are most certain; they are undoubted truths. Therefore, to solve the phœnomenon, we must look another way, and there will be opportunity for that, in speaking to the following conclusions. In the meantime, let these two things be inlaid deeply in our souls, that God is absolutely and every way perfect, so as that, that perfection of his must include the most unalterable eternal righteousness and justice; but that we for our parts are, from our original, impure and polluted creatures, that there may be, accordingly, suitable dispositions in us to acknowledge and adore his righteousness; and to own and abhor our own impurities: to walk humbly in the sense of them as long as we live, and to have so much the more disposition to admire that grace, which hath its exercise towards such creatures as we, when in point of justice there was enough against us to have produced, for ever, all the exercises of such grace.

LECTURE XXXVI.*

II. Now I go on to the next *conclusion*, which is the second in order, namely—That we may be most certain that many things really are, when the manner how they are, or how they came to be, is not understood by the most, or may be of very difficult explication unto any—And to accommodate this to the present purpose I shall proceed by steps.

1. It is very plain that there is a cloud and darkness generally sitting upon, or a veil is generally drawn over the inceptions of things of whatsoever kind, as to how things of any sort, do take their first beginnings. It is observable that, usually, a veil is drawn over those things. Look into all the productions of nature, how things do take their first rise, it is generally very inexplicable, and very unconceivable, at least as to the generality. For such substantial beings as are most sensible to us, as we see with our eyes, or touch with our hands; so that there can be no place or room for any doubt, but that such things are; yet how they came to be, who can give an account? We can none of us be in doubt but there are really these heavens over our heads, which our eyes see from day to day; and this earth underneath us, which we may touch when we please. But if God had not given us a general account of the Genesis, of the beginning of the heavens and the earth, at what a loss would men have been every where? And at what a loss generally are they, how man himself began to be in this world, where they have not the ducture of Revelation in the case, to assist and help them? To think what ridiculous accounts, some of the wise and learned philosophers of this world have given of the very inception of man-

* Preached October 27, 1694.

kind, it shews there is a veil, especially over the beginnings of things, when of the things themselves, there is the greatest certainty imaginable. As who can make any man doubt whether there be such heavens as we behold, or such an earth as we walk upon, though we should never have known, if God had not told us, how they began. And to go a little further,

2. We are most certain of many acts; and abilities and dispositions thereunto; which actions, how they are performed, very few can give an account; and where the dispositions thereunto did arise, they can as little tell. We know that we can see with our eyes, and that we can hear with our ears; and that such actions are performed by those very organs that are used for these purposes. But how few can tell how this act of vision is performed, or can give an account of the structure of that organ of the eye by which it is performed? And so, how the action of hearing is done, and of the aptitude of the organ of the ear thereunto? But we certainly know that we see, and that we hear; and that we see with our eyes, and not with our hands; and hear with our ears, and not with our feet.

And so, for acts of understanding; we know that we do know; we know, and are certain that we do exert acts of reason, that we use thoughts, but who can tell how a thought arises in a man's mind, and how men come to have the seeing, and hearing, and speaking, and reasoning power and faculty transmitted from age to age, and from generation to generation? That there should arise still from age to age such a sort of creatures as have these faculties and powers belonging to them, of that we can give as little account, as how grass, and herbs, and flowers do spring up of their proper seeds upon this earth, from year to year. But of the things themselves, we have the greatest certainty that may be. And to proceed further,

3. Concerning *sinful* acts and dispositions, we can be in as little doubt that such things there really are, though there be here a greater difficulty how they came to be. It is true, that this question vexed some of the wisest, and most learned, and most considering of mankind; before Christianity took place among them; since there was nothing but what was good at first, how should there come to be any such thing as evil in the world? And indeed, the counsel given, was wise and wholesome, rather to consider how sin may be got out of the world, than how it came into it. But there is a necessity upon us, to endeavour, to our utmost, the maintaining and keeping up high and honourable thoughts of God, as that upon which all religion

depends, and without which, men will have a pretence to let it vanish out of the world; yea, and endeavour to make it so to do.

But whatsoever difficulty we may suppose in this case, the matter of fact is plain and evident; that is, we do find that there is such a generation of creatures, that do spring up in the world, from age to age, that are together both reasonable and sinful, as they could not be the latter without being the former. This is plain matter of fact, that a sort of creatures, which do exercise reason, do also sin from age to age, and universally: and that this, their disposition to sin, and their actual sinning, must have a beginning: and it cannot have beginning, but from some common and universal cause, being itself universal; so as that there are no instances to be found where (if there be an opportunity) a disposition to sin, doth not betray itself; so as that men are not more inclined to act rationally, than they are to act irregularly. They act rationally in many instances, they act irregularly in greater instances, and more important, and that constantly, in all times, and all parts of the world. This is plain matter of fact; and men do, therefore, fill their own souls, and fill the world, with confusions and miseries.

This (I say) is all plain matter of fact. We cannot be more certain of any thing, than we are of this; that is, that men have so much reason still remaining, and belonging to their nature, as by which they are capable of knowing they were not self-made, not self-originate, that they came from another, that they owe their all to an infinitely perfect Being; that must have all perfection in itself, and all being originally in itself, and that their interests are someway or other involved within one another. And they are, thereupon, capable of understanding their own obligation to love God above all; and to love one another as themselves. Very plain it is, if men did but act pursuantly to such apprehensions, whereof it is most apparent their nature is capable, they would pass their days, here in this world, in very great tranquillity and felicity, within themselves, and towards one another; and, that it is impossible that those miseries, and those evils and confusions which fill men's spirits, and fill the world, should arise from any thing else but the inclination that is in them to do otherwise; not to love God with a supreme love, and not to love one another with co-ordinate love. So that this is as plain matter of fact, as that there is a world, or that there are reasonable creatures in it. This hath always been a difficulty, how (as to some particular persons especially) sin should have its beginning, when that it hath its continual being in the world proves itself to every one's sad experience and observation, that doth but take notice of himself and the world. But yet,

4. Though, how sin is transmitted to particular and individual persons, from generation to generation, it cannot be so easily told, yet it may, most certainly, be determined how it is not (which most concerns us with reference to our present purpose, to vindicate the righteousness of God) that is, that it is man's creature, and not God's. It is not he that hath infused any thing of evil or malignity into the nature of man, which was originally pure and perfect as it sprang from him, the Author of all nature. This is out of question, that he made man upright, but they have sought and found many inventions. Eccl. 7. 29. This appears, by what that great man, Moses, saith to the people, over whom God had made him a leader and a head, when he was now shortly to take his leave of them; in that much celebrated song which he begins with this, as the design of publishing the name of the Lord, "Because I will publish the name of the Lord, ascribe ye greatness unto our God:" (that, we may take up and accommodate very fully to our own, that is to the common case.) "He is the rock (this is a part of that name of his which he designed to publish in that 32 Deut.) his work is perfect, and all his ways are judgment, a God of truth and without iniquity, just and right is he." But "they have corrupted themselves:" (as in the 4 and 5 verses of that chapter, and onward:) a self-corrupted generation of creatures they are. And concerning this, we may assure our hearts; and ought to do so.

When we are in this case to apologize for God, it is indeed an awful thing that is undertaken; but with the profoundest reverence, and with the greatest veneration, and with a deep resentment of the necessity that men should be so prone to arraign the Almighty: and he be (as it were) put to plead his cause at his own creatures' bar; as the apostle's reading of the words doth imply; and as the former part, even of that clause in the 4 verse of this psalm is understood to signify too: That thou mightest be justified when thou speakest; when thou speakest by way of apology for thyself. It ought to be done with a sincere design, and with a joyful confidence, that he will always overcome and triumph when he judgeth himself, and when men presume to judge him, and pass their censures upon his ways and methods towards the world.

But it is a thing must be done, because there is a proneness in men's minds to admit of, and to have thoughts arise and spring up in them which have a reflecting aspect and look, upon the Most High, and Most Righteous God. As you see, the apostle, in the place where he quotes this text, (Romans 3. 4, 5.) objects this; "Is God unrighteous, who taketh vengeance?" when he was, in the foregoing and following chapters, proving Jew and Gentile to be all under sin. "Is God unrighteous, who taketh vengeance? I speak as a man," *humano more, after the manner of men*, which implies, so men are apt to speak; that is, to raise questions and doubts in their own minds, "How will this or that stand with the righteousness of God?" Therefore, the apostle thought himself concerned to vindicate God's righteousness; and he doth it largely, even there in that mentioned chapter, and afterwards in several others of that epistle; and it ought to be done with a pleasant confidence that there will be an universal applause to the righteousness of God at last, by all his intelligent creatures; that all shall agree and conspire together, in saying, "Holy and true art thou O Lord; just and righteous art thou Lord God Almighty, thou King of nations and of saints."

This I thought fit to say, by way of introduction to what I have further to say to this last mentioned head, that while we may be in some difficulty, how corrupt nature comes to be propagated from man to man, and from age to age, we are yet at a certainty how it is not done; that is, that sin is none of God's creature, and that he never infuses a sinning disposition into any creature whatsoever. The belief of this we ought to establish and settle in our own hearts, as that by which we shall but give God his due, and consult our own peace, and more flourishing and prosperous state of religion in our own souls; that it may have no damps there, or nothing that may tend to extinguish or deaden it in us. And therefore, this I shall evince to you, by some plain considerations; though one would think, indeed, the thing needed no eviction. As,

(1.) That the purity of God's nature cannot but abhor it: it is impossible that a thing so repugnant as sin is to the pure and holy nature of God, can spring from that pure and holy nature. Nothing but what is good can come from the first, the original, the essential, the most perfect Good. And,

(2.) That which he hath forbidden, it is impossible that he should cause or procure; that would be such a contradiction as we could never suspect an honest man of, that he should forbid and procure the same thing.

(3.) Much less is it possible that he should cause that which he punisheth, and punisheth with so terrible severity; the proper wages of sin being no less than eternal death. And,

(4.) It is impossible he should cause that which he hates;

"Do not the abominable thing which I hate, which my soul hateth." Of that he can never be the Author and the Cause. And,

(5.) It can never be, that he should be the Cause or Author of that, which is so highly injurious to him, which doth him the greatest injury imaginable. For though, from the perfection of his own nature, it is impossible it should do him any real harm; yet it doth him the greatest wrong. What a disorder hath it introduced into the creation of God! how hath it spoiled his workmanship, in a great master-piece of his creation, the mind and soul of man made after his image! What deformity hath it introduced in the room of so much beauty and glory! How manifest an attempt is it against his throne, even in the very nature of it! What a violation of the sacred constitution of his government! It is sin that hath set his own creatures against him, disaffected it to him: that is, in itself, in its rooted aversion from God, and hatred of God. It is the most unconceivable thing in the world, that God should make his own nature hate himself, disaffect himsel. It is sin that hath actually torn away so great and noble a part of his creation from him, and plucked it from his obedience and subjection; even all the generations of men from age to age, and so great a part of the heavenly host, and turned them all into rebels against their Maker and Rightful Lord. It cannot be that he should cause so mischievous a thing.

And it is too faint a vindication of God, in this case, to say, that therefore, he cannot cause, because it is a defect, and so not a causable thing, or capable of any other but a deficient cause. This is very true indeed, but very short, for that is no more than to say, God caused it not, than to say, another caused it not; as a thing that cannot be caused, cannot indeed admit of positive causation. That is very true, but we do not do God right if we do not assert also, that he could not bring it about, that it should be any agency of his; not in respect of the object as being an uncausable thing, but in respect of his own nature, as being repugnant to his holiness, and to his sovereignty, and to the sacredness of his government. And as that which he could not but abhor from, and hate, and hate with utmost detestation. And I add to all this,

(6.) To evince that this transmission of sin, cannot be by any direct hand that God hath in it, in that he hath provided so costly a remedy against it, that he should cause that which his own Son came down into our world, and died to destroy. That so wonderful a thing should be, as his descent into this world of ours, "who was the brightness of his Father's glory, and the express image of his person, and who upholds all things by the word of his power, and by whom he made the worlds;" that he should come down and appear once before the end of time, (or upon the declining of time from its fulness,) to put away sin by the sacrifice of himself; (Heb. 9. 25.) that he who sent his own Son to put away sin upon so very expensive terms, by the sacrifice of himself, to throw it out of the world, should have a hand in bringing it into the world, is the most inconceivable thing that can be.

And it is that which all agree in, that however sin came into the world, God was not the Author of it. Every one abhors that thought, men of all sorts, of all persuasions and religions: pagans themselves, in all the descriptions we find in their writings concerning original evil, all agree in this, that God is not the Original of it: all agree to discharge God in the case, though they are put (some of them) upon most absurd imaginations and devices to assoile the matter in themselves; and to avoid one difficulty, run themselves into as great or greater. Some talking, they know not what, of a certain ancient nature, from whence evil must come: some positively asserting two principles, as Manes and his manicheans did, an evil principle, and a good. But this, all have agreed in, by common consent, that God could not be the Author of the sinful evils that have, in so great measure, confounded the world, and spoiled and corrupted the nature of man.

And that being so far clear, we may reckon, that a good step is taken towards the mark that we are aiming at, the vindicating of God's righteousness in reference to this thing. There is the greatest certainty imaginable of the thing itself, while we are uncertain of the manner how sin comes to be transmitted from age to age, or to take its beginning in particular persons in a continual succession. Though there be (I say) a difficulty as to that, there is no difficulty as to the thing; and there is no difficulty as to this, how it did not, though it remain still a difficulty, how it is. It is not from God, sin is none of his creature.

Then I should here subjoin, in the third place, that next conclusion which I design to speak to, namely,

III. That it is the most unreasonable thing that can be, to object uncertainty against certainty. It being certain, that God is immutably holy and righteous, and that his nature is absolutely perfect; it being certain that man's nature is now become sinfully imperfect: and it being again plain, that we may be certain of very many things, when how they come to be, is doubtful, and perhaps, to many or the most inexplicable: but as to this particular thing, we do not know how the corruption of particular persons began, but we know how it began not; that is, that it is impossible to be any way imputable to God: we thence proceed to shew, how unreasonable a thing it is, to object the things about which we are uncertain, against the things that are most certain, that carry the greatest and plainest evidence with them. And of this we may give you instances enough.

If we should argue against the existence of this world, because we have not a particular, distinct account how it took its beginning, how absurd were it? If we may be capable of being puzzled with such questions as these, the great God put to Job. (chapter 38. in several verses of it.) If he should bid us gird up our loins like men, and say he would demand of us, to answer, "Where were you when I laid the foundations of the earth? declare, if you have understanding, Who hath laid the measures thereof, if ye know? or who hath stretched out the line upon them?" If he should expostulate with us, touching our knowledge of the way, how the sea is shut up as within bars and doors; or how ice, and snow, and rain are generated, and would put us upon giving an account of these things, would it not be the absurdest thing in all the world to deny their being, because we cannot give a distinct account of them? If we cannot give a distinct account, (or it may be,) a satisfactory one to ourselves, how matter was moved yet in the unformed chaos, and when the measuring line was stretched forth of this world, and the foundations laid of this mighty work; if we cannot give an account, how light and darkness were severed; which was the parting place, the utmost boundary of light and darkness; if we cannot give an account how the waters of the sea came to be collected and gathered into one place, and to be confined and shut up there, so as not to return and overflow the earth; if we cannot give an account how the rain was generated by its father: "Hath the rain a father? (as it follows here:) how ice and snow came to be condensed into these several substances, wherein we find them; therefore, to say that none of these things are; to oppose the uncertainties about the production of these things, to the manifest undoubted certainty of their existence, is certainly such an absurdity as we could never prevail upon ourselves to be guilty of.

But (as hath been told you before) we cannot be more certain of any thing that we see with our eyes, or of any faculty or power that belongs to ourselves, than we are, that there is a continual transmission of sin in this world. We cannot be more certain that man is a seeing creature, that he is a hearing creature, that he is a reasoning creature, than we can, that he is a living creature. And it would therefore, be the most absurd thing imaginable, to oppose and object that which is uncertain, against that which is so plainly and fully certain.

And I might tell you here, of a great many uncertainties, which they must suppose and take for granted to be very great certainties, who should form a disputation in this case, concerning the production of the corrupt and sinful nature in man. But that would be too large a theme to enter upon now. Yet, all will resolve into this in general, that as to what difficulty men do imagine in this case, it is only from their opposing philosophical uncertainty, to theological verity; and till philosophers be agreed, in other matters, we have very little reason to regard problems, doubtful problems, that may refer to this particular case; of which I may instance at another time, but shall not now. But (I say) let them come to a certainty in other matters first, before they expect to be much regarded in reference to determinate, theological truth, which we reckon, stands unshaken as the foundations of heaven and earth. When they have brought themselves and the world to a certainty about such things as the ebbing and flowing of the sea, the causes of the very centre of our world, the powers of the loadstone; whether it be the sun or the earth, and which it is of these that moves the other about; when they have brought such things as these, and a hundred more that might be mentioned, to a certainty, then, they may, with more pretence, expect to be listened to, as to their determinations which may more directly respect this case.

LECTURE XXXVII.*

Under the opening of the third conclusion, proposed to be spoken to, for the clearing of what I intended in the choice of the text we are upon, namely,—that it is most unreasonable and absurd, to oppose and object dark, and doubtful, and uncertain things, against that which is most evident and certain;—we shewed that there are many uncertainties, that men of philosophical minds, and geniuses, do commendably enough employ their thoughts about, while they do not attempt or offer at such a thing, as to oppose them to manifest, revealed truths. But if they will do so, it is, in all reason, to be expected that they should come to a more general certainty than they do, or are ever like to do, about philosophical matters in general. I in-

* Preached Nov. 6, 1694.

stanced in several, and told you, I would instance in four more which do more directly concern this case, about which, here lies the objected difficulty.

That the human soul cannot be propagated: to suppose it can, would be to expose the doctrine of its immortality, to manifest hazard. It must be supposed, that being immediately created by God himself, it comes pure and sinless out of his hands. The body itself, without the soul, cannot be the seat and subject of sin, as no irrational thing can, which is most evident. Therefore, many think there can be no such thing as propagation of sin from age to age; for how should it be? It cannot be at first found in the soul, which comes pure out of the hand of God. It cannot be seated or subjected in the body, which is not a subject capable of sin, or any mortality, abstractly considered. Here (I say) men do but oppose uncertainty to a certainty; a great many uncertainties to one plain and absolute certainty; that is, that sin doth really descend from age to age; and it is manifest, and in view with every one that observes, that men do not sooner begin to act rationally, than they do begin to act irregularly. But to oppose uncertainties to this plain and evident certainty, is a most unreasonable thing; equally unreasonable as that sophistical reasoning was of the philosopher that would undertake to prove, that there could be no such thing as a local motion: and another undertook to refute him by walking up and down before his eyes. There are too plain and sad proofs, in the walkings of men from age to age, that as soon as ever they begin to move or act as men, they do act sinfully; and so that corruption doth descend and is transmitted. This is certain and evident. But to make this a difficulty, there are a great many uncertainties supposed and taken for granted, about which it concerns ignorant creatures (as we all are) to pronounce nothing one way or other.

It is uncertain when or what time human souls were created, or were not created; whether all at once and at first, or whether at some distance of time, before they become to be united to human bodies. Not that the truth needs a determination of these matters, that way that would seem more favourable to it, as if it be not otherwise defended. But, in the mean time, we ought not to make difficulties greater than they really are, by supposing and taking for granted, that those things are certain, which really are not so.

It is, again, altogether uncertain, by what sort of Divine Agency a human soul comes to be united to a human body, or whether they come into that union electively, yea or no; or whether by a certain sort of fatal necessity; these are uncertainties, and we are not to pronounce concerning them, as if they were certain.

We do not know; philosophy cannot, with certainty, determine the strict, precise limitative bounds, between the sensitive nature, and the rational. We can be at no certainty, what dispositions there may be in the sensitive nature unto sin, though there can be no such thing as formal sin in it, abstractly considered; so that whensoever a reasonable, intelligent spirit, shall come to be united therewith, it will thereupon certainly sin: if it act, it will not act more rationally, than disorderly and irregularly. As if never so skilful a hand do play upon an instrument out of tune, if it sound, it will sound amiss; if never so skilful a horseman ride a lame horse, if he move, he will halt. We are altogether uncertain what of sensitive nature may be propagated with such and such dispositions in it, before the supervention of the reasonable soul.

We are uncertain what orders there are of created spirits, so little do we know; and we ought not to pretend to know of the affairs of the invisible world, so that we ought, in justice, to profess ignorance of such things as these, whether there be any common spirit of nature endowed with a plastic power, that may be immediately concerned about the union of human bodies, and human souls with one another.

These are things, though contraries, whereunto for the most part, men take upon them to determine as certainties; and so make objections against the most certain and unquestionable truths. And the most of the difficulties in this matter do but arise from opposing, doubtful philosophical problems, to unquestionable theological verities. And whereas, there is a very great uncertainty in most parts of philosophy, in natural philosophy, more than in any other part, therefore, the presumptuous determinations of men, about these things, are very unfit to be brought into any competition with the most certain divine truths; that is, to oppose things that are doubtful, that can never be proved, one way or other, unto things that are either most evidently proved, or are in themselves so evident, as to need no proof. And this is the case as to the most of what appears difficult in this affair. But then,

IV. The last conclusion that I am to insist upon, is this, that it is most of all, unreasonable and absurd, to oppose such uncertainties to certainties, to object what is doubtful and dark, against what is plain and evident, when (as hath been evinced already) there is nothing can shake the asserted truth; but there are many considerations may be brought to break the force of such objections, as are raised against it; then, it is most specially absurd. And under this head it was, that I designed to produce and lay before you, the many considerations which tend to break the force of any thing that can be objected against the consistency and agreeableness of the righteous and universal perfection of the Divine Nature, with the continual transmission of the sinful imperfections of the human nature.

The difficulty I need not remind you of, only, that it may lie the more distinctly in your thoughts, it is reducible to two heads; partly somewhat on the part of God, and partly somewhat on the part of man. On man's part first; because he is first to be considered in every thing that is evil, whether it be evil of sin, or evil of misery. And from what hath been said it appears difficult to be conceived, how man can be capable of propagating a sinful soul to another, when the soul, as such, is not propagated: and sin must reside there, inasmuch (as hath been said) as the body cannot be the seat or subject of sin, abstractly considered, and without the soul. On God's part, how it should stand with his righteousness and other perfections, continually to co-operate with second causes in the transmission of a sinful nature from age to age among men; so as thereby to make this world a seedplot of wickedness and misery, to all its inhabitants, from one generation to another; upon which, many have thought themselves necessitated to deny any such thing as the propagation of a corrupted nature, from generation to generation; and so to ascribe the whole business of the continuance of sin from age to age, in the world, only to imitation; one generation learning to be wicked, from another wicked generation, that did precede. But now, I say, as nothing can shake, the truths that have been asserted concerning God's righteousness; and man's unrighteousness continually descending, and transmitted from age to age, so there are many things to be alleged, to break the force of any such objections as these. And,

I shall offer this to consideration, that in reference to God's concern in this matter, (about whose name and honour all our souls ought to be most tenderly and deeply concerned,) there is nothing to be said or thought but this; it were easy for him to have prevented such a descent of sinfulness, from age to age, in this world, by which also misery is continually entailed upon the inhabitants of it. But now (I say) consider these things in reference hereunto.

1. Suppose that men should, hereupon ascribe the whole business of the continued sinfulness of the world, from age to

age, to imitation only, this would no more solve the difficulty, than what is ordinarily asserted; for, even that also, how easy were it for him, the great God, (as we may think,) to have prevented this; that is, to have prevented the descent of sin, from age to age, by imitation? How easily might he have annihilated this world, or annihilated his creature man, either by exerting his power to this purpose, or indeed, by only withholding it! for then all must drop. Or, how easy had it been to him, to have made all perfectly good, and that they should have continued such, from age to age? and then there would have been no bad example for any one's imitation. And we do not know, but that the Divine Agency (such as it may be for ought we can tell) may be as little concerned in transmitting human nature in its corruption, from age to age, as it would be, in sustaining sinful creatures that are corrupted, in co-operating in sinful actions. And without the co-operating influence of the First Cause, we are sure nothing can be done by a sufficient influence; that is, not done by an efficacious and necessitating one. And therefore, it is in vain to allege that, for the solving and expediting this difficulty, which doth itself carry as much of difficulty in it. And again,

2. This is next to be considered, that it is very unreasonable to have been expected from God, that he should annihilate an intelligent creature, upon the account of its having offended him, or upon the account of its being likely to transmit its likeness to those that shall proceed and spring from such a progenitor. It was a most unreasonable thing (I say) that God should, hereupon, annihilate or reduce to nothing such a piece of the work of his own hands; that, had neither been suitable to the wisdom of God, nor his goodness: not to his wisdom, for there had been a direct regression, that he should undo and destroy his own work: because such a creature, the subject and effect of his productive and creating influence, had transgressed the law and rule of its own creation; it was unreasonable that he should, thereupon, reduce it to nothing. And it had been (I say) very disagreeable to his wisdom, as if he were surprised by the fall and lapse of his creature; as if he had not foreseen, as if he had not sagacity enough to apprehend such and such consequences. It hath been always (as we find by the course God hath held) reckoned by him, most worthy of him, and most Godlike, to turn ill events to good; but not to go back. And we shall, in time, come to shew you, how he hath done it in this case, to his own most transcendent glory, and to the advantage of his creatures, such as do not, by their own faulty opposition, stand in the way of his kind and gracious method

towards them. But, that he should annihilate or bring a creature to nothing, that was capable of obeying and serving him, because he did disobey him, and because he is likely to transmit sinful inclinations to those that come of him, or come after him, this is never to be expected from the blessed God: it is a thing disagreeable to his wisdom, that he should do and undo. When he is said to have repented that he made man, as when he brought the flood upon the world; (Gen. 6.) that, as is plain in itself, and all do agree, is spoken *more humano*. And though he did (that he might give one proof of his just displeasancy at the apostasy of the world) bring on that deluge, yet you see he would not destroy the kind, but resolved to continue that, in subserviency to his further great and glorious designs.

And indeed, it could much less have consisted with his goodness, to destroy the capacity which was in that order of creatures, of so high and great things as he designed them to, which should spring up of the human race. That he should prevent himself of that wonderful exercise of his mercy, grace, and good will towards men, of which we shall have occasion to discourse in its proper place, and as the series of things shall lead on. Therefore, that, I would have to be considered, that it was a most unreasonable thing to expect that God should, upon the transgression of his reasonable creatures, and lest sin should be transmitted from age to age, annihilate the kind, and reduce all to nothing. And,

3. It was as little to be expected, that God should at first make all immutably good; that he should have made all his intelligent creatures immutably good at first, both angels in heaven, and men on earth; and so have provided and taken a course that sin should always be kept out of his creation; and that it should be impossible, where there is a nature propagated from age to age, there should be any thing of taint capable of falling into that nature; I say, that God should have done this, was as little to be expected from him.

We may judge of things safely by the event; for that is judging after God; that is judging that to be becoming of God, which he hath done; that course to be most suitable to him, most Godlike, which he hath chosen. And so far as we can discern the reasonableness of the course which he hath taken, we are to take notice of it, and avow it upon all occasions. Now, from the course he hath taken, it appears most suitable to the excellencies of the Divine Being, every way, that he should have made intelligent creatures at first, mutable; not to make them immutably good and happy, which was to be their final state; but that there should be a preparatory, subservient state, introductive to that final sta·e. This appears, upon all accounts, to have been most agreeable to the Supreme Wisdom and Goodness, that his creatures should not arrive to the highest perfection that they were capable of all at once, and at the very first; but that they should undergo a trial, and in that case, (if they must do so,) they must be left to their liberty at first, and being left so, there would be still a possibility that sin should be; and being once, that it should go on and be transmitted from age to age. And therefore, I add,

4. That God's omnipotency, or what his absolute power can do, is not the only measure (abstractly considered) according to which it can be said God can do this or that. It is not fit or proper to say, that he can do whatsoever omnipotency, abstractly considered and alone, could do; because he is not a Being of power alone: power alone gives us but an inadequate conception of God; it doth not give us an intire conception of him, as if he were nothing else but power; for he is wisdom, and goodness, and holiness, and righteousness, and truth, as well as power. And therefore, that only is, in a true sense, possible to God, which is suitable to all his glorious excellencies to do, conjunctly considered; and not what is suitable to his power alone, and separately considered from the rest. When it is said, God cannot lie, and God cannot deny himself, and the like, the meaning is not as if there were a want of mere power to do any such natural act, considered as a natural act; but it is impossible to the divine perfection, (consider him as a Being of universal perfection, wherein all perfections do meet,) to do things so unlike himself, so unworthy of himself.

Therefore, it was never to have been expected from divine power, or because he is omnipotent, that, therefore, he should do all things which that, abstractly considered, could do; as to have put an end to the generations of men lest they should sin on; or to have made all perfectly good at first, so as it should be an impossibility that any such thing as sin should be in the world, which only the possibility of its continuing in the world could, in an ordinary course, be prevented. This (I say) was never to be expected from the infinitely, absolutely, and universally perfect Being, who hath other perfections belonging to his nature besides that of power. But those things are only possible to him, which (all things considered) are most worthy of him, and most suitable to him. And again,

5. We are further to consider, that the course of nature

in the universe, it is most observably fixed and settled; so as (unless it be now and then in single instances) not to admit of change; that is, not to admit of change in an ordinary course. We may observe, that the course of nature is very rarely ever altered. But it were very unreasonable to expect, that it should be statedly or often altered. We find alterations in single instances; as in reference to that great order of day and night; when the sun stood still so long one time; and when it went back so many degrees at another time. And so when the sea did not hold its own course, or do agreeably to its property, as a fluid thing, to overflow all that came within the compass of it, but was bound up as to the Israelites that passed through it. And the fire, it acted not, according to its natural property, to consume and burn what is combustible, in the case of the three children, who were in the fiery furnace unharmed and unhurt.

But we are never to think that the course of nature should be ordinarily or often altered. And that it is not, even because it is not, we ought in great reverence and humility to apprehend there are mighty occult reasons for this. And it should lay an awe upon our spirits, to behold the Author of nature, the God of nature, acting it on, in so stated and unaltered a course, from age to age, through the succession of many ages. If we understood no reason why it should be so, yet our minds should be struck with great reverence when we find, that ordinarily it is so. But we may apprehend very great reason for it too, in reference to the stated course of natural causes, as to what doth concern ourselves. What confusion would it make in the world, if ordinarily, the sun should vary its course, that no man could tell when it would rise, or when it would set, or when to undertake such or such a business? If God's obstructing that course in a single instance or two, should have been often repeated, so as to hold men's minds in a continual suspense, the sad and dismal consequences that would have ensued to this world (though this be but a very minute, inconsiderable part of the universe, the whole creation of God) are obvious to every one's view that considers.

And as to the transmitting of the species of things, and the preserving of the species of all sorts of things, in the world, besides the decorum of it, and that admirable proof that there is of divine wisdom and providence therein, the usefulness thereof to ourselves, is most apparent to any one's notice and view, that through so many thousands of years there should be a preservation of the kinds of things. Go through the several orders of things: the ranks of things that come under our own notice, is an admirable discovery of God's wisdom and providence, and too little considered and reflected on; that the species of things should be unaltered, that what we find was the property of this or that herb, or plant, or tree, continues so. These things have still the same properties that they had. Look to the animals beneath us; we find the same properties the horse to be described by, so many ages ago, are in the same creature still. There is an admirable discovery of the power and wisdom of providence in this, which we ought to contemplate with great admiration, and great reverence, and have our spirits so much the more disposed to acknowledge and adore God the Maker of this world, and the great Author of universal nature. It would do more to preserve a religious impression upon our spirits Godward, than is commonly apprehended, if we did, now and then, allow our thoughts to fix in these contemplations, that whereas there is such a collision in this natural world, there are such antipathies, and contrarieties in the natures of things, that yet their natures are continued, preserved intire, from being confounded; though there is such a vast multiplicity, yet all preserved intire, through so many thousands of years. But then, consider further,

6. That it is most evident, that the course of nature is as settled and constant, in reference to the production of men from age to age, as of any other creature. This is obvious, to wit, that there do spring up, from age to age, creatures of this species, and of the same kind, as there do of any other creatures of any other kind or species. And that, hereupon, we must apprehend a fixedness in the course of nature, not to be altered for a continuance, though it may in single instances, here and there, in reference to this thing, as well as in reference to any thing else that falls under the regulation and measure of the law of nature. And,

7. It is a mighty confirmation of the natural descent of sin with the nature of man, in the ordinary way, that when God designed the incarnation of his own Son, to avoid that corruption of nature descending to him, he there steps out of the ordinary course; a consideration that hath that weight with it, that if any one allow himself to think, it must overbear his mind in that matter, that sure there is some secret, profound reason in the counsel of God, (whether obvious to our view, or not obvious,) that the descent of corrupt nature was in the ordinary way unavoidable: that when God had a design to incarnate his own Son, when it was intended God should

be manifested in the flesh, to avoid that contagion and corruption which, in the ordinary course, is transmitted, he doth in this single instance recede and go off from the ordinary natural course: and so the production is by the Holy Ghost, separating the very matter of the human body which itself, indeed, was not a capable subject of sin, as hath been said, and is plain in itself. But because the human nature had been corrupted, if it had descended in the ordinary way, (and that was inconsistent with the design on which a Redeemer was to come down from heaven into the world,) therefore, the ordinary course of procreation is declined and avoided: a most pregnant demonstration, that, in the ordinary course, sin is always naturally transmitted, in that this must be done on purpose to avoid that taint and contagion that otherwise would have been. But I add, in the next place, and shall go no further now,

8. That men do make the difficulty in this matter greater than they need, by not apprehending and considering aright, wherein the production of a human creature lies. It is plain it doth not lie, though a human creature be a creature of a compounded nature, that hath a terrestrial and celestial part, yet, I say, it doth not lie in the production of either of the parts, but only in the uniting of them substantially with one another. It neither lies in the production of the soul, nor doth it lie in the production of the matter of the body, for all matter is generally apprehended to be ingenerable and incorruptible. But it lies (as I said) in the bringing of these into a substantial union with one another. And do but consider to this purpose, "Wherein doth death lie? wherein doth the death of a man consist?" His death, you will easily apprehend, must stand in direct opposition to his procreation and production. But death doth not lie either in the destruction of the soul, or of the body; but as it is a matter of faith, that the one remains, so it is a matter of sense, that the other remains after death. The soul is gone, but not reduced to nothing; the body remains, and will continue a considerable time the same intire frame that it was, even when the soul is gone. Death, therefore, doth neither lie in the destruction of the soul, nor in the destruction of the body; but in their disunion. So the procreation doth not lie, either in the production of the soul, or in the production of the body; (otherwise than being so and so modified;) but in the union of those two parts, bringing it about, that they should be substantially united with one another.

And if that be duly considered, there is a great deal of room and scope left to apprehend how such a thing may be very possible, (as we find it actual,) the continual descent of sin, and yet the holiness, and purity, and universal rectitude of the Divine Nature, not having any concern unbecoming itself, unsuitable to itself, herein.

There are many more considerations behind, that will not be without weight in this matter: only, now, let us consider and bethink ourselves (as our assembly dissolves) of this one thing; how much more considerable a theme and subject we have for our thoughts, in that which is common to all ages, than can occur to us in what is peculiar to our own time! We are so amused and taken up about the little affairs (in comparison) of our own time, that we do not allow ourselves to consider and look, as we should do, with just intention of mind, upon those things that are great, and of common concern to all time. And we wonder there should be any miscarriage in the conduct of human affairs, and that the perversity of men, here and there, breaks out in this or that instance, forgetting there is a corrupt, human nature still descending from age to age, and from generation to generation, which naturally makes this world a region of impurity, and consequent misery, and gloominess and darkness. And we do not enough reflect upon the intestine cause of all our evils. Every one would be a great deal more ready to fall to self-accusation, than to the accusing of other men. "I have a corrupt nature in myself, out of which nature spring all the confusions and disorders in the world; all the dismal, tragical things that are any where to be found and observed in it." It is very unreasonable to let our minds be confined to the present, when we have such a vast prospect before us, looking forward, looking backward, looking inward, looking on this and that hand; to bind our thoughts when we have so vast a compass of things to look into, this is neither suitable to the reason of a man, nor so suitable as it should be to the more large and concerned mind of a christian, about the great things wherein the Christian Interest is, itself, concerned.

LECTURE XXXVIII.*

Now we shall go on to add further considerations for shewing this *fourth conclusion*. And, thereupon, in the next place,

9. We may further consider, that it is never thought a ble-

* Preached Nov. 17, 1694.

mish to the justice of any government whatsoever, that children should inherit the poverty and rags of their parents that were either poor or profligate, or that had squandered or forfeited all that they had. This was never thought to have been a blemish to the government under which such persons may live, that children are born poor, when their parents had nothing to leave them; and so they have rags and beggary for their patrimony. This doth not use to be, or can be, with any equity, imputed to the government under which such live, as if that were to be blamed. And much less is it imputable in this case; because human governors are debtors to the communities which they govern, and do owe to them their utmost care and providence for them. But God (as hath been formerly shewed you) can be no debtor to any of his creatures, whether considered singly, or in communities, any otherwise than as he hath by any promise made himself debtor. But he never promised, never obliged himself by any promise, to keep sin out of the world, from hurting creatures that can only hurt themselves by it; or from preventing it to descend, or presently to throw it out of the world; though that he will do fully in his own time, and in his own way. And again,

10. There can be no more obligation on the blessed God, to prevent moral defects among his creatures, than natural ones. If he be not obliged to prevent natural defects, he is as little obliged to prevent moral; because moral perfection must be founded in natural; as all morality hath its foundation in the nature of the creatures who are the capable subjects thereof. But plain it is, he can be under no obligation to prevent natural defects, or that his creatures should be naturally perfect: for in what sense will we suppose it requisite that he should make them so? Not with an absolute perfection, perfection in *omni genere;* for that is above the condition of a creature; no creature is capable of being *universally perfect.* That is the peculiar privilege and prerogative of the Original and Uncreated Being, to be absolutely and universally perfect. And therefore, to suppose him obliged to make all his creatures every way perfect, it were to suppose him obliged to have made them all gods; or we must suppose him not obliged to make any thing at all: because it is impossible that a made thing can be absolutely perfect. Or, should we suppose him under an obligation to have made things perfect in any kind above their own? That cannot be thought neither: for that must suppose, then, that there should have been no creatures of any inferior kind, or that all must have been of equal perfection, that every fly or worm must have been a cherubim

or seraphim. Indeed, it is a most accurate discourse that I have taken notice of to this purpose, in a pagan writer, (as it is more generally reckoned,) Plotinus, who saith, that "to find fault with the Author of nature because of such and such defects, in such and such sorts of creatures, or in particular creatures, it were to find fault that he hath made the world an harmonious thing; that there are such orders and gradations in it; that he hath made some inanimate things, and endowed some with a life of sense, and some below them with a life of vegetation, and some above them with a life of reason, and some above them with an angelical nature, and the like." All these comely orders of things should not have been, but all must have been of one order and kind. "And, (as he saith,) it were the same thing as to blame a limner, that he hath not in every thing drawn light colours without any foil; or a comedian, (the author of a comedy,) that he hath not made every person that is to act a part, a king, or a hero; that there should be any that doth sustain the part of mean and inferior persons."

It is plain, and out of doubt, that God is not obliged to make his creatures all, either absolutely perfect, or to give them higher perfections than do belong to their own kind: or (we may add) to give to every one of them those perfections that that kind is capable of. For we find that there are some of greater health, some of less; some of greater strength, some of less, in that order of creatures wherein they are. And we find that there are such things as hereditary diseases, that do descend, and generally are found every where through the human race. But (I say) God can no more be under obligation to prevent moral than natural defects, among his creatures. And again,

11. We are to consider further, that though the descent and transmission of a sinful pravity with the nature of man may appear to have a difficulty with it, yet it is not altogether unaccountable, if we do but consider things as they are, with that compass of thought which we ought. Nay, it is not ordinarily conceivable, how it should be otherwise, if we do but admit into our thoughts, what a concurrence there is of several things to this purpose. As,

(1.) The retirement of the Holy, Divine Spirit from man, having once sinned. And it is certain, that he did retire thereupon, that he hath retired, otherwise than as according to the Redeemer's method he is returned. There was an antecedent retirement and withdrawing, and that, upon the sin of man, upon sin's entering into the world: for do but observe that Gal. 3. 14, 15. " Christ hath redeemed us from the curse of the law, by being made a curse for us; for cursed is every one that hangeth on a tree; that the blessing of Abraham might come upon the Gentiles." (That, which was the blessing of Abraham upon that account, might now be a more diffused blessing, and reach the Gentiles too.) For what? That they might receive the promise of the Spirit (or the promised Spirit) through faith. Now consider what the blessing is, and measure the opposite curse by that: the blessing, you see, is the gift of the Spirit; what is the curse then, but the debasing of the Spirit? And certainly then, that was the curse of the law, the curse of the violated law. As soon as the law was broken, the Divine, Holy Spirit was cursed away from the nature of man; or, man was cursed, so as that thereby this Spirit should be withheld, should be kept off, otherwise than as upon the Redeemer's account, and according to his methods, it should be restored. And then,

(2.) Consider, hereupon, the nature and kind of that corruption that is conveyed and doth descend, and how the Scripture speaks of it, generally under the notion of carnality. That which is born of the flesh is flesh, John 3. 6. That is, now, where there is no divine birth, where nothing is born of the Spirit, or where the work of regeneration hath not taken place, the production is nothing else but flesh, the mere human nature; to wit, the denomination is taken from that which governs: though a man be not all flesh, the denomination is taken from that which prevails. What is the thing produced when a human creature is born? A piece of flesh: as that which is born of the Spirit is spirit, whenever that birth comes to obtain and take place with any soul. That which is born of the flesh is but flesh; not as if the nature of man were nothing but flesh, but because carnality is the prevailing thing in the lapsed state of man, that carries the name, and now he is called nothing but flesh. And,

(3.) This is to be considered, to facilitate our apprehension of this matter, that the sensitive nature, (which only is capable of being propagated,) though it cannot itself be the seat and subject of sin, yet it may be in very great disposition thereunto: or things may be there, in that inferior region, in that disposition, that there cannot but be sinfulness as soon as the intelligent mind and spirit supervene. All things will lie in the sensitive nature, as it is transmitted and conveyed in that state, that when the reasonable and intelligent spirit supervenes, though the sensitive nature (as such) is not capable of sin, yet supervening and coming into union, there cannot but a sinfulness ensue. And,

(4.) We have further to consider to this purpose, how manifest the power of imagination is, every where through the world. And so, how supposable it is, that the power of parental imagination may be great. And we find it is so, very frequently, to make an impression upon the grosser corporeal bulk. There are signatures upon the fœtus, as many unquestionable histories do inform us, that speak of parental imaginations. But much more may it be strong on the more fine sort of vehicles, in which, we have very little reason to doubt, the reasonable soul is lodged, and invested with, whenever it comes into union with a terrestrial body. And it cannot be difficult, to apprehend what signatures parental imagination may make there, when the soul comes to act in a body so and so formed. I do not merely, now, speak of this corporeal external bulk, but that finer indument, that is, that immediate inwrapping of the soul in the body; and which, in all likelihood, it carries away with it out of the body whensoever it leaves it. What signatures may be there easily made by parental imagination, it is not hard for us to apprehend, if we let our thoughts work upon that subject, especially considering what impressions have been made upon the grosser or more corporeal bulk itself. And then consider,

(5.) The natural activity of the intelligent mind and spirit, when it comes into union and supervenes, especially with respect to its cogitativeness, its thinkingness, its power to think; which how soon it doth exert, and put forth its power into act, we do not know: but, to be sure, as soon as its organs are capable, and as soon as it becomes, in its own nature, a cogitative or a thinking thing, nothing is more essential to it than a power of thought; so that as soon as it can use thought, it must: especially the organs that it depends upon, and is to act by, being so and so disposed before, it cannot be but there will be thinking amiss. And according to this course, as the power of using thought grows riper, it will be more and more irregular.

And here are the first ebullitions of corrupt nature. The Lord knows the thoughts of man, that they are vanity. As soon as he thinks, he will think vainly; he will think vanity. Psalm 94. 11.—" And God saw that the imagination of the thoughts of man's heart was only evil, and that continually," in that corrupt state of the world. Genesis 6. 5. And, " out of the heart proceed evil thoughts." Where there is a corrupt heart, the first ebullitions of it are in impure thoughts, vain thoughts, sinful thoughts; that is, that such things, such kind of phantasies are impressed, as do take their rise only from a sensible world: towards an unknown God who is invisible, there are no signatures that can have any power, because they are buried and overwhelmed by such a supervening cloud of sensitive images or imaginations; thereupon, there must be aversion from God, disaffection to him, disinclination towards him, as an unknown, and an unsuitable, and an undesirable Object. And so, here is the very root of all evil. So that he may easily see how it comes to have place, even in the corrupt nature of lapsed man. And then, again,

(6.) We are further to consider, how industrious we must needs suppose the prince of the apostasy to be, for the continuation of that sin in the world, which he introduced into it. And that is a thing less considered in this matter than I think it should be, and doth claim to be. Plain it is, that the whole order of apostate men became apostate, by being accomplices with this great prince of the air. And so sinful men are more universally accomplices with hell, with the apostate prince of the darkness of this world. Nothing is plainer: and do but consider, hereupon, what the parentage of a sinner is, as a sinner; "Ye are of your father the devil, and the works of your father ye will do." John 8. 44. They are the words of him who is truth itself, and who, therefore, cannot deceive us. Now, in what respects do we think that the devil is called the father of sinners? Not in respect of their mere nature, not in respect of their naturals, the substance either of their souls, or of their bodies, but only in respect of their morals, the sinfulness, the corruption, the impurity of them. But is he a father in respect of this? Then, certainly, it must owe its beginnings, in individuals, to him too; as children do owe their beginning, wherein they are children, to their parents.

And let but that context be observed, 1 John 5. 18, 19. "He that is born of God, keepeth himself, that the wicked one toucheth him not." Therefore, this is a divine birth; there is a self-preserving principle conveyed with that divine nature which is new born, that the wicked one shall not touch him; that is, mortally to touch him; not touch him so as to kill him; but he hath touched mortally all the rest. And, therefore, the apostle adds in the very next words, "we are of God," to wit, new-born of God; an eliptical expression: the word *being born*, having been before used, it was enough to say, we are of God; born of God. But how is the case with the rest of the world? They "all lie in wickedness," we read it: in all likelihood, it should be read, "in that wicked one," spoken of before, in that foregoing word: that is, in the wicked one, who can only touch those that are born of God; but doth mortally touch the rest.

And thereupon, we find that the common course of the unregenerate and unconverted world, it is said to be after "the power of the prince of the air, that works in the children of disobedience." Ephes. 2. 2. Whereupon, in the very next words, they are said to be children of wrath too, by nature. Observe how things lie connected; "and are by nature children of wrath." By nature, how so? Inasmuch as there is a corrupt and depraved nature continually descending and transmitted; wherein we are not to suppose him to be without his advantage, or without his agency, who is "the prince of the darkness of this world," and who is also called "the God of this world." 2 Cor. 4. 4.

And it is not, therefore, strange, that men should be, as to all their concerns, so much subject to the diabolical power, because they have been accomplices with him from the beginning, even the first apostasy; when nobody can suppose (that considers matters equally) but that he must be continually intent to keep his ground in this world; and doth all that in him lies, to transmit impurity from age to age. And his advantage, in order hereunto, upon the sensitive nature, cannot but be great. Though he cannot immediately touch the mind and spirit itself, without its own consent, without its own betraying itself; yet, that power variously actuates the sensitive nature; and thereby, the inferior appetite, and whatsoever is in the lower region of the soul; (this is no unapprehensible thing;) to wit, to cherish sin, and to foment and cherish it the same way, by the mediation of sense by which he first introduced it. And, by sense, we are not to understand only the external sense, but we are to understand, under that notion, whatsoever lies within the compass of sensitive nature, imagination and appetite, as well as the external sense. And what signatures he may make upon it, is more easy for us to apprehend as possible, than to conclude as certain: but very likely it is, that his power may go very far; and we are not to doubt but his malice will go as far as his power. And then, I add upon all this,

12. That there being such a sinful pravity conveyed and descending down with our nature, from age to age, this must, in the beginning thereof, be matter of just displeasancy to the blessed God. It cannot be, but there must be aversion in his holy and pure nature, to a nature impure and unholy. And let us but consider this, that we are said to be, (as was taken notice of before,) "by nature, the children of wrath," lying under the divine displeasure, under a *vindicta*, even by nature: Ephes. 2. 2, 3. And pray, let the reason of the thing be a

little discussed and looked into. Consider whether that various inclination and disposition, before actual sin, be not in itself a hateful thing. And that nothing which is asserted, among those that have inquired into, and do profess the truth in this matter, may appear harsh and hard, let us but consider how such matters used to be judged of by human measures, by men; sure, in things wherein they will not censure men, we may think God more uncensurable. If men will allow themselves the liberty of free thought, they cannot deny it. But whereas, there is, such a thing as human justice, pray do but consider how it useth to have its exercise in matter of punishment, and upon what ground. And whereas, all men have some natural notions remaining with them of right and wrong, and they have aversion or propension, according to such notions, more or less, do but consider how these do work among men, considered as men. Let me but set your thoughts on work on the latter of these first: that is, take a virtuous person, one that goes under that common estimate, by all that know him, as a person of strict virtue. Will he not, as such, disaffect an ill man, a vicious and wicked man? And you will say, he instinctively doth so; that is, the wickedness he sees in him. But then, I would inquire, What is it that such a one disaffects, in such another? Is it, I say, any abstract act he doth? That can never be; for that, abstracted or prescinded from an evil inclination, is not the thing that he hates or can hate; that any man can reasonably hate; for an act, an external act, that falls under the notice of another, take it off from an evil inclination, it is but a casual thing; and it is morally neither good nor evil; and therefore, can be no object of a rational hatred. Therefore, whatsoever there is of just hatred in the vilest and most profligate person's course, What is the object of that just hatefulness? Not the external acts, abstractly considered, from a vicious inclination; but as they proceed thence, or as they are supposed to proceed thence. So that it is an ill habit of mind, of a vicious mind, that is the object of hatred, every where, with virtuous men.

And then, consider, what it is that human laws do punish, in the next place. Who do they punish? Do they punish the external action abstractly, from the evil inclination or intention? Never at all: for if it doth appear that there was an action done against the rule of the law, that doth not proceed from an ill inclination or intention, it is looked upon as a casual thing, and not punishable. Therefore, the thing that is punishable, is the ill intention and disposition, only discovering itself by such and such external acts. This is plain in itself.

But now, whereas, we have no way to know the inclinations of men's minds, but by external *indicia*, the disposition and habitude of every one lie immediately open to the divine inspection: there is all the difference. If then, there be a just and reasonable ground to hate an ill disposition, an ill inclination, because it doth discover itself by external acts to us, why is there not the same reason that it should be hated, or that it should be matter of displeasure, whenever it appears, unto him by whom things are immediately seen in themselves, and as they lie without external discovery? And therefore, a sinful generation is called " a generation of vipers." You have poison, you have malignity in your natures. This he can see, that sees all things, and knows all things, before it doth, *se prodere*, before it discovers itself in sinful actions; before it appears to our view, before it can be discerned by us. And therefore, consider further,

13. Which will be a further proof of the former, and contribute further towards our common end, the clearing of difficulties in this matter, that it is plain, that infants, as soon as they come to partake of the human nature, they do need a Redeemer, as much as others: for I hope there is none among us that is such a *durus infantum pater*, so hard and harsh a father of infants, but to admit, that many infants may be saved, may become blessed creatures hereafter. Well, but how shall they come to be so without a Redeemer, without a Christ? Is not he said to be " the Lamb of God that takes away the sins of the world?" Whatsoever sins of the world that are taken away, they are taken away by him. But what? are infants no part of the world? They are said to compose the kingdom of God in this world; that is, concur to the composition. " Suffer little children to be brought unto me, for of such is the kingdom of God." Those that were brought in arms, that were carried, of them it is said, " of such is the kingdom of God;" that kingdom whereof our Lord Jesus Christ is the immediate King. He takes them into his kingdom. They come under the government of the Redeemer; then they did need a Redeemer, and to be dealt with in a way of grace, and not merely upon a natural point. They are a part of that body which he gave himself to purchase and sanctify. Epes. 5. 25, 26. And it is plain,

14. That they do need to be regenerated; they need regeneration as well as redemption; and which, indeed, hath its foundation in redemption: " for that which is born of the

flesh, is but flesh," and no more: but " that which is born of the Spirit is spirit," and that Spirit is the Spirit of Christ: and if we have not the Spirit of Christ, we are none of his. And therefore, I would subjoin to all these considerations, in the last place,

15. That whatsoever God thought fit not to do, by way of prevention of the coming of sin into the world, and of its being transmitted in it, he hath done with more unspeakably glorious advantage, by way of remedy. And the remedy for setting things right, where things were out of course, in the apostate world, it is two ways. The one whereof doth more directly respect us, and the other himself: that is, by redemption, and the penal judgment. These two things will set all things right. I cannot now enlarge as I would: but very true it is indeed, that it must mightily pose, nonplus all our understandings, if there were to be continual descent of our sinful generation one after another in this world eternally. If things were to run on thus to all eternity, it were the most unaccountable thing imaginable. But we find this is not to be; there will be a period put to this course within awhile. This world, and the wickedness of it, must come to an end: and while sin is running on, from age to age, grace hath its exercise too, which runs a parallel, from age to age. And therefore, there is a far more glorious display of all the divine perfections in the appointed means of remedy, than there would have been in the prevention of those great disorders that have been in the world, by sin's once entering into it, and continuing a course in it so long.

LECTURE XXXIX.*

My design (as you have heard) in choosing the text I have been upon for some time, was not to speak of the corruption of human nature abstractly, and in itself, but to consider it here as it stands in connection with the acknowledged justice and righteousness of God; and so to make that my business, to vindicate God's justice in reference to this case,—a continual transmission of a corrupt nature, in this world, from age to age, that draws death and misery after it, and which God permits to run on in such a course; though (as hath been told you) if we did consider his omnipotency abstractly, and ab-

* Preached Nov. 24, 1694.

solutely, it might be supposed easy for him to have hindered it. To this I have spoken at large, and will repeat nothing more, than only to take notice of so much, as the sum of all, that whatsoever is, with the most plausibleness, wont to be alleged against the righteousness of the divine procedure in this matter, doth lie, for the most part, in men's taking such and such things for granted, as if they were certainly so; which are most uncertain, and whereof (whereas all men do all they can) they must be, in a great measure, ignorant: if such had but the modesty to confess the ignorance which they cannot cure or remedy, the justice of God, in permitting all men to come into the world with sinful natures, would appear in glorious light and lustre before their eyes, darkened with no cloud; nor would these dash in the dark one against another, but be easily conceived in their minds, without the least appearance of repugnancy to one another. As we see lie in the Psalmist's, who, in almost the same breath, confesseth the triumphant justice and righteousness of God, and the corruption of that nature that did descend to him, and doth descend from man to man, and from age to age.

But now, it only remains to make *Use* of what hath been said upon this very important subject. And herein, considering one of the things considered and asserted, by itself, to wit, the corruption of the nature, which is conveyed and transmitted down from parents to children. The first use that I shall hereupon make will be this—To shew how greatly they are concerned, who are parents, or who may be so, to their uttermost to strive against this radical evil that is descending and running down, from age to age, in this world which we inhabit, and whereof we are the sinful inhabitants. This is a thing which, in the notion, we generally acknowledge, that there is such a descent of corruption and sinfulness, from age to age, in this world. But even where this truth is admitted, it is a truth hid and shut up in unrighteousness, while the hearts of very few are in any measure suitably affected and influenced to take that course, pursuant and agreeable to so plain and so confessed a truth as this is. It is that which, where it is understood and acknowledged, and were it understood and acknowledged all the world over, it ought universally to have the same effect, ought to startle the world, to awaken men every where, as if there were an universal plague spread over all towns, cities, countries, and kingdoms, at once. And if that were the case, that any poor creature could not tell whither to go, or where to set his foot, secure and free from the danger of meeting such a shaft or arrow that should immediately pierce his very heart, in what a condition were this world, if thus it were with every one? But there is a thousand-fold worse mischief to be feared; and they that think of flying from it, carry it about them, and can no more fly from it than they can fly from themselves, or run away from their own nature. It is not considered, that they carry sin, and death, and hell, about them, even from their very original; things complicated with their natures. Who would pretend to believe so horrid a truth, a truth of so horrid and tremendous import, and not be filled with horror about it? Yet, every one goes on unconcerned, as if there were no fear, no danger, no harm, about them, or before them. But, I say,

First. All should understand, hence, that are, or may be, parents, of how unspeakable concernment it is to them, to counterstrive to the uttermost against this great mischief which they are, or are like to be, instruments of; transmitting sin in this world, and conveying it yet further down from this to another generation in it. And this I take to be a head, upon this occasion, fit to be enlarged upon: and therefore, I shall spend this hour upon it. And therein shall shew you—Wherein such as are, or may be, parents, should use their endeavour to counterwork this radical evil: and then—Upon what considerations they should be awakened and engaged effectually hereunto.

1. Wherein they should endeavour against it, who are, or may be, parents. Why,

(1.) By endeavouring, out of hand, to become seriously godly themselves, so that if ever God call them, or order things so in reference to themselves, and that they become parents, as a corrupt seed will more or less spring from them, they may be the means, also, of raising up a godly seed in this world. The thing which God hath designed even in the first founding of families upon this earth: that whereas, a corrupt nature, if ever they come to be parents, will descend from them, without their design, they may be also instruments, in the hand of God, of conveying his image, his light, his grace, with their own design, in subordination (as all instruments must be) to the Supreme Agent, that alone can make them capable of being effectual ones to such a blessed end.

That, I say, must be their first care in order hereunto; that is, out of hand, to endeavour to become godly themselves; to do what is possible for them to do in order thereunto: not content themselves that they have an empty, spiritless form of godliness about them, that is never likely to be active to such a purpose: but that there be the life and power of godliness, which will be active to the uttermost it is capable of, in pursuance of so high and great a design. As, naturally, men are generally the devil's instruments, to promote his dark and impure kingdom in this world; so if ever God call me to the state and condition of a parent, I will, through his grace, be his instrument, as much as in me, to promote that holy kingdom, which he hath formed, and is intent to promote and propagate in this world, as a counter-kingdom, against the power of that wicked kingdom.

In order hereunto, under that manifestation God is pleased to make of. himself through Christ in the gospel, they ought to surrender and give up themselves to God in Christ: herein becoming godly, doth first begin when, under the convictive and operative light of influence and grace transmitted in the gospel, persons do make a surrender of themselves to God through Christ. "Yield yourselves unto God," as the expression is, Rom. 6. 13. It is but a practical answer to God's claim and challenge—"Yield yourselves to God." He demands his right; he insists upon his interest in you, as you are his creatures, and the work of his hands. And what! will you not yield, not yield him his own? Will you withhold from him what is his? what he hath so indisputably a title to, and interest in? Or, can you ever have a design of helping to raise up a godly seed in this world, if you will never be godly yourself? but remain a continual fighter against God, and a striver against him, under that gospel of peace and grace, wherein he is continually bespeaking you to be his? And then,

(2.) Let such as may be parents of children, lay the more immediate foundation of such an endeavour, as I have been speaking of, in marrying after a godly sort: in marrying holily, whensoever any are called thereunto; that is, with a design for God. He that is the Author, is to be the End of all things. And whereas, that same state is his institution and appointment, it is a most insolent absurdity, for any to take upon them, as if they were to please themselves, or to gratify an inclination, or serve an interest of their own, with neglect of God's great interest. They that enter, or think of entering, into that state, are required to do it in the Lord, as an only thing. 1 Cor. 7. 39. And it is a great deal of pity, that discourses about such matters, and relating to this affair, are so generally confined to a corner only, and that opportunity is not given of speaking to assemblies upon so important a matter as this is; that any undertaking or design, in this kind, is to be done in the Lord, and that as an only thing. Marry they may, only in the Lord. But when they neglect this, they leave out the only thing that can make a blessed marriage; which certainly must argue a very profane mind, when men and women dare venture, and rush upon a matter of so great importance as that, and leave out the very only thing that concerns them in it. This doing of such a thing in the Lord must import,

[1.] A doing it for him, with a design for him; to wit, as one's principal end. And let it be considered, how great an aberration here is from the proper scope, generally, in the world, and even in the Christian world, as to this thing: that the first thing commonly thought of, is some such mean matter as this, in comparison mean, I say in comparison; "I design to change my condition; well, let me think then, how I can please my fancy; let me contrive how I can best satisfy my sensual inclination; and how I can best serve my worldly interest and advantage; where to have a great fortune; and what may set me up into, and promote me in, the most advantageous way of trade, and the like."

What the evangelist says, in another case, of our Lord's animadversion upon the scribes and pharisees, that their religion stood in the tithing of mint, anise, and cummin, neglecting the weightier matters of the law,—judgment, mercy, faith, and the love of God; to wit, that those other things they might and ought to have done, but not to have left the other undone: the like may be said in this case. There is no blame in looking after one suitable, in respect of comeliness, or in respect of fortune, or the like. This may well enough be done; but not to leave the great and most weighty matter and importance: that is, Where shall I have a suitable help, to promote religion in the world, and to plant religion in a family, if it shall please God to make us the founders of a family? one that may help to bear a part with me, in maintaining and keeping up the interest of godliness, in opposition to the common corruption of human nature, which is still descending, from age to age, in this world? How little is thought of among us, so as hereby to design the business of marriage for this in the Lord as the principal thing? When that is not made the principal thing, the very act is idolatry. To be the end of all things is appropriate to Deity: and he must be your Supreme End, even in this thing, or you make yourselves so: and if so, you are an idol of jealousy, set up against God; as if this world were made for you, and you were made for yourself; and as if you might take upon yourself to do what you please here, without reference to the Supreme Ruler and Lord of all. Therefore, it is without question, that he and his interest, in this affair, must be designed in the first place.

[2.] That in subserviency to it, whosoever designs to enter into that state, they must give themselves up, by solemn covenant, to God in Christ first. That is to do this thing in the Lord, which we are told is the only thing in this matter. And that is a most unaccountable piece of presumption, that people will take upon them, to dispose of themselves, give themselves, to one another, before they have ever given themselves to God through Christ, which is the first and most fundamental relation. You all ought to know you are not your own, you have nothing to do with yourselves, you have not yourselves to dispose of otherwise, but from, and by, and under, God. And therefore, give to him your own persons; give yourself to the Lord, in the first place, before you think of giving yourself to another. You have not power over yourselves, nor can dispose of yourselves. None have so much power over themselves, as that they ought to think of giving him, or herself, away without God; but for God: and therefore, the gift must be made to himself first; and that union with him be made fundamental, to that other subsequent and inferior union, much inferior.

But here it may be said, What then, may only godly persons marry? or those only that are in covenant with God in Christ?

To that I will only say in short, and the business will then be clear enough. It is a question that will answer itself. You ought to give up yourselves to God through Christ, every one, the first thing you do, out of hand, without a moment's delay. For till this be done, you are in a state of rebellion against him; he lays his claim to us all upon a natural right, and upon the Redeemer's acquisition too, who died, and revived, and rose again, that he might be Lord, Owner, and Ruler, of the living and dead; to wit, of all most absolutely.

Therefore, this is a thing not to be deferred a moment. So as if the question be, Hath a man sinned then, if he hath married while he was yet ungodly? I say, his sin doth not lie in what he hath done; but it lies in what he hath not done. It doth not lie in this, that you have married; but it lies in this, that you have not taken God for your God, and given up yourselves to God through Christ, to be his: here lies the sin. Marrying, abstractly, and alone, is not a sin; nay, it is, in many cases, a duty: but then, there is a prior duty, a superior duty:

therefore, none sin by marrying, barely, but his sin lies in not giving up himself to God, which he is under continual, momentally obligation to do. So that you are in a rebellion every moment you defer it: you keep from God his own right, his own treasure, that he hath made, and that he should be served by, as his own. And that is the case, which neither deserves, nor needs any further answer. But,

(3.) The design of religion to be, to our uttermost, kept up, from age to age, in this world, is to be served, as much as is possible, by those that have the prospect of being parents in their agreed resolution with themselves, whenever God shall give them posterity, to temper and qualify their complacency herein, with that grief, sorrow, and concern, and fear, which the case itself challengeth, lest there should be a transmitting of corrupt and sinful nature, without a due subsequent endeavour to remedy what they could not prevent. There ought to be, I say, a joint agreement and resolution between such, if ever God give them posterity, to qualify and temper the complacency commonly taken herein, with that just mixture of concern, grief, and fear; that since there is a corrupt nature conveyed, lest it should go alone, or remain alone; and a holy, divine nature not be communicated, too, through any neglect on their part, when God doth give them opportunity of treating and dealing with such, who shall have sprung from them, in order to this end. There ought to be a great and deep concern of mind and spirit to this purpose; that, whereas, commonly, when a child is born, all that is considered in such a case, is, that now such a family is likely to be built up; and they take great complacency in it, that there is an offspring arisen to them: but this complacency is without that mixture and qualification, which the state of the case, as it is in itself, doth challenge. For it ought to be considered, We have been the instruments of bringing into the world a sinful creature, an impure creature, a guilty creature; one that is a child of wrath by nature. The complacency that is taken in having posterity, should not drown or swallow up such just considerations as these are, which, being entertained, may have their due effect, and proper influence, to excite to that subsequent duty which will be incumbent upon such parents. And,

(4.) Such parents ought to endeavour a most entire agreement in, and understanding of, a solemn and early dedication and devoting of such, their issue, to God. This ought to be done understandingly, solemnly, and early. And the parents ought to agree to give God his right in their child; that as it is by nature a child of wrath, it may be; by grace, an heir of mercy; they doing what in them is incumbent in order thereunto; they taking hold of God's covenant, which is not a nullity; and it is profane to think it so. And, indeed, nothing doth more betray the interest of God, and Christ, and Godliness, and Christianity, in the world, than the slight and trifling management of the important affairs of baptism; that it is so little understood; and that men play with it as they do; and as they do also, with that of marriage, as if it were matter of sport, when it is one of the things of the greatest importance in all the world. But it ought to be considered, here is a creature corrupt and impure, it is true, but in which God hath the first and proper right; it belongs to him, and he can make this impure creature a holy creature. And I offer it to him upon his own claim, and challenge, and the engagement of his word, in order thereunto, that he may do so. Herein parents should agree: " We dedicate to thee what thou hast given us, more thine than ours. We have had our contribution to the impurity of it: we can only hope to have it made a pure and holy creature by thy holy, gracious, and vital influences, in thine own way and time imparted, and communicated to it." And it is upon this account, that parents are sanctified to one another; though but one should be a believer, that what springs from them should be holy; that is, by a federal holiness, related to God, and capable of being devoted to him. 1 Cor. 7. 11. And then,

(5.) Pursuantly to such a devoting of their little ones to God, it ought to be a joint agreement between parents, that their first care should be taken about their minds. " Now, here is a little one to be brought up, to be educated:" this should be said, as a fundamental resolution, by agreement and consent of parents. " Our first care shall be about the mind of this little one, if it live to be a capable subject of our education and instruction; that is it we will first be chiefly concerned about For this is an intelligent and immortal part; this is the seat of God's holy image, if ever it shall be produced; and it is itself his natural image: for as it is a mind, or hath a mind, so it is a spiritual and intelligent being, and is like God naturally, and his very offspring, upon this account, who is pleased to style himself, ' the Father of spirits, and the God of the spirits of all flesh;' of those spirits that dwell so meanly as in flesh. And therefore, that ought to be the agreed and resolved first care; that our principal concernment be about the minds of our little ones." The care that is commonly, most of all, taken, is about the outward man, and the external concernments of our posterity: they love to see them fair, comely, beautiful, healthful, strong, vigorous; wish to see them have straight limbs, and the like; but do not care how crooked dispositions they have. This is unaccountable, and detestable, that it should be thus with a reasonable creature; those that are capable of understanding the differences of things; and of how much greater importance one thing is than another. But this, I say, ought to be the first care, and should be the agreement between parents, (with dependance upon the grace of God,) about the minds of our little ones. And,

(6.) In order hereunto, there ought to be a very diligent observation made of them, to see what their natural temper is, or is like to prove, which will discover itself to an observing eye, by early indications, one way or other: that is, whether my child is likely to prove dull or docile; whether it is likely to prove mild and meek, or froward and peevish; whether it is likely to prove tractable or intractable; whether it is likely to prove mean and low spirited, or great and high spirited. These different dispositions will soon and early appear to observing eyes. Such notices should be taken by prudent parents, and must be by conscientious ones, who have a design for the good of their families, that they may know how to acquit themselves in aftertimes accordingly. Some children will discover more of a natural timorousness; others will discover more boldness and venturousness, and that very early. And careful observation should be made of the temper as it doth more early *prodere se, discover itself*, offer itself to view, and observation, that there may be suitable measures taken, for prudent applications afterwards, as the case shall require. And then, again,

(7.) Resolution ought to be taken between parents, and especially the mothers, (whose part will be more about the child in its more tender years,) to watch against any sinful inclinations, one way or other, as they shall discover themselves. If there be any appearance of falsehood, of wrathfulness, of envy, or revengefulness; of pride, or haughtiness in children, to animadvert upon these betimes. And especially of immoderate desires after any thing; only it ought to be distinguished, whether it be the desire of that which is necessary for it; or a desire only of that which curiosity may prompt to desire. That which is necessary for it must be had; but not upon its first signification of a desire; that it may be made to understand betimes, dependance and subjection. And that the less it hath of understanding of its own, the more it is to be managed by the parent's understanding; and the having, even of necessary things, is not to be the reward of demanding them, or asking for them.

But for unlawful inclinations, they are to be checked, with all the care and industry imaginable, very early; any such as I have instanced in, or whatsoever besides can be instanced in; repress the beginnings of these things, as you would the beginnings of a disease that may prove mortal to your child. And it is this neglect; (especially in mothers,) that ripens such evils as these, thus radicated in the very natures of children, till they are incurable; till they be past cure. And that makes so many bills, as in a desperate case, to be sent in to us. It is a far easier thing to send in a bill to a minister, when a child is spoiled and ruined in its tender years, than it is constantly to watch over them, and repress their ill inclinations betimes, and make them understand government, and subjection, and dependance, in their early days. But where the will of the child is the law of the family, and must govern all, no wonder if plagues and mischiefs, of this kind, are introduced and brought into families by this means.

Divine wisdom hath taught us in such cases how to understand the matter aright. "He that spares the rod hates his son:" fond parents think it love; but divine wisdom calls it hatred. And therefore, is the advice, in that same book, Proverbs 19. 18. "Let not thy soul spare for his crying." What! because he cries will you throw him into hell, will you abandon him to destruction? Not that there needs much of frequent severity, where there is a due prudence used in reference to such cases. I have known children brought up to men and women's estate, that never had a blow in their lives; nor was it needful. It would not be needful, if there were a steady awfulness in the deportment of parents towards them, so that they might, upon any thing that were really a miscarriage, understand a frown, a rebuke, a strange look. If there were that prudence used, that might be used, there would be little need of harshness and severity, unless upon very ill temper indeed; and they must be dealt with accordingly.

But where all the care is to indulge a humour, and please the child; and where there is a disposition in parents, many times, to be proud of the ill dispositions of their children, as they appear in them, how many ill tempers are made worse? And how many good tempers are spoiled by this means? And the guilt and future miseries of the children will cry against their parents, not only in this world, but, perhaps, in the other too. And the truth is, parents would shew a great deal more mercy in that which is commonly reckoned harshness and severity: nay, I say, they would not be reckoned so cruel in breaking their childrens' limbs, in tearing their flesh, in pulling out their eyes, as they commonly are, in indulging their vicious, sinful dispositions and inclinations, in them, without a timely endeavour of cure, wherein the seed of those miseries are sown, and spring up so in this world, and in the other too. Again,

(8.) They ought, in pursuance of the mentioned end, to instill the principles of religion betimes. Teach them betimes who made them, that great Supreme Being who is the Maker and Author of all things; teach them reverence and subjection to him: speak awfully before them, so as never to take that great name in vain; so as that your fear, your own fear, of the great God, whose name you bear, may be exemplary to them: as Jacob sware by the fear of his father, Isaac, when the important solemnity of the occasion called for an oath. Jacob had observed what Isaac's reverence of God was, and so called him "my father's fear." O teach your children to know God as their parents' fear. And so the other great principles of religion besides, which they are capable of understanding (if there be a due and diligent application) earlier than is thought; earlier than is commonly thought, at least: but the sooner the better: "Train up a child in the way he should go, and when he is old he will not depart from it." Labour to season him betimes: so the wickedness of a corrupt nature is to be counterwrought. And then,

(9.) Pray much for them. You that are, or may be, parents, as you are so, or upon that prospect, let this be a matter of great concern between God and you. Pour out your souls in your closets, upon this account; especially such of you to whom God hath given children. And be sure,

(10.) To set up and keep up family worship, family religion. Let this be an agreed thing between you; that as holy, good Joshua resolved, "I and my house will serve the Lord, whatever others do, we will serve the Lord." As a corrupt nature comes by birth, and wickedness springs up so, so it is nourished and cherished, in great part, by the ungodliness of parents. In families were there is no calling on the name of the Lord, O how doth it thrive! That wickedness that is natural, how doth it grow and improve in an irreligious family, a profane family! So doth the wickedness of this world grow, the wickedness of England, the wickedness of London. And the misery thereof is growing *pari passu, with an equal pace*. And if dreadful calamities are coming upon us, coming upon the land, coming upon this city, we have reason to apprehend here is the very source of all the mischief, even family profaneness. God is banished out of the families of the most: and what will this come to?

I desire to bless God for it, that the ministers of this city, such as are united, and are wont to meet weekly, about the common concernments of their congregations, are awakened into a sense of this great and growing evil; and they have resolved to use their utmost endeavours to awaken the people of their several charges and congregations, about this very thing. And (God willing) you will have more of it ere it be long; that I believe there will be such a joint, agreed, common cry in London, against the wicked neglect of the worship of God in families, as hath not been for many an age past. I hope there will. And know, it is an agreed thing, that there shall, at some one time and, as near as may be, all about the same time. And so will, I hope, the faithful servants of Christ (at least) deliver their own souls. Yea, I hope God will bless this to be a means of great reformation in this city.

For the evil as is feared (at least it is said to be matter of observation with some, for my part, I know it not, but it is matter of fear with many) is, that a great many professors of religion make no conscience at all of any such thing, as family duty; but prodigally throw away that time otherwise, which should be spent in the solemn worship of God in their families, with those of whom he hath committed the care and charge to them. And if what is designed happen, and do not produce a thorough and general reformation among us, it will produce a vindication of that justice, of that severity, which we are to expect. For God will not be dallied with always; and I doubt, not much longer. That which hath been a seat of religion eminently in the world, in the eye of the past times, that religion should languish and dwindle in it, as it doth by the neglect of family government, even by persons professing godliness, and who would be counted a godly sort of people, is a very sad consideration.

LECTURE XL.*

Secondly. I would now add some considerations to enforce what I have been pleading with you about. And,

* Preached Dec. 8, 1694.

1. That which is obvious in the text—" Behold, I was shapen in iniquity; and in sin did my mother conceive me." Parents, they have transmitted a corrupt nature to their children. Into what agonies of spirit should it put us, to think with ourselves, " I have been an instrument in producing an heir of wrath, and of a divine curse. O! shall I use no endeavour to draw it under a blessing, and make it the subject of blessedness, now that we live under that gospel, in which we are called to blessedness?" But that call must be pursued; and God expects it should be so, in apt and suitable methods and applications, by such as he makes use of as instruments, one way or another, whether in private or more public stations, in order thereunto. And,

2. Consider God's original, supreme, and sovereign interest in families, as he is the Founder of them, and as they are his plantation. " He sets the solitary in families." Psalm 68. 6. Consider this, together with the design of his forming of them; to wit, that he might have a godly seed still arising, from age to age, as you may see in that Malachi 2. 15. It was the very end and design of that fundamental relation in families, and unto families, the conjugal relation: " Wherefore did he make but one, when he had the residue of the Spirit? Why, that he might seek a godly seed." As if it had been said, These plantations are mine. This, the constitution of families, (in which the conjugal relation, is the fundamental relation,) speaks, upon the first design of settling such a constitution as this. There lay open (as we must but be sure) to the foresight of the divine eye, what a general apostasy and defection there would be; and that a corrupt nature would be transmitted, from age to age, from generation to generation. But God did determine with himself, not, therefore, to abandon all to one common ruin: as if he should have said, " I will have an interest in this world, notwithstanding." And therefore, as this was the original design of the constitution of families, that he might have a godly seed, though the apostasy hath intervened, he will not quit his design: for his interest is still the same in its own nature. And therefore, this we must understand him continually to insist upon, as a sacred right to himself; that he will have this design pursued by all that will be subject to him, that will return into their state of subjection, and be willing to serve him in the several stations that he hath set them. He will have all endeavours used for transmitting of religion, as well as corrupt and sinful nature is transmitted, from age to age; though the one is done by a natural, the other is done by instituted means, followed

with a blessing, and by influence from above: he will have this latter design carried on by the mutual and joint endeavours of parents, under the influence of his grace; as well as the former course is carried on unavoidably. But when no care or concern is had about this, the foundations of families are laid in a curse. And then,

3. Consider, that it cannot but concern parents, such as are such, or may be so, to express a natural affection, and to endeavour to have that improved, by having it spiritualized, and improved to a spiritual purpose, as well as they are the means by which a natural corruption is conveyed, and transmitted to their posterity. "They have natural corruption from me; (they ought to think;) and shall there be nothing of natural affection? And shall I not labour to have that natural affection sublimated, and spiritualized, and improved, so as to aim at their spiritual and supernatural good? Shall they have nothing from me, but sin and death? or nothing besides the human nature which they have from me; nothing but what shall corrupt and spoil, make it the subject and seed-plot of sin, against God, and misery to themselves?" If there be any thing of natural affection working downward with the descent of natural corruption, that natural affection should aim at the true good of them whom nature hath so much endeared; and should, upon that account, take in the *auxilia*, draw in the aids and helps from heaven, by which that natural affection will become spiritualized; and so the more sincerely and entirely aim at, and the more fervently pursue, a design for the spiritual and eternal good of those who descended and sprung from us. And,

4. It is to be considered, what an honour this doth derive upon the persons themselves, that shall be instrumental in this design. A glorious thing it is, to be a servant to God in so great a work as this; to recover out of the state of apostasy, those that come into that state by our means; to be an instrument, in the hand of God, to promote his kingdom in this world, in opposition to the dark kingdom of the infernal powers. How glorious a thing is it, to carry on a designed opposition against the work of the devil in this world! that when we know the aim and purpose of the great God, is to have, in all successions of time, a people for his name, I should be instrumental in promoting it! It is an honourable thing, a thing that draws a glory upon the persons, and upon the families, where religion doth thus come to take place, to take root, and is planted, and doth flourish. And again,

5. It speaks an agreement and sameness, in a great mea-

sure, of mind and design, with the Redeemer. For he is to have his seed in this world, from which his word and Spirit are never to depart; Isaiah 59, latter end. And the matter is settled, by everlasting covenant, as you find it there : "This is my covenant, (saith the Lord,) My Spirit that is upon thee, and my words which I have put in thy mouth, shall not depart out of thy mouth, nor out of the mouth of thy seed, nor out of the mouth of thy seed's seed, from henceforth and for ever." And so we know it hath been an agreed thing, as the matter is stated, (Isaiah 53. 11,) between the Father and him, that he shall see his seed, and the travail of his soul, and be satisfied therein : and that, as a recompense for his having undertaken the work of redemption, and accomplishing it, upon terms so painful, so expensive, so dolorous, so ignominious to himself. As if the Father had said to him, " Thou shalt have all this, this reward; thou shalt see thy seed, and the travail of thy soul, and be satisfied therein." Upon this, our Lord Jesus Christ cannot but be most intent to see a continual seed spring up to him, out of a seed of evil doers; out of an apostate race of men. Now, if we be intent upon this thing, it bespeaks a sameness of mind and design, between the Redeemer and us: which, how pleasant, how delightful, how comfortable, should it be to our reflecting thoughts! And again,

6. It is further to be considered, that if there be no such design to promote godliness in families, that that may be transmitted from age to age, (though in a distinct and diverse way,) as the corrupt and sinful nature is transmitted, then, we cannot but be doing our part to the promoting of ungodliness in the world ourselves. We shall do that, and nothing besides, nothing in opposition thereunto. For do but consider, as the case stands between God and man, there can be no medium between being for godliness, and being for ungodliness; we cannot be in an indifferency. If we are not, according to the uttermost of our power and capacity, for transmitting, and continuing of godliness in the world, we must be for the continuing of ungodliness. A horrid and fearful thought, if any would but allow it to take place! They can only be in an indifferency, in reference to any case whatsoever, that have no real concern therein, one way or other. But here, every one is concerned; and he must take a part: he must be for the promoting of godliness, or promoting its contrary. And therefore,

7. According to this state of things in the world, they that do aim to contribute nothing to the transmitting of religion

and godliness in the world, in opposition to the corruption of nature, which is so generally spreading through it, they are continually providing that there may be a war and rebellion continued and kept on foot, against heaven, from age to age, and from generation to generation. "He that is not with me is against me," saith the Lord. If you will not take God's side in this matter, you are fighting against him, and labour to do all that you can, that the rebellion against him, may not cease; but that there may be still a succession of new rebels, new enemies, from one age to another. And,

8. You will herein, too, be constant accomplices and confederates with the prince of the apostasy; he that first fell from God, and that made it his design to involve all the world in the transgression, and in the consequent ruin; you will be continual accomplices with him. And this is, indeed, the state of every one's case, in these matters. Whoever will but consider with himself, if he be come to the use of his understanding, and hath some prospect, (though uncertain,) of a life's time to be run out in this world, he will find the world divided between two great lords, two great masters, two great fathers: that is, the true and Rightful Lord of all, he that made all; and to whom all belong; and that usurping prince of darkness, who is called, "the god of this world," and whose children and seed wicked men (as such) are said to be. Why, every m a upon the prospect of entering upon the scene, the stage of this world, is to think with himself, "I must, in this case, either be with God, or against God. If I be not with God, if I be against him, I am with that horrid, usurped power, that is set up in opposition to him, with this world: and I fall in with that common destroyer, against the common Maker and Preserver of all things." This will be the state of your case, if you be not intent upon a design of counterworking this common corruption, which is descending in this world; you will be looked upon under no other notion but as an accomplice of hell against heaven. And,

9. You will herein, falsify with God, after you have solemnly vowed and covenanted by your Christian parents. You have ordinarily been devoted and dedicated to God in baptism. To deal falsely and treacherously with a man, against the tenor of a covenant, is a horrid thing: but to break faith with God, is much more horrid!

But you will say, You made no such vow; and what your parents did for you, how should that bind you? Why,

(1.) It is very great ignorance to think, that parents cannot bind their children to any thing. Those that have the nearest natural interest in you, and whose understandings and wills are to be employed for you, when you have no understanding and will to use of your own, do you think they, from whom you sprang, have not a natural interest in you? How unreasonable and absurd a thought is that! In reference to all other concerns besides, have parents no disposal of their children? And may they dispose of them, or do for, or with them otherwise, and may they not dispose of them for their spiritual good? And again,

(2.) It is every where counted a very horrid and barbarous thing, to endeavour to rescind the lawful act of a parent, if it were in my power, if I could do it. If I could alienate, or alter, what he hath so and so disposed; and if he have righteously disposed of it for me, to come after and labour to rescind and undo all that he hath done—this is barbarous and infamous, in common estimate, among men. And,

(3.) It must needs be much more so as to God, or if he be concerned in the matter. As now for instance, Suppose a pious person, with an honest mind and design, hath dedicated such a part or portion of his estate to a pious use; suppose it be not mere charity, but a pious charity, that is, not designed for a superstitious use, but for a use truly pious, and to serve the interest of God and religion in the world; and a son comes after, and he labours to undo all this: you that would think it horrid, to alienate a piece of earth, dedicated to God by your parents, ought you not to think it horrid, to alienate a soul from God, which hath, as much as in them was, been dedicated to God by them too? I would not alienate a piece of earth, dedicated to God; but I would alienate myself, my soul, my body, dedicated to him. This no man should (if he had power) alienate. What was dedicated and sacred to a use truly pious, may not be alienated; and if not a portion of his estate, much less himself so dedicated, and given to God. But yet, further,

(4.) It is to be said, that as this was not to be done, if it were in his power, so he cannot have such a thing in his power, to wit, in his rightful power: for every one was a debtor of his whole life and being, his soul and body, and his all, to God, antecedently to any such dedication. And therefore, when such a tender is made to God, it was but to tender and devote to him, what was his own by a more early title. " All souls are mine;" so he lays his claim universally to all the souls of men; and therein to the whole of them; for what are they besides a soul? what that is valuable or considerable besides? " All souls are mine, as well as the soul of the father, as the soul of the son." Ezekiel 18. 4. He hath a nearer interest in them than a parent could have, before any such dedication: for a parent was not the parent of their spirit. They are the fathers of our flesh; but he himself is the Father of spirits; the principal and most considerable thing that we have about us, or that belongs to our being. And therefore, when such a dedication was made, there was only a tender made to God, of what was his before; of what he claims an interest in originally. He is the Father of them, and they are his offspring. And again, further,

(5.) This, in answer to that, is to be considered, that though inclination to good do not descend, yet, obligation to it doth descend, from fathers to children, and from the predecessors in a family, unto their successors. Not only obligations of justice and common right, but obligations of kindness and friendship. As, how ordinary is it for friendships and amities to descend from father to son, in families. And it is looked upon as a rude kind of thing, to be uncivil to my father's friend. And on which side, between families, among whom hath been a friendship, it first begins to fail, it always lies as an imputation upon that side. Great amity there was between such and such families; but now it is at an end, since such and such successors are sprung up there. On whose side the failure is, there commonly lies a very ill character. And it is a thing contrary to the dictates of common wisdom,—yea, and of the divine wisdom. "Thine own friend, and thy father's friend, forsake not." Prov. 27. 10. But how much less then, thy God, and thy father's God? If it be an indecency, and uncomeliness, and a very unfit thing, that is, contrary to the precept of studying whatsoever is lovely, and thinking of those things, to forsake my friend, and my father's friend, how much more horrid must it be to forsake my God, and my father's God? "My father's God shall not be my God!"

And therefore, it is not so light a matter, as is commonly thought, to have the weight of that early dedication, lying upon one's score as a violated thing; as having dealt falsely in that covenant of God. Indeed, it is not only an evidence, but a cause of the languishment of religion in our days, that this is a thing so little thought of among christians: "I was devoted to God early, given up to him with great solemnity; having these venerable names,—the name of the Father, the name of the Son, and the name of the Holy Ghost, named upon me, at my setting forth into the world." It speaks an apprehension of that thing itself, as if it were trivially done at first, if we make a trifle of it all our days afterwards:

as if such a solemn transaction between the great Lord of heaven and earth, and his own dust, his own creatures, the works of his hands, were to be so lightly made of. Therefore, take we the weight of this upon our spirits. If we do not do, in our several stations and capacities, our uttermost to counter-work this descending evil in the world, we do falsify the sacred covenant of God, in which we were early and preventingly bound to him, by the vow of parents concerning us. And then,

10. It is the way, certainly, for us to lose all the comfort of domestical relations, when we are not driving on this design in our several stations: we lose by it, all the comforts of family relations. For what comfort can I take in having such and such relations, in a family, when, in the mean time, there is a contrariety, and a war, maintained and kept up between God and me? So that I can never eat or drink in peace, or converse in peace, or rise up, or lay down in peace; but still I have wrath from heaven upon me? This will infuse gall and gravel into all my enjoyments whatsoever. I am not serving God's design, for the promoting of godliness, in opposition to this growing and descending wickedness in the world: I do nothing towards it. This very reflection is enough to embitter all my comforts. And what are such and such relations to me, but confederates against God? They agree to sin together, and to carry on an interest against God together. For there can be no neutrality in such cases, as was said before. And then,

11. This is but an ill provision for a day of accounting, which will come, whether we sleep, or whether we wake; whether we forget all such considerations, or whether we consider them. "Judgment lingereth not; and destruction slumbereth not." If I eat on, and drink on, and sleep on, judgment comes on with never a whit the slower foot. O! the seriousness of that interwoven counsel, in the discourse of the apostle, even with reference to this business of the matrimonial state. 1 Cor. 7. 29, 30. "But this I say, brethren, the time is short: it remaineth, that both they that have wives be as if they had none; and they that weep, as if they wept not; and they that rejoice, as though they rejoiced not; and they that buy, as if they possessed not; and those that use this world as not abusing it: for the fashion of this world passeth away."

The time is short. That may have reference to families, and the world: families that were spoken of before and after; and the world, in the whole, which is spoken of there in express terms. The fundamental relation in families, it is measured by a short time; by a very short time. Where there hath been such a union lately contracted, it will shortly be broken; time measures it; and that time will have run to its period very speedily. The time is short: it remains, therefore, that they that have wives be as if they had none; and they that rejoice, as though they rejoiced not. They rejoice in having newly contracted such a relation: it is reasonable to understand it so, considering it the subject of the apostle's foregoing discourse; that joy will be as if it had not been, in respect of the grounds: and it ought to be so, in the mean time, in respect of the degree. That rejoicing, in having entered into such a relation, will soon be turned into weeping, as having lost it, or it having lost you, which comes all to one. And it is but a short time that measures all this.

And do you think it strange, that that time would be counted short, which measures the time of a family, as it is made up of such and such persons now coexistent; or that measures the relation of two such conjugal relatives? Do you think it strange, that that should be spoken of, and counted a short time, when it is but a short time that measures the whole, and measures the duration of the whole—the fashion of the world passing away? As persons vanish, and families vanish, so is the world vanishing, all will be gone ere long. As the apostle John speaks in the like place, 1 John, 2. 17. "The world passeth away, and the lust thereof: but he that doeth the will of God abideth for ever."

Now while it is time, and but a short time, that measures all our affairs, and all our enjoyments, and all our designs, under the sun; time that will be soon done, and which will end in a general dissolution of all this world; a day, a time, " when the heavens shall pass away with a great noise, and the elements melt with fervent heat; and the earth, and all things therein, be burnt up and destroyed." I say, sure if this is certain to be the last catastrophe and end of all things, of what concernment is it to us, to consider how we may make a comfortable account when time expires, and when it is to be received, and with it, what I have been, and what I have done, in such or such a state and relation, in which I was placed in this world! There ought to be an account made daily: How can I lie down in peace at night, and not be capable of giving some good account that I have been doing somewhat for God, and for the interest of God, and religion, and godliness, in my station that day? But how shall I lie down in the grave, when a life time is wasted, and spent, and thrown away, and nothing done for God? I have rather served the interest of ungodliness, than religion, all my time in this world: and how shall I think of appearing before the tribunal of the Supreme Judge, when the end of all things cometh; and when I am beset with all the terrors of that day,—the heavens rolling up, and all the powers of them shaken; the earth all on fire, the elements all flaming round about me? And I have a life's time to review and look back upon, spent away in sin and vanity, with no design for God, and for the Redeemer; though I know that he had his design set on foot here in this world, with which I co-operated not, to which I was not subservient—nay, to which I have lived opposite in a stated course.

Let all these things be weighed and put together; and sure we have a great deal to enforce this first instruction; that since corrupt nature is to lie certainly and constantly descending in this world, we would, as we ought, in our several stations and capacities, do our uttermost to counterwork that descending evil.

LECTURE XLI.*

But now I shall carry the matter a little further; and as I have been hitherto shewing what those that are, or shortly may be, parents, ought to do themselves, in reference to their next descendants, that is, those that shall more immediately spring from themselves; so, I will shew you, too, what may and should be done, in order to a further descent, by those that may have the authority to dispose of their children in the conjugal state, with the expectation of a continual descent of human nature by them further and further,—that so, that corruption and pravity which cannot be prevented, to descend with it, may be, as much as is possible, corrected, and redressed in such an after descent.

This that I am now to speak to, will especially concern such as have children to dispose of in the conjugal relation, who are judged meet for that state. And, indeed, it will equally concern such as are loco-parents, that have the parental trust devolved upon them, by the prudence of others, and their own undertaking.

And as to such, I must still insist, that they are to observe the same measures that have been given in reference to persons who are, themselves, now entering the conjugal state, with the prospect of an offspring, to which human nature, when it

* Preached Dec. 15, 1694.

descends, will go accompanied with a sinful pravity. And here, indeed, as to the case I am now to speak to, there are on each side two parties ordinarily to concur, or two persons in each party. There are the persons to be disposed of; and there are the persons that dispose of them. And I shall speak to the part of these that are to be the disposers, parents or loco-parents, guardians, trustees, who are to take care of settling such in the world in the conjugal state. In reference whereto, the things designed, in general, usually are, that mankind may be continued upon the face of the earth; and more especially, more particularly, that such and such families therein, or those that they are concerned or intrusted for, may be built and preserved: and (as the Psalmist speaks) "their houses may endure for ever; and their lands (if possible) still called after their own names;" as in that psalm 49, 11. And this is a thing that may prudently and justly be designed, in its due subordination. If it be substituted in the room of the true and great design of heaven, or carried on without reference to God, and religion, and the transmission of a godly seed here, upon earth, then you see the censure of the Holy Ghost, upon this design, in the same context: "This their way is their folly, though their posterity approve their sayings." Sayings are doings here: the sayings of their minds and designs, together with acting conformably and correspondently thereunto. This their way is their folly; yet one age approves the former herein, and they that come after, run the same course.

Here I must, in reference to this, insist, that their measures ought to be with consideration, that, with human nature, a sinful pravity will descend, and that this may be (as much as is possible) repressed: and so, as that God's design may be carried on concurrently, which he had from the beginning, in settling the conjugal state, and in planting families here on earth; that is, that he might seek a godly seed. Wherefore one, when he might have made many, having the residue of the Spirit, but that he might seek a godly seed? Mal. 2. 15. And this design he hath no more quitted, than he hath disclaimed his interest in this whole lower world, or, saith, "It ceaseth to be a part of my creation, or I cease to be the Lord and Owner of it. But inasmuch as there lies under our present consideration, the duty of such as have children to dispose of, with a prospect that they will have children, and that so a care ought to be extended as far as lies ordinarily within the compass of human endeavour; there ought, indeed, a care extending so far as the desire reacheth, and the main intention of the mind, a great deal further. But so much as I speak to, comes commonly within the compass of actual endeavour. It is ordinary for parents to survive unto the disposal of their children into the conjugal state, with expectation of children from them; and therefore, it is the duty of such that I am now generally to speak to.

And I will tell you, in general, what it is; to wit, that as much as in them is, to endeavour that religion be transmitted and descend, and go down in their families, and in the families for which they are concerned and intrusted. It is true, it cannot descend the same way as human nature, and the sinful pravity doth; that is, not by propagation: but it is to descend by pious education, as the means that God must be supplicated to co-operate with, and bless, for the implantation of a better principle, than could be propagated by nature. This sinful pravity, it comes by nature: this superadded principle must come by grace. But then, there are means of grace in order to the obtaining of that grace: and this is the first and the readiest means; to wit, a pious education. And therefore, it ought to be the care of such as have children to be disposed of in the conjugal state. To speak a little more particularly,

1. To endeavour, as much as is possible, that they may see them godly before they be married. As much, I say, as is possible to endeavour that. It can be very little satisfaction to the heart of a parent, (if it be so tender as the grace of God in it should make it,) to dispose of a child into such a relation, to a human creature, when, as yet, there is no appearance that it is come into a relation to God. "My child hath now a husband, or hath a wife, gotten for it; but hath not a God, not a Christ. This is a sad thought! I have taken care that it might have what is so unspeakably less necessary: but of that which is most necessary, I have taken no care; that is, to see that my child, my son, or daughter, was married to Christ: to see, that before the conjugal covenant, there was the evangelical covenant settled and established between God in Christ, and this poor child of mine." And,

2. Their further care hereon ought to be, finding that there are some good appearances of pious inclinations, they do choose out such for them as will fall in with them, in the design of transmitting piety to their posterity: that I may have one for my son, or my daughter, that I believe, in my conscience, will make it their study and business, to educate their children in the knowledge and fear of God; that religion may run on in the family, and that corrupt nature may not descend alone.

It is a very sad case when this is the very last part of the concern in such a matter as this: when the first thing thought of is, "Where shall I get a great fortune for my son; or how shall I marry my daughter into a great estate?" When this is the first care, is it like that precept of our Lord Christ—"Seek first the kingdom of God?" Matt. 6. 33. This is looked upon as the *unam necessarium*, the one thing necessary; a great fortune, an ample estate, a plentiful income: and as for religion and sobriety, if that be considered, it is considered on the by, collaterally, as if it were but a trifle in comparison. And so, accordingly, are bargains driven on, as formal contracts, as for beasts in Smithfield; even for the very souls of young persons that have not judgment to choose for themselves, and that, (it may be,) have a great deal of reverence for those that are their guides, and have the disposal of them. They think they must trust their care and judgment, and do so. And they concern themselves only, how they may do well in the world, without considering, at all, what shall become of their souls; or how they may be exposed and given up for a prey; or what shall become of those that shall descend from them.

This is so intolerable an evil under the sun, that we have reason to wonder at the divine patience, that it hath not, by vindictive flames, animadverted on such wickedness long ago. But we are to expect it will. And as it is the wickedness of the world, which that final conflagration must animadvert upon, and will, it can be upon no one thing more than this: this way and means by which wickedness hath been propagated in the world, from age to age, without any care or concern, by those that should have driven on a counter-design, in duty to the great Lord and Maker of this world; as if he had given it up to men only to sin in, and to indulge their sinful lusts in, for a short life's time; and then go down into the dust and die. This is a thing so contrary to the reason of mankind, (if that were attended to, and if men would commune with themselves,) that we cannot but wonder that vengeance hath suffered men to live so long upon the face of this earth, at such a rate: and we have no reason to wonder that such a determination is set, that this world shall end, as we are told it shall, by vindictive flames, consuming the inhabitants of this earth from off it.

But I shall here, first, answer a question which may arise about this matter I have been speaking to; and then proceed to enforce that charge or duty which, I have said, doth belong to such whose case and concern I have been speaking of. The question is this: "Why, suppose I that am a parent, or a guardian, do not discern in my child, (son or daughter,) now grown up, and of whom I have some thoughts of disposing into the conjugal state; suppose I do not see in them any thing of a pious inclination; am I to endeavour to settle them, in that relation, with such a one that is judged sincerely pious. And to this I must say,

1. That none ought to be rash and hasty in their judgments concerning others, who are pious, and who are not; at least, there ought to be a very careful abstaining from a positive judgment concerning any, that they are ungodly. What judgment we do pass, it is better, and safer, to err on the most favourable side. But we have a most express rule from our Lord himself not to judge; which is not to be understood, neither, in a simple, but comparative sense. "Judge not, that ye be not judged." We must not judge hastily, not judge rashly, not judge positively, and concludingly, without very clear and full evidence, that such a one is an ungodly man. But we are told afterwards, in the same chapter, Matt. 7. 16. that men are known by their fruits; so that, as we are to be slow and sparing in our judgment concerning others, especially on the severer part, that they are ungodly; so we ought to have, when we do judge, that which may be very clearly evidential: and then (as we do judge that there may be such evidence, as upon which we cannot but conclude so) it is out of question; otherwise, we should not know how to carry it towards such as are put under that mark, according as we are obliged to make distinction; and distinction even between them that have the form of godliness, but appear not to have the power of it, that we may turn away from them. And if there are many other things, mentioned in that context, that are inconsistent with the power of godliness, but do very well agree only with the form, the external form, we are to take our measures from thence, and thereby to endeavour to guide ourselves, as to our carriage and deportment, towards such: "Turn away from them," as the apostle there directeth. And therefore, I say, if matters do evidently appear, such and such do discover, by an habitual stated course and practice, that there is not only no serious godliness, but there is an enmity, a contrariety, an opposition, to it, they cannot comply with rules and ordinary duties that do belong to it; then, upon that, upon that supposition, I say,

2. That they, with whom any such are concerned in such a treaty, will (as they ought to have) have such a design as you ought to have, and therefore will decline you. They will not have such a one for their son, or for their daughter: (if they be such as make conscience of what they do:) and so

your question is answered. They will answer for you: "No, I will not have such a one come into my family, or for my son, or daughter, that appears an enemy to godliness, a rebel against Christ; that hath a fixed, habitual aversion to all serious religion. But,

3. If they should not do so, not make that choice, for those whom they are concerned for, which they ought to make, you, for your parts, ought to do as you would be done unto; according to that general rule of our Lord, which carries so much of equity, so visibly in the face of it, that even some pagans have been fond of it: and one of the pagan emperors would have had Christ owned for a God, purposely upon that account, for that rule: *Quod tibi non vis fieri, alter ne facias what you would not that another should do to you, that do not to him*. Carefully observe that rule in this case; " I would be loath my family, being a godly family, to admit an enemy to God and Christ into it; why then should I endeavour to thrust such a one deceitfully, and when the danger appears not to them, as it doth to me, into a godly family?"

It is true, that if such were married to one another, in that case, this were not a thing that immediately concerns that relation, it not lying against the essential *vinculum*; as the apostle hath determined between christians and avowed infidels: the nuptial bond holds, if it have been entered; but if it be to be made, it ought not to be made: for those that enter into that relation, are to enter it with a design of being "fellow-partakers of the grace of Christ, and helpers of one another heaven-ward;" and such as can comfortably join in prayer, and who are to carry matters so, as that their prayers may not be hindered, and the like. And if I am not to eat with a person visibly ungodly, much less am I to fall into so near a union, and converse with them: that is out of all doubt. And therefore, as I cannot in duty and in prudence, for the good of such as I am concerned for, suffer myself to be imposed upon, in such a case; so I am not to impose upon another. I would be loath to be so imposed upon, to have an enemy to God and godliness brought into my family, or united with my child: and I ought not to obtrude such a mischief as that upon another person, and another family. But when any thing in that kind is done, there must be so much the more serious, subsequent endeavours for redress; there must be the more earnest praying; and so much the more pressing advice given; and so much the more solicitude and care used, that such a one may be plucked out of the snare which, by too much unwariness, they have been betrayed into.

And thus, having answered that question, I will lay before you some considerations that may be given to enforce all this. And pray consider,

1. How little is to be alleged against it, against the carrying on this professed and avowed design, in the disposal of those I am concerned for, whether one's own children, or others that are intrusted to our care; I say, to avow this, as our design, to promote and transmit religion, and the interest of godliness in the world, consider how little is to be said against it. All that can be pretended against it is, that the custom and usage of the world is to look after a suitable match in point of estate, in the first place. It is very true, it is so. And so it is the custom of this world to forget God, and to carry it towards him, as if he were not the Lord of this world; and to cast his fear behind men's back; and to trample upon his interest; and to count religion, (which is the main concern of all men,) instead of their interest, their reproach and dishonour. This is the custom of this world. But let such things as these be put in the balance; and so the other considerations, which I intended, will fall in. As this, in the next place,

2. That God doth manifestly insist upon this design still, of propagating religion in the world. You find that he doth provide that such a design should go on through all the successions of time. Our Lord Jesus Christ hath undertaken to be with them that shall be engaged in carrying on this design, to the end of the world. He hath set up an office on purpose; and therefore, the design is not laid aside, nor ever will be laid aside, of transmitting religion in the world. And how dutiful a thing, and how glorious a thing is it, to offer one's self as an instrument, within the compass of one's own sphere, to serve such a design as this!

For let but conscience be appealed to in the case, Do we not find, that God hath a design to keep religion in the world, from age to age? What doth he continue this world for? Is it only that it may continue in a rebellion against him, from generation to generation, when it is impossible it should subsist an age, or a moment, without his sustaining influence, when we have so much assurance given us, that it is upon the account of Christ's interest, that this world is kept from dissolution all this while? It is by him that all things do subsist, and consist. Therefore, undoubtedly, God hath this design still. What serves that gospel for, that we live under, and the ministry and ordinances of it? And when we know that God hath such a design, shall not that which is his design, be our principal design? or shall we presume to disagree with him about our principal end?

Indeed, it is very true, if he had made a declaration from heaven—"I will have no more to do with this world; I will save no more souls in it; I will leave all to follow the inclination of their own hearts, and to walk and live in that darkness which they love, and will have no more concern with them:" if there had been, I say, such a declaration, then all thoughts and care of this kind, that I am speaking of, would have been superseded. For it is impossible for any to act rationally, with despair. Where there is no hope, there can be no design. But when we know that that is none of the case, but God hath a design to continue religion and godliness in this world, from age to age, I am a wretch, if I will not make his design my principal design; or if any thing shall be greater in mine eyes than that. And again, consider,

3. That if I do not do my utmost, within my sphere and capacity, for the serving this design of God, I do certainly make myself a party against him: for if there be a continual descent of human nature, without a prospect of any means to cultivate it, and correct the exorbitancies of it, in its further descent, this is a continuation of the rebellion against God; when there is only a provision made, that a rebellious nature may descend, and no more; nothing with it, no corrective with it.

But what a monstrous thing is this! when such care is taken to correct the exorbitancies of nature in inferior kinds; vegetative nature, sensitive nature. Men take care of their gardens, of their flowers, of their trees: and (as the divine poet, Herbert, saith) let weeds choke their sun. How monstrous is this! Into what a wilderness doth uncultivated and uncorrected nature grow! You find it in inferior kinds. If nature be not regulated, rectified, even vegetative nature, it will all be over-run with weeds, and better plants grow wild. The protusions of nature, if no way regulated, they become very ungrateful and uncomely. And when we find how the case is, as to rational nature, what cultivation that needs, that it may be susceptible of the implantation of such a better principle that shall be governing, man becoming, without it, "as a wild ass's colt," as the Scriptures speak. O! who can endure the thought, that so it should be with what descends from me; that what descends, shall have descending with it seeds of enmity, and rebellion, against the Majesty of heaven only; but nothing concomitant towards the cure and the remedy of so horrid an evil.

To have a nature poisoned with enmity, an envenomed nature, even against heaven, running on, if I do not use my utmost care and concern, that as there shall be a continual descent of human nature, so that the correctives may accompany it, and go along with it, I do make myself a party against God and godliness. For I am sure that the uncultivated, and impure corrupt nature will be continually carrying on that war, and tumultuating in fresh rebellions, against heaven. And so that makes me, by neglect, a party: I betray the interests of God in that matter. And,

4. Let it be considered too, what horrid cruelty this is towards our own bowels, or such as I have otherwise undertaken the care of, visibly to throw away their souls; to seem not to care what becomes of them; whether they shall have any helps Godward, or heaven-ward, yea or no. No concern that whatever they shall bring forth, in all probability, and according to visible appearance, is only brought forth for the destroyer; all children of perdition only in view. And it is, in the last place, to be added,

5. That if any such persons would allow themselves to consider, that have such a concern upon them, or who are so intrusted with the disposal of young ones, either their own, or others committed to them, that will finally be found most of all cruel to their own souls. For how shall such, at last, lie down in peace, when they come to make up their accounts with God. "Such and such opportunities I had to serve the God of my life in this world, which I have lost; and I have thrown away such, whose souls I was concerned for, to have taken care of, even as my own." For we are to love our neighbours as ourselves: and much more those that are nearly related. O! the wounds and gall, and the terrors of spirit, wherewith (if the matter be reflected on) such must lie down at last. And the case is worse if it be not reflected on.

But then, there is somewhat to be said, too, to the other sort of persons that are concerned in this same case; and that is, the persons to be disposed of. All that I have said hitherto, refers to the disposers. But for them that are disposed of, it is not fit they should come into such a relation as that, till they can use some thoughts of their own, and so be capable of understanding what their duty is in such a case. And,

1. It is manifestly their duty to be very flexible towards parents and guardians, when they see they have a visible design of their spiritual and eternal welfare, in the first place; and that which they are chiefly concerned for. And,

2. It is their duty to be inflexible, if they find that such as are concerned for them, have a design to throw them away;

that they do not care as to what concerns their souls, and their spiritual estate, so as they may marry into an opulent condition in this world. In that case, I say, they ought to be inflexible: but dutifully and submissively, still. They ought to carry it with decorum, and not to be insolent in their refusal of those offers that are made them by parental authority, or in opposition thereunto; but with modesty and humility, still to dissent, still to disagree: "I will not so venture my soul upon an ungodly person; or where there is no hope I shall have help Godward, or heavenward."

LECTURE XLII.*

Thirdly.† It may be of use to *us*, to let us see how reasonable and righteous it is, that the conceptions and births of human creatures should be ordinarily attended, from age to age, with such dolours as we find they are. It is not to be repined at, that when such conceptions and births are in sin and iniquity, they should be also accompanied with terrors, with such pangs and agonies, as are commonly experienced. For it ought to be considered, what the productions are. What are the productions when a human creature is brought forth into this world? Why, a thing shapen in iniquity, and conceived in sin. And abstractly considered, and antecedently to supervening grace, it is a monstrous production. Any such production, it is a monstrous thing. A reasonable, intelligent creature produced into being, with a radical enmity against the infinite and supreme Good, the Fountain of all excellency and perfection. Consider it, I say, antecedently to supervening grace, and every human product is a monstrous one. As reason is yet but radical and seminal, so is corruption, so is malignity against God. "Estranged from the very womb," as that expression is, psalm 58. 3.

Therefore, this lot is to be submitted to, with so much the more equal mind, remembering that this was part of the first sentence, when sin did first spring in the world, that conception and production should be in sorrow. That such sickness, such pangs, such agonies, should so constantly attend human conception and birth; we are not to repine at it, as if it were an unreasonable, an unrighteous thing: but we are to consi-

* Preached Dec. 22, 1694.
†*Secondly*, Should have been inserted at Lec. XLI. p. 532.

der the reason of this and that; God will have a continual memorandum kept on for the putting us in mind, from age to age, what the nature is, that is descending and running down in this world, from age to age.

And that this should be the harder lot of that sex upon which it falls, the apostle gives this account—that that was the first deceived sex, first in the transgression, 1 Tim. 2. latter end. And the indulgence that is superadded, ought to be so much the more gratefully acknowledged; to wit, that there is so particular discovery of grace with reference to that sex: " She shall be saved in child-bearing, if she continue in faith, in holiness, in purity, in sobriety," and in love, the immediate product of that faith; a heart united with God, by that "faith which works by love." We read it, " charity," which commonly is understood to carry a reference especially unto a fellow creature. But there is no reason for that restriction in the native signification of the word itself. If she continue in faith, and love, with holiness and sobriety, she is in a safe state, notwithstanding all the pangs and dolour, and agonies, which, according to the original unreversed sentence, must be expected to be in the way. But again,

Fourthly. We may further learn, hence, by way of use, with what patience, and meekness, and wisdom; and with what considering minds, parents should observe and bear the sickness and death (when that case comes) of their children in their younger and more tender age. It requires much grace, much wisdom, a very serious and considering mind, to carry it equally and aright, in reference to such cases when they fall out: that a poor child, that hath lately peeped into this world, is presently struck with some distemper or another, as soon as it breathes, it languishes, and, it may be, dies; which is, you know, a very common case: the far greater part being hardly thought to outlive infancy, who are born into this world. These languishings end in death more commonly, than in recovery and consistency in health. What is the reason of all this?

Why humanly, indeed, they are apt to think it very strange, who are short-sighted creatures, and measure all things by the short line of time, and confine all those thoughts and apprehensions of things to this present world. But we are to consider, that when such a creature appears first upon the stage, it appears a creature tainted with sin; so it brings death with it, even from its very birth, into this world. " Death passeth over all men, inasmuch as all have sinned:" and sure, infants must be included in that all; and so they must be understood to be sinful creatures; to wit, that this radical evil hath tainted their natures, as soon as they have the human nature.

This is a case, therefore, about which we are not to contend, but which we ought to set ourselves to improve, and turn to gain. Is such a creature, as soon as it is born, a sinful, impure creature? Why, we must consider, that sin refers to eternity. I pray mind, that every thing of sin against God, it implies a reference to eternity, and to another world. Sin never reacheth its end and term here in this world. They that sin in this world, they are to give an account in the other: and that obey, and do comply, and fall in with the terms of the gospel, (the only prescription and relief in the case of having sinned,) they are to have their reward in another world. Sin, if it lie upon the sinner, turns to a miserable eternity in another world. Sin done away by expiation and by satisfaction, turns to a blessed eternity in another world. Do not think, therefore, that such creatures were finally made for this world. It would be an accountable riddle, that infants should but look into this world, and presently fall sick, and (as commonly it doth) that sickness end in death, if human nature were made for this world only. But this is to be considered, when such a creature comes into being, here is a production never to cease; a thing lately come into being, never to go out of being more: and that this world is only a *vestibulum*, an introduction into another world, which never dissolves, and wherein, whether our state be good or bad, they never change.

It ought hereupon to be considered, further, (that so such a case as this may be improved unto advantage,) it is improved to great advantage, if we consider what such a creature was made for; and considering it as a fallen creature, or sinner, what this sin it hath about it, hath reference to. It hath reference to eternity. All sin hath that reference.

But it will be of further improvement, if it be also considered by parents, in such cases, as to what tendency they usually have towards their children, when they are sick, and with what solicitude and fear they used to be vexing and disquieting their minds, lest they should die: yet they ought to be instructed, hence, to have a tenderness in reference to their spiritual maladies, and a like concern and dread of their dying eternally. Here would be a great improvement. "O! what a tenderness have I for my child when it is sick. Why, this distemper doth but attack the flesh, frail, mortal flesh, that was formed out of the dust so newly; and must, sooner or later, return to it again: but my child hath an immortal spirit in it too; and that is tainted with sin: it hath its worst and most dangerous distemper within. O! what cries, what supplications, should I send up to the Father of spirits, and Father of mercies, that he would cure these spiritual maladies?" And whereas, you are afraid that your child will die; you are to be more afraid lest it should die eternally.

And labour to consider aright, the grounds you have of reasonable hope, in reference to this case. It is a case that parents ought not to consider with despair. Those that are themselves in covenant with God through Christ, the promise is to them, and to their seed: and they have a great deal more reason to hope, than they have to despair. And for ought I see, as great reason to hope concerning their children dying in infancy as they have to hope concerning themselves. The covenant of God in Christ doth not signify nothing. And whereas, that age is incapable of covenanting for itself, if such a one, growing to maturity, do not disclaim, but stand to the covenant of his or her parents, it holds firm and unalterable. And, in the mean time, while there is no capacity, or possibility of disclaimer, we have no reason to think there can be any failure on the other part, but, according to the tenour and constitution of God's covenant, the infant, during its infant state, is considered as a branch in the root; and before it be capable of treating and transacting for itself with God, it is treated for acceptably and successfully by a holy and believing parent. And therefore, such a case, when it falls out unto godly parents to have their children languishing, even in their infancy, many times even unto death, they should consider what an admirable, strange thing it is: "This creature, as it came from me, came into this world an impure thing, a polluted thing, a child of wrath by nature; now, how is it numbered among the children of the Most High, and adjoined to the general assembly, (when it is gone from hence,) to the innumerable company of angels, and the spirits of just men made perfect! What a change is this! So impure a creature as it came from me, is become now, all of a sudden, so glorious a creature!"

And it is further to that purpose, to be considered, What did God make such a creature for? Why, what do you think he made it on purpose to please me? If I be the parent, the pleasure I take in it, is but a collateral and secondary thing. But do we yet need to be taught that God made all things for himself? And that it may be good indeed, when such strokes do befal families, children lopt off, one branch after another, (it may be the single one,) to consider whatsoever a providence may specially animadvert upon, and if there be any thing evident in view, it ought to be considered; it ought to be well considered and taken to heart. Yet, it is possible there may be a vulgar error incurred in this matter too: that is, in thinking that the principal design of any such dispensation was, or must be, the affliction and punishment of the holy parent. That ought to be considered, where there is no notorious delinquency to be reflected upon. I say, it ought to be considered as some end, but not as that principal end, of such a dispensation: for as the principal end of God's making such a creature was not to please me; so the principal end of his taking such a creature out of this world, was not to displease me; but to glorify himself: and that end cannot be in this world, for which he hath made such a creature.

And it ought to be considered, that his right in it, is more than mine, infinitely. If any of you should put a child to nurse, and it grows up under the nurse's care, and she is pleased with it, takes complacency in it; and because she doth do so, when you call for your child home, she will not part with it, because it pleaseth her; surely, you would think that your right and interest in the child are superior to her's: and her's (whatever it is) is not to be considered in competition with your's; and, your's is far less to be considered in competition with God's; your's is far more inferior. And therefore, there ought to be a grateful resentment, not without sense, not with stupidity; but with serious and apprehensive minds, and having the state of the case lying in view before you as it is. And therefore, I add,

Fifthly. That the miseries of this world ought not to amaze us. We are not to think it a strange thing, that this lower region should be a region of so much wretchedness and carnality, as it is found to be, from age to age: for is not every one that is born into it, born a sinner? And whereas, none can bring a clean thing out of an unclean, who can hope to bring a quiet thing out of an unclean? Purity and peace, pollution and disturbance go together. Every one brings into this world, not only that which is troublesome to himself, but that which is troublesome to others, too, with whom he hath to do. They bring that with them into this world, which must make it an unquiet, stormy region to them. Our greatest troubles (with every one) are born with us. And this is the common case, and cannot be otherwise, when we consider that sin, which every one brings with him into this world, doth dissolve the union between God and the soul, and breaks it off from God. A sinner, as such, is loose from God. And therefore, this would bring, from age to age, in a state of apostasy and separation from God, that which we see to be the consequent thereof, a universal confusion of our very nature within itself, and of all men (as they fall into any kind of conversation with one another) towards one another too. This cannot but be, hereupon, a heap of confusion, a mere chaos.

How can it be otherwise with creatures fallen from God? If man that is born of a woman be an unclean thing, (as Job 14. 4.) then, (as the 14 chapter begins,) it is not at all strange, that man that is born of a woman should be of few days, and full of trouble. So many such creatures as are produced, and brought forth into being in this world, so many fountains of misery and wretchedness are produced. Think of the vast numbers of the inhabitants of this earth, and every one, even from his very infancy, is a fountain both of impurity and misery. And therefore, it is not strange that so many fountains should deluge this world, from age to age, both with wickedness, so as that it may well be said to lie therein, and (as that which is most connatural thereunto) with misery also.

And it is, hereupon, to be the result of our thoughts, when we consider with ourselves, what a miserable region this world is: this ought, I say, to be the result of our thoughts: it is all natural, it is all most genuine; if we see early discords in families, when a family is planted, young plants springing up in it; if there are quarrellings, janglings, fallings out, perpetual animosities, even among those nearer relatives in families; as the poet observed long ago—*Fratrum concordia rara,* seldom is there any agreement among brethren; those that are branches of the same root. If we look further into larger societies, cities, kingdoms, or nations, they are all continually full of confusion, from age to age; and it is from hence, that the wretchedness of this world, which springs up from as many fountains as there are men and women upon earth, and these fountains, from their very infancy, are "like the troubled sea, whose waters cast forth mire and dirt," as the prophet speaks: "There is no peace saith my God to the wicked." That wickedness which overflows the world, cannot but make it an unquiet and gloomy region. And therefore, again,

Sixthly. We may further learn, how unreasonable and unaccountable a thing it is, that men should be in love with this present world. It is indeed, stupendous to think, that our minds should so cleave to so horrid a thing as this world is; should be set upon it, that they will not run from it; that here we think of taking up our rest! O! think, what we ourselves were, and what the rest of mankind is; "a generation of vipers," poisonous creatures, of an envenomed, malignant nature. If we find that we have a design, any desire, any hope or prospect of a better state, methinks, we should not affect to live among such creatures, and continue ourselves when a cure is to be hoped for; when we understand the design of grace, that it will make such as comply with its methods, pure, and holy, and glorious creatures ere it be long: but not here, but incohatively and imperfectly only. When I consider this, methinks we should be quite out of love with this world, and say with ourselves, "This cannot be our rest, for it is polluted," as in that Micah 2. 10. O! let us be up and begone as soon as we can have a fair exit; and make it our business while we must stay here, as much as is possible for us, to keep from the corruptions that are in this world, and to get, as much as in us lies, this impure fountain of sin dried up; and to be waiting with earnest, and most desirous expectation, for a translation into that place where there shall be no more sin, but perfect purity: nothing to interrupt and hinder the closest union, and sweetest pleasures, and most delightful intercourse, between God and us. "He that hath this hope purifieth himself as God is pure:" the hope of being like God, and seeing him as he is, 1 John 3. 3. referred to the immediately foregoing verse. Which being made like God, and seeing him as he is, we know this present state admits not of.

Seventhly. We may further learn, hence, to admire the divine patience towards this wretched world, that he hath spared it so long, is so indulgent to it; while wickedness is so continually propagating an enmity, rebellion, and war, against himself, from one generation to another. We ought to consider the divine patience in this, both as great and as wise. As great, to look upon it abstractly, it is wonderful patience, that God should bear with such a world, that is transmitting continual wickedness and enmity against himself from age to age, when he hath it so perfectly in his power to put a stop and period to all this, at his own pleasure. It is great patience. It is a very great thing.

But we ought also to consider it, too, that it is the patience of a God; and then it must be wise as well as great. Wise with reference to somewhat else, as well as great in itself. It cannot be, but that the reference of this patience must be to somewhat else, to some God-like design; otherwise, would he sustain a sinful world, and let sinners beget sinners, and propagate a rebellion and war against himself, from age to age, if he had not some great meaning in all this? Why, there will be glorious results out of it, which, by how much the less our understandings are capable of comprehending it, with so much the more patience, and resignation, we should wait for it. It will be found at last a thing worthy of God, to have borne, with so much patience, the wickedness of this world so long. But then,

Eighthly. We are from hence to reckon, too, that this state of things must not last always, when this is the constant course and common case that, from age to age, impure creatures are begotten of impure creatures, conceived in sin, shapen in iniquity, we may conclude upon it, that this course will have an end. And we are not to think it strange, if it should have such an end as the Scriptures of truth, tell us, it will have; that is, that a day will come, "when the heavens shall be rolled up as a scroll, and the elements melt with fervent heat; and all things therein shall be consumed and burnt up, as it is in that 2 Peter, 3. at large. We are not to think this strange or unworthy of God, that he should design such a way, to put a period, at last, to the generations of men on earth, when they are so continually, so long as they last, handing down and transmitting wickedness and war against heaven, from generation to generation. It is never to be thought, that this can last always. Therefore, how much the more wicked we observe the world to be, with so much the more awe, trembling, and dread we should consider what is coming—that day of the perdition, and of the destruction of ungodly men; this world being reserved unto fire against that day. But again,

Ninthly. We are further to learn, how admirable a thing it is, that in the mean time, God should be raising up to himself a divine offspring, out of an impure race of creatures; (Be they as they are, and as they, from age to age, are born in sin, and brought forth in iniquity, yet, saith God, "I will have my part and share among them;") that he should have assigned to a Redeemer his seed, ("He shall see his seed," Isaiah 53. 10,) even out of this corrupt seed, this seed of evil doers. And whereas, according to the natural state of the case, (as it is stated before,) man in his first apostasy being an accomplice with the devil, this world is entirely become the devil's family: "You are of your father the devil." John 8. 44. So men, morally considered, are. In respect of their naturals, (it is true,) God is the Father of their spirits; but in respect of their morals, lapsed, corrupted man, is the devil's seed, and so, antecedently to grace, this world was become the devil's family: but now, that God should raise up to himself a family out of this family; that there should be a diverse and contrary seed springing up, even amidst the other, and out of it, opposite to the other, and having its particular and distinct character, this is admirable! As the apostle tells us, "Herein the children of God, and the children of the devil are manifest." There is a manifest, discernible difference between them. There is no doubt, they must needs differ, beyond all that can be thought, who are of so vastly different parents.

But here is the wonder,—that God should design to raise up to himself such a seed, out of such a world, out of such a race! that he did not rather choose to abandon this (one) when he was gone off from him: and when he could, by a word, have raised up another pure, holy, innocent creature throughout. No: but his design was to defeat the device and contrivance of the devil; he thought to have this seed, all this race of creatures entirely off from God: No, this shall not be; he was resolved he would herein deceive the deceiver; and (as to this design of his) destroy the destroyer;—destroy him that had the power of death, and make a fool of him.

This, (as I noted in the opening of the text to you) was a course most eligible to the Supreme Wisdom, not to make a direct regression of any of his works, by meeting with opposition and a design driven on against him. But he resolves to proceed in the natural course that was laid out at first, and to counterwork that arch-enemy, the first, the grand apostate; and to carry on his own design, against his design; and to turn all to honour and glory at last: even into matter of the highest triumph over the defeated and disappointed destroyer of souls. And this is that which we should consider, with wonder and reverence, that God should have such a design as this in hand, and continually kept on foot, to raise to himself a pure, and holy, and divine seed, (which shall at length be perfectly so,) out of such an apostate degenerate race. And,

Tenthly. This lets us see the necessity of regeneration. Is man such an impure creature, even from his very original, from his conception and birth? Then he must be new made. If any thing shall be made of him to good purpose, he must be made over again. This shews us of how absolute necessity it is, that there should be not only in discourse, but in fact, that great mystery of regeneration, belonging to our religion. Is man now, from the beginning, such an impure thing? (the great God beholding this,) there is nothing to be made of this creature, unless he be new made. Is he born such a thing? he must be new-born. Born he is, of earthly parentage: but "he must be born from above," as that word admits to be rendered, John 3. 5. But yet,

Eleventhly. It also shews the kindness, as well as the necessity, of this regenerating work; by how much the more necessary, by so much the more kind. How admirable grace is there in it; that when the exigency of the case required that this creature should be made and born over again; I say, when the case required such a thing, God should so graciously vouchsafe it? This is admirable grace! "We were sometimes foolish, disobedient, serving divers lusts and pleasures;" slaves in our birth; born slaves. "But when the kindness and love of God appeared, not by works of righteousness which we had done, but according to his mercy he saved us, by the washing of regeneration, and renewing of the Holy Ghost, which he shed upon us abundantly, through Jesus Christ our Lord." Tit. 3. 4, 5. Consider the grace of regeneration, how gracious a work it is, that God, who had no need of such creatures, creatures that could add nothing to him, should condescend to such a thing, to let that holy and pure Spirit of his, come, amidst all their impurities, with his own holy light and influence, upon creatures that he might have abhorred to touch with: that the holy and pure Spirit should shed his light and influences, (so pure things amidst so much impurity,) there to regenerate, there to renew, there to form, there to reform—O what grace is this! And, lastly,

Twelfthly. We may further collect, hence, how glorious a work regeneration or renovation must be, when that shall take effect. "Behold, I make all things new." Rev. 21. 5. Who would expect that such a state of things as this, should come out of such a state as this world was degenerated into, when every particular creature that inhabits it, was a fountain of impurity and misery to itself, and to the rest? That there should be such a thing laid in the divine counsel—" Well, I will new make this world; there shall be such a thing as new heavens, and a new earth, wherein righteousness shall dwell:" With what wonder and transport should we think of this, that God will have so glorious a world, out of a world so lost and sunk in impurity and death, as this world is!

But thus far, we have been considering the state of the apostate children of men—THE FALL OF THE FIRST MAN—

LEC. XLII.) *All men depraved—general inferences.* 551

THE FALLEN STATE OF MEN, and—THE EQUITY AND RIGHTEOUSNESS OF THE DIVINE PROCEDURE IN ALL THIS. It remains, in the next place, to come now to that which I last observed, by way of use, will lead us more directly to consider; and that is, WHAT HATH BEEN DESIGNED, AND WHAT IS DONE, AND IS DOING, IN ORDER TO THE RECOVERY OF THIS IMPURE, THIS LOST, AND LAPSED CREATURE.*

End of the Seventh Volume.

*To be continued in a Supplementary Volume.

Mason, Printer, Chichester.

Lightning Source UK Ltd.
Milton Keynes UK
UKOW07f1831140915

258630UK00010B/309/P